W9-DGL-808

CONTENTS

Acknowledgments

In honor of the addition of Bronfenbrenner's ecological model to this third edition, we'd like to use his theoretical approach to thank those who have helped with and influenced this book. To begin with our microsystems, we'd like to thank our husbands, Brett and Jeff, for their support during the process. We appreciate their patience, understanding, and partnership in making certain that our home lives functioned as normally as possible during the writing of the new edition. Thanks also go to our children, who allowed us to take time away from them so that we could focus on writing. We'd like to extend special thanks to our family and friends who, as part of our mesosystems, helped with child care so that we could work nights and weekends to complete this project on time. Further, we would like to thank Sherith Pankratz at Oxford University Press for her encouragement and guidance in regard to the project.

From an exosystem perspective, we'd like to thank our departments for the supportive context they gave us in helping to complete this work. Specifically, we would like to thank the human development department at Washington State University Vancouver in Vancouver, Washington, and the human development and family science department at Messiah College in Grantham, Pennsylvania. We'd also like to thank the community of scholars who have contributed to this book and its continuing development. Specifically, we want to acknowledge Bron Ingoldsby and Beth Miller, who were co-authors with Suzanne Smith on the first edition of this book. Their time, talents, and efforts helped formulate the first edition on which this edition has been built. They were important scholars, colleagues, and friends without whom this book would never have been originally written. They were not able to participate in the book past the first edition, but what you see now is based on the core of their original writings. In addition, we thank the many colleagues who graciously gave of their time and expertise in reviewing the book as we sought feedback to inform our revisions for the third edition.

- Charles B. Hennon, Miami University
- Ana Lucero-Liu, California State University-Northridge
- Michael Merten, Oklahoma State University
- Richard N. Pitt, Vanderbilt University
- Rhonda A. Richardson, Kent State University
- Katheryn A. Sweeney, Purdue University Calumet

Finally, from a macrosystem perspective, we would like to thank the originators of the theories themselves who offered the various lenses through which we view family life, and the researchers who tested various propositions and further refined our theoretical thinking. Without their insight and ingenuity, we would have a less developed and more incomplete picture of the functioning and processes of families. We hope that today's scholars who are interested in family theory will show the same drive and ambition as these early predecessors, and we look forward to including their work in future editions.

About the Authors

Suzanne R. Smith is Associate Professor of Human Development at Washington State University Vancouver, where she serves as the Associate Chair and Program Director. She earned her Ph.D. from the University of Georgia. In addition to serving as an administrator, she teaches courses on balancing work and family, human development theories, and family diversity. Dr. Smith's primary area of research is parent–child relationships, but she has spent significant time over the last fourteen years living with and researching the Hutterites. She has served as president of both the Northwest Council on Family Relations and the Teaching Family Science Association, as well as having served as a member of the Board of the National Council on Family Relations.

Raeann R. Hamon is Distinguished Professor of Family Science and Gerontology and Chair of the Human Development and Family Science Department at Messiah College in Pennsylvania. Dr. Hamon earned her Ph.D. from Virginia Tech. A Certified Family Life Educator, she teaches courses on family theories, family life education methodology, interpersonal relationships, marital relationships, and aging. Her research is related to intergenerational relationships, families in later life, issues related to the discipline of family science, and Bahamian families. She has served in a variety of professional roles including president of the Pennsylvania/Delaware Council on Family Relations, and board member and 2009 conference chair for the National Council on Family Relations. Dr. Hamon is also an NCFR Fellow.

New to the Third Edition

In addition to minor changes throughout each chapter, the third edition of *Exploring Family Theories* features the following major changes:

- A brand new chapter on ecological theory, including a supplemental reading which utilizes the theory.
- The sections on current areas of research have been updated to reflect the most recent research.
- The majority of supplemental readings now come from more recent publications.
- Supplemental readings are more thoroughly introduced within the chapter prior to the reading so that the connection between the reading and the chapter is more apparent.
- The introductory chapter has been expanded to include a discussion on where theories come from, the functions of theories, how we evaluate theories, and the need for theorizing.
- The epilogue chapter has been expanded to include a more in-depth look at the future of family theories.

INTRODUCTION

"Why do you do that?" "Why does our family insist on doing things that way?" Questions about people's behaviors are the essence of social science inquiry. The focus may be on individuals, families, social groups, communities, or cultures. In order to engage in the process of social science inquiry, you need two things: research and theory. Before we enter into a discussion of social science theory, and specifically family theory, we first need to have a discussion about theory in general.

WHAT IS THEORY?

A theory is a tool used to understand and describe the world. More specifically, a theory is a general framework of ideas and how they relate to each other. Theories can be used to ask and answer questions about particular phenomena. You probably are familiar with many theories already, such as the theory of evolution, the theory of relativity, the theory of the big bang, and the theory of plate tectonics. Theories are also important in the social sciences, particularly those that help us to study families.

Theories have identifiable components that make up their structures. *Assumptions* are beliefs that are taken for granted or believed to be true. They form the foundation underlying the theory. *Concepts* are the terms and specific ideas used in building the theory. *Propositions* are statements that demonstrate how concepts fit together in a context. They are the relationships between the concepts, the "glue" holding the theory together. Thus, a theory is based on assumptions and should be composed of clearly defined concepts that fit together in the form of propositions. For these propositions to be useful, they must be specific enough to help describe, explain, and predict phenomena and to ask questions that would guide their research in deductive ways.

A theory's ability to help us generate questions is known as its *heuristic* value. A theory can help us decide what to research; the results of that research can in turn lead to the development of new theories, which again can lead to new research. In other words, theories need to be empirically testable. Variables and relationships within the propositional statements must be operationalized, and the researcher needs to develop measures to assess the *components* outlined. A theory should also be flexible enough to grow and change, so that new information can be fed back into the theory, causing it to adapt and change in an inductive feedback loop; but a theory also needs to be general enough to apply to a wide variety of specific cases. In short, the usefulness of a theory is determined by its ability to describe more, rather than less, detail; to predict with more, rather than less, accuracy; and to apply to a broader, rather than a narrower, range of specific cases.

It is also true that theories have a certain point of view, or lens. Depending on our emphasis, the perspective may be more broad (macro) or more narrow (micro). The lens we choose is often a function of the question we are asking and so, again, a theory's usefulness depends on the subject at hand. In the social sciences, human situations are complex, and it is difficult to find one theory that can explain or predict every emotion, behavior, interaction, process, and event. Because of this, social theories are those lenses that we can use to help us interpret or focus on the components of human interactions in conceptual ways.

Although theories are abstract, they do serve important purposes in our understanding of social phenomena. Theories provide a general framework for understanding data in an organized way, as well as showing us how to intervene (Burr 1995). In social sciences, it is rare to find anyone who believes that there is only one way to understand social phenomena, particularly those as complicated as individuals and families. Thus, the frustrating but truthful response to many questions in social science is "It depends." Indeed, it does depend on one's point of view, but that is not the same as one's opinion. For example, someone may believe that divorce sets a bad example for children. As scholars, we know that divorce is too complex to be labeled as merely *good* or *bad* and that questions about the effects of divorce on children cannot be easily answered. We need more complex ideas to analyze such situations, and we need to consider multiple elements within families to study aspects of divorce, its development, and its effects. To decide which theory to use, we consider the usefulness of the theory, or how well it enables us to answer the questions at hand. How "well" a theory does in explaining a situation depends on the researcher's point of view, or his or her lens. Thus, two social scientists may each choose a different theory to explain the same situation.

Each theory allows us to look at different aspects of family life. One theory might suggest that we focus on the roles that people play, whereas another might suggest that we focus more on the individual's gains and losses. Looking through the lens of the theory enables us to see how the world looks from that perspective. Each theory has underlying basic assumptions that focus the lens, just as each has concepts and propositions that guide what we analyze. Each theory has been developed within a historical context and has asked different questions; thus, each theory has a different research history. Because of this, each theory can give us a different answer to our question, which is why "It depends."

Where Do Theories Come From?

Theories generally don't emerge fully formed all at once. Instead, they build slowly over time, as scholars gather data through observation and analysis of evidence, relating concepts together in different ways. This type of reasoning, moving from specific bits of information toward a general idea, is known as *inductive reasoning*. Once the theory exists, scholars use the general ideas of the theory to generate more specific questions, often in the form of research questions, thereby moving in the opposite

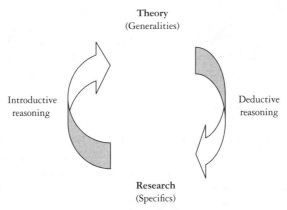

Theory
(Generalities)

Introductive
reasoning

Deductive
reasoning

Research
(Specifics)

The cycle of theory building.

direction. Taking a general idea from a theory and testing it to tease out the details is known as *deductive reasoning*. Both kinds of thinking patterns are common in theory construction and development, and they, once again, demonstrate the linkage between research and theory.

However, as you can see from the figure, "The cycle of theory building," theories are not stagnant. Theories help us to formulate questions that we test via research. The research generates data, which filter back into the cycle and help us to further refine the theory. Such a beneficial relationship is called a *symbiotic relationship*. Research poses questions and then tries to answer them by making observations and collecting data. When enough data have been collected, patterns emerge, and a theory is developed to try to explain the patterns that are observed. Thus, theory helps us explain "what's going on" and can allow us to *predict* "what's going to happen" when certain conditions are present. As our theoretical ideas change, so do our research questions. There is a continuous feedback loop between discovery and confirmation, disconfirmation, or modification. It is also important to remember that theories do not exist in a cultural vacuum, but that they are the products of humans and their experiences. As humans redefine their values, their theories are influenced by those changes. This is particularly evident in theories of social science but can be seen in natural science theories as well. After all, it was once believed that the world was flat and that the earth was the center of the universe.

Radical changes or shifts in scientific views are known as *paradigm shifts* (Kuhn 1970). These shifts occur after significant data that do not fit the current theory have been gathered. Thus, a new theory is needed to explain the data. According to Kuhn, in the natural sciences, paradigm shifts change science dramatically, as did Einstein's theory of relativity or the fact that Columbus did not, in fact, fall off the end of the earth.

In the social sciences, paradigm shifts are not as obvious, because we do not evaluate our theories from the standpoint of truth, but rather on how useful they are. We, as scholars, cannot define what is true for all humans or families, so neither can our theoretical perspectives. At times, significant changes in culture or human experience can change theoretical perspectives in radical ways. For instance, it is not uncommon to see shifts in the most popular theories employed. While reviewing theories in family gerontology during the decade of 1990, Roberto and colleagues (2006) noticed a decline in the use of certain theories and an increase in others. So, over time certain theories can fall out of favor and be replaced by more relevant and helpful frames of reference. You will notice that between the second and third editions of this text, some theories have been used more heavily than others.

What Are the Functions of Theory?

Theories have a variety of functions in helping us to generate knowledge about families. Stan Knapp (2009) identifies the "generative" capacity of family theory in each of the following five functions: descriptive function, sensitizing function, integrative function, explanatory function, and value function. Relative to its *descriptive function*, theories help to name, classify, and organize phenomena in such a way that we can understand them. By articulating basic concepts and the relationship between events, theory helps us to describe what we hope to study. As part of a *sensitizing function*, theory can help us to be aware of processes, events, and phenomena that we may not have otherwise noticed. It sensitizes us to matters that we might have missed without calling our attention to them. The *integrative function* helps us to make connections between events or processes that appear to be quite distinct and unrelated. It identifies the interrelatedness of disparate concepts and propositions, tying together ideas in a new way in order to make sense of data. The *explanatory function* is probably the best-known role of theory. Its unique purpose is to explain data. It attempts to answer the questions "how" and "why," or why do things happen as they do? It also attempts to make predictions about phenomena that can be tested in future research. Finally, theory possesses a *value function*. Knapp notes that theories "become receptacles for valued ideas in making sense of our world" (135). The values embedded in theoretical assumptions, descriptions of concepts, and the like advocate for certain value stances. Thus, it's important to be aware of the underlying values espoused within a particular theory. According to Knapp, we need to see the many functions of theory and not just be consumed by its integrative and explanatory functions, or we will miss the potential to better understand our subject.

How Do We Evaluate Theories?

It is always important to continue to evaluate the theories we are using. How do we do this? Doherty, Boss, LaRossa, Schumm, and Steinmetz (1993, 24–26) delineate seventeen criteria that are helpful in assessing the value and quality of theories in the family field and social sciences in general. Below, we list each and then explain them in more detail.

1. *Richness of ideas* refers to the general appeal that a theory offers to its user. Is the theory original? Does it offer the depth and unique understanding for which a scholar is looking?
2. *Clarity of concepts* relates to the extent to which concepts are well defined. Are the concepts clear and distinctive enough from each other that scholars are able to communicate about them with each other?

3. *Coherence of connections among concepts* refers to the ability of the concepts to logically or intuitively relate well to one another. How easy is it to see the relationships between theoretical concepts?

4. *Simplicity or parsimony* refers to the need to weigh a theory's simplicity against its effectiveness and utility. Does the theory express its ideas parsimoniously without being too reductionistic?

5. *Clarity of theoretical assumptions and presuppositions* relates to how well the originators of the theory have conveyed their philosophy of science and their assumptions about family relationships. What are the authors' underlying assumptions about human behavior and family dynamics?

6. *Consistency with its own assumptions and presuppositions* refers to the extent to which fundamental assumptions are supportive of and related to one another. Is there internal coherence between underlying assumptions and presuppositions outlined in the theory?

7. *Acknowledgment of its sociocultural context* represents the cultural context out of which the theory emerged. What was the cultural context like when the theory was developed? What implications does that have for its use in light of the current cultural context?

8. *Acknowledgment of underlying value positions* refers to the extent to which theorists have made their values known. What are the values represented in this theory? What is good? What is right? What is worthwhile?

9. *Acknowledgment of theoretical forebears* refers to the need to reference the work of those who have contributed to the continuing development of the theory. Whose ideas have contributed to the origination and refinement of this theory? Are there scholars against whom this theorist is reacting in its development?

10. *Potential for validation and current level of validation* refer to the extent to which research observations are able to affirm a theory. Does the theory actually seem to reflect what transpires in the lives of families?

11. *Acknowledgment of limits and points of breakdown* refers to the critical eye needed to identify the limits of the theory and its presuppositions. How does the theory fail to enlighten our understanding of phenomena under consideration?

12. *Complementarity with other theories and levels of explanation* refer to the extent to which a theory is able to interface with other conceptual frameworks that exist within the field. How does the theory fit together with other theoretical frameworks in the field?

13. *Openness to change and modification* refers to the willingness to refine, modify, revise, and even abandon ideas over time, rather than voraciously defend them. Are the theory's proponents willing to discuss its merits and shortcomings with others and modify the theory accordingly?

14. *Ethical implications* relate to the assumptions about morality upon which the theory is based. What impact does this theory have on the rights and responsibilities of families and their members? How can the theory be ethically applied to enhance our understanding of family life?

15. *Sensitivity to pluralistic human experience* refers to the ability of a theory to accommodate a vast range of human and family experiences. To what extent is the theory sensitive to pluralistic human experiences as related to things like gender, race, ethnicity, age, social class, and sexual orientation?

16. *Ability to combine personal experience and academic rigor* refers to the extent to which a theory enables the scholar to move back and forth between lived personal experiences within families and professional reasoning. How able is the theory to accommodate shifting back and forth between personal immersion and academic objectivity and distance?

17. *Potential to inform application for education, therapy, advocacy, social action, or public policy* refers to the theory's ability to help theorizers translate theory and related data into actions that benefit families. Does the theory help to improve the lives of families via education, therapy, public policy, and advocacy? Can the theory be applied to real families?

It is important to recognize that no single theory is likely to measure up on all these items. Nonetheless, these criteria offer one way to more fully appreciate and assess each theory.

The Need for Theorizing

If theories are so important for enhancing our understanding of relationships and the world around us, how does one tackle this assignment? According to Jetse Sprey (1990), "theorizing first and foremost is an intentional activity" (22). We need to commit ourselves to the work of developing and testing theory. Many agree that theorizing is a process, not just a product (Bengtson et al. 2005; Roberto, Blieszner, and Allen 2006). It's something you do, an activity in which you engage.

Many of the world's greatest minds, those whose ideas literally changed the way we understand the world, were theoreticians. For example, we live in a post-Freudian world: Freud's theories revolutionized our understanding of the mind, sexuality, and how we deal with stress. Karl Marx suggested that communism is an alternative to social injustice and oppression and a method by which all humans could achieve a humane and equitable life. Freud and Marx brought about significant shifts in the way we thought about issues in society and human behavior that are still valued today, although we do not believe every aspect of Freudian psychology, and Marx's Communist Manifesto is considered to have its limitations. Similarly, Piaget brought about another paradigm shift in the area of cognitive development with his insight that children think in ways that are qualitatively different from adult processes. His theory has undergone modifications, and many researchers still use his work as a basis for their research, but some of them have also gone beyond his work and expanded on his ideas. In this way, we evaluate theories based on the aspects of them that are useful.

Bengtson et al. (2005) likened theorizing to putting together the pieces of a puzzle. Each puzzle piece is comprised of a bit of family research data. Alone and disorganized, the pieces do not make sense and are perplexing. However, when assembled in a meaningful way, the puzzle provides a more coherent image or picture. Thus, theorizers use ideas or abstractions to make sense of data. Because theories are intellectual constructs that are subject to change as a new puzzle piece or evidence is introduced, theorizers' work is never complete. In fact, it is important to never consider theories to be static and unchanging. Theorizers must always scrutinize theories for their utility and relevance across diverse groups and over the course of time (Bengtson et al. 2005). We need family scholars who commit themselves to theorizing—assembling, disassembling, and then reassembling the puzzles of life. Can you imagine yourself as a family theorizer?

FAMILY THEORY

James White (2005) argues that it is essential to develop family theories that are distinct from those used to examine social groups, as used in the fields of sociology. After all, the family is a unique type of grouping. According to White and Klein (2008), families differ from other social groups in four ways: Families last much longer than most social groups and require lifetime memberships. Families are intergenerational, unlike other social groups, and virtually ensure a range of ages. Although most social groups are primarily based on affinity, families represent biological and affinal (e.g., legal) relationships. Finally, families are connected to larger kinship networks.

So, why study family theory? The family is certainly the most important and enduring of all human social groupings. What, then, could be more fascinating than attempting to understand family dynamics? Nothing affects our personalities and happiness more than our family relationships. Why is kinship always the center of any human society? How do these interactions work, and why are they so influential in our lives?

Because there are so many perspectives to consider, it is not a simple thing to develop a coherent theory of family interaction. Social science is made even more difficult because we are attempting to understand ourselves. Whereas, in the natural sciences, we are examining objects and life forms that are less complex than we are, in human development we do not have the advantage of a higher intelligence than the subject in order to get a good *metaperspective*. With groups like families, there is the added complexity of looking beyond the individual to the relationships between individuals. All of this makes family theory development difficult at best.

We are also hindered by the difficulty of not even having a good and commonly accepted definition of the term *family*. Anthropologist George Murdock (1949) surveyed the world's cultures and came up with this definition:

> The family is a social group characterized by common residence, economic cooperation, and reproduction. It includes adults of both sexes, at least two of whom maintain a socially approved sexual relationship, and one or more children, own or adopted, of the sexually cohabitating adults. (1)

His work (described in greater detail in our chapter on structural functionalism) has generated a half century of ongoing scientific and political debate on what we mean when we say "family." As we will see, each theory has its own variation on the definition.

This is also a good example of why we need more than one family theory. First, there is more than one type and one definition of family. Second, even if you agree on how to define the family, you may disagree on which particular aspect of their interactions or behaviors your attention should be focused. Finally, each theory offers an insight that others cannot provide because of their different lenses.

The purpose of this text is to provide a basic introduction to the major theories pertaining to the family among professionals today. Each addresses different aspects of family life and answers different questions. Humans are extremely complex, and it is difficult to analyze ourselves; therefore, every theory will be imperfect. But each one brings us closer to understanding and being able to make positive change where needed in family life. Each theory has its own basic assumptions and concepts and is a product of its own historical context as well. Each is used in answering specific research questions that other theories may not answer or may answer differently. It will be up to you to try on the lens of each theory and determine how well you think it explains human and family behavior.

TEXT ORGANIZATION

We will discuss ten theories about the family that have been widely used and accepted over the past fifty years. We present these ten theories in a loosely chronological order. It is difficult to be more precise, as most of them experienced a gradual emergence, and some have long histories as general social theories before they were used to study the family as a specific social phenomenon. Our order of placement is determined by the time when significant publications discussing the theory from a family perspective appeared.

Symbolic interaction theory is one of the first and most influential theories in the field of family science. Its roots stem from the pragmatic philosophers of the early 1900s, and it is based on the belief that we construct our own realities. Events and relationships take on different meanings based on an individual's perceptions and the context of a situation. Symbolic interactionism continues to be a very popular family theory today.

Shortly after the Depression and World War II and in the infancy of family theory building, several other theories took center stage. Structural functionalism, which comes from sociology and anthropology, takes a macro view of the family within culture. It looks at the family through the lens of asking what the family does to justify its existence in society.

Family development theory applies basic-stage theory from psychology to families. It considers how families change over time in response to normative family events. Although its widespread use comes later, family stress theory, which looks at how the family as a system deals with challenging situations or events, was developed while studying family reactions to the Depression and later to wartime during World War II.

In the late 1950s and well into the 1960s, several theories took more of an inside look at family communication and interaction. First, family systems theory derived from communication and clinical work. It made a micro analysis of how family members relate to each other in a complex world of multicausality. Rooted in systems theory, ecological theory emerged with the growing recognition of the need to examine individuals and families within their environments, primarily the home. Next, conflict theory came from a sociological perspective and focused on how people and families create stability and instability in their relationships because of differences in status. Then, social exchange theory took its inspiration from behaviorism and economics in analyzing family decision-making as a rational process of choosing between rewards and costs.

Our final two theoretical approaches began to receive significant notice in the 1970s. Feminist theorists began their investigations with the perspective that women's experiences are central to our understanding of families and focused on the influences of social situations and politics. Most recently, the biosocial perspective, with its roots in the work of Charles Darwin, maintains as its general premise that, although humans are driven by innate structures, the family and cultural environment influence their behaviors.

Each chapter begins with a fictional vignette to introduce a way of using that particular theory for understanding an aspect of family life. It is followed by a brief history of the development of the theory, and then an explanation of the basic assumptions that undergird it. The primary terms and concepts used in understanding the theory are provided. The usefulness of each theory is highlighted by examples of research and application within the particular framework. Every theory is critiqued, with its principal problems and strengths discussed. Finally, the reader is provided with a series of questions and exercises designed to relate the implications of the theory to the vignette and to his or her own personal and family life.

A highlight of this book is the integration of research with theory and practice. After each chapter, a professional article is included. Each research article illustrates how new information about families is gained when researchers and practitioners use theories to guide their efforts. Whereas, in the first edition of this text, a classic article was included after each chapter, for this edition, we've chosen more contemporary readings. The Epilogue links the chapters together, using a conceptual model for comparing and contrasting the theories. This model indicates how each theory can be useful for understanding and guiding intervention for particular situations from its viewpoint.

It is important to remember that anyone can collect facts, but being a scholar requires understanding the facts in a way that allows for research, testing, comprehension, and practical application. In order to be useful, data must be ordered within a theoretical framework. Which theories will you enjoy the most and find the most useful? There is only one way to find out!

REFERENCES

Bengtson, V., A. C. Acock, K. R. Allen, P. Dilworth-Anderson, and D. M. Klein. 2005. Theory and theorizing in family research: Puzzle building and puzzle solving. In *Sourcebook of family theory and research*, ed. V. L. Bengtson, A. C. Acock, K. R. Allen, P. Dilworth-Anderson, and D. M. Klein, 3–33. Thousand Oaks, CA: Sage Publications.

Burr, W. R. 1995. Using theories in family science. In *Research and theory in family science*, ed. R. D. Day, K. R. Gilbert, B. H. Settles, and W. R. Burr, 73–88. Pacific Grove, CA: Brooks-Cole.

Doherty, W. J., P. G. Boss, R. LaRossa, W. R. Schumm, and S. K. Steinmetz. 1993. Family theories and methods: A contextual approach. In *Sourcebook of family theories and methods: A contextual approach*, ed. P. G. Boss, W. J. Doherty, R. LaRossa, W. R. Schumm, and S. K. Steinmetz, 3–30. New York: Plenum.

Knapp, S. J. 2009. Critical theorizing: Enhancing theoretical rigor in family research. *Journal of Family Theory and Review* 1: 133–145.

Kuhn, T. S. 1970. *The structure of scientific revolutions* (2nd ed.). Chicago: Univ. of Chicago Press.

Murdock, G. P. 1949. *Social structure*. New York: Free Press.

Roberto, K. A., R. Blieszner, and K. R. Allen. 2006. Theorizing in family gerontology: New opportunities for research and practice. *Family Relations* 55: 513–525.

Sprey, J. (ed.) 1990. *Fashioning family theory*. Newbury Park, CA: Sage Publications.

White, J. M., and D. M. Klein. 2008. *Family theories* (3rd ed.). Thousand Oaks, CA: Sage Publications.

1

Symbolic Interactionism Theory

Keiko and Thanh are leaving the house to attend a cocktail party sponsored by Thanh's company. It's important that he be there because he's up for a big promotion this year and wants to make sure those in charge know who he is and can connect his face with his name, because his name is so unusual in the United States. Keiko is tired from working all day and taking care of the children's needs before they leave the house, so she is dreading the party. Thanh, however, is very excited.

They are greeted at the door by the company vice president and a very loud band. Thanh introduces his wife with pride and accepts champagne for both of them to sip as they mingle in the crowd. He is really in his element, speaking to everyone he passes, introducing his wife, and keeping his hand on the small of her back to make sure she feels comfortable and included. Because she doesn't know anyone there, he wants to make sure she is close so he can introduce her to everyone and make her feel like a part of the group. He is enjoying the music and expensive champagne and can't wait for the dancing to begin. Thanh says to his wife, "Isn't this the best party you've ever been to? And can you believe who is here—all the important people, and I've gotten to talk to all of them. I can't imagine a more perfect evening!"

As Keiko looks at him, he knows something is wrong. He asks, "Aren't you enjoying yourself?" She doesn't know what to say to him. The place is too loud and too crowded, and people are drinking way too much. She wonders how he can stand knowing that everyone he speaks to is judging both of them. And why does he have to be so controlling of her? Everywhere they go, he is right by her side, as if he does not trust her to go out on her own for fear she will say something that would make him look bad. It is one of the worst nights of her life! How can two people at the same party in the same place have such different opinions about what is going on?

So, who was right—was it the best party they had ever been to or a night of feeling controlled and judged? Was the party incredible or incredibly boring? The answer to those questions, according to symbolic interactionism, is that they are both right. People define situations based on their own personal experiences and sense of self. Thus, two people can be in the exact same situation and have different interpretations of what is going on. We'll learn more about this as we discuss this multifaceted and exciting theory.

HISTORY

Important Early Contributions

Of all the theories discussed in this text, symbolic interactionism has probably had the greatest impact on the study of families. Not only is this theory rich in history because it has been in use since the early 1900s, but it is still one of the most commonly used theoretical perspectives in the field today, perhaps because it continues to develop (Fine 1993). The longevity and popularity of this theory are due in part to its emphasis on a conceptual framework that is not only rich in content but also adaptable to any time period. Such success as a theory is also due to the fact that symbolic interactionism was uniquely born out of both qualitative and quantitative research (LaRossa and Reitzes 1993).

Unlike most theories, there is no one person who is most commonly associated with its development. Thus, there are many people whose work needs to be reviewed in order to fully understand the basic assumptions of this theory. Although who is covered in this section will vary from one writing to the next, this particular discussion is based on the guidance of LaRossa and Reitzes (1993).

Symbolic interactionism has its earliest roots in the United States in the pragmatic philosophers of the early 1900s, such as William James, John Dewey, Charles Pierce, and Josiah Royce (Vander Zanden 1987). Not only were these scholars themselves influential in the development of the theory, but perhaps more importantly, they trained their students, who in turn became the primary contributors to the assumptions and concepts that make this theory what it is today. The pragmatists did, however, contribute four important ideas that laid the foundation for the development of symbolic interactionism.

The first important contribution of the pragmatists was to view the world as something that was always changing, rather than as a static structure whose history was predetermined. Second, the pragmatists argued that social structure is not something that is fixed in time, but also something that is constantly changing and developing. Third, they were perhaps the first to suggest that meaning comes not from objects themselves, but rather from our interactions **with** objects. For example, the meaning of a table depends on the person who is viewing or using the table at the time. Finally, "they exhibited an ideological commitment to progress and to democratic values" (La Rossa and Reitzes 1993, 136) that could be advanced through science. Thus arose the notion that we could use research to figure out how societies and people grow and change, and how they do so within the confines of a democratic society that is always evolving.

These four ideas came about at a time in history when people were desperate for information about how the changing structure of society was going to affect them. This was the time of the industrial revolution, when people were going from working at home on the farm to working at the factory, which also meant moving from rural areas to urban areas closer to work (Mintz and Kellogg 1988). Certainly, all these changes left people feeling as though they had little or no control over their lives anymore, which also meant that they probably had little control over society. However, the ideas of symbolic interactionism allowed people to feel as if they gained back a little more of that control, because it was based on the idea that people are not victims of some predetermined course of history, but are instead able to change how things happen in society through communication and interaction (LaRossa and Reitzes 1993).

Not only did these ideas appeal to society in general, they were also accepted by scholars, because they were grounded in research. Symbolic interactionism provided the means by which to study social interactions in a scientific fashion. It was at this time that people began to study the family just as a scientist would study a specimen or an astronomer would study a constellation (LaRossa and Reitzes 1993). This empirical position is still appealing to researchers today and continues to be one of the greatest strengths of the theory (Burnier 2005).

Principal Scholars

As was previously stated, one thing that makes symbolic interactionism unique is that it is a combination of the efforts of many different researchers. Although there are many people who made important contributions to the development of this theory, we will focus on just a few: George Herbert Mead, Charles Horton Cooley, William Isaac Thomas, and Herbert Blumer.

George Herbert Mead. George Herbert Mead, whose primary contributions focused on the self, is probably the most recognized of all those who have influenced symbolic interactionism. He believed that we learn about ourselves through interactions with others that are based on gestures (Mead 1934/1956). A gesture can be thought of as any action that causes a response or reaction in another person. We can all think of certain finger gestures that are sure to create a response in others, but Mead used the term more broadly to include such things as language and facial expressions as well. We develop a sense of self-consciousness when we can anticipate how other people will respond to our gestures. Because of this, it takes interactions with others to fully develop a sense of self.

How does this process take place? Mead believed that there were two stages people follow to develop a sense of self. In the first, the *play stage*, the child tries to use gestures to practice the behaviors associated with different roles, such as that of mother, father, firefighter, or teacher (Vander Zanden 1987). For example, if you have ever watched preschool children play house, you have probably seen a girl imitate things she has seen her mother do, such as cooking dinner, changing a baby's diaper, or helping another child with homework. Boys, on the other hand, if they are in the dramatic play area of the preschool classroom at all, are likely to be doing such things as pretending to drive the family to an event or organizing a play activity for the children. While engaged in this dramatic play experience, children are able to imagine the attitudes of their parent or learn to take on the perspective of another person. During this stage, children usually assume the role of only one person at a time.

In the second stage, however, children begin to take on the perspectives of many people at one time and to see how the individual fits within that group (Mead

1934/1956). This is called the *game stage*, and you can use almost any childhood game as a good example. For instance, when you play soccer, you have to think about not only what you are doing on the field, or the purpose of your position, but also about what everyone else is doing on the field. Another good example is that of the family. During this stage, children can understand what each person's role in the family is, including their own, and how the behavior of one family member affects the interactions of other family members.

The final step in this process is being able to anticipate how one's behaviors affect not only those in our immediate environment, but also those in society at large. Mead (1934/1956) called this being able to take on the role of the "generalized other," which means understanding social norms and expectations so that one can guess how other people will react to a specific gesture or interaction. One example of this is the young man who nervously looks around as he purchases a pornographic magazine. Although he is of legal age, he has internalized the social perception that viewing pornography is lewd and engaged in only by sexual deviants. He is apprehensive that someone he knows will come into the store and see him buying the magazine, thus forming a bad opinion of him.

Finally, Mead (1934/1956) believed that the self is not a thing, but rather a process based on constant movement between the "I" and the "me." The "I" is the spontaneous acts in which we engage; these are unpredictable and unstable. The "me" (the social self), on the other hand, is those learned roles that are determined by interactions with others. In other words, the social self (or "me") is all of our learned experiences, whereas the "I" is our immediate reaction to situations. As Robinson (2007) suggested, the "I" is the response of the individual to the "me," which is a reflection of the social world in which we live and interact.

Charles Horton Cooley. Many of the researchers who developed symbolic interactionism focused on the self. For example, Charles Horton Cooley is perhaps best-known for his idea of the "looking-glass self," which is based on the premise that individuals think about how they appear to others, make a judgment about what the other person thinks about them, and then incorporate those ideas into their own concept of self (Longmore 1998). For this process to take place, we must interact with others. Cooley (1956) believed that most of this learning took place during face-to-face interactions with others, especially in small groups, which he called primary groups. What distinguishes a primary group from other people with whom we come into contact? We do not expect any self-gain or reward from interacting with those in our primary group (Beames 2005). The best example of a primary group is a family. Thus, it is in our families that we learn about ourselves, because families teach us about social expectations for behavior, what talents we may have, and many other thoughts and behaviors that come together to make up who we are.

William Isaac Thomas. So when did the concepts included in symbolic interactionism first start being used in family studies? Most believe it was when William Isaac Thomas and Florian Znaniecki wrote *The Polish Peasant in Europe and America* (1918–1920). This book was one of the first to state that the family has a role in the socialization process (LaRossa and Reitzes 1993). It pointed out that families construct their own realities, so that one's culture, or social structure, influences both family and individual behaviors.

Thomas is also well-known for coining the phrase *definition of the situation*, which is another foundation of symbolic interactionism. According to this idea, you cannot understand human behavior without also understanding the subjective perspectives of the people involved in the interaction. For example, parents are often faced with two siblings who carried on a conversation and then came to the parents for a "final ruling." It becomes obvious during the parents' conversations with each of the siblings that, although they were both a part of the same conversation, each one had a different interpretation of what was said by the end of the discussion. This is because each sibling's reaction to the conversation was based on his or her individual, subjective experience. Thomas took this idea further in what is called the Thomas theorem, which states that "if people define situations as real, they are real in their consequences" (LaRossa and Reitzes 1993, 140). Thus, each sibling in the conversation makes comments based on his or her own interpretation, making each person's subjective opinion valued. So, if they were to ask their parents, "Whose point of view is right?" then, according to Thomas, the parents' answer would be, "They both are because your point of view is based on your interpretation of the conversation, taking into account your own personal experience." This is probably not the answer the disagreeing siblings want to hear! The Thomas theorem also explains why Thanh thinks it's the best party he has ever attended, while Keiko wants to go home.

Herbert Blumer. Herbert Blumer was the first person to use the term *symbolic interactionism*. He is also credited with developing the three primary premises of symbolic interactionism, which are discussed below. Many people consider Blumer's name to be synonymous with symbolic interactionism (Fine 1993). Therefore, the influence of Herbert Blumer (1969) cannot be overlooked in a historical discussion of this theory.

BASIC ASSUMPTIONS

Most people who use symbolic interactionism rely on the three themes developed by Blumer (1969). However, LaRossa and Reitzes (1993) organized these themes around the seven basic assumptions of the theory, and we have followed that organizational structure here. All of these assumptions sprang from the idea that we understand and relate to our environment based on the symbols that we know or those that we learn.

First Overarching Theme

The first overarching theme (Blumer 1969) is that meaning is a central element of human behavior. This is best explained by reviewing the three assumptions that developed from this primary belief.

People will react to something according to the meaning that the thing has for them. In other words, people live in a symbolic environment and will respond to something based on their definition of that symbol. A cigarette, for example, is a symbol of relief and pleasure for one person and a "death stick" to another. Thus, the first person would pick up a cigarette and light it, whereas the second person would probably refuse it. How is this idea reflected in the vignette at the beginning of the chapter? Thanh was excited by the opportunity for networking that the party afforded. Keiko, on the other hand, was uncomfortable with all the drinking and "schmoozing," and so felt bored and excluded.

We learn about meaning through interactions with others. This assumption is drawn from the work of Allen and Doherty (1998). Although different researchers in this area have varying beliefs about the origins of meaning, most would agree that meaning is learned and processed through our social interactions. People make value judgments about which symbols are positive and negative, and react to them based on these values. *As people come into contact with different things and experiences, they interpret what is being learned.* In other words, people are both actors and reactors. We are not passive beings who simply respond to the world around us; instead, we are active beings who choose the parts of the environment to which we respond. So, if we enter a room in which we are uncomfortable, rather than simply standing there and feeling nervous, hoping that someone will come and talk to us, we can actively seek out someone we know and talk to them to put ourselves at ease. In this case, we are taking an active part in controlling our environment.

Second Overarching Theme

The second overarching theme has to do with our self-concept. Because humans are active social beings who interact with others based on their meaning of a situation, they must have a sense of self for this to take place.

A human infant is asocial. This means that infants are not born with predetermined ideas about whom they are, but rather develop these as they interact with people along the way. An example of this is the notion of the looking-glass self (Cooley 1956), which was discussed previously. A symbolic interactionist, then, would not say that a child has misbehaved because of a mischievous temperament, but rather that this child has learned and interpreted this behavior as a result of his or her interactions with the environment.

Once individuals develop a sense of self, this will provide motivation for future behavior. Because humans are reflexive, they will always reflect on what they experience and use this as a guide for future behavior. This process entails not only a sense of self but also a sense of how others view you. For example, people often respond to a situation based not only on their own beliefs and values but also on how they think others will perceive that behavior (whether positively or negatively). This reflexive process requires an understanding of the self as well as the "generalized other" discussed earlier. For example, a group of college students who took part in a ten-week expedition to Ghana found themselves not only more self-aware after the experience, but also more comfortable interacting with people they did not know as a result of both this new self-awareness and the experience itself (Beames 2005).

Third Overarching Theme

The final overarching theme moves from a discussion of the self to a discussion of society. Whereas the previous themes and their underlying assumptions have focused on more individual aspects, this theme is based on the idea that infants are not born into a social vacuum. Instead, the environment of an infant has symbols and values that were assigned at birth. One only has to go into a nursery to see an example of this. If the room is decorated in pink and filled with dolls, what do we assume? We presume, of course, that the infant is a girl. Parents have often used the color pink and dolls as symbols of what is feminine or as an example of the types of things infant girls should come to value.

Individuals are influenced by society. Individuals are influenced not only by their own self-concepts, and the values, symbols, and beliefs of their families, but also by the cultural norms and values of the society in which they live. Perhaps the changing nature of fathering behaviors best exemplifies this. Whereas just a generation ago it was unusual for men to show physical affection to their children, it is now commonplace in today's families. This is because of the changing societal expectations for fathers, which state that both parents should show their children they love them, not only with words but also with actions such as hugs (Smith 1996).

People learn the rules and values of society through everyday interactions within that culture. What is the best way to learn about life in Japan? Although it is helpful prior to a visit to a country to read about their cultural norms, so you do not begin your visit offending people, the best way to learn about Japanese individuals and families is to spend some time living among them. You can learn many things during common daily experiences that can never be taught in a book.

PRIMARY TERMS AND CONCEPTS

There are numerous terms and concepts associated with this theory, many of which have been covered within the previous discussion. Terms commonly associated with symbolic interactionism include, but are not limited to, symbols, interaction, gestures, social norms, rituals, roles, salience, identities, social act, and definition of the situation. Some of these are covered below.

Symbols

The title of this theory combines two terms that are of utmost importance: symbols and interaction. Anything can be thought of as a symbol, with language being the most powerful example (Flint 2006). Symbols are the products of social interaction. This means that we are not free to use symbols in any way we choose. Rather, their meanings are given to us by the ways we see others using them. Thus, the meaning of a symbol in one situation may not be the same in a different situation. For example, how often have you seen professional basketball players swat each other on the buttocks as they come off the court for a timeout? Now, what if you saw a man and woman walking down the street, and the man reached over and swatted the woman on her buttocks? Does the action of slapping the person on the buttocks represent the same thing in each of these situations? Obviously, it does not. We would assume in the basketball example that it is symbolic of encouragement or praise, whereas it might be evidence of intimacy in the example of the couple on the street. How you define the symbol is based on the context of the situation or the current environment, and it is something you learn from interacting with others in this environment.

Interaction

It is difficult to talk about the word *symbols* without also talking about *interaction*, as the two terms are dependent upon each other. Interaction, therefore, is a social behavior between two or more people during which some type of communication takes place, causing each person to react to the situation and, as a result, modify his or her behavior (Burr et al.1979). This communication can be verbal, but it can also be nonverbal.

Gestures

Gestures, a good example of nonverbal communication, are acts that represent something else (Vander Zanden 1987). We all know some popular, and some not so popular, hand gestures that are used in the United States, such as touching the thumb and forefinger together in a circle to represent that something is OK. These gestures and symbols are meaningless if there is not someone around to interpret and react to them, thus making interaction a necessary part of socialization. Think about the gesture Thanh makes in the vignette at the beginning of the chapter, placing his hand on the small of Keiko's back. What does that gesture mean to each of them?

Social Norms

If interactions with others teach us what symbols and gestures mean, this also means that interactions teach us appropriate social norms. Social norms can be defined as expectations about how to act in a given situation. Is your behavior with your friends the same when you are with your parents as it is when you are alone together? A good guess would be that your behavior changes in each of those situations, based on what are appropriate interactions for each of those environments. Interactions with each of these groups, our parents and our friends, teach us what behaviors are acceptable and when, and we adapt our behavior based on the social norms followed within each situation.

Rituals

These ideas come together in families in the form of rituals. For example, think about how your family celebrates holidays such as Thanksgiving. Many of us have elaborate rituals, such as who sits where at the table, who carves the turkey, and whether or not a prayer is said before the meal and, if so, who says the prayer, and so on. Do you eat your big meal in the afternoon or evening? Who does the cooking? Who does the clean-up? What happens after the meal? Each family has its own social norms for how they interact with each other during holidays and which symbols and gestures are an appropriate part of those rituals. Problems can arise when individuals marry and try to negotiate which rituals will be carried out in the new married couple's household, because people often enter into marriage assuming that their own family's traditions will be continued. Thus, it is a good idea to talk about this before marriage, so a couple can decide which behaviors to adopt.

Roles

Another thing that can influence our behavior in any social situation is our self-defined role. A role is a set of social norms for a specific situation, or a "part." Think about actors in a play, each playing a character or a role. The same is true for each of us in life. What are some of the roles you play? Perhaps you are a son or daughter, brother or sister, roommate, athlete, or even a husband or wife. Are the expectations for each of these roles the same? Not only do the expectations differ across roles, they can also differ across people who have the same role. For example, all of you reading this book right now are probably doing so not because of an interest in family theories, but because it was assigned to you in one of your courses in your role as a student. Some people think that the role of a student is to read assigned chapters prior to class, participate in class discussions, study for exams, and complete assignments on time. Others, however, see their role of student as enjoying an active social life, perhaps playing a sport, attending class when it is convenient, and completing assignments when they have time. For still others, the role of student means attending class and completing assignments when time permits after working a forty-hour week and taking care of a family as well. The bottom line is that each person defines for him- or herself what is appropriate behavior for each role that he or she plays.

Salience

So how do you decide which of your roles is most important, or which one is going to receive the most of your time? According to Stryker (1968), we divide our time among each of our roles based on the amount of salience that role has in our lives. The more salient or important a role is to us, the more time we invest in that role. In the previous example, the first student described probably sees his or her role as student as the most salient at the moment, meaning he or she identifies most with the role of a student and will perform those tasks associated with that role first. A student might not go home on a long weekend to see his parents, for example, in order to finish a big paper due the following week at school. One possible explanation for this is that he sees his role as student as more important **right now**, or more salient, than his role as a son.

Although each individual defines for him- or herself the behaviors associated with a role, there are also social norms or expectations for roles. This does not mean, however, that roles are static—we have evidence in many family roles that they do indeed change over time (LaRossa and Reitzes 1993). Perhaps the best examples of this are the roles of mothers and fathers. Although traditionally dads were primarily responsible for the financial support of the family, and mothers were responsible for the care of the house and children, this has been changing in today's society as more women enter the workforce and more men become highly involved fathers. This is true even for nonresidential fathers, as Sano, Smith, and Lanigan (2011) found that role saliency was an important determinant of presence and level of father involvement for those men too. Therefore, roles help us anticipate or predict behavior, but we must never forget that they are also both individual and social constructions.

Because the idea of roles is easy to discern in families, and thought by many scholars to be of utmost importance, an entire theory has emerged based on the concept that families interact based on the assignment of roles. For example, historically males performed the "instrumental role"—being the financial provider for the family—while females performed the "expressive role"—taking care of the house and children (Parsons and Bales 1955). This notion came under attack by feminist scholars, who asserted that it did not account for the role of power and inequality in gendered or socially constructed relationships (Osmond and Thorne 1993). Thus, although role theory is still used today in many ways to discuss the various roles that individuals play within families, it has also changed from its original form to include more modern notions of families.

Identity

Those roles that are most salient for us are also those that most likely define our identities. There are several points to take into consideration here. First, this is a mental process in that our mental events determine our behaviors. Once we have figured out what something means, we use that definition to determine our future behaviors. This determination is made based on its relevance to our identity. Thus, those roles that are most salient to us, or that best identify who we think we are, are given priority in our lives; it is those interactions in which we choose most often to engage and indeed at which we most often attempt to excel (McCall and Simmons 1978).

It is here where we come full circle in our discussion of this theory. Socialization begins with the individual, who is born asocial. Humans begin to learn about their environment, and themselves, through interactions with others, including family, friends, and school. These environments are symbolic representations of meaning. In other words, we are born into a culture and thus must learn what the social norms of a culture are through interactions with others in the same culture. Through this process, people learn about themselves and others, and we learn not only which roles and behaviors are deemed most socially acceptable but also those that best represent each of us as an individual. This helps us decide which roles are most salient to us, or which roles best form our sense of identity. This in turn influences our future interactions with others, as we interpret our own behaviors, and those of others, based on these beliefs. Because of this, some people respond to one thing in a situation, while others in the same situation respond to something entirely different. Our world is, after all, socially constructed.

COMMON AREAS OF RESEARCH AND APPLICATION

There are many areas of research that have used the concepts and assumptions of symbolic interactionism, beginning with the work of the early founders previously discussed. Although some have suggested that symbolic interactionism showed a drop in usage in the 1960s and 1970s (Fine 1993), its use since that time, and even recently, is widely evident. For example, it was used as the theoretical framework for dissertations on topics such as how female rugby players define themselves based on their experiences with, and definitions of, aggression (Baird 2011); how Aboriginal students define their identity (Barnes 2011); how African American men who are leaders of student groups primarily composed of White males create meanings of these experiences (Frazier 2010); and how choosing a simple lifestyle affects how people see themselves and how they present themselves to society (Fox 2010). In addition to being used by developing scholars in this field, this theory is also being used widely today outside of family studies, in fields such as marketing, which uses it to assesses the meanings that products have for consumers (Flint 2006); social work, which uses it to inform their practices across all systems (Forte 2004); forest management, which has used it to assess what nearby wildfires mean to residents (Paveglio, Carroll, Absher, and Robinson 2001); and by the parks service to determine what park visits mean to people and how these perceptions are based on people's own social realities (Jordan et al. 2009).

This section will be organized by using the three overarching themes of symbolic interactionism. Although this review will not be exhaustive, as there has been a great deal of research that has drawn from various aspects of the theory, examples of recent research within each of those assumptions will be reviewed.

Meaning Is a Central Element of Human Behavior

Think about the first overarching theme we discussed, which states that meaning is an important element of human behavior that cannot be overlooked. There was a good deal of research based on this concept in the last several years in the areas of parenting, marriage, identity development, and technology. How people parent, and what defines good parenting, obviously differs from one parent to the next. Sano, Richards, and Zvonkovic (2008) looked at this issue with regard to whether or not rural mothers are gatekeepers when it comes to the involvement of low-income nonresidential fathers. They suggest that parents, whether they live together or not, often disagree on what it means to be a good parent. Thus, perhaps mothers perceive fathers to be incompetent simply because they have differing opinions of what it means to be an effective, involved parent. This disagreement leads them to want to limit the amount of time nonresidential fathers spend with their children, which can be thought of as gatekeeping.

Single parenting was examined from a different angle by Doherty and Craft (2011), who studied how mothers are able to provide "male-positive" attitudes toward men when nonresidential fathers are not involved in their children's lives. They provide examples of messages that mothers can use when talking with their children about both their own fathers and other men in general that are based on a male-positive attitude. These messages help children attribute positive meanings to fathers and men, rather than negative ones, which is important for their future interactions with men both personally and professionally. Interestingly, these authors also suggest that we tend to confuse the term *marital status* with *parental status*, which neglects the fact that some women choose to parent without being married.

Similar to that dichotomy, Cohen and Kuvalanka (2011) studied how women in lesbian couples socialize their children about sexuality because, for them, sex and reproduction are two different entities, much as for single moms, parenting and marital status are separate entities. They found that lesbian mothers use the framework of family diversity to have discussions about sexuality with their children; this allows them to present a wide range of arrangements that can constitute a family. Partners were found to participate equally in the sharing of information about reproduction, sexual orientation, and sex, but were also found to share the information in different ways. Thus, these interactions were guided by the meanings of those words for individual participants, and the conversations were built upon how the meanings of the words differed based on family structure.

One family structure often studied is that of a married couple. Curran, Utley, and Muraco (2010) used a symbolic interactionist perspective to study what marriage means to African Americans. They refer to marriage as a symbol and posit that people enter into marriages with preconceived notions of the meaning of that symbol based on their past experiences and interactions within society. Their sample of 31 African Americans in this exploratory study suggested that marriage is a symbol of commitment, love, partnership/friendship, trust, family, and covenant. Based on their meanings of marriage, participants had positive attitudes toward the symbol of marriage.

The Self

The second overarching theme was more focused on the development of the self. This section will focus on the role of the self in technology, identity development, and perceptions of self. Recent research exploring the role of the self when communicating online suggests that the development of the "I" and the "me" as described by Mead (1934/1956) exists online just as it does offline. Venues such as blogs, MySpace, and eBay's "all about me" pages allow individuals to react to people and environments in cyberspace (the "I") while learning cyber social rules and norms (the "me"). Because of the fast-paced and fluid nature of the online environment, the "I" is constantly redefined as it interacts with the "me" (Robinson 2007). Furthermore, Hogan (2011) found that online tools such as Facebook allow individuals to present an idealized version of self, as they choose what **is** and what **is not** shared as a representation of that self. Additional research on online social relationships suggests that developing a socially constructed sense of community is desired, whether this is done online or offline (Fernbeck 2007). Thus, some people are using the online community as a means of developing the sense of community that they are missing offline. Oksman and Turtianinen (2004) found the same to be true for the use of text messaging in their sample of Finnish teenagers, adding that these online communities are perhaps an important new form of social communities and networks.

People form opinions of themselves based on their interactions with others and how they believe they appear to others. Two diverse studies used this notion to explore how girls/women developed their senses of self. Anderson (2009) looked at how adolescent girls who are disabled used participation in sports to help them develop an identity of which they were proud: that of being an athlete. They were also able to use athletic interactions with others to further their positive self identities outside of the arena of sports. Alarid and Vega (2010) looked at an entirely different population and assessed how women who are incarcerated developed their identities. They found that these women tended to have two reference groups: those who had also been incarcerated and those who had not. The group they were with determined what their identity was, or how they viewed themselves. Thus, how other women saw her affected the way each woman saw herself and affected her identity development.

Finally, how we see ourselves, or our perception of self, can influence our behaviors in many ways. Briscoe and Lavender (2009) found that female asylum seekers and refugees who sought maternity care were greatly affected by their experiences prior to coming to the United States. These experiences shaped their beliefs about themselves, their interactions with health care workers, and their senses of self as someone worthy of medical attention. Similarly, women's experiences with illness, their perceptions of their ability to overcome a cancer diagnosis, and their beliefs about their futures affect how women respond to a diagnosis of gynecological cancer (Roberts and Clarke 2009). Thus, it is important for medical professionals in various fields to realize the importance of the role of the self in treating patients.

The Role of Culture in Social Interactions

The final overarching theme focused on the role of society. We have already said that a sense of self affects medical care, but it's also true that a society's beliefs about medical issues can make a difference. For example, Garcia and Saewyc (2007) studied how immigrant Mexican adolescents viewed health care, especially with regard to mental illness. It was found that, although these adolescents mentioned accessing formal health care for a multitude of problems, they did not mention seeking formal assistance to deal with mental health problems. It is believed this is because of the cultural perception of mental health as being the result of personal behaviors and beliefs, including participating in religiously focused activities. Thus, they would not seek help for this from a formal health care provider, but perhaps they would from a folk healer. Similarly, Yen and colleagues (2010) studied mothers in Taiwan who were caring for adolescent children with schizophrenia. This culture has similar beliefs about the causes of mental illness, including the role of ancestry and inheritance, which can affect the caregiver's reasons for offering care, as well as their feelings of responsibility for the condition, and thus the care of the adolescents.

Finally, culture can determine how we treat other people and our perceptions of when someone has reached adulthood. Dinkha (2010) studied Asian women who were teaching at a university in Kuwait and found that they faced discrimination, such as having their authority challenged, having students be disrespectful toward them, being victims of stereotypes, and not being supported in the academic community by their peers. This was believed to be because students did not treat these professors as professionals, but rather treated them as women of Asian descent, who did not fit the cultural norms of their society. Similarly, Rankin and Kenyon (2008) found that cultures define when someone has entered adulthood differently based on their own social markers. Thus, how people are treated depends on the society of which they are a part, and whether or not they follow the norms of that society.

Methodological Issues

Although some believe Blumer suggested that it is hard to empirically validate this theory because of the difficulty of studying human social life in general, his work seems to suggest that he addressed this problem by using a naturalistic approach (Athens 2010; Hammersley 2010). Assuming we agree that it is possible to study human social life, a final strength of symbolic interactionism that has led to its continued use is its acceptance of both qualitative and quantitative methodologies. This means that researchers are not limited to one means of data collection, such as giving people a survey to find out how they feel about a certain topic. This theory also supports the use of observations, interviews, and, as you would guess, interactions with others to gain a deeper understanding of how people come to define their realities. The use of ethnographies is another example that has gained popularity within this theoretical perspective (Manning 2009). Thus, its history is rich with people who have used a variety of methods to determine what makes individuals and families interact as they do.

CRITIQUE

Although symbolic interactionism has been used for many decades, there are obviously those who have concerns about the theory and its usage. We will review some of the most common criticisms of this theory below. Keep in mind during this discussion that these comments are often directed toward individuals who are using ideas from symbolic interactionism, rather than the entire theory in general.

Stryker (1980) provided a summary of the criticisms of this theory, a few of which will be reviewed here. First, some people found the key concepts confusing because they are difficult to define and thus difficult to test with research. However, as both LaRossa and Reitzes (1993) and Stryker (1987) noted, there has been a plethora of work in this area over the last several decades to address this problem. Thus, although this perhaps was true at the time of Stryker's original writing, it is no longer as valid today.

A related criticism is that the ideas and concepts of individual scholars in this field have not been combined into one central theory. In other words, whereas most theories have a basic set of assumptions, lists of concepts, and organized guidelines, some believe this does not exist in the same sense for symbolic interactionism. Some authors have attempted to develop these theories, but there is no agreement as there is with other theories covered in this text. Thus, for some scholars, symbolic interactionism does in fact have specific guidelines and assumptions, but for others these are not well-developed enough to meet their needs; it depends on one's school of thought. Furthermore, although some scholars see this ambiguity as an asset, because it allows them to pick and choose among the various concepts relevant to their particular research, many would say this is indeed a flaw within the theory in general. This makes it difficult to describe the theory to others in a logical fashion and test its central tenets, because they are so diverse.

Stryker's (1980) third criticism is that symbolic interactionism does not give enough attention to either the importance of emotions or the role of the unconscious. Although few would argue with this statement in a general sense, there are some aspects of this theory that do, in fact, address this issue. Cooley (1956), for example, stated that people have feelings about themselves, or emotions, that drive the looking-glass self. Similarly, recently researchers have started to study the role of emotions in many individual and family contexts using the basic assumptions of symbolic interactionism. Thus, although this criticism holds true for many aspects of this theory, it does not for others.

A fourth criticism, offered by researchers such as Goffman (1974), is that symbolic interactionism places too much emphasis on the ability of individuals to create their own realities and doesn't pay enough attention to the fact that we live in a world that we do not create by ourselves. For example, even though you can spend a lot of time researching how individuals feel about and cope with being removed from their families and sent far away to war, the bottom line is that soldiers must still endure a hostile environment, and their families must still deal with the absence of a loved one. The point to remember from this is that, although concepts such as the definition of a situation are valid and important, one cannot neglect an assessment of the physical realities of the environment as well.

Similarly, Stryker noted in his 1987 writing that the role of power is often neglected in the use of symbolic interactionism. For example, two people can interpret the same situation in different ways, but in any social and political environment, it is likely that one of those people holds more power than the other. Stryker suggests that this point is often neglected in the framework of symbolic interactionism. Athens (2009) reviewed the role of power and domination in human group life and expressed the belief that, while the historical fathers of this theory did address dominance in their writings, they also ignored the role of power.

A current criticism of this theory is its lack of attention to the role of biology. Although there are some scholars who attempt to address the genetic inheritance factor within this framework, as a general rule, symbolic interactionists are more concerned with biology only as it pertains to cognition, which in turn influences social interactions (LaRossa and Reitzes 1993).

Finally, it is best to think of symbolic interactionism as a framework for organizing or influencing research, rather than as a completely integrated theory in and of itself. Although there are obviously some problems with this approach, symbolic interactionism has some valid capabilities that have contributed to its duration in the field. One important capability is its capacity to grow and change with the times, meaning that it is just as applicable today as it was when it began in the 1920s. Another capability of the theory is its focus on family interactions and the roles that individuals play in those social acts. In other words, one cannot look at any situation as being static, but rather must recognize that each person in a situation is viewing things from his or her own perspective and acting with the hope of influencing the outcome of the interaction. Finally, symbolic interactionism reminds us that we are all social beings, playing roles and learning from each other.

APPLICATION

Now that we have covered symbolic interactionism in its entirety and evaluated its strengths and weaknesses, let's see how well you understand this theory by answering some questions about the married couple in the vignette at the beginning of this chapter, and your own lives.

1. Using the concepts and language of symbolic interactionism, explain how the spouses could have such different opinions about the cocktail party they attended.

2. Think about what roles you play. Make a list of them and the behaviors and responsibilities of each of those roles. Which of those roles is most salient for you? How does this influence your behavior?

3. Describe a situation you have been in recently that was similar to the one described at the beginning of this chapter. What was the specific setting? How did you react to the situation? How did the other people involved respond? How did your identity influence your behavior in this situation?

4. What are the social norms for the college or university you attend? How are these norms similar to or different from those of your family? How did you discover what those social norms were? How did you respond initially? List the ways in which your behavior has changed as a result of these social norms and your interactions with others within the college environment.

5. Explain how the concepts of the "I" and the "me" are exemplified in the sample reading that follows. Then, explain how the "generalized other" is used in the reading.

REFERENCES

Alarid, L. F., and O. L. Vega, 2010. Identity construction, self perceptions, and criminal behavior of incarcerated women. *Deviant Behavior* 31(8): 704–728.

Allen, W. D., and W. J. Doherty. 1998. "Being there." The perception of fatherhood among a group of African-American adolescent fathers. In *Resiliency in African-American families*, ed. H. I. McCubbin, E. A. Thompson, A. I. Thompson, and J. A. Futrell, 207–244. Thousand Oaks, CA: Sage.

Anderson, D. 2009. Adolescent girls' involvement in disability sport: Implications for identity development. *Journal of Sport and Social Issues* 33(4): 427–449.

Athens, D. 2009. The roots of "radical interactionism." *Journal for the Theory of Social Behavior* 39(4): 387–414.

Athens, L. 2010. Naturalistic inquiry in theory and practice. *Journal of Contemporary Ethnography* 39(1): 87–125.

Baird, S. M. 2011. Who do you think you are? Constructing self/identity in women's rugby through aggression, control and unacceptable behavior. Ph.d. Diss. *Dissertation Abstracts International, B: Sciences and Engineering,* 71(7): 4536.

Barnes, B. G. 2011. Native students' identity in higher education: Merging, emerging or struggling. Ph.d. Diss. *Dissertation Abstracts International, A: The Humanities and Social Sciences* 71(8): 3015.

Beames, S. 2005. Expeditions and the social construction of the self. *Australian Journal of Outdoor Education* 9(1): 14–22.

Blumer, H. 1969. *Symbolic interactionism: Perspective and method.* Englewood Cliffs, NJ: Prentice-Hall.

Briscoe, L., and T. Lavender. 2009. Exploring maternity care for asylum seekers and refugees. *British Journal of Midwifery* 17(1): 17–24.

Burnier, D. 2005. Making it meaningful: Postmodern public administration and symbolic interactionism. *Administrative Theory & Praxis* 27(3): 498–517.

Burr, W., G. K. Leigh, R. D. Day, and J. Constantine. 1979. Symbolic interaction and the family. In *Contemporary theories about the family*, ed. W. R. Burr, R. Hill, F. I. Nye, and I. I. Reiss. Vol. 2, 42–111. New York: Free Press.

Cohen, R., and K. A. Kuvalanka. 2011. Sexual socialization in lesbian-parent families: An exploratory analysis. *American Journal of Orthopsychiatry* 81(2): 293–305.

Cooley, C. H. 1956. *Social organization.* Glencoe, IL: Free Press.

Curran, M. A., E. A. Utley, and J. A. Muraco. 2010. An exploratory study of the meaning of marriage for African Americans. *Marriage and Family Review* 46(5): 346–365.

Dinkha, J. 2010. Cultural influences affecting Asian women teaching in Kuwait: An analysis of five case studies. *Psychology Journal* 7(1): 31–40.

Doherty, W. J., and S. M. Craft. 2011. Single mothers raising children with "male-positive" attitudes. *Family Process* 50(1): 63–76.

Fernbeck, J. 2007. Beyond the diluted community concept: A symbolic interactionist perspective on online social relations. *New Media Society* 9(1): 49–69.

Fine, G. A. 1993. The sad demise, mysterious disappearance, and glorious triumph of symbolic interactionism. *Annual Review of Sociology* 19: 61–87.

Flint, D. J. 2006. Innovation, symbolic interaction and customer valuing: Thoughts stemming from a service-dominant logic of marketing. *Marketing Theory* 6(3): 349–362.

Forte, J. A. 2004. Symbolic interactionism and social work: A forgotten legacy. Part 2, *Families in Society* 85(4): 521–531.

Fox, J. A. 2010. Voluntary Simplicity and its effects on personal identity, family life, and relationships. *Masters Diss. Masters Abstracts International*, 48(1): 0208.

Frazier, T. L. 2010. African American college men holding leadership roles in majority White student groups. Ph.d. Diss. *Dissertation Abstracts International, A: The Humanities and Social Sciences* 70(7):2409.

Garcia, C. M., and E. M. Saewyc. 2007. Perceptions of mental health among recently immigrated Mexican adolescents. *Issues in Mental Health Nursing* 28: 37–54.

Goffman, E. 1974. *Frame analysis: An essay on the organization of experience*. New York: Harper and Row.

Hammersley, M. 2010. The case of the disappearing dilemma: Herbert Bumer on sociological method. *History of the Human Sciences* 23(5): 70–90.

Hogan, B. 2011. The presentation of self in the age of social media: Distinguishing performances and exhibitions online. *Bulletin of Science, Technology & Society* 30(6): 377–386.

Jordan, D. J., A. Cox, T. Thompson, J. H. Jeon, I. Palacios, A. Patterson, J. Peel, and K. A. Henderson. 2009. An exploration of the meanings of parks in Oklahoma. *Journal of Park and Recreation Administration* 27(2): 17–32.

LaRossa, R., and D. C. Reitzes. 1993. Symbolic interactionism and family studies. In *Sourcebook of family theories and methods: A contextual approach*, ed. P. G. Boss, W. J. Doherty, R. LaRossa, W. R. Schumm, and S. K. Steinmetz, 135–163. New York: Plenum Press.

Manning, P. 2009. Three models of ethnographic research: Wacquant as risk-taker. *Theory and Psychology* 19(6): 756–777.

McCall, G. J., and J. L. Simmons. 1978. *Identities and interactions: An examination of human associations in everyday life*. Rev. ed. New York: Free Press.

Mead, G. H. 1934/1956. *On social psychology: Selected papers*. ed. A. Strauss. Chicago: Univ. of Chicago Press.

Mintz, S., and S. Kellogg. 1988. *Domestic revolutions: A social history of American family life*. New York: Free Press.

Oksman, V., and J. Turtianen. 2004. Mobile communication as a social stage: Meanings of mobile communication in everyday life among teenagers in Finland. *New Media Society* 6: 319–339.

Osmond, M. W., and B. Thorne. 1993. Feminist theories: The social construction of gender in families and society. In *Sourcebook of family theories and methods: A contextual approach*, ed. P. G. Boss, W. J. Doherty, R. LaRossa, W. R. Schumm, and S. K. Steinmetz, 591–623. New York: Plenum Press.

Parsons, T., and R. Bales, eds. 1955. *Family, socialization, and interaction process*. Glencoe, IL: Free Press.

Paveglio, T., M. S. Carroll, J. Absher, and W. Robinson. 2011. Symbolic meaning of wildland fire: A study of residents in the US Inland Northwest. *Society and Natural Resources* 24(1): 18–33.

Rankin, L., and D. Kenyon. 2008. Demarcating role transitions as indicators of adulthood in the 21st century: Who are they? *Journal of Adult Development* 15(2): 87–92.

Roberts, K., and C. Clarke. 2009. Future disorientation following gynaecological cancer: Women's conceptualization of risk after a life threatening illness. *Health, Risk and Society* 11(4): 353–366.

Robinson, L. 2007. The cyberself: The self-ing project goes online, symbolic interaction in the digital age. *New Media Society* 9(1): 93–110.

Sano, Y., L. N. Richards, and A. M. Zvonkovic. 2008. Are mothers really "Gatekeepers" of children? Rural mothers' perceptions of nonresident fathers' involvement in low income families. *Journal of Family Issues* 29(12): 1707–1723.

Sano, Y., S. R. Smith, and J. Lanigan. 2011. Predicting presence and level of nonresident fathers' involvement in infants' lives: Mother's perspectives. *Journal of Divorce & Remarriage* 52: 1–19.

Smith, S. R. 1996. A qualitative investigation of how men come to define themselves as fathers. Ph.D. Diss., University of Georgia, Athens.

Stryker, S. 1968. Identity salience and role performance: The relevance of symbolic interaction theory for family research. *Journal of Marriage and the Family* 30: 558–564.

———. 1980. *Symbolic interactionism: A social structural version*. Menlo Park, CA: Benjamin/ Cummings.

———. 1987. The vitalization of symbolic interactionism. *Social Psychology Quarterly* 50(1): 83–94.

Thomas, W. I., and F. Znaniecki. 1918–1920. *The Polish peasant in Europe and America*. Vol. 5. Boston: Badger.

Vander Zanden, J. W. 1987. *Social psychology*. 4th ed. New York: Random House.

Yen, W., C. Teng, X. Huang, W. Ma, S. Lee, and H. Tseng. 2010. A theory of meaning of caregiving for parents of mentally ill children in Taiwan: A qualitative study. *Journal of Clinical Nursing* 19(1/2): 259–265.

SAMPLE READING

Klunklin, A., and J. Greenwood. 2006. Symbolic interactionism in grounded theory studies: Women surviving with HIV/AIDS in rural northern Thailand. *Journal of the Association of Nurses in AIDS Care* 17(5): 32–41.

This article is about wives and widows in rural northern Thailand who were diagnosed with HIV/AIDS, and how the social construction of the disease in this country impacted them in negative ways. In Thailand, it is seen as a dirty disease that is highly contagious, and people with HIV/AIDS are avoided at all costs. Because of this, they focus on being clean and covered at all times. The stigma also affects family members of the person with the diagnosis. For instance, women often travel long distances to put their children in a school where the mother's diagnosis is not known. This reading addresses some of the issues covered in this chapter, such as the role of the generalized other and the "I" and "me" components of the self.

SAMPLE READING

Symbolic Interactionism in Grounded Theory Studies: Women Surviving with HIV/AIDS in Rural Northern Thailand

Areewan Klunklin, PhD, RN
Jennifer Greenwood, RN, RM, DipN, RNT, DipEd, MEd, PhD

Although it is generally acknowledged that symbolic interactionism and grounded theory are connected, the precise nature of their connection remains implicit and unexplained. As a result, many grounded theory studies are undertaken without an explanatory framework. This in turn results in the description rather than the explanation of data determined. In this report, the authors make explicit and explain the nature of the connections between symbolic interactionism and grounded theory research. Specifically, they make explicit the connection between Blumer's methodological principles and processes and grounded theory methodology. In addition, the authors illustrate the explanatory power of symbolic interactionism in grounded theory using data from a study of the HIV/AIDS experiences of married and widowed Thai women.

Keywords: symbolic interactionism, grounded theory, HIV/AIDS in Thailand, HIV/AIDS in women

It is generally acknowledged that symbolic interactionism and grounded theory are connected (Benoliel, 1996; Strauss & Corbin, 1990), but the precise nature of such connections remains implicit and unexplained. In this report, the authors make explicit and explain these connections. First, they make explicit the connection between Blumer's (1969) methodological principle of direct examination of the social world and the methodological components of grounded theory. Second, the authors make explicit the connections between Blumer's methodological processes of exploration (depiction) and inspection (analysis) and constant comparative analysis, theoretical sampling, and the development and validation of codes, categories, and theories. Third, using data

Areewan Klunklin, PhD, RN, is in the Faculty of Nursing at Chiang Mai University, Thailand.

Jennifer Greenwood, RN, RM, DipN, RNT, DipEd, MEd, PhD, is adjunct professor of nursing at James Cook University, Edmonton, Alberta, Canada.17, No. 5, September/October 2006, 32–41.

derived from a symbolic interactionist grounded theory study into the HIV/AIDS experiences of married and widowed northern Thai women, the authors show the utility of symbolic interactionism as an explanatory framework in grounded theory.

Symbolic interactionism allowed the authors to explain rather than merely describe the relationship of the preemptive strategies used by participants to avoid hurtful discrimination and the distancing strategies used by noninfected people to protect themselves from potential infection. In addition, symbolic interactionism reminded the authors, with considerable force, of the importance of symbolic meaning in social life and that symbolic meaning attaches to differential value systems rather than to social facts, events, and actions per se.

SYMBOLIC INTERACTIONISM

The theoretical basis for grounded theory is derived from the social psychological theory of symbolic interactionism (Benoliel, 1996; Chenitz & Swanson, 1986; Holloway & Wheeler, 1996; Morse & Field, 1996; Stern, 1994), which is a theory of human group life and human conduct (Blumer, 1969). Symbolic interactionism and its related research methods were developed at the University of Chicago School of Sociology between 1920 and 1950. Symbolic interactionism constituted a challenge to the "hegemony of functionalism" (Bowers, 1988; p. 33).

Functionalism views the social world as a whole unit or system composed of interrelating, functioning parts. Parts are generated and adapted based on their functional utility to the whole. Analysis of parts (e.g., individual roles, social groups, and organizations) is significant only in relation to their consequences for the whole. Individuals learn or internalize their functional expectations (roles) through socialization; individuals are determined, therefore, rather than determining (Merton, 1973).

Researchers in the functionalist tradition frame their studies on the functionalist theory of social life; in other words, they begin with a theoretical framework, posing their research questions or problems in terms of the theoretical framework. These questions or problems are then converted into hypotheses, and a study is designed to test these hypotheses (Blumer, 1969). Theories in the functionalist tradition, therefore, are hypotheticodeductively derived from grand theories that are logically derived (what researchers now term *armchair theorizing*).

Social interactionism, a "barbaric neologism" first coined by Blumer in 1937 (Blumer, 1969, p. 1) differs substantially from functionalism in both theoretical perspective and research methods. Symbolic interactionism is theoretically focused on the acting individual; the individual is regarded as determining rather than determined and society is constructed through the purposive interactions of individuals and groups. The theories of symbolic interactionism are empirically and (primarily) inductively derived. The central concepts of symbolic interactionism include the self, the world, and social action (Charon, 1995).

The Self

The self is constructed through social interaction, first with significant others (i.e., those directly responsible for socialization) such as mother, father, and then others in progressively widening social circles. Significant others are important to self-concept because of their confirmatory and validitory feedback on actions and responses (de Laine, 1997). Through interaction with people more generally, the attitudes of the wider community are internalized as the "generalized other," and these interactions then function as an instrument of the self's social control. Religious systems, the legal system, and social norms are elements out of which the generalized other is constituted (de Laine, 1997). Such systems or norms are historical creations linked to contemporary situations; they are therefore subject to social change (de Laine, 1997). For instance, community attitudes to HIV infection change as the community's HIV-related knowledge increases.

Self identity emerges in and through social interaction and is modified as definitions of self, the other, and the situations encountered change (de Laine, 1997). The self is composed of two components, the "I" and the "Me" (Mead, 1934). The I is the active, dynamic interpreting component of the self; it is the reflector, interpreting cues and synthesizing them with the other components of the self. The I relates cues to components of the Me (Bowers, 1988).

The Me is the object of self-reflection, which can be defined to "myself" and others. It is the object of personal, internal conversations and represents "my" self-image. Each individual has multiple Me's, such as mother, person with AIDS (PWA), daughter, seamstress. These multiple Me's can exist simultaneously or consecutively and change over time. Who "I" am at any given time depends on the Me that is called forth by the context in which the I finds itself (e.g., when the child of a Me is diagnosed as HIV-positive, the Me that is mother becomes dominant).

The World

The world in social interactionist theory refers to a world of symbols, but this world is the "object world" (Blumer, 1969). Not all objects are symbols; objects become symbols when meaning is assigned to them by the designator, I. An object is anything that can be designated to the self and reflected upon, such as physical objects (e.g., houses), social objects (e.g., families), and abstract objects (e.g., culture). Symbols, which for the symbolic interactionist include both verbal and nonverbal behaviors, designate objects in the social world (Bowers, 1988). A common language provides people with a stock of ready-made linguistic symbols. Behaviors can be interpreted in relation to gestures, timing, facial and body movements, and intonation. What this implies is that objects possess no inherent or intrinsic meaning; meaning is derived from how others act toward objects, and these meanings are represented symbolically in action and in language. Such symbols indicate to others how particular individuals will act toward the object in question and allow them to adapt or adjust their own actions accordingly. Symbolic interactionism, then, refers to the social processes by which individuals are continuously designating symbols to each other and to themselves.

Participants in social life are continually attempting to determine how others are interpreting their actions to predict their responses and adapt or revise their own courses of action. Feedback from others indicates the relative accuracy of such assessments and whether the chosen course of action should be revised or maintained.

Joint Action

Joint action is accomplished, in particular social contexts, through a complex series of processes whereby participants fit their courses of appropriate action together (Blumer, 1969). Joint action involves each participant attempting to take the role of the other to determine how objects are being designated (to enable prediction of behavior); to select an appropriate action, verbal or nonverbal; and to evaluate from feedback how the selected action is being interpreted by others (Bowers, 1988). Joint action, or meaningful human interaction, is always designed and conducted in complex, dynamic social contexts; to understand it, therefore, requires its observation and interpretation in those complex social contexts. Symbolic interactionism views meanings as social products that are created through the defining activities of people as they interact. The meaning of objects to a particular person arises fundamentally out of the way the objects are defined by those with whom he or she interacts.

Therefore, symbolic interactionists are insistent that social life must be studied through "firsthand observation" (Blumer, 1969, p. 38) of the everyday lives of people in social spheres. Naturalistic inquiry is the only research mode through which to gain an understanding of subjects' realities, the realities of the objects designated as their designator understands them (Bowers, 1988).

Blumer (1969) asserts that the study of social life requires two processes: exploration (depiction) and inspection (analysis). Exploration is a flexible procedure that enables the researcher to become familiar with the sphere of social life that is the focus of the study. Exploration also ensures that subsequent interpretations remain grounded in empirical reality. The line of inquiry, data determination, and analyses all respond flexibly to what is to be found in the empirical data. Inspection essentially refers to establishing the validity of the data analysis. The researcher conceptualizes the data and then carefully examines it for evidence of empirical instances of those conceptualizations.

SYMBOLIC INTERACTIONISM AND GROUNDED THEORY

The theoretical framework of symbolic interactionism guides the principles of grounded theory (Benoliel, 1996, Strauss & Corbin, 1990), yet the specific links between them remain largely implicit. In this section, therefore, the authors will attempt to make such linkages explicit.

According to Blumer (1969), the methodological stance of symbolic interactionism is that of direct examination of the empirical social world. This involves confrontation with the empirical world that is accessible to observation and analysis, the determination of data through disciplined examination of that world, the raising of abstract problems regarding that world, the relating of categories derived from those data, the construction of hypotheses relating to such categories, the weaving of such propositions into a theoretical scheme, and the testing of the categories, propositions and theory constructed by renewed examination of the empirical world. These methodological principles are precisely those recommended by Glaser and Strauss (1967), Glaser (1978), Strauss (1987), and Strauss and Corbin (1990, 1998) in relation to grounded theory methodology (see Table S1.1).

Table S1.1. Symbolic Interactionism—Grounded Theory Methodology

Symbolic interactionism	Grounded theory
Direct observation of empirical world	Participant observation; interviewing; document analysis; videotaping, etc.
Determination of data through disciplined observation	Observation; interviewing guidelines; theoretical sampling
Raising of abstract problems	Analytic, methodologic, personal memoing
Construction of categories	Open coding; axial coding; theoretical coding; properties, dimensions
Construction of theoretical scheme	Core category; categories; subcategories; properties, dimensions; memos; diagrams
Testing of categories	Theoretical sampling; theoretical saturation; literature review; group analysis; member checks

Another more subtle point of association between symbolic interactionism and grounded theory relates to Blumer's (1969) twin research components of exploration (depiction) and inspection (analysis). Blumer's exploration component, or the component that enables the researcher to respond flexibly to what is found in the data, is clearly a function of purposive and theoretical sampling and constant comparative analysis. Indeed, it would be impossible to be flexibly responsive to what is to be found in data in the absence of constant comparative analysis and theoretical sampling. Similarly, Blumer's inspection component, the component in which the researcher conceptualizes (theorizes) the data, then checks those conceptualizations against the data, is strictly consistent with Glaser and Strauss's (1967), Glaser's (1978), Strauss's (1987) and Strauss and Corbin's (1990, 1998) views on the development and validation of analytic elements (i.e., codes, categories and theories). Grounded theory, therefore, is usefully construable as the method of symbolic interactionism.

THE RESEARCH METHOD

The method of grounded theory that was used in this study generally follows that described by Glaser and Strauss (1967) and Glaser (1978, 1992). This research aimed to explore the impact of HIV infection on married or widowed women diagnosed with HIV/AIDS and to understand how they coped with HIV/AIDS. It was conducted in Chiangmai province where HIV infection is highest in women (Cash, Anasuchatkul, & Busayawong, 1995). The researcher chose one subdistrict about 30 kilometers from Chiangmai for a number of reasons. First, the site provides an opportunity to recruit participants from among the infected women who were members of a PWA group. Second, the area consists of rural villages close to the city, where villagers are mainly farmers. Third, there was an active leader of the PWA group who was very cooperative. Finally, the participants were willing to share their experiences. A purposive sample of 24 married or widowed rural women with both symptomatic and asymptomatic disease was included. The age of the participants ranged from 20 to 45 years. Data determination included interviews using interview guidelines and participant observation. The number of interviews conducted with each participant varied from one to four; however, most participants were interviewed at least twice (Foddy, 1993), with the two interviews 3 to 6 weeks apart. Reinterviewing allowed the clarification, elaboration, and verification of information obtained at first interview or cross-checking of information acquired from other sources. In addition, the researcher undertook participant observation when interviewing respondents in their own homes. Field notes were kept of such observations (Russell, 1999), and these helped to inform data analysis. All interviews were conducted in Thai, transcribed in Thai, and analyzed using Thai Ethnograph (Qualis Research, Colorado Springs, CO). The researcher undertook data entry herself; it was very arduous and time-consuming. Data were analyzed using constant comparative method and analysis, and theoretical sampling was facilitated by memoing and diagramming until saturation of categories was achieved. Ethnograph in a qualitative study is useful for analyzing the large amount of textual data. However, in terms of the grounded analytical approach, the computer program cannot assist with the creativity and intuitive nature of qualitative research (Stroh, 2000). For this reason, the researcher not only analyzed the data manually after using the Ethnograph program but also translated six full interviews into English to confirm the credibility of the emergent categories in this study. The study also incorporated group analysis in English (which took place in Australia to reduce researcher bias and enhance analytic validity) as well as "member checks" in Thai (conducted in Thailand) of the substantive theory (Denzin & Lincoln, 1994).

The study was approved by the Human Research Ethics Committee of the University of Western Sydney, Australia (where the principal investigator was enrolled as a PhD student) even though the data were to be determined in Thailand. The study was also approved in northern Thailand by the principal medical officer of the public hospital at which most participants were recruited. Verbal consent is customary in northern Thailand. Consent was obtained from each participant before each episode of data determination.

RESULTS

The basic social problem experienced by participants was surviving with HIV/AIDS, which subsumed a range of physical, psychoemotional, sociocultural, and economic problems. These problems resulted directly from the pathophysiological consequences of the disease but, more particularly, from the social constructions of HIV/AIDS in rural northern Thailand.

The Sociocultural Implications of HIV/AIDS

HIV/AIDS is perceived by northern Thais not only as an incurable infectious disease, but because it is seen as being transmitted through dubious or "bad" behaviors such as intravenous drug use and sexual activity, it is seen as unclean or stigmatizing.

Northern rural Thais live in tightly knit communities in which the closeness of their dwellings reflects the closeness of their social relationships. This closeness, however, impacts negatively on people with HIV/AIDS infection; they have an infectious disease from which relatives and friends fear contagion. Through a range of strategies, therefore, neighbors and friends seek to remove themselves from the risk of infection. Such strategies are perceived by people with HIV/AIDS as social discrimination (Danziger, 1994; Gilmore & Somerville, 1994; Joint United Nations Programme on HIV/AIDS & World Health Organization [UNAIDS], 2005; Songwathana, 1998; Suksatit, 2004). It is also clear that people with the visible signs of HIV infection are subjected to the worst discriminatory practices (Suksatit, 2004; Weitz, 1990).

Northern Thai women with HIV/AIDS infection expect to experience at least some discrimination. They understand how others construe HIV/AIDS through their shared culture by imaginatively taking the role of the generalized Thai village "other." Indeed, at least one participant (P 21) admitted to ostracizing PWA herself before she became infected. Participants not only understood the behaviors and perceptions of the other, but also how to fit their actions to the actions of the other (Blumer, 1969). These women knew, therefore, how HIV/AIDS was designated in northern Thai villages and adjusted their behavior appropriately to concur with this designation.

Discrimination, as examined in this study, took many forms and led to participants feeling different and unworthy. First they were "looked at" very pointedly by village neighbors, and second, they were "kept at a distance" by neighbors, friends, and even some family members. In addition, PWA were looked at and kept at a distance both on an everyday basis and episodically at culturally significant events. The family members of PWA, particularly their children, were also targets of discrimination.

Being looked at. When participants described themselves as "being looked at," they were referring to very pointed looks, the sort they did not elicit before they became known as PWA. Being looked at in this particularly pointed way was to ensure that PWA recognized that they had been designated as undesirable in villagers' object worlds and, because of their shared enculturation, PWA did recognize that they had been designated in this way. Such looks provided the context in which the Me as PWA became painfully salient: "They looked at me as unusual.... The villagers looked at me. I felt uncomfortable" (P 21).

Being kept at a distance. Having looked at PWA in accordance with their designation as abnormal, infectious human objects and to ensure that they appreciated their new designation as ostracized people, villagers used a variety of strategies to avoid the risk of infection from such objects. These strategies were related to both everyday and episodic activities and were all aimed at protecting themselves by keeping their distance from possible infection. "Being kept at a distance" led to the denial of even mundane, everyday courtesies to PWA; even water was withheld. (In rural Thai villages, houses normally have a jar of water and dipper outside that visitors use to refresh themselves): "Some villagers reject me very much. They don't give me any water. They tell me that the dipper doesn't work. I know myself they don't want me to use their dipper. They hide their dipper" (P 16).

Also, on an everyday basis, shopkeepers, particularly those who sold food, kept PWA at a distance. They did this because they were afraid of becoming infected or because they were afraid other customers would stop frequenting their shops: "They reject me. Shopkeepers in some shops tell me to pick the goods by myself and put money on the table. They don't receive money from my hand" (P 16).

Keeping their distance from PWA and food prepared or handled by PWA also extended into culturally significant events such as marriages and funerals:

At [my husband's] funeral, many neighbors came. But no one ate the food. They also stayed away from his coffin...uh...some covered their mouths and noses with a handkerchief. Someone said she was scared the disease was spread by air (P 21).

Families of PWA being kept at a distance. The sociocultural implications of HIV/AIDS also affected the families of PWA; people attempted to keep their distance from the children of PWA and incredibly, their dogs. The most common means of keeping the children of PWA at a distance was to require their withdrawal from school:

My son was not allowed to go to school. A teacher said that my son might catch the disease from his father. She said that my son might bite other students and cause them to catch the disease. If the school took my son, all other parents would take their children out of the school. My son, therefore, had to withdraw from that school (P 17).

And even when children were allowed in school, subtle stigmatization persisted; the personal utensils and equipment of the children of PWA were kept at a distance: "My child can come back to school again. But she has to separate her stuff, for example, her glass, her spoon" (P 21).

Joint Action: An Example

Being looked at and being kept at a distance by noninfected associates were strategies meant to inform PWA that they had been designated by such associates as infectious and "dirty." This designation, however, enabled PWA to interpret, or render meaningful, both the actual and expected distancing behaviors of their associates and, in light of these interpretations and expectations, to plan their own appropriate responses to them. HIV/AIDS is still designated as a seriously stigmatizing disease in northern Thailand; when people become infected they know from their internalization of the generalized, cultural other that they should expect to experience social discrimination and ostracism. They also know that they can expect others in their families to experience discrimination. To avoid such expected discrimination, they "hide out with HIV/AIDS." Hiding out was an appropriate response; indeed, its appropriateness is such that it constituted a mirror image of being kept at a distance. As will become clear in the ensuing discussion, the anticipation of being looked at and especially being kept at a distance by noninfected associates allowed participants to keep themselves and their family members at a distance by hiding out.

Hiding out with HIV/AIDS is a psychologicomotivational orientation that refers to any active strategies used by participants to protect themselves, their children, and their husbands from the discrimination associated with HIV. Clearly, however, the more obvious the manifestations (e.g., lesions) or results (e.g., death) of the disease and the degree of discrimination and ostracism expected, the more participants concentrated on concealing their disease and that of other family members.

What this implies is that the presence of visible and readily recognizable HIV/AIDS-related lesions and symptoms facilitates or expedites the recognition of their bearers as PWA. Participants knew this and accordingly tried to conceal their lesions. Participants found it prudent, in light of the expected distress and discrimination the revelation of the diagnosis would entail, to protect themselves, their children, and their husbands. They told lies to hide out or distance themselves from the truth. They also altered their activities to hide out or distance themselves socially or to physically conceal their own diagnosis or that of close family members from people who they expected would react negatively from the moment the diagnosis was confirmed.

Protecting Herself and Her Husband

Participants told lies and altered their activities to protect the family unit from probable discrimination. They knew that their husbands' positive diagnosis would entail ostracism for themselves, too. They behaved similarly when both partners were infected:

> I talked with my husband, and we decided to quit our jobs. We worked at the same shop in the city. He was a salesman and I was the housekeeper. We could earn around 5,000 baht a month. We decided to quit our jobs at the shop because we were afraid people would reject us if they knew we had AIDS. So we didn't tell the owners of the shop that we got AIDS. They asked us why we were leaving. I told them a lie. I said I wanted to go home (P 10).

Protecting Her Children

Many parents and schoolteachers were afraid that children would become infected through contact with the children of HIV-positive parents. To avoid infection, parents withdrew their children from school. In addition, teachers who feared infection or multiple withdrawals from their school refused to admit the children of HIV-positive people or, if already admitted, to require their withdrawal. Thus, the children of HIV-positive people experienced discrimination. If mothers were unable to shield their children from discrimination, they felt guilty for failing them (Brown et al., 1996). Therefore, to protect their children, HIV-positive mothers lied about their disease:

> When my daughter was two and a half years old, I took her to school near our house. She went to school for around 3 months. The principal of the school told me to withdraw my daughter because four to five students had withdrawn from the school because of her. Two to three months later, the Head asked me to tell my story to other students' parents at one of their meetings. I went there and told them that I had AIDS but I lied about my daughter. I told them I had never tested her blood because I really wanted her to go to school. That's why I told a lie because I knew my daughter had AIDS (P 21).

Parents also found schools that would enroll their children, even if it meant traveling long distances in searing heat: "I send my child to school at [another village]. That school accepted my son; though it is far from home, it is good for my son to study" (P 18).

Protecting Herself

Participants protected themselves from hurtful discrimination, by "avoiding social contact" with people who reacted negatively to them and by "being clean and covered."

Avoiding social contact had three dimensions. The first was engaging in almost reclu-sive behavior, the second was limiting their activities in the village, and the third was resigning from paid employment. Being clean and covered had two dimensions; these were covering skin lesions, dark skin, and weight loss (the common and easily recognized manifestations of advanced disease) and always presenting themselves in public as clean. Both of these strategies are appropriate responses in a culture that still designates HIV/AIDS as a "dirty" disease.

Avoiding social contact. Avoiding social contact includes almost reclusive behav-ior; some participants chose to withdraw almost entirely from village life to pro-tect themselves from hurtful discrimination. Participants recognized that such hurtful behavior was designed precisely to ensure that they did keep their physical distance (hide out). They also recognized that they had been designated as unworthy, dirty, and infectious: "I live alone. I didn't mix with them. I joined some parties sometimes.... I know what I should do" (P 3). "Although other villages treat me badly, I don't care. I live with my son and don't mix with other people" (P 4). "I live only in my house with my daughter. I do not care about anyone. I do not go to join any activities in the village" (P 10).

In addition, participants protected themselves from hurtful rejection by limiting their activities in their villages. Knowing that friends and neighbors still believed that HIV/AIDS can be transmitted in food and food utensils, they selectively avoided engaging in the preparation and cooking of food, both on an everyday basis and at special ceremonial functions. Participants contributed to such events (as all women are traditionally expected to do) by washing and cleaning up. Some participants were so sensitive to the attitudes of others that they refused to eat out at all, always preferring to eat at home.

Participants also chose to hide from possible hurtful discrimination by not going to the temple and by shopping in distant villages where their diagnoses were not known. Participants also made important employment choices to avoid discrimina-tion. They chose to leave factory work to work at home. They also chose not to avail themselves of gainful employment outside their homes.

Being clean and covered. As already indicated, participants tried to conceal the obvious and commonly recognized manifestations of their disease because the degree of discrimination they experienced was associated with visible HIV/AIDS-related symptoms: "I always wear a long-sleeved shirt and pants to cover the nodules on my arms and legs" [she shows her skin lesions on both arms and legs] (P 17).

They also tried to conceal the "dirtiness" of their disease: "When I go anywhere, I will take a bath and put on clean clothes so that others will not think that I am dirty" (P 20).

DISCUSSION

A number of points are worthy of note in the above analyses. First, both PWA and the noninfected share a common understanding of how HIV/AIDS is designated in Thai culture: as a potentially lethal, highly contagious, and dirty disease. This com-mon understanding is a function, as already indicated, of their shared enculturation, and it enables them to fit their behaviors together in joint action. Being "looked at" by noninfected persons is to ensure that PWA understand their designation in the shared object world. It is because PWA expect to be looked at in this very particular way that they strive to hide the most obvious manifestations of their disease by being "clean and covered." They also ensured that any obvious HIV/AIDS-related lesions were covered, because levels of discrimination were associated with the easily recognized or well-known HIV/AIDS symptoms. In both respects, participants behaved as other PWA (Suksatit, 2004; Weitz, 1990) and as cancer sufferers did when cancer was considered a dirty disease (Moneyham et al., 1996). Being clean is to counteract villagers' construal of them as dirty, and being covered is to minimize or limit the amount of being looked at they must face. These behaviors are a perfect fit. In addition, being kept at a distance helps noninfected villagers protect themselves from infection, and hiding out is the PWA response to its expectation.

Second, and related, the behaviors associated with being kept at a distance and hiding out are virtual mirror images; they are almost identical behaviors, and this has some interesting implications. Being kept at a distance is consistent with other HIV/AIDS-related literature. PWA typically experience abandonment and social rejection (Fife & Wright, 2000; Suksatit, 2004). Because they both result in social isolation, financial hardship, and serious inconvenience for PWA, it cannot be the behaviors that are associated with being kept at a distance per se that are problematic for PWA, but what these behaviors mean. For PWA, being kept at a distance subsumes a range of behaviors that mark them as unworthy, lesser people and that evoke the Me that is the PWA. However, when these same behaviors are chosen by PWA themselves (albeit with the same apparently unfortunate consequences), they enable PWA to avoid the hurtful, discriminatory behaviors that mark them as "other." These same behaviors, therefore, mean something different to PWA when they are self-imposed: they mean the exercise of the PWA's self-determining "I."

Implications for Further Nursing Research

The focus of this study has been HIV/AIDS-infected wives and widows in the rural north of Thailand; research into the experiences of other PWA populations in the rural north, therefore, would be useful. Comparative research into the experiences and needs of infected children with parents and those who are orphaned could usefully be undertaken. Another important group whose experiences and needs require investigations is grandparents who, increasingly, are required to support two generations of PWA in their families. Finally, and because the experiences of PWA are directly attributable to community construals of HIV/AIDS, research into the impact of a range of different HIV/AIDS educational programs on the well-being of PWA is needed.

SUMMARY

Symbolic interactionism is theoretically focused on the acting individual, and the individual is regarded as self-determining rather than determined; society is constructed through the purposive actions of individuals and groups. The self is constructed through social interaction and includes the internalization of the beliefs and attitudes of "the generalized other." The self has two components, that is, the "I," the agentic component, and the "Me," the subject component. Individuals and groups interact in object worlds in which meanings are designated symbolically in verbal and nonverbal behavior. Grounded theory is the method of symbolic interactionism. The methodological principles of grounded theory are consistent with the exploration and inspection components of symbolic interactionism. As an explanatory framework, symbolic interactionism really does enable analysts to explain rather than merely describe the behaviors of interactors in local, object worlds.

REFERENCES

Benoliel, J. Q. (1996). Grounded theory and nursing knowledge. *Qualitative Health Research, 6,* 406–428.

Blumer H. (1969). *Symbolic interactionism: Perspective and method.* Englewood Cliffs, CA: Prentice-Hall.

Bowers, B. J. (1988). Grounded theory. In B. Sarter (Ed.), *Paths to knowledge: Innovative research methods for nursing* (pp. 33–60). New York: National League for Nursing.

Brown T., Sittitrai W., Phadungphon C., Carl G., Sirimahachaiyakul W., Jittangkul D., et al. (1996). Risk factors for non-condom use in commercial sex context in Thailand. (Abstract No. Tu.C.2660). *Proceedings of AIDS Research in Thailand, 1993–1997.* Bangkok, Thailand: AIDS Division, Department of Communicable Disease Control, Ministry of Public Health.

Cash K., Anasuchatkul B., & Busayawong W. (1995). *Experimental educational interventions for AIDS prevention among northern Thai single migratory factory workers* (Women and AIDS Research Program, Research Rep. No. 9). Chiangmai, Thailand: Faculty of Education.

Charon J. M. (1995). *Symbolic interactionism.* London: Prentice-Hall.

Chenitz, W. C., & Swanson, J. M. (1986). Qualitative research using grounded theory. In W. C. Chenit, & J. M. Swanson (Eds.), *From practice to grounded theory: Qualitative research in nursing* (pp. 3–15). Menlo Park, CA: Addison-Wesley.

Danziger, R. (1994). The social impact of HIV/AIDS in developing countries. *Social Science and Medicine, 39,* 905–917.

Denzin, N. K., & Lincoln, Y. S. (1994). Introduction: Entering the field of qualitative research. In N. K. Denzin, & Y. S. Lincoln (Eds.), *Handbook of qualitative research* (pp.1–17). Newbury Park, CA: Sage.

de Laine M. (1997). *Ethnography: Theory and applications in health research.* Sydney, Australia: Maclennan & Petty.

Fife, B. L., & Wright, E. R. (2000). The dimensionality of stigma: A comparison of its impact on the self of persons with HIV/AIDS and cancer. *Journal of Health and Social Behavior, 41,* 50–67.

Foddy W. (1993). *Constructing questions for interviews and questionnaires: Theory and practice in social research.* Cambridge, UK: Cambridge University.

Gilmore, N., & Somerville, M. A. (1994). Stigmatization, scape-goating and discrimination in sexually transmitted diseases: Overcoming "them" and "us." *Social Science and Medicine, 39,* 1339–1358.

Glaser B. G. (1978). *Theoretical sensitivity.* Mill Valley, CA: The Sociology Press.

Glaser B. G. (1992). *Basics of grounded theory analysis.* Mill Valley, CA: The Sociology Press.

Glaser B. G., & Strauss A. L. (1967). *The discovery of grounded theory: Strategies for qualitative research.* New York: Aldine De Gruyter.

Holloway I., & Wheeler S. (1996). *Qualitative research for nurses.* London: Blackwell Science.

Joint United Nations Programme on HIV/AIDS & World Health Organization (UNAIDS). (2005). *HIV-related stigma, discrimination and human rights violations: Case studies of successful programmes.* Geneva, Switzerland.

Mead, G. H. (1934). *Mind, self and society.* Chicago: The University of Chicago Press.

Merton, R. (1973). *The sociology of science.* Chicago: The University of Chicago Press.

Moneyham, L., Seals, B., Demi, A., Sowell, R., Cohen, L., & Guillory, J. (1996). Perceptions of stigma in women infected with HIV. *AIDS Patients Care and STDs, 10,* 162–167.

Morse, J. M., & Field, P. A. (1996). *Nursing research: The application of qualitative approach* (2nd. Ed.). London: Chapman & Hall.

Russell, C. (1999). Participant observation. In V. Minichiello, G. Sullivan, & K. Greenwood (Eds.), *Handbook for research methods in health sciences* (pp. 431–448). Sydney, Australia: Addison Wesley Longman.

Songwathana P. (1998). *Kinship, karma, compassion and care: Domiciliary and community based care of AIDS patients in southern Thailand.* Unpublished doctoral dissertation, University of Queensland, Brisbane, Australia.

Stern P. N. (1994). Eroding grounded theory. In J. M. Morse (Ed.), *Critical issues in the qualitative research methods* (pp. 212–224). London: Sage.

Strauss, A. L. (1987). *Qualitative analysis for social scientists.* New York: Cambridge University Press.

Strauss A. L., & Corbin J. (1990). *Basics of qualitative research.* London: Sage.

Strauss A. L., & Corbin J. (1998). *Basic of qualitative research: Techniques and procedures for developing grounded theory* (2nd ed.). Newbury Park, CA: Sage.

Stroh, M. (2000). Computers and qualitative data analysis: To use or not to use...? In D. Burton (Ed.), *Research training for social scientists: A handbook for postgraduate researchers* (pp. 226–243). London: Sage.

Suksatit B. (2004). *Stigma perception and health promoting self-care ability of young adults with HIV/AIDS.* Unpublished master's thesis, Mahidol University, Bangkok, Thailand.

Weitz, R. (1990). Living with the stigma of AIDS. *Qualitative Sociology, 13,* 23–38.

2

Structural Functionalism Theory

Ralph and Alice have been married for about 20 years. Ralph feels that they have a good thing going. He works in construction and is able to provide well for his family. He was able to offer Alice this sense of security when they got married. He is also handy around the house, fixing things as they break or wear out and keeping the place looking nice.

Alice is attractive and a good sexual partner. Rather than working outside the home, she has kept the house clean and prepared meals, and focused her time on the rearing of their four beautiful children. The kids have always appreciated her help with schoolwork and her ability to attend and support their various activities. They have been representative of the traditional, nuclear Western family.

Recently, Alice has grown restless and less satisfied. She would like to get a part-time job in order to have some spending money that she could control. And she would like Ralph to spend more time talking with her instead of working on some project in the garage. Ralph feels that things are just fine the way they are—why do they have to change?

But things are changing. With the children growing up and moving out, the family structure is reverting back to that of a couple. Alice has more free time than she had in the past and would like to focus on some of her own interests. Ralph can see the point in using some of his salary to hire someone to make home repairs—in order to give him more time to watch sports on TV, not to use it for womanly things like shopping and talking about feelings!

Ralph wants both of them to do what he feels they are supposed to do: He works as the provider, and she takes care of him. Alice feels that it makes more sense for both of them to provide and nurture.

HISTORY

Functional theory, as it is often called, is based on the "organic analogy." This is the idea, developed by early social philosophers such as Comte and Durkheim, that society is like the human body. As the body is made up of various parts, such as the organs, muscles, and tissues, that need to work together for it to be healthy, society is also composed of many parts that must function together to work properly. Each part needs to be in a state of *equilibrium*, or balance. Just as the human body has evolved over time, so has society. Comte introduced "positivism"—the view that social science should be based on empirical observations—into social thought. He also focused on terms that later became popular in functional theory, like solidarity and consensus, which refer to the interconnectedness of social life and the source of its unity. Durkheim was also concerned with how social systems are integrated and hold themselves together (Kingsbury and Scanzoni 1993).

The writings of social anthropologist Alfred Radcliffe-Brown (1952) were pivotal in establishing a field of comparative sociology, with structural functionalism as its most important tool. His essay on understanding the role of the mother's brother in certain societies helped to supplant social Darwinism with the new and, at the time, relatively sophisticated framework of structural functionalism.

The leading thinker of functionalism in America was Talcott Parsons (1951), who believed that behavior was driven by our efforts to conform to the moral code of society. The purpose of such codes is to constrain human behavior in ways that promote the common good. The purpose of an organism is to survive. In order for a society to survive, the subsystems (the family and other institutions) must function in ways that promote the maintenance of society as a whole. This is similar to how a person's organs must function in interrelated ways to maintain good health.

For Parsons (1951), the key to societal survival was the shared norms and values held by its individual members. Deviation from those norms leads to disorganization, which threatens the survival of the system. Because the family is the key system in society, according to his view, divorce, teen rebellion, non-marital sex, and single parenthood all threatened the structure and/or the functions of the family and therefore needed to be avoided.

By the 1950s, functionalism had become the dominant paradigm in sociology, and it had a tremendous impact on family studies. For example, family research since the 1930s had adopted the organic model, with its many studies on marital quality and adjustment. Family stability was assumed to be critical to childhood outcomes, and because marital satisfaction was central to that stability, it was seen as one of the most important research questions in the field. Furthermore, the existence of any social structure, such as the family, was explained by the functions it carries out for the greater society (Kingsbury and Scanzoni 1993).

The social upheaval of the 1960s led many to criticize functionalism for its inability to deal with change. Parsons (1951) did not see deviant behavior as contributing to positive change, whereas others, such as Merton (1957), recognized the role of conflict in maintaining equilibrium or leading to a new relationship status. Other writers (Goode 1969) strove to raise the level of theoretical rigor in the discipline. Parsons ignored these ideas, feeling that change always came from the outside (such as industrialization leading to the preeminence of the nuclear family) and that children only learned culturally approved values in the family. He also called on Freudian ideas to support his claim that there were biologically driven roles (instrumental and expressive) that men and women should fulfill within the ideal structure of the nuclear family.

As a result, structural functionalism fell into disfavor with scientists after the 1970s. Holman and Burr (1980) declared it to be a "peripheral" theory with very little to contribute to contemporary thinking. Nevertheless, its organic model and the concept of the family needing to stay in balance are important assumptions in more modern family theories, such as stress and systems theories (Kingsbury and Scanzoni 1993).

In addition, the case has been made (White, Marshall, and Wood 2002) that a considerable amount of present-day family research uses family structure without explicitly recognizing it as a key variable. They concluded, using Canadian data on childhood outcomes, that parenting processes are more important than family structure. There are contemporary scholars, such as Wallerstein and Blakeslee (1989) and Popenoe (1996), who argued that the intact nuclear family is still an important component in healthy child rearing.

Perhaps more important is the fact that family structure continues to play a role in political decision making. White, Marshall, and Wood (2002) indicated that politicians, in making decisions about single parents and welfare, for instance, often overestimate the importance of family structure in creating their policies.

BASIC ASSUMPTIONS

One common criticism of structural functionalism is that it never reached the long-term popularity and usage it could have because its terms, beliefs, and basic assumptions were never fully developed into what we would consider a formalized "theory" (Lane 1994). For this reason, listing the basic assumptions of this theory is difficult, as it depends on which author's work you reference. Therefore, we will discuss only the two basic assumptions that all who use this framework would agree are the central components of the theory itself.

The function of families is to procreate and socialize children. Structural functionalism is basically a theory of social survival. Its key idea is that families perform the critical functions of procreation and socialization of children so that they will fit into the overall society. Theorists ask themselves what is needed for a society to maintain itself and then which institutions or subgroups within that society are providing for those needs. They conclude that the intact nuclear family of husband, wife, and their children is the ideal structure. This is the configuration of individuals in the modern world that works best in meeting the needs of its members, as well as those of the larger society. That is, it functions best, according to this theory.

All systems have functions. Theoretical work has focused principally on the functions carried out by the family and what these functions accomplish. Although other functions are mentioned, the procreation and socialization of children are central. The main function of any social system, including the family, is simply to maintain its basic structure.

Parsons (1951) concluded that the best way to do this was for husbands and wives to play certain roles. Males need to be *instrumental*, which means that they are the ones who provide for the family. Because of this, their abilities should be focused on meeting the physical needs of family members in terms of food, shelter, education, and income. In contrast, females are to be *expressive*, meaning that they should meet the emotional needs of family members by being nurturing and smoothing out problems in relationships. According to this theory, the biological imperatives of motherhood predispose women for this "indoor" work, whereas the greater physical strength of men leads them naturally to the provider role (Winton 1995). These are the roles that Ralph and Alice have been playing throughout their married lives, as indicated in the vignette at the beginning of the chapter.

Parsons (1951) expanded on this notion of instrumental and expressive roles with regard to the functioning of societies and the values and norms that they hold. He believed that our behaviors or actions were driven by the hope of reaching a desirable goal, and what is desirable is defined by the cultural system of which we are a part. He developed five pattern variables that reflect the value orientation of individuals and societies as they make decisions about what actions to take. In each of the word pairings below, the term that comes first is the expressive characteristic and the term that comes second is the instrumental characteristic. The expressive aspects, more often associated with the roles of women, refer to those things that must be done to maintain the culture and our relationships, keep people involved and integrated, and help to manage and resolve internal tensions and conflict. In contrast, the instrumental aspects, associated with the roles of men, are focused on making sure that problems are solved and tasks are accomplished.

The first pattern is *Ascription/Achievement*, and it is based on the concept of what is earned versus what is biologically predetermined. Ascription describes your individual status, or those things with which you were born, such as sex, ethnicity, race, family status, and family composition, whereas achievement refers to those things that you earn based on your performance. For example, we might say that although Oprah Winfrey's ascribed status was one of poverty, her achieved status was one of superstardom and great wealth.

Diffuseness/Specificity refers to the functions of relations, or the nature of our relationships and how broad or narrow their expectations are. If you practice diffuseness, you have a wide variety of relationships that meet a large range of needs, whereas specificity indicates that you develop relationships that meet a specific need. For example, although your friends and family may meet many of your needs, such as support, validation, conversation, and shared activities, other interactions, such as seeing your physician or accountant, satisfy specific needs.

Whereas the previous category dealt with the types of obligations within a role or relationship, *Particularism/Universalism* refers to the range of people with whom we come into contact. Particularism refers to the fact that our behaviors are guided by the person with whom we are interacting and the nature of that relationship. In other words, we act a certain way simply because, for example, we are with our parents and they have a certain set of expectations for our behavior. Universalism refers to the fact that we behave in certain ways based on the norms and values that guide our behavior at a societal level, or that dictate what we should and should not do. The fact that everyone is presumed to be equal in the eyes of the law is an example of this.

Affectivity/Affective Neutrality is based on the quality of our relationships and refers to the amount of emotional expression that is appropriate or perhaps even expected in a given situation. If you have an affectivity approach, then your relationships are based on things such as love, trust, close personal involvement, and other forms of emotion, whereas if your interactions are affective neutral, they are based on what people can do for you, or perhaps on what you can do for them.

Finally, one can focus on *Collectivity/Self* when performing any action. In the first concept, the focus is on the interests of others, or the social group of which one is a part, whereas in the second concept, the focus is on one's own interests. The fact that people do charity work or exhibit altruistic behavior would be explained by the first concept, whereas our economic activities could perhaps fall into the latter category.

PRIMARY TERMS AND CONCEPTS

Structure

Structure refers to the composition of the family, or what members make up the family institution within a particular society. Is it a nuclear or single-parent family? Is the marriage intact, or has there been a death or divorce? Structure can also be used to describe the framework of a society or an organization.

Function

What services does the family provide to society? The family exists for the functions that it serves, which in turn enhance the survival of the larger group. We can best understand the purpose of any organization by examining what it does, or its functions.

Instrumental

Tasks that need to be performed within a family to ensure its physical survival are instrumental in nature. The focus is placed on providing for the material needs of the family members, and it is often assumed from historical analysis that males are best suited for these tasks. This would include earning the family income, paying the rent, and providing for transportation and clothing. These are the tasks that Ralph, from our vignette, feels he should perform.

Expressive

The relationship interactions necessary for the psychological satisfaction of family members are expressive in nature. They include love, communication, and support and are generally assumed, because of biology, to be tasks best suited for females, much the way Alice did throughout her marriage to Ralph in our vignette. Thus, mothers are often assumed to be better able to meet the emotional needs of their children than fathers.

Equilibrium

The assumption here is that any human system will resist change. Even though change comes gradually, family members tend to function best when things are in balance. Parsons (1951) felt that this was most easily achieved when family members shared the same values and goals and when they performed differentiated roles (i.e., each spouse fulfilled a different function, such as an instrumental husband and an expressive wife (Winton 1995).

The Benchmark Family

The benchmark family refers to the traditional nuclear family composed of a husband, wife, and their children, with the husband as breadwinner and the wife as homemaker. (Yes, Ward, June, Wally, and Beaver Cleaver, from the popular television show *Leave It to Beaver* in the 1950s, may come to mind here!) Some Americans consider family structures that differ from this ideal to be less desirable, or even deviant, by comparison (Kingsbury and Scanzoni 1993).

Deviant Behavior

Merton (1957), expanding on the original principles of structural functionalism, developed a typology of deviant behavior to show how behaviors that deviate from the social norms can still play a useful role in the theory, and in society for that matter. His typology was based on five categories that are reviewed below: conformity, innovation, ritualism, retreatism, and rebellion. The examples for each of these are drawn from Kingsbury and Scanzoni (1993), but you could also use examples based on people you know.

Conformity

Nondeviance is the same as conformity. For instance, a husband/father who is a good provider and does so in the approved manner of hard work and achievement has conformed to the social norm of being the family breadwinner.

Innovation

A woman who accepts the goal of material success but attains it in an illegal or otherwise socially unacceptable manner is in this category. She is both conforming and deviant. An example of this would be a mother who tries to have it all but uses drugs in order to have the energy/stamina to get everything done that the "perfect mom" should do. This is a huge social trend.

Ritualism

Ritualism refers to a man who gives up on success but still works hard. No matter how hard he tries, he will not meet his wife's expectations of him as a provider. So, why does he continue to try? He does so because that is his nature, or his ritual.

Retreatism

Retreatism refers to the person who rejects both the normative goals and the means to obtain them. Drug addicts and homeless people are examples of individuals who might fall into this category. They avoid both the rewards of society and the frustrations that come with trying to attain them. In other words, they retreat from cultural norms.

Rebellion

Rebellious individuals are similar to those in the previous category, except that they also attempt to create a new social structure. They might argue that material success is corruptive, and that we should focus on spiritual or other goals instead. This last category in particular allows functionalism to deal with change in ways that Parsons (1951) could not.

COMMON AREAS OF RESEARCH
AND APPLICATION

Structural functionalism has been most useful in guiding comparative research about the family, chiefly as it was carried out by anthropologists and sociologists who were searching for any universals in family life. It has also been used to explore cultural variations among families and societies. This research has provided the foundation upon which much of modern family science is built. Even though this framework has basically not been used since the 1960s or 1970s (Lane 1994), it still influenced much of the work done in the field both prior to and since that time. Below are some of the key areas of knowledge that was attained thanks to the structural functionalism framework.

Family Structure

George Murdock (1949) surveyed 250 societies that were described in the "Human Relations Area Files," an immense collection of ethnographic field notes on cultures around the world. From this research, he concluded that what he called the nuclear family was the basic social structure for humans everywhere. It consists of a husband, wife, and their children. This was the minimum structure, and it was the norm in one-fourth of the societies surveyed. The others were either polygamous or extended families, but they had nuclear families at their cores.

A similar study was done by Crano and Aronoff (1978), which assessed 186 societies that were chosen to reflect a representative sample of the world's societies. They were interested in examining the idea of complementarity in the expressive and instrumental roles in families across these diverse cultures. They found that, while the mother was the principal caretaker for infant children in almost every society, the same was not true as children got older. The father was found to be significantly involved in the expressive functions of the family as children grew up. They concluded that having expressive and instrumental roles as an absolute dichotomy was too restrictive, as men and women in these societies exhibited **both** characteristics.

Family Functions

Historical analysis demonstrates that, across time, the family has provided many important functions for society. In modern times, many of these functions—religion, health care, protection, education, and entertainment—have been taken over by other institutions. Today we have churches, the medical establishment, the police, public and private schools, movies, and other entities to meet these needs. As these kinds of changes occurred, the family adapted and focused on what it does best (Ingoldsby and Smith 1995).

Murdock (1949) concluded that there were four essential functions that the family provides in all societies. The first is *sexual*. All societies have found that this powerful impulse must be restrained in order to avoid chaos. However, it must not be over-regulated or personality problems and an insufficient population would result. The compromise found everywhere is marriage. Although sexual relations do occur outside of marriage, most sexual expression occurs in marriage, and it is the one context in which sexual behavior is always socially acceptable.

The second function is *reproduction*. This follows naturally from the fact that marriage is the primary sexual relationship in all societies. Although many children are born out of wedlock, the majority are born according to society's preference, which is within the family. Such children are usually privileged in terms of acceptance, inheritance, and other factors.

The third function is *socialization*. In addition to producing children, the family must care for them physically and train them to perform adult tasks and adopt the values deemed appropriate by their particular culture. As Lee (1982) pointed out, this is much more than simply learning occupational skills. It involves language skills and the transmission of culture as well. All societies depend on the family to love and nurture their children so that they will become civilized.

The final function is *economic*. This does not mean that the family is the economic unit of production, although it has been in many times and places. Here, Murdock (1949) was referring to the division of labor by gender: "By virtue of their primary sex differences, a man and a woman make an exceptionally efficient cooperating unit.... All known human societies have developed specialization and cooperation between the sexes roughly along this biologically determined line" (7). In other words, because males have greater physical strength and females bear the children, marital pairs have found that their survival is enhanced if they divide responsibilities according to their capacities.

In addition, the functions of rituals and behaviors within the family were also analyzed. Every culture has its own approaches to birthing, parenting, sexual taboos, and other matters. A productive way of understanding these family rules is to investigate what functions they each serve for the family and the society at large.

Origin of the Family

The answers to the questions of how and when the family originated among humans are presently considered to be beyond the reach of science. However, there have been many philosophical and theoretical speculations, and most of them have come to the same basic conclusion: The structure of the family developed as the result of the economic division of labor. Social and technological changes have reduced this traditional (expressive/instrumental) division of labor proposed by the functionalists (Ingoldsby and Smith 1995), but the argument that economic efficiency and sexual attraction are the basis for marriage and family life is still a powerful one. As Lee (1982) explains:

> The family originated among human beings because a certain division of labor between the sexes was found to be convenient or efficient and maximized the

probability of survival for individuals and groups...the logic here implies that the origin of sex roles...coincided with the origin of the family. (54)

Family Universality

Functionalists have wanted to determine if the family exists worldwide as a social institution. If it does, then it can be said that the family may be necessary for the survival of human society. However, if it can be demonstrated that there exists even one culture without the family as we define it, then it must be concluded that, although the family unit is common, there are viable alternatives. Murdock's (1949) research convinced him that the nuclear family is universal and necessary for human social life:

> No society, in short, has succeeded in finding an adequate substitute for the nuclear family, to which to transfer these functions. It is highly doubtful whether any society ever will succeed in such an attempt, utopian proposals for the abolition of the family to the contrary notwithstanding. (11)

Stephens (1963) described the work of Edith Clarke in Jamaica and Melford Spiro with the Israeli kibbutzim, which tells a different story. Clarke argued that fathers are missing from lower-class Jamaican families, and thus the structure there is a mother–child dyad, rather than the father–mother–child triangle of the nuclear family. Similarly, Spiro's work gives the impression that the socialization and economic functions are not provided by the family in the kibbutz. Despite these studies, careful reviews by scholars have rejected these arguments and found in favor of Murdock's ideas instead.

However, Lee (1982) demonstrated that there are a few stable societies, such as the Nayar of India, in which biological fathers do not live with or provide for their families or help socialize their children. Mother–child dyads, typically with help from other male relatives, do exist as the norm in a few places and function much like single-parent families do in the modern Western world. By means of comparison, divorce can be said to provide the important function of enabling adults to escape from difficult relationships, and single parenting may become a necessary adaptation to that situation. In these other societies, however, mother-only parenting is the preferred family structure, even though the couple remains married.

A case could also be made that there are other functions beyond Murdock's four that have emerged as important family contributions to society. The principal one would be providing companionship and emotional support to its members. Although love is not yet found to be essential for marriages everywhere, it is playing an ever greater role in urban, industrialized societies (Ingoldsby and Smith 1995). Given that, in 2007, more than half of the world's population was living in cities, this is becoming increasingly important (Population Reference Bureau 2007).

Marital Structure

Students are often surprised to learn that historically polygyny (multiple wives) is the preferred marital structure in over three-fourths of all societies. This is the case despite the fact that the relatively balanced sex ratio results in most people practicing monogamy. The temptation has always been to blame polygyny on the male sex drive, although functionalists make a very convincing case that it is actually about economics. Societies that engage in light agriculture and animal husbandry tend to prefer polygyny, because the labor of women and children creates wealth and, therefore, these families are better off than monogamous ones. In contrast, polyandrous (multiple husbands) unions, which are very rare, appear to be adaptations to economic poverty attributable to life in a harsh environment (Ingoldsby and Smith 1995).

Working Women

Early functionalists found working mothers to be destabilizing and, therefore, a threat to quality child rearing. Political conservatives who continue to take that position blame "uncaring" and "greedy" mothers in a materialistic society. However, structural functionalism tends to look to outside forces, particularly economics, to explain change—for example, the rise in the number of working mothers since the 1960s has resulted from the shift in the United States from a manufacturing to a service economy. Because these new salaries are much lower than those paid for skilled factory work, couples have found it necessary for both of them to work outside the home in order to maintain a middle-class lifestyle. In this way, many valued benefits for their children, such as music lessons and sports activities, can continue to be provided. This theory always encourages us to look to larger societal forces to explain changes in the family, as it adapts only when there are other factors that require change in order for the family to reestablish equilibrium.

Expressive/Instrumental Roles

As was previously stated, although structural functionalism as a theory in its entirety has not been used for several decades, it is true that concepts from it have been used since that time. A good example of this is the work exploring the existence of expressive/instrumental gender roles in various groups/relationships. For example, Venkatesh (1985) used this concept to address the adoption and use of technology in the home and whether or not such technology is used for instrumental or expressive purposes. He reported that households take both of these purposes into consideration when choosing which technology to purchase, and couples are most likely to choose technology that can provide a high level of functioning in both arenas.

Finley and Schwartz (2006) assessed whether or not the father's instrumental role has changed in the fifty years since Parsons began writing about it by studying an ethnically diverse sample of 1,989 university students who retrospectively reported on their father's behaviors. It was found that, in this sample, the fathering role remained substantially instrumental in nature, although there was some indication that fathers were beginning to show expressive behaviors.

Another interesting, recently conducted study by Caldwell and Mestrovic (2008) concerns the roles of instrumental and expressive behaviors as exhibited by the military personnel involved in the charges of abuse at Abu Ghraib prison in Iraq. They used the language of instrumental/expressive behaviors to explain both the actions at the prison as well as the defenses of two of the military personnel who were charged with these crimes. The military is seen as primarily instrumental in nature and function, and the role of this in the exhibited behaviors was also discussed. The authors concluded by listing eight ways in which you can summarize these experiences from a Parsonian perspective.

Use by Other Fields of Study

Although there are probably many similar fields of study that have benefited from the earlier work of structural functionalism theorists, one field that frequently used this approach was political science (Lane 1994). In fact, Groth (1970) suggested that "among the recent approaches to the study of politics one of the most stimulating as well as influential has been structural functionalism" (485). It is useful for this field because it stimulates research, can fit together puzzle pieces that seem very different, and can help to compare two areas or types of politics that on the surface seem very different. Silverman and Gulliver (2006) further stated that it allows for a comparative analysis of different political systems and aids in the cross-cultural comparison of diverse political structures.

One interesting area of research, especially given the current "graying of America," is in the relationship between aging and cumulative advantage/disadvantage (CAD). CAD is based on the principle that some people are more advantaged when it comes to resources, where they live, financial status, health, and so on, and that the gap between those who are advantaged and those who are not is widening. It also suggests that this is not purely a matter of individual characteristics or abilities, but is also reliant on the society in which one lives and the structures set forth in that society. Thus, it makes sense that structural functionalism might be applied to develop a better understanding of CAD, because it is focused on figuring out how structures that are in place meet the functions needed by a system (Dannefer 2003).

Finally, Chilcott (1998) wrote an interesting article asserting that structural functionalism could be modified to help analyze school systems. If you think of the school itself as a system, with principals, teachers, and students each playing roles within that system, such a framework could be used to better understand why a system does and does not work. You could also research how those roles work together to form an integrated whole. Thus, you can see from this brief review of the literature that, although structural functionalism itself has not been used much in recent research, it has been influential in different ways and modified for many uses over the years, making it an important component in the history of family theories.

CRITIQUE

A number of problems have contributed to the general decline in the acceptance of and use of structural functionalism. The main ones are listed below (see Kingsbury and Scanzoni [1993] and Winton [1995] for a more detailed description).

First, very few scientific ideas can be completely free of the dominant values of society, and structural functionalism is no exception. Historically, it developed in a conservative time and, therefore, values traits that were popular at the time, such as structure, stability, and unity. One must remember that, at the time this theory was developed, it was believed that the family had been growing and changing for decades, and that in the 1950s we had finally arrived at the "normal" American family. Thus, the ideal of the heterosexual couple who is married and raising children based on gender role expectations of the male being instrumental and the female being expressive was the standard that would be followed for decades to come (Scanzoni, 2001). As we know, this standard did not last for long, and women like Alice in the vignette at the beginning of this chapter started wanting to express themselves in both realms. As political views and cultural values changed, support for the theory waned.

At a deeper level, the theory is criticized for confusing "function" with "cause." Even though it may be possible to demonstrate that families perform certain functions that are necessary to society, it does not necessarily serve as a causal explanation for why families exist. The theory does not do a good job of explaining the historical process of how family types come to exist in a given society.

Chilcott (1998) also suggested that structural functionalism does not adequately account for change. Because it is based on a static model of society, explaining change becomes difficult. Similarly, he states that dysfunction is not dealt with in a way that is helpful. Both of these problems, however, have been addressed by people who use this theory as a basis from which to start, rather than as their **only** theoretical framework.

Functionalism also focuses on a macroanalysis of large social systems and assumes that maintaining a steady state is important. Many other theorists feel that understanding the interpersonal struggles that go on in family life is critical and that disagreement must be assumed to be intrinsic to family life.

Finally, some theorists have made the mistake of assuming that, just because something is functional, it deserves to be maintained. Feminists in particular have been offended by the notion that women should always perform expressive tasks, because this is seen as hurting their status within the system. Therefore, the status quo has been dysfunctional for women, even if it has been functional for the rest of the family or the overall society in some times and places. This can be further expanded to include the idea that this theoretical model would be problematic when applied to same-sex relationships. In fact, Parsons considered any family form that was not the benchmark family as deviant and harmful, not diverse. The inability of the theory to allow for the diverse family forms present today has been the source of its most damaging criticism.

However, structural functionalism has a number of strengths that result in its usefulness in family studies today. As mentioned previously, the organic analogy is still used in other, more current theoretical approaches. Family systems theory takes the basic concepts of equilibrium and roles and successfully applies them to a microanalysis of family relationships.

As the research examples in the chapter demonstrate, the theory is very useful for cross-cultural scholarship. No other framework has been as successful in providing us with an understanding of different family forms and why they work at various times and in various places. An example would be the relationship between marital structure (monogamy, polygyny, etc.) and economy (Lee 1982).

Finally, as Pittman (1993) explains, "the presumed moralism allegedly undergirding functionalism with a conservative, consensus-based, status quo bias, is almost certainly the product of the period of theory development (1940s and 1950s) rather than inherent to the theory itself" (221). For example, the theory itself does not demand that all families need to be nuclear, with the husband acting instrumentally and the wife expressively. Researchers using this framework have simply noted the historical and comparative success of this approach in many societies. As times and circumstances—such as social views and economic structures—change, other structures or functions may prove to be more useful. Equilibrium can change and, therefore, be understood as dynamic. The basic theory is neutral in that it looks at stability but does not necessarily value it as superior to other possible forms. More modern interpretations of the theory have attempted to integrate conflict and change into the paradigm.

APPLICATION

1. Think about the couple described in the vignette at the beginning of the chapter. How much can we learn about a family just by analyzing its structure and the functions that are performed? Would this theory be able to help Alice change her situation?

2. Write a short paper listing every member of your own family of origin. What was its basic structure? Who performed the instrumental and expressive tasks? Were there other roles necessary for smooth family functioning, and if so, who carried them out?

3. Think back to a time of family crisis. What changes were taking place? Was a new and different equilibrium reached? Did anyone play a rebellious role in the crisis, and if so, how did that turn out? How strong were societal forces for things to remain the same?

4. How typical are the families that you know? How many do you think meet the criteria for being a benchmark family as described earlier in the chapter? How well, in comparison, do you feel that the less traditional families function?

5. The article that follows is about gendered styles of caregiving. After you read the article, think about other types of behaviors that are gendered in our culture and discuss whether they are similar to or different from what Parsons outlines. How is this similar to or different from what you know about caregiving for children?

REFERENCES

Caldwell, R. A., and S. G. Mestrovic. 2008. The roles of gender in 'expressive' abuse at Abu Ghraib. *Cultural Sociology* 2(3): 275–299.

Carroll, M., and L. Campbell. 2008. Who now reads Parsons and Bales? : Casting a critical eye on the "gendered styles of caregiving" literature. *Journal of Aging Studies* 22: 24–31.

Chilcott, J. H. 1998. Structural functionalism as a heuristic device. *Anthropology & Education Quarterly* 29(1): 103–111.

Crano, W. D., and J. Aronoff. 1978. A cross-cultural study of expressive and instrumental role complementarity in the family. *American Sociological Review* 43(4): 463–471.

Dannefer, D. 2003. Cumulative advantage/disadvantage and the life course: Cross-fertilizing age and social science theory. *The Journals of Gerontology: Series B: Psychological Sciences and Social Science* 58B(6): S327.

Finley, G. E., and S. J. Schwartz. 2006. Parsons and Bales revisited: Young adult children's characterization of the fathering role. *Psychology of Men & Masculinity* 7(1): 42–55.

Goode, W. J. 1969. The theoretical importance of love. *American Sociological Review* 34: 38–47.

Groth, A. J. 1970. Structural functionalism and political development: Three problems. *The Western Political Quarterly* 23(3): 485–499.

Holman, T., and W. Burr. 1980. Beyond the beyond: The growth of family theories in the 1970's. *Journal of Marriage and the Family* 42: 729–742.

Ingoldsby, B., and S. Smith. 1995. *Families in multicultural perspective*. New York: Guilford.

Kingsbury, N., and J. Scanzoni. 1993. Structural-functionalism. In *Sourcebook of family theories and methods: A contextual approach*, ed. P. G. Boss, W. J. Doherty, R. LaRossa, W. R. Schumm, and S. K. Steinmetz, 195–217. New York: Plenum.

Lane, R. 1994. Structural-functionalism reconsidered: A proposed research model. *Comparative Politics* 26(4): 461–477.

Lee, G. 1982. *Family structure and interaction: A comparative analysis*. Minneapolis: University of Minnesota Press.

Merton, R. K. 1957. *Social theory and social structure*. Glencoe, IL: Free Press.

Murdock, G. P. 1949. *Social structure*. New York: Free Press.

Parsons, T. 1951. *The social system*. New York: Free Press.

Pittman, J. 1993. Functionalism may be down, but it is not out: Another point of view for family therapists and policy analysts. In *Sourcebook of family theories and methods: A contextual approach*, ed. P. G. Boss, W. J. Doherty, R. LaRossa, W. R. Schumm, and S. K. Steinmetz, 218–221. New York: Plenum.

Popenoe, D. 1996. *Life without father*. New York: Free Press.

Population Reference Bureau. 2007. *World population data sheet*. http://www.prb.org (accessed January 8, 2007).

Radcliffe-Brown, A. 1952. *Structures and function in primitive society*. Glencoe, IL: Free Press.

Scanzoni, J. (2001). From the normal family to alternate families in the quest for diversity within interdependence. *Journal of Family Issues* 22(6): 688–710.

Silverman, M., and P. H. Gulliver. 2006. "Common sense" and "governmentality": Local government in southeastern Ireland, 1850–1922. *Journal of Royal Anthropology* 12: 109–127.

Stephens, W. 1963. *The family in cross-cultural perspective*. New York: Holt, Rinehart, & Winston.

Venkatesh, A. (1985). A conceptualization of the household/technology. *Advances in Consumer Research* 12: 2–7.

Wallerstein, J., and S. Blakeslee. 1989. *Second chances: Men, women, and children a decade after divorce*. New York: Ticknor and Fields.

White, J., S. Marshall, and J. Wood. 2002. Confusing family structures: The role of family structure in relation to child well-being. Paper presented at the North West Council on Family Relations, Vancouver, British Columbia, Canada.

Winton, C. 1995. *Frameworks for studying families*. Guilford, CT: Duskin Publishing Group.

SAMPLE READING

Carroll, M., and L. Campbell. 2008. Who now reads Parsons and Bales?: Casting a critical eye on the "gendered styles of caregiving" literature. *Journal of Aging Studies* 22: 24–31.

Although there is a lot of depth in this theory, much attention in this chapter has been focused on Parson's notion of expressive and instrumental roles for individuals and for societies. We have also discussed that this theory, once the primary theory in sociology, is now rarely used in the field of family studies or in related fields. The article that follows uses gendered roles as a means of discussing the role of caregiving for elderly parents. They suggest that the work of Parsons is outdated for most of the field, but there is still a good deal of research in the area of caregiving that follows this gendered concept, which they find to be missing the subtleties of caregiving behaviors.

SAMPLE READING

Who Now Reads Parsons and Bales?: Casting a Critical Eye on the "Gendered Styles of Caregiving" Literature

Michael Carroll [a,*]
Lori Campbell [b]

Our concern in this article is with a claim that is either explicit or implicit in much of the gerontological literature on caregiving, namely, that male caregiving is managerial and instrumental while female caregiving is intimately connected with the maintenance of family relationships. We argue that his claim can be seen as a fossilized remnant of a theoretical tradition (the Parsons/ Bales argument relating to an instrumental/expressive division of labor within the nuclear family) that has increasingly gone out of fashion in other areas of sociological research. We then borrow from feminist theories relating to the ideology of intensive mothering to show why claims relating to "gendered styles of care" are problematic. Finally, we use qualitative data from interviews with the wives of caregiving husbands to suggest that the emphasis on "relationship" often found in interviews with female caregivers has less to do with the kinkeeper role typically assigned to women than with the performance of gender.

It is common in the gerontological literature to point out that the care provided to older adults by family members is gendered. Most often this means pointing out that women are far more likely to be caregivers than men (Quadagno, 2005). True, as Calasanti and Slevin (2001) note, some investigators minimize the gender gap here by focusing on spousal care only and/or by failing to make the distinction between primary and secondary caregivers—but in the end, most gerontological investigators do recognize that women, on average, provide more care than men. In the past, there was some tendency to explain this female predominance in purely psychological terms—as resulting, say, from the differences in early infantile experience posited in

[a] *Department of Sociology*, *University of Western Ontario. London, Ontario Canada N6A 5C2.*

[b]*Sociology and Health*, *Aging and Society*, *McMaster University*, *Hamilton, Ontario, Canada L8S 4M4.*

Nancy Chodorow's (1978) well-known argument. Increasingly, however, such psychological interpretations have been set aside in favor of structural explanations which stress the societal devaluation of unpaid care and the unequal power relations between men and women in the larger society (Calasanti & Slevin, 2001).

But, we want to argue, putting aside the matter of simple female predominance, there is a second claim about gender that pervades the gerontological literature on caregiving and it is a claim that has not received much scrutiny. This second claim is that women and men are associated with different "styles of caregiving." What we want to do in this article is (1) tease out from the existing literature just what this claim involves, (2) demonstrate why this claim is problematic in light of recent feminist theory, and (3) bring some qualitative data from a study of filial caregiving to bear on the issues that have been raised.

1. GENDERED STYLES OF CAREGIVING

The suggestion that caregiving style is gendered has been made most explicitly and most forcefully by investigators studying *male* caregiving. Although not every author describes the "male style of caregiving" using precisely the same terms, the general idea is that male caregiving is characterized by an instrumental and managerial orientation that is focused on specific tasks and concerned mainly with maintaining the physical well-being of the care recipient and making sure that the care recipient is happy or content (Thompson, 2002; Russell, 2001; Thompson, 2000; Chappell & Penning, 2005). The instrumental/managerial nature of male caregiving is usually seen to be a carryover from the approach that men adopt in pursuing their jobs in the paid workforce (Harris, 2002; Kaye & Applegate, 1994).

But if males are associated with an instrumental/managerial style of caregiving, what about females? Here it is harder to give a precise characterization because investigators studying female caregiving have not been as forceful in identifying a distinctively female style of caregiving. Nevertheless, we argue, implicit in much of the literature on female caregiving is the claim that female caregiving is intimately bound up (in a way that male caregiving is not) with a distinctively female concern for the maintenance of familial relationships. Such a claim, for example, seems implicit in the commonly-made suggestion that women are the kinkeepers in a family and see caregiving as an extension of their kinkeeping role (Rosenthal, 1985; MacRae, 1995). Conner (2000) provides a particularly succinct statement of this view:

> The care of older family members merges with women's traditional role as the designated kin-keepers....It is through the work of the women of the household that grandchildren, grandparents, aunts, uncles and cousins maintain relationships. The central family position occupied by women and the linkages this position provides causes women to be the caregiver of choice in many American families when the need for elder care arises. (p. 97)

The idea that female caregiving is intimately bound up with the maintenance of family relationships also seems implicit in the claim that female caregivers are more likely than male caregivers to provide care out of felt need to make connections with other family members (Dressel & Clark, 1990); the claim that daughters provide care to their mothers in ways which function to maintain the mother–daughter relationship (McGraw & Walker, 2004); and the claim that sisters, but not brothers, see the caregiving relationship with a parent as intertwined with sibling relationships (Matthews, 2002; Connidis, 2005).

But the caregiving style—involving as it does an emphasis on maintaining familial relationships—associated with female caregivers is not just seen to be different from the caregiving style associated with men; the care that women provide is also seen to be better. Although this valuation is rarely stated explicitly, it is not hard to detect. Consider, for example, how Hillary Rose and Errollyn Bruce (1995) characterize male/female differences in caregiving styles in their study of men and women caring for a spouse with dementia:

> [W]omen grieved for lost persons and for a diminished relationship; they did not take such comfort [as men] in the accomplishment of care...we began to think of men's caring as a pet rabbit relationship. A pet rabbit's survival requires conscientious care; indeed its condition is a source of pride for its carer, and the well cared for pet, or rather its owner, received much admiration. For women, the husband with Alzheimer's fails to become an equivalent pet, so they grieved.

Rose and Bruce go on to qualify their "pet rabbit" metaphor by noting they do not intend to deny the very real suffering experienced by male caregivers and by suggesting that they only want to make the point that men get more credit than women for doing the same caregiving tasks simply because caregiving is expected of women but not men. But even with these qualifications in mind, we suggest that use of the term "pet rabbit" here—a term which suggests that male caregivers dehumanize care recipients by thinking of them as pets—is loaded with negative connotations that cannot be ignored and which function to create a negative impression of male caregiving relative to an implicit contrast with female caregiving. The fact that Rose and Bruce's use of the "pet rabbit" analogy continues to be reproduced uncritically, that is, with no comment on the harshness of the metaphor being invoked (Connidis, 2001; Calasanti & Slevin, 2001), is—we argue—testament to the fact that male caregiving continues to be devalued among gerontological investigators.

2. WHO NOW READS PARSONS AND BALES?

What exists in the gerontological literature on caregiving, then, is a contrast between a male "managerial/instrumental" style of caregiving seen to be a carryover from the male experience in the workplace and a female style of caregiving concerned with the maintenance of family relationship and seen to derive from the fact that women are the kinkeepers in a family. The contrast being drawn here will almost certainly seem familiar to most readers because it matches up so perfectly with the well-known theoretical framework developed decades ago by Talcott Parsons and Robert Bales (1955). Basically, what Parsons and Bales argued is that a nuclear family (and so society itself) functions best when it is characterized by a division of labor in which the husband takes on the role of instrumental leader (which includes working outside the home) and the wife takes on the role of expressive leader (which involves maintaining family solidarity, or kinkeeping). This in turn, so the argument continued, is why society benefits by socializing males to be "instrumental" and females to be "expressive." What makes all this problematic, we suggest, is that functionalist arguments of the Parsons/Bales type, which contrast "instrumental males" with "expressive females," have otherwise gone out of fashion in thinking about gender in sociology—and with good reason.

As Kimmel (2000) points out, during the 1970s and 1980s investigators came increasingly to recognize that there are variety of masculinities and femininities in any given society and so came increasingly to reject all approaches to gender, including the Parsons/Bales approach, that saw gender as a simple binary. Certainly, it is now commonplace in gender studies to note that in any given historical and cultural context not only are there many different ways of "being masculine" and "being feminine" but that some of these masculinities and femininities are privileged over others (Connell & Messerschmidt, 2005; Connell, 1987, 1995). And yet, despite the fact that binary notions of gender are now routinely treated with suspicion in other areas of investigation, just such a binary contrast is still to be found in the caregiving literature. The concern with diversity, in other words, that seems so evident in other areas of gender study is simply absent here.

But the contrast between "managerial male caregivers" and "kinkeeping female caregivers" is more than just a fossilized remnant of an outdated theoretical argument (though it is that). It also serves a political function that needs to be problematized and the easiest way to do that is to borrow from feminist arguments about another sort of caregiving, namely, the care that mothers (should) provide to their children.

3. THE IDEOLOGY OF INTENSIVE MOTHERING

A number of feminist investigators have called attention to the ways in which particular "discourses of mothering" function to maintain gender inequality both within the family unit and within in the larger society (Cowdery & Knudson-Martin, 2005; Elvin-Nowak & Thomsson, 2001; Hays, 1997). Sharon Hays (1997), for example, examined the "expert" advice provided to parents in four bestselling child-rearing manuals. What she found was that in all four cases the authors promoted a style of "intensive mothering" that rested on a claim that was supposedly solidly supported by the evidence: child-rearing proceeds best when a child is raised by a single caretaker and when that caretaker is constantly attentive to the changing needs of the child as the child develops over time. Although none of the books examined by Hays said explicitly that that single caretaker had to be the mother, Hays marshals much evidence suggesting that this message is implicit in the discussion found in those manuals. Hays's larger point, of course, is that by promoting a style of child-rearing in which women are expected to be constantly attentive to their children, these manuals are promoting a style of child-rearing that makes it that much more difficult for women to participate in the paid labor force and so functions to maintain gender inequality.

It seems to us that much of Hays's analysis is directly transferable to the "gendered styles of care" literature. After all, what that literature suggests is that the "better" sort of caregiving is the sort where the caregiver is concerned not simply with attending to the physical and emotional needs of the care recipient in an organized (but limited) manner but is also concerned with maintaining the web of relationships in which the caregiver and care recipient are enmeshed—and in this case, perhaps even more so than in the case considered by Hays, this "better" sort of caregiving is attached to women. What all this means, in other words, is that the caregiving literature is promoting a style of caregiving that impacts women's lives in the same way(s) as the "intensive mothering" style promoted in the bestselling manuals studied by Hays.

It seems clear, for example, that it would be far easier to balance caregiving and an ongoing career in the paid labor force by adopting the sort of limited and compartmentalized caregiving that is coded "male" in the caregiving literature than by adopting the more all-embracing form of caregiving, with its emphasis on maintaining relationships, that is coded "female." By suggesting, then, if only implicitly, that the female style of caregiving is *better*, the existing gerontological literature on caregiving—just like the child-rearing manuals studied by Hays—is promoting a style of caregiving that functions to maintain gender inequality in the larger society. Phrased differently: if child-rearing manuals promote a model of caregiving that makes it difficult for a woman to have a full-time career outside the home at the age when she might have to care for young children, the existing gerontological literature on caregiving does the same thing for women at the age when they might have to care for aging parents. And the fact that relatively more (not fewer) women are taking on the role of unpaid caregiver for adult kin (Moen, Robison, & Fields, 2000) only makes this implicit privileging of the "female" style of caregiving all the more problematic.

4. CAREGIVING AS GENDER PERFORMANCE

One of the most important shifts in feminist writing over the last two decades has involved a movement away from the "sex role socialization" approach, i.e., the view that males and females differ with regard to a number of psychological traits because they have been socialized into different roles. (On the reasons why the sex role socialization approach has been set aside, see Messner, 1998.) Increasingly, investigators—building upon the early work by theorists like Candace West and Don Zimmerman (1987)—have replaced the sex role approach with an approach that sees gender as a performative act, that is, as something that males and females *do* in particular contexts by adopting behaviors that establish themselves as "male" or "female" in the eyes of an audience. (For a sampling of work done in the "doing gender" tradition, see the essays in Fenstermaker & West, 2002.)

Central to this new approach to gender is the idea that what "doing gender" means can vary, even for the same individual, depending upon the context and/or audience involved. In her study of elementary school students, for example, Barrie Thorne (1999) found that in both the schoolyard and in the classroom, gender was bound up with notions of difference. In the schoolyard, however, difference was coupled with opposition and separation whereas in the classroom it was not. The result was that in the schoolyard boys and girls did gender by maintaining separate spaces and by reacting with hostility when members of one group attempted to intrude on the other group's space. In the classroom, by contrast, these same students did gender by engaging in (relatively) friendly competitions.

Although references to the "doing gender" approach do occasionally appear in the literature on caregiving, social gerontologists—as Stoller (2002) points out—have been slow to make use of this approach in any real way when studying caregiving. This is unfortunate, we suggest, because the doing gender approach has the potential to do for the study of gender and caregiving what it has already done for the study of gender generally: to facilitate a greater appreciation of diversity. What that means, more specifically, is that this approach can prove useful in uncovering the diverse ways in which women (and men) relate to the experience of caregiving. The key here lies with what has just been said: the things we chose to do in order to "perform gender" might very well vary by context. Phrased differently, if we grant that what women (or men) "say about caregiving" can be a way of performing gender, then the doing gender approach suggests that what women (or men) "say about caregiving" in one context could be quite different from what they might "say about caregiving" in a different context.

As regards women, the emphasis on "context" in the doing gender approach seems especially relevant to the existing "gendered styles of care" literature because that literature has focused mainly on women in one particular context, namely, women who are actually providing care for their own parent or spouse and/or where the women involved are primary caregivers. But how might women use what they "say about caregiving" to do gender in a quite different context, for example, in a context where caregiving is very salient to them but where the care recipient is not their parent/ spouse and where they themselves are not the primary caregiver? It happens that some data bearing on this issue is available from a larger study on which we have already reported (Campbell & Carroll, 2007).

5. THE WIVES OF CAREGIVING HUSBANDS

The data to be used here consists of interviews with 20 married couples where the husband was a filial caregiver who had participated in a larger study of male caregiving (Campbell & Carroll, 2007). In the larger study, 58 adult sons (38 married, 10 never married and 10 formerly married) who provided care to at least one parent were recruited mainly through health and social service agencies and senior day centers and programs, with a few being contacted through caregiver support groups or newspaper solicitations. All participants lived in or around Hamilton and London (Ontario). Only men who lived within a two hour drive of the older parent's residence were recruited to diminish the potential problem that greater distance might cause for providing care (on the "two hour drive" criterion, see Hallman & Joseph, 1999).

All 38 married sons were asked if their wives would like to be interviewed separately. Of the 38 wives involved, 24 did agree to be interviewed. Since the focus in this larger study was on the male experience of caregiving, the fact that a wife declined to be interviewed did not disqualify her husband from participating in that study. The 20 couples selected for the present study, however, were the couples where (1) the wife agreed to be interviewed and (2) the wife was not the primary caregiver (i.e., where the primary caregiver was the husband or someone else).

The interviews with sons were conducted as a "guided conversation" (Lofland and Lofland 1995), encouraging respondents to share their own experiences in caregiving related to such things as the kind of care and assistance they provided to their parent; the factors they felt influenced their involvement in caregiving; the meaning caregiving had in their lives; the rewards and challenges they experienced in their caregiving role; how the caregiving role fit within the context of their other family and work responsibilities; what advice they would give to others; and so on. The general questions posed to wives were similar, although wives (at least these wives, who were—remember—not primary caregivers) were asked to comment mainly on the care their husbands provided and caregiving in general.

One member of a team of four interviewers conducted each interview; this team included the principal investigator and three (female) research assistants. Interviews lasted between 1.5 to 2 h, and were usually conducted in the respondent's home; some interviews were conducted at another location chosen by the respondent (usually the principal investigator's university office). The interviews were audio-taped and later transcribed verbatim.

Data Analysis

Analysis of the data proceeded in stages. First, each of the authors independently read all the transcripts several times and used a qualitative software program to identify and code every passage that seemed relevant to the themes that show up in the "gendered styles of caregiving" literature. This meant, in particular, identifying passages which described caregiving in purely instrumental terms (as involving the fulfillment of specific tasks) and/or which suggested that the purpose of caregiving was to maintain or promote the physical health or over-all emotional well-being of the care recipient, and passages which in any way suggested that a "relationship" was important in thinking about caregiving. The authors then met to compare notes and to arrive at a shared agreement on the themes in each of the interviews.

Sample Characteristics

The 20 wives who were interviewed ranged in age from 44 to 70, with an average age of 56; their husbands ranged in age from 44 to 73, with an average age of 57. In most cases (13) the care recipient was the husband's mother, and less frequently his father (6) or both his father and mother (1). Care recipients ranged in age from 76 to 97, with an average age of 86. Although many sons were caring for a parent living in a long-term care facility at the time of the interview, for most of these sons the provision of filial care had begun long before the move to a facility. Indeed, for many that move had only occurred very recently.

The Interviews

Although our main concern (in this article) is with the wives who were interviewed, it seems worth pointing out that the husbands in this sample did indeed have an "instrumental" approach to caregiving. Most husbands (17 of 20), in other words, thought of their caregiving in terms of specific tasks that had to be fulfilled in order to keep their parent(s) as happy and healthy as possible. And quite often, this did indeed lead them to say things that—read in isolation—might easily be seen as the sort of things you would say about a pet. For example, in response to the question "What brings [brought] you the most pleasure in providing assistance to your parent[s]," three husbands said:

> Nothing in particular other than the fact that I can say with pride and confidence that given Dad's situation health-wise, he has, I believe the best quality of life. The quality of Dad's life is as good as it can be. [husband, 53; caring for his father, 81]

> Just seeing her smile [husband, 62; caring for his mother, 83]

> Well, just seeing that he's contented. That's—that's all we want. Is that he's contented. But that's the hardest thing to get. I—anything I can do to help him, you know, I don't mind at all. But it's trying to get him contented. [husband, 58; caring for his father, 87]

But of course these (and other similar) remarks cannot be read in isolation; they must instead be read against the evidence (reviewed in Campbell & Carroll, 2007) that the male caregivers in the larger study, including the male caregivers that were part of this study, experienced a range of strong emotions as a result of the caregiving process and were quite willing to share those emotions with the interviewer. These men, in other words, had a strong emotional connection to the care recipient that something like the "pet rabbit" metaphor misses entirely.

Generally, when wives were asked about their *husband's* caregiving, these wives tended to describe that caregiving in the same instrumental terms as their husband. Wives, in others words, just like their husbands, saw the care provided by the husbands as mainly oriented to performing tasks designed to maintain health and happiness of his parent(s). When asked about their *own* role in the caregiving process, most wives routinely said that they saw their primary task to be providing support to their husband. What providing support meant varied from person to person, but generally it meant helping the husband either by taking on a few limited caregiving responsibilities, or by doing certain household tasks so that her husband would not have to do them, or simply offering words of encouragement as necessary.

But what also emerged as a theme in the interviews with wives was that "relationship" should be taken into account in deciding to provide care. Sometimes this meant taking the relationship between parent and child into account in deciding to provide care. For example, asked if she thought that adult sons had an obligation to care for their aging parents, one wife said:

> I think it would depend on their past relationship. If they haven't been close and then all of a sudden you're telling your mother what to do and where to live, I think that would be very, very difficult for both sides. [wife, 48; husband caring for his mother, 89]

In answer to the same question, another wife said:

> Just because it is your parents it doesn't mean that you have to be there taking care of them. You know, I really believe it is nice to do and if you have that type of relationship with your parents. Not everybody does, just because they are your parents doesn't mean they're great people. So I think it all depends on the relationship with them. [wife, 52; husband caring for his mother, 83]

In other cases, "relationship" came up when talking about whether a son-in-law or a daughter-in-law should provide care for their spouse's parent. Talking about sons-in-law, for example, one wife said:

> If a son-in-law is the only one left of the family and they had a good relationship with their mother-in-law, then it should be the same as a parent. A direct parent. As long as that relationship is there. But if it isn't there, then they shouldn't really feel....If it wasn't a good relationship, then I don't think that they have the obligation. It depends an awful lot on the situation. [wife, 62; husband caring for his mother, 95]

In still other cases, wives suggested that "relationship" was the *dependent* variable, that is, in deciding whether or not to provide care to an aging parent or parent-in-law, you needed to take into account the likely impact of this on other relationships. Thus, one wife said:

> You do as much as you can [in] the situation we find ourselves in. I have a friend that's in the process of trying to provide care for the husband's mother. And this woman...whoa! She's making life very difficult. And it's impacting on the whole family. It's on the wife's health, the husband's state of mind, and the kids, the grown kids who are still at home. And I don't think we are asked to put our own families at risk or ignore them. It's just...life is a balance. [wife, 61; husband caring for both of his parents: mother, 78 and father, 80]

Generally, though the particular relationship or set of relationships being discussed might vary, most wives (16 of 20) did link the decision to provide care to "relationship" in some way. By contrast, only a minority (4 of 20) of husbands did anything similar in their interviews.

Notice that all this is not quite what the "gendered styles of care" literature would lead us to expect. That literature, after all, suggests that women are kinkeepers concerned with *maintaining* relationships, and so women make the matter of "*maintaining* relationships" central to the way they think about caregiving. But the wives here did *not* say (as the existing caregiving literature might suggest) that caregiving functioned to maintain the relationship between their husband and his parent, or that caregiving connected the caregiving husband and the care recipient to a larger network of family relationships or that being embedded in a network of family relationships obligated you to provide care. What they said instead was something slightly different: "relationship" is important in thinking about caregiving, but important because you need to think about existing "relationships" when deciding whether or not to provide care in the first place.

As an aside, we note that while most wives (including all those cited above) talked about "relationship" using a familial idiom, this is not the only possible option. One wife, for example, linked "providing care" and "relationship" using a religious idiom. Thus, when asked to comment on whether the care that her husband provided to his father was typical or not, she said:

> I think he's unique [and] I think a lot of that comes from our faith and his personal walk with the Lord, um, I guess in world terms we would be considered religious. I don't know if you know what the term "born again" means but we

consider ourselves born again, which means we have—we feel we have—a personal relationship with Jesus Christ, and that I think makes a big difference in our life because we don't walk to the tune of, well, what feels good to me. We walk to the tune of, ah, sometimes it is self sacrificing, sometimes it's not what either of us want to do. [wife, 44: husband caring for his father, 82]

An emphasis on being born-again and having a personal relationship with Jesus Christ is of course a hallmark of evangelical Christianity, and it might not at first seem surprising that someone firmly committed to this tradition might justify caregiving in these terms. All the more interesting, then, that this woman's husband did not. In his own interview, in other words, although this husband did say vaguely that his caregiving activities "are rooted in my beliefs about Christianity," he at no point mentioned a relationship with Jesus Christ and certainly did not link his caregiving to such a relationship in that way that his wife did.

6. DISCUSSION

One way to make sense of both the findings in the "gendered styles of care" literature and the findings reported above is to suggest that "emphasizing relationship" in *some* way is a way for women to do gender when faced with an audience (which can include a spouse, friends, or an interviewer). When a woman is caring for her own parent, especially when she is the primary caregiver, one obvious way to do this ("emphasize relationship") is to suggest that caregiving is bound up with the maintenance of family relationships—and this is more or less the finding that has been reported in the "gendered styles of care" literature. But this is only one of many ways to "emphasize relationship" in order to do gender. When the care recipient is *not* her own parent (which means, on average, that any pre-existing relationship will be less salient), and when the woman is *not* the primary caregiver (which likely makes it easier to separate out the matter of caregiving in general from the specific case at hand), then other ways of "emphasizing relationship" in order to do gender become feasible. And some of those possibilities are the ones which emerged in the interviews here (e.g., the quality of a relationship should determine whether care is provided; in thinking about whether to provide care you need to think about the effect on other relationships; an obligation to provide care flows from your relationship with Jesus Christ).

We do not mean to suggest of course that the possibilities discussed here exhaust the ways that (statements about) caregiving can be used to do gender. Certainly, further research would be useful. In the larger study from which the present sample was drawn, for example, there were 33 caregiving sons who were married and whose wife was not the primary caregiver. Although 20 of the wives involved did agree to be interviewed (and these are the 20 cases considered here), the fact remains that 13 wives did not agree to be interviewed. What the "missing 13" might have said—if anything—about caregiving and "relationship" is not known. The patterns evident in the material here, in other words, likely do not exhaust the range of possibilities for doing gender when women talk about caregiving.

On the other hand, we do suggest that the results reported here do have wider implications for the study of caregiving. It is common, for example, to suggest that theory building in social gerontology has lagged behind data collection with the result that the discipline is "data rich and theory-poor" (Bengston, Putney, & Johnson, 2005). Typically, this sort of characterization is then immediately paired with a call for more theoretical analysis, as with—to take an example that seems especially relevant to the analysis presented here—Calasanti's (2004) recent call for a greater use of feminist theory in gerontology. What is usually overlooked in these calls for "more theory in social gerontology" however is that a disciplinary culture which attaches little value to theoretical analysis simultaneously attaches little value to critical reflection on the theoretical frameworks that might indeed lurk beneath some particular set of analyses. And *that*, we suggest, leads to what has been uncovered in this article: the continuing use in the caregiving literature of a view of gender, deriving from the work of Parsons and Bales, that has increasingly gone out of fashion (for good reason) in other areas of social research.

Phrased differently, the analysis here suggests that for social gerontology to move forward what is required is not simply "more theory" (though that is certainly needed) but also critical reflection on the "theory" currently being used.

REFERENCES

Bengston, V. L., Putney, N. M., & Johnson, M. L. (2005). The problem of theory in gerontology today. In M. L. Johnson (Ed.), *The Cambridge handbook of age and ageing*. Cambridge, UK: Cambridge University Press.

Calasanti, T. (2004). New directions in feminist gerontology: An introduction. *Journal of Aging Studies, 18, 1–8*.

Calasanti, T. M., & Slevin, K. F. (2001). *Gender, social inequalities and aging*. Walnut Creek, CA: AltaMira Press.

Campbell, L. D., & Carroll, M. P. (2007). The incomplete revolution: Theorizing gender when studying men who provide care to aging parents. *Men and Masculinities, 9 (April)*.

Chappell, N. L., & Penning, M. J. (2005). Family caregivers: Increasing demands in the context of 21st-century globalization? In M. L. Johnson (Ed.), *The Cambridge handbook of age and ageing*. Cambridge, UK: Cambridge University Press.

Chodorow, N. (1978). *The reproduction of mothering*. Berkeley, CA: University of California Press.

Connell, R. W. (1987). *Gender and power: Society, the person and sexual politics*. Cambridge, UK: Polity Press.

Connell, R. W. (1995). *Masculinities*. Berkeley, CA: University of California Press.

Connell, R. W., & Messerschmidt, J. W. (2005). Hegemonic masculinity: Rethinking the concept. *Gender and Society*, 19(6), 829–859.

Conner, K. A. (2000). *Continuing to care: Older Americans and their families*. New York: Falmer Press.

Connidis, I. A. (2001). *Family ties and aging*. Thousand Oaks, CA: Sage.

Connidis, I. A. (2005). Sibling ties across time: The middle and later years. In M. L. Johnson (Ed.), *The Cambridge handbook of age and ageing*. Cambridge, UK: Cambridge University Press.

Cowdery, R. S., & Knudson-Martin, C. (2005). The construction of motherhood: Tasks, relational connection, and gender equality. *Family Relations*, 54, 335–345.

Dressel, P. L., & Clark, A. (1990). A critical look at family care. *Journal of Marriage and the Family*, 52(August), 769–782.

Elvin-Nowak, Y., & Thomsson, H. (2001). Motherhood as idea and practice: A discursive understanding of employed mothers in Sweden. *Gender and Society,* 15(3), 407–428.

Fenstermaker, S., & West, C. (Eds.). (2002). *Doing gender, doing difference: Inequality, power and institutional change.* New York: Routledge.

Hallman, B. C., & Joseph, A. E. (1999). Getting there: Mapping the gendered geography of caregiving to the elderly. *Canadian Journal on Aging,* 18(4), 397–414.

Harris, P. B. (2002). The voices of husbands and sons caring for a family member with dementia. In B. J. Kramer, & E. H. Thompson (Eds.), *Men as caregivers: Theory, research and service implications.* New York: Springer Publishing Company.

Hays, S. (1997). The ideology of intensive mothering: A cultural analysis of the bestselling gurus of appropriate childrearing. In E. Long (Ed.), *From sociology to cultural studies: New perspectives Malden, Mass.*: Blackwell Publisher.

Kaye, L. W., & Applegate, J. S. (1994). Older men and the family caregiving orientation. In E. H. Thompson Jr. (Ed.), *Older men's lives.* Thousand Oaks, CA: Sage Publications.

Kimmel, M. (2000). The gendered society New York: Oxford University Press.

Lofland, J., & Lofland, L. H. (1995). *Analyzing Social Settings.* Belmont, CA: Wadsworth.

MacRae, H. M. (1995). Women and caring: Constructing self through others. *Journal of Women and Aging,* 7(1/2), 145–167.

Matthews, S. H. (2002). Brothers and parent Care: An explanation for sons' underrepresentation. In B. J. Kramer, & E. H. Thompson Jr. (Eds.), *Men as caregivers: Theory, research and service implications.* New York: Springer Publishing Company.

McGraw, L. A., & Walker, A. J. (2004). Negotiating care: Ties between aging mothers and their caregiving daughters. *The Journals of Gerontology: Social Sciences,* 59B(6), S324–S332.

Messner, M. (1998). The limits of "the male sex role": An analysis of the Men's Liberation and Men's Rights movements discourse. *Gender and Society,* 12(3), 255–276.

Moen, P., Robison, J., & Fields, V. (2000). Women's work and caregiving roles: A life course approach. In E. P. Stoller, & R. C. Gibson (Eds.), *In Worlds of difference: Inequality in the aging experience.* Thousand Oaks, CA: Pine Forge Press.

Parsons, T., & Bales, R. (1955). *Family, socialization and interaction process.* New York: The Free Press.

Quadagno, J. (2005). *Aging and the life course: An introduction to social gerontology.* Boston: McGraw Hill.

Rose, H., & Bruce, E. (1995). Mutual care but differential esteem: caring between older couples. In S. Arber, & J. Ginn (Eds.), *Connecting gender and ageing: A sociological approach.* Buckingham, UK: Open University Press.

Rosenthal, C. J. (1985). Kinkeeping in the familial division of labor. *Journal of Marriage and the Family,* 47(4), 965–974.

Russell, R. (2001). In sickness and in health: A qualitative study of elderly men who care for wives with dementia. *Journal of Aging Studies,* 15, 351–367.

Stoller, E. P. (2002). Theoretical perspectives on caregiving men. In E. H. Thompson Jr., & B. J. Kramer (Eds.), *Men as caregivers: Theory, research and service implications.* New York: Springer Publishing Company.

Thompson, E. H. (2000). Gendered arriving of husbands and sons. In E. W. Markson, & L. A. Hollis-Sawyer (Eds.), *Intersections of aging: Readings in social gerontology.* Los Angeles: Roxbury Publishing Company.

Thompson, E. H. (2002). What's unique about men's caregiving? In B. J. Kramer, & E. H. Thomson (Eds.), *Men as caregivers: Theory, research and service implications.* New York: Springer Publishing Company.

Thorne, B. (1999). *Gender play: girls and boys in school.* New Brunswick, NJ: Rutgers University Press.

West, C., & Zimmerman, D. (1987). Doing gender. *Gender and Society,* 1(2), 125–151.

3

FAMILY DEVELOPMENT THEORY

John and Natasha Morrison were looking forward to their retirement in a few years. Their eldest daughter Tamara was just finishing law school and was pregnant with her first child. John Jr., their only son, was doing well in college and planning a career in communications. Their youngest daughter Kamika would soon be graduating from high school. With her college tuition safely tucked away in an education IRA, they were hoping to take retirement in their early sixties. As a couple with active professional careers and three children, they had often dreamed of an extended vacation but had been too busy to take one. They planned to take a grand world tour when they retired.

Natasha's parents, who lived nearby and saw the family regularly, came to visit for Father's Day. The family sat around the picnic table out back and reminisced about the changes in their lives over the years. When the children were young, they all had the same kinds of activities and friends. Now it was as if they were all in their own separate worlds. It was difficult to find time together because each person was so busy and focused on his or her own life. John and Natasha were worried about John's father, who lived 500 miles away and was in poor health. Tamara and her husband were busy getting ready for their first child and establishing their professional careers. John Jr. was beginning to show signs of seriousness about a girlfriend for the first time in his life. Kamika was hardly ever at home anymore, staying busy with her friends and after-school activities. She was particularly interested in dance and recently had made a new friend, Matt, who also wanted to be a dancer.

Everyone gathered around the table to watch John open his Father's Day presents. Kamika seemed very excited. "Daddy, I have the greatest surprise for you! You'll be so excited. I'm going to New York to be a dancer! I've been accepted into a little company in New York where they will train me, and Matt and I are moving there in a month! Isn't that just great?"

HISTORY

Family development theory emerged in the late 1940s, corresponding with the development of the field of family science. It was one of the first family-focused theories, with a separate identity from psychology or sociology. Psychology-based theories, with their narrower emphasis on individuals, did not fully explain what happened in families with competing individual needs. Sociology-based theories, focused on society and culture, were too broad in their analyses. Thus, family development theory originated from the critiques of these two perspectives.

Evelyn Duvall and Ruben Hill (1948) pointed out that families were social groups that were influenced by developmental processes. Like individuals, families experienced life cycles, with clearly delineated stages, each of which required the accomplishment of specific tasks. But families needed to be studied as a dynamic unit, not as a collection of individuals. According to family developmental theorists, the family life cycle had two major stages—expansion and contraction. During expansion, children are born and raised, whereas during contraction, children leave the family home. This cycle of expansion and contraction gave rise to the term *family life cycle* (Duvall 1957).

In 1948, Duvall and Hill first presented their version of the family life cycle in which they identified tasks that were accomplished by both parents and children. These tasks were grouped into eight stages of development across the family life cycle. Later versions of the theory went beyond the demarcation of stages and tasks and began to focus on changes within the family over time, including transitions and social roles. Duvall later codified these in her textbook *Family Development*, first published in 1957. Updated and republished many times (with revised editions in 1962, 1967, 1971, and 1977), it was one of the most widely used textbooks on the subject for the next thirty years. Thus, Duvall's eight stages of the family life cycle are the best-known stages of family development theory.

Other theorists, building on the foundation laid by Duvall and Hill (1948), worked to expand these concepts. In 1964, Roy Rodgers (1964) developed a version of the theory with twenty-four different stages, but its complexity overshadowed its usefulness. Rodgers (1973) further expanded the concept of family interaction by focusing on three dynamics across the family career. He emphasized that families were influenced by institutional norms, by the expectations from the family itself, and by the expectations of the individuals within the family. In contrast, Joan Aldous (1978, 1996) suggested that family development should be considered in four stages, because families are often in several stages of parenting at the same time. She further recommended the use of the term *family career*, rather than *family life cycle*, because families did not return to the way they were at the beginning of their lives as a family.

In the 1970s and 1980s, some family scholars criticized family development theory because it lacked scientific testability. In 1973, Wesley Burr, a renowned theorist and researcher, reviewed many of the major issues in family studies, including the family life cycle. In his book, Burr (1973) wrote: "It has not yet been proved that the family life cycle will turn out to be a very useful concept in deductive theories" (219). His concern with the theory was that the concepts and variables were not well defined and so could not be properly tested in empirical research. Addressing these concerns, James White published a book in 1991 entitled *Dynamics of Family Development: A Theoretical Perspective,* in which he outlined specific testable propositions and variables for family development theory. White is considered one of the major proponents of family development theory today.

At about the same time, a new variant of family development theory—life course perspective, as applied to families—was being described. The life course perspective went beyond the life cycle view by including additional variables, such as multiple views of time (ontogenetic, generational, and historical), micro- and macro-social contexts, and increasing diversity over time (Bengtson and Allen 1993).

Most recently, Tracey Laszloffy (2002) modified family development theory to address two fundamental weaknesses—the assumption that the stages are universally experienced by all families and the bias toward the experience of a single generation. Her revision, called the systemic family development model, conceptualizes the family as a round, multi-layered cake and helps to visualize the impact of family change on complex multigenerational systems.

BASIC ASSUMPTIONS

Aldous (1978), White (1991), and White and Klein (2008) were helpful in outlining the basic assumptions of family development theory.

Just like individuals, families change over time, and these developmental processes are essential for understanding families. Family development theory focuses on the developmental processes of individuals and families over time. Transitions from one stage to the next are usually related to changes in individuals due to maturation and aging, relationships between members, family structure, and norms associated with family roles. Although early theorists believed that families changed in fairly similar and predictable ways over the life course, more-recent thinking assumes greater variation in how these processes manifest themselves in different families.

There are tasks associated with each stage of development. Tasks are defined on the basis of normative expectations. Each stage is delineated by a set of tasks that must be accomplished to prepare adequately for the next stage of development. Failure to complete a task does not necessarily preclude moving to the next stage of development, but it may limit a family's optimal functioning at the next level. For example, parents who pay too much attention to child rearing and not enough to their own relationship may encounter problems with their relationship after the children leave home. Thus, a family's history (including the extent to which it accomplished its responsibilities at each stage) affects its goals, expectations, and future behaviors.

Institutional norms regulate family behavior. These norms control "which events are permitted, required, and forbidden; the order in which families should sequence stages; and the duration of those stages" (White 1991, 57). These social norms or rules also regulate how family members fulfill their roles within their family. For example, it is still the social norm that people will marry first and then have children, although there are more exceptions to this rule than there were in the past.

Development is reciprocal. The individual development of each family member influences other family members, as well as the overall development of the family. Reciprocally, the family's development also influences the critical periods of individual development. Because there is reciprocity in the interaction of the family and individual development, it is necessary to consider them together.

Families must be viewed in multiple levels of analysis. Family development theory requires that family life be considered in the multiple contexts of the society, the family, and the individual. The social context and/or historical period influence both the processes within the family and the developmental issues encountered by individuals within the family. The larger society, for instance, can exert environmental pressures to behave in certain ways at particular points in the family life cycle. Think about the family in the vignette at the beginning of this chapter. The behavior of Kamika and Matt would not have been acceptable in earlier historical periods.

Families should be viewed over time. One of family development theory's core assumptions is that families are not static but change over time. This *changing over time* is the primary focus of the theory. How and when families change, what they accomplish at different points in time, and why they change can be known **only** if one studies families over time.

PRIMARY TERMS AND CONCEPTS

Family

Family developmental scholars have long debated the most appropriate and inclusive definition of family. Duvall (1977) proposed that the family is composed of "interacting persons related by ties of marriage, birth, or adoption, whose central purpose is to create and maintain a common culture which promotes the physical, mental, emotional, and social development of each of its members" (5). More recent formulations have noted that any definition should include the family as a social group; the family as part of a greater institution of marriage and family; and institutional norms that outline family roles and role relationships (Rodgers and White, 1993). White (1991) offered this definition: "A family is an intergenerational social group organized and governed by social norms regarding descent and affinity, reproduction, and the nurturant socialization of the young" (7).

Family Development

Development occurs as families make the transition from one stage to another. According to Rodgers and White (1993), family development can be analyzed at four different levels: "the *individual* family member, family *relationships*, the family *group*, and the *institution* of family" (231). Thus, for the individual, development might be framed as a particular period of family life, such as "retirement." (John and Natasha Morrison, from the vignette at the beginning of the chapter, will need to reconfigure how they spend their time after they retire. As a couple, retirement may signal a new chapter in their lives together, including more time to travel. In terms of the family group, John and Natasha's retirement may signal the acquisition of new expectations for their adult children; for example, their need for caregiving may affect other family members. At the institutional level, norms may prescribe appropriate behaviors for them as retirees.) As we can see, the dynamics of the family may change over time, dependent on the needs of the individuals, the relationships between them, and the impact of society.

Stages

Probably the most unique aspect of family development theory is its focus on the stages of the family life cycle. These stages are periods of "relative equilibrium in which consensus about the allocation of roles and rules of procedure is high" (Hill 1986, 21). In the model developed by Duvall and Hill, stages are the result of major changes in family size, in the developmental age of the oldest child, or in the work status of the breadwinner(s) (Hill 1986). Stages are thought to be qualitatively distinct from each other, often precipitated by normative events that happen with the passage of time, such as marriages, childbirth, and developmental and educational milestones.

Transitions

One cannot study change without studying transitions. Transitions are the processes that form a bridge between the different states when something changes. In family development theory, transitions are the shifts in roles and identities encountered with changes in developmental stages (Hagestad 1988). (For John and Natasha Morrison, their experience of moving into the middle years may be dependent upon their sense of success in their parenting roles, as well as the degree to which they nurtured their own marital relationship in previous stages.) Ease of transition is dependent on the resolution of the stages beforehand, or the degree to which the stage is perceived to be a crisis. As families shift from one stage to the next, their roles, behaviors, and tasks are reallocated in accordance with their new stage. Some families move easily from one stage to the next, and some do not. Depending on how prepared they are for the new stage, families respond to a change as either a crisis or an opportunity (Rapoport 1963). Family stress is usually greatest at transition points between developmental stages.

According to Rodgers and White (1993), family transitions might be operationalized as *events*. "Events are the transition points between stages" (White (1991, 42). Some developmental events that constitute transitions, such as when one's child begins school, are easy to recognize. Other transitions, such as identifying exactly when a child becomes an adolescent, are more difficult for the family to pinpoint and accommodate. Furthermore, crises can create critical transitions—i.e., those that occur in addition to normally expected transitions, such as an unexpected pregnancy. Focusing on transitions helps us to understand what families go through as they move from stage to stage (Duvall 1988).

Change

Something changes when it undergoes a transformation from one state to another. For example, John and Natasha Morrison's experience of family, noted in the vignette at the beginning of this chapter, will be different when the last child Kamika graduates from high school and moves to New York, leaving them with their house all to themselves. Family development theory proposes that family relationships are not static but rather change over time. Catalysts for change can be either internal (such as biological growth) or external (through interaction with the environment). The nature of this interaction is reciprocal—i.e., the organism both elicits and responds to stimuli in its environment.

Change comes with varying levels of acknowledgment and acceptance by family members. Individual changes become the catalyst for family change, causing shifts from one family stage to another. Changes in personal roles within the family are often the result of individual changes and transitions from one stage to the next.

Developmental Tasks

The concept of tasks in family development theory is derived from a similar concept of tasks, as defined by Havighurst (1948, 1953), in individual developmental theory. According to Havighurst, developmental tasks occur at particular points over the life course in response to either physical maturation or cultural pressures and changes. The individual must respond by developing new abilities, roles, or relationships. If the challenge of development is met positively, then the individual will be happier and have more success with later stages of development. If not, then, as with other stage theories of development (e.g., Erikson and Piaget), we would predict that the individual would be less successful.

Using this model, Duvall and Hill (1948) incorporated specific tasks for each of the eight stages of the family life cycle. These tasks focus on what the family, as a unit, must accomplish, while also taking into account the individual needs of the parents and children. For example, Duvall (1957, 1977) outlined the tasks (as an individual) that a child would have to achieve to optimally develop. She further linked those individual tasks to the tasks that the family must achieve as it assimilates the individual child into its unit. For example, when a newborn moves into the toddler stage, the family must create a safe physical environment for the toddler to explore. Later, when a young adult enters into the launching phase or plans to leave home, the family's task is to provide a secure base while recognizing that the young adult's reliance on the family may be more economic than physical at this point. Each stage of development requires the family to change and accommodate the needs of the children as they grow up (Duvall 1977).

Rodgers and White (1993) challenge the utility of the *family developmental task*, as they find the concept problematic. Although there certainly might be "relatively common family patterns" (227) that occur during a developmental stage, they wonder if it is possible to truly define "success" and "failure" at mastering tasks, and if such mastery is indeed critical prior to movement to the next stage.

Norms

Each stage of development is related to behaviors or tasks that would normally be expected to occur during that stage. Norms govern both group and individual behaviors, often defining the roles that people play. It is important to note that these norms are socially defined and change over time as cultural mores change. There are two types of norms: static and process. Static norms regulate behavior and expectations within a particular stage. For instance, a static norm might dictate the appropriate age or stage for consumption of alcoholic beverages. Although children may not legally drink, upon reaching the age of 21 (or other legally defined age), young adults are allowed the choice to consume alcohol. Similarly, a static norm would mandate that a father protect and provide for children in the home. Process norms regulate timing and sequencing of expectations and behaviors over the family life course. For example, in many Western cultures, it is expected that love will precede marriage. Another process norm might be that marriage will precede childbearing.

Timing

When something happens has an impact on family life. Time is multifaceted. *Timing as normative* recognizes that social prescriptions exist as to *when* individuals and families are to engage in particular behaviors or accomplish certain tasks. Pressure exists for family life events to occur "on time," rather than "off time" (Neugarten, Moore, and Lowe 1965). *Age timing* notes the chronological demarcation of a beginning event. For the individual, that beginning is a birthday, just as an anniversary might denote the age of a relationship. *Event and stage sequencing* suggests that the order in which a family approaches events and stages has ramifications for family development. In other words, it makes a difference to the family when a child is born, when a couple marries, when someone retires, or when someone moves out of the house. This is particularly apparent when there are multiple events occurring at or near the same time. For instance, many traditional-aged college students often note that parents and others hold expectations about the normative order in which they should do things; first, they should finish their education, then get a job, and only then get married.

The life course perspective theorists introduced the concept of different qualities of time into family development theory. *Ontogenetic time* refers to the time one recognizes as one grows and changes through one's own lifetime (one's personal awareness of time—like an "internal clock"). *Generational time* refers to how time is experienced within one's social group (as in one's family or in a cohort). *Historical time* refers to how time is experienced in the social context or greater historical period (e.g., living during the Great Depression in contrast to being a baby boomer; Bengtson and Allen 1993). Thus, one can experience one's adolescent period as a unique stage in one's developmental history (ontogenetically speaking). But it might matter whether one's adolescence was experienced during the turbulent Vietnam era or the recession of 2009 (generationally speaking). Similarly, it might make some difference if one becomes a first-time parent at the age of seventeen or at the age of forty-four.

COMMON AREAS OF RESEARCH AND APPLICATION

The Family Life Cycle

Evelyn Duvall's eight-stage model (see Table 3.1) is one of the original versions of the family development theory. As with all stage theories, there are specific tasks associated with each stage. The chart provided by Duvall and Miller (1985)[1] provides a delineation of those eight stages, corresponding family positions, and associated developmental tasks.

Table 3.1 Stage-Sensitive Family Developmental Tasks through the Family Life Cycle

Stages of the family life cycle	Positions in the family	Stage-sensitive family developmental tasks
1. Married Couple	Wife Husband	Establishing a mutually satisfying marriage Adjusting to pregnancy and the promise of parenthood Fitting into the kin network
2. Childbearing	Wife-mother Husband-father Infant daughter or son or both	Having, adjusting to, and encouraging the development of infants Establishing a satisfying home for both parents and infant(s)
3. Preschool age	Wife-mother Husband-father Daughter-sister Son-brother	Adapting to the critical needs and interests of preschool children in stimulating, growth-promoting ways Coping with energy depletion and lack of privacy as parents
4. School age	Wife-mother Husband-father Daughter-sister Son-brother	Fitting into the community of school-age families in constructive ways Encouraging children's educational achievement
5. Teenage	Wife-mother Husband-father Daughter-sister Son-brother	Balancing freedom with responsibility as teenagers mature and emancipate themselves Establishing post-parental interests and careers as growing parents
6. Launching Center	Wife-mother-grandmother Husband-father-grandfather Daughter-sister-aunt Son-brother-uncle	Releasing young adults into work, military service, college, marriage, and so on, with appropriate rituals and assistance Maintaining a supportive home base
7. Middle aged Parents	Wife-mother-grandmother Husband-father-grandfather	Refocusing on the marriage relationship Maintaining kin ties with older and younger generations
8. Aging Family Members	Widow or widower Wife-mother-grandmother Husband-father-grandfather	Coping with bereavement and living alone Closing the family home or adapting it to aging Adjusting to retirement

Each of the stages can be more thoroughly examined in an effort to better understand the events and developmental tasks associated with it.

Stage 1: Establishment phase—courtship and marriage. Stage 1 is known as the *establishment phase* because couples are focused on establishing their home base. There are many tasks associated with the establishment phase of relationships, and as in individual developmental models, the accomplishment of future tasks relies heavily on the successful negotiation of the previous stage's tasks. If couples can blend their individual needs and desires, find workable solutions to conflicts, and maintain good communication and intimacy patterns, then they are better able to handle the tasks associated with the next stages.

Individuals thinking about forming a couple need to learn about each other's desires, dreams, expectations, and style of living. They need to find out more about each other's habits and hobbies, ways of interacting with their friends and families, and likes and dislikes, from foods to movies to household decor. In addition to these pragmatic considerations, couples also have to develop intellectual and emotional communication patterns, patterns of behaviors and preferences, and a jointly workable philosophy of life and set of values. Some couples, frequently encouraged by clergy or marriage educators and counselors, participate in a marriage preparation program in order to be certain that the most important issues have been discussed. Once these topics are explored, the marriage ceremony is an outward and clearly demarcated symbol of status change for couples. It receives both legal sanction and public recognition and, in many instances, religious validation. Before cohabitation became more common, the marriage ceremony also signaled the end of individuals living separately.

The new marital tasks for the couple include developing systems for acquiring and spending money, establishing daily routines, and creating a satisfying sex life. Both partners must also create new and appropriate relationships with relatives and old friends while establishing new friendships as a couple.

Many of the tasks associated with early marriage focus on the establishment of a home suitable for children. Some of these tasks include developing family-planning strategies, agreeing on the timing of pregnancy, arranging for the care of the baby, acquiring knowledge regarding parenthood, and adapting the home to accommodate children.

Stage 2: Childbearing families—families with infants. The arrival of an infant brings about a new set of tasks for the family to face. The new roles of "father" and "mother" appear. The couple must now negotiate how they will share the new responsibilities of caring for the child and must reallocate previously assigned household responsibilities.

Parents must provide food, clothing, shelter, and medical care for their infant, as well as nurture their infant's cognitive and emotional needs. Infants require a safe and stimulating environment, which can include car seats, diapers, cribs, and toys. The couple might have to expand their household space by moving to a new home or rearranging their current space and how they use it.

All of this, of course, costs money, which places an additional financial demand on the family. These stressors can be damaging to the couple's relationship, so the couple must continue to practice effective communication strategies to maintain a strong bond. They should also remember to pay attention to their own relationship while they attend to their infant's needs.

Stage 3: Families with preschool children. Preschoolers need structure in their play and activities, and they benefit from intensive parental involvement. When there is more than one child, parents need to manage greater physical needs and adjust to individual differences and temperaments of the children. Infants and toddlers also need a lot of physical attention, with diaper changes and feedings, as well as emotional and cognitive nurturing.

Just as in Stage 2, there are the issues of additional physical space and additional financial demands. The more children there are, the more difficult it becomes for the couple to meet their own developmental needs and continue to grow as a couple. Despite demands on the resources of time, energy, and money, the couple still needs to spend meaningful time together.

Stage 4: Families with school-aged children. School represents an expansion of the family to other social systems that influence the family system in significant ways. Parents relinquish some authority to the school. Their parenting skills and their children's behaviors are judged in this public forum as well.

Families with school-aged children must provide for their children's activities inside and outside of school; these often include sports, music, and religious and social interactions. Parents must work to develop relationships with teachers, religious leaders, and parents of other children. They must develop strategies for accomplishing tasks around the home, particularly if schedules require the parents and children to be away from home more frequently, and find ways to appropriately delegate family tasks to various family members. Parents must also determine what the appropriate expectations are for their children (who may be at different developmental stages) for helping around the house, developing responsible behavior, watching television, or listening to music. Parental monitoring is important. For instance, R-rated movies may be prohibited in one ten-year-old's household but may be allowed at her friend's house. One reason for this may be that, as their children's physical autonomy increases, many parents increase their level of parental monitoring.

Stage 5: Families with adolescents. As in Stage 4, individual development drives the family in Stage 5. Adolescence is a time of rapid physical (sexual), cognitive, and psychosocial change. Parents must allow adolescents to establish their own separate identities, which sometimes may be in conflict with the family's values and ideas. Duvall (1957) states that open communication helps parents and adolescents learn from each other and helps to bridge the generation gap.

The adolescent may express a need for more space, both physical and emotional, more freedom to choose activities, and more activities to do, along with the need for more money to do those things. In addition, many adolescents and their parents have concerns about their futures, including the cost of tuition for college or technical training.

Adolescents are able to share more of the responsibilities of family living, perhaps cooking meals, making repairs around the house, or looking after younger children. This enables many parents to work longer hours and earn more money without having to spend money on child care for younger children. Thus, families can find ways to develop cooperative and symbiotic interactions.

Stage 6: Families with young adults—the launching stage. This stage begins when the oldest child leaves home and ends when the last child has left. During the launching stage, the family experiences the cycle of contraction.

Whenever one member leaves the family, the family must adapt, and this includes reallocating responsibilities, duties, and roles among the family members who remain at home. At times, there is a reallocation of physical facilities and resources, such as when bedrooms are shifted after the oldest child moves away. More frequently, there is a reallocation of financial resources, because the oldest child's move may entail financial burdens such as tuition, room and board at a university, a large wedding, or supplementing the oldest child's finances until he or she "gets situated."

As the children leave the physical home, communication patterns change. Daily casual communication or chatting around the dinner table gives way to phone calls or text messages. The nature of the communication might also change to include crisis management and questions about how to cope with being on one's own. When good communication patterns between parents and children have been established in previous stages, young adults can rely on their parents to support them during the launching stage.

With launching comes an ever-widening family circle where friends and new family members enter into the family setting. From a roommate who visits on Thanksgiving to a potential life partner, young adults' relationships bring a new dimension into the family structure. Similarly, their new interactions may also bring divergent life philosophies into the family. Reconciling these differences can bring about major family changes.

Stage 7: The middle years. The middle years refer to the time after all the children have launched, but before the parents retire. One of the associated tasks is ensuring security for later years by increasing retirement accounts. The couple must reallocate household responsibilities once again, as they are no longer serving as "shuttle services" for their busy teens. They need to work to maintain a comfortable home, but they may look for a smaller one that requires less maintenance and space, given that their children have moved out. Although the children are not physically there, emotional ties still exist, of course, so parents must develop new methods of extended family contacts, which can include increased phone contact, electronic communication, or visits. Their children begin to have children during this stage, and now the couple can begin to develop relationships with their grandchildren.

So what is a couple to do when they stop being caretakers of their children? For many couples, this is a major transition, as they have just lost the job of parenting that they had for 20 to 25 years. Couples who neglected their own relationships during the child-rearing years may be at risk during this time. Or, couples might take the opportunity to renew their relationship with their partner and become more involved in community life by pursuing political office, volunteer work, or mission work. They may also simply indulge themselves, for example, by eating out more frequently. Most importantly, the couple must work to maintain their own communication, as they consider what they want to accomplish during the remainder of their lives.

Stage 8: Aging family members. According to Duvall (1957 [rev. ed. 1977]), this last stage "begins with the man's retirement, goes through the loss of the first spouse, and ends with the death of the second" (385). This stage includes the task of adjusting to retirement, including the reduced income that retirement frequently brings. If there is illness or physical limitation, couples may seek a new home arrangement that is more satisfying or safe, such as a retirement village, long-term care facility, or moving in with one of their children. All such transitions require a shift in household routines.

Aging adults continue to spend time with their adult children and grandchildren. Some of these couples may need to care for their elderly relatives, as well as their grandchildren. As the couple ages, they encounter the deaths of family and friends more frequently. Older relatives die, and then friends of their own generation whom they may have known for years, or even decades, begin to die. As they face bereavement, the couple must prepare for their own death and the death of their partner. The family cycle is complete when the last partner dies.

The Family Career

Aldous (1978, 1996) built on the concept of the family life cycle, but noted that not all families followed the cycle from beginning to end, as in the case of divorced or remarried families. She preferred the term *family careers* to indicate that families followed stages that were somewhat predictable but not cyclical in nature. Moreover, she combined Duvall's (1957) stages of parenting into one stage, because parents were often in several stages of parenting at the same time (depending upon the ages of their children). Thus, Aldous's family career had only four stages—the establishment of the marital relationship, the parental role, the return to the couple relationship, and the aging couple.

Aldous's model did not focus exclusively on the family, however, but went further to include dimensions of family interdependency and social networks. For example, in addition to her analysis of the family career, she also considered the parent-child career and the sibling career, and how these interactions changed over the lifespan of the family. Expanding on the sibling career, Cicerelli (1994) indicated that the sibling relationship was, for many individuals, likely to be the longest bond experienced in their lifetimes.

The Dynamics of Family Development

White (1991) and his colleagues (Rodgers and White 1993; Watt and White 1999) expanded the family development theory to provide a more contextualized perspective. The stages of family development are driven not only by the ontogenetic development of the individuals, but also by the contexts in which the development occurs. These changing contexts make the family development stages dynamic rather than static. This perspective still takes into account stages over time but recognizes that, in this social context, all families do not follow the exact same path at the exact same time (White 1991). Understanding the family as a dynamic process encourages researchers to see fluidity and interrelationships between the process of development, the individual, and the context of the development (Fuller and Fincham 1994).

Interestingly, Watt and White (1999) found that the family development perspective created a structure for analyzing how computer technology pervades family life. Through each family developmental stage, computers serve as inexpensive tools for education, recreation, and communication. For example, computers affect mate selection by creating a "space" for cyber dating. Computers assist newly married couples with financial planning and career enhancement. When children leave the home, computers can help parents fill the "empty nest" with e-mail or allow them to pursue educational and occupational interests.

It is not enough, according to White (1991), to simply note that computers are used differently in each stage, but their use must also be studied based on context. For example, are boys more likely to use computers than girls? Does differential computer use/competency create a hierarchical status in the family? What are the effects of spending long hours on the computer? How is family life affected? And—more to the point of development theory—does it matter to the family *when* those hours are spent? Is there a different consequence if a young adult, early in his or her married career, spends hours on the computer, compared to an older, retired adult? These are all interesting questions to consider.

White (1999) also used family development theory to examine satisfaction with work–family balance over the course of the family career. Particular attention was devoted to the sequencing of family and work demands of married couples with at least one child under the age of fifteen years living at home. White suspected that dual-earner families would be more synchronized with societal and institutionalized norms and expectations than single-earner families. Surprisingly, however, single-earner families had significantly higher work–family balance than did dual-earner families. Similarly, both females and males in part-time dual-earner families experience higher work–family balance than those in full-time dual-earner families. Mothers experienced greatest satisfaction in work–family balance when they were able to spend more time at home and less time at work when children were in the home. Men, generally, seemed to have higher satisfaction when their wives were in the labor force, although satisfaction with work–family balance tended to be higher when female labor force participation was reduced. White's work reiterates the need to understand the impact of family stages on work–family balance.

Erickson, Martinengo, and Hill (2010) have examined work–family interface across six family life stages—before children, transition to parenthood, youngest child preschool-aged, youngest child school-aged, youngest child adolescent, and empty nest. Using a large sample of IBM employees in 79 countries, they examined the extent to which work and family role demands across the stages of family life affected work–family experiences. Work–family and family–work conflicts were highest among employees with preschool-age and school-age children, while work–family conflict was lowest among those in later family stages. Although work role demands increased linearly over the life course, role demands and work–family conflict were greatest during the transition to parenthood stage. The authors suggest that job flexibility is most likely to reduce work–family conflict for those entering the parenting years and family–work conflict for those during the preschool child stage. Thus, family development theory offers important insights about the work–family experiences of employees over the life course, details that might be lost without utilizing such a framework. In addition, examining phenomena across family life stages has a variety of ramifications for policy developments, particularly those in the workplace.

The Life Course Perspective

Bengtson and Allen (1993) expanded our thinking about family development by applying the *life course perspective* to the study of families. They contended that the life course perspective has a number of advantages over the family life cycle perspective in that it takes into account the dynamic versus the static nature of the concept of the family life cycle. Rather than emphasizing fixed hierarchical stages, the life course perspective recognizes more contextual variations. It also introduces the notion of *continuity* in addition to change, such that family values, obligations, rights and exchanges can be examined over time. The perspective also offers insights on three different kinds of time: ontogenetic, generational, and historical. Each element of the theory adds richness to our understanding of how families exist in time, space, context, and process. It enhances our understanding of the social meanings that people give to their own developmental and family life (Bengtson and Allen 1993).

Elder and Giele (2009) noted that a life course perspective incorporates four important paradigms: *historical and geographical location, social embeddedness, human agency,* and *variations in timing.* When and where one is born, as well as the historical events occurring at various points during one's life, are significant in shaping the life course. Social ties or *linked lives* (Elder 1994, 6) reflect the fact that humans are interdependent upon one another, embedded in social relationships with family and friends. Personal control, or agency, acknowledges the ways in which individual and family decisions and behaviors shape the life course, within certain constraints. Timing, or when events or transitions occur, affects the life course as well.

In the context of families, then, the life course perspective encourages the consideration of the multiple social contexts of family development. Although our families are our primary socialization agent, we are also influenced by our peers, schooling, faith systems, government, culture, and historical context. The diversity of culture should be included in any analysis of the life course, as the differences of our ethnic, racial, geographic, socioeconomic, and religious heritage play out in our families and our lives. Similarly, the historical context in which family events take place, as well as the critical experiences or events that occur before and after each developmental stage, impacts the family's current state and future possibilities (Bengtson and Allen 1993).

Consider widowhood as an example. As individuals, we mourn the deaths of those we love in a multitude of ways. Thus, we have an *individual response* to death. Placed within a *time context*, the death of a spouse is likely to be experienced differently depending on how old one is when widowhood occurs. Some people believe that, as one grows older, death is easier to accept, although it is difficult to gather hard data on such a belief. What about *family context*? Is the death of a spouse processed differently if the children are grown, or if the spouses spent most of their time together (as in a family-run business) compared to less time together? Next, consider the *social context*. Is the death processed differently if both partners worked and neither was totally dependent on the other for family income? Finally, contemplate the *meaning* associated with death. Is the death processed differently if it is the result of a long illness? Is it different for those who ascribe religious meanings to death, such as the possibility of "eternal life"?

The life course perspective has been successfully applied in examining the consequences of becoming a father on the life courses of men, particularly in regard to personal growth and identity, social relationships, health and well-being, and work and education (Settersten and Cancel-Tirado 2010). The authors found that, rather than solely investigating the impact of fathers on the development of their children, it is imperative to study how fatherhood changes the lives of men in order to enhance the performance of men in the fathering role and ultimately enrich the quality of their own lives. Settersten (2006) also acknowledged the value of assuming a life course perspective when considering the impact of wartime military service on a variety of life course outcomes related to marriage and family, friendships, occupation, education, income, and mental and physical health. Bucx, Raaijmakers, and van Well (2010) also utilized life course stage in better understanding intergenerational congruence in family values among those in the young adult stage. They discovered that intergenerational congruence on attitudes about marriage, cohabitation, divorce, and gender roles within the family decreased when young adults leave the family home, but increased as they become parents themselves. All of this work reminds us of the ways in which unique personal and historical events and experiences distinctly impact the family life course.

Carter and McGoldrick Model

Family development theory has found support in family therapy, particularly when it defines family more broadly (e.g., remarried families, multigenerational families, gay and lesbian families) and is expanded to include varied developmental trajectories. Betty Carter and Monica McGoldrick (1999) analyzed the individual, from a therapy perspective, in terms of his or her place in the larger context of the family life cycle. Table 3.2 reflects the therapeutic focus of this version of the theory.

For each family life cycle stage, fundamental emotional processes and requisite second-order changes are noted. For these therapists, however, recognition of a variety of trajectories is essential. Table 3.3 outlines an example of an additional stage in the developmental course for families who encounter divorce.

As a therapeutically focused model, the Carter and McGoldrick version helps therapists to consider how problems or symptoms develop in individuals and families over time. In addition to developmental stages, they recognize several different levels—the individual, immediate household, extended family, community and social connections, and larger society—useful in assessing families. At the individual level, clinicians might focus on such things as individual temperament, class, genetic makeup, and religious and spiritual values over time. The immediate family level of analysis might include an exploration of emotional climate, communication patterns, ethnicity, family structure, and boundaries and triangles. When assessing the extended family, such things as relationship patterns, loss, family secrets, work patterns, and dysfunctions are of interest. When examining a family's connection to the community, attention might be given to friends and neighbors, volunteer work, and other links to organizations. Finally, both the individual and the family need to be considered relative to their positions within the larger sociocultural context. Thus, it is important to recognize the existence of any societal or contextual biases based on class, sex, race, sexual orientation, family structure, and so forth. Carter and McGoldrick provide an example. The birth of a child is naturally a taxing event on a couple, producing "the normal stresses of a system expanding its boundaries at the present time" (Carter and McGoldrick 1999, 7). If there was excessive turmoil in the family of origin for one or both of the parents, then there might be heightened anxiety for the couple as new parents. Relational distress might also arise if there is a mismatch between the temperaments of the parents and the new child. Similarly, if the child is born with a major defect, and the larger society encourages abandoning or institutionalizing such child, the parents may encounter considerable turmoil. Finally, additional disorder might

Table 3.2 The Stages of the Family Life Cycle.

Family life cycle stage	Emotional process of transition: key principles	Second-order changes in family status required to proceed developmentally
Leaving home: single young adults	Accepting emotional and financial responsibility for self	a. Differentiation of self in relation to family of origin b. Development of intimate peer relationships c. Establishment of self in respect to work and financial independence
The joining of families through marriage: the new couple	Commitment to new system	a. Formation of marital system b. Realignment of relationships with extended families and friends to include spouse
Families with young children	Accepting new members into the system	a. Adjusting marital system to make space for children b. Joining in child rearing, financial and household tasks c. Realignment of relationships with extended family to include parenting and grand parenting roles
Families with adolescents	Increasing flexibility of family boundaries to permit children's independence and grandparents' frailties	a. Shifting of parent/child relationships to permit adolescent to move into and out of system b. Refocus on midlife marital and career issues c. Beginning shift toward caring for older generation
Launching children and moving on	Accepting a multitude of exits from and entries into the family system	a. Renegotiation of marital system as a dyad b. Development of adult-to-adult relationships between grown children and their parents c. Realignment of relationships to include in-laws and grandchildren d. Dealing with disabilities and death of parents (grandparents)
Families in later life	Accepting the shifting generational roles	a. Maintaining own and/or couple functioning and interests in face of physiological decline: exploration of new familial and social role options b. Support for more central role of middle generation c. Making room in the system for the wisdom and experience of the elderly, supporting the older generation without overfunctioning for them d. Dealing with loss of spouse, siblings, and other peers and preparation for death

Table 3.3 An Additional Stage of the Family Life Cycle for Divorcing Families

Phase		Emotional process of transition: prerequisite attitude	Developmental issues
Divorce	The decision to divorce	Acceptance of inability to resolve marital tensions sufficiently to continue relationship.	Acceptance of one's own part in the failure of the marriage.
	Planning the breakup of the system	Supporting viable arrangements for all parts of the system.	a. Working cooperatively on problems of custody, visitation, and finances. b. Dealing with extended family about the divorce.
	Separation	a. Willingness to continue cooperative co-parental relationship and joint financial support of children. b. Work on resolution of attachment to spouse.	a. Mourning loss of intact family. b. Restructuring marital and parent-child relationships and finances; adaptation to living apart. c. Realignment of relationships with extended family; staying connected with spouse's extended family.
	The divorce	More work on emotional divorce: overcoming hurt, anger, guilt, etc.	a. Mourning loss of intact family; giving up fantasies of reunion. b. Retrieval of hopes, dreams, expectations from the marriage. c. Staying connected with extended families.
Post-divorce	Single parent (custodial household or primary residence)	Willingness to maintain financial responsibilities, continue parental contact with ex-spouse, and support contact of children with ex-spouse and his or her family.	a. Making flexible visitation arrangements with ex-spouse and family. b. Rebuilding own financial resources. c. Rebuilding own social network.
	Single parent (non custodial)	Willingness to maintain financial responsibilities and parental contact with ex-spouse and to support custodial parent's relationship with children.	a. Finding ways to continue effective parenting. b. Maintaining financial responsibilities to ex-spouse and children. c. Rebuilding own social network.

be introduced if the child's birth occurred during a natural disaster, like the Japanese tsunami, or during a time of political upheaval, such as when the parents might be refugees living outside their own country.

This model is particularly useful in exploring life cycle stressors and how these interact with family stories, themes, triangles, and roles over time. It further emphasizes a balance between connectedness and separateness, as individual identity is understood in relation to significant people, relationships, and contexts.

The Systemic Family Development Model

Most recently, Tracey Laszloffy (2002) proposed a new model that incorporates aspects of family systems theory, family stress theory, and a multigenerational perspective of family development theory. Laszloffy's efforts address two perceived shortcomings in the original theory: the assumption that all families develop similarly (universality) and the bias toward a single generational experience/focus of the life cycle (for example, labeling a stage the *launching stage* emphasizes the parental experience, whereas naming it *launching and leaving* acknowledges this as a multigenerational interchange). The systemic family development (SFD) model proposes, just like other developmental theories, that families experience transitions and shifts in family roles. Unlike other theories, though, that attempt to generalize patterns of family development over time, SFD states that each family's developmental pattern is unique. An analysis of a family must account for the combination, specific to the family being analyzed, of all the factors influencing it, including socioeconomic status, race, religion, gender, sexual orientation, politics, and sociocultural values. Laszloffy describes the family as a layer cake, with each layer representing a generation within the family. Each layer is at a different stage within the family cycle (aged adults, parents, adolescents, preschoolers, and others), having to deal with its own issues and developmental tasks. Laszloffy argues that, in order to fully describe the family, one must study the interrelationships between the layers and describe the complexities that result from the family dealing with emerging stressors.

At this particular time (or slice of "cake") in the life of the Morrison family (from the vignette at the beginning of the chapter), there is concern about the health and well-being of John's father, a member of the third generation. John and Natasha (second generation) are anticipating retirement and the opportunity to travel. Each of their three children (first generation)—Tamara, John Jr., and Kamika—is dealing with a variety of issues including preparation for a first child, the completion of college, and graduation from high school. Depending upon when the next slice is removed from the Morrison family cake, there is likely to be four generations, the anticipated birth of Tamara's child as well as the possibility of other grandchildren for John and Natasha. Assuming they are still alive, Natasha's parents would become generation four, John and Natasha would be generation three, their three children would be generation two, and Tamara's child and any other grandchildren would become generation one. Again, each generation would be examined for its developmental issues and stressors. Consideration would also be given to the way in which these events affected the total family system. From a systems perspective, families are process-oriented. Although there is a great deal of variability in the timing and type of family stressors they encounter, all families experience stressors and the need to change and adapt.

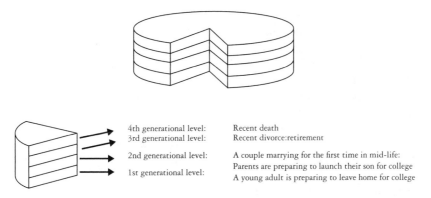

4th generational level: Recent death
3rd generational level: Recent divorce:retirement

2nd generational level: A couple marrying for the first time in mid-life:
                               Parents are preparing to launch their son for college
1st generational level: A young adult is preparing to leave home for college

FIGURE 3.1 The Systemic Family Development Model as illustrated by the round-layered cake.

Therefore, even normative developmental transitions cause stress for the family unit. The family's response to its stressors will vary according to its resources, as predicted by stress theory. The more difficult a transition is, the more intense the stress will be. If the family has many resources, and the developmental transition is normative (and therefore expected), it will be easier to handle. When the family successfully negotiates the transition, stress is relieved, and the family returns to stability. For the SFD model, "it is the complex interplay between the nature and timing of stressors that makes family development highly idiosyncratic" (208).

The SFD model provides a way for family scholars, family life educators, and family therapists to view the family in multiple developmental cycles concurrently while respecting the various social contexts (e.g., race, ethnicity, and socioeconomic status) that influence development. It allows us to investigate the influences across, as well as within, generations. It may also prove to be an important research tool, because scholars can use the same theory to explain a family both at a point in time (a cross-sectional view, or the vertical slice of the cake) and over a span of time (a longitudinal view, or a layer of the cake).

CRITIQUE

A primary criticism of family development theory is that it best describes the trajectory of intact, two-parent, heterosexual nuclear families. For example, Duvall's (Duvall and Miller 1985) eight-stage model was based on a nuclear family, assumed an intact marriage throughout the life cycle of the family, and was organized around the oldest child's developmental needs. It did not take into account divorce, death of a spouse, remarriage, unmarried parents, childless couples, or cohabiting or gay and lesbian couples. In so doing, it "normalized" one type of family and invalidated others. Today's family experiences and structures are more varied. For example, launching comes later in life for many families and is less complete than when Duvall first described these stages (Qualls 1997). Similarly, Dykstra and Hagestad (2007), in examining the impact of childlessness on older adults, expose the way in which parenthood is deemed to be a critical "organizer of the life course and a major factor in social integration" (1275) in family development, disadvantaging those who do not have children, whether by choice or circumstance. Slater and Mencher (1991), too, acknowledge the exclusion of lesbian families from most family life cycle models and the need to afford such families rituals that delineate important markers of family life and connect them to the larger society.

Family development theory has also been criticized by many as being only descriptive and not heuristic (research generating). Critics said it lacked a sense of usefulness as a theory because it had little predictive power. It described only one particular kind of family (middle class, heterosexual, lifelong couples and their children), and it did not provide much insight into what governed their patterns of behavior (Bengtson and Allen 1993; Burr 1973; Falicov 1988). In fact, in the early 1980s, some researchers pronounced it a "minor" theory (Holman and Burr 1980). Because of these criticisms, White (1991) worked to formalize the theory in a more scientific way, with testable propositions that could be used to predict family functioning.

Mattessich and Hill (1987) worked to expand the theoretical structure, but it was still deemed too descriptive and broad (Aldous 1990). In other words, the theory suffered from trying to explain too much, so it could only explain things simply in order to avoid being overwhelmingly complex. Furthermore, although family development theory described the stages of the family life cycle, it did not describe the relationship between the stages or how they formed a total pattern of the family's development (Breunlin 1988).

In addition, early renderings of family development theory failed to include family identity factors such as race, socioeconomic status, ethnicity, and family structure (Bennett, Wolin, and McAvity 1988; Dilworth-Anderson and Burton 1996; Winton 1995). Bengtson and Allen's (1993) development of the life course perspective specifically includes these factors and lends itself to testable hypotheses. Carter and McGoldrick's (1999) family therapy perspective actually includes even more family identity structures (e.g., stepfamilies, divorcing families, never-married families, multigenerational families) and ethnic and racial differences. Laszloffy's (2002) systemic family development model broadens the theory's scope to include not only families of different structure, race, ethnicity, and sexuality, but also multiple generations of families at the same time. The continued viability of family development theory will depend on its ability to incorporate diverse families and varied family experiences.

APPLICATION

1. Using the scenario of the Morrison family at the beginning of the chapter:

a. Identify the assumptions in the scenario.

b. Outline the different life cycle stages represented by the Morrison family. Note the different tasks that each must accomplish.

c. Create a family genogram of the Morrison family to help record family information in a more concise and visual way.

d. Analyze the tasks that each family member must accomplish in terms of different social and personal constraints. Can some tasks be avoided altogether? Must some tasks be addressed within a limited time frame?

e. Indicate how the concept of change can be seen in this vignette. How do you think the family might cope with these changes?

f. Indicate how this family provides examples of the effect of social changes.

g. What might be some unique insights that the life course perspective as applied to families and the systemic family development (SFD) model might offer to this family analysis?

2. Think of an intimate relationship in which either you or people close to you have been involved. How has being in the intimate relationship changed this person? What kinds of changes have you noticed? What kinds of changes have been noticed by your family and friends? Can you identify any of the establishment tasks in this relationship?

3. Draw pictures of your family at the time you entered it; when you were in elementary school; when you graduated from high school; your family as it is today; and your family as you expect it to be five years from now.

a. How did your family change over time?

b. Compare and contrast your drawings and reflections with others in class.

4. In the sample reading for this chapter, Martinengo, Jacob, and Hill (2010) identify several differences between working mothers and fathers over the family life course. Identify them. How does the family development theory afford insights that might be masked without using this theoretical perspective? If you were in the human resources department of IBM or another workplace, how might this information shape the policies you develop for your employees? Consider *yourself* in each family life cycle stage and how working might impact *your* work–family balance. What types of strategies do you imagine yourself and your partner (if you choose to have one) employing in order to manage the responsibilities of both home/family and work?

NOTE

1. The edition that Duvall edited with Brent Miller was the last edition of Duvall's *Family Development* textbook. She died in 1998.

REFERENCES

Aldous, J. 1978. *Family careers: Developmental change in families*. New York: Wiley.

———. 1990. Family development and the life course: Two perspectives on family change. *Journal of Marriage and the Family* 52: 571–583.

———. 1996. *Family careers: Rethinking the developmental perspective*. Thousand Oaks, CA: Sage.

Bengtson, V. I., and K. R. Allen. 1993. The life-course perspective applied to families over time. In *Sourcebook of family theories and methods: A contextual approach*, ed. P. G. Boss, W. J. Doherty, R. LaRossa, W. J. Schumm, and S. K. Steinmetz, 469–499. New York: Plenum.

Bennett, L. A., S. J. Wolin, and K. J. McAvity. 1988. Family identity, ritual and myth: A cultural perspective on life cycle transitions. In *Family transitions: Continuity and change over the life cycle*, ed. C. J. Falicov, 211–234. New York: Guilford.

Breunlin, D. C. 1988. Oscillation theory and family development. In *Family transitions: Continuity and change over the life cycle*, ed. C. J. Falicov, 133–155. New York: Guilford.

Bucx, F., Q. Raaijmakers, and F. van Wel. 2010. Life course stage in young adulthood and intergenerational congruence in family attitudes. *Journal of Marriage and Family* 72: 117–134.

Burr, W. R. 1973. *Theory construction and the sociology of the family*. New York: Wiley.

Carter, B., and M. McGoldrick. 1999. *The expanded family life cycle: Individual, family and social perspectives*. 3rd ed. Needham Heights, MA: Allen and Bacon.

Cicerelli, V. 1994. The sibling life cycle. In *Handbook of developmental family psychology and psychopathology*, ed. L. L'Abate, 44–59. New York: Wiley.

Dilworth-Anderson, P., and L. M. Burton. 1996. Rethinking family development theory. *Journal of Social and Personal Relationships* 13: 325–334.

Duvall, E. M. 1957 and the revised editions 1962, 1967, 1971, 1977. *Family development*. New York: Lippincott.

———. 1988. Family development's first forty years. *Family Relations* 37: 127–134.

Duvall, E. M., and R. L. Hill. 1948. *Reports of the committee on the dynamics of family interaction*. Washington, DC: National Conference on Family Life.

Duvall, E. M., and B. C. Miller. 1985. *Marriage and family development*. 6th ed. New York: Harper and Row.

Dykstra, P. A., and G. O. Hagestad. 2007. Roads less taken: Developing a nuanced view of older adults without children. *Journal of Family Issues* 28:1275–1310.

Elder Jr., G. H. 1994. Time, human agency, and social change: Perspectives on the life course. *Social Psychology Quarterly* 57(1): 4–15.

Elder Jr., G. H., and J. Z. Giele. 2009. Life course studies: An evolving field. In *The craft of life course research*, ed. G. H. Elder Jr., and J. Z. Giele, 1–24. New York: Guilford Press.

Erickson, J. J., G. Martinengo, and E. J. Hill. 2010. Putting work and family experiences in context: Differences by family life stage. *Human Relations* 63(7): 955–979.

Falicov, C. J. 1988. Family sociology and family therapy contributions to the family developmental framework: A comparative analysis and thoughts on future trends. In *Family transitions: Continuity and change over the life cycle*, ed. C. J. Falicov, 3–51. New York: Guilford.

Fuller, T. L., and F. D. Fincham. 1994. The marital life cycle: A developmental approach to the study of marital change. In *Handbook of developmental family psychology and psychopathology*, ed. L. L'Abate, 60–82. New York: Wiley.

Glick, P. C. 1977. Updating the life cycle of the family. *Journal of Marriage and the Family* 39: 5–13.

Hagestad, G. 1988. Demographic change and the life course: Some emerging trends in the family realm. *Family Relations* 37: 405–410.

Havighurst, R. J. 1948. *Developmental tasks and education*. Chicago: Univ. of Chicago Press.

———. 1953. *Human development and education*. New York: Longmans and Green.

Hill, R. 1986. Life cycle stages for types of single parent families: Of family development theory. *Family Relations* 35: 19–30.

Holman, T. B., and W. R. Burr. 1980. Beyond the beyond: The growth of family theories in the 1970s. *Journal of Marriage and the Family* 42: 729–742.

Laszloffy, T. A. 2002. Rethinking family development theory: Teaching with the systemic family development (SFD) model. *Family Relations* 51: 206–214.

Mattessich, P., and R. Hill. 1987. Life cycle and family development. In *Handbook of marriage and the family*, ed. M. B. Sussman and S. K. Steinmetz, 437–469. New York: Plenum.

Neugarten, B., J. Moore, and J. Lowe. 1965. Age norms, age constraints, and adult socialization. *American Journal of Sociology* 70: 710–717.

Qualls, S. H. 1997. Transitions in autonomy: The essential caregiving challenge. *Family Relations* 46: 41–46.

Rapoport, R. 1963. Normal crises, family structure and mental health. *Family Process* 2: 68–80.

Rodgers, R. 1964. Toward a theory of family development. *Journal of Marriage and the Family* 26: 262–270.

———. 1973. *Family interaction and transaction: The developmental approach.* Englewood Cliffs, NJ: Prentice-Hall.

Rodgers, R. H., and J. M. White. 1993. Family developmental theory. In *Sourcebook of family theories and methods: A contextual approach*, ed. P. G. Boss, W. J. Doherty, R. LaRossa, W. R. Schumm, and S. K. Steinmetz, 225–254. New York: Plenum.

Settersten Jr., R. A. 2006. When nations call: How wartime military service matters for the life course and aging. *Research on Aging* 28(1): 12–36.

Settersten Jr., R. A., and D. Cancel-Tirado. 2010. Fatherhood as a hidden variable in men's development and life courses. *Research in Human Development* 72(2): 83–102.

Slater, S., and J. Mencher. 1991. The lesbian family life cycle: A contextual approach. *American Journal of Orthopsychiatry* 61: 372–382.

Watt, D., and J. M. White. 1999. Computers and the family life: A family development perspective. *Journal of Comparative Family Studies* 30: 1–15.

White, J. M. 1991. *Dynamics of family development: A theoretical perspective.* New York: Guilford.

White, J. M. 1999. Work–family stage and satisfaction with work–family balance. *Journal of Comparative Family Studies* 30(2): 163–175.

Winton, C. A. 1995. *Frameworks for studying families.* Guilford, CT: Dushkin Publishing.

SAMPLE READING

Martinengo, G., J. I. Jacob, and E. J. Hill. 2010. Gender and the work–family interface: Exploring differences across the family life course. *Journal of Family Issues* 31 (10): 1363–1390.

Using a large international sample of IBM employees, the authors evaluated how men and women compare in their experience of the work–family interface during six family life stages—before children, transition to parenthood, preschool child[ren], adolescent child[ren], and empty nest. The family life cycle perspective afforded a valuable lens through which to examine gender differences across various stages of family life. Several important findings emerged. For one, the greatest gender differences in job hours occurred among parents of young children or teenagers, when men worked more hours than women. When children are young, women appear to increase their commitment to family responsibilities, while men intensify their dedication to paid work. Even though both men and women worked outside the home, women experienced more family–work spillover as they held primary responsibility for child care and home-related matters, particularly when the children were young.

SAMPLE READING

Gender and the Work–Family Interface: Exploring Differences across the Family Life Course

Giuseppe Martinengo[1],
Jenet I. Jacob[1], and E. Jeffrey Hill[1]

This study examines gender differences in the work–family interface across six family life stages using a global sample of IBM employees in 79 countries (N = 41,813). Family life stage was constructed using the age of respondent and age of youngest child. Results revealed that having young children at home was the critical catalyst for gender differences in the work–family interface. The greatest gender differences were found in the central stages of life when children require more temporal and economic resources from their parents. When life stage was not considered, the first and last stages tended to offset each other, concealing major gender differences during the central stages of family life. These findings signify that life stage is an important concept to consider in research related to gender and the work–family interface. Implications to the development of work policies attentive to shifts in work–family linkages during the life course are discussed.

Keywords: gender, work–family interface, life stage, family life course

INTRODUCTION

Issues of gender have been a central focus of work–family scholarship in the past three decades. Yet explorations of gender differences in work–family conflict to date have been inconclusive. Many studies indicate that men and women report similar levels of work–family conflict (Barnett & Gareis, 2006) but seem to exhibit different behavior patterns in response to this conflict (Mennino & Brayfield, 2002; Mennino,

[1]Brigham Young University, Provo, Utah
Corresponding Author: Giuseppe Martinengo, Brigham Young University, School of Family Life, 2052 JFSB, Provo, UT 84602. Email:giuseppemartinengo@gmail.com

Rubin, & Brayfield, 2005). Other studies have identified gender differences in work–family stress, generally showing significantly more conflict for women than for men (Dilworth, 2004; Duxbury & Higgins, 1991).

Recent work–family research has called for "a life course reframing," concluding that gender may best be understood in the context of family life stage (Moen & Sweet, 2004, p. 209; Grzywacz, Almeida, & McDonald, 2002). Findings from a range of research studies support this perspective. Entering parenthood, for example, presents striking changes in roles and responsibilities that is a harbinger of significant differences between men and women in work and family life (Kaufman & Uhlenberg, 2000). Across the intensive child-rearing years gender differences in caregiving responsibilities, and the increase in work responsibilities associated with career building, have also been associated with significant gender differences (Moen & Roehling, 2005). Changes in family responsibilities, as well as goals of personal development as workers take on eldercare responsibilities and children leave the home, suggest continued gender differences as workers age (Staudinger & Bluck, 2001).

Yet further research is needed to empirically validate the extent to which family life stage is associated with gender differences in the strengths of relationships among variables in the work–family interface. Studies have largely treated life stage as a *noise* variable rather than a *focus* issue in explorations of gender differences (Barnes-Farrell & Matthews, 2007). Studies that have explored gender differences across life stages have generally focused on differences in one life stage, or differences between workers with and without children (Dilworth, 2004; McElwain, Korabik, & Rosin, 2005; Mennino et al., 2005). These weaknesses reflect the challenge of accessing data with sufficient size and range to allow for statistical comparisons between men and women across multiple life stages on the same work and family variables.

The purpose of this study is to empirically evaluate how men and women in six family life stages (before children, transition to parenthood, preschool child[ren], school-age child[ren], adolescent child[ren], and empty nest stages) differ on the same measures of the work–family experience. The study draws on a large international sample of workers to compare a previously validated model of the work–family interface for men and women within and across each family life stage. Job and family factors are explored as predictors of conflict in the work–family interface, and conflict is explored as a predictor of work, individual, and family outcomes (Aryee, Fields, & Luk, 1999; Frone, Russell, & Cooper, 1992; Hill, Yang, Hawkins, & Ferris, 2004). The means of each of the factors and the strengths of the relationships among them are compared across six family life stage groups using structural equation modeling.

Placing life stage at the center of explorations of gender differences has the potential to reduce the fragmented nature of knowledge about how men and women differ in their experience of work and family life across the life course (Barnes-Farrell & Matthews, 2007). Comparing the strengths of work and family relationships at different family life stages provides points of contrast from which to more effectively theorize about gender differences in the work–family interface. Grounding the study of gender differences in work and family life with a family life course perspective may facilitate more effective work policies and programs responsive to the diverse work and family needs of men and women across the family life cycle.

DEFINING THE EXPERIENCE OF WORK
AND FAMILY LIFE

The model used for comparison explores conflict in the work–family interface, and the work, personal, and family outcomes associated with that conflict. Conflict is defined as a type of interrole stress that results from incompatible demands in the work and family domains (Greenhaus & Beutell, 1985). Because interrole conflict may originate from either the work or family domain, a distinction has been made between work–family conflict and family–work conflict (Gutek, Searle, & Klepa, 1991). Work-related factors, such as job responsibility, are explored as sources of work–family conflict, conflict in which work pressures are incompatible with family demands. Family-related factors such as household labor are explored as sources of family–work conflict, in which pressures from family life are incompatible with work demands.

This study distinguishes between time-based work–family conflict, in which work responsibilities compete with time and attention for family responsibilities, and family–work spillover, in which workers experience emotional drain at work because of family pressures. The combination of time-based conflict and emotional spillover from one domain into another provides a more comprehensive view of conflict in the work–family interface (Moen & Roehling, 2005). Work–family conflict and family–work spillover are explored as predictors of work–family fit, an assessment of the difficulty of managing work and family life that consider both sources of conflict. Work–family fit is explored as a predictor of work, personal, and family success.

CONCEPTUAL FRAMEWORK

The concepts of family life cycle are useful for exploring gender differences in the experience of work and family life across the life course. From a family life cycle perspective, families in the same stages experience similar events, face similar crises, and accomplish similar developmental tasks (Mattessich & Hill, 1987). Stages are distinguished by their structural complexity, which are defined by the numbers of persons involved; the number of interpersonal relationships and density (age homogeneity); the cognitive and prosocial competency of the members; the allocation of power, tasks and affection; the ratio of instrumental and expressive resources to member needs; efficiency in the management of time, energy, and space; and links to work, schools, and support systems of kinship and friendship networks (Mattessich & Hill, 1987, p. 458). These life stage factors are reflected in work and family role demands.

Gender is a central concept in the factors that define the complexity of each family life stage (Moen & Sweet, 2004). Indeed, biological sex and social–psychological gender create a context that permeates every aspect of the unfolding work and family life course. As a result, the connection between work and family is likely to operate differently for men and women across the life course (Hinze, 2000). The social expectation of women-as-caregivers and men-as-providers, for example, presents a context that continues to exert a strong, normative influence on the experience of work and family life (Orrange, 1999). Furthermore, the linked nature of men's and women's lives means that the work and family expectations and experiences of one may support and constrain the work and family lives of the other (Elder, 1996).

The context of gender is closely tied to the cultural and national context, which presents socially constructed and institutionalized norms for work and family roles and relationships (Moen & Sweet, 2004). Societal norms around maternal employment, for example, create a context that influences public work–family policies and trends in mothers' labor force participation (Treas & Widmer, 2000). The current study does not analyze cross-cultural differences but attempts to empirically validate gender differences across family life course stages for individuals from a range of nationalities. This lays the ground work for future analyses of the influence of national context on gender differences across the life course.

RELATED RESEARCH

The following review presents empirical and theoretical evidence for gender differences across family life stages. Previous studies have not explored the same variables in the work–family interface and the strength of the relationships among these variables for men and women across the spectrum of family life stages. But findings from previous studies provide a framework of hypotheses for empirically validating gender differences in the work–family interface across family life stages. Research and theoretical perspectives on the work and family experiences of workers in the following life stages are reviewed: transition to parenthood, preschool child(ren), school-age child(ren), adolescent child(ren), and empty-nesters.

Transition to Parenthood

Explorations of the relationship between parenthood and the work–family interface suggest that parenthood transforms the work and family lives of men and women (Moen & Roehling, 2005). For women, the transition to parenthood has been associated with striking increases in the amount of time spent on family care and a prioritization of the family role by adjusting work identities "to accommodate" family responsibilities (Bielby & Bielby, 1992, p. 784; Hinze, 2000). For men, parenthood has been associated with increased work hours and stronger prioritization of work roles (Kaufman & Uhlenberg, 2000; Nock, 1998). New fathers who have not established themselves financially and occupationally in their careers may experience particular pressure to work longer hours to provide for their families (Lundberg & Rose, 1999). Employed new mothers may experience a "double bind": increased responsibilities for care work and the simultaneous expectation to build career to obtain income and advancement (Moen & Roehling, 2005).

Research findings indicating a drop in marital satisfaction in the transition to parenthood suggest that negotiations of increased household labor and child care responsibilities put additional strains on marital quality that may in turn influence work and family life (Cowan & Cowan, 2000). Negotiations in household labor and child care responsibilities have been negatively associated with marital quality for both men and women, and marital quality has been related to the conflict in which family concerns intrude on the capacity to perform work responsibilities (Aryee, 1992; Nomaguchi & Milkie, 2003).

The exposure to increased role responsibilities in both work and family domains suggest the potential for increased conflict in the work–family interface in the transition to parenthood. Previous studies have not distinguished work–family conflict for men and women in the transition to parenthood stage from those with preschool- and school-age children. But findings indicated that new mothers and mothers of young children were more likely to experience increased family–work spillover, including feeling drained at work because of caregiving demands (Higgins, Duxbury, & Lee, 1994). In contrast, new fathers may be likely to experience work–family conflict in the form of time and energy constraints as they prioritize work responsibilities and work longer hours (Nock, 1998).

Job flexibility and work–family programs that enable new parents to more successfully meet role demands have been identified as more important for new parents, relative to workers who are not parents, and particularly for mothers of young children (Hill et al., 2008). The current analysis will expand on these findings by exploring whether the strength of those relationships differs for women and men in the transition to parenthood stage and how those relationships compare with later stages.

Preschool-Age Child Stage

Studies exploring work–family conflict for parents with preschool-age children suggest that work and family role demands may increase for men and women in this life stage. Men and women with a child under the age of 6 years had higher levels of negative spillover from family to work associated with caregiving responsibilities than parents of older children (Grzywacz et al., 2002). Mothers with preschool-age children seemed to be particularly vulnerable to work–family and family–work conflict (Moen & Roehling, 2005). The presence of preschool children predicted significantly greater family– work spillover for self-employed mothers (Hundley, 2001), and mothers of young children were more likely to miss work as a result of family demands than men or women in other life stages (Dilworth, 2004). Fathers' reports of conflict, however, were not related to ages of their children (Higgins et al., 1994; Marshall & Barnett, 1993).

Caregiving and housework responsibilities were identified as important predictors of greater family–work spillover for mothers of young children (Crouter, 1984). But recent analyses of the National Study of the Changing Workforce indicated that hours in housework and caregiving were not significant predictors of family–work spillover for mothers (Dilworth, 2004). The current analysis will allow further exploration of the relationship between mothers' household labor and perceptions of conflict across family life stages.

Theoretical perspectives suggest that perceived success in meeting work and family demands during this life stage is likely to be strongly related to perceptions of success in other dimensions of life (Jung, 1971; Staudinger & Bluck, 2001). Mothers of young children, in particular, may experience more negative perceptions of life and personal success when they do not feel they are effectively meeting family role responsibilities. Women reported more emotional distress than men when they felt work prevented them from spending enough time with their spouse or children, and more so than men

(Nomaguchi, Milkie, & Bianchi, 2005). But the relationship between work–family conflict and family and life satisfaction was equivocal for men and women in research on full-time professionals (McElwain et al., 2005). The current analysis will allow further exploration of how the context of family life stage may influence the relationship between work and family conflict and perceptions of success.

Access to and use of flexible work arrangements has consistently been associated with reduced conflict in the work–family interface but further research is needed to analyze whether flexibility is more effective for men and women in particular family life stages (Hill, Jackson, & Martinengo, 2006; Hill, Martinson, & Ferris, 2004). Men and women from a large sample of employed and self-employed workers who had greater access to flexible work arrangements were significantly more likely to report low levels of work–family conflict (Bond, Thompson, Galinsky, & Prottas, 2002). Job flexibility was identified as particularly valued by mothers with young children, but it is not known whether its effectiveness reducing conflict in the work–family interface differs by gender and life stage (Hill et al., 2008; Jacob, Bond, Galinsky, & Hill, 2008).

School-Age Child Stage

Studies of workers with elementary school-age children indicated lower caregiving demands relative to workers with preschool-age children. But as Moen and Roehling (2005) concluded, having school-age children may require "a real juggling act" for employed parents (p. 95). Finding appropriate child care, for example, becomes more complicated as children move into elementary school and child care needs become less consistent from week to week (Moen & Roehling, 2005). These and other factors may help explain why women with school-age children experienced higher rates of family–work conflict than childless workers or workers in later family life stages (Higgins et al., 1994; Moen & Roehling, 2005).

Work–family conflict, however, may actually be lower for mothers and fathers of school-age children. Women who were parents of school-age children reported lower work–family spillover than workers of comparable ages who did not have children (Roehling, Moen, & Batt, 2003). Women with children in elementary school "may have learned to compartmentalize the stresses and strains of their jobs," strengthening their ability to prevent negative spillover from work to family (Moen & Roehling, 2005, p. 96). Workers without children may have greater difficulty justifying the protection of personal and family time from the intrusion of work responsibilities. Whether or not workers have children, success in managing work and family is likely to continue to be strongly related to other perceptions of success (Jung, 1971).

Adolescent Child Stage

Entering the adolescent child family life stage has been associated with a decrease in conflict in the work–family interface for both men and women relative to earlier family life stages. Roehling et al. (2003) found that for highly involved families, family life can serve as "a haven" to escape the pressures of work when children enter the teenage years and no longer require constant care. Some evidence suggests a "life course" for work–family conflict, with decreasing conflict as workers' youngest children enter adolescence (Grzywacz et al., 2002; Higgins et al., 1994). Women in the adolescent child stage reported less work–family spillover and family–work spillover than women in previous family life stages, and the same levels as their male counterparts (Higgins et al., 1994).

But concerns about adolescents may also predict greater conflict in this stage, particularly for men. The presence of older children was associated with greater family–work conflict for men, whereas preschool-age children predicted greater family–work conflict for women (Hundley, 2001). At the same time, workers in this family life stage may be more focused on subjective perceptions of role experiences rather than meeting societal work and family role expectations (Jung, 1971). As a result, perceived success in fulfilling work and family roles may not be as strongly related to perceived success in other domains compared to earlier family life stages.

Empty Nest Stage

Workers who no longer have dependent children have reported less conflict in the work–family interface than workers in earlier family life stage. Recent trends, however, suggest that older workers face a great deal of change in their family lives including children moving out, parents or spouses becoming ill, and possible divorce and remarriage that contribute to greater family role demands. Mature workers today are more likely than any other age group to have an elderly parent needing care and also be responsible for young children or grandchildren (Simon-Rusinowitz, Krach, Marks, Piktialis, & Wilson, 1996). Women have been most likely to shoulder these caregiving responsibilities. Entmacher (1999) found that nearly 75% of caregivers of the elderly were women, and most likely to be ages 50 to 64. Men who were caregivers were as likely as women who were caregivers to experience family–work conflict due to caregiving, but women were much more likely to be caregivers (Barrah, Shultz, Baltes, & Stoltz, 2004).

Nevertheless, work and family role demands that have been related to conflict in the work–family interface for younger workers may not be as strongly related to conflict for mature workers. Mature workers are also likely to have developed more effective coping mechanisms throughout a lifetime of communicating, solving problems, and integrating knowledge with practical experience (Baltes & Young, 2007; Sterns & Huyck, 2001). Changes in central life interests and emotional functioning contributed to a decrease in negative affect among mature workers as they adjusted from overly idealistic aspirations to realistic ones (Sterns & Huyck, 2001).

Marriage may also be particularly beneficial in reducing conflict in the work–family interface for workers in the empty nest stage. Married workers had reduced conflict in the work–family interface in an analysis of a large multinational sample (Hill et al., 2004), and mature workers reported paying more attention to their marriages than younger workers who reported focusing more on challenges with children (Baltes & Young, 2007). But male mature workers are more likely to be married or living with a partner than female mature workers who are more likely to be divorced or widowed (Bond, Galinsky, Pitt-Catsouphes, & Smyer, 2005). Mature workers who are women may be less likely than men to benefit from a marriage relationship in which there is a spouse or partner at home taking care of home and family responsibilities.

Flexibility in the work domain may become increasingly important in later family life stages. Surveys of both male and female mature workers have consistently identified a strong preference for being able to use a range of different "flexible work options" (Pitt-Catsouphes & Smyer, 2006). Evidence suggests that mature workers want to do meaningful work but do not want to work long hours and have inflexible demands in their work role responsibilities (Moen, Erickson, Agarwal, Fields, & Todd, 2000). Thus, flexibility may be more strongly related to reduced work–family conflict and family–work conflict and success in meeting work and family role expectations for workers in later family life stages.

RESEARCH HYPOTHESES

In the current study, potential differences in the work–family interface by gender and family life stage are explored through the following research questions and hypotheses:

Hypothesis 1: The means of work–family interface model variables will differ for men and women at different family life stages. Differences across family life stages will reflect a curvilinear dynamic in which work and family role demands increase across early family life stages and then decrease as children leave the home. Gender differences will be smallest prior to parenthood, will increase during the family life stages of early parenthood, and then decrease as children grow and leave the home.

Hypothesis 2: The strength of the path coefficients in the work–family interface model will differ for men and women at different family life stages. Work and family role demands will be more strongly related to work–family and family–work spillover during the family life stages of early parenthood. Work role demands will be more predictive of work–family conflict for men in the early parenthood stages, and family demands will be more predictive of family–work spillover for women in the early parenthood stages.

METHOD

The source for the data in this study is the IBM 2004 Global Work and Life Issues Survey. It consists of more than 100 questions asked of 97,644 employees in 79 countries designed to help IBM address employee needs related to work and personal and family life. Altogether, 41,769 responded, for a participation rate of 43%. Participants were from Europe (42%), the United States (26%), Asia/Pacific (19%), Latin America (8%), and Canada (6%). Respondents from Latin America had a higher response rate (55%) than the overall average (43%), whereas respondents from Asia had a lower response rate (37%). The overall sample was 60% male and 40% female, with an average age of 43, an average tenure with IBM of 13 years, and an average of 1.97 children. The sample represented the distribution of job levels among IBM employees: professionals (77%), managers (13%), and executives (9%). The types of jobs reported were indicative of the high level of skills needed: hardware, software, and other engineers (25%); information technology professionals (19%); sales and marketing (11%); product support (11%); finance (5%); consultants (5%); human resources (3%); manufacturing (3%); and other job categories (18%). These jobs typically require high levels of university education and are generally compensated with above-average salaries.

Measures

Family life stage. Family life stage was operationalized into six groups: before children (workers age 35 years or less without children), transition to parenthood (only one child age 1 year or less), preschool-age child (youngest child age 2 to 5 years), school-age child (youngest child age 6 to 12 years), adolescent child (youngest child 13 to 17 years), and empty nest stage (workers age 50 years or more without children living at home). Individuals between ages 35 and 50 years with no dependent children were not categorized into any family life stage because of the ambiguity of their life stage characteristics. Although they had no dependents, their age and experience precluded their being categorized in the same life stage as those who were younger than age 35 years without dependents. They could not be categorized in the empty nest stage because of the difference in age and experience and their potential to yet have dependents in the future.

Most methods for determining family life cycle stages use the age of the oldest child in addition to a measure of the age of the parent(s). The current study used the age of the youngest child to demarcate family life stage. Previous findings have suggested that as the youngest child gets older, child care demands decrease, resulting in increased levels of control and lower stress for parents (Dilworth, 2004; Higgins et al., 1994). As a result, the youngest child's age has been identified as a better predictor of the work–family interface than the oldest child's age.

Work characteristics. Job responsibility was measured by the question "Which of the following best describes your job?" Responses were coded 1 = *professional*, 2 = *manager*, or 3 = *executive*. Professionals included employees such as programmers and marketers who had no people management responsibilities. Managers supervised groups of employees, and executives supervised groups of managers. Job hours was measured by the question "How many hours per week do you TYPICALLY work for IBM? (Please make an average per week estimate covering the last 6 months)?"

Job flexibility was a latent construct with three indicators (α = .75). The first indicator was measured by reverse-coding the question "How much flexibility (personal control) do you have in selecting WHERE you do your work (home customer, IBM office, etc.)?" Ratings ranged from 1 = *no flexibility* to 5 = *complete flexibility*. The second indicator used this same response scale and asked, "How much flexibility (personal control) do you have in selecting WHEN you do your work (scheduling the hours you work, the time of day, etc.)?" The third indicator was measured by the question "Working from home at least one day per week is acceptable in my work group." Ratings ranged from 1 = *strongly disagree* to 5 = *strongly agree*. Knowledge and use of work–family programs was measured by reverse-coding the question "Which statement best describes your awareness and use of company 'work/ life' options?" (1 = *I am aware of them and have used them*, 2 = *I am aware of them but have not used them*, 3 = *I am not aware of IBM's work/life options*).

Family characteristics. Time spent in household chores was measured by the question "Estimate how many hours you spend in [household chores] during a typical week. (Make an average per week estimate covering the last 6 months.)" Marital status was measured by the question "Which best describes your current relationship with a spouse or partner?" (0 = *not married or remarried*, 1 = *married or remarried*).

Outcomes. Work–family conflict was a latent construct with five items (α = .75). The question stem was, "In the last 6 months, how many times, if any, have the following happened to you?" Items included: missed a significant personal/family obligation for work reasons; missed all or part of a scheduled vacation for work reasons; been interrupted at home by phone calls during weekends or off hours on work-related matters; missed dinnertime because of work; and missed sleep because of work-related stress. Frequency ranged from 1 = *never* to 2 = *once*, 3 = *twice*, 4 = *3–4 times*, 5 = *5–9 times*, 6 = *10–19 times*, 7 = *20–29 times*, 8 = *30–49 times*, and 9 = *50+ times*. Family–work spillover was measured by a single item: "How often do you feel drained when you come to work because of pressures and problems at home?" Ratings ranged from 1 = *never* to 5 = *always*.

Work–family fit was measured by a single item: "How easy or difficult is it for you to manage the demands of your work and personal/family life?" Ratings ranged from 1 = *very easy* to 5 = *very difficult*. Job satisfaction was measured by reverse-coding the question "Considering everything, how satisfied are you with your job?" Ratings ranged from 1 = *very satisfied* to 5 = *very dissatisfied*. Work success, Life success, Marital Success, and Parenting Success were measured with single items following the stem "All in all, how successful do you feel in each of the following: (1) your work life, (2) your personal life, (3) your relationship with your spouse/partner, (4) your relationship(s) with your child(ren)." Items were reverse coded and rated on a 7-point Likert-type scale from 1 = *extremely successful* to 7 = *extremely unsuccessful*.

Plan of Analysis

An effect size cutoff of .20 was used to determine meaningful differences by gender and life stage on the variables included in the model. The large sample size meant differences in means may have been statistically significant but not meaningful (Cohen, 1988). Effect size (ES) was calculated using the formula ES = $(M_2 - M_1) / SD_p$, where M_1 and M_2 represent the means of variable for the two groups and SD_p represents the pooled standard deviation.

Structural equation modeling (SEM) was used to estimate the work–family interface model proposed in this study and make comparisons across gender and family life stage groups. First, a single-group model was estimated with all the respondents ignoring any heterogeneity in the paths that could stem from gender or life stage. The models' goodness-of-fit indices, comparative fit index (CFI > .90) and root mean square error of approximation (RMSEA < .05), indicated that it was generalizable to the total sample of all IBM employees. The model was then reestimated with the two gender groups. The freely estimated model without equality constraints on the paths across the gender and life stage groups served as the baseline model to be compared with the subsequent equality model (in which all paths were the same for the groups) and with subsequent models that each had one path constraint and the others freely estimated. The chi-square differences between the baseline model and other models provided the tests of the path equality across gender and life stage groups.

RESULTS

Hypothesis 1

Table S3.1 presents the means and standard deviations of the variables modeled for each of the six family life stages. Effect sizes of mean differences between men and women at each family life stage were calculated. Gender differences with effect sizes greater than .20 were identified for all of the predictors except job flexibility.

Work characteristics. Gender comparisons for job responsibility across the six life stages found significant differences between men and women with a youngest child in elementary school. In all other life stages, men had greater, but not significantly greater, job responsibility. Gender comparisons of job hours found that men worked significantly more hours in almost every life stage, with women showing greater fluctuation in work hours across the life stages. The greatest gender difference in job hours was between men and women with a youngest child in elementary school. Gender comparisons of job flexibility indicated no significant gender differences across family life stages. Men had higher mean levels in all stages except in the stages with a youngest child in elementary school, or a youngest child who was a teenager. Gender differences in access to and use of work–family programs indicated significantly higher levels for women across all family life stages except the first parenthood stage. The greatest gender differences were between men and women with a youngest child in elementary school, or a youngest child who was a teenager.

Gender comparisons of work–family conflict indicated that men had significantly greater work–family conflict in almost every life stage, with the greatest gender differences between men and women with a youngest child in elementary school. There were no significant gender differences for men and women in the first parenthood stage, or those who were empty-nesters. In contrast, women reported significantly greater family–work conflict in the life stages of being younger than age 35 years with no children, having a youngest child in elementary school, or having a youngest child who was a teenager.

Family characteristics. Gender comparisons for time in household chores showed the greatest effect size differences, with significantly higher levels for women across all family life stages. The greatest gender differences were between men and women with a youngest child in elementary school, a youngest child who was a teenager, or men and women who were empty-nesters. Gender comparisons of marital status indicated that men were significantly more likely to be married across all family life stages.

Outcomes. There were no mean differences with effect sizes greater than .20 for the outcome variables of work, life, marital, and parenting success or job satisfaction. Gender comparisons for work–family fit identified one significant difference. Women with a youngest child who was a teenager had significantly greater fit than men in that life stage.

Hypothesis 2

The proposed work–family interface model fit the global data (see Figure S3.1). The χ^2 was significant ($\chi^2 = 13,312$, $df = 149$, $p < .000$), and the CFI, Tucker–Lewis

Table S3.1. Means Comparing Men and Women in Different Life Stages on Variables of the Work–Family Interface

Variables	No children (age < 35 years), n = 9,949			First parenthood (child ≤ 1), n = 1,009			Youngest child preschool aged (2–5 years), n = 6,827			Youngest child elementary school aged (6–12 years), n = 6,441			Youngest child teenager (13–17 years old), n = 7,062			Empty–nester (age > 50 years), n = 2,610		
	Male	Female	Effect size	Male	Female	Effect size	Male	Female	Effect size	Male	Female	Effect size	Male	Female	Effect size	Male	Female	Effect size
Job characteristics																		
Job responsibility	1.05	1.06	-0.04	1.12	1.08	0.13	1.23	1.14	0.20[a]	1.30	1.22	0.15	1.33	1.22	0.19	1.20	1.20	0.00
Job hours	50.04	49.08	0.11	50.30	46.10	0.43[a]	50.97	43.68	0.65[a]	51.23	46.07	0.48[a]	50.39	48.65	0.18	48.01	48.91	-0.10
W–F conflict	3.63	3.35	0.19	3.80	3.18	0.42[a]	3.90	3.18	0.49[a]	3.83	3.31	0.36[a]	3.59	3.31	0.19	3.12	3.11	0.01
Job flexibility	3.05	2.93	0.09	3.20	3.13	0.07	3.31	3.35	-0.04	3.40	3.44	-0.04	3.40	3.32	0.08	3.40	3.39	0.01
Program access/use	1.86	1.96	-0.14	2.02	2.24	-0.29[a]	2.08	2.48	-0.52[a]	2.16	2.53	0.50[a]	2.16	2.42	-0.36[a]	2.20	2.38	-0.26[a]
Family characteristics																		
F–W conflict	2.22	2.21	0.01	2.46	2.55	-0.10	2.43	2.62	-0.23[a]	2.37	2.54	-0.21[a]	2.28	2.42	-0.17	2.09	2.28	-0.24[a]
Time in household chores	3.65	3.9	-0.20[a]	3.72	4.32	-0.47[a]	3.52	4.42	-0.64[a]	3.47	4.55	-0.76[a]	3.49	4.58	-0.78[a]	3.63	4.44	-0.60[a]
Outcomes																		
Married (% Yes)	31	31	0.00	92	85	0.23[a]	91	86	0.16	89	80	0.26[a]	90	73	0.46[a]	79	55	0.51[a]
W–F fit	2.63	2.67	-0.04	2.58	2.58	0.00	2.60	2.60	0.00	2.37	2.54	-0.21[a]	2.81	2.85	-0.04	2.95	2.95	0.00
Job satisfaction	3.57	3.58	-0.01	3.59	3.74	-0.18	3.65	3.73	-0.10	3.71	3.79	-0.09	3.71	3.79	-0.09	3.69	3.80	-0.13
Work success	4.73	4.66	0.07	4.74	4.71	0.03	4.84	4.71	0.13	4.88	4.84	0.04	4.92	4.90	0.02	4.97	4.97	0.00
Life success	4.89	4.94	-0.04	5.24	5.26	-0.02	5.10	5.12	-0.02	5.03	5.09	-0.06	5.10	5.13	-0.03	5.21	5.21	0.05
Marital success	5.30	5.44	-0.11	5.60	5.52	0.07	5.30	5.22	0.07	5.25	5.17	0.07	5.44	5.33	0.09	5.65	5.58	0.06
Parenting success	4.66	4.53	0.11	5.66	5.60	0.05	5.49	5.58	-0.08	5.40	5.57	-0.16	5.45	5.59	-0.13	5.60	5.79	-0.18

Note: F-W = family–work; W-F = work–family.
a. Indicates a statistically significant difference (effect size > .20) between men and women in the family life stage.

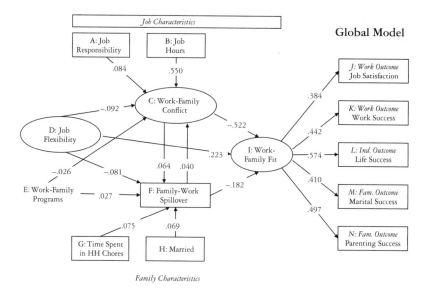

FIGURE S3.1. Structural equation modeling standardized parameter estimates for the model of the work–family interface (global sample)

index (TLI), and RMSEA were within acceptable ranges (CFI = .942, TLI = .910, RMSEA = .0460; Kline, 1998). All 18 paths were significant in the predicted direction. The same work–family interface model also fit 6 two-group models based on gender and family life stage. Table S3.2 presents the structural equation modeling standardized parameter estimates for the six life stage groups. Model comparisons treating the six groups together identified significant gender differences in all of the paths except work–family programs to work–family conflict, work–family programs to family–work conflict, time in household chores to family–work conflict, and work–family fit to job satisfaction, work, life, marital, and family success.

Work characteristic paths. The strength of the relationship between job responsibility and increased work–family conflict was greatest for women in the first parenthood stage, and women who had a youngest child in elementary school. Significant gender differences were identified between men and women in the first parenthood stage, and those who were empty-nesters. The strength of the relationship between job hours and work–family conflict was greatest for women with a youngest child in elementary school, a youngest child who was a teenager, and those who were empty-nesters.

Significant gender differences were identified between men and women with a youngest child who was in preschool, or those with a youngest child who was in elementary school.

The strength of the relationship between job flexibility and reduced work–family conflict was greater for men across all of the family life stages except for men under age 35 years with no children. The greatest gender differences were between men and women with a youngest child in elementary school, a youngest child who was a teenager, and those who were empty-nesters. Similarly, the strength of the relationship

Table S3.2. Structural Equation Standardized Parameter Estimates for Gender and Life Stage Models

Variables	No children (age < 35), n = 9,949		First parenthood (child ≤ 1), n = 1,009		Youngest child preschool aged (2–5 years), n = 6,827		Youngest child elementary school aged (6–12 years), n = 6,441		Youngest child teenager (13–17 years old), n = 7,062		Empty-nester (age > 50 years), n = 2,610	
	Male	Female	Male	Female	Male	Female	Male	Female	Male	Female	Male	Female
(a) Job responsibility	.041[a]	.066	.056[a]	.148[b]	.086	.109	.096	.136	.049[a]	.079	.055[a]	.141[b]
(b) Job hours → W-F conflict	.540	.536	.536	.560	.526	.562[b]	.524	.576[b]	.535	.596	.548	.587
(c) Job flexibility → W-F conflict	−.078	−.116	−.149[a]	−.099	−.105	−.099	−.154	−.049[a,b]	−.156	−.049[a,b]	−.132	−.017[a,b]
(d) W-F programs → W-F conflict	−.035[a]	−.015[a]	−.110[a]	−.118[a]	−.046[a]	−.013[a]	−.032[a]	−.026	.003[a]	−.005[a]	−.034[a]	−.015[a]
(e) Job flexibility → F-W conflict	.076	−.064	−.056[a]	−.031[a]	−.101	.108	−.097	−.076	−.089	−.045[a,b]	−.085[a]	−.046[a]
(f) W-F programs → F-W conflict	−.034[a]	.003[a]	.043[a]	−.051[a]	.015[a]	.038[a]	.010[a]	.012[a]	−.006[a]	.043[a]	.052[a]	.043[a,b]
(g) Time in HH chores → F-W conflict	.028[a]	.030[a]	.061[a]	.100[a]	.052[a]	.052[a]	.092	.056[a]	.065	.099	.064[a]	.150[b]
(h) Married → F-W conflict	.044[a]	.032[a]	−.010[a]	.090[a]	.018[a]	−.021[a]	−.037[a]	−.073	−.022[a]	−.035[a]	−.040[a]	−.005[a,b]
(i) W-F conflict → F-W conflict	.194	.085[b]	.231[a]	.102[a,b]	.148	.040[a,b]	.008[a]	.084[a,b]	.148	.043[a,b]	.150[a]	.030[a,b]

(Continued)

Table S3.2. (Continued)

Variables	No children (age < 35), n = 9,949		First parenthood (child ≤ 1), n = 1,009		Youngest child preschool aged (2–5 years), n = 6,827		Youngest child elementary school aged (6–12 years), n = 6,441		Youngest child teenager (13–17 years old), n = 7,062		Empty-nester (age > 50 years), n = 2,610	
	Male	Female	Male	Female	Male	Female	Male	Female	Male	Female	Male	Female
(j) F-W conflict → W-F conflict	-.024a	-.007a	-.127a	.129a	-.032a	.036a	.008a	.084a,b	-.043a	.060a,b	-.054a	-.117a,b
(k) Job flexibility → W-F fit	.218	.200b	.201	.151a	.244	.232b	.226	.235	.226	.244	.190	.203
(l) W-F conflict → W-F fit	-.503	-.561b	-.555	-.552	-.535	-.486	-.521	-.500	-.526	-.548	-.492	-.534
(m) F-W conflict → W-F fit	-.122	-.150	-.215	-.173	-.200	-.250b	-.162	-.207b	-.526	-.548b	-.140	-.139
(n) W-F fit → job satisfaction	.353	.368	.423	.360	.345	.394	.407	.394	.368	.380	.397	.403
(o) W-F fit → work success	.391	.392	.509	.517	.439	.450	.464	.457	.454	.456	.452	.437
(p) W-F fit → life success	.551	.545	.614	.446	.591	.588	.598	.608	.598	.578	.533	.533
(q) W-F fit → marital success	.414	.396	.473	.570	.399	.466	.519	.543	.497	.465	.405	.353
(r) W-F fit → parenting success	.542	.554	.531	.514	.519	.543	.497	.436	.430	.436	.430	.436

Note: F-W = family–work; W-F = work–family.
a. Indicates that the path was not statistically significant.
b. Indicates statistically significant difference between men and women in the family life stage.

between job flexibility and reduced family–work conflict was greater for men, with the most pronounced gender differences between men and women with a youngest child who was a teenager.

Family characteristic paths. The relationship between time in household chores and family–work conflict was not significant for men or women in any family life stage. Marriage significantly predicted reduced family–work conflict only for men who were empty-nesters.

Work–family interface outcomes. The strength of the relationship between job flexibility and increased work–family fit was significant for men and women in every life stage, but stronger for men. Significant gender differences were identified between men and women younger than age 35 years with no children, and those with a youngest child in preschool. The strength of the relationship between work–family conflict and reduced work–family fit was significant for men and women in every family life stage. Similarly, the strength of the relationship between family–work spillover and reduced work–family fit was significant for men and women in every family life stage. Significant gender differences, with a more strongly negative relationship for women, were identified for those with a youngest child in preschool, a youngest child in elementary school, or a youngest child who was a teenager.

DISCUSSION

The purpose of this study was to empirically evaluate the influence of family life stage on gender differences in the experience of work and family life across six family life stages. As hypothesized, the model fit the data at a global level. It also fit the data by gender, across life stages, and across life stages by gender. However, significant differences in the means of the model variables and in the size and direction of the relationships among the variables revealed important differences by gender and family life stage. Findings confirmed the usefulness of a life course perspective in exploring gender differences in the work–family interface (Moen & Sweet, 2004). Within-gender differences were as important as between-gender differences in understanding men's and women's experiences of the work–family interface.

Gender Differences in the Work–Family Interface

Several important gender differences emerged, irrespective of family life stage. Men on average worked more hours than women, were less aware of and used fewer family programs, spent less time in household labor, and experienced more work–family conflict including missing family obligations and dinners and reporting interruptions at home because of work. Women, in contrast, reported greater family–work spillover, particularly when they had a youngest child who was in elementary school or was a teenager. In spite of these differences, men and women reported similar levels of work, life, and family success with differing levels of work–family and family–work spillover.

Gender Differences by Family Life Stage in the
Work–Family Interface

The inclusion of life stage in the analysis provided a more informative and detailed picture of these gender differences. Some gender differences were temporary, limited to one or few life stages. Parenthood presented the strongest gender differences. Parents of young children seemed to organize the division of labor inside and outside the home to respond to the new demands of children. In gendered ways, women continued to have primary responsibility for their homes and child care, whereas both men and women focused on work and earning an income.

With job hours, men consistently worked more hours, but the greatest gender difference was for men and women with young children or teenagers. The gender gap in job hours augmented to almost 3 times the gender difference in the over-all sample for men and women with children under age 12 years, whereas there were almost no gender differences for men and women in the first stage (no children and age 35 or less) or in the last stage (empty nest stage). Similarly, men as a group reported more work–family conflict than women but the greatest differences were for men and women with young children at home. For those with a youngest child in preschool, the gender difference was nearly 2 times the gender difference for the entire sample. All of these gender differences reflected a curvilinear relationship. The greatest differences emerged during the intensive child-rearing years, whereas the earlier and later family life stages showed smaller or no gender differences.

With family–work conflict, the lack of gender differences found when comparing men and women without regard to life stage was misleading. Although there were no significant gender differences in the first life stage (no children), women with preschool and elementary school-age children reported significantly higher levels of family–work conflict than men. The gender difference in time spent in household chores was also significantly greater during these life stages. The gender gap in household chores, with women spending greater time, was 4 times larger for those with children under age 12 years at home than the average difference. Women seemed to increase their concern and commitment toward family responsibilities particularly when children were young, whereas men increased their commitment toward paid work.

The gender differences in work–family conflict and family–work spillover are consistent with Mennino and Brayfield's (2002) conclusion that men in male-dominated occupations are more likely to make trade-offs in which work is allowed to interfere with family plans or time. These findings suggest a privileging of employment responsibilities over family responsibilities (Mennino et al., 2005). Women, on the other hand, are more likely to experience spillover in which task, time, and emotional reactions in the home spill over into the work sphere, especially when they have young children (Roehling et al., 2003).

This suggests parallel curvilinear relationships of work–family conflict and family–work spillover for men and women. Men increase in work–family conflict across the early parenting life stages and decrease as children grow and leave the home, whereas women follow a similar pattern, but with family–work spillover. The relationship between family–work spillover and decreased work–family fit is also curvilinear for women. Feelings of spillover from family to work are more strongly related to perceptions of successful management of work and family relationships across the intensive parenting years. In contrast, work–family conflict does not differ in its relationship with work–family fit for men across family life stages. These findings confirm previous conclusions that women's experience of work and family life is more strongly related to children's ages and needs than men's (Higgins et al., 1994).

Job hours were consistently a strong predictor of women's experience of work–family conflict, especially women with a youngest child in elementary school, a youngest child who was a teenager, and those who were empty-nesters. But the flexibility that would presumably reduce the experience of time-based conflicts between work and family life was more effective for men across all family life stages, including the intensive parenting and empty nest stages. Mennino et al. (2005) found that a family-friendly workplace culture was more effective in reducing negative spillover than formal company policies. Women may be particularly likely to benefit from a culture of flexibility in addition to formal flexibility policies. Previous studies also suggested that reduced work hours may be most effective in reducing work–family conflict for women. This may be particularly true for women who are mature workers. Studies of mature workers indicated that mature women preferred working fewer hours and found job responsibilities more emotionally draining than mature men (Pitt-Catsouphes & Smyer, 2005).

Implications

Having young children at home emerged as the critical catalyst for gender differences in the work–family interface in this analysis. Greater gender differences were found in the central stages of life when children require a great deal of temporal and economic resources from their parents. When life stage was not considered, the first and last stages seemed to offset each other, concealing major gender differences in the central stages of family life. Thus, although there has been an increase in cultural emphasis on gender equality in the work and family realms, the findings indicated that gender differences persist. This does not mean that the current generation is not more egalitarian, but suggests that becoming a parent has more influence than other cultural norms. Men and women seemed to focus on their work and roles somewhat differently, particularly during the central stages of family life. Sanchez and Thompson (1997) emphasized that mothers continue to be primarily responsible for the household and that "contemporary fatherhood" has not altered this pattern in spite of change in other social relations.

Findings from this study suggest that these persistent differences may be working for men and women, at least in their perceptions of personal and family success. But in interpreting these findings, it is important to recognize that the sample reflects upper-middle-class men and women. Thus, the fact that persistent differences seem to be working for upper-middle-class men and women from IBM does not suggest similar results for women in more oppressed or economically difficult circumstances. Furthermore, the small number of success perception measures and common method variance suggest that strong conclusions cannot be drawn about men's and women's well-being from these measures.

Limitations

There are several limitations to consider in interpreting these results. Because of the use of cross-sectional data, differences may be conflated with cohort effects. Longitudinal data is necessary to evaluate how work–family linkages shift over the life course. The study presents an essential first step toward understanding differences in the experience of the work–family interface for workers at various family life stages. Future longitudinal research will be able to build on this foundation to further isolate life stage effects from potential cohort effects.

It is also crucial to acknowledge that the data came from only one corporation, and IBM employees tend to be more highly educated, have higher salaries, and have more experience with computer technology than the general population (Hill et al., 2004). These features may limit generalizability of the findings. Furthermore, the corporate sponsor required that the study contain a limited number of questions, which prevented using established work–family scales for all the variables in the analysis. It is unlikely that single items were as reliable in capturing the complexity of these constructs. This trade-off was necessary to gain access to broad corporate data, which allowed group comparisons on a range of factors that would have been impossible with a more common data set (Hill et al., 2004). The corporate nature of the data also limited the availability of couple data, which is essential to explorations of how women's choices and work and family realities are influenced by their husband's circumstances and vice versa. Fuller exploration of the "linked lives" contribution of the life course perspective is limited.

Finally, in interpreting these relationships, it is important to recognize that national differences are masked by the group analysis of the data. But it is very likely that national context influences the means of these work–family variables and their relationships across the family life course. Based on work by Aryee et al. (1999), nations may be categorized based on their collectivist/familistic or individualistic cultures. Collectivistic/familistic cultures are those in which the tendency is to place family interests above those of the individual. This is in contrast to individualistic cultures in which "self-development and family development are posed as counter to the demands of work" (Aryee et al., 1999, p. 494). This cultural difference in orientation is likely to influence interpretations of work–family conflict and family–work spillover. Furthermore, societal norms around maternal employment and the public work–family policies that reflect those norms are likely to influence gender differences in the experience of work–family conflict across the life course, as well as access to flexibility and work–family programs. The current analysis provides empirical evidence for how men and women differ on the same measures of the work–family experience across the life course. These findings serve as a baseline for future explorations of the influence of national context on gender differences across the family life course.

CONCLUSION

This analysis provided an important first step toward a better understanding of similarities and differences between male and female workers across the life course. The findings indicate that children strongly influence the work and family lives of men and women and that parenthood creates or maintains a more gendered work and family life. This lends empirical support to the assertion that work–family linkages are deeply embedded within life course location and temporal and social structural contexts (Grzywacz et al., 2002; Moen & Sweet, 2004). It is imperative that life stage be included in work and family analyses to better understand the shifts in effect sizes and directions of effect across gender.

The findings also suggest that men and women may need different work and family options even when they are in the same family life stage. For example, when children are young, men may benefit from more job flexibility in when and where they work, whereas women may need more reduced hour or part-time options. Unfortunately, there may be limits to the real possibilities offered to workers, because their work-life strategies are constrained by structural options. In organizations that are committed to work–family programs, greater awareness of the differences in the needs of men and women at different life stages could improve work–family fit and work, family, or life success for a variety of employees.

ACKNOWLEDGMENTS

We thank International Business Machines Corporation (IBM) for providing the support and cooperation needed to collect the data used in this article. We also thank the Family Studies Center of the BYU School of Family Life for its support of this project. Ideas expressed are the opinions of the authors, not necessarily of IBM or BYU.

DECLARATION OF CONFLICTING INTERESTS

The authors declared no conflicts of interests with respect to the authorship and/or publication of this article.

FUNDING

The authors appreciate funding from the Family Studies Center of the Brigham Young University School of Family Life and the College of Family, Home, and Social Sciences.

REFERENCES

Aryee, S. (1992). Antecedents and outcomes of work-family conflict among married professional women: Evidence from Singapore. *Human Relations, 45*, 813–837.

Aryee, S., Fields, D., & Luk, V. (1999). A cross-cultural test of a model of the work–family interface. *Journal of Management, 25*, 491–511.

Baltes, B., & Young, L. M. (2007). Aging and work/family issues. In G. Adams & K. Shultz (Eds.), *Aging and work in the 21st century* (pp. 7–23). Mahwah, NJ: Lawrence Erlbaum.

Barnes-Farrell, J. L., & Matthews, R. (2007). Age and work attitudes. In G. Adams & K. Shultz (Eds.), *Aging and work in the 21st century* (pp. 7–23). Mahwah, NJ: Lawrence Erlbaum.

Barnett, R. C., & Gareis, K. C. (2006). Role theory perspectives on work and family. In M. Pitt-Catsouphes, E. E. Kossek, & S. Sweet (Eds.), *The work and family handbook: Multidisciplinary perspectives and approaches* (pp. 209–221). Mahwah, NJ: Lawrence Erlbaum.

Barrah, J. L., Shultz, K., Baltes, B., & Stoltz, H. E. (2004). Men's and women's eldercare-based work-family conflict: Antecedents and work-related outcomes. *Fathering, 2,* 305–330.

Bielby, W. T., & Bielby, D. D. (1992). I will follow him: Family ties, gender-role beliefs, and reluctance to relocate for a better job. *American Journal of Sociology, 97,* 124–167.

Bond, E. M., Galinsky, E., Pitt-Catsouphes, M., & Smyer, M. A. (2005, November). The diverse employment experience of older men and women in the workforce. Boston: Families and Work Institute, the Center on Aging and Work at Boston College.

Bond, J. T., Thompson, C., Galinsky, E., & Prottas, D. (2002). *Highlights of the national study of the changing workforce.* New York: Families and Work Institute.

Cohen, J. (1988). *Statistical power analysis for the behavioral sciences.* Hillsdale, NJ: Erlbaum.

Cowan, C. P., & Cowan, P. A. (2000). *When partners become parents.* Mahwah, NJ: Lawrence Erlbaum.

Crouter, A. C. (1984). Spillover from family to work: The neglected side of the work-family interface. *Human Relations, 37,* 425–442.

Dilworth, J. E. L. (2004). Predictors of negative spillover from family to work. *Journal of Family Issues, 25,* 241–261.

Duxbury, L. E., & Higgins, C. A. (1991). Gender differences in work-family conflict. *Journal of Applied Psychology, 76,* 60–74.

Elder, G. H., Jr. (1996). The life course paradigm: Social change and individual development. In G. J. Elder Jr., P. Moen, & K. Luscher (Eds.), *Examining lives in context: Perspectives on the ecology of human development* (pp. 101–139). Washington, DC: American Psychological Association.

Entmacher, J. (1999). Testimony before the Subcommittee on Social Security of the House Committee on Ways and Means: Hearing on the impacts of the current social security's protections for women. Washington, DC: National Women's Law Center.

Frone, M. R., Russell, M., & Cooper, M. L. (1992). Prevalence of work–family conflict: Are work and family boundaries asymmetrically permeable? *Journal of Organizational Behavior, 13,* 723–729.

Greenhaus, J. H., & Beutell, N. J. (1985). Sources of conflict between work and family roles. *Academy of Management Review, 10,* 76–88.

Grzywacz, J. G., Almeida, D. M., & McDonald, D. A. (2002). Work–family spillover and daily reports of work and family stress in the adult labor force. *Family Relations, 51,* 28–36.

Gutek, B. A., Searle, S., & Klepa, L. (1991). Rational versus gender role explanations for work–family conflict. *Journal of Applied Psychology, 76,* 560–568.

Higgins, C., Duxbury, L., & Lee, C. (1994). Impact of life-cycle stage and gender on the ability to balance work and family responsibilities. *Family Relations, 43,* 144–150.

Hill, E. J., Jackson, A. D., & Martinengo, G. (2006). Twenty years of work and family at International Business Machines Corporation. *American Behavioral Scientist, 49,* 1165–1183.

Hill, E. J., Jacob, J. I., Shannon, L. L., Brennan, R. T., Blanchard, V. L., & Martinengo, G. (2008). Exploring the relationship of workplace flexibility, gender, and life stage to family-to-work conflict, and stress and burnout. *Community, Work, and Family, 11,* 165–181.

Hill, E. J., Martinson, V., & Ferris, M. (2004). New-concept part-time employment as a work–family adaptive strategy for women professionals with small children. *Family Relations, 53,* 282–292.

Hill, E. J., Yang, C., Hawkins, A. J., & Ferris, M. (2004). A cross-cultural test of the work–family interface in 48 countries. *Journal of Marriage and Family, 66,* 1300–1316.

Hinze, S. W. (2000). Inside medical marriages: The effect of gender on income. *Work and Occupations, 27,* 464–499.

Hundley, G. (2001). Domestic division of labor and self/organizationally employed differences in job attitudes and earnings. *Journal of Family and Economic Issues, 22*, 121–139.

Jacob, J. I., Bond, J. T., Galinsky, E., & Hill, E. J. (2008). Flexibility: A critical ingredient in creating an effective workplace. *The Psychologist-Manager Journal, 11,* 141–161.

Jung, C. G. (1971). *The portable Jung.* New York: Viking.

Kaufman, G., & Uhlenberg, P. (2000). The influence of parenthood on the work effort of married men and women. *Social Forces, 78*, 931–949.

Kline, R. B. (1998). *Principles and practice of structural equation modeling.* New York: Guilford.

Lundberg, S., & Rose, E. (1999). Parenthood and the earnings of married men and women. *Labour Economics, 7*, 689–710.

Marshall, N. L., & Barnett, R. C. (1993). Work–family strains and gains among two-earner couples. *Journal of Community Psychology, 21*, 64–78.

Mattessich, P., & Hill, R. (1987). Life cycle and family development. In M. B. Sussman & S. K. Steinbmetz (Eds.), *Handbook of marriage and the family* (pp. 437–465). New York: Plenum.

McElwain, A. K., Korabik, K., & Rosin, H. M. (2005). An examination of gender differences in work-family conflict. *Canadian Journal of Behavioral Science, 37*, 283–298.

Mennino, S. F., & Brayfield, A. (2002). Job-family trade-offs: The multidimensional effect of gender. *Work and Occupations, 29*, 226–256.

Mennino, S. F., Rubin, B. A., & Brayfield, A. (2005). Home-to-job and job-to-home spillover: The impact of company policies and workplace culture. *Sociological Quarterly, 46*, 107–135.

Moen, P., Erickson, W., Agarwal, M., Fields, V., & Todd, L. (2000). *The Cornell Retirement and Wellbeing Study.* Ithaca, NY: Bronfenbrenner Life Course Center at Cornell University.

Moen, P., & Roehling, P. (2005). *The career mystique: Cracks in the American dream.* New York: Rowman & Littlefield.

Moen, P., & Sweet, S. (2004). From "work–family" to "flexible careers": A life course reframing. *Community, Work, and Family, 7*, 209–226.

Nock, S. (1998). *Marriage in men's lives.* New York: Oxford University Press.

Nomaguchi, K. M., & Milkie, M. A. (2003). Costs and rewards of children: The effects of becoming a parent on adults' lives. *Journal of Marriage and Family, 65*, 356–374.

Nomaguchi, K. M., Milkie, M. A., & Bianchi, S. M. (2005). Time strains and psychological wellbeing: Do dual-earner mothers and fathers differ? *Journal of Family Issues, 26*, 756–792.

Orrange, R. (1999). *Work, family and meaning in life: Thoughts of professionals in transitioning to work.* Ithaca, NY: Cornell University Press.

Pitt-Catsouphes, M., & Smyer, M. A. (2006). *One size doesn't fit all: Workplace flexibility.* Boston, MA: Families and Work Institute, the Center on Aging and Work at Boston College. Retrieved from www.bc.edu/agingandwork

Roehling, P. V., Moen, P., & Batt, R. (2003). When work spills over into the home and home spills over into work. In P. Moen (Ed.), *It's about time: Couples and careers* (pp. 101–121). Ithaca, NY: Cornell University Press.

Sanchez, L., & Thomson, E. (1997). Becoming mothers and fathers: Parenthood, gender and the division of Labor. *Gender & Society, 11*, 747–772.

Simon-Rusinowitz, L., Krach, C. A., Marks, L. N., Piktialis, D., & Wilson, L. B. (1996). Grandparents in the workplace: The effects of economic and labor trends. *Generations, 20*, 41–44.

Staudinger, U. M., & Bluck, S. (2001). A view on midlife development from life-span theory. In M. E. Lachman (Ed.), *Handbook of midlife development* (pp. 447–486). New York: John Wiley.

Sterns, H. L., & Huyck, M. H. (2001). The role of work in midlife. In M. E. Lachman (Ed.), *Handbook of midlife development* (pp. 447–486). New York: John Wiley.

Treas, J., & Widmer, E. D. (2000). Married women's employment over the life course: Attitudes in cross-national perspective. *Social Forces, 78*, 1409–1436.

4

FAMILY STRESS THEORY

Marsha and Sean Peabody have been married for five years; this is the second marriage for both. Sean has a child from his previous marriage (eight-year-old Billy) who spends every other week, holidays, and one month during the summer with them, but they have wanted to have their "own" baby for some time. After trying to become pregnant for several years, they started infertility treatment, which worked. Marsha, a corporate manager at a large software company, had to leave work six weeks early because of a difficult pregnancy; she's having twins. Sean, a salesman at a television station, spent three weeks running back and forth between work and the hospital. Finally, Alicia and Barry were born, but five weeks prematurely, which led to health complications for both but especially for little Barry. Although Alicia was able to come home after just two weeks, Barry was in the hospital for one month. Thus, Marsha and Sean spent a lot of time running back and forth between work, home, and the hospital. This also affected Billy's visitation schedule, which left him feeling unwanted and angry.

Marsha was not able to return to work because of the health needs of the twins and the fact that child care for two would consume most of her paycheck. Sean kept his job but was able to take off only one week once the twins were born. Needless to say, life has been stressful for the Peabody family!

The twins are now three months old and getting stronger every day. They still wake up every three hours to be fed, and each is taking different medications that must be administered at different times. Marsha's parents live nearby and are taking turns spending the night and helping with the feedings. Other friends and family members come over during the day to help Marsha take care of the twins. Both parents are still exhausted and constantly worry about the health of the twins. They often turn to prayer when they feel overwhelmed and find that it comforts them. They are also both very optimistic people and take it all in stride. They were so desperate to be parents that the lack of sleep and complete loss of any activity outside of taking care of the twins seems like no big deal in comparison to the joy that Alicia and Barry bring them. Now if they could just convince Billy how wonderful it is to be a big half brother!

HISTORY

Although families have experienced stress since time began, the scientific study of how families deal with stress is a relatively recent phenomenon. The Great Depression of the 1930s was the impetus for this research, as Angell (1936) and Cavan and Ranck (1938) sought to discover how families were dealing with the loss of household income and the stress associated with unemployment. Angell discovered that a family's reaction to the sudden loss of income during the Depression was based on two things: integration and adaptability. Integration means how close or unified a family feels and how economically interdependent they are, whereas adaptability means how flexible families are in talking about problems, making decisions as a group, and modifying existing patterns, roles, and rules. Angell found that families who are both integrated and easily able to adapt their family roles to meet the needs of the situation are most capable of dealing with stress, such as that caused by job loss during the Depression. Similarly, Cavan and Ranck studied families both before and after the Depression and found that those who were organized and cohesive prior to the Depression were best able to deal with economic losses, whereas disorganized families faced further breakdown.

Koos (1946) also researched how families deal with economic loss, building upon Hill's (1949) "roller-coaster profile of adjustment to crisis" (14). According to Hill's model (see Figure 4.1), families go through four stages when faced with a stressful situation: crisis, disorganization, recovery, and reorganization. The crisis phase is obviously the stress-provoking event that sent the family into crisis. This can be anything from the birth of a new child to the death of a family member. Once the family is faced with a crisis, a period of disorganization follows as family members attempt to cope with the situation. For example, new parents attempt to develop a schedule of feeding and/or waking up with the child at night so that each parent is able to get some sleep. They also must attempt to cope with little sleep, meeting the needs of the infant, and changing how they view each other now that they are parents as well as spouses.

As families figure out how to handle the situation, they enter the stage of recovery, which can be either fairly quick or long. According to Hill (1949), families will eventually reach a new level of organization; for some it will be the same as the

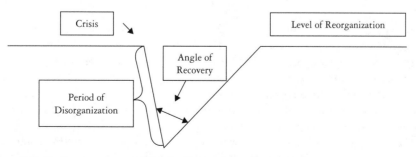

FIGURE 4.1 Roller-coaster profile of adjustment.

Source: Hill, R. 1949. Roller-Coaster Profile of Adjustment. In *Families Under Stress,* 138. New York: Harper & Brothers.

previous level of organization; for others it will be better than it was before; and for still others things will become stable but not as good as they were prior to the stressful event. Thus, some new parents eventually find a schedule that fits all of their needs and are able to continue much as they did prior to the birth of their child. Other first-time parents become closer and find that their marital relationship is better because they have bonded over the birth of their child. This may also lead to better communication skills as a result of figuring out how to manage a newborn. Unfortunately, some parents find having an infant in the home overwhelming and never really learn to adjust. In these families, lines of communication break down, resentments and jealousies form, and often divorces occur, because the couple is not able to return to a satisfactory level of interaction.

The roller-coaster model of adjustment to crisis was the predecessor to Reuben Hill's (1949) ABC-X model of family stress, which is the foundation of family stress theory. His early research on how families attempted to adjust to the crisis caused by separation and reunion during wartime led to the development of a theory that has remained virtually unchanged over the last five decades. Although other scholars have added to it (McCubbin and Patterson 1982), attempted to simplify it (Burr and Klein 1994), or built on it (Lazarus and Folkman 1984), the basics of this theory, as Hill wrote them, have remained primarily unchanged. The rest of this chapter discusses Hill's ABC-X model.

BASIC ASSUMPTIONS

The basic assumptions of family stress theory revolve around the central components of the model. This section focuses on the theory itself, and then we will focus more specifically on defining each of its components. As previously stated, stress theory is based on the ABC-X model, with A being the stressor event, B the family resources or strengths, and C the family's perception of the event, or how they define or attribute meaning to the event. If the event or stressor is such that the family cannot immediately figure out how to solve the problem, this will lead to crisis, the X component of the model (Hill 1949). Because of the nature of this theory, the format for this chapter is slightly different.

Stressor Events (A)

Now, let's look at each component of the model a little more closely, beginning with the stressor. It's critical to realize that the stressor event itself is neither positive nor negative, because events or situations are neutral before we interpret them. It is also important to remember that both positive and negative events can cause stress. For example, although it is obvious that events such as the loss of a family member are stressful, the birth of a much-wanted child or winning the lottery can also cause stress, even though both events are causes for celebration.

Many people have come up with ways to categorize or define stressors, and we will review just a few. Lipman-Bluman (1975) came up with ten criteria that affect the degree to which a stressor will impact a family, eight of which are commonly used in stress theory and are addressed here.

1. The first criterion is whether the stressor is internal or external to the family. An example of this would be a mother who chooses to return to work after the birth of a child versus the mother who loses her job following the birth of her child. In the first case, the mother makes the choice to quit her job to take care of her child, so this is a decision made internally. In the second case, however, the mother is fired because she is always late to work and is falling asleep on the job; thus, external circumstances control the decision.

2. Whether a stressor is focused on one member of the family or all members of the family can make a difference. For example, a stressful workplace might cause one family member to come home unhappy, which might then disrupt the family. In another example, a recession might cause both spouses to lose their jobs, forcing the entire family to deal with a loss of income.

3. Suddenness versus gradual onset revolves around how much time a family has to anticipate a stressor's arrival. Whereas an unexpected illness might cause immediate crisis, pregnancy gives couples time to adjust to the idea of being parents.

4. The severity of a stressor can also make a difference. Are you dealing with the death of a child or the purchase of a new home, for example?

5. How long families have to adjust to a stressor can affect how they cope. The first day of kindergarten happens only once, but learning how to care for a spouse with cancer is a long-term stressor event.

6. Whether the stressor is expected or not can also make a difference. We can expect to have difficult times while our children are adolescents, but we do not expect to be the victim of a road-rage crime.

7. The seventh criterion is whether the stressor is natural or artificial/human-made. For example, are you trying to deal with the damage left behind by Hurricane Katrina, or are you dealing with the loss of a job because of increased technological advantages at your canning plant?

8. Finally, the family's perception of whether or not they are able to solve the crisis situation can determine how they react to the stressor. It is much easier to respond to something like being a member of a blended family than it is to deal with a terrorist attack, over which we have little control.

When looking at the *A* component of ABC-X model, use these eight criteria to determine how to define and describe the stressor event in determining how it will affect the family.

Similarly, three types or kinds of stressor events were identified by Boss (2002). The first is whether the stressor is normative or non-normative. Something that is normative is expected, like entering puberty or having to deal with the death of a grandparent, whereas being in a serious car accident is not predicted, or not normative. The second stressor descriptor is either ambiguous or clear. If a stressor is ambiguous, we don't know the basic details (when, where, why, how long it will last, who it will happen to, etc.), whereas things that are clear (non-ambiguous) can be anticipated, such as the death of someone who has been diagnosed with terminal cancer. The third type of stressor is something that is volitional or non-volitional. Volitional stressors are things that we want to happen and that we work to make happen, such as starting a new business or adopting a child, whereas non-volitional stressors are things that just happen to us, such as losing a job due to company downsizing.

Finally, people often describe stressors based on how long they last, or as being either chronic or acute. A chronic stressor is one that you expect to last a long time. It is usually not the chronic stressor itself that leads to crisis; it is the resources that are being used (and depleted) to deal with the chronic stressor that make people more vulnerable to other types of stressors. Dealing with a chronic illness is an example of this, because it is often the limitations caused by the illness that cause stress, not the illness itself per se. In contrast, an acute stressor happens quickly and does not last very long, but it is intense when it is happening. Dealing with a natural disaster, such as a forest fire that destroys your home, is an acute stressor. They are often more difficult to deal with even though they are shorter in duration, because they tend to be more severe in nature (Weber 2011).

Resources (B)

Once a stressor has affected a family, the family must figure out how to deal with the event or situation. One way of doing this is by accessing resources, the B component of this model. Recall the work of Angell (1936), who described the ideas of family integration and adaptability. The abilities to pull together as a family and be flexible based on the circumstances are both resources. These two resources were further developed into a more complex model by Olson and McCubbin (1982), but the premise remains the same: Family members must learn to balance being cohesive and remaining individuals while also finding ways to retain their boundaries as a family, unless doing so brings harm to the family. In other words, family members should stick together as a cohesive unit when facing a crisis and pull together to help one another, but they also need to learn when they should go outside the family and seek help.

McCubbin and Patterson (1985) stated that we should think of resources as falling within three categories: individual, family, and community. For example, one way to deal with the loss of a job is to figure out what you can do to solve the problem or find another job. In this case, individual resources would be level of education, job experience, perseverance, and work ethic. One can also use family resources to deal with unemployment by being supportive and encouraging to one another, making contacts with those you know in the job market, helping your spouse with a résumé, and sharing household responsibilities to allow more time for a job search. Finally, one can also turn to the community for help (job relocation services, headhunters, having people at church help you make contacts and keep you in their prayers, and having friends help with some of your current tasks to allow you more time to search for a job). The more resources you have available, the better you are able to cope. Thus, the best response to stress is to use a variety of resources.

According to McKenry and Price (2000), social support is one of the most important resources we can access. This can be provided by families instrumentally (i.e., with household chores or writing a résumé), emotionally, and through the building of increased social networks. Being supported also has the added benefit of building one's self-esteem, because our feelings of self-worth increase when others are willing to help us—it is seen as a sign of love and support. We can also receive social support from community resources, such as increased networking, help with problem-solving skills, and providing assistance in accessing valuable resources.

The role of social support is so strong that Kotchick, Dorsey, and Heller (2005) suggested that it can act as a buffer for single African American mothers living in low-income, environmentally hazardous conditions with their children. In their family stress model, the neighborhood is the stressor that decreases the mother's psychological functioning, which in turn leads to impaired parenting. However, having good social support from friends, neighbors, and family can lead to more positive parenting practices and can minimize the effects of environmental stress.

Definition of the Situation (C)

Lazarus and Launier (1978) suggested that what individuals think about or how they interpret the stressor is as important as accessing resources when determining how a family will react to a crisis. This is often assessed in research about coping with a chronic illness like cancer. Cognitive appraisal and coping processes are thought of as mediators of individual psychological responses to stressors, such as being diagnosed and living with cancer (Folkman 1999; Lazarus and Folkman 1984). Optimism, or the belief that more good things will happen than bad, helps a person to view a stressor as more challenging than threatening, which has been associated with more positive outcomes in breast cancer patients (Carver et al. 1993; Epping-Jordan et al. 1999). The appraisal process in turn influences the thoughts and behaviors used to manage stress—coping. Thus, individuals with cancer who are optimistic about their chances of survival are better able to deal with their diagnosis than those who see it as an insurmountable problem (Smith and Soliday 2001).

The self-fulfilling prophecy, which is "a prediction of behavior which biases people to act as though the prediction were already true" (Papalia and Olds 1996, 487), also influences our perceptions of stressors. Burr (1982) related this to stress theory by saying that individuals and families who believe that a stressor cannot be solved are dooming themselves to failure. By contrast, those who can cognitively reframe the problem as something they can handle are better able to manage the stressor. For example, if a student convinces herself that she cannot pass an exam, she is less likely to study than she would otherwise, which may lead her to actually fail the exam. In contrast, if she had confidence that she could pass the exam, or her perception was that she was able to pass the exam, she would probably study more, which would more likely lead to success.

An important part of this process is how the stressor is broken down into manageable tasks. For example, rather than looking at the problem in its entirety, such as moving to a new town to take a new job, one might make a list of things that have to be done in each location. That way only one item is focused on at a time, and the individual is not overwhelmed with all that has to be done. Cognitive reappraisal is a part of this process as well; we attempt to decrease the intensity of the emotions surrounding the situation as much as possible. Rather than viewing a move as tearing you away from a place you love, one might focus on the adventures that await in a new town and work environment. This changes the emotional energy from negative to more positive. Finally, family members should encourage each other to maintain their normal lives, rather than allow a problem to consume them. In this example, that would mean spending time with friends you care about and doing things in your community as a family, while still working toward completing the tasks necessary to make the move.

Stress and Crisis (X)

Whether or not a family will enter a state of crisis is determined by the previously discussed components of the ABC-X model. A crisis is reached when the family is no longer able to maintain its usual balance because of the stressor event. It is important to note that not all stressors lead to crisis. In addition, just because a family faces a crisis does not mean the family will be broken apart because of it. In fact, families often function better and are more cohesive after a crisis than they were before, as was shown previously, when the roller-coaster model of adjustment to crisis (Hill 1949) was discussed in the example of how different couples adjust to having a newborn.

PRIMARY TERMS AND CONCEPTS

Stressors

Now that we know the basics of the theory, it is important to define a few of the concepts in more detail, which will be done following the ABC-X model. Olson, Lavee, and McCubbin (1988) defined stressors as "discrete life events or transitions that have an impact upon the family unit and produce, or have the potential to produce, change in the family system" (19). Notice that this definition uses the word *discrete*, which implies that stressors are singular. In other words, in this model, we deal with one stress-producing event at a time. It is also important to note that stressors are neither positive nor negative by themselves, but become one or the other based on how we define the situation. What is negative for one person might be a positive event for another. Becoming pregnant may be perceived differently by a 15-year-old with plans to attend medical school compared to Marsha and Sean (from the vignette at the beginning of this chapter), who have taken extraordinary measures to become pregnant. Both families are faced with the same event, pregnancy, but what is a painful and difficult predicament for the teenager is a cause for celebration for the Peabody family. The sample reading for this chapter is based on ambiguous loss as a potential stressor for families (Betz and Thorngren 2006). This refers to types of losses, physical or psychological, that are not as commonly understood or accepted as something like the death of a spouse. It includes losses such as a missing family member (i.e., due to war or child abduction), a miscarriage, or having a parent who is suffering from dementia and no longer able to recognize you. Cacciatore, Schnebly, and Froen (2009) studied the importance of social support in decreasing anxiety and depression among mothers dealing with stillbirths, another type of ambiguous loss. Falicov (2007) described transnational migration as a similar type of ambiguous loss, because the length of time away from family, the ability to survive in a new country, and the challenges faced during the migration itself are examples of a multitude of potential stressors.

As is discussed at the end of this chapter in the critique, it should come as no surprise that stressors typically do not happen in isolation. Although this model is formulated to deal with one stressor at a time, unfortunately we often must deal with many stressors at once. This has lead to the concept of *pileup*, which refers to the idea of multiple stressors occurring at the same time (Patterson 1988). Much research has been done based on the pileup notion. One example is a study by Darling et al. (2008) that focuses on whether or not people diagnosed with bipolar disorder adhere to their medication regimen. They found that one cannot understand medication adherence (or lack thereof) without also understanding the other stressors associated with living with this disorder (the physical and mental effects of the disorder, medication side effects, and family stress and general life contentment). Similarly, Willoughby, Doty, and Malik (2008) assessed parental reactions to a child's disclosure of minority sexual-orientation status and found that, although using the ABC-X model is useful in understanding how parents react, it's also important to take into consideration the other types of demands being made on the family when disclosure takes place. They suggest that a parent already coping with a multitude of stressors will be less equipped to deal with disclosure than will a parent with fewer stressors.

Normative Event

While stressors can be both positive and negative, they can also be normative or non-normative. A normative event has three primary components: It is something that occurs in all families, you can anticipate its occurrence, and it is short-term rather than chronic (McCubbin and Patterson 1983). Examples of normative stressors would be the birth of a child, learning how to deal with a teenager, buying your first home, and facing retirement. We are better able to deal with stressors that are normative, because we have had some time to think about how we will handle the situation or what resources we can access. Non-normative stressors, such as losing an infant to sudden infant death syndrome or the separation of family members due to war, are not anticipated and thus more likely to lead to a crisis.

Resources

The *B* component of the model—resources—includes characteristics, traits, or abilities of individuals, families, or communities, as was discussed earlier (McCubbin and Patterson 1985). One resource not already mentioned is that of *coping*, which is what we do in an attempt to deal with a stressor. Coping is really an interaction of our resources and perceptions, because we choose the resources we draw upon based on our perceptions of what will work and what won't. For example, if a student has a big paper due on Monday, and it's now Sunday night, he is sick, and hasn't started the paper yet, there is a problem. One way for him to cope with the problem is to simply admit to himself that the paper will not be his best work, but that he can still get it done if he locks himself in his room with his reference materials and computer. With this response, he has defined the problem as solvable and has used the resources at his disposal—his work ethic, self-confidence, and creativity—to write the paper. If, on the other hand, he decides that he just can't get it done and will explain it to his professor tomorrow, he might cope by going to bed, which in turn is likely to result in a failing grade on his paper.

Lazarus and Folkman (1984), among others, believe there are three primary ways to define how families cope: using direct actions, intrapsychically, or by controlling the emotions associated with the stressor itself. *Direct actions* mean actually doing something, such as searching the community for resources, writing a new résumé, or seeking counseling to help deal with a problem. *Intrapsychic coping* refers to cognitively reframing the problem so that it does not seem so overwhelming or insurmountable. Finally, although some people control the emotions caused by a stressor in positive ways, such as talking to a friend or going to a religious service, others use more destructive means, such as turning to alcohol or drugs in an attempt to dull the pain or alleviate the emotions. Regardless of how a family copes, the ultimate goal is to return the family to its previous state of functioning—in other words, solving the problem so that things can return to normal.

Crisis

Here it is important to make a distinction between stress and crisis. Whereas *family stress* is something that causes a change in the family or upsets their sense of normalcy, *crisis* is a state or period of disorganization that rocks the foundation of the family. One should also bear in mind that, although families can experience different degrees of stress, a family is either in crisis or not. When does stress become crisis? Families are in crisis when they can no longer maintain the status quo using their existing resources, or when they are so overwhelmed as to be incapacitated (Boss 1988).

Adaptation

The level of family adaptation is usually thought to fall somewhere between *bonadaptation*, a positive result to the crisis, and *maladaptation*, an unhealthy or dysfunctional resolution of the crisis. For example, whereas some families deal with the job loss of one spouse by pulling together and pooling resources until a new job is found (bonadaptation), other families fall apart in this situation, fighting with each other, and turning to substances like drugs and alcohol to cope with the loss (maladaptation).

COMMON AREAS OF RESEARCH AND APPLICATION

Family stress theory is still being used in the field of family science. One indicator of this is the number of dissertations and theses that have used this theoretical approach in recent years. For example, Bonneau (2011) used this theory to study how wives of firefighters deal with the stress associated with having a husband in this line of work by focusing on the meaning they associate with that stressor, as well as the use of social support systems. Similarly, Wilson (2011) used family stress theory to assess how adult children of clergy dealt with the stressors associated with being the child of someone in that line of work. We will review other studies that focused on clergy families in this section. Huber (2011) used this model to look at how mothers who have a child with ADHD deal with the stress of this caregiving responsibility. As we will find in the literature review to follow, caregiving is an area that has been rich with this theoretical underpinning. We start with a brief review of the role of family stress theory in research on military families in the last few years.

Military Families

The use of family stress theory in the study of military families has a long history. After all, this theory was based on Hill's (1949) study of how families were able to deal with separation and then reunion during times of war. Although the nature of war times has changed today, Wadsworth (2010) indicates there are still multiple reasons why family scholars should research the effects of war and terrorism on families. First, wars and terrorism are still having effects in our global world that impact us locally. Second, this theory and research have benefited from such work in the past, and third, studies in this area have led to the development of new and effective ways of helping families cope with stressful life events. Wadsworth provided a discussion of research utilizing this approach in recent years that guided the inclusion of the following articles in this section.

Researchers have used family stress theory to assess how families deal with deployment and which factors can determine their success in this process (Wiens and Boss 2006). Many researchers have also looked at deployment from a different angle. It has been suggested that, while soldiers are away from home, they are physically absent, but because family members think about them, they are still psychologically present. However, sometimes when they come home from war, the opposite happens. In other words, although they are now physically present at home with their families, they may not be psychologically present because of the mental stresses suffered during war. This is primarily the result of boundary ambiguity, in which both those who go to war and those who stay home have to change their roles. Once military personnel return home, roles have to once again be renegotiated, which can create a great deal of stress for families. However, Faber et al (2008) found that this ambiguity decreased over time, which also helped to decrease stress. Similarly, Huebner et al. (2007) studied the effects of parental employment on youth and how it basically creates a sense of ambiguous loss. In other words, the family member is not there playing his or her normal role, but the person is still a part of the youth's family; this creates boundary ambiguity.

Clergy Families

The previously discussed research suggests that having a family member in the military is stressful, but another occupation that can create stress for the family is that of the clergy. Several studies in the last few years have assessed the role of stress and support for clergy and their spouses to determine if they cope with the stress of the job in the same way, despite their obviously different roles. Such studies have also sought to determine the effects of stressors from this occupation on the quality of their lives. Darling, Hill, and McWey (2004) found that clergy families that experienced lower levels of stress experienced a higher quality of life. They found clergy and their wives to be similar in their experiences, with the exception being that clergy spouses tended to be more affected by family stress than the clergy themselves. They believe this is because dealing with family issues fell more frequently to the spouse, so that the clergy member could tend to the stressors of his or her congregation. Lee (2007) also found similar results across spouses, with the addition of the finding that clergy/pastors have more presumptive expectations placed on them than do their wives; this leads to higher levels of stress. The greater the level of stress there was for the clergy member, the greater the impact was on all family members.

Does having children affect clergy families positively or negatively? Darling, McWey, and Hill (2006) surveyed clergy and their spouses to determine if children affected the quality of life for their families and used the ABC-X model as a basis for a predictive model for determining whether clergy families had children in the house or not. It was found that those households with children experienced more stress than those without, perhaps due to increased time demands on spouses whose partners were often called away from home for work. Despite this, spousal quality of life was found to be the same whether or not children were present in the home.

Although not directly related to clergy families, an interesting analysis was done by Wilmoth and Smyser (2009) that used the ABC-X model of family stress to analyze the Book of Philippians in the Bible. They provided a thorough description of the theory, and then used the language of the theory to describe how Paul basically used the same model in the Bible in his speech to the Philippians. The authors suggest that this analysis could help both clergy and laymen when they counsel people who are Christians, as it would help them understand how the model works so they could apply it to their own lives, and also because it teaches that problems are not insurmountable. They suggest that, although family stress theory is somewhat recent as a field of study, its strategies have been around and used for centuries.

Non-normative Caregiving

Occupational stressors such as those related to being a member of the military or clergy are only two examples of ways in which the ABC-X model has been used in recent years. This section reviews some of the non-normative or unexpected situations that require a caregiver.. For example, Provencher et al. (2000) reviewed measures using a family stress theory framework that is available to assess how caregivers of individuals with schizophrenia cope. Primary emphasis was placed on the fact that, although much of the literature in this area identifies how caregivers respond to the stress of caring for the behavioral needs of individuals with schizophrenia, there is little study of how caregivers perceive their roles or how they cope with caring for the individual. It seems obvious that each of these components would influence the behaviors of caregivers as discussed in the ABC-X model.

This model has been used with other types of disabilities as well. Norizan and Shamsuddin (2010) used family stress theory to assess the impact of stress on mothers in Malaysia who parent children with Down syndrome, a congenital birth outcome that can lead to higher levels of parental stress than are found among parents of typically developing children. The role of culture was important in this study, as they discovered that the primary means of coping were first religious, then acceptance, and finally active coping. This study points to the role not only of culture, but also to the need to assess multiple stressors outside of those directly related to the parenting difficulties associated with Down syndrome, such as marital status, economics, maternal characteristics, and number of children in the house. Being depressed and not having accepted that your child has Down syndrome were the primary predictors of parental stress for the mothers in this study.

Caregiving can be stressful in many situations. Hardesty et al. (2008) studied caregivers (primarily grandparents) who were caring for children following the violent deaths of their mothers at the hands of their intimate partners. In addition to the stressors such as lack of financial resources, ambiguity around terminology for what to call each other, and limited resources during retirement years, for grandparents raising grandchildren, you now have children who were typically exposed to domestic violence prior to the homicide, and many of whom saw the murders take place or were there for the aftermath. Some of these children then watched the family members of the victims and perpetrators fight over what should be done with them. The ABC-X model was an excellent tool in this study for understanding the experiences of both the children and their caregivers.

Another area of non-normative caregiving is taking care of someone with, or living with, a chronic illness. As was stated earlier, much of the research in the area of chronic illness uses a stress theory approach to determine how individuals and families cope with the diagnosis of a chronic illness such as cancer. This is especially difficult when the form of cancer is extremely rare, as in the case of carcinoid cancer (Soliday et al. 2004). Much of the stress for these patients comes from uncertainty about the disease itself, as well as the knowledge that there is currently no cure. It was found that the perception of the diagnosis as either a death sentence or something that can be coped with by living life to the fullest affected patient levels of depression. In addition, coping strategies differed widely from one individual to the next, again supporting the need to address **both** individual and family reactions to stressors, as well as to make inferences to large populations **only** with extreme caution (Smith and Soliday 2001).

Sometimes illnesses that are initially acute in nature become more chronic, increasing the level of stress for families and caregivers. Oktay et al (2011) studied women suffering from post-treatment fatigue (as the result of receiving treatment for breast cancer) and their caregivers. The perception of the fatigue was the main focus of the research, because most patients and family members did not expect symptoms, especially to this degree, to last so long after treatment. This can keep them from resuming their previous family roles, as well as create longer-term hardships for other family members. How family members come to define and explain the fatigue helps determine their abilities to cope with its chronic existence.

Similarly, Darling, Olmstead, and Tiggleman (2009) studied individuals with AIDS and their caregivers to determine the effects of stress on life satisfaction. In this case, there is not only the physical stress associated with the disease itself, but also the psychological stress associated with being part of a stigmatized group. Special focus was given to their perception of the stressor for this reason. They found that how individuals and their caregivers handled stress historically and their current levels of family stress impacted their current level of life satisfaction. Female caregivers were also found to experience greater stress than males. As hypothesized, the biggest predictor of greater life satisfaction was their perception of the stressor.

Family Ambiguity

Family systems theory states that families have boundaries that determine who is or is not a part of the family system, and/or what roles people play within the family. When those positions or roles are unclear, family boundary ambiguity exists (Boss and Greenberg 1984). Researchers have integrated this concept into family systems theory as being the cause of stress (the A component) or as being defined by the perceptions of the individual family members (the C component). So, for example, integrating a stepparent into the home may cause family members to have to share resources, change rituals, or reevaluate their boundaries, and these could all be potential stressors. How they perceive this person, however, will also influence the level of boundary ambiguity. Family stress research and therapeutic practices have benefited from the integration of boundary ambiguity into the ABC-X model of family stress in areas such as MIA family members, death of a family member, divorce, remarriage, stepfamilies, family health care issues, and research on clergy families (Carroll, Olsen, and Buckmiller 2007).

If there is one thing we can conclude from this review of current literature based on family stress theory, it is that the theory is as relevant today as it was in its inception in the 1930s. One would predict that, as people face more and more stressors in their lives and society becomes increasingly complex, the use of this theory will remain strong. Perhaps the most common approach will be a combined theoretical orientation as authors discuss issues, such as those in the previous paragraph, using this theory in addition to other theoretical approaches more specific to their topics of study.

CRITIQUE

Despite the fact that this theory has been widely used since its introduction in the 1930s, many have identified problems in the theory. Perhaps the most well-established problem is the fact that this is a linear model trying to explain complex families and situations. In other words, it is usually not one single event that causes a family to become stressed to the point of crisis but rather an accumulation of events. To address this problem, McCubbin and Patterson (1982) developed the double ABC-X model (see Figure 4.2), based on their research on families who had a member either captured during, or unaccounted for after, a war. The model begins with the traditional ABC-X

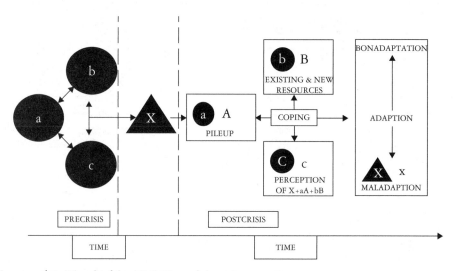

FIGURE 4.2 The double ABC-X model.
Source: McCubbin, H. I., A. E. Carble, and J. M. Patterson. 1982. *Family Stress Coping and Social Support*, 46. New York: Brunner/Mazel.

structure and treats this as the precipitating event. However, it adds a post-crisis period of adjustment, which takes into consideration the fact that families must respond not just to the initial crisis itself but to the events that precede and follow it as well. With that in mind, the double ABC-X model uses the traditional structure as its base and then replicates this with a different interpretation to represent post-crisis adjustment.

The Double A Factor: Stress and Change

There are three components to the double *A* factor: the initial stressor, changes in the family, and stressors resulting from attempting to cope with the initial stressor. Therefore, if one is attempting to deal with the loss of a job, the initial stressor event, there are often other things that happen at the same time to compound the stress. Perhaps the family has to change roles to accommodate the husband now being at home while the wife is the only parent working. In this case, the father must now take on housework and child-care responsibilities, which can be stressful for him as he learns to balance those duties while also searching for employment. It is also possible that the resources one can access to help deal with the loss of a job, such as having an in-law come and help out with the kids because child care can no longer be afforded, are in and of themselves a source of stress. Having multiple stressors at one time is called stressor pileup.

The Double B Factor: Family Resources

The initial stressor caused the family to access those resources that were immediately available, but frequently those resources are not enough to keep the family from entering a crisis state. When those resources fail or prove to be insufficient, families must turn to new sources, learn new skills, or strengthen old skills in order to cope. Thus, the double *B* factor takes into account the fact that sometimes those resources on which we rely cannot help us solve the problem, in which case we must seek out new opportunities.

The Double C Factor: Family Perception

The double *C* factor component is concerned not only with the family's response to or beliefs about the initial stressor, but also with how they interpret their previous responses to the crisis situation itself. For example, a family faced with the death of a child will assess how they interpret the death of the child and then how they assess their ability to cope with that loss. How a family perceives its ability to respond to situations such as this can determine how they will continue to cope with the ramifications of this event.

The Double X Factor: Family Crisis and Adaptation

In the double X factor, the post-crisis adaptation hinges on how the family has adapted to the initial crisis, as well as how it has adapted to the new level of family functioning. In other words, does the situation break the family apart or build it up? This time, however, we are referring to the entire family system, rather than to how the family responds to one event or situation. The family's outcome can range from bonadaptation to maladaptation.

Mundane Extreme Environmental Stress (MEES) Model

It was thought by Peters and Massey (1983) that family stress theory does not truly represent the experiences of those who experience oppression on a continual basis as, for example, African American family members do. In fact, these researchers thought that racism and discrimination were so much a part of their daily lives that they were not an **additional** stressor as implied by Hill's (1949) model, but were instead a part of everyday life. So, they developed the mundane extreme environmental stress (MEES) model, which adds three components to the original ABC-X model. The first addition is an *A* factor, which represents constant exposure to racial discrimination, most of which is both chronic and unpredictable. In this case, it's not another stressor but simply a piece of the puzzle that must be examined when studying African American family stress. The second addition is the *D* factor, which is the pervasive environmental stress associated with being of a minority status in the United States. This is more anticipated because it is a part of daily living. Finally, the *Y* factor is the lens through which crisis situations must be viewed for African American families, because their experiences are different from those of majority status. Thus, this model simply builds upon the traditional family stress theory by adding the need to take racial discrimination into account when studying African American families.

Family Adjustment and Adaptation Response (FAAR) Model

A final extension of family stress theory that addresses critics who say that this is only an individual theory focusing on one specific topic is Patterson's (1988) FAAR model, which basically expands the previous theory to be more inclusive of family systems. In this framework, families attempt to balance the demands they face with their capacity to deal with them, as influenced by the family meaning or definition/interpretation of the situation. When these demands are beyond the family's ability to deal with them, the family experiences crisis. Thus, the model looks at the processes families use in an attempt to restore balance while also condidering what is added by individual family members, the family unit itself, and the community.

This model has been further tested in the field of family resiliency (Patterson 2002). Resiliency means thriving or succeeding despite adverse circumstances. The focus here is on why some families do well while others are torn apart by stressful or high-risk situations. It is hoped that, by determining the process that allows some families to thrive, we can help other families that are unable to balance their demands on their own.

Another common criticism of family stress theory is that it focuses on only one issue: stress. Because of this, the theory will perhaps never be considered a grand theory or a theory that one can apply to any discipline or situation. However, this should not overshadow the primary strength of this theory, which is its applicability to real-life situations. There is a great deal of literature using this theory as a basis for therapy. For example, you can help a couple deal with their lack of communication by having them analyze each component of the ABC-X model in an attempt to keep them from entering crisis, or if they're already in crisis to help them adapt positively. Similarly, this theory is helpful when studying any issue that produces stress with the potential to lead to crisis for an individual or a family. In addition, this is one of the few theories reviewed that has shown continual development, as is illustrated in this critique. Although it may not have reached the status some would like in order for it to be included in a textbook on family theory, it is a great example of an evolving theory with more and more applications to family situations in modern times. Thus, although the scope of the theory is perhaps limited to dealing with stress, its applicability is far-reaching.

APPLICATION

1. Think about the story of the Peabody family at the beginning of this chapter. How does the ABC-X model apply to their lives? What are the family's stressors, resources, and definition of the situation? How are they coping? Would one of the other models covered be more useful here? If so, why?

2. Name three things that are causing you stress right now in your life. How would you use the ABC-X model to analyze each situation and figure out how to keep those stressors from leading to crisis?

3. Look at your list of stressors again. Which of these would be better explained by using the double ABC-X model? Analyze the situation again using this model.

4. Early family stress research was focused on the Great Depression and the effects of war on families. What are some events in society today that could benefit from research using this theory? Outline the basic components of the model as they apply to current events.

5. What do you think the ABC-X model is missing? How do current models address or fail to address these issues? How would you further modify the model?

6. Entering college exposes you to many potential stressors (Darling et al. 2007). A freshman has come to you because he is dealing with some of these stressors. How would you use the ABC-X model to help him deal with these issues?

7. Think about the eight criteria that Lipman-Bluman (1975) developed to determine how much a stressor will impact a family. Pick a form of ambiguous loss as described in the following sample reading, and see how each of these eight criteria applies to it. How will these factors affect the family's ability to cope?

REFERENCES

Angell, R. C. 1936. *The family encounters the depression.* New York: Charles Scribner.

Betz, G., and J. M. Thorngren. 2006. Ambiguous loss and the family grieving process. *The Family Journal* 14(4): 359–365.

Bonneau, K. L. 2011. Marriage, children and the fireman's wife: A qualitative study. *Dissertation Abstracts International, A: The Humanitites and Social Sciences* 71(7): 2658.

Boss, P. 1988. *Family stress management.* Newbury Park, CA: Sage.

Boss, P. 2002. *Family stress: A contextual approach.* Thousand Oaks, CA: Sage.

Boss, P., and J. Greenberg. 1984. Family boundary ambiguity: A new variable in family stress theory. *Family Process* 23: 535–546.

Burr, W. R. 1982. Families under stress. In *Family stress, coping, and social support*, ed. H. I. McCubbin, A. E. Cauble, and J. M. Patterson, 5–25. Springfield, IL: Charles C. Thomas.

Burr, W. R., and S. R. Klein. 1994. *Reexamining family stress: New theory and research.* Thousand Oaks, CA: Sage.

Cacciatore, J., S. Schnebly, and J. F. Froen. 2009. The effects of social support on maternal anxiety and depression after still birth. *Health and Social Care in the Community* 17(2): 167–176.

Carroll, J. S., C. D. Olson, and N. Buckmiller. 2007. Family boundary ambiguity: A 30-year review of theory, research, and measurement. *Family Relations* 56(2): 210–230.

Carver, C. S., C. Pozo, S. D. Harris, V. Noriega, M. F. Scheier, D. S. Robinson, A. S. Ketcham, F. L. Moffat, and K. C. Clark. 1993. How coping mediates the effect of optimism on distress: A study of women with early stage breast cancer. *Journal of Personality and Social Psychology* 64: 375–390.

Cavan, R. S., and K. H. Ranck. 1938. *The family and the depression.* Chicago: Univ. of Chicago Press.

Darling, C. A., E. W. Hill, and L. M. McWey. 2004. Understanding stress and quality of life for clergy and clergy spouses. *Stress and Health* 20: 261–277.

Darling, C. A., L. M McWey, and E. W. Hill. 2006. The paradox of children in clergy families. *Journal of Family Issues* 27(4): 439–463.

Darling, C. A., L. M. McWey, S. N. Howard, and S. B. Olmstead. 2007. College student stress: The influence of interpersonal relationships on sense of coherence. *Stress and Health* 23: 215–229.

Darling, C. A., S. B. Olmstead, V. E. Lund, and J. F. Fairclough. 2008. Bipolar disorder: Medication adherence and life contentment. *Archives of Psychiatric Nursing* 22(3): 113–126.

Darling, C.A., S. B. Olmstead, and C. Tiggleman. 2009. Persons with AIDS and their support persons: Stress and life satisfaction. *Stress and Health* 26: 33–44.

Epping-Jordan, J. E., B. E. Compas, D. M. Osowiecki, G. Oppedisano, C. Gerhardt, K. Primo, and D. N. Krag. 1999. Psychological adjustment in breast cancer: Processes of emotional distress. *Health Psychology* 18: 315–326.

Faber, A.J., E. Willerton, E. Clymer, S. M. MacDermid, and H. M. Weiss. 2008. Ambiguous absence, ambiguous presence: A qualitative study of military reserve families in wartime. *Journal of Family Psychology* 22: 222–230.

Falicov, C. J. 2007. Working with transnational immigrants: Expanding meanings of family, community, and culture. *Family Process* 46(2): 157–171.

Folkman, S. 1999. Thoughts about psychological factors, PNI, and cancer. *Advances in Mind-Body Medicine* 15: 236–259.

Hardesty, J. L., J. C. Campbell, J. M. McFarlane, and L. A. Lewandowski. 2008. How children and their caregivers adjust after intimate partner femicide. *Journal of Family Issues* 24(1): 100–124.

Hill, R. 1949. *Families under stress: Adjustment to the crisis of war separation and reunion.* New York: Harper and Brothers.

Huber, J. S. 2011. The mediating effects of sibling warmth on parental stress in families with children who have attention deficit hyperactivity disorder. *Dissertation Abstracts Internation, A: The Humanities and Social Sciences* 71(8): 3053.

Heubner, A.J., J. A. Mancini, R. M. Wilcox, ,S. R. Grass, ,and G.A. Grass. 2007. Parental deployment and youth in military families: Exploring uncertainty and ambiguous loss. *Family Relations* 56: 112–122.

Koos, E. L. 1946. *Families in trouble.* New York: Kings Crown Press.

Kotchick, B. A., S. Dorsey, and L. Heller. 2005. Predictors of parenting among African American single mothers: Personal and contextual factors. *Journal of Marriage and Family* 67(2): 448–460.

Lazarus, R. S., and S. Folkman. 1984. *Stress, appraisal, and coping*. New York: Springer.

Lazarus, R. S., and R. Launier, R. 1978. Stress-related transactions between person and environment. In *Perspectives in interactional psychology*, ed. L. A. Pervia and M. Lewis, 360–392. New York: Plenum.

Lee, C. 2007. Patterns of stress and support among Adventist clergy: Do pastors and their spouses differ? *Pastoral Psychology* 55: 761–771.

Lipman-Bluman, J. 1975. A crisis framework applied to macrosociological family changes: Marriage, divorce, and occupational trends associated with World War II. *Journal of Marriage and the Family* 3: 889–902.

McCubbin, H. I., and J. M. Patterson. 1982. Family adaptation to crisis. In *Family stress, coping, and social support*, ed. H. I. McCubbin, A. E. Cauble, and J. M. Patterson, 26–47. Springfield, IL: Charles C. Thomas.

———. 1983. Family transitions: Adaptation to stress. In *Stress and the family: Coping with normative transitions*, ed. H. I. McCubbin and C. R. Figley. Vol. 1, 2–25. New York: Brunner/Mazel.

———. 1985. Adolescent stress, coping, and adaptation: A normative family perspective. In *Adolescents in families*, ed. G. K. Leigh and G. W. Peterson, 256–276. Cincinnati, OH: Southwestern.

McKenry, P. C., and S. J. Price. 2000. Families coping with problems and change: A conceptual overview. In *Families and change: Coping with stressful events and transitions*, ed. P. C. McKenry and S. J. Price, 1–21. Thousand Oaks, CA: Sage.

Norizan, A., and K. Shamsuddin. 2010. Predictors of parenting stress among Malaysian mothers of children with Down syndrome. *Journal of Intellectual Disability Research* 54: 992–1003.

Oktay, J. S., M. H. Bellin, S. Scarvalone, S. Appling, and K. J. Helzlsouer. 2011. Managing the impact of posttreatment fatigue on the family: Breast cancer survivors share their experiences. *Families, Systems, and Health* 29(2): 127–137.

Olson, D. H., and H. I. McCubbin. 1982. Circumplex model of marital and family systems V: Application to family stress and crisis intervention. In *Family stress, coping, and social support*, ed. H. I. McCubbin, A. E. Cauble, and J. M. Patterson, 48–72. Springfield, IL: Charles C. Thomas.

Olson, D. H., Y. Lavee, and H. I. McCubbin. 1988. Types of families and family response to stress across the family life cycle. In *Social stress and family development*, ed. D. M. Klein and J. Aldous, 16–43. New York: Guilford.

Papalia, D. E., and S. W. Olds. 1996. *A child's world: Infancy through adolescence*. 7th ed. New York: McGraw-Hill.

Patterson, J. 1988. Families experiencing stress: The family adjustment and adaptation response model. *Family Systems Medicine* 5(2): 202–237.

Patterson, J. M. 2002. Integrating family resiliency and family stress theory. *Journal of Marriage and the Family* 64(2): 349–360.

Peters, M. F., and G. Massey. 1983. Chronic vs. mundane stress in family stress theories: The case of black families in white America. *Marriage and Family Review* 6: 193–218.

Provencher, H. L., J. P. Fournier, M. Perreault, and J. Vezina. 2000. The caregiver's perception of behavioral disturbance in relatives with schizophrenia: A stress-coping approach. *Community Mental Health Journal* 36(3): 293–306.

Smith, S. R., and E. Soliday. 2001. The effects of parental chronic kidney disease on the family. *Family Relations* 50(2): 171–177.

Soliday, E., J. P. Garofalo, S. R. Smith, and R. R. P. Warner. 2004. Psychosocial functioning of carcinoid cancer patients: Test of a stress and coping medicated model. *Journal of Applied Biobehavioral Research* 9(3): 156–171.

Wadsworth, S. M. M. 2010. Family risk and resilience in the context of war and terrorism. *Journal of Marriage and Family* 72(3): 537–556.

Weber, J. G. 2011. *Individual and family stress and crises.* Los Angeles, CA: Sage Publications.

Wiens, T. W., and P. Boss. 2006. Maintaining family resiliency before, during and after military separation. In C. A. Castro, A. B. Adler, and T. W. Britt (eds.), *Military life: The psychology of serving in peace and combat, Vol. 3: The military family* (13–38). Westport, CT: Praeger.

Willoughby, B. L., N. D. Doty, and N. M. Malik. 2008. Parental reactions to their child's sexual orientation disclosure: A family stress perspective. *Parenting Science and Practice* 8: 70–91.

Wilmoth, J. D., and S. Smyser. 2009. The ABC-X model of family stress in the Book of Philippians. *Journal of Psychology and Theology* 37(3): 155–162.

Wilson, C. B. 2011. Understanding stress and the quality of life for adolescent children of clergy: A retrospective study. *Dissertation Abstracts International, A: The Humanities and Social Sciences* 71(8): 3055.

SAMPLE READING

Betz, G., and J. M. Thorngren. 2006. Ambiguous loss and the family grieving process. *The Family Journal* 14(4): 359–365.

This article uses the ABC-X model as a therapeutic tool to help families who are dealing with an ambiguous loss. An ambiguous loss is one not typically socially recognized, such as a family member whose whereabouts are unknown or having a spouse with Alzheimer's disease who no longer knows who you are despite the fact that you are providing care on a daily basis. They describe two types of ambiguous loss, and take you through the application of the ABC-X model when dealing with a loss. They utilize narrative therapy as a means of helping people work through their losses; this basically means having people write about their losses by putting the process of grief into writing.

SAMPLE READING

Ambiguous Loss and the Family Grieving Process

Gabrielle Betz
Jill M. Thorngren
Montana State University

Ambiguous losses are physical or psychological experiences of families that are not as concrete or identifiable as traditional losses such as death. Ambiguous loss could include anything from miscarriage to losing one's spouse to Alzheimer's disease while he or she is still living. Ambiguous loss may include not knowing whether or not a loved one is living or dead, such as cases of child abduction or military personnel who are missing in action. Ambiguous loss is inherently characterized by lack of closure or clear understanding. This article defines types of ambiguous losses and details some of their characteristics. A model for counseling families who are experiencing ambiguous loss is described. Specifically, the model combines family stress theory with narrative therapy techniques to help families define their losses, assess their resources, and develop meaningful narratives about the loss.

Keywords: ambiguous loss; grief; family stress; narrative therapy

CHARACTERISTICS OF AMBIGUOUS LOSS

When Grandmother dies, it is a clear and recognizable form of loss. Although it is terribly painful to lose a loved one, the passing of an elderly person is viewed as a natural part of life. There are prescribed rituals such as the receipt of the death certificate, the

Gabrielle Betz is a recent graduate of the marriage and family counseling program at Montana State University.

Jill M. Thorngren, College of Education, Health and Human Development, is an associate professor and assistant dean at Montana State University. She serves as program leader of the marriage and family counseling program.

reading of a written will that allocates finances and possessions to certain individuals, and an obituary in the newspaper, and there is typically a funeral where friends and family members gather to lay the deceased to rest. It is often unquestionable that family will take time off from work, and they will receive condolences, cards, and flowers from sympathizers. Many find comfort in their religion and hope to be reunited with their loved one after death. These cultural practices and social support systems help to facilitate the grieving process. Because their loss is publicly recognized and legitimized, family members are more likely to receive support from the community.

There are numerous losses families experience on a daily or ongoing basis that are not recognized or legitimized by society. Many losses are not as clearly definable as death. It may not even be certain as to what was lost. Loss may involve a person, an object, an experience, or an event. Such ambiguous losses may include divorce or the ending of a relationship, infertility, miscarriage, abortion, unemployment, migration, sexual abuse, chronic illness or disability, adult children leaving home, or mental illness (Boss, 1999; Knauer, 2002; Rycroft & Perlesz, 2001). Boss (1999) identifies two types of ambiguous loss. The first is when a person is physically absent yet psychologically present. A child who is given up for adoption, a soldier who is listed as missing in action, or a divorced father who is no longer living with his children are all examples. Family members may not know if the person is still alive or the state of his or her well-being. Although the person is not physically present, he or she is still very much a part of the psychological family and continuously in family members' thoughts. The second kind of ambiguous loss involves someone being physically present but psychologically absent. A mother who is slowly deteriorating because of Alzheimer's disease, a brother whose life is consumed by alcoholism, or a husband who is preoccupied with his career and spends little time with his family are examples. Psychological absence is confusing because the emotional bond appears to be missing or gradually slipping away. As with Alzheimer's, the sufferer may no longer recognize loved ones or resemble the person he or she used to be. Family members may question whether the person who is psychologically absent is even a part of the family anymore. This may bring up further questions regarding role shifts in the family.

For the family who experiences ambiguous loss, the situation is stressful and oftentimes cruel in its unending torment. Because the loss is intangible or uncertain, the mourning process for family members becomes complicated. Ambiguous loss is characterized by factors that inherently impede the grieving process (Boss, 1999, 2002). For example, it is cognitively difficult to understand what has happened or why. The family of a child who has been kidnapped may endure for years not knowing if that missing child will ever return. The natural progression of their lives stops the day the child is abducted. Parents may berate themselves for not having protected their child and jump at every phone call hoping that it may be news of their child's whereabouts. A surviving child may harbor guilt for fighting with his or her sibling, wondering if he or she is to blame or if he or she may be abducted as well. The family may be terrified of betraying their missing member by considering the child dead when they should be out searching. The typical stages and rituals related to grieving no longer apply.

When faced with ambiguous loss, family members may get stuck in the same roles or no longer know what their roles entail. For the mother who has given up her child for adoption, she is uncertain how to answer the question when posed as to how many children she has. She may feel confused as to whether or not she is a mother at all if she is not raising her child. A family whose member is physically absent but psychologically present may go on with daily life as if the person is still with them. They may set a place for the missing person at the dinner table or buy gifts for the holidays. Family members may feel on edge, afraid to talk about what is happening or how they really feel. They become trapped in their helpless roles. Other losses such as divorce, infertility, chronic illness, and disability can cause one to view the self as less than ideal, a failure as a man or woman (Tshudin, 1997).

Loss is a reminder that life is not always kind or fair (Boss, 1999). Tragic circumstances can strike the happiest and healthiest of families. The family is put in a no-win situation, and their questions may never be resolved. Ambiguous loss leaves people feeling powerless in their lives and insecure in their future. For example, a woman who suffers a miscarriage may wonder if she did something wrong. Others may not understand or recognize the depth of her loss—the death of a child, the ending of a dream and future, and the unfilled expectation of being a mother (Werner-Lin & Moro, 2004). Comments such as "you can always have another one" or "it was meant to be" invalidate the experience as an important loss. Perhaps if she miscarried early in the first trimester, she may not have told others yet about the pregnancy and subsequent miscarriage. She can become isolated in her grief. Loss forces the individual to recognize that there are some things that cannot be controlled.

Grieving often involves an examination of one's values and beliefs and calls into question who one truly is. Losing a job may prompt the unemployed person to consider his or her self-worth if he or she is not contributing or supporting his or her family financially. He or she may feel incapable, helpless, angry, ashamed, rejected, betrayed, and useless (Tshudin, 1997). It is customary in American culture to define oneself by a person's career. When people ask, "What do you do?" they are really asking, "Who are you?" Job loss affects a person's identity and role in society. When people lose their previous state of health because of illness or injury, they may no longer be able to do the things most important to them such as traveling, recreating, or socializing. They lose their identity and way of being in the world. They may question if life is even worth living. The recently deceased Christopher Reeve expressed his desire to die after he was paralyzed in a horseback riding accident. It was only through a painful grieving process that he redefined himself and became a passionate advocate for stem cell research. Losses such as death can trigger associated ambiguous losses. The death of an elderly mother may cause the adult daughter to grieve for her own lost youth and realize her own mortality (Tshudin, 1997). She mourns the loss of her role as daughter or caretaker and a connection to her past. She may feel that her relationship was not what she had hoped and sense the loss of the opportunity to resolve past differences or issues. She may regret that her children no longer have a grandmother.

If not dealt with, ambiguous loss can exacerbate family stress tremendously. Although stress in all families is inevitable and the stress related to ambiguous loss can be particularly depleting, family stress theory contends that the family's response to stress determines the degree of its impact (Madden-Derdich & Herzog, 2005). Utilizing Hill's (1958) ABC-X model of family stress is one method for helping families who are experiencing ambiguous loss recognize their grief and harness the resources they have for coping with such loss. Although Hill's original work is somewhat dated, adaptations of the model are still very much used in working with contemporary family issues (McKenry & Price, 2005). The ABC-X model of family stress contends that the intensity or severity of stress is comprised of three components. The actual stress (A), plus the available resources for coping with the stress (B), plus the perceptions of each family member about the stress (C) equals the actual degrees of stress (X).

Because of the inherent nature of ambiguous loss, there is no one-size-fits-all model for helping families cope with its multifaceted stressors. One must cope differently when still caring for a spouse with Alzheimer's than one would cope with the ambiguous loss that accompanies losing a spouse through divorce. Rituals surrounding a terminally ill child are probably different than those related to coping with a child who is missing. The first step, therefore, in applying this model to ambiguous loss would entail determining what the actual stress is or defining the loss. Is the loss physical or psychological? What or who exactly is lost or missing? How does the loss redefine relationships, roles, and responsibilities? For some family members, simply defining their experience as loss and worthy of grief may be comforting. Because their loss is not typical, it may be that they have not allowed themselves the same empathy that they would allow for an actual death or more readily identifiable loss.

In conjunction with identifying the loss, an exploration of available resources must also be conducted. Social support may be difficult for the family to find (Boss, 1999). People are afraid to face their own fears about loss and do not have the language to discuss ambiguous loss. Caretaking of a chronically ill person may go on for years, so friends and neighbors may not have the stamina or desire to make such a long-term commitment. Most often, people do not understand the trauma of loss—especially when that loss is unclear and uncertain (Rycroft & Perlesz, 2001). When the loss is not acknowledged socially, family members may be denied their right to grieve (Werner-Lin & Moro, 2004). This is especially true if the loss is socially stigmatized, such as if a loved one suffered from AIDS. Lesbian, gay, bisexual, and transgendered people may not have their losses validated because they are a marginalized group. The loss of a relationship or death of a partner may not be recognized if the couple had not been open about their relationship or did not receive public recognition as a married couple. Often the surviving partner has few, if any, legal rights and may lose his or her home, possessions, and children. When mourners are socially isolated, they tend to believe that they do not have a right to their feelings (Rycroft & Perlesz, 2001). Such invalidation prevents people from understanding their loss and asking for help (Werner-Lin & Moro, 2004).

Although resources may be limited when dealing with ambiguous loss, counselors still need to explore what family members are already doing to cope with the loss. The assumption is that in his or her own way, each family member is doing things to help him or her function in the face of loss. This exploration is important for two reasons. First, as family members hear what each is doing, they may develop new ideas about how to better support one another and gain new respect or understanding for what others around them are experiencing. Acting out or misbehavior may make more sense in this light. Second, the family counselor can develop an awareness of both the strengths and weaknesses in the coping strategies. Healthy behaviors such as seeking out friends or journaling can be encouraged, whereas less healthy behaviors such as turning to substances or ignoring feelings can be empathized with and then a search for more healthy coping skills can begin. In addition to assessing what resources are already being used, counselors will also want to assess what or who could be a resource that the family is not utilizing. Perhaps family members have not thought to tap potential resources, or perhaps there are negative beliefs in the family about seeking help. Accessing resources, in sum, involves looking at the behaviors related to the ambiguous loss. What are members doing or not doing, and what could be done differently in terms of coping are questions to ask.

Exploring the family's beliefs about seeking help is related to Hill's (1958) third component of stress: beliefs or perceptions family members have about the stressor. Here it is important to explore each member's thoughts and feelings about the loss. Some family members may believe that they are responsible for the loss. Others may only be expressing a limited amount of emotion regarding the loss because they are not sure what feelings they are entitled to have regarding it.

Contributing to the perceptions and emotions family members have about their loss is the fact that for most ambiguous losses, there are no rituals for mourning (Boss, 1999; Rycroft & Perlesz, 2001). A child of divorced parents is expected to adjust to his or her parents' new lifestyles. He or she desperately misses his or her old life when his or her family was all together. For the woman who has an abortion or a miscarriage, there is no body to bury or a funeral to attend (Werner-Lin & Moro, 2004). The father who experiences "empty nest syndrome" may regret not spending more time with his child and does not have a ritual to help him release the past and embrace the future (Boss, 1999). With the absence of ritual or social support, family members believe that they are unjustified in their emotions. They may try to suppress their grief and move on as they are socially expected without giving themselves permission to mourn their loss.

Counselors can help each family member tell the story of his or her loss from his or her perspective and each should be allowed an opportunity to express a wide range of feelings applicable to the loss. From this exploration of the family's stories about their losses can arise new rituals that honor the past yet also embrace the future and present. For example, the child who is experiencing the loss of his or her parent's marriage can be encouraged to mourn what he or she misses about the past and having his or her parents together and also to develop new rituals in each of his or her new homes or for staying in contact with the parent he or she less frequently sees. The woman who gives up her baby for adoption can share the mixed feelings she has regarding this decision and decide to do something that honors that child regardless of where the child now lives.

A never-ending rollercoaster, ambiguous loss takes its toll on family members physically, cognitively, behaviorally, and emotionally (Boss, 1999; Weiner, 1999). Physically they may experience fatigue, sleep disruption, headaches, or stomachaches. Cognitively they may experience a preoccupation with the loss, forgetfulness, dreaming about the loss, or worrying. Behaviorally they may experience talkativeness, quietness, crying, hyperactivity, inactivity, sighing, support seeking, withdrawal, dependence, or avoidance. Emotionally they may experience loneliness, yearning, anxiety, depression, fear, anger, irritability, apathy, or relief (Weiner, 1999). For years, they may go through cycles of hope only to be disappointed once again. The unpredictable nature of an uncertain future leaves family members in a reactive position. The family may feel tremendous guilt and may be unable to make decisions, fearing that the wrong choice will be made. Family members experience an onslaught of conflicting emotions—love and hate, hope and despair, joy and sadness, anger and frustration. Something is wrong, and the family does not know how to fix it. Family members likely differ in their views and emotions. They may withdraw from one another furthering their sense of isolation. Their grief can be exhausting.

Although working with families who are experiencing ambiguous loss is similar to working with those who are struggling with more typical grief scenarios, the biggest differences lie in defining the losses and creating meaningful narratives about the loss. Losses are more readily identifiable in traditional grief work. Those who are experiencing ambiguous loss may need additional help with defining their loss. They may also struggle with understanding that although their losses are ambiguous in nature, this makes them no less real than more tangible losses.

Although it is clear that ambiguous loss is a complex phenomenon that presents many different scenarios to which families can and do react very differently, family stress theory (Hill, 1958; McKenry & Price, 2005) provides counselors with some useful parameters within which their work can be loosely structured. In sum, these guidelines include defining the loss, assessing resources, and exploring the perceptions or meanings members have about the loss.

EFFECTS ON FAMILIES

In spite of the 2-month allotment for bereavement of the *Diagnostic and Statistical Manual of Mental Disorders* (American Psychiatric Association, 2000), mourning is a natural and lifelong experience. Grief does not disappear after one has accepted the loss. Mourning a loss is a unique and complicated experience for the individual and the family. Grieving is a physical, emotional, intellectual, spiritual, and social event (Tshudin, 1997). Rycroft and Perlesz (2001) stated that grief is misunderstood within the counseling field. Grief counseling is considered a specialization; yet all counselors deal with grief and loss at some level with their clients. The grieving process in American culture is constricted and denied, viewed as something to avoid or to get through quickly. The language used surrounding loss often implies judgment and societal expectations. For example, when someone asks if the loss was expected, it often implies that an expected loss should be easier to deal with than an unexpected loss (Hedtke, 2002).

The ABC-X model of family stress (Hill, 1958; McKenry & Price, 2005) is an example of a broad systemic approach that is appropriate for counselors to take when working with grieving families. It allows room for consideration of cultural and religious practices and beliefs, the family support system, the environment, and multigenerational relationships and issues. Counseling should focus on the family's strengths and coping strategies that have already been working for them (Shapiro, 1994). When working with families from diverse backgrounds, it is important to consider their culture or family history. Cultures vary greatly in their perceptions, beliefs, and rituals about death and other types of losses (Weiner, 1999). Entire nations and groups of people can be seriously affected by ambiguous loss (Boss, 1999). Jews who survived the Holocaust, Native Americans whose cultures have become decimated by disease and Anglo American oppression, or African Americans who were slaves and separated from their families of origin are examples. The residual effects of ambiguous loss—grief surrounding the loss of a way of life and cultural identity—are passed down through the generations.

People are expected to move on with their lives after a loss. With ambiguous loss, the family simply cannot just move on. Their immobility or inability to deal effectively with the situation is not the result of the family's failure; it is the impossibility of the situation that may leave them powerless (Boss, 1999). Especially early in the counseling process, family members may need to tell their stories over and over. It is through telling stories that meaning is made. "People make meaning; meaning is not made for us" (Drewery & Winslade, 1997, p. 33). If we make meaning through talking and language, then meaning can also be changed through talking and language (Drewery & Winslade, 1997). By telling their story over and over, family members can create new meanings about their losses and discern what they need to heal (Tshudin, 1997).

The counselor needs to help the family identify the ambiguous loss and label it as such. The counselor can help to normalize the family members' experiences even if the situation is not typical. Family members may hesitate to share their grief with others because of shame, fearing judgment, or believing that they should just get over it (Shapiro, 1994). Feelings are not inherently good or bad; it is the clients' perception that labels them such. When the counselor assures the family that no matter how they have responded to the loss, their feelings and behaviors are understandable given the situation. The family is less likely to be resistant in therapy if they feel validated by the counselor. The counselor should help family members accept and explore their wide range of emotions. By practicing mindfulness, the clients may learn to observe their thoughts and emotions passively without judgment, censorship, or action (Tshudin, 1997).

Death or loss interferes with the family's natural developmental process. The family is thrust into crisis and seeks stability (Shapiro, 1994). With ambiguous loss, the crisis is ongoing and the family may be unable to adjust on some levels. According to Shapiro (1994), "Grief is a crisis of both attachment and identity, disrupting family stability in the interrelated domains of emotions, interactions, social roles, and meanings" (p. 17). The grief process includes an adjustment and redefining of identity and roles. Families want to derive meaning from the loss to restructure and define their roles. The therapist can help facilitate the process of reorganizing the family structure and adjusting roles (Rycroft & Perlesz, 2001).

In counseling, the family may not be able to resolve the situation but can create ways to deal with the stress so that the loss does not devastate the family (Boss, 1999). The therapist provides a safe holding environment for the family to discuss their issues and air emotions that may have become suppressed (Rycroft & Perlesz, 2001). All family members need to have the time to express their views, what they believe is happening, and what the loss means to them personally. By pointing out similarities, the therapist can help family members find common ground when there is conflict and disagreement. However, the family does not need to agree to improve intimacy. The therapist should encourage family members to validate one another, listening and drawing closer, even when they disagree. The therapist's task is to help the family members reduce isolation within the family. By giving the loss a name, family members have the opportunity to change relationships, roles, and interactions.

Family members can learn to compromise with each other about those changes. Boss (1999) states that "overcoming the solitude of ambiguous loss is the first step on the road to healthy change" (p. 103).

Grief is a complicated emotion. It surfaces as sadness, shock, anger, confusion, apathy, and guilt. It is common for individuals to experience a variety of conflicting feelings such as love and hate or joy and despair (Tshudin, 1997). For individuals who are depressed, unresolved grief may be at the root of their symptoms, and loss may have been unrecognized by health care professionals (Boss, 1999; Knauer, 2002). It can be helpful for the therapist to point out to the clients that their mixed and strong emotions are a part of grief. Grief is multidimensional and not just limited to sadness. If the counselor can help normalize those feelings, the client may learn to embrace and accept the full spectrum of emotions (Tshudin, 1997).

Families are faced with many important decisions. When there is uncertainty about how to proceed, the family resists change while waiting for some kind of resolution. Boss (1999) calls it the family gamble when the family makes an educated guess about the most likely outcome of a situation and creates a plan. It is risky because the family may make the wrong decision or may never know if they have gone in the right direction. The family may fear that a wrong decision will finalize the loss. Part of the healing process is for the family to give up the idea of perfection and absolute truth. They may have to make some difficult decisions based on very little information. At some point, the family must be willing to live with their decisions. Although the family may have to come together to make decisions, each individual should consider for themselves what will work for them and how to personally deal with the loss.

Family members may enter counseling blaming themselves or each other for their situation. Boss (1999) believes that blame is toxic and only interferes with the grieving process. Family members must learn to forgive themselves and each other. Ambiguous loss leaves the family struggling to understand the causes of their pain. Searching for meaning despite a lack of answers is important to the family's grieving process (Boss, 1999). Discussions do not need to always focus on the negative aspects of the loss. The family should be encouraged to share individual memories and experiences. Clients need to tell their family stories—traditions, how they celebrate holidays, rituals, relationships, and roles. Through storytelling, family members can begin to piece together their lives and figure out what place the loss should take (Rycroft & Perlesz, 2001).

NARRATIVE THERAPY AND AMBIGUOUS LOSS

When working with families who are experiencing ambiguous loss, it is suggested that counselors use a broad, systemic approach such as the ABC-X model of family stress (Hill, 1958; McKenry & Price, 2005). This model encourages counselors to help families define all aspects of their loss, assess what resources they are currently using and what other resources they could use to cope with their losses, and provide families with ways to share their perceptions and beliefs about their losses. This last piece, sharing perceptions about loss, lends itself to further therapeutic work in the form of helping families redefine or create new meanings and rituals surrounding their losses.

From an early age, children learn family rules such as those concerning what can and cannot be openly discussed, what emotions are acceptable, and what roles family members play. This becomes part of their family story. When family stories do not provide for adequate means to grieve or cope with stressors related to ambiguous losses, the family may function in less than healthy ways. Often there are triangles created in grieving families in an effort to protect themselves and manage anxiety. Loss can become debilitating in families whose anxiety is high and differentiation is low. Symptoms such as behavioral disorders, compulsions, marital conflicts, or mental illness may reflect the family's inability to adjust to loss (McGoldrick, 2004). If families can share their current stories related to their loss and have the experience of being heard, in a nonjudgmental and accepting manner, they may also be able to tell their stories again in new ways that capture different nuances of their experiences. This does not change the facts of the experience or loss, but it can change the meanings that family members assign to their losses and to their part of the loss.

Narrative therapy (Freedman & Combs, 1996; White, 1989; White & Epston, 1990) provides a way for clients to be heard and validated and also to explore alternate meanings around their experience of ambiguous loss. Narrative therapy assumes that each individual is the author of his or her life. Within each life is a multitude of stories that could be told about our experiences. Some stories are more meaningful and useful than others. For example, stories told about loss could have plots of blame or guilt or plots of hope and good memories.

Using elements of narrative therapy in conjunction with the ABC-X model of family stress (Hill, 1958; McKenry & Price, 2005) allows counselors to help family members articulate and define their losses, explore current and potential resources, and therapeutically define and redefine the meaning assigned to losses.

Identifying the stressor can be accomplished by asking each family member to tell his or her story of what he or she has lost. Perhaps it is something or someone tangible; perhaps it is a feeling or part of a relationship. Each client should be encouraged to recall the memories of who or what he or she has lost, including positive and negatives. He or she can then be encouraged to name the loss or the stressors associated with the loss. Perhaps the name is something like "missing grandma" or "readjusting to life without him." When problems or stressors are named, they can be externalized (White, 1988/1989), which means that although they are still part of the person's life, they are not the person. This allows clients to be able to step outside of their losses and stressors and look at them more objectively with less blaming of themselves.

In writing about illness narratives, Weingarten (2001) borrows from Frank's (1995) classification system to describe three types of stories that can be told in relation to illness. Restitution narratives are told from the perspective of diagnosis and treatment. Modern medicine and science are the key players in this plot. Chaos narratives are told from the perspective of the patient who is experiencing the turbulence of conflicting emotions, thoughts, and physical experiences. Quest narratives are those that allow for fate to be turned into experience and meaning to be extrapolated from the turbulence. Restitution, chaos, and quest narratives could all be articulated in relation to ambiguous loss.

As stories about illness or other ambiguous losses are told, it may be helpful to introduce two of Weingarten's (2001) and Frank's (1995) classifications of narratives. Is the story being told from a factual (restitution) perspective of what actually happened and what is being done to alleviate the loss? Perhaps a narrative of chaos more clearly depicts the range of emotions and thoughts that are occurring. Weingarten notes that chaos narratives are the most difficult to hear because of their rawness and poignancy. These may be the most important stories to hear as they encapsulate the myriad of feelings and beliefs associated with ambiguous loss.

In addition to naming and describing the problem, the narrative technique of mapping the problem (White 1988/1989) can also be used in relation to the loss. Here, clients are asked to describe all the ways in which the loss affects them. Included may be school and employment issues, changes in relationships with friends and other family members, changes in family rules and routines, and so on. This exercise is conducted to help normalize the experiences that family members are having that they may not connect to the loss they are experiencing. It is helpful for families to become aware of how they are being affected and how their experiences are affecting one another. Empathy is typically engendered when members begin to understand how others are feeling and what is influencing their behaviors.

As the losses are named and mapped, it is then important to begin assessing the resources available for coping. White (1988/1989) uses "exception" questions to ferret out when people are able to cope healthily despite their feelings of grief. For example, "When was the last time you allowed yourself to rest despite your ongoing worry?" is an exception question that points out that family members are coping and allowing themselves to do healthy activities despite their grief. Another strategy is to discuss what the person who is physically or emotionally absent might name as strengths of the family if he or she were present. As families create maps of their loss and the influences of the loss, members can be encouraged to notice who else is feeling similarly to them and to ascertain ways in which the members can help one another. No potential resource, however small, should be overlooked.

Finally, an assessment of the perceptions that each family member has about the loss should be conducted. This includes an exploration of not only what is being experienced by each person but what each is telling himself or herself about the loss. Previous activities focused more on the present and past. Here is an opportunity to discuss the future. The quest (Frank, 1995; Weingarten, 2001) category of narrative may be used to extrapolate issues such as "What will the loss mean to the family?" How will it affect their future goals and plans? How can they continue to function in a healthy manner while still honoring the loss? Now is the time to gently lay to rest the guilt and blame that family members may be experiencing and help them construct a new meaning system that incorporates what they have learned about themselves and each other. To paraphrase Weingarten, "How can fate be turned into experience?" It is important to help family members develop rituals that allow each to move on developmentally but still provide for remembrance and celebration of his or her loved one.

The assessment of the family's stressors, resources, and perceptions thus also becomes a treatment strategy. Through exploring ambiguous loss using narrative techniques, counselors can become more aware of the intensity and context of the stressors, and family members can become more aware of their resources and potential ways to reframe their perceptions. This model can be used flexibly, of course. The primary premises include letting family members share their stories, empathizing with their feelings, and encouraging them to take authorship of new and more meaningful stories about their losses.

CONCLUSION

Ambiguous loss can complicate the grieving process. Rycroft and Perlesz (2001) state that counseling can help the family "to find a balance between grieving and living, between the past and the future, and between despair and hope" (pp. 63–64). Even when a family member is lost either psychologically or physically, remembering that person and maintaining a connection is important to the family. The loved one does not have to be forgotten to move forward in life. Family members should be encouraged to share individual memories or stories about their loved one (Hedtke, 2002). Storytelling can transform grief into a growth process rather than leaving the family stuck. Whether the loss involves a person, event, object, or experience, the same principles of expression, exploration, and connection apply. Change becomes possible when families are willing to let go of the need to be in control (Boss, 1999). Mourning does not have to unfold in neat stages. Family members may need to revisit their ambiguous loss many times through the years and continue to grieve. The biggest risk for the family is to move forward even when they are unsure of the way.

REFERENCES

American Psychiatric Association. (2000). *Diagnostic and statistical manual of mental disorders* (4th ed). Washington, DC: Author.

Boss, P. G. (1999). *Ambiguous loss: Learning to live with unresolved grief.* Cambridge, MA: Harvard University Press.

Boss, P. G. (2002). Working with families of the missing. *Family Process, 41,* 14–17.

Drewery, W., & Winslade, J. (1997). The theoretical story of narrative therapy. In G. Monk, J. Winslade, K Crockett, & D. Epston (Eds.), *Narrative therapy in practice: The archaeology of hope* (pp. 32–52). San Francisco: Jossey-Bass.

Frank, A. W. (1995). *The wounded storyteller: Body, illness and ethics.* Chicago: University of Chicago Press.

Freedman, J., & Combs, G. (1996). *Narrative therapy: The social construction of preferred realities.* New York: Norton.

Hedtke, L. (2002). Reconstructing the language of death and grief. *Illness, Crisis, and Loss, 10,* 285–293.

Hill, R. (1958). Social stress on the family: Genetic features of families under stress. *Social Casework, 39,* 139–150.

Knauer, S. (2002). *Recovering from sexual abuse, addictions, and compulsive behaviors: "Numb" survivors.* New York: Hawthorne.

Madden-Derdich, D. A., & Herzog, M. J. (2005). Families, stress, and intervention. In P. C. McKenry & S. J. Price (Eds.), *Families & change: Coping with stressful events and transitions* (3rd ed., pp. 403–425). Thousand Oaks, CA: Sage.

McGoldrick, M. (2004). Echoes from the past: Helping families deal with their ghosts. In F. Walsh & M. McGoldrick (Eds.), *Living beyond loss* (2nd ed., pp. 310–339). New York: Norton.

McKenry, P. C., & Price, S. J. (2005). *Families & change: Coping with stressful events and transitions.* Thousand Oaks, CA: Sage.

Rycroft, P., & Perlesz, A. (2001). Speaking the unspeakable: Reclaiming grief and loss in family life. *The Australian and New Zealand Journal of Family Therapy, 22*(2), 57–65.

Shapiro, E. (1994). *Grief as a family process.* New York: Guilford.

Tshudin, V. (1997). *Counselling for loss and bereavement.* Philadelphia: Bailliere Tindall.

Weiner, I. (1999). *Coping with loss*. Mahwah, NJ: Lawrence Erlbaum.

Werner-Lin, A., & Moro, T. (2004). Unacknowledged and stigmatized losses. In F. Walsh & M. McGoldrick (Eds.), *Living beyond loss* (2nd ed., pp. 247–271). New York: Norton.

White, M. (1988/1989, Summer). The externalizing of the problem and the re-authoring of lives and relationships. *Dulwich Centre Newsletter*, 3–20.

White, M. (1989). *Selected papers*. Adelaide, Australia: Dulwich Centre.

White, M., & Epston, D. (1990). *Narrative means to therapeutic ends*. New York: Norton.

Weingarten, K. (2001). *Working with the stories of women's lives*. Adelaide, Australia: Dulwich Centre.

5

FAMILY SYSTEMS THEORY

Alexa and Cassie affirmed their love and commitment for each other in a civil union ceremony three years ago. For the most part, the women do not have any serious disagreements, or at least none that they can really put a finger on. But sometimes Alexa says or does something that offends Cassie. Alexa then feels somewhat guilty for what she has done, but she does not feel that it is totally her fault and doesn't like the superior attitude Cassie sometimes has when Alexa does apologize. So, Alexa acts defensively instead, giving the impression that she is now responding to a revengeful reaction on her part, even though she has not (at least yet) given one. Cassie can't understand why Alexa was mean to her and is angry but doesn't want to show it, so she acts indifferently. Alexa notices the indifference and wonders if it is feigned or deliberate. Alexa is afraid to apologize because it would be embarrassing and even more hurtful if the apology were rejected or used to advantage by Cassie. Besides, it wasn't as though Cassie hadn't done something to her earlier that precipitated the offense. Meanwhile, Cassie wants to hear an apology but isn't sure that it will be enough. Cassie would like restitution but isn't sure that she can demand it. So, neither apologizes nor forgives and the relationship spirals downhill. They eventually stop talking to each other without really understanding why and are urged by their friends to seek counseling.

This continuous circular interaction, where each person is responding to her perception of the other, is at the heart of family systems theory and illustrates its complexity.

HISTORY

It is generally believed that family systems theory emerged primarily in the 1960s. However, the basic concepts that would eventually lead to a coherent theory were being discussed a long time before that. For example, in 1926, Ernest Burgess made a presentation to the American Sociological Association that became a landmark publication. He referred to the family as "a unity of interacting personalities." He explained that this means that the family is much more than its formal or legal definition; instead, it is a living, growing "super personality" that has as its essence the interaction of its members.

Burgess (1926) went on to describe two basic family types: the highly integrated and the un-integrated. The first is characterized by rituals, discipline, and interdependence; the second is characterized by a lack of those features. He discussed the importance of the roles played by each family member, how problems result when they conflict, and how one member can be identified as the "family problem."

These insights are all elaborated upon in Chapter 2 of Waller's (1938) classic textbook on the family. This chapter, titled "The Family as an Arena of Interacting Personalities," begins by discussing how the family is basically a closed system of social interaction. It also discusses how the family is the greatest source of influence on a child and that the child's personality also affects the parents. And perhaps most importantly, Waller explores the idea that family experiences are repetitive and are based on patterns of interaction.

During the late 1920s, Austrian biologist Ludwig von Bertalanffy (1969) was beginning to develop the basic ideas of general systems theory. However, for the most part, systems theory as it relates to families remained hidden as a part of structural functionalism until after World War II. At that point, family therapists (Bateson et al. 1956) began to seek explanations for the transactions between family members that seemed to be at the heart of the dysfunctions with which they were dealing, rather than focusing on the faults or qualities of individual family members. The therapeutic application of general systems theory is also referred to as family process theory (Broderick 1993). In general, family systems theory has its greatest utility in communication and clinical applications, although there has been a plethora of activity using systems theory in addressing a variety of family issues in both scholarship and therapy.

BASIC ASSUMPTIONS

The whole is greater than the sum of the parts. A family is much more than a collection of individuals who live together and are related to each other; it has a holistic quality. As a natural social system, it possesses its own characteristics, rules, roles, communication patterns, and power structure. It represents an integration of parts such that individual members can be understood only within the context of the whole.

A common analogy to illustrate wholeness can be depicted by a cake. While the individual ingredients (e.g., flour, sugar, milk, butter, baking soda, eggs) are the component parts, what is removed from the oven (i.e., the cake) is of a very different quality; it is more than each of its individual elements. An insignificant member (e.g., a small amount of baking soda) has the potential to impact the whole by influencing whether the cake rises or is flat.

Similarly, Alexa and Cassie (the couple in the vignette at the beginning of this chapter) are more than their individual personalities or beings. Their system creates a new and distinctive entity or whole. Who they are with each other is different than who they might be with someone else. One can no longer consider Alexa without also thinking about Cassie, as the individual women cannot be examined in isolation from each other; they are connected. Their relationships with their families-of-origin, their future children (should they decide to have them), and to each other shapes this new entity and gives their family unique properties.

The locus of pathology is not within the person but is a system dysfunction.
Systems theory requires a *paradigm shift* in the way we think about the world. Most
social science theories have taken what we call an intrapsychic viewpoint, in which
the individual is the unit of study, and problems are presumed to be "in the head"
of that person. However, with systems theory, the *locus of pathology*, or the location of
the problem, is not within the person. Rather than saying that an individual has a
disease, we say that the system of which he or she is a part is *dysfunctional* (i.e., problems are seen as being a function of a struggle between persons). Think of a family
as being represented by a circle for each member, with lines connecting them. The
lines represent the communication patterns—the ways they speak to and act toward
each other—between the members. Systems theorists believe that the problems are
in the lines, rather than in the circles. This applies, of course, to normative or functional behaviors as well, even though clinical applications tend to focus on problems.
Another way of thinking about it is to compare a system to a child's mobile hang-
ing over a crib. A number of interesting objects are connected by strings or wires.
Whenever one is hit, it causes the others to move. If you remove one of the objects,
the entire system becomes unbalanced.

This interpersonal rather than intrapsychic perspective considers all behavior to
be a part of ongoing, interactive, and recurring events, with no real beginning or end
points. Therefore, a person who manifests some symptomatic behavior is seen as representing a dysfunctional system. Some are disturbed by this, taking it to mean that
individuals are not responsible for their behavior and that they can, therefore, blame
their problems on their family or society. Actually, according to systems theory, time
is not wasted on assigning blame, because the beginning points of a conflict typically
cannot be found. We are then free to focus on how to resolve the problem, rather than
being distracted by trying to find someone to punish for it. It is recognized that individuals are ultimately responsible for their own behaviors, but that no behavior can be
understood in isolation. One's behaviors, emotions, and interactions make sense only
within the context of their social world or the environment in which they occur.

For example, a teen's eating disorder may have resulted in part from her mother's
tendency to control her behavior. So is the teen's behavior the mother's fault? Before
we answer, assume that the mother became controlling in part because of living with
an abusive father, who himself grew up under similarly abusive conditions, which is
where he learned that pattern of interaction. Pretty soon, we discover that the family
ancestors who may have started the behavioral patterns are all deceased. So, rather than
attempt to trace the behavior to its roots in order to place blame, a family therapist
can focus on finding ways to break the present chains of interaction that are maintaining the symptoms.

This paradigm, which is more than a therapeutic approach and actually a new
way of conceptualizing human problems and understanding behavior, requires its own
epistemology. This term refers to the way that knowledge is gained and how conclusions
are made. The relationship outlook shifts the attention from content to process, or
from the behavior itself to how it is maintained.

Circular causality guides behavior. With *linear causality*, the focus is on content.
If you believe that one event causes the next in a straight-line, stimulus-response
fashion, as an observer, you will be distracted by what a couple is arguing about and
how it got started. By contrast, *circular causality* is the idea that, with human social

interactions, there are a number of forces moving in many directions simultaneously. It is all about process. That is, it doesn't matter whether the couple is fighting about money or child rearing—it is the repetitive pattern of interaction that is of interest. The focus is on *how* they interact, regardless of the topic, and what can be done to change that pattern into a more functional one (i.e., one that leads to happiness rather than unhappiness or relationship satisfaction versus dissatisfaction).

Take as an example a young, recently married couple. Desiring to be autonomous, they resent and avoid their parents and in-laws for calling and visiting too often and giving unwanted advice. From their viewpoint, they are running away from the parents because the parents are running after them. However, the parents see it differently—they would not have to call and visit so often if the adult children would just see them occasionally. Each sees themselves as reacting to the other and believes that the other one "started it." Are the children avoiding the parents because they are intrusive, or are the parents intrusive because the children are avoiding them? Humans tend to think linearly, but behaviors are circular. Reciprocal causality exists in that the exchange occurs within a context of mutual influence.

Rules result from the redundancy principle and are critical in defining a family. Couples begin to create the rules of their relationship as soon as they meet. Families cannot have an infinite reservoir of possible behavioral responses for every situation, so a few are selected and used over and over again. This is the *redundancy principle*, which results in family rules. These repetitive patterns of interaction are the rules by which a family lives. Some rules are dysfunctional (such as when a husband withdraws every time his wife wants to discuss their money problems), but once established, they tend to remain. Positive change is made in a family by helping them to change their dysfunctional rules.

A few rules are clear and overt—that is, you can ask family members what the rules are, and they can consciously identify and agree on them. They might include a curfew for the teenagers and not talking back to mom or dad. Many rules are implicit, or outside of conscious awareness. Examples of unspoken rules might include where everyone sits at the dinner table or that dad gets to control the TV remote. The most powerful rules are the ones that are covert and unstated. They might include such things as the fact that mom can get mad, but dad may not; brother can get away with poor school performance, but not sister; or that, in an argument, one person blusters while the other ignores it.

A family's rules differentiate it from other family systems and delineate its boundaries. Such rules, which might insist that its members observe certain religious practices, enact certain gender roles, maintain a certain standard of job performance, reserve Saturday afternoons for family functions, and treat one another with respect, distinguish it from other families whose rules may be different.

So, how do these ideas work in therapy? An example will further explain the basic ideas. A couple comes for counseling because of a problem with domestic battery. The husband is defensive and blames his wife for forcing him to be mean to her because she won't do as she is told. She responds apologetically that if she were just a better housewife, the marriage would be OK. Putting the specific content or the presenting behavioral problems aside for the moment, the therapist determines the following repetitive sequence of events: (1) The husband has strict expectations about what his wife should be and when she should have things ready for him; (2) he has been drinking; (3) she fails to meet an expectation, such as arriving late from work when he has been waiting to pick her up; (4) he becomes angry and berates her; (5) she withdraws—becomes quiet and makes no eye contact in the hope that it will blow over; (6) this makes him more upset, so he escalates his abusive behavior to force a reaction from her; and (7) she finally responds, either with an apology or anger. Either way, this ends the sequence, and all is well until it starts again.

Systems thinking does not excuse individual family members for their behavior (Whitchurch and Constantine 1993); however, it considers these behaviors as circular. They represent some of their family rules that are repeated over and over again. The therapist would choose to intervene at the point where it appears the couple would be most likely to be able to make changes. It could be with the husband's attitudes or drinking behavior or it could be with the wife's tendency to withdraw before responding. Regardless, it is the process that must be dealt with, not just the physical abuse.

Feedback loops guide behavior. A family system corrects itself or tries to regain homeostasis through the use of feedback loops. *Negative feedback* occurs when a family member begins to move outside the accepted limits of family behavior and others enact corrective measures to get that member back in line. The family tries to restore the member to the proper way of acting. For instance, when a teen "sasses," a parent might give negative feedback by grounding the teen or by giving a "look." The same would occur when breaking a dysfunctional rule, so "negative" does not refer to good or bad, but suggests that no change in behavior is permitted.

Positive feedback is a rewarding response for the deviation, promoting change in the family. In this case, the person is encouraged to break out of the homeostatic balance. Therapists will often give positive feedback for attempts to replace dysfunctional rules with functional ones. Also, family members receive positive feedback for behaviors that stay within the rules, whether they are functional or not. Thus, the focus of systems theory is on the quality of communication among family members.

Pathological communication contributes to relationship problems. Emotional illnesses have generally been considered to be "in the head" of the patient, although we now understand the important role of genetics in these disturbances. Early family therapists, however, discovered some important family connections. For example, a young person would be hospitalized for schizophrenia and receive behavioral and psychoanalytic therapy. As a reward for getting better, his family would be allowed to visit him, but then he would relapse. They initially thought that it had to do with having interactions once again with a cold, rejecting mother and coined the term *schizophrenogenic mother* to describe this situation. This, in combination with a passive, ineffectual father, was believed to result in sons, more so than daughters, who could become confused and feel inadequate, and thus become schizophrenic.

As the communication theorists refined their work, it became clear that the primary source of dysfunctions such as schizophrenia was communication patterns, rather than gender and parental behavior issues. *Pathological communication* refers to the various kinds of unclear and confusing ways of relating that can cause problems in a relationship. One is mystification, in which the speaker denies the reality of a situation by perhaps saying that nothing is wrong when there clearly is. Another is indirect communication, or "beating around the bush" instead of coming out and clearly stating one's desires. Volumes have been written about these and other difficulties in communication.

One of the most prominent concepts in systems work is the *double bind*. It is a special form of contradictory communication. Whenever someone speaks, he or she sends two messages: the verbal and the nonverbal. In other words, there is both **what** you say and **how** you say it. When someone says "I love you" in the proper tone of voice and in an appropriate circumstance, then he or she "affirms" the verbal portion of the communication. That is, when the two parts of the message are congruent, the message is clear and more believable. This is functional because a person sends the message he or she intended to send, and it is received appropriately. However, levels of messages sometimes contradict each other, leaving the recipient to decide what the truth is and how to respond. This is particularly difficult for children, who can be stressed into dysfunctional behaviors as a result. It also predictably leads to conflict in adult relationships.

When the two contradicting messages are commands, a double bind occurs (i.e., the individual is told to do two things but cannot do one without disobeying the other). Either way, he or she will be punished—the classic "damned if you do, damned if you don't" situation. The person feels compelled to respond, and the family rules are such that one may not comment on the contradiction or leave the situation. It is like the classic joke where the child is given two shirts for his birthday and puts one on. His mother then responds: "What's the matter, you didn't like the other one?" No matter which shirt he does or does not put on, he is in trouble.

Returning to the case described in Goldenberg and Goldenberg (2008), a schizophrenic son is visited by his mother. Happy to see her, he goes up and gives her a hug. In response, she stiffens, so he withdraws, to which she responds by asking why he doesn't love her anymore. He can hug her and be rejected or not hug her and still be rejected. If he points out what she is doing, she will deny it. Instead, he can choose the "schizophrenic way" and withdraw from reality so as not to be responsible for making any decisions. In other words, "crazy" behavior is the logical way to respond to a system with dysfunctional rules. Therefore, the identified patient is often the person in the family who is the healthiest, in the sense of not wanting to endure dysfunctional rules. Even though it is well-known now that most serious emotional disturbances have a genetic basis, as with any other illness, it is also true that such disorders are most evident in families with the highest levels of communication deviance. That is, pathological communication patterns are stressful and make things worse, whereas healthy rules result in a calmer family life and, therefore, fewer symptoms in its members.

Systems clinicians such as Virginia Satir also see a loop between self-esteem and ability to communicate. Dysfunctional communication patterns among family members result in low self-esteem. People tend to defend themselves from threats to their esteem by using defensive and dysfunctional communication styles. Therefore, one leads to the other in a downward spiral. Satir (1964) goes back to the family-of-origin causes and helps the clients to "reframe" (i.e., consider less negative motivations for the behaviors of others) their childhood experiences into more positive and generally truthful memories and then teaches congruent and value-building communication styles that raise self-esteem. As self-esteem rises, so does a person's ability to communicate in a functional manner (Satir 1964).

All family members take on roles. Family roles are defined as "recurring patterns of behavior developed through interaction that family members use to fulfill family functions" (Galvin, Bylund, and Brommel 2012, 150). Through dialogue and inter-actions with one another, families create shared meanings or expectations about how various roles should be played. Although children may be given explicit instructions about how to enact the role of daughter or son, adults might utilize their observation of roles in their family of origin as starting points in role negotiation (Galvin et al. 2011). The fact that we all tend to play out certain roles is part of the redundancy principle. In addition to being a parent, child, student, or athlete, there are common psychological roles that family members take on. Refusing to play one's role can upset the family equilibrium and result in negative feedback.

In their classic work *Inside the Family*, David Kantor and William Lehr (1975) identified "four player parts" in the family. The *mover* initiates action. The *opposer* disapproves of the mover's action and tries to block it. The *follower* approves of the mover's action or the opposer's reaction, and thus empowers the side with whom he or she allies. The *bystander* witnesses the action of the mover, but is passive about overtly aligning with the mover or the opposer. Instead, the bystander remains on the periphery of family functioning.

Dysfunctional families, particularly alcoholic families, reveal certain roles that are found to some degree in most families (Winton 1995). The parent with the chemical dependency (in this example, the father) plays the role of the *dependent* person. His job is to bring grief to the family while blaming others for his abuses. For example, in his mind, if you did what he asked, then he wouldn't have to drink. He manipulates others and denies his problems in order to perpetuate them. His wife is the *enabler* (also referred to as the *codependent*), who helps him to avoid the consequences of his behavior. She may call in sick to work for him or encourage the children to stay away from him when he "gets like that." Perhaps there were alcohol-ics in her family of origin, and her husband was drawn to her because of her traits of covering for others. She often has psychosomatic symptoms due to her repressed feelings of anger and guilt.

The firstborn child is often the *hero*. He or she is the ideal student and caretaker who appears to have it all together. This is a stressful role but one that is difficult to give up because it has many rewards. The second child is the *delinquent*. This is the scapegoated child, who does poorly in school or manifests other acting-out behaviors. It is a negative approach to getting dad to change because the hope is that, by turning attention to the child, it will alleviate the need of the father to drink. The next child is the *invisible child*, who just keeps a low profile in the hope that it will help lessen family tensions. This child, who basically stays out of the way and thus never deals with emotions, is the most likely to suffer from an emotional illness. The last child is the *clown*, who attempts to use humor in dealing with family problems.

For any one person to change, the entire system must be changed. Instead of focusing on why the father became an alcoholic and how bad that is, a therapist would help some of the others, particularly the enabling spouse, to give up their supportive roles. All this occurs at more subtle levels in families with less serious problems. For example, a young woman might marry into an extended family at whose reunions she is expected to babysit all the children while the other adults socialize. No one knows how this happened, or would even admit to it being the case, but trouble ensues if she refuses to play her role. Another might be selected as the family rebel, or star, and be the focus of the same family reunion.

Family types are based on the rigidity of family boundaries. Some researchers (Kantor and Lehr 1975) have identified three basic family types, based on the rigidity of family boundaries and rules. *Open families* are basically democratic, and the rights of individuals are protected and interactions with outsiders are permitted. There is also consensus and flexibility, and family members are bound together by love and respect. This is often called mutuality, and healthy children and patterns of interaction are common in these families.

The second type is the *random family.* Here there are almost no boundaries; few rules exist about defending the "family's territory." The members are seen as *disengaged*, and their commitments to and investments in the family are *transitory*. Children often see this level of freedom as a sign of a lack of love and concern from their parents, and social problems are common. In fact, as adolescents, they often yearn for the rules imposed on their peers by their parents, because they see the rules as an indication of love, care, and concern. The final type is the *closed family.* In this one, family members are *enmeshed* or overly involved in each other's lives. Individual identities are not allowed, and family boundaries close off much of the outside world. Such families might value privacy, even secretiveness, and limit exposure to media or other external influences. Emotional illnesses can result from this family configuration, because individuals cannot think or function on their own behalf.

A family's response to their children's friends might offer a simplified illustration of these family types. A closed family is likely to discourage children from inviting their friends to the family's home at all, whereas an open family might help their children to discriminate between "good" and "bad" friends. Only friends with desirable traits that are in line with the family's values and rules are invited to the family's home. In a random family, any of a child's peers can exit and enter the family's home indiscriminately.

PRIMARY TERMS AND CONCEPTS

Whitchurch and Constantine (1993), Broderick and Smith (1979), and White and Klein (2008) provided us with explanations for the key concepts of systems theory.

System

A system is essentially any set of objects, with their attributes, that relate to each other in a way that creates a new "super entity." The family is a social system (Winton 1995). It is a boundary-maintained unit composed of interrelated and interdependent parts such that an alteration in one part affects all components of the system. Family systems are typically composed of one or more subsystems (e.g., parental, spousal, sibling), smaller units that serve various functions within the family system.

Boundaries

Boundaries are lines of demarcation that distinguish a system from its environment and affect the flow of information and energy between the two (Broderick and Smith 1979; White and Klein, 2008). A family maintains its boundaries by filtering out any external elements that seem hostile to the goals and policies of the family while at the same time incorporating those that are deemed beneficial. Kantor and Lehr (1975) identified this process as "bounding." This is similar to the role of the placenta during pregnancy. In addition to the boundaries for the overall household kin group, boundaries exist between family subgroups or subsystems, such as those between parents and children. Family boundaries typically can be classified as falling between two extremes on a continuum from open (highly interactive with outside environment) to closed (extremely private with little external interchange), depending on how permeable or flexible the boundaries are.

Pauline Boss (2002) introduced the concept of *boundary ambiguity*, the inability to determine who is in and out of the family. It typically occurs when there is incongruence between *physical presence* (person is bodily present in the home) and *psychological presence* (physically absent person is emotionally present in family members' minds). For instance, a family whose father/husband is MIA (missing in action) may experience boundary ambiguity in that, although he is physically absent, he is still very much on their minds and in their hearts.

Hierarchy

The hierarchy of a family system reflects its arrangement of layers according to delegation or power. Miller's (1978) concept of *echelon* is useful here. For instance, for most families the parental subsystem would be located above the offspring subsystem, or in the system's upper echelon, as it has more power to make decisions that affect the offspring subsystem. Because individuals within families also constitute systems, individuals could be arranged in a hierarchy in such a way as to reveal who has the most power and authority in the family. A family's hierarchical arrangement is related to its organization, communication patterns, decision-making processes, and the like.

Entropy

Entropy is the natural tendency of a system to move from order to disorder. Without attention, a marriage or family system will move toward disorganization or disrepair. Energy—new information or input—is the lifeblood of systems. A family must be able and willing to incorporate energy into its system in order to thrive. Open and permeable boundaries make the flow of energy into a system more likely. Interchange with the environment is critical for the viability of a system.

Family Rules

Family rules are the repetitive behavioral patterns, based on the *redundancy principle*, that regulate family functioning by offering guidelines for future family interactions (Goldenberg and Goldenberg 2008). Rules develop over time and become "calibrated," or set. Rules help families know how to regulate conformity to their standards and deal with input and change. Rules can be *explicit*, clearly articulated, and acknowledged by the family; or *implicit*, invisible, and not discussed (Satir 1972). If families do not have rules in place that allow them to respond appropriately to new situations, they may either adjust or simply break down. The typical response is to fall back on an already existing rule, even when it is insufficient to solve the problem. However, families do have *meta-rules*—rules about the rules—that dictate how families might interpret, enforce, change, or create new rules.

Feedback

Feedback refers to the response a family member makes to the behavior of another person, particularly when it deviates from existing patterns of interaction. It may be *positive* or deviation-amplifying in that it encourages more of the stimulus or input from the other, or *negative* in that it discourages change and is deviation-dampening. Positive feedback encourages further change, whereas negative feedback tries to restore the system to a previous, steady state. There are continuous "feedback loops" as each member speaks to and affects the behaviors of the others. When positive feedback is present and system alterations occur, *morphogenesis* is the result. If the family maintains the status quo through negative feedback, *morphostasis* is the outcome. For a system to survive, it is best to have a balance between positive feedback loops—that allow innovation and change—and negative ones—that suppress alterations, as too much change could become chaotic or unstable for a system.

Equilibrium

There is a tendency for any system to seek a balance between stability and change in the variety of its behaviors and rules. This natural inclination to maintain the status quo and resist change is usually referred to as *homeostasis*, which means that the system has equilibrium. Families essentially have a range of limits within which they function. Just like the body maintains its temperature within a few degrees, so the family attempts to maintain itself by balancing inputs with outputs. Cassie and Alexa, from the vignette, want to find a way to reach equilibrium once again, as they are currently out of balance.

Clinical Concepts. There are additional concepts that must be understood when applying the theory, particularly in therapy. These are important for understanding how family members affect the emotional lives of each other (Goldenberg and Goldenberg 2008).

Circular Causality Versus Linear Causality

Humans tend to "punctuate" behavior sequences in order to make sense of interactions, assigning "cause and blame to individuals instead of focusing on the problematic pattern" (Galvin et al. 2012, 63) between family members. A wife might say that she nags because her husband withdraws, while the husband claims that he withdraws because his wife nags. Each is suggesting that one event causes the next in unidirectional stimulus-response fashion or linear causality. Systems theory, however, recognizes the futility of trying to assign cause and effect, because many forces impact the relationship system simultaneously. There is a continuous series of circular feedback loops in which everyone influences everyone else in the family without any clear beginning or ending points. Because of this, you cannot identify a specific beginning cause or event. Instead, emphasis is upon the reciprocity and shared responsibility of *what is transpiring*, not *why* it is occurring (Becvar and Becvar 2008).

In the vignette at the beginning of the chapter, Cassie would like to blame Alexa for her offensive comments and/or insensitivity in their relationship. Alexa would like to blame their problems on Cassie's indifference to her, as well as her sense of superiority when Alexa does apologize for how she has hurt Cassie's feelings. The two seem caught up in trying to identify a linear explanation for their relationship hardships. From a systems perspective, however, the two might accomplish more by examining their relational patterns when each feels offended by the other and considering how they might resolve things differently.

Identified Patient

Often one person may manifest more symptoms, or is believed by the others to be the major cause of family problems and is, therefore, sent for counseling. We call this individual the "identified patient." In actuality, that individual is simply the symptom bearer in a dysfunctional family, or the one who carries much of the family burden. In family therapy, then, the entire family is the focus of attention rather than a particular individual member. The key to understanding a family is to refrain from paying attention to the individual members and, instead, to focus on the family's behavioral exchanges.

Double Bind

A double bind is a kind of pathological communication in which a person is given two commands that contradict each other and, given that the contradiction is concealed and denied, he or she is not allowed to comment on the existence of incongruent messages. If you obey one request, then you are in trouble for disobeying the other. This confusion leads to emotional or mental distress. Such is the case, for instance, when an adult child tells an aging parent, "We will help you to remain independent. But if you refuse our help (by not following all our advice and directives), it will be a sign to us that you are unable to continue living independently" (Herr and Weakland 1979, 147).

Family Cohesion

Family cohesion is the degree of closeness or emotional bonding family members have for one another. According to Olson (2000), there are four levels of family cohesion. At one extreme is disengagement, when family members are insufficiently involved in each other's lives and members hold a high degree of individuality and little sense of togetherness. Enmeshment, represented by extreme togetherness and high dependence, exists at the opposite end of the continuum. Enmeshment can be characteristic of a closed family, and it often results in psychosomatic symptoms due to the lack of personal autonomy.

Family Flexibility

A family's adaptability to new and/or stressful situations represents a family's flexibility. Like cohesion, Olson (2000) identifies four levels of flexibility. At one end of the continuum are rigid families, those that are characterized by little or no ability to change their roles, rules, or relationship patterns. At the other extreme are chaotic families. Such families evidence little or no constancy to the point that family members have a difficult time knowing what to expect. Given the external and developmental changes that occur within individuals and families, some degree of flexibility is essential for healthy family functioning.

Mutuality

Mutuality is found in open families in which everyone is accepted and loved, despite differences of opinion. The opposite is *pseudomutuality* in which a family gives the surface impression that it is open and understanding when, in fact, it is not.

COMMON AREAS OF RESEARCH AND APPLICATION

Originally, systems theory was most commonly found in research on family communication and family therapy. However, with the introduction of more sophisticated methodological and statistical techniques, the use of systems theory as a theoretical frame is extending into new topical areas, examining ever-more complex family systems dynamics.

Communication and Family Typologies

David Olson (2000) has helped to link theory with research and practice by developing his circumplex model of marital and family systems. The model includes three dimensions: family cohesion, flexibility, and communication. It assumes that very high or very low levels of cohesion and/or flexibility are problematic for couples and families. Moderate or balanced levels of these two factors are the ideal, promoting healthy family functioning. Communication, the third dimension of the model, serves a facilitating role in that it helps families move around in the other two dimensions. By using communication skills such as active listening, respect, and clarity, families are better able to achieve balanced levels of cohesion and flexibility. The family adaptability and cohesion evaluation scale (FACES) IV is an instrument designed to measure family cohesion and family adaptability, based on the circumplex model. The assessment tool is a reliable and valid measure that is helpful for research and clinical work with couples and families (Olson 2011). Therapists use the information to help couples and families move to a balance between the two traits that is characteristic of well-functioning families. Family scholars have used the instrument in hundreds of research articles to examine all types of family relationships and problems (Kouneski 2000).

More recently, Julie Harris and colleagues (2010) used a family systems perspective, and the family adaptation and cohesion measures from FACES II, to examine the extent to which families communicated about melanoma risk. The authors noted that since HIPPA regulations now make it difficult for health professionals to share pertinent medical information directly with family members, it is essential to better understand conditions under which families are likely to share critical information with one another. They discovered that persons in adaptable and cohesive families were more likely to employ an open style of communication regarding melanoma risk.

Family Health and Illness

Systems concepts are particularly useful in understanding families and health matters. For example, given that obesity is one of the gravest health concerns today, numerous scholars utilize family systems theory to better comprehend the dynamics surrounding obesity and family interventions that might help reduce the incidence of being overweight, along with the deleterious health conditions associated with it. Heather Kitzman-Ulrich and colleagues (2010) assessed the effectiveness of 21 weight loss intervention programs for youth and 25 programs designed to improve physical activity and healthy diet in normal weight children, each of which included a family component. The authors discovered that many of the successful weight loss programs deliberately included information on parenting styles (encouraging authoritative parenting), parenting skills (e.g., reinforcement, monitoring), child management tips (promoting positive behaviors), and family functioning qualities (e.g., cohesion, adaptability, satisfaction) (249). The activity and diet programs frequently included the family through group-based approaches, often located in schools or communities, but rarely assessed the effectiveness of the family component of their programs. The authors suggest that parenting skills, parenting styles, and healthy family functioning characteristics are essential in shaping children's behavior and in making environmental changes within the home that promote healthy weight among offspring. Hooper, Burnham, and Richey (2009) identified family system correlates of current weight status of a sample of 77 predominately non-Hispanic Black adolescents and their parents. The authors discovered that, as concern over parents' own weight status, family conflict, and family resources increased, so did the adolescents' weight status. Consequently, like many other scholars and practitioners, they encourage providers of health promotion and obesity treatment programs to consider the family system in which the child or adolescent is embedded.

According to Yang and Rosenblatt (2007), systems theory constructs are instrumental in understanding the emotional distancing and couple rage frequently encountered when a partner is dying. They delineate how terminal illness alters internal system boundaries, explicit and implicit contracts in couple systems, and system rules for engaging in conflict and dealing with loss, as well as how a system's morphostatic tendency affects the couple's ability to say goodbye. One or both of the partners might use rage or emotional distance to create sufficient psychological distance in order to say goodbye and change the couple system to accommodate its loss.

Family Dynamics and Functioning

A variety of studies examine the impact of various dimensions of family functioning on some aspect of life for individual members or for the family as a whole. For instance, there is a great deal of interest in the impact of family functioning on children's school adjustment. Vanessa Johnson (2010) conducted triadic-level observations on 66 two-parent families, when their oldest child was in kindergarten and again when that child was in ninth grade, in order to determine if there was any relationship between family functioning and school behavior. Using Minuchin's four patterns of family functioning—cohesive families, separate families, detouring families, and triangulated families—Johnson discovered that family types were not consistent across time. For instance, among the 23 families who were deemed to be cohesive during the kindergarten evaluation, 9 families remained cohesive, and 14 were determined not to be cohesive nine years later, when their eldest child was in ninth grade. Importantly, children in families assessed as cohesive during the kindergarten years were rated by their ninth-grade teachers as more academically competent and less aggressive/hyperactive than their peers in mother–child allied families. Father–child allied families, as assessed during the kindergarten years, were rated as more academically competent, less aggressive/hyperactive, and less anxious/withdrawn than those in mother–child allied families (321). Johnson's work reaffirms the importance of formulating healthy family interaction patterns during early childhood and their impact on children's ninth-grade adjustment and school behavior. Her research suggests that family life education prevention programs should promote strong family functioning, with particular efforts aimed at enhancing the mother–father alliance, as well as the father–child relationship. Similarly, Johnson also recommends that the entire family be included in any attempts to improve children's behavior, focusing on co-parenting and not just techniques for managing the troublesome behavior of children.

Sturge-Apple and her colleagues (2010) also employed family systems theory in examining the impact of family functioning on children's adjustment to school trajectories. Using interparental, parent–child, and triadic assessments of 234 kindergarten children and their parents over three years, the authors identified three family typologies of functioning: cohesive, enmeshed, and disengaged. Children in enmeshed families experienced more internal symptomology and demonstrated more challenges in negotiating emotional adjustment to school than those from cohesive families. Children from disengaged families had more classroom engagement difficulties (e.g., inability to adhere to rules) and externalizing problems (e.g., aggression) than those from the other two groups. Children from both disengaged and enmeshed families displayed a greater tendency to internalize symptoms and encounter difficulties in emotional adjustment to school than those in cohesive families.

Systems theory was also instrumental in Buehler, Franck, and Cook's (2009) examination of early adolescents' triangulation in married parents' disputes and its impact on peer relationships. Using a 4-wave longitudinal research design, the authors collected data from 416 families during early adolescence. It turns out that triangulation—offspring involvement in marital conflict—was a risk factor for both sons and daughters. More specifically, early adolescents' triangulation into married parents' disputes was associated negatively with perceived support from friends and positively with perceived peer rejection. Thus, when parents violate marital subsystem boundaries, they place their children at risk for developing strong and supportive social relationships with their peers.

Guided by systems theory, Ngu and Florsheim (2011) studied 60 young, high-risk fathers and their co-parenting partners relative to their paternal functioning, with particular attention to the young mother's role in her partner's paternal competence. Data were collected during the second trimester of pregnancy and two years after the birth of the child. Results revealed that high-risk fathers with relationally competent partners improved in relational competence over time, and these gains were associated with more positive paternal functioning. Fathers whose romantic partnerships with the mother of their child endured that two-year period exhibited higher levels of nurturing behavior, but less warmth, than co-parenting fathers no longer romantically linked to their child's mother. The authors suggest that, rather than directing parenting education programs to groups of young fathers, it might behoove us to develop programs for dyads—fathers and the mothers of their children—with an emphasis on relationship skills.

Clinical Contexts

Family systems theory and its related concepts are especially useful within therapeutic contexts. Heiden Rootes, Jankowski, and Sandage (2010) applied Bowen family systems theory to better understand the relationship between triangulation and religious questing—a struggle with existential questions about sacred matters—among 77 college students. Recognizing that triangulation is a potentially damaging relational pattern thought to occur when one family member engages a third member into a dysfunctional relationship in order to manage dyadic relational anxiety, the authors anticipated a positive relationship between differentiated functioning and religious questing. The authors discovered, however, that religious questing—particularly in regard to asking existential questions—peaked at moderate levels of intergenerational triangulation. They suggest that students with higher levels of triangulation may be immobilized to differentiate, and those with lower levels of triangulation may reveal less urgency to differentiate. Heiden Rootes and her colleagues offer numerous suggestions for therapists who might provide clinical services to questing young adults and their families. These and other studies reveal how the family context, with all of its unique system qualities, impacts family subsystems and individual developmental processes.

Bettinger (2005) examined how a family systems approach is helpful when doing couples therapy with openly gay male couples. He asserts that systems concepts like boundaries, homeostasis, rules, and roles are critical in understanding and accepting gay male sexuality, including the practice of "polyamory," defined as "responsible non-monogamy" (151), which frequently occurs among gay male couples.

A family systems lens is also helpful in working with families in which one or more members struggle with addictive disorders. For example, Curtis (1999) notes that altering interaction patterns, establishing new roles, and reworking family structures are critical objectives in treating families with chemical dependency. Mercado (2000) examined how systems concepts are helpful in providing therapeutic intervention with Asian American substance abusers and their families, as well.

Beyond couple and family therapy, Matthew Paylo (2011) advocates for the inclusion of a family systems perspective in school counseling curricula. From his point of view, it is essential to make a paradigm shift from "individual thinking to systems thinking" (141), because, after all, long-term change requires an examination of how the family and other systems could be helping to maintain behaviors. Thus, competent school counselors must be able to navigate within school and family systems, promoting collaboration between these contextual domains for developing children and adolescents.

CRITIQUE

There are some legitimate criticisms of systems theory. White and Klein (2008) summarized three principal concerns. The first is the belief that systems theory is more of a model or flowchart for conceptualizing, and that it does not qualify as a true theory. The major concepts seem to be too vague for true testing, and they do not predict in the sense of deducing from propositions. This is a valid criticism if you are coming from the dominant epistemology of science, which is the hypothetical-deductive model of empirical testing. However, systems advocates counter that the worldview most appropriate for this theory is the *constructivist* position, in which different models may be useful for different purposes.

The second criticism is that systems theory is too global and abstract, and is therefore virtually meaningless. In other words, it is too "general" to pick up important distinctions that would make it worthwhile. The defense here is that the world is very diverse and that systems theory can make connections between the natural and social worlds that discipline-specific theories are not capable of doing.

Finally, some critics claim that family process theorists in particular make the mistake of reifying the idea of system. That is, instead of remembering that it is just a model for understanding, they slip into considering the system to be reality. They confuse the "model" with the "thing." The response from systems apologists is that all theories have their naive claims and that systems theory is no less prone to reification than any other theory.

One finds validity in these criticisms because of the relative lack of useful mathematical models and predictive propositions that have emerged over the years from this approach. It may be that the kinds of interactions attended to by systems theory are simply too complex for the traditional scientific method to deal with in an understandable fashion. As a result, the theory has been most useful in the areas of family communication and family therapy. Broderick and Smith (1979) list the following as the most productive types of issues for examination by systems theorists:

1. *Sequential patterns of interaction.* Other disciplines, such as economics, have benefited for many years by utilizing such concepts as feedback loops, escalation, and dampening in the context of temporal patterns of everyday life. Systems theory can use the same conceptual tools to understand family interactions.

2. *Communication and control.* Traditional family literature tends to see communication as a variable that ranges in amount and satisfaction, but little else. The family process therapists have accumulated considerable evidence that controlling behavior is the most important aspect of communication.

3. *Goal orientation.* The dynamics of system goal achievement and its relationship to control and family rules appears to be a topic unique to systems theory literature.

4. *Boundary maintenance.* The importance of maintaining systems boundaries is more important to systems theory than it is to any other theory. There is considerable evidence now that whether a family boundary is relatively open or closed is crucial to its effectiveness.

5. *Complex relationships.* Finally, most other theoretical approaches utilize causal models that are linear, avoid too many interaction effects, and tend to average outputs into mean results. Systems theory recognizes that life is nonlinear, with multiple causal paths and outcomes. Therefore, its models emphasize branching, rather than averaging.

APPLICATION

1. Answer these questions based on the vignette at the beginning of the chapter:

   a. Consider Alexa and Cassie's communication exchange from a linear perspective (punctuation) versus a circular perspective. Why does it make a difference?

   b. How might this couple employ positive feedback to alter this unfruitful pattern of interaction?

2. One of the best ways to understand systems concepts is to apply them to your own family life. The following are some good exercises adapted from Goldenberg and Goldenberg (2008):

   a. List the roles that you currently play in their order of importance. How many are family (family versus career or other) roles? Which role is the most integral to your sense of self?

   b. What homeostatic or corrective feedback do you engage in when dealing with conflict with a loved one? How do they respond to it?

   c. List some behaviors of friends or family members that irritate you. Now, try to reframe their motivations into more positive possibilities. Does this change your feelings toward the person?

   d. Most communications between people have a "command" aspect as well as the content of the message. For instance, asking where the salt is at dinner implies a command to get it. List some common comments in your family that have implicit commands in them.

   e. Identify multiple rules that your family enforces. Are the rules implicit or explicit? What rule has someone most recently attempted to change, and how has the family responded (feedback)?

   f. In reference to the vignette at the beginning of this chapter, list examples of circular causality from your own family. What are some examples of endless arguments in which each person blames the other for "starting it"?

3. The sample reading (Bacallao and Smokowski 2007) shows that Mexican immigrant families lose contact with extended family because of geographic separations and, therefore, find a variety of ways to cope. What do you think are some of the long-term effects of these coping mechanisms on the family system? What are other ways in which the families attempted to restore family equilibrium? What implications do the findings in this research have for development of family policy or family life education programs?

REFERENCES

Bateson, G., D. Jackson, J. Haley, and J. Weakland. 1956. Toward a theory of schizophrenia. *Behavioral Science* 1: 251–264.

Becvar, D. S., and R. J. Becvar. 2008. *Family therapy: A systemic integration.* 7th ed. Boston: Pearson Education.

Bertalanffy, L. 1969. *General systems theory: Essays in its foundation and development.* New York: Braziller.

Bettinger, M. 2005. A family systems approach to working with sexually open gay male couples. *Journal of Couple and Relationship Therapy* 4: 149–160.

Boss, P. 2002. *Family stress management: A contextual approach.* 2nd ed. Thousand Oaks, CA: Sage.

Broderick, C. 1993. *Understanding family process.* Newbury Park, CA: Sage.

Broderick, C., and J. Smith. 1979. The general systems approach to the family. In *Contemporary theories about the family,* ed. W. R. Burr, R. Hill, F. I. Nye, and I. L. Reiss. Vol. 1, 112–129. New York: Free Press.

Buehler, C., K. L. Franck, and E. C. Cook. 2009. Adolescents' triangulation in marital conflict and peer relations. *Journal of Research on Adolescence* 19(4): 669–689.

Burgess, E. 1926. The family as a unity of interacting personalities. *The Family* 7: 3–9.

Curtis, O. 1999. *Chemical dependency: A family affair.* Pacific Grove, CA: Brooks/Cole.

Galvin, K. M., C. L. Bylund, and B. J. Brommel. 2012. *Family communication: Cohesion and change.* 8th ed. Boston: Pearson Education.

Goldenberg, I., and H. Goldenberg. 2008. *Family therapy: An overview.* 7th ed. Belmont, CA: Brooks/Cole.

Harris, J. N., J. Hay, A. Kuniyuki, M. M. Asgari, N. Press, and D. J. Bowen. 2010. Using a family systems approach to investigate cancer risk communication within melanoma families. *Psycho-Oncology* 19: 1102–1111. DOI: 10.1002/pon.1667

Heiden Rootes, K. M., P. J. Jankowski, and S. J. Sandage. 2010. Bowen family systems theory and spirituality: Exploring the relationship between triangulation and religious questing. *Contemporary Family Therapy* 32: 89–101. DOI: 10.1007/s10591–009-9101-y

Herr, J. J., and J. H. Weakland. 1979. Communications within systems: Growing older within and with the double bind. In *Aging parents,* ed. P. K. Ragan, 144–153. Los Angeles: Simon & Schuster Adult Publishing Group.

Hooper, L. M., J. J. Burnham, and R. Richey. 2009. Select parent and family system correlates of adolescent current weight status: A pilot study. *The Family Journal: Counseling and Therapy for Couples and Families* 17(1): 14–21. DOI: 10.1177/1066480708328460

Johnson, V. K. 2010. From early childhood to adolescence: Linking family functioning and school behavior. *Family Relations* 59: 313–325. DOI: 10.1111/j.1741–3729.2010.00604.x

Kantor, D., and W. Lehr. 1975. *Inside the family.* San Francisco: Jossey-Bass.

Kitzman-Ulrich, H., D. K. Wilson, S. M. St. George, H. Lawman, M. Segal, and A. Fairchild. 2010. The integration of a family systems approach for understanding youth obesity, physical activity, and dietary programs. *Clinical Child Family Psychological Review* 13: 231–253. DOI: 10.1007/s10567–010-0073–0

Kouneski, E. F. 2000. *The Family Circumplex Model, FACES II, and FACES III: Overview of research and applications.* Retrieved from http://www.facesiv.com/pdf/faces_and_circumplex.pdf

Mercado, M. M. 2000. The invisible family: Counseling Asian American substance abusers and their families. *The Family Journal: Counseling and Therapy for Couples and Families* 8: 267–272.

Miller, J. G. 1978. *Living systems.* New York: McGraw-Hill.

Ngu, L., and P. Florsheim. 2011. The development of relational competence among young high-risk fathers across the transition to parenthood. *Family Process* 50: 184–202.

Olson, D. H. 2000. Circumplex model of marital and family systems. *Journal of Family Therapy* 22: 144–167.

Olson, D. H. 2011. FACES IV and the Circumplex Model: Validation study. *Journal of Marital and Family Therapy* 37(1): 64–80.

Paylo, M. J. 2011. Preparing school counseling students to aid families: Integrating a family systems perspective. *The Family Journal: Counseling and Therapy for Couples and Families* 19(2): 140–146. DOI: 10.1177/1066480710397130

Satir, V. 1964. *Conjoint family therapy*. Palo Alto, CA: Science and Behavior Books.

Satir, V. 1972. *Peoplemaking*. Palo Alto, CA: Science and Behavior Books.

Sturge-Apple, M. L., P. T. Davies, and E. M. Cummings. 2010. Typologies of family functioning and children's adjustment during the early school years. *Child Development* 81(4): 1320–1335.

Waller, W. 1938. *The family: A dynamic interpretation*. R. Hill, rev., 1951. New York: Holt, Rinehart, and Winston.

Whitchurch, G. G., and L. L. Constantine. 1993. Systems theory. In *Sourcebook of family theories and methods: A contextual approach*, eds. P. G. Boss, W. J. Doherty, R. LaRossa, W. R. Schumm, and S. K. Steinmetz, 325–352. New York: Plenum.

White, J., and D. Klein. 2008. *Family theories*. 3rd ed. Thousand Oaks, CA: Sage.

Winton, C. 1995. *Frameworks for studying families*. Guilford, CT: Duskin Publishing Group.

Yang, S., and P. C. Rosenblatt. 2007. Couple rage and emotional distancing when a partner is dying. *Journal of Loss and Trauma* 12: 305–320. DOI: 10.1080/15325020601138799

SAMPLE READING

Bacallao, M. L., and P. R. Smokowski. 2007. The costs of getting ahead: Mexican family system changes after immigration. *Family Relations* 56: 52–66.

Based on qualitative interviews with 14 parents and 12 teenagers from 10 undocumented Mexican immigrant families, the authors explore the impact of immigration on family dynamics, with particular attention to parent–adolescent relationships. More specifically, the authors addressed three major questions: (1) how do undocumented families from Mexico change after coming to the United States, (2) how do these changes affect individual family members, as well as the family's dynamics, and (3) what variables contribute to the adjustment of undocumented families in this new country? Grounded theory methods helped to explain the many stressors and adjustments that these Mexican families had to make to their family systems. For instance, many of the families became dual-earner households and, as a result, experienced a decrease in shared family time. A variety of coping strategies were employed, including parents becoming stricter in an attempt to protect their children from negative aspects of American culture, as well as the promotion of greater familism or family cohesion. The article affords a deeper understanding of postimmigration adjustment.

SAMPLE READING

The Costs of Getting Ahead:
Mexican Family System Changes
after Immigration[*]

Martica L. Bacallao
*Paul R. Smokowski**[**]

This study explored how immigration influenced Mexican family relationships. Qualitative interviews were conducted with 12 adolescents and 14 parents from 10 undocumented Mexican families. Participants immigrated to North Carolina within the past 7 years. A conceptual model derived from the data using grounded theory methods suggested that, after immigration, parents had less time to spend with children because of demanding new jobs and mothers entering the work force. Decreased time as a family was associated with adolescents' loneliness, isolation, and risk-taking behavior. In response to perceived environmental threats, Mexican parents became authoritarian, precipitating parent-adolescent conflict. Parent-adolescent acculturation gaps were viewed as an asset as adolescents helped parents navigate within the new cultural system. Families coped with postimmigration changes by maintaining high levels of familism and enacting cultural traditions.

Keywords: acculturation, familism, family systems, Latinos, migration

[*]The authors wish to thank the Latino families who participated in this study. This study was supported by grants from the Center for Disease Control's National Injury Prevention Center (R49/CCR42172–02) and from the Centers for Disease Control's Office of the Director (1K01 CE000496–01).

[**]Martica L. Bacallao is an Assistant Professor in the Department of Social Work at the University of North Carolina—Greensboro, P.O. Box 26170, Greensboro, NC 27402–6170 (m.bacallao@ uncg.edu). Paul R. Smokowski is an Associate Professor in the School of Social Work at the University of North Carolina at Chapel Hill, 301 Pittsboro Street, CB # 3550, Chapel Hill, NC 27599–3550 (smokowsk@email.unc.edu).

Family Relations, 56 (January 2007), 52–66. Blackwell Publishing.
Copyright 2007 by the National Council on Family Relations.

Mexico, lindo y querido, si muero lejos de ti, por siempre te extrañare. Para siempre. {Mexico, beautiful and beloved, if I die far away from you, know that I will always miss you. Always.}—Yariela, Mexican female adolescent, age 12, living in United States for 1 year

Researchers from the Pew Hispanic Center estimate that 11 million undocumented individuals currently live in the United States; a 30% increase from the 8.4 million estimated in 2000. Six million of these undocumented individuals are Mexican. The same researchers estimate that one-sixth of this population, or 1.7 million people, are younger than 18 years (Passel, 2005). Although there is clearly a large group of undocumented Mexicans living in the United States, we know little about these families and how they function. It is important to learn more about the unique challenges faced by undocumented families who, compared to legal immigrants or refugees, live in fear of deportation and cannot easily travel back and forth to Mexico.

Most of the research on Latino immigration, acculturation, and adjustment has been conducted with adults, leaving us with scant information on adolescents and even less on family relationships (García Coll & Magnuson, 2001). Little attention has been given to the *1.5 generation*, that is, children and adolescents who were born and socialized in a foreign country and subsequently immigrated to the United States (Hirschman, 1994; Portes & Rumbaut, 2001). Notwithstanding the emphasis that acculturation research has placed on comparisons between different generations within immigrant families (e.g., U.S.-born children vs. their immigrant parents), these 1.5 generation children arguably experience the most upheaval of the family system and are most likely to either become bicultural or get caught between cultural systems (García Coll & Magnuson; Hirschman).

This study focused on understanding family system dynamics in undocumented Mexican families and the changes that parents and adolescents experience after immigration. We contribute to the body of knowledge on Latino immigrant families by exploring three fundamental questions that have not received adequate attention in the previous research on undocumented Mexican immigrant families: (a) how do undocumented Mexican families change after immigration, (b) how do these changes affect family members and their interactions, and (c) what factors explain postimmigration family system adjustment in undocumented families?

The immigration experience and stressors that arise therein such as learning a new language, finding jobs, and coping with discrimination can lead to both acculturation stress and familial stress. Depending upon the reasons for relocation, as well as the exiting and entering environments, immigrant families often experience significant upheaval during migration, shifts in socioeconomic status, loss of social networks, and disorienting cultural changes in the new land (Hernandez & McGoldrick, 1999). We sought to delineate how these challenges influence undocumented Mexican family system functioning and family relationships.

Past research suggests that after immigration (a) acculturation differences (i.e., gaps) between parents and adolescent children precipitate family stress (Hernandez & McGoldrick, 1999; Szapocznik & Kurtines, 1980) and (b) the strong sense of family cohesion (i.e., familism) many Mexican families arrive with erodes over time (Cortes, 1995; Rogler & Cooney, 1984). These changes may be considered what we currently know about the "costs" of getting ahead in the United States. However, few studies have used qualitative data to examine the processes behind these family system dynamics. The following sections describe sensitizing concepts—acculturation gaps and the erosion of familism—that provided a foundation for the present study.

Acculturation Gaps

Normative conflicts between parents and adolescents can be exacerbated by acculturation stress, creating intercultural as well as intergenerational difficulties between family members (Coatsworth, Pantin, & Szapocznik, 2002). Children commonly acculturate faster than adults, creating an acculturation gap between generations that precipitates family stress (Hernandez & McGoldrick, 1999; Szapocznik & Kurtines, 1980). Because of this cultural clash, Latino families' external boundaries often become rigid to preserve culture of origin beliefs and norms (Hernandez & McGoldrick). This conflict can fuel adolescent rebellion, alienate parents and adolescents, and contribute to the development of adolescent behavioral problems (Coatsworth et al., 2002; Szapocznik, Santisteban, Kurtines, Perez-Vidal, & Hervis 1986).

Familism

Familism involves a deeply ingrained sense of the individual being inextricably rooted in the family. The term encompasses attitudes, behaviors, and family structures within an extended family system and is believed to be one of the most important factors influencing the lives of Latinos (Cooley, 2001; Parra-Cardona, Bulock, Imig, Villarruel, & Gold, 2006). This strong sense of family orientation, obligation, and cohesion has noteworthy protective effects. For example, Cooley found familism to be an important factor associated with less child maltreatment in both Latino and non-Latino families. Gil, Wagner, and Vega (2000) reported familism to have a highly significant, negative association with acculturation stress, though this relationship was stronger for immigrant Latino adolescents than it was for U.S.-born Latino adolescents.

Familism is thought to decrease as acculturation progresses. Cortes (1995) found levels of familism decreased with higher levels of education and were higher for children and adolescents who were older when they arrived in the United States. Rogler and Cooney (1984) found that second generation adult children were less familistic than their first generation parents.

To summarize, current research on Latino families suggests that acculturation gaps between family members contribute to intergenerational stress, and familism tends to erode over time spent in the United States. These sensitizing concepts further underscore the need for the present study.

METHOD

Participants and Procedure

Participants. The first author conducted in-depth, semistructured interviews with 10 undocumented Mexican immigrant families. Families were recruited from

Latino communities in North Carolina as a part of a large mixed-methods study (Bacallao & Smokowski, 2005). Recruitment was conducted through churches, English as a Second Language programs, and at Latino community events. The 10 participating families consisted of undocumented Mexican immigrants with adolescents who were born in Mexico and had come to the United States in late childhood or adolescence. Within these 10 families, one adolescent and one parent were interviewed. In two of the families, two adolescent siblings were interviewed. Both parents were interviewed in four of the families, fathers only in three, and mothers only in the remaining three. Interviews provided qualitative data on 12 adolescents and 14 parents. Interviews were conducted with seven mothers and seven fathers, lasted 4–5 hours, and were conducted in the participants' homes in Spanish, the participants' preferred language. Participants' names were changed to protect confidentiality.

On average, adolescents were 14 years of age and had been in the United States for an average of 4 years when interviews were conducted in 2004. Forty percent (4 of 10) of the undocumented families had mothers and fathers who obtained only an elementary school education in Mexico, although 30% (3 of 10) of the families had at least one parent who had attended some high school in Mexico. The remaining 30% of families had at least one mother or father who had graduated from high school in Mexico. All of the families had two parents and lived in trailer parks or crowded apartment buildings. The average annual family income was $21,000.

Interview protocol and analyses. The semistructured interview protocol contained open-ended questions. To prompt participants to discuss acculturation, family members were asked the following questions: "In what ways are you Mexican? In what ways are you American?" To solicit information on coping and adaptation, family members were asked: "What have you overcome? What has it been like for you to adjust to life in the U.S.?" The following questions were asked to prompt participants to discuss personal and interpersonal relationship changes: "What is your relationship like with your parents (for parents: with your adolescent child) since you've been here? How have you (for parents: has your child) changed since coming to the U.S.?" These semistructured interview questions often generated lengthy narratives that were the focus of our analyses.

Parents were interviewed first, enabling them to hear the questions that their child would be asked. In every participating family, parents allowed the first author to privately interview their adolescent child. Consequently, all interviews occurred separately so that parents and adolescents did not influence one another's answers. All interviews were conducted in Spanish and translated into English during transcription by the first author.

This study used grounded theory methods (GTM) for the analyses of interview data (Charmaz, 2000). We specifically sought to explain undocumented Mexican family system adjustment after immigration, using GTM to build a conceptual model from "concepts" and "indicators" that emerged from the data (LaRossa, 2005). We used Atlas/ti version 4.1 for Windows to code text files. Following the stages of analyses in ground theory, we used open, axial, and selective coding to derive the concepts and indicators in the conceptual model (LaRossa).

During open coding, the authors broke the text down into discrete parts or units of analyses called concepts. In vivo coding was carried out similarly when participants' own words were used as a code or concept. For example, an adolescent saying "I just can't stop thinking about how my life was in Mexico" was coded "thinking about the past after immigration" during open coding; whereas a mother saying "family separations made us do things differently" initiated an in vivo code called "family separations." Open and in vivo codes were clustered into more abstract categories or variables with multiple indicators theoretically saturating each category (LaRossa, 2005). Our sensitizing concepts, familism and acculturation gaps surfaced as open codes and categories.

Axial coding followed open and in vivo coding by examining relationships between and among categories or variables (Charmaz, 2000). Using the constant comparison method, we compared codes, concepts, and categories from different adolescents, parents, and families to examine their universality and to identify cases where they did not fit. Code notes, theory notes, and process notes were kept in memos attached to the data files to record the potential relationships between codes and categories (Parra-Cardona et al., 2006). Finally, selective coding was used to craft the story line (LaRossa, 2005). In our case, the story line emerged as articulating the costs of getting ahead and how undocumented Mexican families coped with these costs. A conceptual model was finalized to describe postimmigration adjustment in undocumented Mexican families, and exemplars were identified to illustrate the concepts and indicators in the final model.

Trustworthiness of the analysis. Qualitative researchers emphasize rigor in their studies by examining trustworthiness of the results. Triangulation of methods, sources, analysts, and perspectives are strategies for enhancing credibility in qualitative research (Patton, 2002). In this study, we used all of these triangulation methods. We triangulated information from multiple sources in the interviews with adolescents and their parents. Informal discussions with participating families after the interviews confirmed what was included in the formal interviews. With 7 of 10 families, the first author talked with both parents when the interviews were completed, gaining multiple perspectives from the same family. She also spoke with five siblings. These conversations were documented in field notes, providing multiple perspectives from which we could view the data.

In addition, as part of a large mixed-methods study, the authors discussed themes from the qualitative analyses with research staff who conducted quantitative assessments to confirm themes and integrate feedback. We shared our conceptual model with consultants and audiences at local, state, and national conferences to gain insights from other professionals working with undocumented Mexican families.

Positionality. Qualitative researchers believe that it is critical to understand and make overt the positionality, or personal beliefs and biases, brought to the research endeavor (Patton, 2002). The first author, who conducted the interviews and led the analyses, is a bicultural mental health social worker with an emphasis on the importance of family and social support, qualities that influenced her positionality. In every interview except for one, she went beyond the interview protocol to provide guidance, information, and links to local resources. We believe that this positionality enhanced the study by encouraging families to provide detailed information about their experiences.

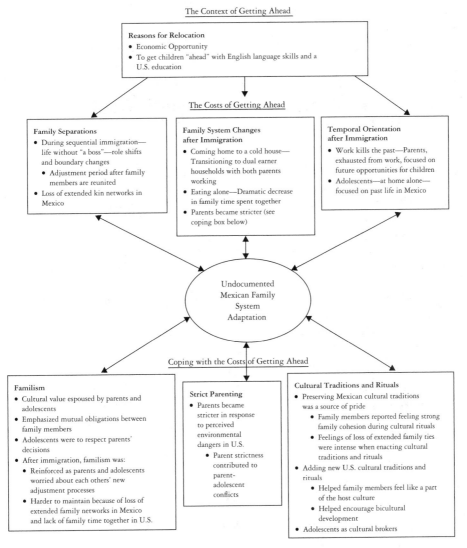

FIGURE S5.1. Getting Ahead: Mexican Family Systems after Immigration.

RESULTS

Figure S5.1 shows the conceptual model generated in the GTM analyses. The bold titles within each box are abstract concepts underpinned by the indicators shown in each bulleted list. These concepts and indicators were salient for all of the families for both adolescent and parent data. Each concept and indicators cluster captured at least 20 single-spaced pages of thick description text from the families; the overall model characterizes over 200 pages of thick description. All of the concept and indicators clusters were associated with overall adjustment in the undocumented Mexican families. This conceptual model of postimmigration undocumented Mexican family adjustment guides the presentation of findings. We use exemplars from adolescents and parents to illustrate each element in the model. As stated above, pseudonyms are used in quotations.

THE CONTEXT OF GETTING AHEAD

Relocation as a Means to "Grow Toward the Light"

The Mexican families interviewed for this study immigrated to the United States for two primary reasons. First, all of the families thought better job opportunities existed in the United States to support their family members who immigrated and those who stayed in Mexico. Four families wanted to save enough money to return to Mexico to start businesses. All of the families discussed escaping chronic poverty in Mexico and considered the most basic living conditions in the United States a marked improvement. The second reason for relocation was to seek a better future for their children, to try to "get our children ahead." Getting children ahead meant educating them in the United States and having them learn English to enhance future opportunities. This was an organizing theme for all of the parents, making immigration-related difficulties worthwhile. Future dreams for children provided inspiration during stressful times. One mother offered this metaphor:

> Diocelina (mother): I did not come here [to the U.S.] to become rich. I didn't even come here to be happy, no. I came here to get my children ahead. I tell my children that we came here for them, and to become better persons. We work like burros here. This is not a happier life. My father told me when I was seven that everything grows towards the light. We are here to grow towards the light even when we think that darkness surrounds us. In this family, under these circumstances, we are seeds in the soil trying to grow towards the light.

THE COSTS OF GETTING AHEAD

There were significant costs associated with the possibility for getting ahead. Immigration brought serious family system changes along with economic opportunities in the United States and enhanced prospects for children's futures.

Family Separations

Life without "a boss": Sequential immigration and shifting family roles. Having family members immigrate at different times (i.e., sequential immigration) was a common experience that disrupted family functioning. Eight fathers relocated first in order to find work and lay the groundwork for bringing other family members. The fathers contributed as much as they could to the family in Mexico by sending money home. At the same time, family homeostasis or equilibrium, members' roles, and patterns of functioning were influenced by the father's absence.

The severity of separation problems appeared to depend upon the length of the separation. When the separation was short, 6 months to a year, families said they were able to cope with the stress. In the father's absence, mothers and children typically lived with and received support from extended family members. Although families originally believed that the separation from the father would last only a year, in six of eight families the separation lasted considerably longer (3 years or more). Fathers did not return to visit the family because of their undocumented legal status, the inherent risk in being smuggled across the border, and the high cost of the travel—reported to be $4,000 for one undocumented person. Family members said that long separations brought significant changes in family roles and patterns of functioning, contributing to family stress.

In the father's absence, the family left behind restructured itself and established new patterns of functioning. In three families, both parents immigrated, leaving their children with grandparents, aunts, or uncles. The loss of key parent relationships sometimes allowed adolescents, especially young males, to drift into high-risk situations, such as getting involved with antisocial peers or in illegal activities. Adolescents said these separations prompted the family to reconfigure itself around the single parent or surrogate parents that remained—a dynamic that was helpful for coping with the absence, but one that commonly created difficulties when the family was reunited. One adolescent male, Manuel, reported that he became strongly attached to his resilient mother during his father's absence. Manuel described his mother as the greatest influence in his life. His relationship with his father after separation was never the same.

> Manuel (male adolescent): My mom probably influenced me the most. I got really close to her when my dad wasn't with me. She was like the head of the family, and somehow, even though my dad's with us now, that's never been restored. She's still the head of this family. Nothing against him, it's just the way she is as a figure head. We grew up with her for six years while Dad was here [in the U.S.]. She takes charge.

Another adolescent male experienced the same intense bonding with his mother. His parents divorced after immigrating. The father returned to Mexico to get the boy when he heard that his son stopped going to school and was associating with delinquent peers. Father, son, and the father's second wife began to live together for the first time in 8 years. The son explained the difficulties he experienced in the situation.

> Jaime (male adolescent): We were separated seven or eight years. When I was...six, he [the father] left [for the U.S.]. And he returned to get me when I was 13. I had little memory of him when he came back. Even though it's been 3 years that I'm here with him, it's still difficult for me to adapt to him, his way of being. Now I finally know how to control things better. Back there [in Mexico], there was no boss. My older brother was here. My stepfather was living in Chicago. There was no boss. It was difficult adjusting to a boss in this house. He told me when I got here that he was the boss. He didn't talk. But he would tell me to talk to my brother. Call my mother [in Chicago]. Talk to my sister. With my mother, I had a lot of trust. My father was more closed. I couldn't talk with him like I do with my mother. Well, he would tell me one thing: Use condoms.... That would

be the only thing he'd tell me. My mother would explain everything to me....I haven't developed that sense of trust with anyone else....I'm still getting to know my father.

Once families were reunited after immigration, they described an adjustment period in which structural changes created new configurations of roles, boundaries, and communication processes, as well as a stormy period after reuniting. In three families, the father would argue with his wife, yell, and use foul language when speaking with the children. Family members, especially mothers, said that it took at least 1 year to readjust to living with each other. Others, like Jaime, said they were still struggling to readjust to family changes.

The loss of extended kin in Mexico. In addition to family separations during sequential immigration, there were also separations between family members who immigrated and extended kin who remained in Mexico. Given the importance many Mexicans place on familism, adolescents and parents said that the loss of close relationships with extended family members (e.g., grandparents, aunts, uncles, cousins) was hard to bear. Parents missed the companionship, support, and help extended family members provided. They also worried about aging relatives in Mexico and were limited in their ability to go back to visit. One father said that he felt closer to his daughter because they had only their nuclear family in this country; this was an uncommon contrasting view. All the other parents and adolescents said they missed the extensive family support that characterized their lives in Mexico. Adolescents reported missing family members in Mexico as much as or more than their parents. For adolescents, the family members remaining in Mexico were strongly linked to memories of childhood in Mexico, especially if the relatives had served as surrogate parents during sequential immigration family separations. During the difficulties of adjusting to life in the United States, most adolescents thought of happy times with family members in Mexico. This focus on the past made adolescents feel ambivalent about their new lives in America.

> Elena (female adolescent): The United States. I think of it with many dollars but the people are sad. You have everything, but you don't have your family. It's not like in Mexico where you visit with your grandparents and your other relatives. In Mexico, you don't have money but you're much better because you're with your family. I know that my parents do this for our well-being, so we're here. But I think all the people in Mexico are happy because they are with their family. You see, here, it is mostly sadness. I feel like crying instead of feeling good. We used to always be with my family, that's who I miss.

Thinking about loved ones left behind saddened adolescents, making some adolescents yearn to return to Mexico. Nostalgic memories were particularly enticing when adolescents felt lonely, isolated, and friendless. These memories and attachments sustained one adolescent during the difficult adjustment to life in America when she was depressed and suicidal. The interviewer asked if she was thinking of hurting herself.

> Teresa (female adolescent): Sometimes—I've felt that way when I feel shut in, when there are problems, when I've just had a fight with my mom or dad, things like that. The only thing I do is I get into my room and I make myself think. I just try to let it pass. I used to be a happy person. So, I just try to let this thing

pass. [She started to cry.] I think about my grandparents, my uncles, my friends [back in Mexico]. I haven't seen my uncles and grandparents for so long that I feel like I hardly know them. But I think about them and how they would suffer if this happened to me [if she hurt herself attempting suicide]. So, no, I can't let them down. They would suffer so much.

Memories of her family in Mexico fueled this adolescent's sense of family loyalty and prevented her from hurting herself. Yet, feelings of loss associated with separation from family in Mexico also contributed to adolescents' depression. This young girl's experience of shifting from being "a happy person" to being depressed provides a bridge to broaden our discussion of family separations to postimmigration family system stress.

Mexican Family System Changes After Immigration

Coming home to a cold house: The transformation into dual-earner households. Fathers played the role of family provider in Mexico, maintaining low-paying employment and shouldering financial responsibilities for the family. Mothers managed the home and took primary responsibility for raising children. Parents and adolescents described traditional gender roles reinforced by Mexican cultural norms, prompting mothers to be at home with their children spending time together and fathers to feel proud of their role as sole providers for their families.

After immigrating, Mexican families reconfigured themselves into dual-earner households. In 7 of 10 families, both parents worked. Financial stress and the higher U.S. cost of living prompted five of seven mothers to enter the labor force for the first time. This change helped family finances but was a difficult adjustment for family members. Mexican men who were invested in traditional gender roles said they found it particularly distressing because it was now publicly displayed that the father, as head of the household, could not solely provide for his family. Women found jobs in factories, cafeterias, restaurants, or hotel housekeeping services. According to both parents and adolescents, the amount of time the family now had to spend together decreased dramatically. All families reported that this change took a toll on both the marital relationship and parent–child relationships. In addition, adolescents were commonly left with much more unsupervised time on their own. One father described his difficulty with the changes.

Carmelo (father): In Mexico, I would come home with my little briefcase, and my kids would come greet me when I came home. They'd say, "Dad! Dad! What do you bring?" I have this or I have that. . . . Now, no, I come home to an empty and cold house. Empty and cold, because there's no one here. We only share our time together for a little while. We miss out on some conversation, something we may need to say to one another. In Mexico, I had my worries from work, but as soon as I go home, my bad mood would be gone. The aggravations from work would go away because people are waiting for you. My wife would tell me, "Look, I just made you your favorite dish," or simply, "I made you your cup of coffee how you like it." In the U.S., we both come home from work with the same bad mood.

How work kills the past: Parents' stress from demanding jobs. Dual-earner families described being overloaded and having little flexibility to absorb additional stressors. In the quotation below, one mother described the conflict she felt having to work, while she worried about her adolescent children and her ailing mother, who lived nearby. Her work demands did not allow her the time to support her family members in the ways she would have liked.

> Alicia (mother): I would like my daughter to talk to someone. She doesn't have papers, but she needs to talk to someone...like a psychologist. I'm not home to be with her. I had to work. The jobs here are tiring, very tiring. But we must keep our eyes on our children, and get them ahead. My husband and I have three teenagers, and one married daughter....We have to sacrifice so many things to get the family ahead. There are so many more worries about our children here. I just want to sit here and cry, but my children, they lift me.

Family stress seemed to be worsened by the nature of the parents' work, which was physically exhausting and emotionally stressful. This may be one reason that parents did not seem to mourn family separations with extended kin in Mexico as much as adolescents did. Exhausted parents had little time to reminisce. They focused on the multiple tasks of daily life, struggling to support both their families in Mexico and in the United States. One parent described what it was like to be consumed by work.

> Miguel (father): Work kills all your concentration on what used to be. By working, you don't realize anything but what is in front of you, the job ahead of you. I concentrate so much on myself and on my job. That's how I adapted. You learn about the ways here at your job.

In addition to the demanding physical labor, parents found that their work skills did not translate to work settings in America, requiring quick acquisition of new skills, often without the benefit of adequate communication with supervisors. The language barrier made this occupational adjustment particularly difficult. Four men described having to learn complicated skills, such as furniture assembly or using new machinery, after watching it done only once or twice. All fathers and four of the working mothers described being frustrated and unable to advance themselves at work because of their limited English language skills. This frustration was compounded by daily experiences of discrimination, such as being told to go back to Mexico. However, parents said they did not measure their success by their work. Work, and the stress inherent in their jobs, was a sacrifice made to provide for their families. Success for parents meant helping their children get ahead.

Eating alone: Family relationships and the decrease in shared family time. Parents' stress from work in dual-earner households influenced parent–adolescent relationships, family dynamics, and communication processes. Seven parents worked 12-hour days, 6 days per week. Two adolescents had jobs at fast food restaurants to help their parents with finances. Family members said that these work schedules, along with both parents working, reduced the amount of time family members could spend with one another. Four parents said they would not see their adolescents for 1–3 days because of conflicting work and school schedules. There was markedly less shared family time in the United States than in Mexico. Parents often worked for hourly pay; more hours worked meant more financial gain for the family. A female adolescent commented on the impact of work on family life.

Nohemi (female adolescent): My relationship with my parents has changed because, in Mexico, mom was always at home while we were at school. She would do the housework... ironing. When I came home from school, everything was ready, the food would be prepared, the clothes were washed and ironed and all that, you know? I would sit down with mom and dad to eat. And in the U.S., sometimes I don't see my dad for three days. Living in the same house, you know? For example, I go to school, then I go to work and sometimes, I get home late at night, and he's already sleeping when I come home. And the next day, it's the same thing. I don't get to see him until the third day. That's changed our relationship when you don't eat with each other every day.

Less time spent together meant adolescents had to handle problems on their own. This increase in the time they spent alone may have contributed to adolescents missing the close relationships they had in Mexico. Five female and two male adolescents described feeling isolated, lonely, and depressed in their homes. Feelings of sadness seemed to stem from grieving the loss of time spent with their parents and family in Mexico reflected in the words of a female adolescent:

Reyna (female adolescent): I just stay in my room. I like to draw.... Sometimes, I'll sleep. There's no one in the house. I don't go out of my bedroom for anything except to brush my teeth and wash myself. My mother is always working or going to church. My mother and sister are gone, so, here is where I pass the time. Alone. Always alone.

The amount of unsupervised time also allowed adolescents the opportunity to get into trouble. One immigrant father described the difficulties he had with his son who habitually skipped school after coming to the United States. On one occasion, the police escorted the adolescent home after he was found in an abandoned house partying with his Mexican gang associates. After a great deal of effort and structure from his father, this adolescent began to attend school regularly. The father commented:

Victor (father): He's changed 100%. When he lived in Mexico, he did not go to school. I decided I had to go to Mexico and bring him here. He is relatively intelligent, and had to get out of that situation in Mexico.... Since he's been here, he has been told that he has to go to school, and if he doesn't go to school, he will get me in trouble. And if he doesn't obey me, he will get both of us in trouble, in trouble with the law. His behavior can either protect us, or can get us into problems. Also, he doesn't have his mother near him since he left Mexico. That has been difficult for him. He's had to adapt to being more on his own in the house. When I come home from work, I have to pay more attention to where he's going, what he did that day, if the homework is done. It's difficult because I work all day, and then, this at home.

Both parents and adolescents seemed greatly affected by the loss of maternal supervision, decreased family time together, fatigue from physically demanding jobs, and relationship changes because of sequential immigration and the loss of extended kin in Mexico. These new family system stressors had different psychological impacts on parents and adolescents. One of the differences was the temporal orientation after immigration.

Temporal orientation after relocation. Although all family members understood the reasons for relocation, parents and adolescents had dramatically different temporal orientations in the postimmigration adjustment process. Parents focused on the future, on getting their children educated, and anticipated the enhanced opportunities they perceived that their children would have with bilingual skills and a U.S. education. In contrast, adolescents focused on the past, mourning the loss of the lifestyle, family, and friends they left in Mexico. The following quote captures one adolescent's ambivalence.

> Juana (female adolescent): I feel sad because I had to leave a place that I loved very much for something that's better, better in that, if we were to go back [to Mexico], I'd have more opportunities because I'd know another language, and maybe we'd be able to get better jobs. But, I miss my family, my cousins [in Mexico].

If the metaphor for family relocation was indeed Diocelina's "plant growing toward the light," it seemed adolescents' thoughts centered on the roots under the soil that they could no longer see, whereas parents' dreamt of the future buds they hoped would bloom. These contrasting temporal orientations were one important way in which parents and adolescents went through different processes in their postimmigration adjustment to life in the United States. This provides a helpful bridge to shift our focus onto how parents and adolescents coped with these costs of getting ahead.

COPING WITH THE COSTS OF GETTING AHEAD

Parental Strictness as a Means to Counter Americanization

Both parents and adolescents reported that parents tended to become stricter with their children after immigrating to the United States. This was both an important change in parent–adolescent dynamics and a strategy for coping with new family stressors. Parents had little time to spend with their children and were worried about dangers they perceived in the environment (e.g., drug use, pulling away from the family, having too much freedom). In this new context for parenting and without the network of support from extended family members, parents did not allow their adolescents many opportunities to explore their new environment. Parents also reported feeling vulnerable to the effects of their adolescents' behavior. Families in the United States without legal papers were especially worried about being involved with the police, which may be one of the reasons parents restricted their adolescents' freedom outside the home. Participation in school-affiliated activities was uncommon. Parents and adolescents said that rules were stricter for daughters than sons, permitting daughters little latitude to recreate outside of the home. Sons generally had more freedom than daughters but were more frequently told to obey the law and keep out of legal trouble. A female adolescent commented on her understanding of the strict parenting:

> Eva (female adolescent): I think for us Latinos there are more restrictions at home because our parents do not exactly know how it is out there, and how other [American] people are.... They feel better if we stay home. Maybe because they do not want us to behave like [Americans] that we are [Mexicans] in other words that we don't become so liberal but rather that we remain like we were before we left Mexico. So we do not change our way of being. When you are too liberal many things can happen to you. One of them is using drugs, or having trouble with your studies. Those are things the parents fear that will happen here. They do not want that to happen, so they do not want you to go out.

Adolescents said that parental strictness caused the most parent–child conflict. Seven adolescents disagreed with the restrictions but acquiesced to their parents' decisions. It was difficult for adolescents to question their parents' decisions because these Mexican family systems strongly valued familism and respect for parents (respeto). This left the adolescents quietly simmering with conflict against parents who set the restrictive rules. Several parents reported that having their children question their decisions brought home to them the extent to which the adolescents were becoming "Americanized." One mother commented on her daughter's Americanized attitude:

> Zunilda (mother): Eva will say to me..."Well, why is that not good?" And I'll repeat, "Why is that not good?" At her age, I wouldn't dare question my parents. I wouldn't even think of it. She's questioning her parent [facial expression widened with disbelief]. I say these kids are Americanized in those ways. But I will tell her "I don't have to answer that question because I am your mother. You don't ask me to explain 'why.'" I think that correction is needed because our customs are this way.

Cultural Assets and Family Strengths After Immigration

Familism: Connection makes me Mexican. Immediate family members relied on family cohesion, trust, and mutual support to cope with stressors in the new cultural system. The concept of familism refers to a strong sense of family orientation, obligation, loyalty, and cohesion (Parra-Cardona et al., 2006). One adolescent captured the concept of familism when he expressed his devotion to his family.

> Juan (male adolescent): I think it's being close to my family. That's always a really big part of the Hispanic population, being close to the family, and the family being a priority all the time. My friends, they've always got time for school sports, being at school after school. For me, it's my family. And it's not strange. I have people say, "Why do you want to go to a party where your family's at? Don't you want to get away from them?" You know, I don't really get tired of them. I've always been really close to them. That connection to my parents, that trust that you can talk to them, that makes me Mexican.

Familism was an important cultural asset for the Mexican adolescents. Adolescents said they recreated and relaxed physically and emotionally with family members unlike with anyone else. There was a pervasive sense that the families supported the adolescents, especially during difficult times. At the same time, there were important obligations to be met. Parents said they expected respect and obedience from their children. There was a clear hierarchical structure in which parents were responsible for making decisions that adolescents were required to obey. There was a shared sense of success and failure. Parents believed their success and accomplishments were for their children. Conversely, parents would feel like they had failed if their children did not succeed. At the same time, adolescents said that their own failure becomes their parents' failure.

Both parents and adolescents said that familism provided initiative for at least some family members to become bilingual and bicultural in order to help other family members interact with the host culture. Adolescents were proud that they could help their parents navigate the new cultural system. Parents were proud of their adolescents' new cultural skills, seeing these skills as a sign their children were getting ahead. However, parents worried about how their adolescent's biculturalism would affect the family in the future. Parents were highly invested in keeping their family together and worried that the family might end up living in two different countries. One mother remarked:

> Adriana (mother): Now, if the children want to stay here, and the parents have finished educating their children and want to return to their land, that is difficult because the family doesn't stay together after all this....We come here to grab...economic security for our children, and then the family separates in two countries?...That is worrisome. And it happens at the end, when the obstacles have been overcome.

All of the parents and adolescents described familism as a core value in Mexican family life both before and after immigration. However, during the postimmigration period, familism became complex and reflected a dialectic. On the one hand, familism appeared to be strengthened after immigration because adolescents were worried about their parents' vulnerability in the new cultural system and strived to acquire new cultural skills to help their families. At the same time, family ties were more difficult to maintain because of new family circumstances with both parents working multiple jobs, distance from family left in Mexico, and uncertainty over where adolescents would live after they adjusted to life in the United States. Familism was at the heart of this ongoing dialectical tension described by both parents and adolescents.

Cultural traditions and rituals. Mexican cultural traditions and rituals were important to both parents and adolescents because they intensified the families' collective pride and identity. Adolescents said that they felt Mexican because of the traditions that they practiced. Parents said that they would never let go of their traditions and rituals that helped to build family identity and unity. Traditions and rituals centered on religious holidays. Some holidays, like Christmas, were the same religious holidays practiced in the United States, but they were celebrated differently in Mexico. There were also Mexican holidays, such as *Dia de los Muertos* [Day of the Dead] to honor deceased ancestors, and *Posadas*, which were typically not celebrated in the United States. Families tried to replicate their Mexican traditions in their homes and sometimes in their churches. The holidays did not feel quite the same without their family members who remained in Mexico. One mother shared her insights about the importance of family traditions:

> Graciela (mother): Customs and traditions have changed, yes, in the sense that I don't have my whole family here. We do celebrate Christmas, but it is not the same. Still, I wouldn't let go of my Mexican traditions. Now I must think of my family as my husband and my children. When there is a celebration where traditional foods are made, we really enjoy ourselves. There is much happiness. The traditions that I've brought from Mexico, how we celebrate holidays is very different. There is no Christmas here like there was in my town. We would begin Christmas festivities the 16th of December and continue them until January.

Maintaining cultural rituals and traditions was one way that families described staying close to their Mexican culture. Adolescents said that practicing these traditions and rituals helped them preserve their Mexican cultural identities, their history, sense of familism, and ethnic pride even as they experienced stress and pressure to assimilate from social systems outside of their homes. At the same time, the postimmigration adjustment process prompted families to adopt new traditions and rituals. Adopting and adapting U.S. cultural traditions and rituals helped the Mexican families take part in the host culture. One adolescent explained how learning celebrations and traditions was a key aspect of feeling one is a part of the host culture and was a sign of growing bicultural competencies.

> Eva (female adolescent): I like to learn about the things that the [U.S.] culture likes to celebrate, its traditions. Halloween, St. Patrick's Day, Mother's Day, all of those. These holidays are different and that is why you learn and feel a part of them, even if you are not too much a part, but you feel a part of this culture. You learn your culture and you learn other cultures, and you mix the cultures, and you can make something new out of one and the other, or you can pick the way that you like how things are done.

A mother from a different family expressed the same sentiment, explaining how her family adapts new cultural customs to participate in the host culture.

> Adriana (mother): My daughter is learning a little more English, and we can start grabbing some of their [American] customs. Like here, the first year we heard, "No work tomorrow. It's Thanksgiving." And we say among ourselves, "What's Thanksgiving?" Then the second year, we started knowing a little more of what Thanksgiving is. Little by little, we learn the customs. We know that we give thanks to God on Thanksgiving. We said, "We can do that here at home." We start grabbing a little of their customs because we live here. I think we must learn their [American] customs, and celebrate what we can of them.

Adolescents as cultural brokers. Parent–adolescent cultural differences (e.g., acculturation gaps) did not just contribute to conflicts in some of the families. All of the parents said they welcomed some aspects of acculturation in their adolescents because this helped the family meet daily needs. Adolescents paid bills, provided translation for their parents, and advised their younger siblings when their parents did not. Adolescents' growing knowledge of English placed them in a highly valued position in the family. One male adolescent commented on his new family role:

Manuel (male adolescent): My parents didn't really have to adapt because of us [pointed to himself]. We are there as their mediator between the two cultures, and when they need something, they'll say, "Can you help us out?" We don't tell them that we need this or that. We go to the bank, the doctor, the store. We [children] help them. Like at the bank, they'll say, "Say this for us." They didn't need to adapt too much. They live their way here, and when they want something from the outside, they come to us, and that's just how it is. We help them out.

Adolescents said that along with this new power came the responsibility inherent in using new cultural knowledge and language skills to assist parents. Nearly all of the adolescents said they worried about their parents being vulnerable in the new cultural system. The majority of these adolescents used this new role as cultural brokers to take a step toward maturity.

DISCUSSION

This study sought to explore three major questions: (a) how do undocumented Mexican families change after immigration, (b) how do these changes affect family members and their interactions, and (c) what factors explain postimmigration family system adjustment in undocumented families? A conceptual model explaining undocumented Mexican family adjustment was created using GTM. Past research on Latino immigrant families contends that acculturation gaps precipitate parent–adolescent relationship stress and that familism decreases with time spent in the United States (Coatsworth et al., 2002; Cortes, 1995; Szapocznik & Kurtines, 1980). If these dynamics were indeed occurring, we wanted to illuminate why they were taking place and what underlying processes were fueling these changes in parent–adolescent relationships and the family system as a whole using the conceptual model that emerged from the data.

The conceptual model shown in Figure S5.1 delineated three major domains related to postimmigration adjustment of Mexican families—the context of getting ahead, the costs of getting ahead, and coping with the costs of getting ahead. In the "context for getting ahead," all of the participating parents and adolescents said they had relocated to the United States for work opportunities and to get their children ahead by providing them with English language skills and a U.S. education. Families in this study also described a number of costs or challenges associated with getting ahead. Adolescents and mothers said that family relationships, especially relationships with fathers, were often strained and roles needed to be redefined because of lengthy separations during sequential immigration. After immigration, parents lamented having less time to spend with their children because of demanding new jobs and mothers entering the work force. Parents endured these new challenges by focusing on the future and on how their children would get ahead. In contrast, adolescents reported that decreased family time together, coupled with the loss of relationships with family members left in Mexico, left them focused on the past, feeling lonely, and mourning the losses they had experienced. The costs of getting ahead influenced Mexican family system adjustment.

Families compensated by developing strategies to cope with the costs of getting ahead. After immigration, a complex dialectic surfaced around familism. All parents and adolescents said familism continued to be of utmost importance and was even reinforced after immigration because of the new challenges to family unity. Adolescents expressed worries about their parents' vulnerability in the new cultural system, whereas parents made major sacrifices to get their children ahead. Although parents and adolescents were highly invested in familism, maintaining strong family cohesion seemed increasingly difficult while facing the challenging costs of getting ahead.

Our conceptual model helps to explain why past researchers have found familism to erode over time spent in the United States (Cortes, 1995; Rogler & Cooney, 1984) and posits new theoretical propositions for future research. Geographic separations cut family members off from the extensive network of family relationships they enjoyed in Mexico. Parents reported reluctantly having to redefine their notion of the family to emphasize relationships with immediate, nuclear members. Parents coped by focusing on the future of their children. Adolescents spent time mourning their losses but had to adjust to the new living circumstances. Their new lives in the United States consisted of nuclear family members juggling multiple jobs with far less external social support and little time to devote to one another. Despite dynamics that made it particularly difficult to maintain high levels of familism, parents and adolescents continued to stress the importance of this cultural value in their new environment. Our model suggests that family system changes (e.g., family separations, becoming a dual-earner household, spending less time together) are more strongly connected to postimmigration changes in familism than adoption of American cultural norms. Future research should examine this new proposition as an alternative to traditional assimilation hypotheses (Hirschman, 1994).

Our conceptual model also proposes that parent–adolescent acculturation gaps are more complex than previously hypothesized. Hernandez and McGoldrick (1999) reported that parent–adolescent conflicts arose from parents' insistence on maintaining culture of origin traditions in the face of their children's acculturation to the host culture—that is, from the acculturation gap (see also Szapocznik & Kurtines, 1980; Szapocznik et al., 1986). Coatsworth et al. (2002, p. 118) also asserted that parent–adolescent conflict because of acculturation gaps contributed to Latino parents having low investment in their children. In contrast, we found parent–adolescent acculturation gaps to be less problematic and no evidence to link these gaps with low parental investment. All of the parents and adolescents in this study said they wanted to maintain their Mexican traditions and reported little conflict directly because of acculturation. Instead, conflicts revolved around parents' fears of the dangers they perceived in the U.S. environment. In these families, conflicts arose when adolescents requested—and were consistently denied—permission to recreate with their Latino friends outside the home. From the adolescents' perspective, these conflicts with parents were complex because they wanted to recreate in the U.S. environment with Latino friends who shared similar cultural ways. Adolescents were not necessarily rapidly adopting U.S. cultural behaviors. Nine of 10 of the adolescents maintained high levels of involvement with their Mexican cultural norms, values, and traditions. This dynamic makes the acculturation gap between parents and adolescents more complex than if adolescents were eagerly assimilating. We propose that postimmigration parent–adolescent conflict is due more to increasingly restrictive parenting styles adopted in response to perceived dangers in the families' new environments than to acculturation gaps caused by the rapid assimilation of children.

Although the literature on parent–adolescent acculturation gaps has focused on how these gaps precipitate family stress, we found that acculturation gaps may also serve an adaptive purpose. In our interviews, all of the parents wanted their adolescents to become bicultural. Adolescents who learned English were called upon to help other family members navigate the host culture, creating a valuable new role in the family. Theoretically, we posit that adolescent development of new bicultural skills in the host culture (e.g., becoming cultural brokers) is encouraged by the family as one way to foster family system adjustment and cope with the costs of getting ahead. Future research should examine the relative contributions of these competing explanations, examining how acculturation gaps are connected to both stress and adaptation in Mexican immigrant families.

Limitations

We relied on interview data from multiple family members for this study. Family interactions were chronicled in field notes before, during, and after the interviews. Using constant comparison methods, we took great care to triangulate the data from multiple informants. Even so, there are alternative qualitative methods, such as conducting family observations, which would have yielded helpful data. Including multiple data types, such as journals and school records, would further have strengthened this study's design and should be included in future studies.

Implications for Clinical Practice and Policy for Mexican Families

Our findings support the need for the development of prevention and intervention programs for Mexican immigrant families. These programs should work to decrease acculturation stress, help families cope with postimmigration changes (e.g., becoming dual-earner households, maximizing the little time spent together), and promote cultural assets such as familism and ethnic traditions. Programs for Latino immigrant families have been developed and show promising results (see Bacallao & Smokowski, 2005, for a review; see also Coatsworth et al., 2002; Szapocznik et al., 1986) but require dissemination and further testing. Two programs in particular, Familias Unidas developed by Szapocznik et al. (Coatsworth et al.) and Entre Dos Mundos developed by Bacallao and Smokowski, adopt a family focus to address parent–adolescent cultural conflicts and enhance coping skills for handling acculturation stressors. Clinicians facilitating these programs should pay special attention to the accumulation of losses and the grieving process family members experience in being separated from family in Mexico. Clinicians should help family members address relationship issues that develop during sequential immigration and aid in creating adaptive new roles to meet postimmigration challenges.

Finally, social policymakers should consider initiatives, like guest worker programs, that would decrease acculturation stress by allowing undocumented families to come out of hiding. Many proposals for reforming immigration policies focus on border enforcement, making safe travel back and forth from Mexico increasingly difficult and dangerous. Our findings suggest that this approach increases the stress of family separations, contributing to difficulties in the postimmigration period.

CONCLUSIONS

This study delineated the ways in which the costs of getting ahead influenced the postimmigration adjustment in undocumented Mexican families who immigrated to North Carolina. Parents chose to relocate to the United States for their families' economic security and to get their children ahead with bilingual skills and a U.S. education. Immigration was a difficult and protracted event that disturbed the family's homeostasis, often requiring profound changes in the Mexican family system to reestablish equilibrium. After immigration, these families mourned the loss of family connections and familial support both in Mexico and in the United States. Families also had to adjust to becoming dual-earner households, juggling multiple jobs and stressful work conditions, which left little time for family relationships. Parents became more authoritarian in order to shield their adolescents from perceived dangers in the U.S. environment. Without extended family support that protected children in Mexico, parents were reluctant to let their adolescents recreate in the new U.S. environment with Latino friends, and this generated conflict in parent–adolescent relationships.

The families' sense of familism and maintenance of cultural traditions helped buffer families coping with the costs of getting ahead. Although familism became more difficult to maintain after immigration, this cultural value provided families with a sense of mutual obligation that delineated roles and responsibilities in meeting the challenges in their new living situations. Cultural traditions and rituals also helped families preserve their ethnic pride and develop bicultural competencies.

Because the number of undocumented immigrants continues to rise, we need to learn more about how undocumented families function. Having a deeper understanding of undocumented family processes will guide efforts to help individuals and families like these who are trying to "get ahead" and will aid in fashioning programs and policies for reducing the costs of getting ahead.

REFERENCES

Bacallao, M. L., & Smokowski, P. R. (2005). Entre Dos Mundos: Bicultural skills training with Latino immigrant families. *Journal of Primary Prevention, 26,* 485–509.

Charmaz, K. (2000). Grounded theory: Objectivist and constructivist methods. In N. K. Denzin & Y. S. Lincoln (Eds.), *Handbook of qualitative research* (2nd ed., pp. 509–535). Thousand Oaks, CA: Sage.

Coatsworth, J. D., Pantin, H., & Szapocznik, J. (2002). Familias Unidas: A family-centered ecodevelopmental intervention to reduce risk for problem behavior among Hispanic adolescents. *Clinical Child and Family Psychology Review, 5*(2), 113–132.

Cooley, C. (2001). The relationship between familism and child maltreatment in Latino and Anglo families. *Child Maltreatment, 6*(2), 130–142.

Cortes, D. E. (1995). Variations in familism in two generations of Puerto Ricans. *Hispanic Journal of Behavioral Sciences, 17,* 249–256.

García Coll, C., & Magnuson, K. (2001). The psychological experience of immigration: A developmental perspective. In M. M. Suarez-Orozco, C. Suarez-Orozco, & D. Quin Hilliard (Eds.), *Interdisciplinary perspectives on the new immigration: Vol. 4. The new immigrant and the American family* (pp. 69–110). New York: Routledge.

Gil, A., Wagner, E., & Vega, W. (2000). Acculturation, familism, and alcohol use among Latino adolescent males: Longitudinal relations. *Journal of Community Psychology, 28,* 443–458.

Hernandez, M., & McGoldrick, M. (1999). Migration and the family life cycle. In B. Carter & M. McGoldrick (Eds.), *The expanded family life cycle: Individual, family, and social perspectives* (3rd ed., pp. 169–184). Needham Heights, MA: Allyn & Bacon.

Hirschman, C. (1994). Problems and prospects of studying immigrant adaptation from the 1990 population census: From generational comparisons to the process of "becoming American." *International Migration Review, 28,* 690–711.

LaRossa, R. (2005). Grounded theory methods and qualitative family research. *Journal of Marriage and Family, 67,* 837–857.

Parra-Cardona, J. R., Bulock, L. A., Imig, D. R., Villarruel, F. A., & Gold, S. J. (2006). "Trabajando duro todos los dias": Learning from the experiences of Mexican-origin migrant families. *Family Relations, 55,* 361–375.

Passel, J. S. (2005). Estimates of the size and characteristics of the undocumented population. Retrieved March 3, 2006, http://pewhispanic.org/files/reports/44.pdf

Patton, M. (2002). *Qualitative research and evaluation methods* (3rd ed.). Thousand Oaks, CA: Sage.

Portes, A., & Rumbaut, R. G. (2001). *Legacies: The story of the immigrant second generation.* Berkeley: University of California Press.

Rogler, L. H., & Cooney, R. S. (1984). *Puerto Rican families in New York City: Intergenerational processes.* Maplewood, NJ: Waterfront.

Szapocznik, J., & Kurtines, W. M. (1980). *Acculturation, biculturalism and adjustment among Cuban Americans.* In A. Padilla (Ed.), Acculturation: Theory, models, and some new findings (pp. 139–159). Boulder, CO: Praeger.

Szapocznik, J., Santisteban, D., Kurtines, W. M., Perez-Vidal, A., & Hervis, O. (1986). Bicultural effectiveness training (BET): An experimental test of an intervention modality for families experiencing intergenerational/intercultural conflict. *Hispanic Journal of Behavioral Sciences, 8,* 303–330.

6

HUMAN ECOLOGICAL THEORY

Maneeya is 25 years old with two young children, a daughter named Ansley who is 3 years old and a son named Najac who is 11 months of age. Maneeya is a housekeeper for a large hotel in Haiti. Prior to the earthquake, Maneeya and her children lived with her mother Yanik, a widow, in a very modest two-room house in Port-au-Prince. The house was deteriorating and located in a crime-infested part of the city, but there were people who were worse off. Before the earthquake, Yanik tended Ansley and Najac while Maneeya put in long hours cleaning rooms at the hotel. Yanik was able to make crafts to supplement their income. Their life was hard, without a doubt, but the earthquake has made it unbearable. Although they recognize that they were among the fortunate ones to have survived the massive rumblings, Maneeya and her family now reside among a plethora of make-shift tents in which millions of others huddle. The children have only a couple of small toys, and not an hour goes by that Maneeya and Yanik don't fear for their safety. There have been multiple reports of sexual assaults on children and adults alike. With massive damage to the hotel, Maneeya has not been able to work. The disruption in Maneeya's miniscule income has made her and her mother feel more desperate.

HISTORY

Human ecology theory concentrates on the interaction and interdependence of humans—as biological and social entities—with the environment (Bubolz and Sontag, 1993). Rooted in a systems perspective, ecological theory acknowledges the interrelatedness among components of human systems. Thus, individuals and families need to be examined within the context of their environments, recognizing that each influences and is changed by the other.

Ecological sciences emerged in the late 1800s, about the time of Darwin's evolutionary theory. In fact, in 1873, Ernest Haeckel proposed the need for a science "to study organisms in their environment" (Clark 1973, 39). A German zoologist and early evolutionist who coined the names of about 12 new sciences, Haeckel named this science "oekologie," the Greek root *oik* meaning house or place to reside.

Although Haeckel never developed the science of oekologie himself, American chemist Ellen Swallow Richards did. As the first female student at MIT, Swallow Richards was a pioneer in proposing a science of the environment, with primary emphasis on home and family. With her chemistry background, she began by studying water quality (e.g., streams, water supply, sewage, water purity), and later added air quality and circulation; sanitation and waste disposal; preservation, handling, storage, additives, and cooking of food; nutrition; clothing appropriate to one's environment; and efficient and economic furnishing and housing. Among her many accomplishments, Swallow Richards was appointed the first female science consultant to industry, where she pioneered innovative health, safety, and environmental quality measures. She also crusaded for women's access to higher education; publicly proclaimed the science of oekology in 1892; introduced "nutrition lunches" in schools and other public facilities; was among the original home oekologists at Lake Placid in 1908 when they voted to call themselves home economists; and served as the first president of the American Home Economics Association (Clarke 1973). Most importantly, Ellen Swallow Richards envisioned oekology as a means to improve people's lives within their environments and focused many of her educational efforts on women.

In 1916, five years after Swallow Richards's death, Robert Wollcott and C. V. Shreve founded the Ecological Society of America, which provided an interdisciplinary professional home to those in life sciences and other traditions (Clark 1973). In the early 1920s, Robert E. Park and Ernest W. Burgess embraced "human ecology" in the field of sociology (Hook and Paolucci 1970). However, during the 1960s and 1970s, there was a more generalized, resurgent international interest in the relationship between life and the environment, with a growing awareness of global population growth, the degradation of the environment, and the depletion of natural resources. As a result, although Ellen Swallow Richards is credited as the founder of human ecology and home economics as the field of its origin, many social sciences came to embrace an ecological perspective (Bubolz and Sontag 1993).

As a professor within the College of Home Economics at Michigan State University, Beatrice Paolucci was instrumental in rejuvenating an ecological perspective in the study of families. Hook and Paolucci's (1970) seminal article, entitled "The Family as an Ecosystem," enumerated a variety of concepts that became foundational for future applications of ecological theory in family studies. They viewed the family as a "life support system," dependent upon the natural environment for physical sustenance and social environments for fostering humanness and furnishing quality and meaning to life (316). Paolucci and colleagues (1977) went on to develop an ecological model for family decision making that highlights the interdependence of the microenvironment (family decisions) with decisions in the macroenvironment. Through the decisions they make, families affect both their own destiny and that of all humanity.

Urie Bronfenbrenner (1979, 1989) was the Jacob Gould Schurman Professor in Human Development at Cornell University and one of the most well-known contributors to the ecological theory of human development. He raised awareness of "contextual variation in human development" and the need for "ecological validity" in human development research (Bronfenbrenner 1977, 515; Darling 2007, 203). He envisioned ecological environments as an arrangement of nested structures, similar to Russian *matryoshka* dolls, with each contained within the next. Particularly concerned about child development, Bronfenbrenner examined the interface of children and their multiple environments (i.e., home, school, and community). Bronfenbrenner helped to enlarge the study of children from concentrating on their genetic and biological capacities to how they are also affected by the influences of their home, school, and neighborhood environments.

Bronfenbrenner outlined four basic systems that make up the ecological environment. The first, the *microsystem*, represents the immediate environment of the developing person. For a child, microsystems would include the family, school, day care center, and religious center. The environment itself interacts with the age, health, sex, genetic predispositions, and other aspects of the individual child. Because of this, a child's behavior will vary based on the microsystem or the environment. The second level, the *mesosystem*, recognizes the links that exist between two or more microsystems. Various components of the developing person's environment are not independent, but interact with each other and with the components of the next system as well. So, an adolescent may learn something at school that will make the home environment better. Or an adopted child's biological and adoptive families may interface in ways that affect the child, ultimately also shaping these familial contexts.

The *exosystem* is composed of those settings or institutions not experienced directly by the child, but which affect his or her development in less direct ways. Examples include the neighborhood, government agencies, the work world, informal social networks, communication and transportation systems, and the media. So, if a parent has a bad day at work, even though the child never entered that workplace or environment, he or she may be affected by the bad mood of the parent when the parent gets home. Beyond that is the *macrosystem*, which includes the customs, attitudes, ideologies, values, and laws of the culture in which the developing person lives. It encompasses all the other systems. Individual lives are affected on a daily basis by laws such as speed limits, over which there is no personal control. All of these systems must be understood and taken into account if one is to have a full understanding of a child's development.

Bronfenbrenner's theoretical work continued to evolve over his academic career. One important refinement integrated the notion of *time*. Development within the individual and within the environment occurs throughout the entire life course. More specifically, future personal development must be examined in relation to an individual's developmental history, as well as the changes in their environment over time. Thus, development occurs within the context of a *chronosystem*.

Concerned that researchers lost sight of the developing **person** in their emphasis on **context**, Bronfenbrenner's later works examined more closely the impact of genetic influences on development. Introducing a "Process-Person-Context-Time (PPCT) model," Bronfenbrenner (1995) encouraged the simultaneous investigation of the variability in developmental processes as a function of process, person, context, and time. Tudge and colleagues (2009) offer a succinct overview of the PPCT model. Progressively more complex reciprocal interchanges between an evolving, dynamic person and the objects, persons, and symbols in the external environment constitute *proximal processes*. As primary facilitators of development, proximal processes are enduring patterns of interaction, particularly within parent–child and child–child activities, like group or solitary play, reading, and learning new skills.

While engaging in these activities and interactions, children "make sense of their world and their place within it, changing the prevailing order while fitting into the existing one" (200). *Person* denotes the personal characteristics (biological, genetic) that an individual carries into any social situation. There are three types of personal characteristics: *demand* characteristics (variables like age, gender, personal appearance, and skin tone that act as an immediate stimulus to those encountered); *resource* characteristics (mental and emotional characteristics, like skills and intelligence, that are not immediately apparent but can emerge from demand characteristics); and *force* characteristics (differences in motivation, persistence, and temperament that impact developmental trajectories). *Context* or environment represents the four nested systems outlined earlier: the microsystem, mesosystem, exosystem, and macrosystem. *Time* represents the constancy and change for the individual and environments. *Micro-time* represents what is happening during a particular activity or interaction. *Meso-time* is the degree to which activities and interactions occur with some regularity within particular environments. *Macro-time*, or the chronosystem, represents the historical events (e.g., act of terrorism, economic depression) happening at particular ages that might ultimately affect the development trajectory of individuals in different cohorts.

In his final major work, published the year of his death, *Making Human Beings Human: Bioecological Perspectives on Human Development*, Bronfenbrenner (2005) transitioned from using the term *ecology* to the term *bioecology*. One possible reason for this change in term usage is that it "re-emphasizes the interaction between the biological and the ontological character of development with the social character of development" (White and Klein, 2008, 260).

BASIC ASSUMPTIONS

White and Klein (2008) and Bubolz and Sontag (1993) articulated the following key assumptions of ecological theory.

Human beings and groups are a product of both genetics and environment. Both biology and the spatial and biophysical environment affect the developing person, affirming the importance of both nature and nurture. Maximal human development is dependent on successful nature–nurture interaction. Based on this notion, if you have two people of equal intelligence, it is no wonder that the one who has unlimited access to resources such as money, education, and mentorship will follow a very different occupational path than the one who is often hungry, lacks role models, and is unable to attend college. Although their genetic tendencies might be the same, their lives may have very different outcomes based on the richness (or lack thereof) of their environments. Environments have the capacity to enhance possibilities for individuals and families, as well as impose limits and constraints on their behavior and development as just noted.

Humans are dependent upon their environment to meet their biological needs. Although technological advances have enhanced the possibility of human survival in some pretty desolate and uninviting environments, people still need air, water, food and other basic amenities in order to live in particular geographical contexts. It can also be said that the quality of human life is interdependent with the quality of the environment. Thus, individuals and families should make careful decisions relative to attaining their goals in order to preserve environmental assets. The earthquake in the vignette at the beginning of this chapter has put Maneeya and her family at risk of not being able to meet their biological needs in their current environment.

As social beings, humans are dependent on others. Human beings have the capacity to enrich environments by caring for one another and developing capacities, like language, that are essential to human interactions. All of the world's peoples are interdependent as well, because the continuation of the earth's life-sustaining resources is dependent on the consumption patterns and decisions made by individuals, families, and nations. The need to live together, both with other human beings and the environment, has generated some basic moral values of human ecology. This is why people in some countries come to the aid of people in other countries when catastrophes strike and needs are great. For instance, we hope that people like Maneeya and her family will experience international relief support after the earthquake in Haiti as people of the world unite in mutually caring for others in need.

Human beings are finite, such that time is both a limitation and a resource. Over the course of the life cycle, there are universal changes common to human beings (ontogenetic development). Within this context, time constrains and enables the evolution of a population, and helps us better understand individual behaviors and social arrangements. An ecological perspective facilitates the examination of how individuals and families carry out their various functions for themselves and society's greater good over time. Families are semi-open, dynamic, and goal-directed, capable of changing and modifying their environment as well as adapting to it.

Humans organize their interactions within their spatial environments. Distinct spatial arrangements channel human interactions in particular ways. For instance, masses of housing in one area of a city, industrial parks in another, and arrangements of streets and sidewalks route humans in particular ways within their human-built environment. Physical and biological laws of nature (e.g., entropy) and human-derived rules (e.g., social norms, resource consumption, power distribution) guide family–environment interactions. Thus, the behavior of someone in a rural village in Africa is perhaps different than the behavior of someone in downtown Chicago because of their different spatial environments. Behaviors acceptable in one environment would probably not be acceptable in the other one.

Human behavior can be comprehended on at least two levels: individual and population. At the individual level of analysis, researchers might be interested in the extent to which individuals adapt or fail to adapt to their environment. An organism's failure to modify itself or adapt in response to its environment might result in the organism's death. At the population level of analysis, attention might be given to the spatial organization or distribution of characteristics among groups. The evolution of a healthy gene pool and the ability to continue to survive on available environmental resources would be of concern and represent natural selection.

PRIMARY TERMS AND CONCEPTS

Bubolz and Sontag (1993) offer the following helpful delineation of primary concepts.

Human Ecosystem

A human ecosystem is an organism that operates as a unit in interaction with its environment. More specifically, a family ecosystem, a type of human ecosystem, contains a particular family system in interaction with its environment. However, human ecosystems can also be analyzed at the community, societal, or global levels (Bubolz and Sontag 1993). Bronfenbrenner's (1979) delineation of the individual or family as "nested" systems (i.e., microsystem, mesosystem, exosystem, and macrosystem) continues to serve as one of the most useful conceptions of the interrelationships of human ecosystems.

Niche

Niches exist within human ecosystems. Within niches are reiterative patterns of stable sets of activities. These actions provide functions for those within a niche, so that they can adapt to the environment. According to White and Klein (2008), the family inhabits a niche in all human systems by nurturing and supporting its members, while also maintaining reproductive, economic, and social organization for the larger society. A niche is akin to Bronfenbrenner's (1979) notion of molar activity.

Environment

An environment "consists of the totality of the physical, biological, social, economic, political, aesthetic, and structural surroundings for human beings and the context for their behavior and development" (Bubolz and Sontag 1993, 432). The environment offers essential elements for the maintenance of life (Hook and Paolucci, 1970). There are three types of environments with which humans interact. The natural physical–biological environment includes elements of nature like animals, climate, soil, plants, air, minerals, water, and sources of food and energy. The human-built environment represents the ways in which humans have altered or transformed the natural physical–biological environment (e.g., bridges, roads, dense housing, logging, cultivated land, hydroelectric plants) to survive or to sustain themselves. The socio-cultural environment includes other human beings (e.g., other children who make up a particular class in school), abstract cultural constructions (e.g., language, laws, morals, cultural values), and social and economic institutions (e.g., marriage, political systems, economic markets).

Ontogenetic Development

Change generated from within the organism itself is often precipitated by ontogenetic development. It represents the biologically inclined or genetic part of development or aging. Ecological theory posits, however, that internal or ontogenetic development is intimately linked to environmental factors that enhance or diminish developmental capabilities. Thus, one cannot easily disentangle the relationship between genetics and the environment.

Adaptation

As the core concept of ecological theory, adaptation represents the ways in which human organisms (e.g., individuals, families) modify their systems to accommodate to and/or alter their environments to obtain particular outcomes. Human values, decision-making processes, actions, and selective perception affect adaptation, because continuing survival, quality of life, and environmental conservation all depend on the ways and means by which humans attain their goals and satisfy their needs (Bubolz and Sontag, 1993). Thus, as a result of adaptation, human systems are changed, as are their environments.

Needs

Needs are the requirements essential for survival and adaptation. Allardt (1976) identified three types of needs: the need for having, the need for relating, and the need for being. The need for having suggests that possessing information and resources necessary for sustenance is essential. The need for relating encompasses being loved and loving, being valued and accepted by others, and being able to communicate with others. The need for being includes growth, development, fulfillment, and a sense of satisfaction with one's identity and life. The needs of individuals and families must be analyzed within the contexts of their respective ecosystems.

Values

Values are human appraisals of what is desirable, worthwhile, and proper. Values articulate what is beautiful (aesthetic values), what is useful (pragmatic values), what is profitable (economic values), what is correct and decent behavior (moral values), and what is beyond human life and understanding (spiritual values) (Jacobson 1970, 1). It is essential to identify individual and family values, as well as those present within the social-cultural environment in which they exist, in order to better understand decisions made and actions taken. Values lend meaning to life and help to shape goals and provide direction.

Management

Management entails all of the processes surrounding the acquisition, distribution, and utilization of resources essential for attaining human goals. Families make decisions about which goals are set, how plans are implemented, and how evaluative feedback is utilized in future management decisions.

Decision-making

Decision-making is a key aspect of family functioning. Fundamental decision-making processes include "(1) recognizing that a decision is needed, (2) identifying, comparing, and evaluating alternatives, and (3) choosing an acceptable alternative" (Bubolz and Sontag 1993, 436). In the vignette at the beginning of the chapter, Maneeya and Yanik needed to make numerous decisions in a relatively short period of time in response to the earthquake. They had to decide where to take the children and themselves. They also had to figure out how they were going to obtain their basic needs, like shelter and food. In the process, Maneeya and Yanik had to evaluate the limited number of options before them and choose the most acceptable ones.

Human Development

Human development is the process that maturing persons undergo as they perceive, differentiate themselves from, and behave in relation to their environment in increasingly complex ways (Bronfenbrenner, 1979). Both developing individuals and the environments in which they find themselves are dynamic, each changing in response to the other. For individuals, the family is a crucial microsystem for development, just as mesosystems (e.g., relationships between home and work), exosystems (e.g., neighborhoods), and macrosystems (e.g., values, social conditions) are influential forces on human development.

Quality of Human Life and Quality of Environment

For human beings, quality of life is determined by the adequacy of basic needs and the attainment of goals. Quality of life can be evaluated, both subjectively and objectively, at individual (e.g., feelings of satisfaction versus dissatisfaction, personal health indicators), familial (e.g., marital satisfaction, housing quality), and societal levels (e.g., rates of unemployment and poverty, access to health care). High-quality environments for humans would likely be secure, rich in resources, supportive, and aesthetically pleasing, among other things. In the chapter's opening vignette, the current quality of environment for Maneeya, Yanik, and the children is, by most objective measures, poor. Their housing is inadequate, the community is not safe, and they are feeling desperate.

COMMON AREAS OF RESEARCH AND APPLICATION

Scholarship utilizing an ecological perspective has been prolific over the last decade. As was noted in the history section, Bronfenbrenner's theory evolved over the years as he sought to modify, expand, and enhance it. Still, much of the work done uses the more traditional form of his theory. Because of the breadth of this theory, the review of research for this chapter is organized first on the part/version of the theory being used and then by topical areas. We first review articles that focus on parts of the theory, then on those areas that have utilized the entire systems of context, and we close with a few articles that apply the PPCT model.

Microsystem and Environmental Interactions

One area that utilized an ecological model is the study of how one's definition of family changes over the life cycle for a woman who never marries. Although our cultural norm has been that of courtship and marriage as a natural part of the life course, this is not a reality for some women. A recent article reflects on the microsystem explanations for this, such as a tendency for these women to have parents who died before they were 25 years of age, as well as other family members who never married, thus providing a positive role model for this behavior. The participants in this study had high levels of self-esteem, were confident and happy in their lives, and felt that perhaps a change in the chronosystem beliefs concerning perceptions about women in their 40s who never married is in process (McDill, Hall, and Turrell, 2006). McDill, Hall, and Turrell (2006) suggested that there may be an intergenerational pattern in that women who never married often have family members who have been positive role models for this life choice.

Similarly, Sipsma, Biello, Cole-Lewis, and Kershaw (2010) suggest that an intergenerational cycle of adolescent fatherhood exists. Although there is a good deal of research on adolescent parenting from the female's perspective, this is a unique look at the topic from the fathers' perspective. An ecological perspective suggests that individual variables, such as delinquency and dating at an early age, interact with family variables, such as maternal education, to increase the chances of adolescent fathering. The interactions of the microsystems were used to explain risk behaviors and increased probability of adolescent fathering (Sipsma et al. 2010).

Regardless of the age of the parent, the transition to parenting can be a complex and stressful time. Perry-Jenkins and Claxton (2011) studied the transition to parenthood using an ecological model to examine the microlevel proximal processes that take place as couples transition to becoming parents, as well as the cultural influences on this developmental period. It is well known that women experience a decline in marital satisfaction after childbirth, and although this has been explored at a microlevel, the authors suggest that these variables need to be explored within the context of the environment. Thus, while work hours, leisure time, social support, and division of labor are important considerations, things such as religiosity, ethnicity, racial differences, social class, and gender are important moderators. Using an ecological model helps us to understand the interactions of these variables.

A final example of research primarily using a microlevel perspective is a study that focuses on adolescents in self-care, which means that they are at home alone for at least part of the day after school. Shumow, Smith, and Smith (2009) found that adolescents in self-care were more likely to have academic and school behavior problems. This is true whether or not self-care is the primary arrangement after school. It was also found that they tend to have more problems with grades than they do with behavior problems, and the authors suggest that it is because of the roles, relationships, and activities within the microsystems, as these are the things that influence child development.

Ecological Systems Theory

Program Development/Intervention

Bronfenbrenner's ecological systems theory has been used a great deal to study the development and usefulness of various programs and interventions. For example, Duerden and Witt (2010) used this model to explain how practitioners could ensure that their programs are developmentally appropriate, engaging, and effective by looking at each level of the system and providing suggestions for program enhancement.

They provide key components of programs for youth, questions that should be considered, and examples of best practices within each level of the model.

Other researchers have looked at specific programs and used ecological theory to assess the success of a particular program. For example, Martin (2010) reviews the Early Start project in Ireland for its ability to improve academic and social outcomes for students who are at risk of being disadvantaged in the educational system. This is similar to the work done by others in the United States studying Head Start programs (Sigel 2004). The authors found great support for the use of such programs, because of their ability to show long-term, positive outcomes for children, as well as their ability to show the importance of the inclusion of programming that considers the impacts on children within each level of the ecological model. Similar work was done by Lin and Bates (2010) in the United States on just one aspect of the Head Start program—home visits. They found that, although home visits exist within the mesosystem (the interaction of home and school), they have significant impact on the teacher's understanding of each child's exosystem and macrosystems as well. Such insights can help teachers provide a more effective classroom environment for their students.

There are many other types of programs that have been assessed using this model across a wide variety of topics and fields of study. For example, Campbell, Patterson, and Fehler-Cabral (2010) used an ecological model to assess the effectiveness of a sexual-assault nurse-examiner program, which is developed and delivered by individuals embedded within the community rather than by researchers. It is their position that interventions should come from within the community rather than from outside. Whereas most programs start at the individual level and work outward through the model, this approach begins at the community level and works inward. They suggest that the most effective programs are those that are based on the naturally existing interdependence of the systems of which we are a part. Leu (2008) uses the same basic idea—that each of the systems of which we are a part should be included when developing a program—to study the effectiveness of music education in Taiwan. She outlines the benefits of music education for children within each system and provides recommendations for educational policies and practices in this area.

Multidimensional Constructs

Although this theory is useful in analyzing programs because of its ability to look at a wide variety of systems and potential influences, this benefit also extends to the exploration of other complex problems. Thus, research on multidimensional constructs, such as challenges related to the adoption of special-needs children and the role of physical appearance in Latino adolescents' ethnic identity, was conducted. Schweiger and O'Brien (2005) examined the interactions of Bronfenbrenner's ecological systems as they pertain to the adoption process for special-needs children, as well as providing suggestions for adoption services both before and after adoption takes places. This theoretical model is especially helpful because of the complex interactions between individuals, adoptive families, school and community environments, and legal systems. This is made even more complex by the cultural beliefs about adoption in general and, more specifically, children with special needs. The same complex interplay across the levels of analysis exists when studying the attainment of ethnic identity for Latino youth, because there are adjustments at the individual level, numerous mesosystem interactions, the role of the environment, and the laws that predicate the immigration of this population. Gonzales-Backen and Umana-Taylor (2010) focus specifically on the bidirectional nature of the individual variables and the multiple contextual variables that affect this process.

Violence and Abuse

A good deal of research has used an ecological model to understand the role of violence and abuse in a wide variety of cultural environments. The work of Hong, Lee, Park, and Faller (2011), based on a study conducted in Korea, exemplifies research on why children are mistreated. They used an ecological model because, although there is a good deal of research in this culture on the risk factors for an individual associated with child maltreatment, there is less research that looks at other contextual variables across the levels of the environment. This study looks at risks factors within each system and provides suggestions for developing more effective interventions. Similarly, Hong, Kim, Yoshihama, and Byoun (2010) assessed the issue of why wife-battering takes place in South Korea. They expanded previous research on individual risk and protective factors of batterers and victims to include social and cultural factors that contribute to this behavior, while also advocating for the necessity of providing intervention and education for those within other systems levels that are affected by this national social problem.

Intimate partner violence, such as that examined in South Korea, is often misunderstood, because women in this situation are often criticized for "allowing" the behavior to happen and for not simply leaving an unsafe environment. Bliss, Cook, and Kaslow (2006) address this question by studying women who have been victims of partner violence to determine their strategic responses to the violence and the influence of each system on their behaviors. Their study reveals, as one would expect, that this is a very complex issue that cannot be understood by looking only at individual, or microlevel, variables.

But does one have to experience physical violence to be affected by it? Interesting research by Cummings et al. (2010) on the effects of political violence in Northern Ireland on children's adjustment suggests that being exposed to violence, even if not directly, can affect children's adjustment. Although they focused specifically on political violence, one might suggest that these findings could be extrapolated to children exposed to situational violence in other contexts, such as those described for Maneeya's children in the vignette that starts this chapter. This research would suggest that Maneeya's children, even though not yet directly victims of violence, will suffer from feelings of anxiety, depression, stress, problems with school, increased participation in aggressive and violent acts, and emotional insecurity and internalizing problems, much as the children who lived in an area threatened by political violence did.

Process-Person-Context-Time (PPCT) Model

Whether because little is known about it or because it has yet to be sufficiently empirically tested and applied, the latest refinement of Bronfenbrenner's model, PPCT, is not frequently used in the field (Tudge, Hatfield, and Karnik, 2009). However, there were two studies that utilized this version recently to study diverse topics.

Berzin et al. (2006) used this framework to assess the role of poverty on child outcomes. They explain that it is not only poverty itself that affects children, but also the process by which poverty occurs. They use this as a backdrop to study how parental reliance on welfare during childhood impacts the child's subsequent transition to adulthood. Interestingly, Holt et al. (2007) used this same idea of parental influence within the backdrop of a larger context to examine the role of the effects of parental behavior on youth's participation in competitive sports. It is not just the parent's level of involvement that matters, but also their involvement in other areas, such sports team policies, verbal supportiveness, whether or not parents were empathetic with their children, the intensity of the crowd, and the parent's knowledge of the sport. Although these are drastically different topics of study, they were able to employ the same theoretical grounding because of its ability to address the importance of context.

This is just a sampling of the research that is out there using the diverse manifestations of ecological theory. This demonstrates the utility of the theory, its ability to provide context for complex topics, and its usefulness in research, program development, and program evaluation.

CRITIQUE

The use of ecological theory in all of its variations continues to be prominent in the field of family science, as is evident in the extensive diversity of research topics just covered. However, just because a theory is frequently used does not mean that it is without potential shortcomings. This review, though not exhaustive, covers those areas of concern stated most frequently in the literature.

As you can tell from reading this chapter, ecological theory is one of the most broad and inclusive theories in human development. Although this is frequently cited as a strong point of the model, some also feel this is a weakness. The inclusion of so many systems, concepts, terms, and assumptions leaves one wondering what is outside the boundaries of this theory and what limits, if any, have been set for its applicability.

Similarly, the use of so many frequently abstract, terms, concepts, and primary assumptions leads to the possibility of confusion and repetition. For example, this chapter provides only a basic outline of the theory as it has progressed over the years and focuses on those terms and assumptions most commonly used throughout the field. However, a more in-depth exploration of the theory presents a plethora of concepts that were not reviewed here. Some of these terms are similar in nature, and some of them are not. All of this leads to a theory that is both very wide in its scope and has some terms and concepts that are difficult to understand and apply. The use of a more common core of terminology that is clearly defined would help solve this problem.

Another potential problem with a theory so all-encompassing is that it can be difficult to test using traditional research methods (Bubolz and Sontag 1993). Of particular concern is the issue of how to choose the unit of analysis when conducting research (Klein and White 1996). If one is going to focus on the entire context of a situation, should the unit of analysis be each individual, the family, the school system, or the geographic region? The theory one uses guides the research questions, including the unit of analysis. In this case, the theory does not give us clear guidance on which system is most important or which system should be the focus of the study, making it difficult in some situations to determine the appropriate unit of analysis.

Similarly, if one is to truly assess each system within the context, data collection becomes a very complex process. Theoretically, data should be included from each part of the system. Do you have to use the same methods with each system? How do you develop studies that adequately and similarly address the issues of importance across multiple settings and multiple types of participants? Do we have statistical models that are sophisticated enough to handle this many levels of analysis? Many researchers answer these questions by doing a mixed-methods study, but this presents its own challenges when it comes to synthesizing and analyzing data (Bubolz and Sontag, 1993).

It was stated in the history section and mentioned again in the research section that this theory has gone through several revisions over the years, which is one of its strengths. Bronfenbrenner was known for being very critical of his own work, and he made changes and modifications throughout his career to the core of his original theory that was developed in 1979 and is the work primarily presented in this chapter (Tudge, Mokrova, Hatfield, and Karnik 2009). Using theoretical underpinnings in research is one of the primary ways in which theories grow and develop over time, and one of the purposes of using a theoretical perspective when we conduct research is to foster this growth. However, this theory has undergone so much modification and development that it is not often evident at first glance which version of his theory is being used in any research that states it is based on ecological theory. The Common Areas of Research and Application section is a perfect example of this; it is first broken down by whether scholars used parts or all of the theory, and then by whether the research used the four different contextual systems or the PPCT model. Tudge et al. conducted a literature review in 2009, which found that, although the PPCT model is the newest version of this theory, only 4 of the 25 papers they reviewed used it in its entirety. So, when you see the term "ecological theory," keep in mind that there are many ways it can be represented in the literature.

Despite these issues, this is a theory that is still being used in the field, especially in the area of child development. Although there are methodological issues and complications with research design, it gives us the ability to study complex issues across multiple systems that allow for the development of more descriptive and encompassing explanations for human experiences. Whether one uses Bronfenbrenner's classical version of the theory or the newer version, which adds the importance of process to the equation, ecological theory provides a framework for the exploration of the interactions of genetics, individuals, and their various environments.

APPLICATION

1. Using the sample reading that follows as a guide, think of a problem or situation in your life that involves more than just you. How could you use the different contextual systems to help you deal with this situation? How could the addition of the PPCT model strengthen your analysis?

2. Answer the following questions based on the vignette at the beginning of this chapter:

   a. Discuss the importance of the chronosystem, and provide some examples of it in this family. If you were to place the family in a different time period, would it change their situation? Why or why not?

   b. Imagine what their microsystems, mesosystems, exosystems, and macrosystems are like and describe them.

   c. Consider the physical–biological, human-built, and sociocultural environments for Maneeya's family. Describe them.

   d. Using several measures of quality of human life and quality of environment, assess Maneeya's situation.

   e. Describe the ontogenetic developmental capacities of each of the family members and how the environment impacts those outcomes.

   f. Based on the assumption that "humans are dependent on each other," articulate why we should feel compelled to be concerned about and responsive to the welfare of others.

3. How do you feel about the basic assumption that "human beings and groups are a product of both genetics and environment"? Does this theory provide enough support for the idea that both of these are important, in your opinion? What parts of the theory support this notion? What do you wish the theory addressed with regard to this concept?

4. Bronfenbrenner refers to the family as having a niche. How is this niche different now than it was 100 years ago? Do you think this niche will be different 100 years from now? If so, how would you predict it will change?

5. Humans are said to have three needs. Using the language of the theory, what could happen if these needs are not met? How would this affect the individual across each contextual system?

6. List as many of your "values" as possible. Identify how these values affect your life and choices within each ecosystem. How have your values affected your interactions with your environments? How have your values affected your adaptation?

REFERENCES

Allardt, E. 1976. Dimensions of welfare in a comparative Scandinavian study. *Acta Sociologica* 19: 227–239.

Berzin, S. C., A. C. De Marco, T. V. Shaw, G. J. Unick, and S. R. Hogan. 2006. The effect of parental work history and public assistance use on the transition to adulthood. *Journal of Sociology and Social Welfare* 33(1): 141–162.

Bliss, M. J., S. L. Cook, and N. J. Kaslow. 2007. An ecological approach to understanding incarcerated women's responses to abuse. *Women and Therapy* 29(3): 97–115.

Bronfenbrenner, U. 1977. Toward an experimental ecology of human development. *American Psychologist 32*: 513–531.

Bronfenbrenner, U. 1979. *The ecology of human development: Experiments by nature and design.* Cambridge, MA: Harvard University Press.

Bronfenbrenner, U. 1989. Ecological systems theory. In R. Vasta (Ed.), *Annals of child development* (Vol. 6, pp. 187–249). Greenwich, CT: JAI.

Bronfenbrenner, U. 1995. Developmental ecology through space and time: A future perspective (pp. 619–647). In P. Moen, G. H. Elder, and K. Luscher (Eds.), *Examining lives in context: Perspectives on the ecology of human development*. Washington, DC: American Psychological Association.

Bronfenbrenner, U. (Ed.). 2005. *Making human beings: Bioecological perspectives on human development*. Thousand Oaks, CA: Sage.

Bronfenbrenner, U., and A. C. Crouter. 1983. The evolution of environmental models in developmental research. In P. H. Mussen (Ed.). *Handbook of child psychology: Vol. 1. History, theory and methods* (4th ed.) (pp. 357–414). New York: Wiley.

Bubolz, M. M., and M.S. Sontag. 1993. Human ecology theory. In P. G. Boss, W. J. Doherty, R. LaRossa, W. R. Schumm, and S. K. Steinmetz (Eds.), *Sourcebook of family theories and methods: A contextual approach* (419–448). New York: Plenum Press.

Campbell, R., D. Patterson, and G. Fehler-Cabral. 2010. Using ecological theory to evaluate the effectiveness of an indigenous community intervention: A study of Sexual Assault Nurse Examiner (SANE) programs. *American Journal of Community Psychology* 46(3–4): 263–276.

Clark, R. 1973. *Ellen Swallow: The woman who founded ecology*. Chicago: Follett Publishing.

Cosner-Berzin, S., A. C. De Marco, T. V. Shaw, G. J.Unick, and S. R. Hogan. 2006. The effect of parental work history and public assistance use on the transition to adulthood. *Journal of Sociology and Social Welfare* 33(1): 141–162.

Cummings, E. M., C. E. Merrilees, A .C. Shermerhorn, M. C. Goeke-Morey, P. Shirlow, and E. Cairns. 2010. Testing a social ecological model for relations between political violence and child adjustment in North Ireland. *Development and Psychopathology*, 22(2), 405–418.

Darling, N. 2007. Ecological systems theory: The person in the center of the circles. *Research in Human Development* 4(3–4): 203–217.

Duerden, M. D., and P. A. Witt. 2010. An ecological systems theory perspective on youth programming. *Journal of Park and Recreation Administration* 28(2): 108–120.

Gonzales-Backen, M. A., and A. J. Umana-Taylor. 2010. Examining the role of physical appearance in Latino adolescents' ethnic identity. *Journal of Adolescence* 34: 151–162.

Holt, N. L., K. A. Tamminen, D. E. Black,. Z. L. Sehn, , and M. P. Wall. 2008. Parental involvement in competitive youth sport settings. *Psychology of Sports and Exercise* 9(5): 663–685.

Hong, J. S., H. Cho, and A. Lee. 2010. Revisiting the Virginia Tech shootings: An ecological systems analysis. *Journal of Loss and Trauma* 15(6): 561–575.

Hong, J. S., S. M. Kim, M. Yoshihama, and S. Byoun. 2010. Wife battering in South Korea: An ecological systems analysis. *Children and Youth Services Review* 32(12): 1623–1630.

Hong, J. S., N. A. Lee, H. J. Park, and K. C. Paller. 2011. Child maltreatment in South Korea: An ecological systems analysis. *Children and Youth Services Review* 33(7): 1058–1066.

Hook, N.C., and B. Paolucci. 1970. The family as an ecosystem. *Journal of Home Economics* 62(5): 315–318.

Jacobson, M. 1970, November. *Values I* (Extension Bulletin E-647). East Lansing MI: Michigan State University Cooperative Extension Service.

Klein, D. M., and J. M. White. 1996. *Family theories*. Thousand Oaks CA: Sage Publications.

Leu, J. C-Y. 2008. Early childhood music education in Taiwan: An ecological systems perspective. *Arts Education Policy Review* 109(3): 17–26.

Lin, M., and A. Bates. 2010. Home visits: How do they affect teachers' beliefs about teaching and diversity? *Early Childhood Education Journal* 38(3): 179–185.

Martin, S. (2010). An early childhood intervention programme and the long-term outcomes for students. *Child Care in Practice* 16(3): 257–274.

McDill, T., S. K. Hall, and S. C. Turell. 2006. Aging and creating families: Never-married heterosexual women over forty. *Journal of Women and Aging* 18(3): 37–50.

Perry-Jenkins, M., and A. Claxton. 2011. The transition to parenthood and the reasons "momma ain't happy." *Journal of Marriage and Family* 73: 23–28.

Paolucci, B., O. A. Hall, and N. Axinn. 1977. *Family decision making: An ecosystem approach.* New York: Wiley.

Richardson, J. W., and L. J. Juszczak. 2008. Schools as sites for health care delivery. *Public Health Reports* 123(6): 692–694.

Schweiger, W. K., and M. O'Brien. 2005. Special needs adoption: An ecological systems approach. *Family Relations* 54(4): 512–522.

Shumow, L., T. J. Smith, and M. C. Smith. 2009. Academic and behavioral characteristics of young adolescents in self-care. *Journal of Early Adolescence* 29(2): 233–257.

Sigel, I. (2004). Head Start—Revisiting a historical psychoeducational intervention: A revisionist perspective. In E. Zigler and S. Styfco (Eds.), *The Head Start debates* (pp. 45–60). Baltimore, MD: Paul H. Brooks Publishing Co.

Sipsma, H., Biello, K.B., Cole-Lewis, H., and T. Kershaw. 2010. Like father, like son: The intergenerational cycle of adolescent fatherhood. *American Journal of Public Health* 100(3): 517–524.

Tudge, J. R. H., I. Mokrova, B. E. Hatfield, and R. B. Karnik. 2009. Uses and misuses of Bronfenbrenner's bioecological theory of human development. *Journal of Family Theory and Review* 1: 198–210.

White, J. M., and D. M. Klein. 2008. *Family theories* (3rd ed.). Thousand Oaks, CA: Sage.

SAMPLE READING

Hong, J. S., H. Cho, and A. S. Lee. 2010. Revisiting the Virginia Tech Shootings: An Ecological Analysis. *Journal of Loss and Trauma* 15(5): 561–575.

This article is unique to this textbook because it is a reflection of theoretical work, rather than empirical work. However, because not all of us will be conducting research as a part of our future professions, it's important that we also know how to use theories to analyze different issues or situations that may arise in either our professional or personal lives.

This article is a good example of how to use the ecological model to analyze what could have led to the shootings at Virginia Tech on April 16th, 2007, and how we can use this information from an ecological perspective for future assessment, intervention, and prevention. Hong, Cho, and Lee look at the risk factors of the shooter, with special attention on minority status, and provide an assessment of how things could have been done differently with the possibility of a different outcome. Of primary importance is the ability to use this information for prevention efforts in an attempt to minimize the potential for this type of travesty in the future.

SAMPLE READING

Revisiting the Virginia Tech Shootings: An Ecological Systems Analysis

Jun Sung Hong[a], Hyunkag Cho[b], and Alvin Shiulain Lee[c]

School shooting cases since the late 1990s have prompted school officials and legislators to develop and implement programs and measures that would prevent violence in school. Despite the number of explanations by the media, politicians, organizations, and researchers about the etiology of school shootings, we are not united in our understanding of the risk factors, particularly those relevant to racial minorities and immigrants. This article examines the Virginia Tech shooting incident using Bronfenbrenner's ecological systems theory. We assess a number of risk factors that operate within five system levels (the micro, meso, exo, macro, and chrono systems) and draw implications for assessment and intervention.

On April 16, 2007, a school shooting tragedy befell the Virginia Tech campus, leaving 33 people, including the gunman, dead and countless others seriously injured.

Jun Sung Hong *is a doctoral student in the School of Social Work at the University of Illinois at Urbana-Champaign. His research interests include school violence, school-based intervention, juvenile delinquency, child welfare, and cultural competency in social work practice. He is currently a Council of Social Work Education Minority Fellowship Program fellow.*

Hyunkag Cho *is an assistant professor in the School of Social Work at Michigan State University. He received his Ph.D. in social work from Florida State University. His research interests include the intersection between domestic violence and criminal justice systems among immigrants and cross-national studies on policy and multicultural competence. He teaches human behavior and the social environment; social work macro practice with groups, organizations, and communities; and research and statistics classes.*

Alvin Shiulain Lee *received his B.A. in psychology from California State University at Long Beach and his M.S.W. at the University of Pennsylvania School of Social Policy and Practice. He is currently a doctoral student at the Boston University School of Social Work. His research interests include youth and adolescent mental health, mental health access and utilization, and cultural factors that impact mental illnesses and service utilization. He is currently a Council of Social Work Education Minority Fellowship Program fellow.*

[a]School of Social Work, University of Illinois, Urbana Champaign, Urbana, Illinois, USA
[b]School of Social Work, Michigan State University, East Lansing, Michigan, USA
[c]School of Social Work, BostonUniversity, Boston, Massachusetts, USA
Address correspondence to Jun Sung Hong, School of Social Work, University of Illinois, Urbana Champaign, 1010 W. Nevada St., Urbana, IL 61801, USA. E-mail: jhong23@illinois.edu

The lone gunman was identified as Seung-Hui Cho, 23, a senior at Virginia Tech. The nation was once again gripped with trauma, sadness, and disbelief, desperately searching for answers to what provoked Cho to carry out what is now known as the "worst school shooting in American history." In the days, weeks, and months that followed, school officials, policymakers, psychiatrists, and researchers took to the media spotlight, theorizing why violence and shootings are plaguing school districts and higher education institutions.

Unlike other headline-grabbing school shooting cases that mostly involved White, suburban teenage boys (e.g., the Columbine shooting), the perpetrator in this case was an immigrant student from South Korea. Korean communities in Virginia and across the country were shocked that the perpetrator of America's worst school shooting was one of their own. Fearing potential backlash against Koreans in the United States, schools, universities, and Korean community leaders sent e-mail messages and distributed flyers to Korean students and residents, urging them to take precautions and report any possible hate crimes to the police. Shock and dismay also traversed across South Korea, and South Korean president Roh Moo Hyun offered his condolences to the survivors of the shooting (Steinhauer, 2007).

Much has been speculated about Cho's motivation for the shooting based on testimonials by Cho's family and relatives, interviews with students and classmates, school officials, and a self-made videotape of Cho (which he sent to a television station) in which he expressed his resentment against his perceived mistreatment. As this case demonstrates, much is still unknown about youth violence, particularly that involving racial and ethnic minorities. The Report to the President on Issues Raised by the Virginia Tech Tragedy found that school officials, health care professionals, law enforcement personnel, and researchers were not disseminating information on Seung-Hui Cho and those likely to pose a danger to themselves or others (Leavitt, 2007). Moreover, the majority of the studies on the Virginia Tech case (e.g., Vieweg et al., 2008) have focused on the aftermath rather than on the etiology of the shooting. As a result, much of our energy and resources have been directed toward intervention programs and policy measures, which have been far more costly than prevention efforts.

Bronfenbrenner's ecological systems model is ideal in integrating segmented parts into understandable pieces and allows for a more complete analysis of social–environmental factors that impact human behavior—in this case, violence. This model can facilitate our understanding of the unknowns surrounding the Virginia Tech shooting incident. This article examines the multiple risk factors associated with the incident using ecological systems theory. Practice and policy implications are also discussed.

APPLICATION OF ECOLOGICAL SYSTEMS THEORY TO SCHOOL VIOLENCE

In recent years, a number of researchers have taken the ecological approach as a framework for violence prevention by examining the complex interplay of individuals, families, peers, schools, and the communities where violence occurs. The interactions of the various spheres of influence are important in our understanding of how the spheres of human interaction cultivate an environment that fosters school violence (Verlinden,

Hersen, & Thomas, 2000). Bronfenbrenner's ecological systems theory, which facilitates a broader understanding of school violence, represents a reaction to the limited scope of research being conducted by social scientists. This theory eschews the tendency to focus exclusively on a youth's individual characteristics; rather, it depicts school violence as a result of interactions among multitudes of factors directly and indirectly affecting the individual. Ecological systems theory posits that individuals are part of five interrelated systems: the micro, meso, exo, macro, and chrono systems (Bronfenbrenner, 1994). The following sections examine the Virginia Tech shooting case within each system of ecological systems theory.

MICRO SYSTEM

The most direct influences are within the micro-system level, which consists of individuals or groups of individuals with whom the person has interactions. Bronfenbrenner (1994) depicts the micro system as a pattern of activities, social roles, and interpersonal relations experienced by the individual in a direct setting (e.g., family) with particular physical, social, and symbolic features that would invite, permit, or inhibit engagement in sustained, progressively more complex interactions with the immediate environment. Three micro-system-level factors in this case are individual characteristics, the parent-child relationship, and peer victimization.

Individual Characteristics

Individual characteristics of school shooters have been identified by psychologists, educators, and law enforcement. In recent years, the FBI's Behavioral Science Unit and the U.S. Secret Services have "profiled" youth who are potentially at risk of violence at school (U.S. Department of Education, 2002). Despite their best intentions, however, profiling potential school shooters has been a problem in that the accuracy of such profiles is questionable. Reddy et al. (2001) note the erroneous assumption that all of the perpetrators were White, when in fact a small number were not. Nevertheless, two individual-level characteristics (i.e., gender and mental health status) are risk factors relevant to the Virginia Tech shooting committed by a racial minority individual.

Virtually all of the infamous school shootings have been committed by males (Leary et al., 2003), who are typically perceived as the more aggressive gender (e.g., Coie & Dodge, 1998), more prone to violent behavior, and more likely to engage in fights than females (Espelage, Mebane, & Swearer, 2004). Males are also four times more likely to perceive violence as a legitimate way to resolve conflicts (Kimmel & Mahler, 2003), which can be explained by gender role socialization theory. This theory posits that males are socialized to be dominant, powerful, and aggressive; males experience greater social pressure than females to conform to socially prescribed gender roles as independent, self-reliant, and tough (Martin, 1995). This is true for the perpetrator of the Virginia Tech shooting. Cho came from a country with traditionally strong male-dominant values, which are normally transmitted from one generation to the next. Korean Americans, as with most ethnic minorities, preserve their own cultural values, which they reinforce to the next generation (Min, 1999). Although gender appears to be a risk factor, it is shaped by sociocultural influences.

For instance, since it is strictly prohibited in South Korea for citizens to possess a gun, Cho would not have committed a mass killing had he remained in South Korea.

A number of school shooters have also been identified as having mental and emotional distress (e.g., Immelman, 1999). It has been reported, for example, that many of the shooters underwent counseling sessions for depression, impulsivity, and antisocial behavior (Tappan & Kita, 1999). Mental health issues were also a risk factor in the Virginia Tech case. Cho was referred to the school educational screening committee during his elementary school years because his teachers felt that his lack of communication stemmed from emotional issues. During his middle school years, he was referred to the Center for Multicultural Human Services, a mental health facility for low-income immigrants and refugees. Psychiatrists diagnosed him as having social anxiety disorder and emotional problems. Tests administered by mental health professionals evaluated Cho as socially immature and lacking verbal skills, although his IQ was above average (Virginia Tech Review Panel, 2007).

Subsequent to the massacre, a number of forensic psychiatrists diagnosed Cho as suffering from anger and depression, similar to most of the school shooters profiled. A study conducted by the Secret Service found that 98% of the high-profile school shooters had experienced loss, grief, or sense of failure (Cullen, 2007). According to a roommate Cho confided in, he was dreaming of a supermodel girlfriend. In real life, he stalked a number of women who refused his advances and contacted the police. He rarely expressed his emotions directly but rather was bottling up his anger (e.g., "You have vandalized my heart, raped my soul, and torched my conscience") (Cullen, 2007).

Lack of Parent–Child Relationship

As reported by the Virginia Tech Review Panel (2007), a major issue between Cho and his family was lack of relationship and communication. Cho spoke very little to his parents and avoided eye contact. Although his parents urged him to open up, he isolated himself from his family, which generated a high level of family stress. The lack of a parent–child relationship was attributed to the fact that both of Cho's parents worked long and extended hours at their dry cleaning business. Such situations can create child-rearing difficulties and decrease parent–child interactions. Both Cho and his sister reportedly felt isolated due to lack of interaction with their parents (Virginia Tech Review Panel, 2007).

Strong parent-child relationships can potentially be a protective factor against violence. Unfortunately, few studies have specifically examined the association between parent–child relationships and violent behavior (Hawkins et al., 2000). A number of researchers in South Korea report that a negative parent–child relationship or the lack of such a relationship is significantly associated with violent and suicidal behaviors among youth (e.g., Oh, Park, & Choi, 2008). Parents' employment and working hours can also influence child behavior because parents have less time to form attachments and interact positively with their children (Eamon, 2001). Several researchers have found an association between parents' employment and negative child outcomes. Han, Waldfogel, and Brooks-Gunn (2001), for example, report that children with working mothers are likely to exhibit behavioral problems.

Attachment theory (Bowlby, 1977), which emphasizes the importance of children's emotional bonds with their caretakers during their early years, might explain why negative parent–child relationships are related to violent behavior. Children with negative parental attachment have problems relating with others and are likely to engage in violence (Kennedy & Kennedy, 2004). Attachment theorists also suggest that parents must form a positive attachment with their children, which will facilitate children's healthy social development.

Peer Victimization

Former classmates at Westfield High School recalled Cho being mocked and bullied for his poor English skills, as well as his inaudible manner of speaking (Kleinfield, 2007). He only whispered if pushed to speak by his teachers. Cho's sister also reported that both she and her brother were subjected to harassment by classmates throughout their school years since their immigration to the U.S. (Virginia Tech Review Panel, 2007). Cho expressed his resentment at his perceived mistreatment by his classmates. In a QuickTime video of himself, he said, "You...decided to spill my blood. You forced me into a corner and gave me only one option" (Kleinfield, 2007).

As mentioned earlier, only a limited number of studies shed light on the association between peer victimization and racial minority status, despite the fact that Asian American youth are frequently subject to racial harassment from peers in school. Moran and colleagues (1993) found that 50% of the bullied Asian children in their study (compared to none of the bullied White children) had been harassed due to their race. Chin (2008) cites federal statistics showing that the percentage of Asian American youth who report being bullied at school has increased in recent years, from 2.5% in 1999 to 6.8% in 2003. Statistics from 2005 also indicate that Asian-Pacific Islander, American Indian, and Alaska Native youth more frequently report being targeted for verbal harassment (11.8%) than White (10.3%) and Hispanic (10.5%) youth but not African American youth (15.0%). Although there was no difference in the frequency of peer victimization between ethnic minorities and Whites (Moran et al., 1993), the consequences are more likely to be severe for the former, who tend to have fewer resources to deal with victimization than the latter.

Harassment against Asian American youth often stems from racial stereotypes. Because Asians are stereotypically perceived as silent, docile foreigners who rarely cause problems, they are easily targeted for peer harassment that often results in bicultural stress, which has been found to be associated with depressive symptoms (Romero et al., 2007). These stereotypes are internalized by many Asian American youth and are also associated with negative outcomes such as delinquency and violent behaviors (Huang & Ida, 2004).

MESO SYSTEM

The meso system consists of the interrelationships between two or more micro systems that directly affect the individual (Bronfenbrenner, 1994). Interactions in one micro system, such as family environment, may influence interactions in another, such as peer relationships in school, or vice versa (Eamon, 2001). The association between parent–child relationships and peer relationships is a meso system-level example in the Virginia Tech shooting case. Lack of a parent–child relationship can result in the child developing ineffective social skills, which leads to peer rejection and bullying in school (Orpinas & Horne, 2006). Likewise, victimization in school can unduly influence family relationships. It was reported that Cho's sister witnessed students taunting him when he walked down school hallways; however, he never opened up to his family about his experiences of being ridiculed at school and further distanced himself from his family (Virginia Tech Review Panel, 2007).

EXO SYSTEM

The exo system consists of interrelationships between two or more micro systems or settings, but the individual is contained in one (Bronfenbrenner, 1994). One relevant exo-system-level factor is media coverage of school shootings. It has been a major public concern that at-risk youth exposed to media violence (e.g., media coverage of school shootings) may be influenced to act out violently for their perceived mistreatment and injustice in school. Cho expressed his admiration for Columbine shooters Eric Harris and Dylan Klebold. In his letter, he wrote, "We martyrs like Eric and Dylan will sacrifice our lives to & you thousand folds for what you apostles of sin have done to us" (ABC News, 2007). Studies reveal that exposure to media coverage of violence increases the likelihood of immediate and long-term violent behavior. Media violence primes existing aggressive scripts and cognitions, increases physiological arousal, and triggers an automatic tendency to imitate observed behavior (Anderson et al., 2003). Social learning theory can also explain the relationship between media and violence; violent behavior can potentially result from observing a model acting violently.

MACRO SYSTEM

The macro-system level is considered a "cultural blueprint," which may determine the occurrence of social structures and activities in the immediate system levels (Bronfenbrenner, 1994). The macro system refers to cultural beliefs, opportunity structures, and hazards that affect the particular conditions and processes in the micro system. Macro-system-level factors relevant to this case are cultural barriers to mental health services and access to guns.

Cultural Barriers to Mental Health Services

Following the recommendation from the elementary school, Cho's parents reluctantly sought counseling for their son. However, Cho and his parents had to overcome several obstacles, including cultural barriers to mental health services (Virginia Tech Review Panel, 2007). In South Korea and in Asian American communities, mental or emotional problems are commonly perceived as signs of shame (Kramer et al., 2002). Leong and Lau (2001) reviewed a number of studies on mental health services for Asian Americans. These studies found a number of barriers to mental health services for this population, including conflict between Asian American cultural values and Western-based mental health systems (Atkinson & Gim, 1989); also, traditional, Western-based psychotherapy emphasizes open verbal communication as opposed to the allocentric values held by Asian Americans (Sue & Sue, 1977). In addition, many Asian American immigrants encounter language barriers, lack of information on mental health services, and lack of affordable mental health services within their ethnic community (e.g., Ingram, 2007).

Access to Guns

In the aftermath of the shooting, then-President George W. Bush signed into effect the first major federal gun control measure. This measure requires states to enter the names of people declared by a court as mentally ill into an FBI database, which would prohibit the purchase of guns (Cochran, 2008). According to the Brady Center to Prevent Gun Violence, Cho would be prohibited from purchasing a gun since he posed a danger to himself and others. Regrettably, Virginia did not send Cho's mental health information to an FBI database (Cochran, 2008), which might have prevented Cho from purchasing guns. Studies have shown that homicide rates among youth have significantly increased since 1985, which has been attributed to an increase in the availability of firearms to young people (Blumstein & Cork, 1996).

CHRONO SYSTEM

The chrono-system level is characterized as change or consistency over time in the characteristics of the individual and the environment in which the individual is embedded. The chrono system encompasses both individual (e.g., life transition) and environmental change (e.g., divorce, historical events, social conditions) (Bronfenbrenner, 1994). Immigration to the United States is an example of a chrono-system-level factor. In South Korea, Cho had few friends that he played with. Cho was introverted and spoke little; however, reticence is regarded as a positive trait in South Korea, one that is often equated with scholarliness (Virginia Tech Review Panel, 2007). In 1992, Cho's family immigrated to the United States to provide educational opportunities for Cho and his sister. Cho's family reported that after their arrival, Cho appeared to be more socially withdrawn and isolated than he had been in South Korea. These observations suggest that historical events over the life course can affect the individual.

PRACTICE AND POLICY IMPLICATIONS

As this analysis indicates, the risk factors among racial and ethnic minorities as identified in the Virginia Tech case are complex and multifaceted. Unfortunately, several of these major risk factors for Cho's violent behavior were overlooked by counselors at the Virginia Tech Cook Counseling Center who had interactions with Cho ("Mental Health," 2009). Because different configurations of risk factors are associated with particular behaviors, identifying and understanding these factors can inform effective and relevant intervention and prevention strategies (Gorman-Smith, Tolan, & Henry,

2000). The following sections draw assessment, prevention, and intervention implications for school shootings in relation to the Virginia Tech case.

Micro System

The micro-system-level analysis suggests that assessment must consider the individual's relationships with parents and peers. Proper assessment and intervention strategies also require examining gender and mental health status, which are relevant to the individual. Gender-specific issues (e.g., masculinity) and mental health status should be included in the assessment. Educating parents, teachers, and school officials about the early signs of distorted gender images and misconceptions concerning mental health needs to be a part of prevention efforts. Referral and notification systems among schools, mental health professionals, and law enforcement regarding potential perpetrators may be critical.

Depending on the assessment, practitioners should utilize skill-building programs for communication, problem solving, and conflict resolution between parents and youth. The inclusion of parent education programs that enhance prosocial parenting practices (e.g., Doh et al., 2003) has been successful in improving the relationship between the parent and the youth. In addition, assisting parents in creating a supportive, caring family structure would be effective. Interventions should also consider parents' work-related stress in attempts to enhance parenting practices (Eamon, 2001). Moreover, assessing factors that weaken the parent–child bond can provide needed information for selecting interventions that promote healthy family relationships.

Establishing a safe school environment that promotes a sense of belonging would decrease the likelihood of youth violent behavior. Providing students with social activities is important for developing and maintaining friendships and social support networks. Because teachers and school staff members have the most frequent contacts with youth, teacher and school staff involvement in peer conflict resolution is crucial (Espelage & Swearer, 2003). We also suggest a systematic reporting system for bullying in school and strengthening of multicultural curricula in the classroom, which can foster a sense of school connectedness among Asian and racial minority students and reduce their likelihood of becoming victimized in school. School administrators might develop after-school programs and youth mentoring programs, which have been proven to have positive youth outcomes (e.g., Posner & Vandell, 1994).

Meso System

Negative parent–child relationships may result in negative peer relationships in school, which potentially result in violent behavior. Thus, assessing meso-system-level factors can facilitate selecting the appropriate system in which to intervene (Eamon, 2001). Assessments at the meso-system level need to consider the interrelations between parents and the school and between parents and their children's peers. Teachers and school administrators need to encourage parents to be involved in their children's school activities and provide an arena in which parents can meet with teachers and other youth. School administrators should also establish networks for parents such as parent–teacher associations and other activities where parents can be aware of their children's academic and social life in school.

Exo System

Assessment should include examining the amount of violence viewed by youth, as well as the link between parents' employment and parenting practices. Schools should incorporate media viewing into school curricula, provide a balanced view on violence via school newsletters and student discussion forums, and develop educational materials for parents about the detrimental effects of exposure to media violence on youth.

Macro System

Bonnie and colleagues (2009) argue that more thorough assessments and evaluations of mental health background are necessary. They note that in the Virginia Tech case, although Cho was ordered to undergo outpatient treatment by a judge, he never complied with this order, which went unnoticed. Assessments and interventions are likely to be effective if they are relevant to a family's lifestyle and cultural beliefs (Eamon, 2001). Although cultural values and practices are difficult to change, proper intervention requires practitioners to assess cultural barriers to seeking mental health services for immigrant families. Practitioners must consider the feasibility of mental health services to their clients' cultural values and beliefs. Effective intervention strategies should include culturally sensitive psychoeducational techniques, which are designed to facilitate clients' and their families' adaptation to mental health services. One study on the effectiveness of a psychoeducation program for mentally ill Korean Americans found that the program enhanced participants' knowledge of mental illness and available treatment (Shin & Lukens, 2002).

Practitioners should also actively collaborate with school officials to implement a program that addresses gun violence in school. Gun control programs that involve collaboration between schools and the community, such as the Baton Rouge Partnership, have proven to be effective in reducing gun-related violence (Lizotte & Sheppard, 2001). Schools must also enforce strict rules against weapon carrying on school property.

Chrono System

Practitioners have little direct influence over chrono-system-level factors, such as historical events and life transitions (e.g., immigration), that may create problems (e.g., violence). However, practitioners and professional organizations must collaborate to advocate on behalf of immigrant youth and families by educating government-elected representatives about the relations between social conditions and negative outcomes for immigrants. They also must advocate for social services to assist immigrant youth and families in coping with events that create problems within micro systems.

CONCLUSION

Extensive research has been done on school shootings, producing invaluable knowledge, information, and implications. However, many of these studies have focused on the aftermath of the shooting or on interventions rather than etiology or prevention efforts. Racial minorities have been largely ignored by the vast majority of literature on school violence. This study attempted to fill these gaps by reviewing the existing studies, newspaper articles, and commentaries on the Virginia Tech shooting incident, which occurred within the complicated context of multiple social systems. Untangling these complexities requires a comprehensive framework. We utilized ecological systems theory to identify the risk factors at various levels of social systems that were associated with the shooting case. We found this theory to be effective in enhancing our understanding of these risk factors, which have major implications for assessment, prevention, and intervention for at-risk racial minorities.

While most of the risk factors identified can be relevant for various racial and ethnic groups, the dynamics of these risk factors vary among minorities. For instance, micro-level risk factors, such as mental health problems, are interrelated with macro-level risk factors, such as cultural barriers to mental health services. Cho's parents, like many Koreans in the United States, had to work long hours in order to establish themselves as immigrants, sacrificing crucial interactions with their children. Peer victimization, a micro-level risk factor, might not have led to the shooting had the parents established a strong relationship with their son, the would-be shooter.

We provided several suggestions for practitioners and policymakers based on our understanding of the complexity surrounding this incident. We acknowledge that implementing all of these suggestions may not be practical or feasible. However, one of the strengths of ecological systems theory is that it allows us to start where we are ready to start. The theory posits that any changes in a particular system create entirely different dynamics in all other systems (Bronfenbrenner, 1994). However, it is also true that initiating changes may not be effective without a comprehensive understanding of the complicated interactions among the multiple systems. Ecological systems theory as applied to this study enables practitioners in various fields to utilize information on risk factors and interactions between multiple systems to effectively address the problem of school violence. While much work needs to be done to reduce and eventually end violence in school, an ecological understanding of this case, as demonstrated here, can contribute not only to a better understanding of this problem but also to developing better approaches.

REFERENCES

ABC News. (2007). *Killer mails letter, photos, video to NBC.* Retrieved November 23, 2009, from http://abcnews.go.com/GMA/story?id=3055889&page=1

Anderson, C. A., Berkowitz, L., Donnerstein, E., Huesmann, L. R., Johnson, J. D., Linz, D. et al. (2003). The influence of media violence on youth. *Psychological Science in the Public Interest, 4,* 81–110.

Atkinson, D. R., & Gim, R. H. (1989). Asian American cultural identity and attitudes toward mental health services. *Journal of Counseling Psychology, 36,* 209–212.

Blumstein, A., & Cork, D. (1996). Linking gun availability to youth gun violence. *Law and Contemporary Problems, 59,* 5–24.

Bonnie, R. J., Reinhard, J. S., Hamilton, P., & McGarvey, E. L. (2009). Mental health system transformation after the Virginia Tech tragedy. *Tragedy and Reform, 28,* 793–804.

Bowlby, J. (1977). The making and breaking of affectional bonds: I. Aetiology and psychology in the light of attachment theory. *British Journal of Psychiatry, 130,* 201–210.

Bronfenbrenner, U. (1994). Ecological models of human development. In T. Husen & T. N. Postlethwaite (Eds.), *The international encyclopedia of education*, 2nd ed., (pp. 1643–1647). New York: Elsevier Science.

Chin, W. Y. (2008). School violence and race: The problem of peer racial harassment against Asian Pacific American students in schools. *The Scholar: St. Mary's Law Review on Minority Issues*, 10, 333–372.

Cochran, J. (2008). New gun control law is killer's legacy. *ABC News*. Retrieved November 24, 2009, from http://abcnews.go.com/Politics/Story?id=4126152& page=1

Coie, J. D., & Dodge, K. A. (1998). Aggression and antisocial behavior. In W. Damon (Series Ed.) & N. Eisenberg (Vol. Ed.), *Handbook of child psychology: Vol. 3. Social emotional and personality development*, 5th ed., (pp. 779–862). New York: Wiley.

Cullen, D. (2007). Psychopath? Depressive? Schizophrenic? Was Cho Seung-Hui really like the Columbine killers? *Slate*. Retrieved November 23, 2009, from http://www.slate.com/id/2164757

Doh, H. S., Kwon, J. I., Park, B. K., Hong, S. H., Hong, J. Y., & Hwang, Y. E. (2003). The development of intervention programs based on characteristics of children victimized by peers: Focus on parent education and social skills training programs. *Korean Journal of Child Studies*, 24, 103–121.

Eamon, M. K. (2001). The effects of poverty on children's socioemotional development: An ecological systems analysis. *Social Work*, 46, 256–266.

Espelage, D. L., Mebane, S. E., & Swearer, S. M. (2004). Gender differences in bullying: Moving beyond mean level differences. In D. L. Espelage & S. M. Swearer (Eds.), *Bullying in American schools: A social-ecological perspective on prevention and intervention* (pp. 15–35). Mahwah, NJ: Erlbaum.

Espelage, D. L., & Swearer, S. M. (2003). Research on school bullying and victimization: What have we learned and where do we go from here? *School Psychology Review*, 32, 365–383.

Gorman-Smith, D., Tolan, P. H., & Henry, D. B. B. (2000). A developmental-ecological model of the relation of family functioning to patterns of delinquency. *Journal of Quantitative Criminology*, 16, 169–198.

Han, W., Waldfogel, J., & Brooks-Gunn, J. (2001). The effects of early maternal employment on later cognitive and behavioral outcomes. *Journal of Family and the Marriage*, 63, 336–354.

Hawkins, J. D., Herrenkohl, T. I., Farrington, D. B., Catalano, R. F., Harachi, T. W., & Cothern, L. (2000). *Predictors of youth violence*. Washington, DC: U.S. State Department.

Huang, L. N., & Ida, D. J. (2004). *Promoting positive development and preventing youth violence and high-risk behaviors in Asian American-Pacific Islander communities: A social ecology perspective*. Washington, DC: U.S. Department of Health and Human Services.

Immelman, A. (1999). *Indirect evaluation of Eric Harris*. Retrieved August 2, 2009, from http://www.csbsju.edu/uspp/Research/Harris.html

Ingram, E. M. (2007). A comparison of help seeking between Latino and non-Latino victims of intimate partner violence. *Violence Against Women*, 13, 159–171.

Kennedy, J. H., & Kennedy, C. E. (2004). Attachment theory: Implication for school psychology. *Psychology in the Schools*, 41, 247–259.

Kimmel, M. S., & Mahler, M. (2003). Adolescent masculinity, homophobia, and violence: Random school shootings, 1982–2001. *American Behavioral Scientist*, 46, 1439–1458.

Kramer, E. J., Kwong, K., Lee, E., & Chung, H. (2002). Cultural factors influencing the mental health of Asian Americans. *Western Journal of Medicine*, 176, 227–231.

Leary, M. R., Kowalski, R. M., Smith, L., & Phillips, S. (2003). Teasing, rejection, and violence: Case studies of school shootings. *Aggressive Behavior*, 29, 202–214.

Leavitt, M. O. (2007). *Report to the president on issues raised by the Virginia Tech tragedy*. Washington, DC: U.S. Department of Justice.

Leong, F. T. L., & Lau, A. S. L. (2001). Barriers to providing effective mental health services to Asian Americans. *Mental Health Services Research*, 3, 201–214.

Lizotte, A. J., & Sheppard, D. (2001). *Gun use by male juveniles: Research and prevention.* Washington, DC: U.S. Department of Justice, Office of Justice Programs.

Martin, C. L. (1995). Stereotypes about children with traditional and nontraditional gender roles. *Sex Roles*, 33(11–12), 727–751.

Mental health files of Virginia Tech gunman released. (2009). *CNN.com.* Retrieved March 23, 2010, from http://www.cnn.com/2009/CRIME/08/19/virginia.tech. records

Min, P. G. (1999). A comparison of post-1965 and turn-of-the-century immigrants in inter-generational mobility and cultural transmission. *Journal of American Ethnic History*, 18, 65–94.

Moran, S., Smith, P. K., Thompson, D., & Whitney, I. (1993). Ethnic differences in experiences of bullying: Asian and White children. *British Journal of Educational Psychology*, 63, 431–440.

Oh, H. A., Park, Y. R., & Choi, M. H. (2008). The effects of parent-adolescent communication and depression on suicide ideation. *Journal of the Korean Academy of Child Health*, 14, 35–43.

Orpinas, P., & Horne, A. M. (2006). *Bullying prevention: Creating a positive school climate and developing social competence.* Washington, DC: American Psychological Association.

Posner, J. K., & Vandell, D. L. (1994). Low-income children's after-school care: Are there beneficial effects of after-school programs? *Child Development*, 65, 440–456.

Reddy, M., Borum, R., Berglund, J., Vossekuil, B., Fein, R., & Modzeleski, W. (2001). Evaluating risk for targeted violence in schools: Comparing risk assessment, threat assessment, and other approaches. *Psychology in the Schools*, 38, 157–172.

Romero, A. J., Carvajal, S. C., Valle, F., & Orduna, M. (2007). Adolescent bicultural stress and its impact on mental well-being among Latinos, Asian Americans, and European Americans. *Journal of Community Psychology*, 35, 519–534.

Shin, S. K., & Lukens, E. P. (2002). Effects of psychoeducation for Korean Americans with chronic mental illness. *Psychiatric Services*, 53, 1125–1131.

Steinhauer, J. (2007, April). Korean Americans brace for problems in wake of killings. *New York Times.* Retrieved November 24, 2009, from http://www. nytimes.com/2007/04/19/us/19korea.html?ei=5088&en=70f60d0db807fd95&ex=1334635200&partner=rssnyt&emc=rss&pagewanted=print

Sue, D. W., & Sue, D. (1977). Barriers to effective cross-cultural counseling. *Journal of Counseling Psychology*, 24, 420–429.

Tappan, M., & Kita, B. (1999, November). *The Columbine tragedy: A sociocultural perspective.* Paper presented at the annual meeting of the Association for Moral Education, Minneapolis.

U.S. Department of Education. (2002). *Threat assessment in school: A guide to managing threatening situations and to creating safe school climates.* Washington, DC: Author.

Verlinden, S., Hersen, M., & Thomas, J. (2000). Risk factors in school shootings. *Clinical Psychology Review*, 20, 3–56.

Vieweg, S., Palen, L., Liu, S., Hughes, A., & Sutton, J. (2008). *Collective intelligence in disaster: An examination of the phenomenon in the aftermath of the 2007 Virginia Tech shooting.* Paper presented at the 5th International ISCRAM Conference, Washington, DC.

Virginia Tech Review Panel. (2007). *Mass shootings at Virginia Tech April 16, 2007: Report of the review panel.* Arlington, VA: Author.

7

CONFLICT THEORY

Deborah and Jackie live together with their mother and children in Chicago. Deborah, the older sister, works as a licensed practical nurse on the evening shift at a downtown hospital. Her two boys stay with their grandmother when they get home from school. They do not see their father. Jackie, the younger sister, works the day shift at the local bakery and occasionally picks up an extra shift on the weekends. Her daughter goes to the day care center down the street from her house and spends the weekends with her father.

Deborah and Jackie are out shopping. They want to buy some new clothes for their children for Christmas but do not have the money to shop at the fanciest clothing shops in the mall. In fact, they drive 40 miles out of town to an outlet mall to find some bargain shops. As Jackie drives, she laments their financial state.

Jackie: I wish that, for once, I could just go to the mall and tell all those snooty salespeople to wrap up anything I want for the kids and us. I know that the kids feel badly because they don't have the "coolest" clothes. And I'd love to buy Mom a cashmere sweater. Just think—I could tell them to wrap it up and deliver it! Wouldn't that be great?

Deborah: Yeah, Sis, it would be, but you know it isn't ever going to happen. We were born poor and we're always going to be poor. All we can hope for is that our children will go to college somehow and maybe get good jobs and not have to always worry about money.

Deborah and Jackie have a fun afternoon shopping together, but having stayed too late, they drive home too fast. A police officer pulls them over for speeding, and despite their pleas, they receive a ticket for $150. On the drive home, Jackie and Deborah begin to argue with each other.

Jackie: We went all that way to save money and look what happened! We don't have the money to pay this ticket. Why does this stuff always happen to us? Now we're going to have to work overtime just to pay for this speeding ticket.

Deborah: What do you mean *we*? You were the one who was driving! How can you be so irresponsible? You should have been watching your speed more carefully!

Jackie: I wasn't driving that fast. Did you see that Mercedes pass us? He was doing 85 miles per hour and he didn't get pulled over. I bet if we'd been driving a BMW, we wouldn't have been stopped either! You know I can't afford to pay this ticket. How am I supposed to get overtime when they are laying off people? I thought I could count on you to help cover this—after all, you were in the car with me!

Deborah: This is just the kind of thing you always do. You get yourself in over your head and you always expect me to bail you out. I'm tired of it. This was clearly your fault, and this time you are on your own!

Jackie: You are the worst sister in the world!

By this time, both sisters are emotionally overwrought and drive the rest of the way home in silence.

HISTORY

Conflict theory is rooted in sociology where it is used to explain differences between classes within society and the competition for scarce resources, including economic wealth, political power, and social status. In some earlier (as well as some current) societies, people were born into their roles in society as defined by their social class (such as slave, serf, working class, or aristocracy) and remained there for life. Some social theorists believed that, if conditions were right, eventually those who were in the lower classes could move into the higher classes, but this would happen only as the result of conflict.

The famous social philosopher Karl Marx (1818–1883) is sometimes referred to as the father of conflict theory. His thinking was profoundly influenced by an earlier German philosopher, Georg Wihelm Friedrich Hegel (1770–1831). Hegel's theory about the evolution of ideas, known as the Hegelian dialectic, postulated that an accepted idea (the thesis) would eventually be challenged by its opposite (the antithesis) until a stable middle ground was reached that combined aspects of both extremes (the synthesis). The synthesis would then become the new thesis, and the whole pendulum process would begin again (Russell 1945/1972).

Whereas Hegel's philosophy focused on the conflict of ideas, Marx focused on much more pragmatic issues—the economic well-being of individuals in society. Marx took Hegel's approach and applied it to a theory of social and economic change. He studied social change throughout history and proposed that such change followed a dialectical form. He maintained that ruling classes in a society (the ones controlling the economic wealth and the political power) were always overthrown by the oppressed classes through conflict, after which they in turn became the ruling classes and were likewise eventually overthrown by those classes that they had oppressed (Russell 1945/1972; Turner 1998).

Marx envisioned a time when the laborers (the oppressed and exploited proletariat) would unite their forces and overthrow the capitalist landowners and industrialists (the oppressive and exploitative bourgeoisie) and create a world where everyone had equal access to resources. This was the basic idea in his now famous *Communist Manifesto*

(1848). But before a communistic society could prevail, there had to be many years of class conflict in which the focus was on how the distribution of scarce resources played out and who ultimately maintained the power in those communities.

Although Marx was a major proponent of conflict theory, his focus was primarily on the economic impact of the theory. Later sociologists focused on its interpersonal uses, most notably Max Weber, Georg Simmel, and Lewis Coser. Simmel (translated 1998) added interpersonal dimensions of love, ownership, valuing, and jealousy to the perspective of conflict in families, noting that, although we seem to move from one extreme to the other in interpersonal relationships, we find a synthesis in our need for loving. Human interaction has, within its structure, components of inequality (Sprey 1999). Coser said that conflict can solidify and unify a group, as well as promote cohesion and adaptability within groups. This is because dealing with conflict brings flexibility to a system's structure and increases its capacity to change (Turner 1998).

Although these sociologists were important in helping us understand the uses of conflict in society at large, one theorist has been most important in helping define the need for understanding conflict in families—Jetse Sprey. Sprey (1969, 1979, 1999) wrote that conflict was a part of every relationship, including those in families. He outlined how conflict may be understood in families by specifying the components of the theory, by helping researchers to generate ways in which to classify conflict in families, and by distinguishing conflict in families as unique from other types of conflict.

BASIC ASSUMPTIONS

Conflict theory focuses on the explanation of orderly as well as disorderly societal processes. In the context of marriage and family studies, it explains "how and why stability and instability occur, and under what conditions harmonious interpersonal bonds are possible" (Sprey 1979, 130). All humans engage in conflict situations, and understanding the management of conflict will lead to an understanding of stability and instability in marriage and family.

The nature of humans is that they are self-oriented. Conflict theorists make certain assumptions about human nature. They assume that the individual is self-oriented, or focused on self-interests. They believe that individuals are symbol-producing, which means that they are able to ascribe value to things (such as a corner office, shares of a piece of cake, or praise from parents). This ability sets up the system of scarce resources for which individuals are in competition. In light of limited resources, family members employ a number of strategies to achieve their personal goals and interests, and might even resort to interpersonal aggression, if necessary (Olson, Fine, and Lloyd, 2005). Conflict theorists also believe that humans have unlimited potential to hope, which means they have unlimited potential to desire power, prestige, and privilege, thereby setting up relationships with other humans as real or potential competitors (Farrington and Chertok 1993; Sprey 1979).

Societies operate under a perpetual scarcity of resources. Conflict theorists also make certain assumptions about the nature of society. Societies represent organized systems for species survival. They operate under a perpetual scarcity of resources, and this leads to perpetual confrontations. According to conflict theorists, such confrontations keep societies in a state of flux and lead to upheaval, social change, and growth. Like structural functional theorists, conflict theorists recognize that inequality is an inevitable aspect of most relationships; unlike other theorists, conflict theorists try to manage the inequality rather than resolve it. In our opening scenario, Deborah and Jackie recognize the differential distribution of scarce resources. They lament that "we were born poor and we're always going to be poor," though they wish for more. They believe that their children may be able to access a greater share of these limited resources if they are able to obtain a higher education and get good-paying jobs.

Group dynamics are different in families than in other groups. When applying conflict theory, one must recognize the differences between groups and families. The demand for resources varies between groups and families because some crises can drain family resources. For example, an illness in a family can cause a family to stress its resources to the maximum, whereas an illness in a group will generally not. Membership in a group is voluntary, whereas membership in a family is generally involuntary. If membership in a voluntary group becomes too intense or too competitive, a member may choose to leave. However, it is more difficult to leave a family than it is to leave a group. For instance, despite their current level of outrage with each other, Deborah and Jackie (from the vignette at the chapter's beginning) are not likely to dissolve their relationship because they are sisters and their lives are intertwined. Relationships in a family are by definition more intense, because they are closer in proximity and generally have a longer history. Also, dissolution of a family is more threatening than the dissolution of a group. It takes two to form a group, but only one to break it up. Thus, the person with the least interest has the most power. The ability to dissolve a family group is a great power indeed, so families generally tolerate a higher degree of conflict than groups (Sprey 1979).

The power differentials are also different in voluntary groups. Groups often consist of just one sex, so there is more equality of status. Also, group power remains rather static for the life of the group, but power changes over the life cycle of the family. As children age, they gain more power; as adults age, they lose power. These changes keep the family dynamics of power continuously fluid (Farrington and Chertok 1993).

Conflict is a confrontation over control of scarce resources. Conflict is categorized as either internal or external. Internal conflict is conflict originating from inside the social system (be it between individuals, families, or societies). In closely knit groups, members may suppress conflict. Negative emotions may accumulate and deepen, a phenomenon that social psychologists refer to as "gunny-sacking." When the conflict finally boils over, it is intensified. Not only is the conflict a problem, but it is also compounded and magnified by the expression of conflict. Thus, one outcome of conflict theory is the study of conflict management.

External conflict is conflict originating from outside the social system. One cannot deal with internal conflict while also using energy to fight external conflict. An example might be the conflict between political parties over tax policies (an internal conflict with respect to the country). But if war is declared on a foreign aggressor, the parties put aside their differences to concentrate on dealing with the war against another country (an external conflict). Likewise, a couple may be going through a difficult time and feeling as though their marriage is "on the rocks." Then they learn that their young child has a life-threatening illness, and they bond together for the sake of the child to fight the aggressor—in this case, the disease. The scenario between

Deborah and Jackie represented both types of conflict. The sisters were united in their fight against external conflict as they long for greater access to money and the things that it can buy, similar to what is available to those in higher social classes. However, internal conflict emerged as it became apparent that the sisters did not agree that they should share equal culpability for the speeding ticket. Deborah's comment suggests deeper internal conflict than the present hardship of how to pay for the ticket; historically, she has felt that her sister expects her to bail her out of situations in which she should have displayed greater personal responsibility.

One of the advantages of conflict is that, in the context of discussions, arguments, negotiations, and management, people come to new understandings of one another. This is often the case in families when couples or parents and their children learn about each other in the course of an argument. Thus, conflict can produce new or different values and revitalize existing norms. For example, in a disagreement with her 14-year-old daughter, a mother might learn that the curfew of 9 p.m. every night was too early to allow her to see even the early movie with her boyfriend. The mother, while still maintaining strict control over her adolescent daughter's dating habits, might be willing to negotiate a 10 p.m. curfew for weekends while maintaining the 9 p.m. deadline for all other nights. The negotiation maintains social structure in that the mother retains the power, although neither mother nor daughter is truly satisfied with the outcome (the mother probably doesn't want her daughter to date at all; the daughter probably doesn't want any curfew), but the social order is maintained. Furthermore, the conflict allows for growth to occur in the relationship between the daughter and mother as they both learn something about power, negotiation, family relationships, growing up, letting go, and communication skills.

Conflict can be classified. There are two major ways of classifying conflict in families—from a macrosocial perspective and from a microsocial perspective. Depending on one's educational orientation (more sociological or more developmental), the questions and focus (and related research) are different. Conflict theory is one of the few theories that can be used in both ways, although it does make the theory a bit more complex to fully understand.

As noted above, the conflict perspective allows us to see society as a place that generates and perpetuates inequality, which leads to conflict and change. Unlike structure functionalists, who see society as basically finding its own equilibrium, conflict theorists see that, as a society, we ascribe meaning and value, and stratify people into unequal roles, with varying levels of power and access to resources (Farrington and Chertok 1993). When we apply the theory to families, we analyze how families are classified based on their access to scarce resources and determine who has the power to maintain those value structures. For example, conflict theorists analyze the unequal distribution of power and social status based on social class, gender, race, ethnicity, and education.

From the macrosocial perspective, conflict theorists look at issues of conflict between classes of people who have privilege or dominance and those who are disadvantaged—the "haves" versus the "have nots"—(e.g., men versus women, rich versus poor, Whites versus Blacks, those with access to health care versus those without, employed versus unemployed, heterosexuals versus gays and lesbians, adults versus children, married versus single, married versus divorced, etc.). This is not to imply that any one individual has more or less than another, but rather that a group as a whole has more privilege than another group, and those privileges impact families and their opportunities and choices. Conflict theorists are concerned with how people manage the discrimination and stigma they face, how they negotiate their inequality in the face of unyielding privilege, and how society creates a shared value about what people "deserve" (Seccombe 1999, 2000).

A conflict theorist who studies families from this perspective might, for example, study how adoption placements are made. Consider the various levels of privilege and disadvantage of the following five potential parents for an adoption placement: a White, married, upper-income heterosexual couple; a White, middle-class lesbian couple; a Hispanic, single, upper-class gay man; a single, upper-class Black woman; and a White, previously divorced, lower-class married couple. If you were the adoption caseworker, how would you rank the order of placement, if all other factors were equal? What aspects of stratification enter into that decision? Generally, it is not the case that families fit neatly into stereotypical distinctions and, at times, values about certain families are based on myths rooted in class consciousness.

From a macrosocial perspective, conflict theorists help to deconstruct and analyze the ways in which our society ascribes values and how this leads to inequality in the family. They focus on broad social issues, such as economic inequities between men's and women's salaries, differing societal expectations of men's and women's responsibilities for child-rearing, and the acceptance of violence toward women and children. Family conflict theorists make the link between these broad social issues and family dynamics. In this way, feminist family theory and conflict theory share common goals.

From the microsocial perspective, conflict theorists look within the family system at the elements that can bring about conflict. Two major structural distinctions in families are gender and age. These structural differences bring about a distinct asymmetry in member resources and authority (Farrington and Chertok 1993). Regardless of the intent of the family members, society gives them access to resources in different ways. Adults have access to resources that children do not have (e.g., money, freedom, and power); males frequently have access to resources that females do not have (e.g., physical power, higher salaries, and opportunities). In addition, children have an involuntary membership in families. In most other societal groups, membership is voluntary or is the result of one's behavior. But children join families without any consultation. Thus, despite their perspective on membership, they must stay within the group and be governed by those in authority within the group.

The family life cycle also affects the long-term balance of resources within the family. Resource utilization and contribution may be different at various stages of the life cycle. In the earlier stages of the life cycle, parents have the power while children have little power. But in the later stages of the life cycle, the children typically gain power while the parents often lose power. This power shift may create conflict.

The interplay between the various macrosocial influences on intrafamily dynamics can be seen in the example of how power shifts over the life course. In our culture, power tends to decrease as one approaches old age. People are valued by their ability to contribute financially, and older adults are often thought of as being "past their prime" in this regard. In some other cultures, power tends to increase as one approaches old age. The wisdom and experience acquired over the years is regarded as a valuable resource, and so older adults are held in high esteem, even if their physical abilities are not what they once were.

Marital conflict is the most dramatic form of conflict in families in many ways. First, although it takes two to make a relationship, it takes only one to end it. So, as in exchange theory, the person with the least interest in maintaining the relationship has the most power in the relationship. Secondly, marital conflict can be intense simply because it is dyadic; in a twosome, there are no other allies. Third, marital conflict can also be intense because the marital relationship can come to an end. In contrast, other family relationships are for life. Whenever the stakes are high, the level of conflict can easily escalate.

The outcomes of marital conflict can be assessed in two ways. The first method is to determine the patterns of "winning" and "losing"—i.e., "keeping score." The idea of keeping score includes calculating the **importance** of battles won and lost, as well as the **number** of battles won and lost. The second method is to answer the question "What are the consequences for the relationship after conflict?" Conflict in a relationship ends either constructively or destructively. Marital dissolution affects the family as a whole but does not end it. At any given point, families are seen in the midst of their life course, at different points of conflict, growth, and change along the way (Sprey 1999).

Conflict has positive aspects. Conflict theorists believe that, ultimately, conflict is good, which is to say that the aftermath (the result) of conflict is beneficial. They argue that conflict is actually at the root of progress and change. (This is the legacy of Marx.) Conflict brings about the process of assimilation and compromise. It brings solidity and unity within groups and challenges the values and power we ascribe to those in other groups.

We learn as we change and grow in families. The process of learning to negotiate, communicate, and manage conflict is a positive aspect of development in families. Indeed, in close relationships, it is less important that there **are** conflicts, than **how** the conflicts are handled (Mace and Mace 1980). Facing conflict can bring relationships to new levels of intimacy, relieve tension and resentment, help to identify problems, increase understanding, and bring about a renewed appreciation for the relationship (Farrington and Chertok 1993; Stinnett, Walters, and Stinnett 1991). We would hope, for instance, that Deborah and Jackie (from the vignette) can work out a mutually satisfying resolution in handling the speeding ticket that will allow Jackie to take personal responsibility, while at the same time permitting them to be supportive of one another. Macrosocial conflict theorists believe that conflict theory promotes change by identifying the inequities in society and families and by promoting a reflection and critique of the structures and values that perpetuate oppression.

PRIMARY TERMS AND CONCEPTS

Competition

Sprey (1979) defined conflict as the "state of negative interdependence between the elements of a social system" (134). When one member of the family or group gains, others lose. Groups that exist over time, such as families, have highly honed abilities to function within a system of competitiveness and to recognize their interdependence. They realize that they can take turns winning and losing and make decisions whereby members jointly win or lose, depending on their willingness to negotiate, cooperate, and seek compromise.

Conflict

Conflict is the direct confrontation between individuals or groups over scarce resources. It occurs when people use controversial means to obtain their goals, or when they have incompatible goals, or some combination of these. Conflict implies a direct confrontation between opponents, whereas competition is more indirect and less personal. Conflict behavior can include physical force and litigation or the use of other external powers to achieve one's goals. Conflict can end only when both parties reach a mutually recognized agreement (e.g., one party gives up, a settlement is negotiated, or a peace treaty is signed). This does not, however, eliminate the underlying competitive basis.

Conflict Management

Conflict management involves dealing with the conflict while acknowledging the continued existence of the underlying competitive structure. It requires recognizing that (1) there are at least two competing perspectives, (2) there are scarce resources, and (3) each side should have an opportunity for access to those resources. Through negotiation and bargaining, conflict management can help competitors decide whether they wish to participate in a reciprocal sequence of access to resources (win–lose now, but lose–win later), a compromise in which both lose some resources, or a win–win option in which both sides jointly win. Conflict management does not negate the conflict, but it seeks ways to keep it from escalating.

Conflict Resolution

Conflict resolution refers to both the end state of conflict and the process of a given conflict's ending. Conflict resolution is different from conflict management, in which the conflict is maintained but negotiated into a stable state. In conflict resolution, the parties no longer see the issue as competition for scarce resources; there is no more conflict (on a particular matter), and resolution is the outcome. This may require redefining the situation, so that conflict is no longer perceived as being present.

Let's consider the difference between conflict management and conflict resolution by examining a rather common conflict in new relationships: money. A young couple begins their relationship with two separate bank accounts. Each pays half of the bills for housing, food, and other shared expenses; they spend the rest of their incomes on whatever they choose. But conflicts arise as their relationship begins to change and they want to buy a house, invest in expensive furniture, and save for their future. Who should be responsible for giving up their "fun" money for clothes, itunes, or going out? A conflict-managed solution might be for the couple to continue to pay one-half of the bills and for each to put some percentage of their extra funds into a shared account for future expenses (e.g., a down payment for a house, furniture, and other items) and continue to maintain control of the rest of their money. A conflict resolution would have occurred if this couple decided to combine their incomes into a joint checking account and then set up saving funds for their long-term goals. All the bills are paid, but now they are jointly focusing on their goals together, rather than seeing themselves as competitors. Because of a shift in their perspectives, money is no longer seen as an individual resource to be hoarded, but rather as a resource that has shared value for them as a couple.

Consensus

Consensus refers to a stable state in which society, groups, or families exist, sharing common awareness or knowledge of given issues, values, and norms. Consensus is reached when all parties "see things the same way." Unanimity, reached during deci- sion- making and negotiation, is a special case of consensus that occurs when all par- ties agree to a given course of action or perception of a situation. Conflict management seeks the consensus of the involved parties.

Negotiation and Bargaining

According to Sprey (1979), much conflict behavior is actually focused on negotiation and bargaining rather than fighting per se. These terms refer to the exchange process designed to reach a collective agreement on a disputed issue. Although the exchange may be heated or passionate as individuals and groups explain their positions, the underlying position is that they are trying to maintain access to their share of scarce resources and must, at least for the purposes of this exchange, perceive those "on the other side" as adversaries who seek to take scarce resources away from them. At times, negotiation and bargaining can be associated with hostility, but that is not always the case.

Power

Power refers to the ability to control the direction or course of action of others. It may apply to individuals or groups. It is a particularly salient concept in the analysis of families, because structures in families give authority to parents over children, and society has historically and culturally given power to men over women and boys over girls. Power can also be a function of personality and temperament, because some people tend to be more persuasive (or overpowering interpersonally, regardless of age, gender, or status). Conflict theory looks at the degree to which interpersonal uses of power enter into reciprocal interactions, identifying ways in which power can be used either positively, as a resource (e.g., authority or privilege), or negatively (e.g., to unduly control others).

Assertion and Aggression

Assertion is acting in a way that affirms one's rights and positions but does not nec- essarily do so at the expense of others. This is in contrast to aggression, which is a behavioral use of power to get others to behave to one's own advantage, even at the expense of others. Whereas assertion is most typically used in verbal statements, aggression can escalate to the psychological and physical overpowering of others.

Threats and Promises

Threats are messages, not behaviors, that communicate the delivery of punishment if demands are not met at some point in the future; promises are messages, not behaviors, that communicate the delivery of something positive or rewarding if demands are met at some point in the future. These messages, verbal or otherwise, require shared understandings of symbols and meanings, making them sometimes more meaningful to groups and families who have had similar shared experiences and less meaningful to outsiders who do not see their inherent power. For example, a wife may threaten to ruin her husband's reputation if he leaves her, or a husband may threaten to leave his wife poor and destitute if she leaves him. Both of these constitute threats, are coercive, and have a negative impact on the relationship by maintaining power, although no physical aggression is used.

COMMON AREAS OF RESEARCH AND APPLICATION

Conflict Management

For people studying conflict theory, it is often difficult to separate the difference between having a conflict with someone and seeing a relationship in the context of conflict. We all know that being in conflict with someone is draining, frustrating, and often disheartening. In intimate relationships, it is difficult to figure out if there are winners or losers—both partners lose when conflict is destructive. Although it seems intuitive that conflicts need to be resolved for relationships to be stable, conflict theorists believe that growth and change are necessary to achieve true stability. Thus, conflict theorists reject the notion that conflict between partners should focus on resolution, and instead believe that the focus should be on conflict management (Alberts 1990; Cahn 1990; Sprey 1979). The focus then turns to how couples and families communicate their needs and manage their individual desires as a group.

Power in the marital dyad has been studied extensively, and some classic works are included here because they remain important. Blood and Wolfe (1960) used the concept of power to understand decision-making between husbands and wives. Goode (1964) defined a negative authority as someone who could prevent someone else from doing something and indicated that this hidden power was often found in the husband's role. Cromwell and Olson (1975) defined three types of power in intimate relationships: power bases, power processes, and power outcomes. *Power bases* are what we bring into the relationship, or our personal assets such as knowledge or skills that might serve as a reward for the other partner. *Power processes* refer to the techniques we use to gain control in relationships. These might include our abilities to be assertive, persuade, solve problems, or coerce. *Power outcomes* refer to the final decisions that are made. These elements of power have been used to evaluate many components of family dynamics and decision-making.

Although other factors, such as money, education, and employment, contribute to the balance of power in social conflicts, communication seems to be one of the key factors in interpersonal conflict (Richmond, McCroskey, and Roach 1997). One of the best-known researchers in the past 30 years in the field of couples' communication is

John Gottman. Research by Gottman and his associates (Gottman 1979; Gottman et al. 1976; Gottman and Notarius 2000) has demonstrated the differences between the ways distressed and nondistressed couples communicate, illustrating that those who have negative communication patterns also have higher degrees of marital dissatisfaction and conflict. However, even highly distressed couples who reported high levels of conflict could be taught to manage their conflict in more positive and satisfactory ways, leading to more positive outcomes and higher marital satisfaction. Conflict management, then, is not a static skill, but rather one that improves over time (Gottman 1979; Mackey and O'Brien 1998). The Gottman team's research was so precise that they could predict the outcome of a disagreement 96 percent of the time by the amount of criticism and negative emotion apparent at the beginning of the conflict (Gottman and Notarius 2000). Furthermore, they found that the single most important predictor of divorce is when negative emotion escalates in a disagreement (e.g., anger is met with contempt). More recent work by Madhyastha, Hamaker, and Gottman (2011), suggests that the amount of positivity or negativity each partner brings to the conflictual exchange, as well as each individual's ability to "self-influence" their own emotional state during the interchange, might play an increasingly important role in helping couples manage conflict. As a result, they propose that interventions that focus on self-influence rather than mutual influence might be fruitful in future clinical work with couples.

Though not explicitly employing conflict theory per se, Timothy Smith and colleagues (2009) studied affect (e.g., anger, anxiety), cognitive appraisals of spouse (e.g., submissive, dominant), and behavioral responses of 300 middle-aged and older couples under two conditions: a disagreement exercise about a current conflict and a collaborative exercise involving planning errands. Overall, couples reported experiencing more anger and anxiety, and perceived their spouses as less friendly and more controlling, during the disagreement exercise than during the collaboration exercise. Couples were more friendly in their control and submission during the collaboration activity than during disagreement, and more controlling, hostile submissive, hostile separate, and assertive during disagreement than during collaboration. Although it appeared that older couples experienced the disagreement condition as less distressing than middle-aged couples, the disparities disappeared when marital satisfaction was controlled. Thus, there is a lot to be learned about how couples of all ages and relationship durations manage conflict.

When coupled with the concept of power, negative communication takes on additional meaning. For example, some people have a higher tolerance for conflict than others and can use that power to escalate a conflict. Those partners would be classified as *demanders*, and their partners are often *avoiders*. Researchers used to see those labels simply, with the demanders having more power in the relationship than the avoiders. But more careful analysis of communication and power clarified several points. First, couples who avoided conflict entirely were less satisfied with their relationships than those who confronted one another (Gottman and Krokoff 1989). Second, avoidance was not always found to be a negative or deficient element in a relationship; it was found to be a beneficial skill used by couples to postpone discussions until they had the time and energy to discuss issues (Alberts 1990). Combining power dimensions with communication also is one of the emerging avenues of research on domestic violence and power discrepancies (Babcock et al. 1993).

Gender is also an important variable in the assessment of power in relationships. In fact, conflict theory forms the basis of some aspects of feminist theory, because it underscores the inevitability of conflict between men and women who have unequal access to resources in our society, which is often reflected in the power relationships of intimate relationships. This is discussed in much more detail in the chapter on feminist theory.

Divorce

Obviously, not all conflicts can be managed, and divorce is the result when marital conflicts cannot be resolved. Historically, conflict theory was used to examine divorce, although nothing has been published more recently on the topic that employed the theory. Researchers studying divorce have identified various processes that correspond to the divorce experience, including the emotional, economic, and societal divorce (Shehan and Kammeyer 1997). These processes represent resources that affect the couple differentially and will impact the divorce experience for each partner differently. For example, if one partner has more emotional power by having more emotional closeness with the children, then custody arrangements might be of the greatest importance for that person in the divorce proceedings. If the couple has vast economic holdings and no children, perhaps the economic settlement may be the most important. If the couple lives in a small community, the social aspect of the divorce may carry the most weight. In the worst-case scenarios, these resource issues collide as one partner spreads rumors of drug use or child molestation in order to ensure child custody, or another partner declares bankruptcy in order not to have to pay child support to retaliate for the ex-spouse winning child custody. Obviously, in these conflict-habituated relationships, conflict did not lend itself to the positive growth and change that the theorists envisioned but still demonstrated the use of competition, power, and attempts to access scarce resources.

Developmental Changes

Of particular interest to developmental family scholars is how family dynamics change over the life course and how power differentials change as people age. For example, parents and adolescents are generally expected to have more conflict than parents and children, because adolescents are seeking to gain power as individuals (Smetana and Gaines 1999; Steinberg 1989). Before their children reach adolescence, parents have all the power, but as adolescents age, they have increased power, through increased access to social and financial networks and, particularly for males, increased physical power. Yet, for most families, the conflicts are generally about minor things—daily activities such as chores, keeping rooms clean, and choice of foods and snacks (Dacey and Kenny 1997). The research on parent–adolescent conflict also reflects, though, that the frequency and magnitude of conflict in parent–adolescent relationships depend on whom one asks. When adolescents were surveyed, they reported that adolescence was not particularly conflicted (Gecas and Seff 1990), but parents reported adolescence as more turbulent (Pasley and Gecas 1984). Despite this difference in perspective, it is important to remember that conflict can serve to teach adolescents how to appropriately manage and negotiate conflict as they grow up and leave home.

The interplay between developmental issues and macrolevel social issues can be seen in families as they struggle to negotiate the myriad of pressures that adolescents face. One level of conflict is found in the internal conflicts within emerging adolescents as they enter formal operational thought. For example, their cognitive ability to consider the real versus the ideal enables them to imagine idealized versions of themselves, their families, and their society. A second level of conflict exists as the adolescent seeks to individuate from the family while still maintaining some connection to it. A third level of conflict exists as the adolescent seeks to connect with society at large but does not have the resources to do so. Finally, a fourth level of conflict exists if the adolescent can, in fact, connect with society but must "leave the family behind" to do so.

Family Violence

Conflict theory has frequently been used in family studies to clarify issues in family violence and abuse. The clear dynamics of conflict and power are a part of abusive relationships, and family scholars have analyzed these relationships to determine how and why violence occurs, what the predetermining factors are, why people stay in abusive relationships, and what motivates people to leave such abusive relationships.

Typically, when we consider couple violence, we often consider physical strength as the power in the relationship, but conflict theorists broaden our perspective. The 1950s picture of domestic violence was of a strong man telling "his woman" what to do, and forcing her, if necessary, to bend to his will. The 21st-century picture of domestic violence must take into account dating and courtship violence, cohabiting violence, violence perpetrated on men by women, same-sex relationship violence, and our increasing knowledge of the many forms of abuse (Johnson and Ferraro 2000; Miller and Knudsen 1999). *Wife abuse* is no longer a term sufficient to include the types of abuse found in intimate relationships today. Even such labels as partner abuse, child abuse, and elder abuse are not sufficient. Within couples, we must now distinguish between common couple violence, intimate terrorism, and violent resistance (Johnson and Ferraro 2000). Conflict theorists have helped us to analyze the complexity of the many forms of violence perpetrated in families.

One of the most important predictors of domestic violence is inequity in power (Sagrestano, Heavey, and Christensen 1999). Couples with more egalitarian distributions of power in their relationships are less likely to report violence than those with unequal power (Coleman and Straus 1986). Furthermore, the severity of the abuse toward a female is dependent on the abuser's perception of her power (Claes and Rosenthal 1990). Power differentials can be seen in communication patterns, because verbal coercion can be a form of emotional abuse and a precursor to physical abuse (Babcock et al. 1993). Ironically, despite the hope that women would be empowered by educational and occupational achievements, violence against women is greater in couples when the woman's economic, educational, or occupational status is higher than the man's (Claes and Rosenthal 1990; Sagrestano, Heavey, and Christensen 1999).

Siblings can also resort to the use of violence to resolve conflicts resulting from such things as sibling jealousy or competition for parental attention, distribution of household chores, and the need to share space and possessions. Recognizing that most family violence occurs between siblings, Hoffman, Kiecolt, and Edwards (2005) used conflict, feminist, and social-learning theories to ask 651 first-year college students about their experience of physical violence with siblings. As might be expected from a conflict theory perspective, sibling violence, particularly among males, was more prevalent when parents elevated one child as a standard for other children. Such resentments exacerbated sibling arguments and also made it more difficult for siblings to share property.

Professional Practice and Policy

In some instances, conflict theory has been helpful for practitioners and clinicians in the work that they do. For example, Vodde (2001) applies a linguistic theory of conflict in working with couples in therapy, particularly in the treatment of marital conflict. Vodde recognizes that power differentials exist within couples, and that language is a means to express symbolic power. By making assessments or judgments about the nature of one's partner or one's marital relationship, a more powerful person exerts a certain narrative, legitimizing the structure and governance of the relationship or the distribution of resources. As Vodde states, "simply put, any statement defining the other or one's relationship with the other is considered a statement that attempts to define, unilaterally, one's position of authority with that person" (75), thus normalizing the control. Positioned within this larger field of power (e.g., gender, economics, vocation), couples struggle, not necessarily over resource distribution, but over "legitimizing a particular description of what is happening" (77). He encourages therapists to consider the power disparities that might exist between couples and how roles and power are decided both internally and externally to the relationship. The therapist should pay particular attention to "strategies of condescension" (81), as such tactics silence the other partner, while often appearing as agreement. When working with couples in conflict, therapists should not assume "dialogical equality," as it may not be safe for one of the partners to share his or her version of the truth. If social justice is to become a reality within the family, the therapist must expose the power imbalance that exists within dysfunctional marital conflict.

Conflict theory has been used to consider the competing forces encountered by human service professionals functioning within their employment contexts. Fogler (2009) used conflict theory to outline the dilemma encountered by nursing home social workers when they are confronted by competing interests of the nursing home industry and governmental policy in making discharge plans related to long-term care for older adults. Conflict theory is helpful in identifying vying superstructures at the macrolevel and their related interests. In this case, the for-profit nursing home industry wants nursing home social workers to maintain population so that homes operate as close to capacity as possible. At the same time, government, which is concerned about cost-containment, encourages social work discharge planners to maximize the utilization of home- and community-based services, which tend to be less expensive than institutionalization. These disparate interests create the potential for real confusion and conflict for discharge planners, particularly when they ultimately need to keep the best interests of the older adult in mind. This and other research reveal how conflict theory is helpful in examining competing needs within family relationships, as well as between social structures.

Conflict theory also helps professionals analyze various social problems. For instance, Patterson and Wolf (2010) used conflict theory, social construction theory, and ethnomethodology to evaluate HIV/AIDS and alcohol and drug use. According to the authors, conflict theory recognizes that many chronic drug users are structurally disadvantaged individuals; they are politically less powerful and often from low-income families and disorganized neighborhoods. Conflict theory, and its attentiveness to power relations and those with authority within society, helps us recognize the impact of decisions made by policy makers and medical professionals relative to who deserves health care and what those health care options will include. Consequently, the authors conclude that, to combat HIV transmission and the spread of alcohol and drug dependency among those with HIV infection, both individual and macrolevel risk factors need to be considered. Conflict theory helps to identify those opposing forces.

CRITIQUE

One of the criticisms of conflict theory is that it analyzes families in destructive, negative terms (i.e., conflict, power, and competition). Many family theorists prefer to focus on constructive and positive terms (i.e., cooperation, equity, and compassion). In other words, it simply does not fit our ideal of what relationships "ought" to be, and therefore provides a less positive model for study.

Another criticism is that conflict theory, once it has described relationships in terms of its components of competition, power, and access to resources, does not propose how families can improve. Other theories focus on order and being able to make predictions about families. Conflict theory, by definition, does not engender a static view of families, but rather an always changing perspective. Thus, conflict theory does not lend itself to research or application outcomes that are immediately transferable to skill-building. One exception is the work by Gottman, but his focus has been on conflicts at the interpersonal level and not at the social level.

Some scholars may wish for families that are safe and happy places, but conflict theory does, in fact, describe situations where families are not. Conflict theory raises our awareness of situations that families face regarding inequities in health care, income, access to education, and equal opportunity (both legally and in other, more subtle ways). It encourages us to see families within their complex social systems. In addition, conflict theory takes into account the ever-changing elements brought into families by development, social events, social pressures, and internal and external forces.

APPLICATION

1. Using the vignette at the beginning of the chapter, answer the following questions:

a. How is Deborah and Jackie's socioeconomic status illustrated in the story? What elements of class conflict are apparent in their situation?

b. How might the elements of class conflict that are expressed by Deborah and Jackie earlier in the day be a part of the interpersonal conflict experienced between the sisters later in the day?

c. Find an example of each basic assumption in the story.

d. There were examples of both conflict and competition in this story. Identify some of them, and discuss how socioeconomic, educational, gender, or power components combine to make the situations more complex.

e. Discuss your perspective on the conflict between Jackie and Deborah. Is it positive or negative? Is it good or bad for the relationship? How? What could they do at this point to manage the conflict better?

f. Discuss some of the consequences of the conflict between the sisters on the family as a whole. What if the children had been present during the argument? Would that have made a difference? In what other ways, aside from observing parents arguing, do children learn how to manage conflicts in their lives?

g. In this family, there are three generations living together. What additional issues of power and conflict management does this family face because of the extended family arrangement?

2. Over what resources has your own family experienced competition and/or conflict? How has your family managed the conflict? Are there any issues around which conflict was resolved? Describe how, and under what circumstances, your family has sought consensus, exhibited power, and employed the use of negotiating/bargaining, assertion and aggression, and threats and promises.

3. Answer the following questions after reading the sample reading (Recchia, Ross, and Vickar 2010):

a. How are each of conflict theory's basic assumptions represented in the article?

b. How does the relative power of dyadic partners affect parent–child, marital, and sibling conflict? Have you witnessed any of these same power dynamics during conflict exchanges within your own family?

c. Differentiate between constructive strategies for conflict resolution, like problem-solving, and less productive strategies, like opposition.

d. The authors make connections between their results and conflict theory in the discussion section. What additional points would you include?

e. If you were creating a parenting program on helping parents to be better communicators with their children, what information and skill-enhancing elements would you include in the section on "Managing conflict with your child"?

REFERENCES

Alberts, J. K. 1990. The use of humor in managing couples' conflict interactions. In *Intimates in conflict*, ed. D. D. Cahn, 105–120. Hillsdale, NJ: Lawrence Erlbaum.

Babcock, J. C., J. Waltz, N. S. Jacobson, and J. M. Gottman. 1993. Power and violence: The relations between communication patterns, power discrepancies, and domestic violence. *Journal of Consulting and Clinical Psychology* 61: 40–50.

Blood, R. O., and D. M. Wolfe. 1960. *Husbands and wives, the dynamics of married living.* New York: Free Press.

Cahn, D. 1990. *Intimates in conflict: A communication perspective.* Hillsdale, NJ: Lawrence Erlbaum.

Claes, J. A., and D. M. Rosenthal. 1990. Men who batter women: A study in power. *Journal of Family Violence* 5: 215–224.

Coleman, D. H., and M. A. Straus. 1986. Marital power, conflict, and violence in a nationally representative sample of American couples. *Violence and Victims* 1: 141–157.

Cromwell, R. E., and D. H. Olson. 1975. *Power in families*. New York: Wiley.

Dacey, J., and M. Kenny. 1997. *Adolescent development*. 2nd ed. Madison, WI: Brown and Benchmark.

Farrington, K., and E. Chertok. 1993. Social conflict theories of the family. In *Sourcebook of family theories and methods: A contextual approach*, ed. P. G. Boss, W. J. Doherty, R. LaRossa, W. R. Schumm, and S. K. Steinmetz, 357–381. New York: Plenum.

Fogler, S. 2009. Using conflict theory to explore the role of nursing home social workers in home- and community-based service utilization. *Journal of Gerontological Social Work* 52: 859–869.

Gecas, V., and M. A. Seff. 1990. Families and adolescents: A review of the 1980's. *Journal of Marriage and the Family* 52: 941–958.

Goode, W. 1964. *The family*. Englewood Cliffs, NJ: Prentice Hall.

Gottman, J. M. 1979. *Marital interaction: Experimental investigations*. New York: Academic Press.

Gottman, J. M., and L. J. Krokoff. 1989. Marital interaction and satisfaction: A longitudinal view. *Journal of Consulting and Clinical Psychology* 57: 47–52.

Gottman, J. M., and C. I. Notarius. 2000. Decade review: Observing marital interaction. *Journal of Marriage and the Family* 62: 927–947.

Gottman, J., C. Notarius, J. Gonso, and H. Markman. 1976. *A couple's guide to communication*. Champaign, IL: Research Press.

Hoffman, K. L., K. J. Kiecolt, and J. N. Edwards. 2005. Physical violence between siblings: A theoretical and empirical analysis. *Journal of Family Issues* 26: 1103–1130.

Johnson, M. P., and K. J. Ferraro. 2000. Research on domestic violence in the 1990's: Making distinctions. *Journal of Marriage and the Family* 62: 948–963.

Mace, D., and V. Mace. 1980. Enriching marriages: The foundation of family strength. In *Family strengths: Positive models for family life*, ed. N. Stinnett, B. Chesser, J. DeFrain, and P. Knaub, 89–110. Lincoln, NE: University of Nebraska.

Mackey, R. A., and B. A. O'Brien. 1998. Marital conflict management: Gender and ethnic differences. *Social Work* 43: 128–141.

Madhyastha, T. M., E. L. Hamaker, and J. M. Gottman. 2011. Investigating spousal influence using moment-to-moment affect data from marital conflict. *Journal of Family Psychology* 25(2): 292–300.

Miller, J. L., and D. D. Knudsen. 1999. Family abuse and violence. In *Handbook of marriage and the family*, ed. M. Sussman, S. K. Steinmetz, and G. W. Peterson. 2nd ed., 705–741. New York: Plenum.

Olson, L. N., M. A. Fine, and S. A. Lloyd. (2005). Theorizing about aggression between intimates: A dialectical approach. In *Sourcebook of family theory and research*, ed. V. L. Bengtson, A. C. Acock, K. R. Allen, P. Dilworth-Anderson, and D. M. Klein. 315–331. Thousand Oaks, CA: Sage Publications.

Pasley, K., and V. Gecas. 1984. Stresses and satisfactions of the parental role. *Personnel and Guidance Journal* 2: 400–404.

Patterson, D. A., and S. Wolf. 2010. Analyzing HIV/AIDS and alcohol and other drug use as a social problem. *Journal of Gay and Lesbian Social Services* 22: 211–225.

Richmond, V. P., J. C. McCroskey, and K. D. Roach. 1997. Communication and decision-making styles, power base usage, and satisfaction in marital dyads. *Communication Quarterly* 45: 410–426.

Russell, B. 1945/1972. *A history of Western philosophy*. New York: Simon and Schuster.

Sagrestano, L. M., C. L. Heavey, and A. Christensen. 1999. Perceived power and physical violence in marital conflict. *Journal of Social Issues* 55: 65–79.

Seccombe, K. 1999. *"So you think I drive a Cadillac?" Welfare recipients' perspectives on the system and its reform*. Boston: Allyn and Bacon.

————. 2000. Families in poverty in the 1990s: Trends, causes, consequences, and lessons learned. *Journal of Marriage and the Family* 62: 1094–1113.

Shehan, C. L., and K. C. W. Kammeyer. 1997. *Marriages and families: Reflections of a gendered society*. Boston: Allyn and Bacon.

Simmel, G. (trans. Mark Ritter and David Frisby). 1998. On the sociology of the family. *Theory, Culture and Society* 15(3–4): 283–293.

Smetana, J., and C. Gaines. 1999. Adolescent–parent conflict in middle-class African American families. *Child Development* 70: 1447–1463.

Smith, T.W., C. A. Berg, P. Forsheim, B. N. Uchino, G. Pearce, M. Hawkins, N. J. M. Henry, R. M. Beveridge, M. A. Skinner, and C. Olsen-Curry. 2009. Conflict and collaboration in middle-aged and older couples: I. Age differences in agency and communion during marital interaction. *Psychology and Aging* 24(2): 259–273.

Sprey, J. 1969. The family as a system in conflict. *Journal of Marriage and the Family* 31: 699–706.

————. 1979. Conflict theory and the study of marriage and the family. In *Contemporary theories about the family*. Vol. 2 of *General theories/theoretical orientations*, ed. W. R. Burr, R. Hill, F. I. Nye, and I. L. Reiss, 130–159. New York: Free Press.

————. 1999. Family dynamics: An essay on conflict and power. In *Handbook of marriage and the family*, ed. M. Sussman, S. K. Steinmetz, and G. W. Peterson. 2nd ed., 667–685. New York: Plenum.

Steinberg, L. 1989. *Adolescence*. 2nd ed. New York: Knopf.

Stinnett, N., J. Walters, and N. Stinnett. 1991. *Relationships in marriage and the family*. New York: Macmillan.

Turner, J. H. 1998. *The structure of sociological theory*. 6th ed. Belmont, CA: Wadsworth.

Vodde, R. 2001. Fighting words and challenging stories in couples work: Using constructionist conflict theory to understand marital conflict. *Journal of Family Social Work* 6(2): 69–86.

SAMPLE READING

Recchia, H. E., H. S. Ross, and M. Vickar. 2010. Power and conflict resolution in sibling, parent–child, and spousal negotiations. *Journal of Family Psychology* 24(5): 605–615.

As we know, conflict is a normal part of family life. Recchia, Ross, and Vickar examine conflict occurring within three different family subsystems—that between siblings, parents and children, and spouses. In particular, they look at the extent to which conflict strategies—like planning and opposition—are used, as well as the type of resolutions that occur—standoff, win-loss, or compromise. The authors assume that the power differentials existing within these various subsystems will make a difference in the types of strategies (processes) employed, as well as the resultant outcomes. Using a sample of 67 families with two children, dyadic pairs were assigned discussion tasks, and their actions were coded. After you read the authors' hypotheses, pause and reflect for a moment. Would you anticipate the same findings? After you read the results section, consider the implications of these findings for relationships between parents and their children, between spouses, and between siblings. How might power be used more positively in resolving conflict in each of these contexts? What specific steps might you propose for family life educators or family therapists working with each family dyad?

SAMPLE READING

Power and Conflict Resolution in Sibling, Parent–Child, and Spousal Negotiations

Holley E. Recchia
University of Utah

Hildy S. Ross
University of Waterloo

Marica Vickar
University of Toronto

This study used a within-family observational design to examine conflict strategies (planning, opposition) and resolutions (standoff, win-loss, compromise) across family subsystems, with an emphasis on power differences between parents and children during relatively symmetrical within-generation (spousal, sibling) and relatively asymmetrical between-generation (parent–child) dyadic interactions. Up to six dyads in 67 families (children's ages ranging from 3 to 12 years) discussed an unresolved conflict. Results revealed that within-generation discussions ended more in standoff, whereas between-generation discussions ended with more win-loss resolutions. Multilevel

Holly E. Recchia, Department of Psychology, University of Utah; Hildy S. Ross, Department of Psychology, University of Waterloo; Marcia Vickar, Ontario Institute for Studies in Education, University of Toronto. Correspondence concerning this article should be addressed to Hildy S. Ross, Department of Psychology, University of Waterloo, Waterloo, ON, Canada N2L 3G1. Email: hross@uwaterloo.ca

The project described was supported by Grant Number HD38895 from the National Institute of Child Health and Human Development (NICHD) and Grant Number 410–2005-1018 from the Social Sciences and Humanities Research Council of Canada (SSHRC). Its contents are solely the responsibility of the authors and do not necessarily represent the official views of either NICHD or SSHRC. We thank the families who generously participated in this study, Nancy L. Stein, Tom Trabasso, and Michael Ross, co-PIs; along with Hildy S. Ross, on the NICHD grant; Marc Hernandez, Krista Gass, Alex North, and Lauren Chance, who coordinated data collection and coding; Jonathan Santo and Jonathan Butner, who provided advice on data analyses; and research assistants in Chicago and Waterloo.

analyses indicated that parents engaged in more planning and opposition than children; however, they opposed more and planned less with their spouses than their children. In general, more planning and less opposition were associated with achieving resolutions rather than failing to resolve differences. Some effects were qualified by within-family differences between mothers versus fathers and older versus younger siblings, as well as between-family differences in younger siblings' age. Implications for theories of power and family relationship dynamics are discussed.

Keywords: conflict, negotiation, spouses, siblings, parent–child relations

Across the lifespan, relationships with siblings, spouses, parents, and children are among our most enduring interpersonal connections. Furthermore, spousal, sibling, and parent– child subsystems in the family are reciprocally interdependent (Minuchin, 1985), and many studies of family conflict have focused on these connections among family subsystems (e.g., Rinaldi & Howe, 2003) or the impact of family conflict on children's adjustment (e.g., Goeke-Morey, Cummings, & Papp, 2007). This research has convincingly demonstrated that family conflict processes have clear implications for both later relationships (Whitton et al., 2008) and children's development (Cummings, Fair-cloth, Mitchell, Cummings, & Schermerhorn, 2008).

Yet family subsystems also exhibit unique characteristics that follow from the particular roles that family members assume within different relationship contexts. With research focused on individual differences between families, within-family variability in conflict resolution among subsystems has seldom been addressed. The emphasis in the literature on associations between family subsystems does not directly assess fundamental structural differences in conflict processes between different family relationships, or how interactions in each relationship constitute distinct contexts for children's development. That is, the features of relationships between husbands and wives versus parents and children may be predictably linked to differences in the constructiveness of adults' conflict strategies and conflict resolutions during interactions with their marital partners and their children. Similarly, children's conflicts with siblings and parents provide very different affordances for learning about constructive conflict resolution (Dunn, Slomkowski, Donelan, & Herrera, 1995). With these issues in mind, the goal of this study was to elucidate how discrepancies and similarities in power between family members are related to conflict resolutions in spousal, sibling, and parent–child relationships. Using a within-family design, we examined conflict strategies (opposition and planning), resolutions (standoff, win-loss, and compromise), and links between strategies and resolutions as family members discussed and attempted to resolve issues in their relationships.

SOURCES OF POWER IN FAMILY CONFLICT

One central dimension that differentiates between- and within-generation family relationships is the relative power of dyadic partners. In parent–child interactions, parents have more power than do their children (Emery, 1992). Parental power is derived from a variety of sources (French & Raven, 1959; Perlman, Siddiqui, Ram, & Ross, 2000):

their greater physical strength and control of family resources are obvious sources of parents' power, but their recognized expertise and sophisticated reasoning abilities also contribute to parents' dominance in parent–child relationships. In comparison to parent–child dyads, various sources of power may be relatively more equivalent between siblings and spouses, but importantly, neither of these relationships is entirely symmetrical. Age differences between siblings provide earlier-born children with greater ability to control sibling interaction (Perlman et al., 2000), and spousal interactions reveal asymmetrical roles between partners (e.g., Dunbar & Burgoon, 2005). Yet, in comparison to parent– child dyads, various sources of power are relatively more equivalent between siblings and spouses. As such, our study set out to capture both sources of variability (i.e., within-dyad and between-dyad differences in the family) by observing multiple family members (mothers, fathers, older and younger siblings) across multiple contexts (i.e., spousal, sibling, and parent–child interactions).

RESOLUTIONS AND STRATEGIES IN FAMILY CONFLICTS

Conflict theorists have noted that conflict resolutions reflect the contrast in relative power that differentiates symmetrical from asymmetrical relationships (Perlman et al., 2000). In relationships where power is asymmetrical, more powerful opponents tend to achieve their goals. Indeed, dyadic power theory suggests that it may not even be necessary for powerful opponents to engage in explicit control attempts to prevail in conflict (Dunbar, 2004). In contrast, when power is more equal between partners, reciprocal control attempts are more likely, and conflict resolutions are less predictable. If both arguers are unable to coerce or persuade the other and neither is willing to give up ground, negotiators will fail to resolve their differences. In contrast, if both arguers are willing to revise their initial positions so that each person partly achieves his/her goals, compromise resolutions can be reached. The distinction between these two plausible resolutions in relatively equal power dyads may depend on family members' orientation as they attempt to resolve issues, and especially the strategies that they use to do so.

Methods used in many studies of family conflict fail to separately assess both conflict strategies and resolutions, or confound variables related to processes and outcomes of negotiations. However, for our purposes, separately examining each individual's conflict strategies as well as the dyadic resolution is critical, because it provides a window into how family members exercise and experience power as they resolve interpersonal problems in different relationships. For instance, although children may engage in problem-solving with their parents, it may be parents' constructive strategies that are particularly associated with mutually agreeable solutions in this context.

In general, certain types of conflict strategies are more or less conducive to achieving constructive conflict resolutions such as compromise. Deutsch (1973) differentiated between constructive and destructive conflict strategies, a distinction that has been echoed in the spousal (Gottman, 1994; Stanley, Markman, & Whitton, 2002), sibling (Perlman & Ross, 2005; Ram & Ross, 2001), and parent–child conflict literatures (Rinaldi & Howe, 2003; Rueter & Conger, 1995). In these studies, one key set of constructive strategies, often labeled "problem-solving," is defined by future-oriented planning (Cummings et al., 2008) aimed at seeking ways to integrate the goals of both parties via compromise (Stein & Albro, 2001). In turn, oppositional tactics focus on making the other yield to one's own position through disagreements, accusations, or persuasive contentious arguments, and tend to interfere with the achievement of mutually agreeable resolutions (Forgatch, 1989; Stanley et al., 2002). Across family relationships, oppositional strategies predict family members' failures to resolve their differences, whereas future-oriented planning has been linked to constructive conflict resolutions such as compromise (Forgatch, 1989; Ram & Ross, 2001; Vuchinich, 1999). These two sets of strategies (i.e., planning and opposition) are particularly relevant for our purposes, because each reflects a distinct source of power that individuals may use to achieve their conflict goals (French & Raven, 1959). Specifically, less constructive forms of coercive power may be exercised though oppositional strategies whereas expertise is manifested when more sophisticated family members control the planning process that resolves differences.

Although conflict processes among siblings, spouses, and parent–child dyads have each been well researched, the relative frequencies of specific conflict strategies between subsystems are rarely compared directly. Only a few studies have compared children's conflict *strategies* using the same observational methodologies across family relationships, generally finding more negative emotionality and unreasoned opposition between young siblings than within mother–child dyads (Dunn & Munn, 1987; Dunn et al., 1995). Although theory on adults' family conflict strategies suggests a similar pattern of greater opposition between spouses than with children (Vuchinich, 1984), this comparison has not been systematically addressed in the literature. In contrast, the relative frequencies of different conflict *resolutions* across family relationships have been more clearly delineated. Most studies reveal that when family members do not compromise, in spousal or sibling relationships, disputants typically fail to entirely resolve their differences (Goeke-Morey et al., 2007; Siddiqui & Ross, 1999; Vuchinich, 1987). In contrast to sibling or spousal interactions, parent–child relationships are characterized by substantial differences in power. Thus, not surprisingly, when parents and children engage in conflict, parents typically prevail (Stein & Albro, 2001; Vuchinich, 1987). Parent–child discussions may be oriented differently than sibling or spousal discussions; these interactions are primarily aimed at producing a concession by the child or maintaining the family power structure (Emery, 1992; Vuchinich, 1984), rather than finding a way to satisfy both parties' interests.

The Current Study

In this study we systematically explored variability in family conflict resolution using a within-family design. We used discussion tasks that have been developed to assess conflict strategies in various family subsystems (Gottman, 1994; Rueter & Conger, 1995; Smith & Ross, 2007). In 67 families with two children, we asked all available dyadic combinations of family members to discuss an unresolved conflict. That is, parents were observed resolving conflicts with their spouses and each of their two children, and children were observed with their siblings and each parent. For each dyad, we coded the resolution achieved (i.e., compromise, win-loss, or standoff) as well as the use of future-oriented planning (i.e., developing solutions) and oppositional strategies (i.e., accusing, challenging, counterarguing) by each partner in particular family subsystems. In our view, power can be considered both in terms of resolutions (i.e., achieving one's own personal goals during conflict resolution) and process (the extent to which each individual's strategies influence conflict resolutions). Thus, the resolutions achieved, the strategies that family members use to influence one another, and the relative effectiveness of each individual's strategies in influencing conflict resolutions across family relationships frame our analysis of family conflict negotiations.

Hypotheses

We expected conflict resolutions to differ across family relationship contexts (H1a). Specifically, we expected that the relative asymmetry of parent–child relationships would be linked to more win-loss resolutions in this dyad (Stein & Albro, 2001; Vuchinich, 1987), whereas sibling and spousal conflicts would be more often left unresolved (Siddiqui & Ross, 1999; Vuchinich, 1987). Furthermore, when win-loss resolutions did occur, we expected parents to overwhelmingly emerge as the winners during interactions with their children, whereas the distributions of wins and losses would be relatively equitable between siblings and spouses (H1b), although older siblings may achieve their conflict goals more often than younger ones (Perlman et al., 2000).

Following from dyadic power theory (Dunbar, 2004), we expected family members to engage in more oppositional behavior during spousal and sibling discussions than during parent–child interactions (H2). Although parents do use power assertive techniques with their children and in turn, children oppose their parents (Hastings & Grusec, 1998; Kuczynski, Kochanska, Radke-Yarrow, & Girnius-Brown, 1987), oppositional strategies may be more frequent during interactions in relatively symmetrical family relationships. In contrast, we expected parents to engage in more future-oriented planning during parent–child interactions than during discussions with their spouses, given their role as socialization agents for their children (H3).

Finally, across all family relationships, we expected more planning and less opposition to be associated with compromise resolutions that considered both negotiators' goals (Forgatch, 1989; Ram & Ross, 2001; Stanley et al., 2002; Vuchinich, 1999; H4). However, we expected these associations to vary as a function of relative power in different family subsystems. Consistent with parents' leadership roles and relative expertise in conflict management, we expected that the strategies adopted by parents would be more strongly related to resolutions than those of their children (H5a). Similarly, we expected that older siblings' conflict strategies would be more strongly related to conflict resolutions than those of younger siblings (H5b).

Although our emphasis was on within-family differences, some studies suggest that family conflict processes may vary as a function of child age (e.g., Ram & Ross, 2001), although others do not (e.g., Goeke-Morey et al., 2007). As relevant, age effects were tested as potential between-family moderators of the predicted associations.

METHOD

Participants

Data for this investigation were drawn from a more extensive intervention study of family relationships. The entire procedure consisted of 14 sessions in families' homes that included interviews, observations, and, in some randomly assigned cases, conflict training. The data for these analyses came from the pre-test sessions of the intervention study (i.e., prior to assigning families randomly to groups).

Participants were recruited through 20 middle-class, ethnically diverse elementary schools in metropolitan Chicago. Letters sent home invited families with two children between 4- and 12-years of age who were not experiencing serious developmental delays or physical or mental health problems to participate. Eighty-five families who responded to invitations met these criteria; however, 18 families decided to discontinue their participation after one or two sessions when the full extent of the time commitment became clear to them.

The 67 families with available observational data for conflict discussions included six single-parent households (all mothers) and 61 two-parent households. The sample included 55 Caucasian, 6 African American, and 3 Latino families, as well as 3 families of mixed ethnicity. All families spoke English at home. Children's ages ranged from 3.55 to 12.39 years (younger sibling $M = 5.76$ years, $SD = .96$, range = 3.55 to 7.93; older sibling $M = 8.82$, $SD = 1.22$, range = 5.38 to 12.39). The average age difference between siblings was 3.07 years ($SD = 1.17$, range = 1.00 to 5.39). The sample included 31 same-gender pairs (9 female, 22 male) and 36 mixed-gender pairs (22 older female and 14 older male). Mothers' M age was 37.96 years ($SD = 4.57$, range = 26 to 48 years), and fathers' M age was 39.57 years ($SD = 5.19$, range = 30 to 56 years). Parental education ranged from high school (5 mothers, 4 fathers) to advanced degrees (21 mothers, 23 fathers), with most parents having received some college education (14 mothers, 14 fathers) or completing a college degree (27 mothers, 20 fathers). Family incomes ranged from under $15,000 to over $75,000 per year. None of these characteristics significantly differentiated the sub sample of 67 participating families from the initial sample of 85 families. Each family received a $330 honorarium for their participation.

Procedure

During the first visit to the family's home, parents provided written informed consent on behalf of themselves and their children; children verbally assented to all procedures. Families were made aware of mandatory reporting in cases of suspected abuse or maltreatment. During the second and third visits, each participant completed scales assessing the quality of family relationships, behavior problems, and well-being (see Ross, Stein, Trabasso, Woody, & Ross, 2005).

During the third to fifth visits to the home, each participant was interviewed privately about conflicts with one of their family members with the order counterbalanced across families. Then dyad members were brought together, and the interviewer briefly described the unresolved conflicts nominated by each family member. Once it was ascertained that both dyad members remembered the events referred to, the dyad was asked to select one of the conflicts for discussion. In all cases, dyads were able to mutually agree on a conflict for discussion. Family members were then left alone to discuss the problem for up to 13 min, but they were also asked to notify the researcher when discussions ended earlier. In each case, spouses, siblings, or parent–child dyads were asked to talk together and "work out some sort of solution that you're both happy with." All discussions were videotaped.

Conflict issues across all dyads were related to family members' everyday attempts to control one another's behavior; for example, parents trying to teach their children rules and conventions, children trying to control their siblings' access to property, and spouses attempting to resolve differences in their individual goals. Very few conflicts (only 8%) involved issues of physical, verbal or emotional harm and none of these occurred between spouses.

Measures and Coding

Verbatim transcripts of all verbal conflict strategies along with records of nonverbal actions relevant to the interaction (e.g., nodding, shaking hands, pointing, threatening gestures, intonation or gestures that changed the meaning of the utterance) were prepared from video records. To permit the calculation of kappas for interrater reliability, coding was done from transcripts which were parsed into the smallest meaningful units of verbal and nonverbal behavior (i.e., subject-verb clauses, or single actions). Transcripts were coded for planning and oppositional strategies. Frequencies of each strategy were computed for each family member in each dyad. Generally, the unit of analysis for coding was a clause, although if consecutive clauses received the same code, the behavior was scored only once. Nine trained undergraduate coders coded the data, and all coders participated in establishing interobserver reliability, based on a sample of discussions including equal numbers of all dyad types. Reliability was established on 34% of the data. Weighted mean Cohen's kappa for parsing of codable units was .85 and kappa for the type of conflict strategy was .84. Kappas for all pairs of coders exceeded .70.

Planning was coded when family members generated, assessed or adopted plans for resolving similar issues in the future (Cummings et al., 2008; Ram & Ross, 2001). This included proposing plans (e.g., "We should take turns."), modifying plans (e.g., "Except we should each get double turns."), asking about plans (e.g., "Who would go first?"), justifying plans (e.g., "That would make it fair."), and requesting assent to plans (e.g., "So you agree with that?"). Opposition was coded when family members advanced their own positions or versions of past events while countering or dismissing the arguments of the other (Forgatch, 1989; Stanley et al., 2002). Oppositional strategies included accusations (e.g., "You barged right into my room."), disagreements (e.g., "No, I don't think so."), counterarguments (e.g., "That plan is too complicated."), challenges (e.g., "Are you trying to say *that's* a good plan?"), and dismissals (e.g., "I don't actually care what you think.").

Each discussion was coded globally for the resolution reached by the dyad in light of their conflict goals. To increase the validity of associations between strategies and resolutions, resolutions were scored by a different team of coders. If family members successfully resolved their conflict, dyadic resolutions were scored as compromise (i.e., both participants achieving at least some of what they wanted) or win-loss (i.e., only one participant's goal being realized) resolutions. In the latter case, the winner was noted. If family members failed to resolve their differences, the resolution was coded as a standoff. Cohen's kappa, established among four coders on 21% of the data, was .71.

RESULTS

How Do Conflict Resolutions Vary Across Different Dyads in the Family?

To begin, we conducted nonparametric tests to examine patterns of dyadic conflict resolutions across family dyads (H1; Table S7.1). As expected, resolutions varied across dyads, $X^2(10, N = 376) = 61.22, p < .001$, Cramer's $\Phi = .29$. Family subsystems differed largely in terms of whether discussions ended in standoff or win-loss resolutions (H1a). Stand-offs occurred in 35% of both the sibling and spousal discussions, but in fewer than 8% of the 254 discussions between parents and children. In contrast, parents and children ended their discussions with win-loss outcomes fully 50% of the time, whereas within-generation discussions ended with wins and losses only 23% of the time for siblings and 18% of the time for spouses. In contrast, the rates of compromise were more consistent across dyad types; Siblings and spouses compromised 42% and 47% of the time respectively, and parents and children compromised on average in 43% of their discussions. As expected (H1b), win-loss resolutions in each parent–child dyad overwhelmingly favored the parent (all $ps < .001$; only 4/126 these win-loss resolutions favored the child). In contrast, the binomial tests for siblings (10/14 win-loss resolutions favored older siblings) and spouses (6/11 resolutions favored the mother) were not significant, although the low frequency of such resolutions may account for the lack of significance for siblings.

How Do Conflict Strategies Vary Across Different Individuals and Dyads in the Family, and How Are They Associated With Conflict Resolutions?

We used multilevel models to examine individual, dyadic and family effects on opposition and planning (H2, H3), as well as links between these conflict strategies and dyadic resolutions (H4, H5). Primary analyses were performed in HLM, a multilevel modeling program that allows the simultaneous analysis of relationships between multiple, interdependent actors such as are found within families (Bryk & Raudenbush, 1992). Individuals' frequencies of conflict strategies were nested within dyad at L2 and family at L3. Initial models containing only the dependent variable were used

Table S7.1. Frequencies of Conflict Discussion Resolutions in Different Dyads within the Family

	Discussion resolution			
Dyad	Compromise	Win-loss	Standoff	Total
Siblings	26	14	22	62
Spouses	28	11	21	60
Mother–Older sibling	34	27	6	67
Mother–Younger sibling	31	34	2	67
Father–Older sibling	24	32	5	61
Father–Younger sibling	19	33	7	59
Total	162	151	63	376

to describe how the variability in strategies was distributed across different levels of analysis (i.e., individual-, dyad-, and family-level effects). In subsequent steps, model comparison tests (i.e., X^2 tests of reduction in deviance) were used to determine whether the inclusion of each significant fixed and random effect improved the model. Any effects that did not improve the model at entry were removed in subsequent steps. To examine whether opposition and planning strategies varied across dyad types (i.e., within- and between-generation discussions) and whether there were associations between conflict strategies and resolutions within family dyads, we computed two sets of nested multi-level models (one set for each conflict strategy). In each case, we first tested differences between parents and children within dyadic interactions (L1), and whether family members' conflict strategies varied across dyad types (L2). Then, we tested links between individuals' conflict strategies and dyadic conflict resolutions (L2). Finally, we examined whether these effects differed for mothers and fathers, and similarly, whether they differed for older and younger siblings. Although our primary emphasis was on within-family effects, between-family variables (specifically, each child's age as well as the interaction between children's ages) were tested at L3 as moderators of lower-level effects for relevant coefficients with significant L3 random variance components. To control for the length of discussions, the main effect of each individual's verbal on-topic clauses (subtracting the number of clauses that captured the strategy of interest, to avoid controlling for the variable being analyzed) was entered at L1. For example, in the prediction of opposition, nonoppositional clauses were included as an L1 control variable.

There were up to 12 data points per family (i.e., 6 dyads × 2 actors per dyad) or a potential total of 804 data points for each conflict strategy across all families, although only 751 scores were available because of missing data occasioned largely by the inclusion of single-parent families in our sample. For clarity, alphabetic superscripts are included throughout the subsequent sections to identify the specific model effects in Tables S7.2 and S7.3 that are being reported in the text. Predicted Ms reported in the text are computed based on model coefficients, with other variables held constant either at the mean or at 0, as appropriate. For significant effects, we report a simple measure of effect size (ES), computed as model coefficient/SD of the outcome (Cooper & Hedges, 1994).

Explaining Variability in Family Members' Use of Opposition

The unconditional model revealed that 26% of the total variability in opposition was between actors within dyads (L1; σ^2), 61% was between dyads within families (L2; τ_Π), and 13% was between families (L3; τ_β). Multilevel models for opposition are presented in Table S7.2. Model A tested whether children (0) and parents (1) differed in their conflict strategies in within-(0) and between-generation (1) discussions. Overall, the effect for parents[a] (ES = .41) revealed that they (M = 10.28) were more oppositional than children (M = 7.71; superscripts correspond with tables). Partially confirming H2, whereas children's use of opposition did not vary across contexts (i.e., ns effect of between-generation discussion [BWGEN] on the intercept[b]), the Parent ×BWGEN[c] interaction (ES =-.32) revealed that parents were more oppositional with their spouses (M =11.78) than with their children (M =8.77). Furthermore, the age of the younger sibling moderated family members' use of opposition in between-generation (but not

Table S7.2. Multilevel Models Explaining Variability in Family Members' Oppositional Conflict Strategies

	Model A	Model B	Model B1
Fixed effect	B (SE)	B (SE)	B (SE)
Intercept	7.51 (.77)***	7.54 (.71)***	6.93 (.70)***
BWGEN (L2)[b]	.40 (.62)	.82 (.64)	.85 (.62)
× YS age (L3)[d]	.84 (.39)*	.80 (.36)*	.74 (.36)*
WC (L2)[e]		-1.79 (.55)**	-2.35 (.65)***
SW (L2)[f]		-1.49 (1.05)	-1.38 (1.03)
Parent (L1)[a]	4.27 (1.33)**	3.75 (1.25)**	4.44 (1.23)***
× BWGEN (L2)[c]	-3.41 (1.39)*	-2.07 (1.29)	-2.04 (1.29)
× SW (L2)[g]		-3.78 (1.50)*	-4.38 (1.59)**
YS (L1)[h]			1.14 (.50)*
× WC (L2)[i]			2.00 (.93)*
Clauses (L1)	.09 (.01)***	.09 (.01)***	.09 (.01)***

	Model A	Model B	Model B1
Random effect	Variance component	Variance component	Variance component
Intercept (L2)	14.97***	10.41***	11.38***
Intercept (L3)	37.25***	26.73***	26.46***
BWGEN (L3)	17.64**	6.78*	5.94*
SW (L3)		8.31†	7.62†
Parent × SW (L3)		44.97*	46.82*
Clauses (L3)	0.004***	.005***	.005***

Note. BWGEN = between-generation discussion; YS = younger sibling; WC = win-loss/standoff (−) vs. Compromise (+); SW = standoff (−) vs. win-loss (+). Predictor variables are indented when they denote higher-level moderators of lower-level effects. Alphabetic superscripts link effects to the pattern of associations described in the text. Clauses and L3 variables were entered as grand mean centered predictors. HLM equations are available upon request from the first author.

† p < .10. * p < .05. ** p < .01. *** p < .001.

within-generation) discussions (i.e., BWGEN ×younger sibling [YS] age[d];ES =.08). As the chronological age of the younger sibling increased, families exhibited more opposition in parent– child discussions.

In Model B, two orthogonal contrast codes were added at L2 to distinguish between dyadic conflict resolutions: (a) Win-Loss/Standoff vs. Compromise (WC) and (b) Standoff vs. Win-Loss (SW). These contrast codes were chosen because they distinguished constructive compromise solutions from other endings. As expected (H4), the effect for WC on the intercept[e] (ES =-.17) revealed that family members engaged in less opposition when discussions ended in compromise (M =8.11) than when they did not (M =9.90). Although the association between children's opposition and win-loss resolutions vs. standoffs was not significant (effect of SW[f] on intercept ns), the Parent ×SW interaction[g] (ES =- .36) revealed a pattern that partially supported H5a. That is, whereas children's opposition distinguished between compromise and win-loss/standoff, parents' opposition distinguished between failure to resolve issues (i.e., standoff; M =13.89) and both compromise and win-loss resolutions (Ms =9.47 and 8.62, respectively). With conflict resolutions accounted for, the effect of dyad type on parents' conflict behavior[c] was no longer significant.

Our next two models tested whether distinguishing between older vs. younger siblings (Model B1) and mothers vs. fathers (Model B2; not included in Table S7.2) added to the prediction of opposition. Distinguishing between older (0) and younger siblings (1) improved Model B. The effect for younger siblings[h] (ES =.11) revealed that they (M = 8.29) engaged in more opposition than older siblings (M = 6.95). Further, as expected (H5b), unlike the pattern for older siblings, the YS × WC interaction[i] (ES =.19) revealed that younger siblings' opposition did not distinguish compromises from other conflict resolutions. In contrast, distinguishing between mothers and fathers did not improve the model, or moderate any of the effects in Model B. Thus, mothers' and fathers' use of opposition across dyad types appeared to be similar, as did their associations between conflict resolutions and opposition.

Explaining Variability in Family Members' Use of Planning.

The unconditional model revealed that the vast majority (99%) of the total variability in planning was between individuals within dyads (L1). Nevertheless, various L2 and L3 predictors significantly improved the model for planning. Results are presented in Table S7.3. Our first analysis (Model A) tested overall differences between parents' and children's planning in within-and between-generation discussions. In general, the effect for parents[j] (ES =.49) suggested that they (M =11.82) engaged in more planning than children (M = 4.82). However, supporting H3, the Parent × BWGEN[k] interaction (ES =.66) revealed that whereas children planned equally with their parents and siblings, parents planned more with their children (M = 14.69) than their spouses (M = 8.95). The model also revealed that the younger sibling's age moderated the Parent ×BWGEN interaction[l] (ES =-.19); in families with chronologically older laterborns, parents engaged in less planning during interactions with their children.

Next, we added contrasts between dyadic conflict resolutions (Model B). Partially supporting H4, the two resolution contrast codes predicting the intercept in Model B (i.e., WC[m] and SW[n];ES =.39 and .43, respectively) revealed that compromise (M =9.97) was associated with slightly more planning than win-loss resolutions

Table S7.3. Multilevel Models Examining Variability in Family Members' Future Oriented Planning

	Model A		Model B		Model B1		Model B2	
	Fixed effect	B (SE)	Fixed effect	B (SE)	Fixed effect	B (SE)	Fixed effect	B (SE)
	Intercept	4.76 (.65)***	Intercept	5.00 (.57)***	Intercept	5.89 (.63)***	Intercept	9.41 (1.18)***
	BWGEN (L2)	.11 (.53)	BWGEN (L2)	−1.02 (.56)†	BWGEN (L2)	−1.03 (.56)†	BWGEN (L2)	4.28 (1.40)***
							× YS age (L3)	−1.93 (.51)**
			WC (L2)[m]	3.36 (.52)***	WC (L2)	3.31 (.52)***	WC (L2)	3.45 (.51)***
			SW (L2)[n]	3.66 (.76)***	SW (L2)	3.67 (.74)***	SW (L2)	4.09 (.73)***
	Parent (L1)[j]	4.19 (1.17)**	Parent (L1)	3.37 (1.05)**	Parent (L1)	2.54 (1.09)*	Child (L1)	−4.37 (1.34)**
	× BWGEN (L2)[k]	5.63 (1.21)***	× BWGEN (L2)	6.17 (1.12)***	× BWGEN (L2)	6.13 (1.13)***	× BWGEN (L2)	−5.39 (1.42)***
	× YS age (L3)[l]	−1.65 (.49)**	× YS age (L3)	−1.82 (.49)**	× YS age (L3)	−1.80 (.48)***	× YS age (L3)	1.58 (.58)**
					YS (L1)[o]	−1.85 (.37)***	Dad (L1)[p]	−1.21 (1.29)
							× BWGEN (L2)[q]	.55 (1.37)
							× WC (L2)	−4.11 (1.51)**
							× WC × BWGEN (L2)[r]	6.69 (2.02)**
	Clauses (L1)	.06 (.01)***	Clauses (L1)	.07 (.01)***	Clauses (L1)	.07 (.01)***	Clauses (L1)	.07 (.01)***

Model A		Model B		Model B1		Model B2	
Random effect	Variance component	Random effect	Variance component	Random effect	Variance component	Random effect	Variance component
Intercept (L2)	5.77	Intercept (L2)	3.69	Intercept (L2)	4.10	Intercept (L2)	3.63
Intercept (L3)	2.17**	Intercept (L3)	1.14**	Intercept (L3)	1.06**	Intercept (L3)	5.91***
Parent × BWGEN (L3)	4.54†	Parent × BWGEN (L3)	5.27*	Parent × BWGEN (L3)	5.54*	BWGEN (L3)	5.48*
						Dad (L3)	12.19***
Clauses (L3)	.002***	Clauses (L3)	.001***	Clauses (L3)	.001***	Clauses (L3)	.003***

Note. BWGEN = between-generation discussion; YS = younger sibling; WC = win-loss/standoff (−) vs. compromise (+); SW = standoff (−) vs. win-loss (+). Predictor variables are indented when they denote higher-level moderators of lower-level effects. Alphabetic superscripts link effects to the pattern of associations described in the text. Clauses and L3 variables were entered as grand mean centered predictors.
† $p < .10$. * $p < .05$. ** $p < .01$. *** $p < .001$.

(M =8.44). However, relative to the other two resolutions, standoffs were especially associated with a lack of planning (M =4.78). These effects did not differ for parents and children, thus disconfirming H5a.

Finally, we tested whether distinguishing between older vs. younger siblings (Model B1) and mothers vs. fathers (Model B2) would add to the prediction of planning. In both cases, these contrasts improved the models. The effect for younger siblings in Model B1 (ES = -.22) revealed that they (M = 4.31) planned less than older siblings (M = 6.16). However, the lack of significant interaction effects suggested that older and younger siblings did not differ in terms of (a) planning during within vs. between-generation discussions or (b) associations between planning and conflict resolutions (disconfirming H5b). In contrast, the pattern was substantially more complex for differences between mothers and fathers (Model B2). Testing differences between mothers' and fathers' planning required reversing the reference group in the analysis, thus inverting the model coefficients involving the distinctions between parents and children. Although fathers did not differ in their overall levels of planning from mothers (i.e., main effect of Dad[p] ns), differences between mothers and fathers qualified a number of the above associations. Overall, fathers showed the same pattern in which they engaged in more planning with their children than with their spouses (Dad × BWGEN[q], ns), but for fathers, planning was positively associated with compromise only during discussions with their children (Dad × WC × BWGEN[r]; ES =.78; father–child Ms =17.07, 13.09, and 9.00, for compromise, win-loss, and standoff, respectively). In contrast to mothers, during spousal discussions, fathers' planning was selectively associated with win-loss resolutions favoring either spouse, rather than compromise resolutions (planning Ms for mothers in spousal discussions ending in compromise, win-loss, and standoff =11.72, 10.32, and 6.22, respectively; comparable planning Ms for fathers in spousal discussions =7.76, 10.46, and 6.37, respectively).

DISCUSSION

In this study, we used an innovative observational research design that included 376 negotiations capturing the conflict strategies of each dyadic combination of family members. The dramatic differences in resolutions and the distribution of variation in future-oriented planning and opposition revealed in the unconditional models suggested that our emphasis on within-family differences in conflict processes was apt. In each case, the majority of the observed variability was associated with differences between actors within dyads and/or differences between dyads within the family, rather than between families.

This strategy revealed various novel findings that contribute to our understanding of how the relative power of family members influences conflict dynamics. Our results reveal substantial and largely unexplored differences in conflict strategies across actors and contexts within the family. First, we found differences between parents' and children's conflict strategies as well as between parents' behavior in spousal and parent–child discussions. Second, the conflict resolutions of within-and between-generation dyads differed in predictable ways. Third, in line with our hypotheses, conflict strategies and resolutions were associated, although the nature of these links differed among actors in the family.

Differences in Conflict Strategies and Resolutions Between
Parents and Children Within- and Between-Generations

As expected, we found that conflict resolutions varied across dyad types. Whereas parent–child discussions were likely to end in win-loss resolutions that overwhelmingly favored parents (Stein & Albro, 2001; Vuchinich, 1987), more spousal and sibling conflicts were left unresolved (Siddiqui & Ross, 1999; Vuchinich, 1987). This difference is in line with theory suggesting that conflicts may be more difficult to resolve in symmetrical relationships, as "power struggles" are more likely to ensue (Dunbar, 2004; Perlman et al., 2000). Thus, even in light of our request that family members attempt to resolve their differences in a mutually satisfying way (a goal that may not always be salient in naturalistic family conflict), the proportional frequencies of win-loss resolutions and standoff reflected clear differences between family subsystems.

Parents and children also differed in terms of their conflict strategies. With the length of discussions accounted for, we found that parents engaged in more future-oriented planning as well as more opposition than their children. However, more interestingly, these differences between parents and children varied considerably as a function of relationship context. As expected, with their spouses, adults engaged in more opposition and less planning than with their children. This pattern suggests that during parent–child discussions, parents typically modeled constructive patterns of strategies for their children. Our request that parents solve conflicts with their children during a reflective discussion most likely brought adults' child-centered parenting goals to the fore (Hastings & Grusec, 1998). Furthermore, various sources of power favor parents during interactions with children (French & Raven, 1959; Perlman et al., 2000). As such, parents largely controlled the process and planned the resolution of parent–child issues. In contrast, with their spouses, adults were more likely to engage as equals; disagreement and heated debate may be relatively normative behaviors during marital interactions (Gottman, 1994). The observed between-family effects of the younger sibling's age were also consistent with an interpretation of findings in terms of relative power: in families with older and increasingly sophisticated children (Ram & Ross, 2001), parents' less constructive strategies during interactions with their children reflected these differences in relative symmetry (Dunbar, 2004).

Yet contrary to expectations, we did not find that children's planning or opposition differed between discussions with their siblings and their parents. Previous research suggests that children are less upset and more constructive during conflicts with parents than with siblings (Dunn & Munn, 1987; Dunn et al., 1995). However, rather than naturalistic observations of preschoolers, our study assessed conflict strategies during family discussions of previously unresolved issues, and also included somewhat older children. This divergence from previous research may reflect changes in parent–child relationships across development, differences between brief naturalistic squabbles and discussions of especially memorable issues, as well as dissimilarities between our measured variables (i.e., verbal planning and oppositional strategies) and those assessed in other studies (e.g., emotionality).

The within-family patterns of results for parents and children have implications for family conflict theory, in that they suggest that parents' relative power in the family may be exercised more via future-oriented planning than opposition during interactions with their children. This reflects the use of expert and informational power, rather than coercion (French & Raven, 1959), to produce solutions that are in one's own interests. It seems that parents are largely charting the course of resolution during parent–child discussions and are not as effective in eliciting plans from their children, although children do participate in the planning process to a limited degree. Interestingly, the observed birth order effects for siblings are also in line with this argument, in that older siblings engaged in more planning (but less opposition) than younger siblings. That is, older siblings appear to be exercising more power in family conflict discussions than their younger counterparts, consistent with findings on asymmetry in siblings' conflict roles (Perlman et al., 2000).

Associations Between Conflict Strategies and Resolutions

Conflict resolutions varied considerably within, in addition to between dyad types, and this variability was associated with the conflict strategies employed by family members in the discussion task. As expected, less opposition by older siblings (but not younger siblings) was associated with compromise resolutions that considered both family members' goals. It may be that younger siblings' strategies were least diagnostic because of their less sophisticated conflict skills (Ram & Ross, 2001), and thus they were less able to influence the direction that conflict discussions would take. In turn, parents' opposition was linked to more standoffs (i.e., fewer win-loss and compromise resolutions). In other words, both compromises and wins by parents were associated with less opposition in comparison with standoffs. This pattern provides the novel insight that less opposition by parents promotes resolution, whereas less opposition by older siblings may be particularly relevant to the achievement of compromise. This divergence makes more sense when one considers that parents achieve their goals in both compromise and win-loss outcomes, whereas children's goals are realized largely in compromises, as they very rarely emerge as the sole winners of conflict discussions. Thus for both parents and children, opposition appears to impede their achievement of their own goals in resolving differences.

In turn, both parents' and children's planning was particularly associated with fewer standoffs. Further, although fathers' and mothers' planning with their children was linked to resolving differences (especially via compromise), it appeared to be mothers' planning that was selectively linked to compromise between spouses. Interestingly, relative to standoffs, husbands' planning with their wives was positively related to win-loss, but not with compromise resolutions. This unanticipated finding for win-loss resolutions should be interpreted cautiously, due to the relatively low frequency of these outcomes among spouses. The literature also suggests that spouses may exercise power by withdrawing from spousal conflicts (e.g., Dunbar & Burgoon, 2005), an option that did not exist in our mandated discussions.

Other research on family conflict suggests that both planning and oppositional conflict strategies tend to be reciprocated in kind (Vuchinich, 1984), leading to either constructive or destructive pathways. For example, studies in both the sibling (Perlman & Ross, 2005) and spousal (Gottman, 1994) conflict literatures reveal that conflict negotiation trajectories depend on how these discussions begin. Consistent with our results, opposition has been shown to interfere with the achievement of resolutions, leading to negative affect which in turn precludes constructive problem-solving behavior (Forgatch, 1989). In contrast, future-oriented planning shifts the discussion away from past blame to dealing effectively with future recurrences of the issues and achieving goals (Stein & Albro, 2001; Vuchinich, 1999). It is important to note that the links between parents' and children's strategies and resolutions observed in our study were generally consistent across dyad types, suggesting relatively uniform patterns of association across family subsystems. In sum, our results corroborate past research on family conflict suggesting the constructiveness of future-oriented planning and the potential destructiveness unmitigation of opposition.

Limitations and Implications

In this study, we asked each dyad within the family to discuss an actual unresolved conflict. Although this procedure provides insight into conflict strategies for the issues that are meaningful to siblings, spouses, and parent–child dyads, it may also lead to heterogeneity between the topics of conflict nominated in each dyad type. It is known that conflict issues are related to the strategies used to resolve disputes (e.g., Papp, Cummings, & Goeke-Morey, 2009). Thus, our results may partly reflect variability associated with the different issues implicated in sibling, spousal, and parent–child conflicts. On the other hand, it is not reasonable to expect that the same issues are present across relationship types, and indeed it would be artificial to force that equivalence.

In this study, we only focused on two conflict strategies that have been theorized to reflect constructive and destructive conflict management as well as power dynamics. These strategies are not exhaustive, and within-family analyses of other conflict dimensions (e.g., emotionality, perspective-taking) may further contribute to our understanding of power dynamics in the family. In addition, we observed each dyad in the family resolving only one conflict. By observing each dyad on multiple occasions as they attempt to resolve different conflict issues, future studies could clarify how patterns in each dyad vary as a function of the characteristics of particular conflicts. Due to the relatively low number of standoffs (in parent–child dyads) and win-loss resolutions (in sibling and spousal dyads), investigating associations between strategies and resolutions could also benefit from a study including a larger number of discussions. That said, our findings are based on observations of 376 conflict discussions that do provide a substantial sample for this initial within-family investigation of conflict. Finally, our study revealed some intriguing and novel differences between fathers' and mothers' conflict behavior in the family. As such, a more focused investigation of parents' conflict strategies and dyadic resolutions appears to be warranted, with particular emphasis on the mechanisms that may underlie the differences observed here. For instance, recent research on spouses reveals that power may differ between spouses, but contrary to earlier studies, that these asymmetries may not consistently favor husbands (Papp et al., 2009). As such, directly measuring perceptions of within- and between-family differences in spousal power may be a fruitful avenue for further study.

In this investigation, we attempted to capitalize on the strengths of both the family psychology and conflict negotiation literatures by simultaneously examining multiple sources of variability in family conflict strategies and resolutions. The adult conflict negotiation literature has developed sophisticated theories and methods to explain dyadic conflict strategies and resolutions during structured negotiation tasks, yet only recently has research in that field begun to consider relationship contexts as critical determinants of dyadic conflict strategies (Barry & Oliver, 1996). Our findings elucidate family conflict processes both between- and within-subsystems that may inform interventions aimed at promoting constructive conflict management in the family. For instance, across all family dyads, future-oriented planning strategies were linked to mutually agreed-upon conflict resolutions. At the same time, our results provide support for the notion that individual family subsystems vary in their conflict dynamics, consistent with predictions based on the sources of power that exist in the family. That is, power differences between parents and children in parent child dyads were evident in the unequal resolutions achieved in this subsystem. In contrast, conflict resolutions in sibling and spousal dyads reflected more equal power between individuals. Within the family, parents exerted their authority by selecting constructive strategies to resolve issues with their children. Yet it was also clear that, within generations, individual siblings and spouses did not take on identical roles. Younger siblings were more oppositional, whereas older siblings engaged in more planning and appeared to have greater ability to influence conflict resolutions. Similarly, mothers' planning was a more potent correlate of equitable spousal conflict resolutions than that of fathers. Thus, family conflict dynamics appear to be more nuanced than can be accounted for by basic comparisons of within- and between-generation dyads and both adults and children experience conflict differently within specific dyadic contexts. Further, our study suggests that tracking differences in the associations between conflict strategies and resolutions in different relationships may also add substantially to our understanding of how to promote constructive conflict resolution across family subsystems.

REFERENCES

Barry, B., & Oliver, R. L. (1996). Affect in dyadic negotiation: A model and propositions. *Organizational Behavior and Human Decision Processes, 67,* 127–143.

Bryk, A. S., & Raudenbush, S. W. (1992). *Hierarchical linear models.* Newbury Park, CA: Sage.

Cooper, H., & Hedges, L. (1994). *The handbook of research synthesis.* New York: Sage.

Cummings, E. M., Faircloth, W. B., Mitchell, P. M., Cummings, J. S., & Schermerhorn, A. C. (2008). Evaluating a brief prevention program for improving marital conflict in community families. *Journal of Family Psychology, 22,* 193–202.

Deutsch, M. (1973). *The resolution of conflict: Constructive and destructive processes.* New Haven, CT: Yale University Press.

Dunbar, N. E. (2004). Dyadic power theory: Constructing a communication-based theory of relational power. *Journal of Family Communication, 4,* 235–248.

Dunbar, N. E., & Burgoon, J. K. (2005). Perceptions of power and interactional dominance in interpersonal relationships. *Journal of Social and Personal Relationships, 22,* 207–233.

Dunn, J., & Munn, P. (1987). Development of justification in disputes with mother and sibling. *Developmental Psychology, 23,* 791–798.

Dunn, J., Slomkowski, C., Donelan, N., & Herrera, C. (1995). Conflict, understanding, and relationships: Developments and differences in the preschool years. *Early Education and Development, 6,* 303–316.

Emery, R. E. (1992). Family conflicts and their developmental implications. In C. U. Shantz & W. W. Hartup (Eds.), *Conflict in child and adolescent development* (pp. 270 –298). New York: Cambridge University Press.

Forgatch, M. S. (1989). Patterns and outcome in family problem-solving: The disrupting effect of negative emotion. *Journal of Marriage and the Family, 51,* 115–124.

French, J. R. P., & Raven, B. H. (1959). The bases of social power. In D. Cartwright (Ed.), *Studies in social power* (pp. 150 –167). Ann Arbor, MI: University of Michigan.

Goeke-Morey, M. C., Cummings, E. M., & Papp, L. M. (2007). Children and marital conflict resolution: Implications for emotional security and adjustment. *Journal of Family Psychology, 21,* 744 –753.

Gottman, J. M. (1994). *What predicts divorce: The relationship between marital processes and marital outcomes.* Hillsdale, NJ: Erlbaum.

Hastings, P. D., & Grusec, J. E. (1998). Parenting goals as organizers of responses to parent–child disagreement. *Developmental Psychology, 34,* 465– 479.

Kuczynski, L., Kochanska, G., Radke-Yarrow, M., & Girnius Brown, O. (1987). A developmental interpretation of young children's noncompliance. *Developmental Psychology, 23,* 799–806.

Minuchin, P. (1985). Families and individual development: Provocations from the field of family therapy. *Child Development, 56,* 289 –302.

Papp, L. M., Cummings, E. M., & Goeke-Morey, M. C. (2009). For richer, for poorer: Money as a topic of marital conflict in the home. *Family Relations, 58,* 91–103.

Perlman, M., & Ross, H. S. (2005). If-then contingencies in children's sibling conflicts. *Merrill-Palmer Quarterly, 51,* 42– 66.

Perlman, M., Siddiqui, A., Ram, A., & Ross, H. (2000). The role of power in children's conflict interactions. In R. S. L. Mills & S. Duck (Eds.), *The developmental psychology of personal relationships* (pp. 155–174). New York: Wiley.

Ram, A., & Ross, H. S. (2001). Problem-solving, contention, and struggle: How siblings resolve a conflict of interests. *Child Development, 72,* 1710 –1722.

Rinaldi, C. M., & Howe, N. L. (2003). Perceptions of constructive and destructive conflict within and across family subsystems. *Infant and Child Development, 12,* 441– 459.

Ross, H., Stein, N., Trabasso, T., Woody, E., & Ross, M. (2005). The quality of family relationships within and across generations: A social relations analysis. *International Journal of Behavioral Development, 29,* 120 –128.

Rueter, M. A., & Conger, R. D. (1995). Interaction style, problem-solving behavior, and family problem-solving effectiveness. *Child Development, 66,* 98 –115.

Siddiqui, A. A., & Ross. H. S. (1999). How do sibling conflicts end? *Early Education and Development, 10,* 315–332.

Smith, J., & Ross, H. (2007). Training parents to mediate sibling disputes affects children's negotiation and conflict understanding. *Child Development, 78,* 790–805.

Stanley, S. M., Markman, H. J., & Whitton, S. W. (2002). Communication, conflict, and commitment: Insights on the foundations of relationship success from a national survey. *Family Process, 41,* 659–675.

Stein, N. L., & Albro, E. (2001). The origins and nature of arguments: Studies in conflict understanding, emotion, and negotiation. *Discourse Processes, 32,* 113–133.

Vuchinich, S. (1984). Sequencing and social structure in family conflict. *Social Psychology Quarterly, 47,* 217–234.

Vuchinich, S. (1987). Starting and stopping spontaneous family conflicts. *Journal of Marriage and the Family, 49,* 591– 601.

Vuchinich, S. (1999). *Problem solving in families: Research and practice.* Thousand Oaks, CA: Sage.

Whitton, S. W., Waldinger, R. J., Schulz, M. S., Allen, J. P., Crowell, J. A., & Hauser, S. T. (2008). Prospective associations from family-of-origin interactions to adult marital interactions and relationship adjustment. *Journal of Family Psychology, 22,* 274 –286.

8

SOCIAL EXCHANGE THEORY

Nicholas and Alyssa have been dating for about a year—exclusively for the last eight months or so. They are both juniors in college and have been thinking about whether or not they should get married. Alyssa frequently discusses the possibility with her roommates, and they debate the pros and cons. "He is so handsome and nice to me, and we are totally in love," says Alyssa. However, she wishes that he were majoring in something more substantial than history—business or law, perhaps. And she knows that he will want them to move back to his rural hometown in the West, which bothers her because she is a city girl. On the other hand, her friends point out that he is nice to children and (they have been told) is a great kisser. But is she really ready to give up dating and settle down?

For Nicholas it is a more private process, but he is also trying to decide. He loves Alyssa and wants to be with her all the time. Their physical relationship is wonderful, and he enjoys her intellect. He is afraid he might not be good enough for her, and that if she knew what he is really like, she might think that she can do better. He has no solid job or income to offer and needs to be in school for at least two more years. She gets upset when he doesn't want to talk about his feelings, and he worries about having to endure that pressure forever. And with the divorce rate as high as it is, is marriage even worth the effort?

Both of them are trying to be logical about this most important life decision, but it is hard to do. Feelings of love and hormonal urges get in the way. Isn't it too calculating to weigh the pros and cons of the relationship? Won't that just kill the romance? Can they even know what the most important considerations are before they get married?

HISTORY

Philosophers have been discussing the ideas relevant to modern social exchange theory for the last two centuries. The basic concept is that human social relationships can be understood as revolving around the exchange of resources valued by the participants. Utilitarian writers such as Adam Smith taught that people tend to act rationally in ways designed to maximize their profit economically. In the early twentieth century, anthropologists such as Bronislaw Malinowski and Claude Lévi-Strauss demonstrated how many cultures engage in the exchange of various goods and services as a central aspect of their social life. The latter took the collectivist position that one's behavior in social relationships tends to be a function of the social system of which one is a part (Ekeh 1974). In other words, the social norms, customs, laws, and values of the culture help to regulate the exchanges.

These early anthropologists explored the relationship between social norms and individual behaviors. James George Frazer (1919) concluded that many social structures result from the economic needs of the individuals within the system. He was investigating the tendency of Australian aborigines to marry cross, rather than parallel, cousins and concluded that because the men were too poor to provide a bride price, they would trade a sister or other female relative for their bride.

Sociologists began to seriously consider the exchange model in the context of human societies and families with the groundbreaking writings of John Thibaut and Harold Kelley (1959), George Homans (1961/1974), and Peter Blau (1964). These writers took us beyond the concepts of economic exchanges and into the more complex world of the social marketplace where individuals negotiated to maximize their profits. In addition to trading such things as food, money, and other services, humans in relationships make exchanges that are harder to quantify, such as status, attractiveness, and love. Even though each had a somewhat different emphasis, they all agreed that what people want and need can be obtained only through exchanges with others, and that we will try to get those things at the lowest possible cost to ourselves (Turner 1991). Thus, dyadic exchanges are influenced by the costs and rewards associated with them.

Among their many contributions to the development of social exchange, social psychologists Kelley and Thibaut (1959, 1978) outlined an interdependence theory in their book *Interpersonal Relations: A Theory of Interdependence* (1978). They distinctly noted that actors not only try to maximize rewards that they personally receive from a relationship exchange, but they also take into account the needs of their partner. Because relationships are interdependent, both parties rely on the relationship to provide them with rewards. Attraction and dependence in relationships will depend on how individuals assess the degree to which a relationship meets their expectations, and how it compares to alternative relationships. More will be said about Kelley and Thibaut's concepts of dependence, commitment, comparison level, and comparison level for alternatives in the concepts section of this chapter.

George Homans is probably the most influential scholar in bringing social exchange theory to general sociology, as he provided an articulation of exchange theory in his book *Social Behavior: Its Elementary Form* (1961/1974). Essentially adapting the principles of behaviorism, he alleged that reinforcement and punishment were the driving forces in human behavior and that sociology should pay more attention to how individuals choose to act within social situations. In his own study of cross-cousin marriages (Homans and Schneider 1955), Homans rejected the collectivist orientation of Lévi-Strauss. He took the position that societal norms result from the needs of individuals, rather than that society regulates interpersonal behavior. Richard Emerson (1976) made important contributions to the application of social exchange theory for family studies by proposing that the unit of analysis in the theory is not the individual, but the relationship between people and the networks in which those exchange relationships are embedded (Collett 2010). His concepts of "dependence, power, and balance" are not individual properties; instead, they are relational properties that help us focus on interpersonal processes (Sabatelli and Shehan 1993).

Ivan Nye (1978, 1979) summarized the concepts of the exchange model, calling it a choice and exchange theory. By labeling it as such, "Nye saw exchange as something that was more relevant within a relationship (e.g., doing favors for a partner), whereas choice (e.g., of partners, benefits) was an important component of deciding whether to enter a specific relationship" (Collett 2010, 283). Nye also showed how exchange concepts could be applied to a large number of research questions in family science, and offered a series of theoretical propositions and testable hypotheses. His work completed the evolution of exchange from economic to sociological to family science theory. It has been and continues to be a widely used framework in analyzing family issues since the publication of his chapter in *Contemporary Theories about the Family* (1979).

Building upon Kelley and Thibault's (1978) interdependence theory, Caryl Rusbult (1980, 1983) developed an investment model to better understand commitment and persistence in relationships. The model asserts that, as one becomes increasingly dependent upon a relationship, commitment to that relationship strengthens, and allegiance is established. Thus, referring to our couple in the vignette at the beginning of the chapter, we would anticipate that as Nicolas and Alyssa become increasingly dependent on each other, their commitment to one another will increase, and they will feel psychologically attached to one another. As a result, their relationship is likely to persist. More will be said about commitment in the concepts section.

BASIC ASSUMPTIONS

We will now examine the basic assumptions that undergird social exchange theory. We draw from the writings of Sabatelli and Shehan (1993) as well as White and Klein (2008) in this section. Although social exchange theory is built upon the principles of behaviorism and economics, it goes beyond just explaining individual behavior. It focuses on the dynamics of relationships and how they are formed, maintained, and dissolved. As a result, there are assumptions about the nature of both individuals and relationships that are embedded in the framework.

People are motivated by self-interest. The first assumption is that people are motivated by self-interest. This means that we seek those things and relationships that are beneficial to ourselves. Another way of saying this is that we seek rewards and avoid punishments or costs. Thus, we are most likely to engage in interactions that we find rewarding while avoiding those we do not like.

Individuals are constrained by their choices. The second assumption is that individuals are constrained by their choices, and it is within that range of possible choices that we strive to understand one's motivations. Nye (1979), in fact, concluded that the theory is more about choice than exchange. Social structure leads us to conclude that family life is rewarding to most individuals, because this is a choice most people make.

In interacting with others, individuals will seek to maximize their profits while minimizing costs. Because the actual outcome of an interaction cannot always be known, humans will use their expectations in making their decisions. This means that we enter into situations we believe will be rewarding, based on our past experiences.

Humans are rational beings. Another important assumption is that humans are rational beings. This means that we have the analytical ability to calculate the ratio of rewards to costs. Based on information that we possess, we consider the alternatives before acting and choose the outcome that is deemed to be the most profitable or the option that carries the least cost. Exchange theorists also accept the fact that how rewards and costs are evaluated varies from one person to another as well as across time. Therefore, what Nicholas finds rewarding may not be rewarding to Alyssa. Similarly, what Nicholas finds rewarding in his relationship with Alyssa today may not be the same as what he considers rewarding in his relationship with her ten years from now.

Social relationships are also characterized by interdependence and reciprocity. This means that, in order to gain a profit in an exchange, we must provide the other person with rewards as well. All parties must expect some rewards in order to continue the relationship or interaction. And finally, social exchanges are regulated by the expectations or norms of reciprocity and fairness. Thus, we expect others to meet our needs if we attempt to meet their needs, and we expect them to do so based on what is right or fair.

PRIMARY TERMS AND CONCEPTS

The principal concepts used in social exchange theory are listed by Nye (1979), who draws heavily from Thibaut and Kelley (1959).

Rewards

All of the things in a person's physical, social, and psychological world that are experienced as pleasurable are considered rewards. A reward can be any satisfaction, gratification, status, or relationship that one enjoys, and therefore, would like to experience with greater frequency (Thibaut and Kelley 1959). It includes anything that the individual would choose in the absence of added costs. What is rewarding will vary from one person to the next. Rewards positively reinforce behavior.

Blau (1964) identified six commodities that are capable of rewarding another during interpersonal exchanges: personal attraction, social acceptance, social approval, instrumental services, respect/prestige, and compliance/power. Foa and Foa (1980) added six more: love, status, services, goods, information, and money. Nye (1979) contributed autonomy, security, value and opinion agreement, and equality.

In our opening vignette, Nicholas's good looks and kindness are rewards for Alyssa. Nicholas finds his love for Alyssa, his appreciation for her intellect, and his enjoyment of their time together as rewarding aspects in his relationship with her. They are drawn to each other because of these rewarding capacities.

Costs

In contrast, any status, relationship, or feeling that the individual does not like is considered a cost. A cost is a factor that would deter an activity, and it can be classified into three categories (Blau 1964). Investment costs are time and energy that an individual will expend in order to gain a new skill that can be used to reward another. Opportunity costs consist of those rewarding feelings or positions that must be given up when selecting some competing alternative. Finally, direct costs are resources that are used up in an exchange. This could be giving up money for a good or service, such as a weekly housekeeper, or marrying an intelligent person who isn't all that attractive.

Both Alyssa and Nicholas incur costs as a result of choosing to be in a relationship with one another; for one, their exclusivity means that they are not free to engage in a similar love relationship with another partner. For Alyssa, Nicholas's desire to live in a rural area and his inability to talk about his feelings are costly to her. Her desire to live in the city and discontent with his choice of college major are costs for him associated with this relationship.

Profit

Profit refers to the outcome in terms of rewards and costs. People strive to gain the most rewards with the fewest costs. When they do so, they have profited. We all try to maximize profits and minimize costs in our relationships and interactions. Generally, most rewarding outcomes have some costs attached to them, which must, therefore, be weighed and considered.

Alyssa is weighing the costs and rewards in her relationship with Nicholas. Some things, like his kindness and his strong affection for her, may outweigh some of the potential negative aspects of this relationship, such as his desire to live in a rural area. Nonetheless, just like Alyssa, people make determinations about how profitable or desirable their relationships are to them based on the ratio of costs and rewards.

Comparison Level

The evaluation of the profitability of our relationships against what we feel we deserve is our comparison level (Thibaut and Kelley 1959)—that is, we compare the rewards and costs we are experiencing in a relationship and judge our feelings about them based on our ideas of what should be the fair outcome for us. We might also look at how well we think others in similar positions, such as other newly married or nice people, are doing in comparison to what we are experiencing. We expect our rewards to be similar to those of others in comparable situations. The notion of comparison level affects one's satisfaction in a relationship.

Comparison Level for Alternatives

Thibaut and Kelley (1959) also note that individuals will compare their outcomes in a particular relationship with alternative relationships that may be out there. For instance, Nicholas, fifteen years from now, may meet another woman who is more physically attractive and exciting than his wife Alyssa. Because he determines that divorce, having to share custody of his children, and changing locations and families involve considerable expense, Nicholas may decide that leaving his marriage to Alyssa to be with a beautiful new woman is not worth the cost after all. It is assumed that a new relationship must be sufficiently superior to compensate for any costs incurred in moving from one relationship to another. A subjective assessment, the comparison level for alternatives, then is "the lowest level of outcomes a member will accept in the light of alternative opportunities" (Thibaut and Kelley 1959, 21); it determines the stability of a relationship.

Dependence, Commitment, and Persistence

Dependence is the extent to which a person needs or is reliant upon a particular person for a desired relationship outcome. In Kelley and Thibault's (1978) interdependence theory, dependence grows when a partner experiences a high level of satisfaction in his/her relationship and when potential alternative relationships are undesirable.

According to Rusbult's (1980, 1983) investment model, feelings of commitment arise with growing dependence. Commitment is a "long-term orientation toward a relationship, including feelings of psychological attachment and intentions to persist through both good and bad times" (Cox, Wexler, Rusbult, and Gaines 1997, 80). Rusbult (1980, 1983) asserts that commitment is enhanced by three variables. First, a high level of satisfaction with the relationship is important. When a partner meets one's needs (e.g., companionate, intellectual) and expectations for the relationship, based on experience or comparison with others, satisfaction is likely to be good. Second, commitment is stronger when alternatives are perceived to be unavailable or unattractive. Third, commitment becomes stronger depending upon the investments each has made in their partner and the relationship. For instance, partners may invest resources (e.g., effort, self-disclosure, identity, time) directly into the relationship and experience other resources (e.g., mutual friends, children, shared memories, possessions, changed name) that become linked to the relationship. These investments increase the likelihood that a relationship will persist, elevating the costs to terminate the relationship (Cox, et al. 1997; Rusbult, Johnson, and Morrow 1986). Rusbult and colleagues (1998) developed an investment model scale to measure commitment, satisfaction level, quality of alternatives, and investment size. It is useful in examining commitment and dependence in close relationships.

Norm of Reciprocity

A cornerstone of social exchange theory, the norm of reciprocity is the social expectation or rule that dictates that people should help those who have helped them, and that they should not injure those who have helped them (Blau 1964). This is an important norm because an effective, ongoing society cannot function without it. For social interactions, including but not limited to those found in family life, to take place and continue, they must be rewarding to all of the individuals involved. Others will typically not allow us to reward ourselves at their expense; so, to gain rewards, we must give rewards to others. As the saying goes, "You scratch my back and I'll scratch yours."

Rule of Distributive Justice, Norm of Fairness, and Equity

Homans (1961/1974) and Blau (1964) worked with concepts similar to reciprocity and other social norms that offered guidelines about exchange behavior. These relate to the idea that a relationship between two people needs to be roughly equal. If one person is receiving most of the rewards while the other pays the costs, the latter individual will feel angry or used and may try to end the exchange. The partner doing most of the receiving is likely to feel guilty. On the other hand, when one gives and receives about the same, satisfaction is likely to be the result. In other words, an individual will perceive his or her situation as fair—and distributive justice will exist—when "personal investments in another are equivalent to the personal profits derived from the relationship" (Sabatelli and Shehan 1993, 403). Equity theory, an extension of social exchange theory, posits that equity exists when both parties in a relationship are equally dependent upon their relationship. This balance in contributions made to and rewards received from the relationship promotes greater well-being among the partners (Walster, Walster, and Berscheid 1978). Although who gives the most may alternate between partners across time, both partners must feel that the overall balance of give-and-take is equal for exchange relationships to be successful. Relationships are sustained and trust develops as partners reciprocate obligations and rewards.

COMMON AREAS OF RESEARCH AND APPLICATION

Nye (1979), in his seminal summary of the choice and exchange theory, formulated 120 propositions that he deemed outgrowths of the research utilizing the theory. They are in the areas of maternal employment, marital timing and parenthood, sexual behavior, communication, marital dissolution, social networks, intergenerational relations, men's work, family violence, social class, and parental behavior. Although many of his hypotheses have yet to be adequately tested, social exchange theory has proven very useful for studying relationship dynamics. We review a few key areas in which social exchange has been used to explore family relationships below.

Relationship Formation

The concept of the *"marriage market,"* which is used commonly in regular conversation today, comes from exchange thinking. It is the idea that people make choices about a companion based on what that other person has to offer them that will lead to their happiness. It also implies that the person seeking a companion must have things to offer as well. Therefore, single people list what rewards they want from a relationship, what costs they are willing to incur, and what they have to offer a possible mate.

Winton (1995) noted how romantic love is seen as resulting when one feels that he or she is getting a high ratio of rewards with little cost (i.e., the reward/cost ratio affects how we feel about other people). We come to like or love those whose interactions with us are rewarding. Being in love is a very rewarding state of being that can even have addictive qualities (Brown 1990). Similarly, we fall out of love with those who cost us too much of ourselves.

Couple formation or mate selection is another topic studied using exchange principles. It assumes that Nicholas (from the chapter's opening vignette) comes to the marriage market with a certain value, which is the sum of what he has to offer in terms of family status, physical appearance, intelligence, and other factors. He will seek someone who is similar to him, because he would lose interest in someone of lesser value and fear being rejected by someone of greater value.

Over the years, considerable research has been conducted attempting to identify and rank the various traits that are important to couple formation. There is an implication that partners, like material objects, will tend to be discarded when they are no longer of sufficient value to an individual. Cross-cultural research (Ingoldsby, Schvaneveldt, and Uribe 2003) indicates that there are many apparent universals. Women tend to prefer a man who is older, taller, and with good income potential, whereas men value youth and beauty in a mate. Everyone desires positive traits, such as kindness and intelligence, and seeks to avoid ending up with a partner who is violent or drug-addicted.

Personal ads are often indicative of the attributes that individuals find rewarding in a partner and reflect the ways in which people evaluate relationship options. Smith, Konik, and Tuve (2011) analyzed 617 personal newspaper and website advertisements to compare partner preferences among butch and femme lesbians and heterosexual men and women. In terms of requests for attractiveness, no differences existed between the groups. Heterosexual women, however, were much more likely to offer physical attractiveness, with butch lesbians the least likely to do so. Heterosexual men were most likely to offer, and heterosexual women were most likely to request, financial status and height. Both butch and femme lesbians were significantly more likely to offer and request honesty. Thus, social exchange theory is useful in considering the characteristics people seek in romantic partners.

Fitzpatrick, Sharp, and Reifman (2009) used social exchange theory and the marriage market concept to consider the willingness of midlife singles to date partners who are different from themselves (e.g., different race or religion, much less financial wealth). In middle age there may be a more limited supply of eligible partners, so those in midlife may need to alter their preferences in order to expand their available options. The authors discovered that men, never-married adults, and younger middle-aged (40–59 years) people expressed greater willingness to date partners with heterogeneous characteristics. Women were less likely to date partners who made less money, however. These scholars point out that it is important to note how perceptions of rewards and costs in relationships can be modified by extenuating contextual circumstances, like availability.

Social exchange theory has also been used to examine intermarriage. An early hypothesis suggested that people who have a lower status or disadvantage in one area, as compared to their partner, tend to have an advantage or higher status than their partner in another domain. For instance, a physically attractive but socioeconomically disadvantaged woman may want to marry a man with high status and earnings who can improve her standard of living, and she may use her physical appearance as a resource in doing so. Kalmijn (1998) posited that intermarriage was the result of a preference for a partner with resources, the influence of a social group or interfering third parties, and constraints of the marriage market. In contrast, Rosenfeld (2005) argued against status–caste exchange, or the prediction that one partner will exchange socioeconomic status for the other's racial caste status. Kalmijn (2010) has since counter-argued, suggesting that "status homogamy is in fact weaker in mixed-race couples than in same-race couples" (1253). So, the status–caste debate has provided a lively forum for discussing exchange principles.

Influenced by the research in this area, Chen and Takeuchi (2011) analyzed interview data from 589 Vietnamese, Filipina, and Chinese women who were married or cohabiting to determine the consequences of intermarriage on ethnic identity and perceived social standing. They wanted to determine the extent to which intermarriage actually increased the social standing of Asian women. These authors concluded that intermarriage was not associated with higher social standing, thus downplaying this aspect of social exchange.

Commitment

Rooted in interdependence (Kelley and Thibaut 1978) and social exchange theories (Homans 1958), there is a growing and rich literature on commitment in romantic relationships. Rusbult's (1980) investment model, which links interdependence to enhanced commitment has also generated research on the topic.

Johnson and colleagues (1999) outlined three dimensions of commitment: personal, moral and structural. Personal commitment represents the desire to stay married to one's partner. Moral commitment denotes the values and morals that underlie one's feeling of obligation to remain married. Structural commitment addresses the constraints that encourage one to remain in the relationship, such as quality and availability of alternatives, costs associated with ending the relationship, and the amount of investment in the relationship. Stanley and Markman (1992) identify two key processes in commitment: dedication ("want to") and constraint ("have to"). Their dedication component is very similar to Johnson's personal commitment, and their constraint component is synonymous with Johnson's structural (e.g., shared possessions, economic investment) and moral aspects of commitment (e.g., belief that divorce is wrong, belief that you must complete what you started). Knoester and Booth (2000) examined a variety of constraints, or barriers, that might prevent divorce, but discovered that most were ineffective deterrents. They recommended that greater attention be devoted to the quality of marital relationships and the existence of attractive alternative relationships.

Viewing commitment as a dynamic process, Byrd (2009) employed social exchange theory and a life history interview methodology in understanding the social construction of marital commitment among 40 women and 35 men between the ages of 28 and 35. About one-third of her participants perceived of marital commitment as a life-course goal. About one-quarter deemphasized the value of marital commitment, instead focusing on alternative options of personal fulfillment. Most participants perceived of marital commitment as a necessity, something that must be achieved because it has value as a lifestyle option. However, most recognized the challenges or barriers to doing so. Some obstacles to achieving commitment included: material obstacles (e.g., concerns over economic well-being and career attainment); social group membership obstacles (gender, age, religion, social class, race, and ethnic background) and social pressure obstacles (e.g., lack of social support to marry); psychological-emotional barriers (e.g., lack of emotional readiness for marital commitment); and physical obstacles (e.g., concerns about addictions, illness, infertility, physical location).

Stanley, Rhoades, and Whitton (2010) offer a review of the psychological construct of commitment, examine the role that commitment plays in securing romantic attachments, and outline how common patterns of premarital relationship development can undermine commitment. Connecting commitment to attachment styles, Stanley and colleagues posit that, as a person becomes increasingly satisfied with a relationship, anxiety grows in response to the potential loss of one's partner. Commitment serves to stabilize the relationship and heighten a personal sense of security. Individuals are most likely to communicate commitment and foster a sense of security by express-ing dedication. Examples of dedication include criticizing alternatives, consistently assuming a couple identity, and conveying a desire to be with the partner for the long haul. Ideally, commitment expressions must be mutual and clear in order to secure romantic attachment. Otherwise, relationship imbalance and power differential will result. Although romantic attachment "implies only depth of emotional connec-tion...commitment (dedication and constraint) highlights an intention to persist in the relationship" (249). Engagement and marriage are two cultural emblems of com-mitment. Finally, Stanley and colleagues assert that couples who *slide* into cohabitation before deliberating about their relationship will experience constraints before dedica-tion. Without dedication first, couples are likely to have a more difficult time sustain-ing internal commitment. We anticipate a continuing, rich generation of findings and ideas on the topic of commitment.

Sexual Behavior

White and Klein (2008) draw on the work of Nye (1979) to argue the case that males are more likely to exchange rewards (money and marriage in particular) for sexual access. Assuming that the biological drive is equal for the two genders, the theory would posit that sex is more profitable for males than it is for females. This is because pregnancy is more costly for women than it is for men, and males achieve orgasm more consistently than do females. As a result, males must make sexual relations more prof-itable for females by offering them additional rewards. Baumeister and Vohs (2004) afford a thorough examination of how sex has exchange value for women and not men in the heterosexual marketplace. This value of sex for women is particularly salient in the work done by Hattori and DeRose (2008). Using interview data collected from 1,483 unmarried women in urban Cameroon, Hattori and DeRose discovered that the youngest women and those who had not yet reached secondary school expressed the greatest difficulty in their perceived ability to refuse sex with a man who has paid for their school fees. So, despite the high prevalence of HIV in Cameroon, many young women incur the costs of potential HIV infection in an effort to attain the reward of access to education.

Basow and Minieri (2011) tested another context in which women's sexuality is also often deemed to have exchange value—on dates. More explicitly, the authors thought that social exchange theory might predict that, when a man pays for an expensive date with a woman, he is more likely to expect sexual favors in return. Using a sample of 185 undergraduate students, Basow and Minieri presented four vignettes describing an acquaintance rape situation, with the cost of the date and who paid for the date varying. Results revealed that, when the male paid for an expensive date, men agreed more than women that sexual intercourse should have been expected. When the costs of an inexpensive date were shared, both male and female respondents blamed the perpetrator. Regardless of conditions, however, men tended to blame the victim more and the perpetrator less for the sexual intercourse than did the female respondents. More attention needs to be paid to the potential economic power that men might attain as a result of paying for an expensive date, as well as their general expectations for reciprocity in such dates.

Van de Rijt and Macy (2006) used social exchange to examine "labors of love" and discovered that the most intimate of behaviors—sex—has exchange value in close relationships. Sexual effort (e.g., partner's willingness to engage in a variety of sexual activities that would confer sexual pleasure) received and attachment to partner were critical predictors of sexual effort. In other words, sexuality between intimates appears to be governed by the norm of reciprocity.

Decision-Making

Another area of utility for the theory is decision-making (see Kieren, Henton, and Marotz 1975). The social exchange perspective can make the logic of the process followed in important family-related decisions explicit. Using an organized approach that highlights the pros and cons of each alternative should increase the likelihood of coming to a rational conclusion with greater final profit. Hunts and Marotz-Baden (2004) have developed the flowchart in Figure 8.1 for this process.

In their example, a young woman is trying to decide whether or not to accept a marriage proposal. She loves the young man but is concerned because he does not approve of her career decision. With the help of concerned classmates, she goes through the steps of considering each alternative. What would it be like to be married to him and give up her career? Can she talk him into changing his mind? What would it be like to discontinue the relationship? At certain stages, activities are tried and then evaluated. Sometimes, it may be realized that the particular situation is hopeless without new resources, and at other times the goals are reached.

Donnelly and Burgess (2008) employed social exchange to analyze the decision to stay in an involuntarily celibate relationship. The authors were interested in the ways in which participants evaluated the costs and rewards of remaining in such a relationship, as well as their perceptions with regard to what they thought they deserved or was normal (comparison level), and the likelihood of getting something more rewarding from an alternative relationship (comparison level for alternatives). Donnelly and Burgess developed a model depicting the process of involuntary celibacy, including the following components: causes of involuntary celibacy, types of involuntary celibacy, consequences of involuntary celibacy, and making the decision to stay. In sum, the participants in this study stayed because the benefits of staying outweighed the costs of leaving. Participants gleaned alternative, nonsexual benefits (e.g., best friends); had few appealing alternatives; were invested in their relationship (e.g., shared children, home, and finances); and were influenced by social prescriptions and expectations to stay in their relationship. Participants also made decisions about how to cope with their sexless relationships.

People make all sorts of decisions. McDonough (2010) applied social exchange to battered women's cognitive deliberations when deciding to stay in or leave violent relationships. Twenty-eight battered women and 30 women who had not experienced

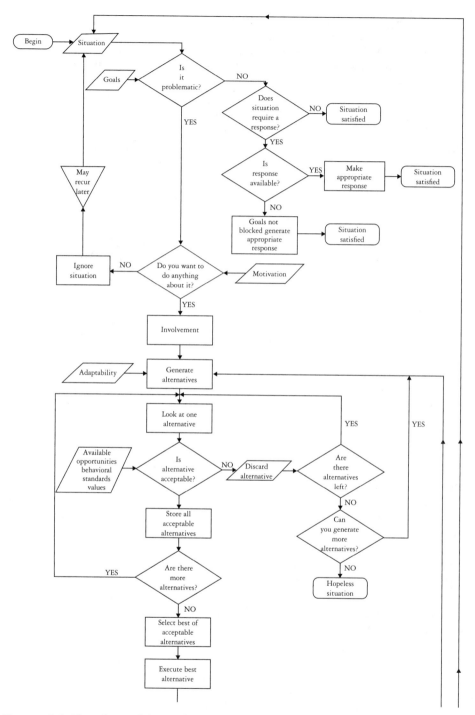

FIGURE 8.1 Flowchart of the problem-solving process.

Source: Hunts, H., and R. Marotz-Baden. 2004. The GO Model: A new way of teaching problem solving in context. *Journal of Teaching in Marriage and Family* 4: 27–58.

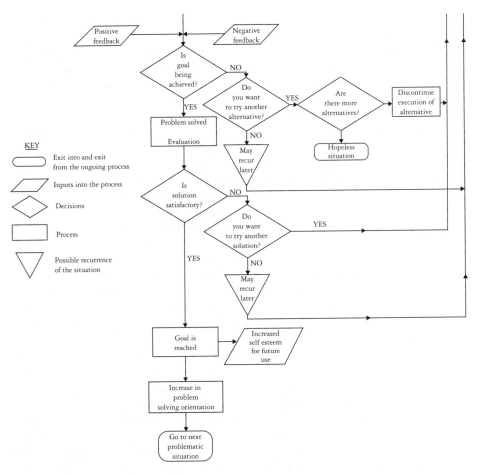

FIGURE 8.1 (Continued)

violent relationships answered a series of questions and responded to vignettes about violent relationships. Both battered and nonbattered women related that they would not stay in a violent relationship, when responding to the vignette, noting that violence intensity was the strongest and primary cue for the need to leave the relationship. Battered women did, however, report more costs, fewer rewards, and a stronger yearning for alternatives than women who did not report a history of relationship violence.

By recognizing that life is about social exchanges, with their resultant rewards and costs, one can take the time to carefully and clearly evaluate one's logic and decision-making. In this way, the theory goes beyond merely analyzing what we do and helps us make good decisions. Any time you have made a list, either physically or mentally, of the pros and cons of a decision, you have utilized the principles of social exchange theory.

Caregiving and Intergenerational Exchanges

Filial relationships are impacted by social exchange norms. Many societies assume that parents will be "reimbursed" for the costs of bearing and rearing children (time, money, worry, and other costs) when they are old and their adult children take care of them. If adult children do not fulfill their filial obligations, however, aging parents may feel that distributive justice has been violated, and their morale may suffer. Similarly, if siblings fail to equitably share in the care of an aging parent, concerns about equity arise, and the sibling relationship can be negatively affected (Whiteman, McHale, and Soli 2011). Thus, social exchange concepts have been helpful in assessing caregiving and intergenerational exchanges in later life.

A good deal of research has been devoted to reviewing the costs of caregiving, with some—though less—attention given to the rewards that caregivers also receive in the process. For instance, using a national sample of 978 spouse and child caregivers, Raschick and Ingersoll-Dayton (2004) employed social exchange theory to explore the costs and rewards of caregiving, particularly as related to the gender and relationship of caregiver. The authors found that caregiving women—whether wives or daughters—experienced greater costs associated with caregiving than did men. This may be due to the greater societal expectations and norms for women to assume filial responsibilities. In addition, even though adult children encountered more rewards as a result of caregiving than did spouses overall, spouses (particularly wives) found receiving companionship and gifts from the care recipient as most rewarding for them. This finding suggests that the companionship that care-recipient husbands provide to their caregiving wives is a particularly valued type of reciprocity.

Social relationships require reciprocity. From a social exchange perspective, receiving something from another obligates the recipient to return the favor. Beel-Bates, Ingersoll-Dayton, and Nelson (2007) conducted interviews with 31 residents, 85 years or older, and who lived in an assisted living facility to see how increasingly dependent older adults might offer reciprocity in their relationships with family and staff. An analysis of qualitative data suggested that these relatively frail, oldest adults used four types of deference as a form of social exchange: participation, pleasantness, cooperation, and gratitude. Although these various forms of deference become an important resource for exchange in light of shrinking exchange resources, the authors note that deference has psychological costs, as well as rewards, for older adults.

Lowenstein, Katz, and Gur-Yaish (2007) used a cross-national sample of 6,000 urban residents from Norway, England, Germany, Spain, and Israel to determine the effects of intergenerational exchanges on life satisfaction of older adults. As social exchange and equity theory would predict, older adults who were able to reciprocate in exchange relations with their adult children experienced greater life satisfaction. However, parents who were "under-benefited," providing more help than they received, had the highest levels of life satisfaction, followed by those in balanced intergenerational exchanges, and then those in "over-benefited" relationships. Probably because they have extensive public service networks for older adults, elders in Norway and Israel had the lowest proportion of over-benefited exchange relationships. Higher proportions of balanced exchanges occurred in Spain and Israel, where adult children provided very little instrumental support (e.g., transportation, shopping). Overall, older adults received more instrumental support (e.g., house repairs, shopping) and provided more financial support. The authors conclude that the continuing ability to reciprocate in parent–child relationships is important for aging adults and their life satisfaction.

CRITIQUE

The social exchange model does an impressive job of providing a context for predicting and explaining a great deal of human behavior in social contexts. It is just one way of looking at families, but it has a straightforward methodology that is appealing to many scholars. It is clear and relatively easy to "get a handle on," compared with some of the other approaches. Much of its power comes from its emergence from behaviorism; however, the individualistic focus also results in certain limitations.

The assumption that the family is just a collection of individuals is too simplistic for many theorists. For some, the family has too many unique and long-lasting aspects to be reduced basically to an economic system with interchangeable characters (White and Klein 2008).

In addition, the key assumption that humans act rationally in decision-making is criticized by many. Since Freud's time, practitioners and other scholars have made the case that humans are emotional beings who rarely act in ways that could be classified as truly rational and objective. Family life, in particular, is an emotional world in which many decisions do not seem to make sense rationally. The case can be made (Beutler, Burr, and Bahr 1989) that the rational focus of the theory makes it impossible for it to deal with love and the other emotional elements that make up family life. Nye (1979) responded to this criticism by stating that people act in accordance with the best information available to them. Because such information is often lacking, they may appear to be less rational than they actually are.

Social exchange theory can also be criticized for the way in which it assumes that people are looking out for their own best interests. Although it might be reflective of basic human nature, Hamon (1999) argued that this and other key assumptions are problematic from a Christian faith perspective. It would be interesting to measure social exchange concepts against other faith traditions, as well.

It has also been said that social exchange theory, like some other theories, suffers from a tautology in which terms are defined by each other and thus make it impossible to scientifically disprove conclusions. For example, we cannot find a situation in which one's behavior is not a function of reward, because the definition of a reward is the behaviors that one chooses (Turner 1991). So, too, what is rewarding or costly to one person may not be deemed the same by another. Similarly, determining relative value of various rewards and costs is problematic, making the treatment of marital couples within the context of social exchange theory challenging (Nakonezny and Denton 2008).

Feminist theorists also point out a masculine bias in social exchange theory, which seems to assume a "separate" rather than a "connected" self. As a result, the theory is less capable of understanding behaviors that support the group over the individual. The assumption of maximizing profit ignores altruistic behavior, for instance. It elevates the traditionally masculine and modern Western notion that autonomy and independence are more functional than caring and sharing (England 1989). Exchange theorists respond that individuals do engage in group supportive behaviors when the social approval is rewarding.

Social exchange theory has been used considerably by family scholars over the last quarter century. Collett (2010) makes a strong case that social exchange theory is a dynamic perspective with a great deal to offer family scholars and those theorizing about families.

APPLICATION

1. In a small group, play out the roles of Nicholas and Alyssa from the vignette at the beginning of the chapter. Weigh the pros and cons of the relationship, and decide if the two should get married, and why. What important ways of viewing the relationship are missed by just focusing on the rational aspects?

  a. Use Stanley and Markman's (1992) key process of dedication to delineate some tangible behaviors in which Alyssa and Nicholas can engage in order to demonstrate their growing commitment to one another.

  b. Discuss why it is important for their commitment to be mutual and clear.

  c. What cultural emblems of commitment might they use in order to demonstrate the persistence of their relationship?

2. Analyze a relationship in your own immediate family with which you are at least somewhat uncomfortable. What are the rewards you are exchanging? Remember that this includes such intangibles as kindness and humor, in addition to goods (buying clothes) and services (fixing dinner). Now, what does it cost you to be in this relationship? After you make this list of costs associated with relating to the other person, can you identify the costs that he or she must endure to be with you? Now, are there ways that the relationship could be made more equitable, and therefore more rewarding, for both of you?

3. Divide into small groups within your class and use the problem-solving model found in the chapter. Take a real problem from one of the members and use the process to see if a solution to the relationship difficulty can be reached.

4. Have you ever been in a romantic relationship where you felt exploited or where you were the exploiter? Use social exchange theory concepts to write up an understanding of the dynamics of that relationship and what could have been done to make it fair. What aspects of the relationship are ignored by just looking at it through the lens of social exchange theory?

5. Respond to the following questions based on the sample reading (Yabiku and Gager 2009):

  a. Evaluate the basic exchange theory assumptions outlined in this chapter in light of their finding that cohabitors are significantly more likely than married couples to dissolve their relationship when they experience low sexual frequency.

  b. The authors conclude that "cohabitation is not so much an incomplete institution but better described as a more narrow institution—both structurally and emotionally" (997). Delineate the ways in which cohabitation is a more narrow institution.

c. Based on the authors' findings, outline the rewards and costs that appear to be apparent in both marital and cohabiting relationships.

d. What implications does this research have on relationship formation?

e. What connections can you make between these findings and the notions of attachment, security, and commitment, particularly as related to dedication and constraints?

REFERENCES

Basow, S. A., and A. Minieri. 2010. "You owe me": Effects of date cost, who pays, participant gender and rape myth beliefs on perception of rape. *Journal of Interpersonal Violence* 26: 479–497.

Baumeister, R. F., and K. D. Vohs. 2004. Sexual economics: Sex as female resource for social exchange in heterosexual interactions. *Personality and Social Psychology Review* 8: 339–363.

Beel-Bates, C. A., B. Ingersoll-Dayton, and E. Nelson. 2007. Deference as a form of reciprocity among residents in assisted living. *Research on Aging* 29(6): 626–643.

Beutler, I., W. Burr, and K. Bahr. 1989. The family realm: Theoretical contributions for understanding its uniqueness. *Journal of Marriage and the Family* 51: 805–816.

Blau, P. 1964. *Exchange and power in social life*. New York: John Wiley.

Brown, E. 1990. *Patterns of infidelity and their treatment*. New York: Brunner/Mazel.

Byrd, S. E. 2009. The social construction of marital commitment. *Journal of Marriage and Family* 71: 318–336.

Chen, J., and D. T. Takeuchi. 2011. Intermarriage, ethnic identity, and perceived social standing among Asian women in the United States. *Journal of Marriage and Family* 73: 876–888.

Collett, J. L. 2010. Integrating theory, enhancing understanding: The potential contributions of recent experimental research in social exchange for studying intimate relationships. *Journal of Family Theory and Review* 2: 280–298.

Cox, C. L., M. O. Wexler, C. E. Rusbult, and S. O. Gaines Jr. 1997. Prescriptive support and commitment process in close relationships. *Social Psychology Quarterly,* 60(1): 79–90.

Donnelly, D. A., and E. O. Burgess. 2008. The decision to remain in an involuntary celibate relationship. *Journal of Marriage and Family* 70: 519–535.

Ekeh, P. 1974. *Social exchange: The two traditions*. Cambridge, MA: Harvard University Press.

Emerson, R. 1976. Social exchange theory. In *Annual review of sociology*, ed. A. Inkeles, J. Coleman, and N. Smelser. Vol. 2, 335–362. Palo Alto, CA: Annual Reviews.

England, P. 1989. A feminist critique of rational choice theories: Implications for sociology. *The American Sociologist* 20: 14–28.

Fitzpatrick, J., E. A. Sharp, and A. Reifman. 2009. Midlife singles' willingness to date partners with heterogeneous characteristics. *Family Relations* 58: 121–133.

Foa, E. B., and U. G. Foa. 1980. Resource theory: Interpersonal behavior as exchange. In *Social exchange: Advances in theory and research*, ed. K. J. Gergen, M. S. Greenberg, and R. H. Willis, 77–94. New York: Plenum.

Frazer, J. 1919. *Folklore of the old testament*. New York: Macmillan.

Gelles, R., and M. Straus. 1988. *Intimate violence*. New York: Simon and Schuster.

Hamon, R. R. 1999. Social exchange and the Christian faith: Is a satisfactory marriage possible? *Journal of Psychology and Christianity* 18: 19–27.

Hattori, M. K., and L. DeRose. 2008. Young women's perceived ability to refuse sex in urban Cameroon. *Studies in Family Planning* 39(4): 309–320.

Homans, G. C. 1958. Social behavior as exchange. *American Journal of Sociology* 63: 597–606.

Homans, G. C. 1961/1974. *Social behavior: Its elementary forms*. New York: Harcourt, Brace & Jovanovich.

Homans, G. C., and D. Schneider. 1955. *Marriage, authority, and final causes: A study of unilateral cross-cousin marriage*. New York: Free Press.

Hunts, H., and R. Marotz-Baden. 2004. The GO Model: A new way of teaching problem solving in context. *Journal of Teaching in Marriage and Family* 4: 27–58.

Ingoldsby, B., P. Schvaneveldt, and C. Uribe. 2003. Perceptions of acceptable mate attributes in Ecuador. *Journal of Comparative Family Studies* 34: 171–186.

Johnson, M. P., J.P. Caughlin, and T. L. Huston. 1999. The tripartite nature of marital commitment: Personal, moral, and structural reasons to stay married. *Journal of Marriage and the Family* 61:160–177.

Kalmijn, M. 1998. Intermarriage and homogamy: Causes, patterns, trends. *Annual Review of Sociology* 24(1): 395–421.

Kalmijn, M. 2010. Educational inequality, homogamy, and status exchange in black-white intermarriage: A comment on Rosenfeld. *American Journal of Sociology* 115(4): 1252–1263.

Kelley, H. H., and J. W. Thibault. 1978. Interpersonal relations: A theory of interdependence. New York: Wiley.

Kieren, D., J. Henton, and R. Marotz. 1975. *Hers and his: A problem-solving approach to marriage*. Hinsdale, IL: Dryden.

Knoester, C., and A. Booth. 2000. Barriers to divorce: When are they effective? When are they not? *Journal of Family Issues* 21: 78–99. DOI: 10.1177/019251300021001001004

Lowenstein, A., R. Katz, and N. Gur-Yaish. 2007. Reciprocity in parent–child exchange and life satisfaction among the elderly: A cross-national perspective. *Journal of Social Issues* 63(4): 865–883.

McDonough, T.A. 2010. A policy capturing investigation of battered women's decisions to stay in violent relationships. *Violence and Victims* 25(2): 165–184.

Nakonezny, P. A., and W. H. Denton 2008. Marital relationships: A social exchange theory perspective. *The American Journal of Family Therapy* 36: 402–412.

Nye, I. 1978. Is choice and exchange theory the key? *Journal of Marriage and the Family* 40: 219–233.

———. 1979. Choice, exchange, and the family. In *Contemporary theories about the family*, ed. W. R. Burr, R. Hill, F. I. Nye, and I. L. Reiss. Vol. 2, 1–41. New York: Free Press.

Raschick, M., and B. Ingersoll-Dayton. 2004. The costs and rewards of caregiving among aging spouses and adult children. *Family Relations* 53: 317–325.

Rosenfeld, M. J. 2005. A critique of exchange theory in mate selection. *American Journal of Sociology* 110(5): 1284–1325.

Rusbult, C. E. 1980. Commitment and satisfaction in romantic associations: A test of the investment model. *Journal of Experimental Social Psychology* 16: 172–186.

Rusbult, C. E. 1983. A longitudinal test of the investment model: The development (and deterioration) of satisfaction and commitment in heterosexual involvements. *Journal of Personality and Social Psychology,* 45: 101–117.

Rusbult, C. E., D. J. Johnson, and G. D. Morrow. 1986. Predicting satisfaction and commitment in adult romantic involvements: An assessment of the generalizability of the investment model. *Social Psychology Quarterly* 49(1): 81–89.

Rusbult, C. E., J. M. Martz, and C. R. Agnew. 1998. The investment model scale: Measuring commitment level, satisfaction level, quality of alternatives, and investment size. *Personal Relationships* 5: 357–391.

Sabatelli, R., and C. Shehan. 1993. Exchange and resource theories. In *Sourcebook of family theories and methods: A contextual approach*, ed. P. G. Boss, W. J. Doherty, R. LaRossa, W. R. Schumm, and S. K. Steinmetz, 385–417. New York: Plenum.

Smith, C. A., J. A. Konik, and M. V. Tuve. 2011. In search of looks, status or something else? Partner preferences among butch and femme lesbians and heterosexual men and women. *Sex Roles* 64: 658–668. DOI: 10.1007/s11199–010-9861-8

Stanley, S. M., and H. J. Markman. 1992. Assessing commitment in personal relationships. *Journal of Marriage and the Family* 54: 595–608.

Stanley, S. M., G. K. Rhoades, and S. W. Whitton. 2010. Commitment: Functions, formation, and the securing of romantic attachment. *Journal of Family Theory and Review* 2: 243–257.

Thibaut, J. W., and H. H. Kelley. 1959. *The social psychology of groups.* New York: Wiley.

Turner, J. 1991. *The structure of sociological theory.* 5th ed. Belmont, CA: Wadsworth.

Van de Rijt, A., and M. W. Macy. 2006. Power and dependence in intimate relationships. *Social Forces* 84: 1455–1470.

Walster, E., G. W. Walster, and E. Berscheid. 1978. *Equity: Theory and research.* Boston: Allyn and Bacon.

White, L., and A. Booth. 1991. Divorce over the life course: The role of marital happiness. *Journal of Family Issues* 12: 5–21.

White, J. M., and D. M. Klein. 2008. *Family theories* (3rd ed.). Thousand Oaks, CA: Sage Publications.

Whiteman, S. D., S. M. McHale, and A. Soli. 2011. Theoretical perspectives on sibling relationships. *Journal of Family Theory and Review* 3: 124–139.

Winton, C. 1995. *Frameworks for studying families.* Guilford, CT: Duskin.

SAMPLE READING

Yabiku, S. T., and C. T. Gager. 2009. Sexual frequency and the stability of marital and cohabiting unions. *Journal of Marriage and Family* 71: 983–1000.

Using data from the National Survey of Households, Yabiku and Gager employed social exchange theory to examine the importance of sexual activity to the stability of cohabiting and marital relationships. Results indicated that sexual frequency was more strongly associated with relationship termination for cohabitors than for those who were married. The authors suggest that there are a number of differences that exist between cohabiting and marital relationships, many of which have to do with expectations for their relationship. They conclude that "cohabitation is not so much an incomplete institution but better described as a more narrow institution—both structurally and emotionally" (997). As you read the article, delineate the ways in which cohabitation is a more narrow institution. Also consider the rewards and costs that appear to be apparent in both marital and cohabiting relationships.

SAMPLE READING

Sexual Frequency and the Stability of Marital and Cohabiting Unions

Scott T. Yabiku
Arizona State University

Constance T. Gager
Montclair State University*

Prior research found that lower sexual frequency and satisfaction were associated with higher rates of divorce, but little research had examined the role of sexual activity in the dissolution of cohabiting unions. We drew upon social exchange theory to hypothesize why sexual frequency is more important in cohabitation: (a) cohabitors' lower costs of finding sexual alternatives, (b) cohabitors' lower barriers to ending the relationship in the form of union-specific economic and noneconomic capital, and (c) cohabitors' higher expectations for sexual activity. Using the National Survey of Families and Households (N = 5,902), we examined the relationship between sexual frequency and union dissolution. Results indicated that low sexual frequency was associated with significantly higher rates of union dissolution among cohabitors than married couples.

Prior research finds that sexuality within marriage is an important component of marital quality and stability. Typically, studies found that higher sexual satisfaction or frequency is positively associated with marital stability (Edwards & Booth, 1994; Oggins, Veroff, & Leber, 1993; Veroff, Douvan, & Hatchett, 1995; White & Keith, 1990; Yeh, Lorenz, Wickrama, Conger, & Elder, 2006). The relationship between sexual activity and union stability in cohabitations has received less research attention, but the existing research found that sexual satisfaction in nonmarital unions also promotes stability (Sprecher, 2002).

Keywords: cohabitation, dissolution, divorce, marriage, sexual frequency

Center for Population Dynamics and School of Social and Family Dynamics, Arizona State University, PO Box 873701, Tempe, AZ 85287–3701 (scott.yabiku@asu.edu).
*Department of Family & Child Studies, Montclair State University, One Normal Avenue, Montclair, NJ 07043.

Although it was previously established in separate studies that sexual activity was associated with union stability for both marriage and cohabitation, no studies compared the importance of sexual activity across marital and nonmarital unions. Because partners in these two types of unions have different expectations, histories, and responsibilities (Giddens, 1992), there is good reason to believe that sexuality within these unions may have differential stabilizing roles. The role of sexual frequency in relationships is an important area of study, as recent research found that sexual relations ranked as the second most problematic issue (after balancing job and family) among a national sample of young married couples (Risch, Riley, & Lawler, 2003).

In this paper, we develop a theoretical framework that links sexual activity to union stability. We examine how the importance of sexual activity varied across marital and cohabiting unions. To empirically test our hypotheses, we used the first and second waves of the National Survey of Families and Households (NSFH).

THEORETICAL ISSUES

It has been well established in the literature that positive, healthy sexuality within marriage is associated with several dimensions of marital well-being, including marital satisfaction and happiness (Blumstein & Schwartz, 1983; Edwards & Booth, 1994; Henderson-King & Veroff, 1994; Perlman & Abrahmson, 1982; Yeh et al., 2006). Research has also found that low sexual satisfaction can promote marital instability (Edwards & Booth; Oggins et al., 1993; Veroff et al., 1995; White & Keith, 1990). For example, Edwards and Booth found that declines in sexual satisfaction among married couples from 1980 to 1983 were associated with a higher likelihood of divorce 5 years later. White and Booth (1991) wrote that reports of sexual problems among married couples increased the likelihood of divorce, net of other relationship quality variables. Fewer studies focused on the role of sexual satisfaction in cohabiting or dating relationships. One exception was Sprecher's (2002) study of the quality and stability of dating couples. She found that couples who reported higher sexual satisfaction scores were more likely to stay together than couples with lower scores.

Social and Biological Factors Linking Sexual Frequency and Dissolution

There are several explanations for the link between lower sexual frequency or lower sexual satisfaction to higher rates of union dissolution. One explanation is selection. It may not be that reduced sexual activity causes union dissolution, but that as partners experience other nonsexual problems and difficulties in the relationship, their level of intimacy and sexual activity drops as well. Findings from prior studies are consistent with this reasoning. For example, alcoholism is likely to cause both low sexual frequency and higher rates of dissolution (O'Farrell, Choquette, & Birchler, 1991). Also, much research has demonstrated that poor communication is linked to low levels of sexual satisfaction. Poor communication may also account for higher rates of relationship dissolution (Thachil & Bhugra, 2006). In sum, this literature suggested that any research studying the relationship between sexual activity and union stability must control for potential confounding causes of both sexual frequency and dissolution in order to avoid spurious associations.

A second explanation of the relationship between sexual frequency and union stability is a causal one: The sexual act promotes social attachment between individuals. Research from both the biological and social sciences also is consistent with this explanation. The social sciences usually focus on behavioral models of attachment, and biological sciences have investigated neuroendocrine models (Carter, 1998). Neuroendocrine models of attachment point to neurochemical mechanisms that aid the formation of social bonds. Neurochemicals such as oxytocin and vasopressin, for example, are released during sexual activity and may help to increase social attachment (Carter; Insel, 1997). Although these processes have not been conclusively identified in humans, animal studies strongly suggested that neurochemicals released during sex promote social attachment through biochemical mechanisms in the brain (Insel).

From a social science perspective, the relationship between sexual activity and union dissolution can be studied with social exchange theory. Social exchange theory has been used to analyze a broad range of social interactions (e.g., Blau, 1964; Homans, 1961; Sprecher, 1998), on the basis of the assumption that in a given interaction, each individual weighs the costs and benefits of various interpersonal behaviors. This approach provides a useful basis for making predictions about how people will choose to act. Specifically, social exchange theory can help explain how sexual interaction occurs or does not (Lawrance & Byers, 1995) and more generally how sexual interactions may influence relationship disruption decisions (Levinger, 1979).

Levinger (1979) laid out a general theory of union dissolution that informs the specific role that low sexual frequency may play. He presented a three-category typology: (a) attractions to the relationship, (b) barriers to ending the relationship, and (c) the availability of attractive alternatives. An individual's attraction to the relationship is positively associated with the perceived rewards and inversely associated with costs. Rewards are defined as positive outcomes deriving from the relationship including love, sex, money, status, support, and security. Costs might include time, energy, or other expenditures associated with the demands of the relationship. Partners continuously weigh the rewards and costs of their relationship, and dissolution may occur when perceived costs outweigh perceived rewards, especially if this imbalance continues over the long term.

Barriers refer to both actual and perceived outcomes that keep relationships intact. For example, barriers might include individuals' expectation of a decline in their standard of living or fear of spending their life alone. Another example is the marriage contract, which binds spouses both legally and normatively. Although the stigma of divorce has lessened, marital bonds remain stronger than cohabiting ones. For example, Kravdal (1999) suggested that married individuals may not want to break up their union because of the public nature of the commitment. Thus, even if marital attraction becomes negative, barriers can act to secure the relationship. Last, alternative attractions refer to relationships with persons outside the marriage. Again, these may be real or perceived. If partners believe that their alternatives outside the marriage exceed their current ones, then the relationship may dissolve, especially when the costs of staying in a relationship consistently outweigh the rewards and barriers are seen as surmountable.

Extending this theoretical framework to low sexual frequency and relationship dissolution, social exchange theory suggests that when continuing a relationship with low sexual frequency (a cost) begins to outweigh perceived love or security (rewards), an individual may seek to end the relationship. Further, when faced with low sexual frequency, we argue that cohabiting couples may assign a higher cost to low sexual frequency and face fewer barriers to leaving a relationship. Using social exchange theory, we generated several hypotheses to predict why the impact of sexual frequency on union stability will differ for cohabitation versus marriage.

Differences Between Marital and Cohabiting Unions

To better understand differences between cohabiting and marital unions in relation to sexual frequency and dissolution, we first explicate the more general differences between marriage and cohabitation. Broadly, marriage and cohabitation involve different levels of institutionalization. Specifically, cohabitation has been described as an incomplete institution compared to marriage (Brown & Bulanda, 2007; Smock & Gupta, 2002). The concept of an incomplete institution was first used by Cherlin (1978) to argue that remarried families with children lack a clear set of norms and thus proscriptive solutions to problems that may emerge. For example, the role of a stepparent in rearing stepchildren is less clear than the role of a biological parent. Nock (1995) extended this idea to argue that cohabitation also falls within the definition of an incomplete institution. The norms about marriage are clearer and more specific than those surrounding cohabitation because cohabitation is a much newer relationship form and thus not governed by a clear set of consensual norms. Because the rules and norms governing cohabiting relationships are less clear, it has been suggested that partners face greater negotiations over their roles in the relationship than married couples (Brown & Bulanda), although direct evidence of this is scant.

Perhaps even more salient, Nock (1995) noted that cohabitation is not governed by formal law as marriage is. This partially explains why marriage and cohabitation have different time horizons (Waite & Joyner, 1992). Although both marriage and cohabitation are viewed as monogamous relationships, cohabiting involves less long-term commitment compared to marriage, as cohabitations are more easily dissolved. Married couples expect to and do stay together longer than cohabiting couples (Bumpass & Lu, 2000; Bumpass, Sweet, & Cherlin, 1991). Thus, cohabitation, unlike marriage, carries no explicit social or legal commitment to stay together for the long term.

On a more social-psychological level, cohabiting couples likely have lower levels of interrelatedness compared to married couples—in other words, they occupy a different location on "the continuum of relatedness" (Levinger, 1979). According to Levinger's schema, the degree of interdependence among couples "refers to a complex of joint property, joint outlook or knowledge, capacities, behaviors, feelings, joint memories and anticipations" (p. 39). Extending this concept to cohabitors, shorter relationship time horizons likely translate into less joint property and fewer memories and anticipations; thus cohabiting couples likely have lower levels of interdependence compared to married ones.

Given these broad differences between marriage and cohabitation, we propose several hypotheses to explain why the impact of sexual frequency on union stability differs between marriages and cohabitations. First, cohabitors might have higher expectations and demands for sexual activity than married partners. In other words, sex represents a greater attraction to the relationship for cohabitors than married couples (Levinger, 1979). The literature suggests multiple dimensions on which cohabitors' values, expectations, and norms differ from married spouses. For example, cohabitors are usually more individualistic than people in marital unions (Teachman, 2003), and these individualistic tendencies can interfere with the development of commitment to the relationship and its intrinsic rewards (Scanzoni, Polonko, Teachman, & Thompson, 1989). An additional dimension on which cohabitors and married partners might differ is their expectations of sexual frequency. Researchers found that cohabitors reported higher sexual frequency per month compared to married couples (Michael, Gagnon, Laumann, & Kolata, 1994). For example, although over 40% of married couples reported having sex 2 – 3 times per week, well over 50% of cohabiting couples had sex 2 – 3 times per week (Michael et al.). Similarly, Byers and Heinlein (1989) found that, compared to married partners, cohabitors more frequently attempted to initiate sexual activity.

We hypothesize that cohabitors expect and derive more relationship satisfaction from sexual activity than married partners do. Given the many differences between cohabitors and married couples, sexual frequency may be more closely associated with relationship satisfaction for cohabitors because sex may be more highly prioritized in their evaluations of relationship satisfaction and dissolution decisions. Although research showed that relationship happiness mediated the link between sexual satisfaction and instability for married couples (Yeh et al., 2006), low sexual frequency may play a lesser role in evaluations of marital quality compared to cohabiting quality. Married couples may have a greater number of areas from which to seek relationship satisfaction—such as raising biological children or owning and caring for a home together—which lessens the focus on sexual activity.

Second, cohabitors face fewer barriers to ending the union because they have fewer shared investments in economic and noneconomic union-specific capital (Brines & Joyner, 1999). This lower level of investments produces lower interrelatedness (Levinger, 1979). Children can be viewed as a form of noneconomic, union-specific capital. Cohabiting couples are less likely to have children present in the household compared to married couples. Furthermore, in married couples with children, the children are more likely to be the biological offspring of both parents compared with children in cohabiting families. In sum, it is still the case that cohabitors are less likely to have children than married couples and that a larger proportion of these cohabiting couples did not have these children together. Thus, compared to married couples, cohabitors have fewer barriers to dissolve the union because of a higher likelihood that no children are present or that only one of the partners is the child's biological parent.

In contrast to noneconomic union-specific capital, home ownership represents economic union-specific capital. A home represents a substantial economic asset that would have to be divided if the union were to end (Rindfuss & Van den Heuvel, 1990). In general, cohabitors do not pool together financial resources to the same degree as married partners (Morrison & Ritualo, 2000). Thus, married couples are more likely to face substantial barriers such as selling a large asset or losing touch with biological children than are cohabitors. In terms of social exchange, although low sexual frequency may lower the rewards of the union for both marriage and cohabitation, married individuals will face more barriers to leaving the relationship; thus the impact of low sexual frequency may be weaker.

Third, cohabiting couples who are contemplating dissolution have greater availability of attractive alternatives (Levinger, 1979) with regards to sexual activity. When a marriage or cohabitation ends, sexual activity with the partner also ends: One of the costs of dissolving the union is lost sexual activity. Partners may seek to replace this lost sexual activity with a new partner, but there are search costs to finding a new partner (Oppenheimer, 1988). These search costs are probably lower for cohabiting than married individuals because cohabitors may face fewer barriers to seeking an alternative sexual partner, as they are likely younger and have spent less time out of the dating market compared to married persons. For example, married individuals may have less access to the opposite sex than cohabitors because of restricted freedom to meet potential mates while married (Kravdal, 1999). Dolcini et al. (1993) reported that although only 2% of married individuals had more than one sexual partner in the past year, 12% of cohabitors did. Other research showed that cohabitors were twice as likely to have been unfaithful in the past year (Treas & Giesen, 2000). We hypothesize that cohabitors will have more ready access to a replacement sexual partner, which increases the likelihood that they will end the union.

In sum, we expect that lower sexual frequency will be associated with higher rates of union disruption in both marriage and cohabitation. We hypothesize, however, that lower sexual frequency will have a stronger effect on union instability in cohabitation than marriage. Potential reasons include cohabitors' lower attractions to the relationship because of their greater expectations for sexual activity, lower barriers of ending the relationship in the form of union-specific economic and noneconomic capital, and higher availability of sexual alternatives.

METHOD

To test our hypotheses, we used data from the first two waves of the National Survey of Families and Households. Wave 1 of the NSFH collected a variety of family, household, and demographic data from a nationally representative sample of individuals in 1987–1988. NSFH data were collected from a randomly selected adult in each household surveyed and from the respondent's spouse or partner. Respondent data were collected through both face-to-face interviews and self-administered questionnaires; spouses and partners were asked to complete a shorter, less detailed questionnaire (Sweet, Bumpass, & Call, 1988). Wave 2 data were collected in 1992–1994, and Wave 3 data were collected in 2001–2003, but did not follow up with all respondents. Thus, our analysis was based on the Wave 1 sample of married and cohabiting couples in which the primary respondent was reinterviewed at Wave 2. Our sample included 5,440 marital unions and 462 cohabiting unions. We took advantage of the couple data by including measures of variables for both partners.

Dependent Variable: Union Dissolution

As is typical in discrete-time event history (Allison, 1995), for every month that the union was intact the dependent variable was coded 0. In the month in which the couple either divorced (marriages) or dissolved (cohabitations), the dependent variable was coded 1, and the couple no longer contributed observations to the data set. Couples who remained together until Wave 2 were censored and did not experience dissolution. Cohabiting couples who married were considered intact unless their marriage ended.

Independent Variable: Sexual Frequency

Our primary independent variable of interest was sexual frequency. Although subject to social desirability bias (Leridon, 1996), researchers have been confident that reports of coital frequency are valid and fairly reliable (Smith, Morgan, & Gager, 1994). This confidence came from a set of empirical observations. First, respondents were willing to provide answers. Second, frequency distributions seemed reasonable given consistency with distributions obtained using other data collection procedures such as interviews or diaries (Kinsey, Pomeroy, & Martin, 1948; Kinsey, Pomeroy, Martin, & Gebhard 1953). Some expected correlates of coital frequency were confirmed across studies using a variety of data collection techniques. For example, in all surveys, mean sexual frequency was found to decline with age and marital duration (Kinsey et al., 1948, 1953; Laumann, Gagnon, Michael, & Michaels, 1994; Udry, Deven, & Coleman, 1982).

Recall is one potential problem with such retrospective reports of sexual frequency. For example, Udry (1993) contended that the use of a diary for data collection was superior to retrospective reports, especially when trying to map out the rhythmic aspects of coitus. He argued that respondents answered the retrospective question concerning monthly coital frequency by looking back over the past week, counting how often they had intercourse, and then multiplying that number by 4. Although retrospective recall of sexual frequency will contain measurement error, this error is most likely to introduce Type II error (failing to reject the null when the null hypothesis is false), thus making our estimates more conservative.

The NSFH question on sexual frequency asked married respondents, "About how often did you and your husband/wife have sex during the past month?" A similar question was asked of cohabiting respondents. The scale for this survey question was the number of times, from 0 up to a maximum of 95. Because the NSFH interviewed partners of respondents, answers to these questions were also available from the partners. We took the average of both partners' responses because Smith et al. (1994) found little difference between husbands' and wives' reports of sexual frequency. In our sample, the average difference in reports of monthly sexual frequency between partners was 0.11 times per month for cohabitors and 0.21 for married partners. The correlation between partners' reports was $r = .74$ in cohabitations and $r = .71$ in marriages. Although this correlation was strong, it might have obscured important differences. To investigate how partners' differential perceptions of sexual frequency might have affected our results, we repeated our analyses (not shown) with four variations of the dependent variable: the wife's report, the husband's report, the lowest of the two partners' reports, and the highest of the two partners' reports. The substantive findings were similar to the couple average models.

In addition, we transformed the sexual frequency measure with a logarithmic function by adding 1 and taking the natural log. The log transformation compressed the distribution at the higher range more than at the lower range. For example, a difference between 5 and 10 times per month was given more importance than the difference between 20 and 25 times per month. This log transformation was appropriate because there is likely a threshold effect of sexual intimacy. In other words, additional sexual activity at higher levels is not as important as increases in sexual frequency at lower levels (Blanchflower & Oswald, 2004).

Attractions to the Relationship

As we discussed above, sex may be a greater attraction to the relationship for cohabitors. Thus relationship satisfaction may mediate the relationship between sexual frequency and dissolution more for cohabitors than married partners. Relationship happiness has been shown to be positively correlated with sexual frequency and negatively correlated with divorce (Blumstein & Schwartz, 1983; Edwards & Booth, 1994; Sprecher, 2002). Respondents were asked, "Taking things all together, how would you describe your marriage?" Responses were on a 7-point scale, from 1 (*very unhappy*) to 7 (*very happy*). A similarly worded question was asked of respondents in cohabiting relationships.

Barriers to Ending the Union: Union-Specific Capital

One possible reason why sexual frequency is more important for the dissolution of cohabitation compared to marriage is that cohabitors have less union-specific capital. Thus, cohabitors may find it easier to end the union than married couples. We used two measures of union-specific capital: one was economic; the other is noneconomic. The first was home ownership. Although the NSFH asked respondents about multiple assets, we focused on home ownership because a primary residence constitutes the single most valuable asset for most American couples (Keister & Deeb-Sossa, 2001). Home ownership was coded 1 if the couple owned a home and 0 otherwise. Because of the survey question design of the NSFH regarding home ownership, we had to make several assumptions. If a couple was married, the home ownership question was asked only of the primary respondent; it was assumed that both partners shared ownership because they are married. If a couple was cohabiting, the question was asked of both the respondent and partner, but it remained unknown whether they had joint ownership of the same house. Thus, we assumed that if both cohabiting partners said they owned a home, both partners were referring to the same house. The second measure of union-specific capital was the presence of biological children common to both partners in the home. We coded the presence of young children (aged 0–4) and older children (aged 5–18) with dummy variables if there was at least one child in the household within each age group who was biologically related to both partners and 0 otherwise. We divided children into these age groups on the basis of prior research on sexual frequency (Call, Sprecher, & Schwartz, 1995) and the finding that age of the child was differentially associated with union stability (Waite & Lillard, 1991).

Availability of Attractive Alternatives

If cohabitors have fewer barriers to ending the union, then they have little reason to stay in a union if they become dissatisfied as a result of low sexual frequency.

Perceiving few barriers to leaving a relationship, however, may not be enough to lead to relationship dissolution, as individuals may also consider their "alternative attractions" (i.e., their potential sexual alternatives). If partners believe their sex lives will suffer greatly if their union ends, then the union may be less likely to dissolve, even if one partner perceives low sexual frequency. It may be that married spouses have fewer potential sexual alternatives than cohabiting partners. For married individuals, low sexual frequency may not be as strongly linked to dissolution because these individuals may be less confident of their ability to find a replacement sexual partner. We measured potential sexual alternatives with a question that asked both partners, "Even though it may be very unlikely, think for a moment about how various areas of your life might be different if you separated." The survey asked how they thought their "sex life" would change: *much worse, worse, same, better,* or *much better.* This variable was coded from 1 to 5, with higher values meaning the respondent thought his or her sex life would become better if the current union would end. We used separate measures of this question for each partner.

Controls

Age of each partner was included, given the consistent findings that older age is associated with less coital frequency. Lower coital frequency occurs among older couples and those in longer marital unions (James, 1974; Jasso, 1985; Rao & DeMaris, 1995; Udry, 1993; Udry & Morris, 1978; Westoff, 1974). Declines in coital frequency by age and marital duration are attributed to the aging process and include increases in illness and decreases in male physical ability and male and female hormone levels, although age cannot fully explain the pattern of the decline (Greenblat, 1983; Udry et al., 1982).

We also included control variables previously shown to be correlated with sexual frequency and divorce or the dissolution of cohabitation, including religion, race and ethnicity, couple income, education level, self-rated health, and hours in the paid workforce (Call et al., 1995; Michael et al., 1994; Teachman, 2003). Because prior work documented differences in the frequency of sex and the likelihood of divorce by religious affiliation (Call et al.; Lehrer & Chiswick, 1993), we included the religion of the couple. We based our measurement of religion on the work of Lehrer and Chiswick, who also used the NSFH to study marital stability. Taking advantage of couple-level data, we measured whether both partners were (a) ecumenical Protestant, (b) exclusivist Protestant, (c) Catholic, (d) an interfaith marriage involving two different religion categories, or (e) all other categories. Although not ideal, it was necessary to combine many different faiths in an "all other category" because the sample of cohabitors was not large enough to distinguish between these different faiths. The race/ethnicity of the couple was coded as (a) both non-Hispanic White, (b) both non-Hispanic Black, (c) both Hispanic, (d) both other race/ethnicity, or (e) interracial marriage. Income was measured as the couple's total income, including investments, as reported by the respondent. Because this measure was skewed, we used a log transformation. Education of the partners was measured in years, with a maximum of 17 for respondents who achieved more than a Bachelor's degree. Hours per week spent in the paid work force was included in the models as it may jointly affect sexual frequency and the likelihood of divorce. It was measured with a continuous variable.

We included two different measures of health and well-being. Prior research found that poor physical health interfered with the ability to engage in sexual activity, and depression and anxiety may have inhibited desire for sex (Channon & Ballinger, 1986; Heiman, 2000; Laumann, Paik, & Rosen, 1999). The overall health measure asked, "Compared with other people your age, how would you describe your health?" Respondents replied on a scale from 1 (*very poor*) to 5 (*excellent*). Individual mental well-being was assessed with a global happiness question that asked, "First taking things all together, how would you say things are these days?" Respondents answered on a scale from 1 (*very unhappy*) to 7 (*very happy*). Although the NSFH contained more detailed measurement of mental well-being using a more standard assessment of mental health, this more detailed measurement was available only for the primary respondent, not spouses and partners. Thus we used a general measure of overall well-being, which was asked of both partners.

Because premarital cohabitation has been identified as a risk factor for divorce (Holley, Yabiku, & Benin, 2006; Smock, 2000), in the analysis of married couples, we included a control for whether or not the marriage started as a cohabitation. Because couples who cohabited prior to marriage might have been very different than married couples who did not cohabit, a single additive term may not capture these differences. Therefore, we also explored models in which we interacted our key independent variables to test if they varied by premarital cohabitation experience.

Another important potentially confounding factor was the length of sexual relationship. Prior research suggested that some of the decline in sexual frequency is attributed to habituation, which is defined as the loss of interest or novelty of a sexual partner (James, 1974, 1981). Important for our analysis was the finding that the effects of habituation were strongest early in relationships (Call et al., 1995). Because most cohabitations are short, an apparent greater effect of sexual frequency on dissolution of cohabitation could result mostly from habitation. Although the NSFH did not ask respondents when the sexual relationship with their partners began, we addressed this issue in three ways. First, our controls for both partners' ages and their relationship duration (as captured by the baseline hazard) partially captured the processes of habituation and aging. Second, we conducted additional analyses that compared the dissolution rates of marriages in their first year and cohabitations in their first year. Although sample sizes were greatly reduced, this closely matched comparison better controlled for length of sexual relationship.

Methods of Analysis

We used discrete-time event history analysis to model the rate of union dissolution for marriages and cohabitations between Wave 1 and Wave 2. Event history methods are ideal for studying family behaviors that may be censored, such as divorce (Teachman, 2003), marriage (Yabiku, 2004), or contraceptive use (Axinn & Yabiku, 2001). Because a couple's union dissolution was measured to the nearest month, the time unit of risk was the couple-month. Logistic regression applied to a couple-month file, with variable numbers of observations contributed per couple, was the method we used to estimate our discrete-time event history models (Allison, 1995). To preserve the proper time ordering of independent variables measured at Wave 1, couples became at risk of dissolution and contributed observations starting at NSFH Wave 1. It was necessary to specify the functional form of the hazard in a discrete time model, and we used a quadratic function of the duration since the date of marriage or date of the beginning of cohabitation. For married couples who began their union as a cohabitation, their duration began at the date of their cohabitation. This modeling approach can be described as left truncation or delayed entry (Allison, 1995), because couples were already married or cohabiting at Wave 1 but the duration measure began prior to Wave 1. We also estimated an alternative specification using dummy variables to represent time periods of risk, which did not force the hazard into a predetermined shape. This alternative specification yielded similar results, and thus we present the quadratic models only.

An additional methodological concern in our analysis was missing data. There are many ways to handle missing data, and Call et al. (1995) tried numerous strategies for dealing with missing reports of sexual frequency. Currently, a well-accepted practice is to use multiple imputation techniques (Allison, 2002). The critical assumption for this missing data is that the data are missing at random, conditional on other nonmissing attributes. Although this assumption cannot be tested, the assumption can be strengthened by including all relevant predictors in an imputation model. In our multiple imputation approach to deal with item missing data, we created five complete data sets for Wave 1 respondents who were also interviewed at Wave 2. We then analyzed the imputed data sets with complete-data methods. The results of these complete-data analyses were combined to arrive at a single estimate that properly incorporated the uncertainty in the imputed values. We used SAS PROC MI and PROC MIANALYZE to create the data sets and combine the multiple analyses.

RESULTS

Descriptive statistics are presented separately for cohabiting and marital unions in Table S8.1. From NSFH Wave 1 to Wave 2, 47% of cohabitations dissolved, but only 10% of marriages did. Sexual activity was higher in cohabitation, at about 12 times per month compared to only 6 times per month for marriages. Relationship happiness was lower for cohabitors than married couples, which was consistent with prior literature (Brown & Booth, 1996; Nock, 1995). Cohabiting couples were less likely to have a shared biological child in the household (49% of cohabitors had a child 18 or younger, compared to 65% of married partners). Home ownership clearly represented a greater potential barrier for married couples who had high proportions of home ownership (79%) compared to only 21% among cohabitors. Perceptions of how each partner's sex life would change if the union ended varied by union type and gender. If the current union ended, men were more optimistic about the improvements in their sex lives than women, and cohabitors were more optimistic about possible improvements in their sex lives than married partners.

Many of the differences in the control variables between the two types of unions were expected and consistent with the prior literature. For example, compared to married partners, cohabitors were younger, had lower income, worked more hours in the labor force, and had less traditional gender ideologies. Cohabiting women had lower self-rated health than married women, which might have seemed unexpected, given that cohabiting women were much younger than married women. The self-rated health question in the NSFH, however, asked respondents to compare themselves to

Table S8.1. Descriptive Statistics (n = 462 Cohabiting Unions and n = 5,440 Marital Unions)

Variables	Cohabiting Unions		Marital Unions		
	M	SD	M	SD	
Experienced dissolution by wave 2	0.47	0.44	0.10	0.32	X
Sexual frequency (prior month)	12.16	9.03	6.48	6.38	X
Woman's relationship happiness	5.83	1.18	6.02	1.35	X
Man's relationship happiness	5.85	1.00	6.07	1.29	X
Couple has biological child age 0–4	0.21	0.36	0.23	0.45	
Couple has biological child age 5–18	0.28	0.39	0.42	0.53	X
Couple owns home	0.21	0.35	0.79	0.43	X
Woman's belief sex improves if separated	2.08	0.92	1.87	1.03	X
Man's belief sex improves if separated	2.45	0.89	2.23	1.11	X
Controls					
Woman's age	29.11	7.93	43.08	15.36	X
Man's age	31.76	8.38	45.74	15.82	X
Woman's education	12.49	2.11	12.74	2.84	X
Man's education	12.62	2.23	12.85	3.25	X
Couple's income	$36,202	$33,578	$44,944	$48,558	X
Woman's paid work hours	26.35	16.77	19.18	20.45	X
Man's paid work hours	37.52	15.82	34.27	21.79	X
Couple both White	0.72	0.39	0.84	0.40	X
Couple both Black	0.12	0.28	0.07	0.27	X
Couple both Hispanic	0.06	0.20	0.05	0.24	
Couple both other race	0.01	0.08	0.01	0.10	
Couple interracial	0.10	0.26	0.04	0.20	X
Couple both ecumenical Protestant	0.09	0.25	0.24	0.45	X
Couple both exclusivist Protestant	0.11	0.28	0.20	0.42	X
Couple both Catholic	0.19	0.34	0.20	0.43	
Couple both other religion	0.10	0.26	0.09	0.31	
Couple interfaith	0.51	0.44	0.27	0.48	X
Woman's self-rated health	3.97	0.74	4.08	0.83	X
Man's self-rated health	4.09	0.67	4.07	0.88	
Woman's global happiness	5.43	1.17	5.63	1.36	X
Man's global happiness	5.36	1.08	5.58	1.34	X
Woman's traditional gender ideology	11.16	2.50	12.34	3.09	X
Man's traditional gender ideology	12.27	2.39	13.36	2.96	X
Duration of union as of wave 1 (years)	2.82	2.84	19.71	15.10	X

Note: X in the rightmost column indicates that means are different at the .05 level.

others of similar age. Controlling for age, prior research has found that cohabitors had lower health than married individuals (Brown, 2000; Brown, Bulanda, & Lee, 2005; Ren, 1997).

Duration of the union as of NSFH Wave 1 was much longer for marriages (19.7 years) than cohabitations (2.8 years). This was expected, as cohabitation is much less stable than marriage. The average length of cohabitation in our sample, however, was longer than what was found for national averages (Bumpass & Lu, 2000). This was likely because of the NSFH Wave 1 sample being slightly biased toward longer cohabitations (Smock & Manning, 1997). Another possibility was attrition from Wave 1 to Wave 2. Of the marriages and cohabitations at Wave 1, the primary respondent of the union (who may or may not still be in the union at Wave 2) needed to be reinterviewed in order for the couple's experiences to be included in our analysis. Selective attrition, therefore, made the analytic sample less representative of the experiences of all cohabitations.

In Table S8.2, we present the multivariate analyses of sexual frequency and union dissolution. Analyses were conducted separately for cohabitations and marriages. The results are presented as odds ratios, which are the exponentiated coefficients from the logistic regression models. A coefficient with an odds ratio greater than 1 represents a positive effect—one that accelerates the rate of union dissolution. An odds ratio less than 1 represents a negative effect—one that slows dissolution. Because odds ratios are multiplicative, an odds ratio equal to or not significantly different from 1 is a null effect (i.e., the variable has no effect on the rate of dissolution). Pairs of models were estimated separately for cohabitors and married couples. An additional column next to each pair of models indicates with an "X" if the coefficient significantly differed (at the .05 level) across the two models. The determination of significant difference across the two models was conducted by estimating fully interactive models in which predictors were interacted with union type.

In Model 1, we examined the relationship between logged sexual frequency and the rate of dissolution among cohabitors. Sexual frequency was significantly and negatively associated with relationship dissolution of cohabitors: When partners had higher sexual frequency, the rate of cohabitation dissolution was significantly lower. In Model 2, we also found a significant negative relationship between logged sexual frequency and the rate of marital dissolution. This relationship between logged sexual frequency and dissolution, however, varied between cohabitors and married partners: The association was significantly more negative for cohabitors. This supports the hypothesis that sexual frequency has a stronger association with union dissolution for cohabitors.

Although the controls were not a focus of the analysis, we note that significant predictors of relationship dissolution included the married women's age, cohabiting men's age, both cohabiting and married women's global happiness, married men's global happiness, and married women's traditional gender ideology. Women's age was protective against marital dissolution, as was women's global happiness in both types of unions. Men's global happiness was negatively associated with union dissolution, but only for marriages. Women's traditional gender ideology was associated with lower rates of marital dissolution. And in the marital sample, premarital cohabitation was significantly associated with higher rates of divorce. Note that some control variables in our models were not significant or had effects somewhat weaker than what was found in the literature. This might have been a result of the numerous control variables. We had a considerable number of controls, all entered simultaneously. Some controls, such as self-rated health and paid work hours, were likely to share complex associations in which causal ordering was unclear. We included a large number of controls in order to reduce possible spurious relationships between sexual frequency and union dissolution, and we did not focus on identifying the independent or overlapping contributions of each of the controls in explaining variation in our outcome.

Given that a significant difference in the association between sexual frequency and dissolution existed for cohabiting and marital unions, the remaining models in Table S8.2 attempted to test some identified mechanisms that may have accounted for this difference. Models 3 and 4 introduced measures of relationship happiness. If sexual activity was more important for the happiness of cohabiting than marital unions, then relationship happiness could mediate the association between sexual frequency and

Table S8.2. Summary of Discrete-Time Event History Analysis Predicting Union Dissolution for Cohabiting (n = 14,758 Couple Months) and Marital Unions (n = 36,487 Couple Months)

Predictor	1 C	2 M	3 C	4 M	5 C	6 M	7 C	8 M	9 C	10 M	11 C	12 M
			X				X				X	X
Logged sexual frequency	0.649*** (−3.357)	0.880* (−2.107)	0.698* (−2.541)	0.950 (−0.791)	0.644*** (−3.409)	0.861* (−2.416)	0.641*** (−3.452)	0.875* (−2.190)	0.668** (−3.122)	0.954 (−0.718)	0.675** (−2.733)	0.965 (−0.508)
Woman's relationship happiness			0.756** (−2.944)	0.744*** (−8.954)							0.785* (−2.339)	0.756*** (−7.924)
Man's relationship happiness			0.920 (−0.753)	0.847*** (−5.041)							0.900 (−0.849)	0.865*** (−4.133)
Couple has biological child age 0–4					0.768 (−1.021)	0.753** (−3.050)					0.793 (−0.868)	0.749** (−3.087)
Couple has biological child age 5–18					1.123 (0.510)	1.037 (0.388)					1.137 (0.553)	0.997 (−0.033)
Couple owns home							0.552 (−1.142)	0.877 (−1.356)			0.566 (−1.194)	0.881 (−1.282)
Woman's belief sex improves if separated									1.232* (2.259)	1.175*** (3.656)	1.091 (0.827)	1.070 (1.461)
Man's belief sex improves if separated									0.948 (−0.535)	1.171*** (4.060)	0.897 (−0.974)	1.101* (2.371)
Controls												
Marriage formed from cohabitation		1.535*** (4.924)		1.499*** (4.672)		1.536*** (4.919)		1.523*** (4.828)		1.479*** (4.471)		1.462*** (4.337)
Woman's age	0.999 (−0.067)	0.941*** (−5.582)	0.997 (−0.130)	0.939*** (−5.606)	0.995 (−0.256)	0.936*** (−6.019)	0.999 (−0.041)	0.942*** (−5.468)	1.001 (0.061)	0.943*** (−5.472)	0.997 (−0.139)	0.936*** (−5.934)
Man's age	0.961* (−2.094)	1.009 (0.908)	0.957* (−2.228)	1.008 (0.806)	0.960* (−2.118)	1.008 (0.827)	0.963 (−1.941)	1.009 (0.935)	0.956* (−2.300)	1.008 (0.899)	0.955* (−2.254)	1.007 (0.760)
Woman's education	0.964 (−0.642)	0.965 (−1.606)	0.976 (−0.430)	0.967 (−1.475)	0.959 (−0.743)	0.967 (−1.550)	0.967 (−0.574)	0.967 (−1.516)	0.960 (−0.697)	0.969 (−1.428)	0.972 (−0.481)	0.972 (−1.254)

(Continued)

Table S8.2. (Continued)

Predictor	1 C	2 M	3 C	4 M	5 C	6 M	7 C	8 M	9 C	10 M	11 C	12 M
Man's education	0.994	0.968	1.012	0.967	0.996	0.968	1.001	0.967	1.008	0.975	1.023	0.970
	(−0.111)	(−1.727)	(0.218)	(−1.650)	(−0.081)	(−1.716)	(0.026)	(−1.745)	(0.145)	(−1.336)	(0.388)	(−1.512)
Couple's income, logged	1.087	0.996	1.047	0.973	1.077	0.993	1.097	1.009	1.093	0.990	1.054	0.984
	(0.732)	(−0.062)	(0.375)	(−0.401)	(0.656)	(−0.099)	(0.772)	(0.133)	(0.786)	(−0.151)	(0.418)	(−0.246)
Woman's paid work hours	1.000	1.001	0.999	1.001	0.999	0.999	1.000	1.001	0.999	1.001	0.998	0.999
	(−0.001)	(0.388)	(−0.270)	(0.271)	(−0.217)	(−0.275)	(−0.052)	(0.452)	(−0.107)	(0.521)	(−0.393)	(−0.205)
Man's paid work hours	0.992	0.997	0.992	0.997	0.992	0.997	0.993	0.998	0.992	0.997	0.993	0.997
	(−1.316)	(−0.960)	(−1.274)	(−1.188)	(−1.313)	(−1.020)	(−1.043)	(−0.865)	(−1.262)	(−1.025)	(−1.052)	(−1.157)
Couple both White[a]	0.832	0.807	0.958	0.818	0.818	0.822	0.835	0.820	0.863	0.847	0.926	0.873
	(−0.574)	(−1.353)	(−0.130)	(−1.273)	(−0.607)	(−1.228)	(−0.556)	(−1.251)	(−0.458)	(−1.048)	(−0.226)	(−0.848)
Couple both Black[a]	0.866	1.110	0.964	1.035	0.870	1.124	0.885	1.112	0.884	1.009	1.019	1.022
	(−0.334)	(0.513)	(−0.085)	(0.172)	(−0.324)	(0.572)	(−0.292)	(0.525)	(−0.285)	(0.044)	(0.045)	(0.110)
Couple both Hispanic[a]	0.995	0.691	1.038	0.656	1.014	0.701	1.023	0.683	1.016	0.687	1.116	0.663
	(−0.009)	(−1.474)	(0.069)	(−1.659)	(0.025)	(−1.416)	(0.040)	(−1.525)	(0.030)	(−1.484)	(0.191)	(−1.628)
Couple both other race[a]	0.576	0.503	0.640	0.564	0.598	0.487	0.535	0.501	0.697	0.485	0.650	0.532
	(−0.366)	(−1.282)	(−0.307)	(−1.047)	(−0.347)	(−1.346)	(−0.406)	(−1.292)	(−0.243)	(−1.339)	(−0.294)	(−1.153)
Couple both ecumenical Protestant[b]	1.714	0.949	1.810	1.009	1.720	0.917	1.657	0.949	1.762	0.981	1.813	0.969
	(1.070)	(−0.299)	(1.161)	(0.049)	(1.070)	(−0.495)	(1.033)	(−0.300)	(1.107)	(−0.113)	(1.176)	(−0.176)
Couple both exclusivist Protestant[b]	1.475	0.996	1.398	1.017	1.435	0.962	1.437	0.997	1.324	1.031	1.282	0.991
	(0.713)	(−0.023)	(0.608)	(0.091)	(0.662)	(−0.207)	(0.712)	(−0.014)	(0.524)	(0.161)	(0.467)	(−0.049)
Couple both Catholic[b]	0.887	0.846	0.847	0.941	0.904	0.824	0.869	0.845	0.867	0.866	0.844	0.906
	(−0.271)	(−0.995)	(−0.370)	(−0.359)	(−0.229)	(−1.141)	(−0.310)	(−1.002)	(−0.321)	(−0.852)	(−0.361)	(−0.578)
Couple interfaith[b]	1.749	0.936	1.841	0.951	1.754	0.912	1.737	0.936	1.774	0.948	1.863	0.919
	(1.356)	(−0.379)	(1.530)	(−0.283)	(1.364)	(−0.520)	(1.352)	(−0.378)	(1.402)	(−0.309)	(1.586)	(−0.478)
Woman's self-rated health	1.254	1.087	1.228	1.083	1.246	1.100	1.254	1.089	1.246	1.081	1.236	1.095
	(1.664)	(1.379)	(1.560)	(1.332)	(1.620)	(1.548)	(1.700)	(1.410)	(1.576)	(1.280)	(1.592)	(1.472)
Man's self-rated health	0.929	0.969	0.924	0.971	0.929	0.968	0.941	0.968	0.925	0.971	0.942	0.969
	(−0.554)	(−0.584)	(−0.599)	(−0.532)	(−0.559)	(−0.589)	(−0.452)	(−0.590)	(−0.582)	(−0.531)	(−0.447)	(−0.585)
Woman's global happiness	0.847*	0.810***	0.984	0.963	0.836*	0.807***	0.843*	0.811***	0.867	0.835***	0.974	0.966
	(−2.218)	(−6.854)	(−0.174)	(−1.026)	(−2.329)	(−6.955)	(−2.194)	(−6.776)	(−1.856)	(−5.706)	(−0.272)	(−0.913)

(Continued)

Table S8.2. (Continued)

Predictor	1	2	3	4	5	6	7	8	9	10	11	12
	C	M	C	M	C	M	C	M	C	M	C	M
Man's global happiness	0.917	0.876***	0.998	0.993	0.917	0.876***	0.926	0.879***	0.925	0.902**	0.989	1.001
	(−1.024)	(−3.799)	(−0.021)	(−0.185)	(−1.011)	(−3.787)	(−0.897)	(−3.726)	(−0.892)	(−2.901)	(−0.113)	(0.032)
Woman's traditional gender ideology	0.978	0.964*	0.986	0.971	0.976	0.964*	0.972	0.964*	0.972	0.971	0.983	0.976
	(−0.515)	(−2.262)	(−0.321)	(−1.826)	(−0.545)	(−2.266)	(−0.597)	(−2.289)	(−0.626)	(−1.748)	(−0.359)	(−1.531)
Man's traditional gender ideology	0.998	1.005	1.002	1.000	1.000	1.005	0.994	1.006	0.999	1.004	0.999	1.001
	(−0.043)	(0.265)	(0.045)	(−0.028)	(−0.000)	(0.293)	(−0.128)	(0.309)	(−0.027)	(0.202)	(−0.020)	(0.057)
Duration of union	0.803**	1.015	0.820**	1.005	X 0.809**	1.012	X 0.812**	1.018	X 0.813**	1.011	X 0.840*	1.008 X
	(−3.195)	(0.918)	(−2.877)	(0.343)	(−3.050)	(0.687)	(−2.904)	(1.116)	(−2.984)	(0.665)	(−2.412)	(0.425)
Duration of union-squared	1.008*	0.999*	1.006	0.999	1.008	0.999*	X 1.008	0.999**	X 1.007	0.999*	X 1.005	0.999
	(2.016)	(−2.546)	(1.547)	(−1.929)	(1.888)	(−2.202)	(1.833)	(−2.699)	(1.766)	(−2.344)	(1.209)	(−1.848)
Constant	0.905	0.348	1.320	1.049	1.293	0.499	0.781	0.316*	0.524	0.084***	1.487	0.594
	(−0.076)	(−1.917)	(0.221)	(0.082)	(0.186)	(−1.231)	(−0.187)	(−2.071)	(−0.474)	(−4.004)	(0.261)	(−0.740)

Note: Coefficients are odds ratios, with *t* statistics in parentheses. C: model for cohabitors; M: model for marrieds. X indicates coefficients are significantly different ($p < .05$) across cohabitation and marriage models.

[a]Reference is interracial. [b]Reference is both other religion.

* $p < .05$. ** $p < .01$. *** $p < .001$, two-tailed tests.

dissolution for cohabitors. Relationship happiness was associated with significantly lower rates of dissolution for both cohabitating and married women; men's relationship happiness was associated with significantly lower rates of dissolution, but only for married men. The coefficients for sexual frequency were slightly reduced in the cohabiting model and became insignificant in the married model. The difference in the coefficients for sexual frequency in the two union types also became insignificant, but at the $p = .08$ level. Thus there was little evidence that relationship happiness provided substantial mediation of the differences in sexual frequency between cohabitations and marriages.

In Models 5 and 6, the presence of shared biological children in the household at Wave 1 was examined. Shared biological children—a form of noneconomic union-specific capital—were hypothesized to act as barriers to ending a union. Biological children in the home, however, were not related to the dissolution of cohabitation. For married couples, children age 4 and under were associated with lower rates of divorce. This finding was consistent with prior literature suggesting that young children were stabilizing factors for marriage (Waite & Lillard, 1991). The coefficients for logged sexual frequency, however, remained significant, and the coefficient for sexual frequency in cohabitation was significantly more negative than in marriage.

In Models 7 and 8, we examined an additional form of union-specific capital: home ownership. Although the coefficient for home ownership was negative on the rate of dissolution for both types of unions, it was not significant. Home ownership, too, failed to decrease the association between logged sexual frequency 993 and the rates of dissolution, which remained significantly stronger in cohabitations.

In Models 9 and 10, we examined a specific type of cost to ending the union. If partners believed their sex lives would not suffer if the union ended—or if they believed their sex lives would improve—then it might have been easier to leave a union because of low frequency of sexual relations. In marriages, the perception that one's sex life would improve increased the risk for divorce. For both men and women, each point on this 1–5 scale raised the rate of divorce by about 17%. A similar pattern was observed for cohabiting women. Despite the fact that the coefficient for logged sexual frequency was not significant for married couples, the coefficient for logged sexual frequency remained significantly more negative for cohabitors compared to married individuals. This suggested that sexual alternatives did not explain the difference in the role of sexual frequency for marital and cohabitation union stability. Models 11 and 12 estimated all the predictors of prior models in a single model, yet the conclusions were the same: Significant differences in the effects of sexual frequency on union dissolution remained, with these effects being significantly stronger for cohabiting than marital unions.

Finally, we performed additional analyses to test the sensitivity of our results to different approaches. First, we limited our sample to only those couples at Wave 1 who had first formed the union with their partner in the previous 12 months. Although this reduced the sample size considerably (only 218 cohabiting and 205 married couples), this approach may have better controlled for the length of sexual relationship in the two unions. Even in this reduced sample, the association between sexual frequency and dissolution was significantly different between cohabitation and marriage ($p = .04$). This evidence was consistent with the premise that the unmeasured length of sexual relationship might not have been confounding the associations we reported for the full sample. Second, we estimated additional models on the married sample in which we interacted premarital cohabitation experience with our key independent variables (sexual frequency, relationship happiness, children, home ownership, and the belief that one's sex life would improve upon separation). None of these interactions were significant at the .05 level, suggesting that the experience of premarital cohabitation did not significantly alter the effects of these variables for the union dissolution of married couples.

DISCUSSION

Drawing upon social exchange theory, we developed a theoretical framework and hypothesized that sexual frequency would have a stronger influence on the dissolution of cohabitation than marriage. The results indicated that although sexual frequency was negatively associated with dissolution for both types of unions, the association was significantly more negative for cohabitations. This initial finding supported our hypothesis. We investigated several factors that might explain these differences between married and cohabiting couples on the basis of Levinger's (1979) typology: relationship happiness, two measures of union-specific capital, and a measure of perceived alternative attractions to the current union in the form of perceived sexual alternatives. None of these measures, however, substantially reduced the magnitude of difference in the association between sexual frequency and marital and cohabitation dissolution.

Our findings contributed to a larger debate in the research literature that has identified the important differences between cohabitors and spouses but has recently documented more and more commonalities (for a review, see Smock, 2000). For example, research documented differences as varied as the ideal fertility—cohabitors expected to have fewer children than married couples—(Rindfuss & Van den Heuvel, 1990) to attitudes about sexual fidelity and gender roles—cohabitors expected less fidelity and more equality (Clarkberg, Stolzenberg, & Waite, 1995; DeMaris & McDonald, 1993). Most importantly, however, cohabitors were less likely to view their relationship as one that would last a lifetime, and few cohabiting couples continued for a lifetime without marriage (Bumpass & Lu, 2000; Bumpass et al., 1991). Thus, cohabitation, as a newer relationship form, has been described as less institutionalized compared to marriage (Waite & Joyner, 1992) and as an incomplete institution (Nock, 1995; Smock & Gupta, 2002).

A common stereotype proclaims that marriage is associated with low sexual frequency. Our results, however, suggested that low sexual frequency was not as problematic for married couples. Instead, it was cohabiting couples who faced more problematic outcomes of low frequency. In other words, sex appeared to be more important to cohabitors, as low sexual frequency was more detrimental to relationship success among cohabitors. It may be that cohabitors still expected an active sex life. When they did not experience it, cohabitors were more likely than married couples to leave the relationship.

Thus, we might conclude that cohabitation is not so much an incomplete institution but better described as a more narrow institution—both structurally and emotionally. In terms of structure, marriage typically involves a broader range of activities than cohabitation. More often than cohabitors, married partners engage in procreation, childrearing, sharing of financial assets, and closer relationships with in-laws. For example, as cohabitation is less institutionalized than marriage, kin relations can be far more problematic, which could reduce cohabitors' relations with in-laws (Milan, 1998). Because marriage encompasses more activities, sexuality occupies a less prominent role for married partners compared to cohabitors. Past research is consistent with this reasoning: Liu (2000) applied a rational choice framework to marital sex and proposed that marital unions make consumption choices from a broader set of familial goods and services. Marital sex decreased because couples reallocated resources from sex to other activities (Liu).

Although we tested several mechanisms in an attempt to explain the differential link between sexual frequency and union dissolution in marriage and cohabitation, none of these measures substantially reduced these differences. Because sex is a highly emotional and intimate activity, it may be that a focus on the emotional dynamics of the dyadic relationship is needed. In addition to being a more narrow institution, cohabitation may also be more emotionally narrow than marriage. As Levinger (1979) pointed out, a continuum of relationship closeness ranges from superficial contact to profound closeness and many dyads dissolve long before they reach any "appreciable depth." Our results suggested that many cohabitations were on a lower end of this continuum compared to marital relationships. Waite and Joyner (1992) suggested that a long-term marital contract facilitated emotional investment, but that cohabitors may be less likely to make such emotional investments in general, thus hindering the development of relationship-specific capital. Cohabitors were found to have lower levels of commitment than married couples (Nock 1995). Scanzoni et al. (1989) proposed that, initially, intimate relationships were often based on extrinsic rewards—partners continued the relationship in order to obtain sex—but over time the relationships developed intrinsic rewards—partners continued the relationship out of feelings of commitment and solidarity. These intrinsic rewards helped to maintain the relationship by diversifying the factors in partners' cost/benefit calculations (Scanzoni et al.). Compared to marriage, cohabitation may be more heavily based on extrinsic rewards, and sex may play a greater role. Thus, cohabitors might rely more upon sexual activity as opposed to long-term emotional attachment to keep their unions together. When sexual activity decreases in cohabitation, there is a lack of emotional investment to keep the partners together. In contrast, when sexual frequency in a marriage is low or of poor quality, there are other shared concerns or bonds that may keep a marriage together. In sum, it may be that the differential impact of sexual frequency on union dissolution between cohabitors and marrieds could be explained by emotional and relational factors.

Lastly, we note that a selection explanation might be proposed as a counterargument to our findings. The argument would state that sexual frequency is not causally linked to union dissolution, but that low sexual frequency is the consequence of some other relationship problem. Although observational data cannot conclusively answer these questions, we argue that a simple selection argument is not sufficient to completely explain our results. We found that the effect of sexual frequency significantly varied across marriage and cohabitation. Thus, even if it were true that selection drove almost all of the effect between sexual frequency and dissolution, the degree of selection apparently varied between marriage and cohabitation. Even if not completely causal, this difference across the two types of unions still points to important differences in the role of sexual frequency in marriage and cohabitation.

REFERENCES

Allison, P. D. (1995). *Survival analysis using the SAS system.* Cary, NC: SAS Institute.

Allison, P. D. (2002). *Missing data.* Thousand Oaks, CA: Sage.

Axinn, W., & Yabiku, S. T. (2001). Social change, the social organization of families, and fertility limitation. *American Journal of Sociology, 106,* 1219–1261.

Blanchflower, D. G., & Oswald, A. J. (2004). Money, sex and happiness: An empirical study. *Scandinavian Journal of Economics, 106,* 393 – 415.

Blau, P. M. (1964). *Exchange and power in social life.* New York: Wiley.

Blumstein, P., & Schwartz, P. (1983). *American couples: Money, work, sex.* New York: William Morrow.

Brines, J., & Joyner, K. (1999). The ties that bind: Principles of cohesion in cohabitation and marriage. *American Sociological Review, 64,* 333–355.

Brown, S. L. (2000). The effect of union type on psychological well-being: Depression among cohabitors versus marrieds. *Journal of Health and Social Behavior, 41,* 241–255.

Brown, S. L., & Booth, A. (1996). Cohabitation versus marriage: A comparison of relationship quality. *Journal of Marriage and the Family, 58,* 668–678.

Brown, S. L., & Bulanda, J. R. (2007). Relationship violence in young adulthood: A comparison of daters, cohabitors, and marrieds. *Social Science Research, 37,* 73 – 87.

Brown, S. L., Bulanda, J. R., & Lee, G. R. (2005). The significance of cohabitation: Marital status and mental health benefits among middle-aged and older adults. *Journal of Gerontology: Social Sciences, 60,* S21–S29.

Bumpass, L., & Lu, H. (2000). Trends in cohabitation and implications for children's family contexts in the United States. *Population Studies, 54,* 29–41.

Bumpass, L., Sweet, J., & Cherlin, A. (1991). The role of cohabitation in declining rates of marriage. *Journal of Marriage and the Family, 53,* 4913–4927.

Byers, E. S., & Heinlein, L. (1989). Predicting initiations and refusals of sexual activities in married and cohabiting heterosexual couples. *Journal of Sex Research, 26,* 210–231.

Call, V., Sprecher, S., & Schwartz, P. (1995). The incidence and frequency of marital sex in a national sample. *Journal of Marriage and the Family, 57,* 639–652.

Carter, C. S. (1998). Neuroendocrine perspectives on social attachment and love. *Psychoneuroendocrinology, 23,* 779–818.

Channon, L. D., & Ballinger, S. E. (1986). Some aspects of sexuality and vaginal symptoms during menopause and their relation to anxiety and depression. *British Journal of Medical Psychology, 59,* 173–180.

Cherlin, A. (1978). Remarriage as an incomplete institution. *American Journal of Sociology, 84,* 634–650.

Clarkberg, M., Stolzenberg, R. M., & Waite, L. J. (1995). Attitudes, values, and entrance into cohabitational versus marital unions. *Social Forces, 74,* 609–634.

DeMaris, A., & McDonald, W. (1993). Premarital cohabitation and marital instability: A test of the unconventionality hypothesis. *Journal of Marriage and the Family, 55,* 399–407.

Dolcini, M. M., Cantania, J., Coates, T., Stall, R., Hudes, E., Gagnon, J., & Pollack. L. (1993). Demographic characteristics of heterosexuals with multiple partners: The national AIDS behavioral surveys. *Family Planning Perspectives, 25,* 208–214.

Edwards, J. N., & Booth, A. (1994). Sexuality, marriage, and well-being: The middle years. In A. S. Rossi (Ed.), *Sexuality across the life course* (pp. 233–259). Chicago: The University of Chicago Press.

Giddens, A. (1992). *The transformation of intimacy*. Stanford, CA: Stanford University Press.

Greenblat, C. S. (1983). The salience of sexuality in the early years of marriage. *Journal of Marriage and the Family, 45,* 289–299.

Heiman, J. (2000). Psychologic treatments for female sexual dysfunction: Are they effective and do we need them? *Archives of Sexual Behavior, 31,* 445–450.

Henderson-King, D. H., & Veroff, J. (1994). Sexual satisfaction and marital well-being in the first years of marriage. *Journal of Social and Personal Relationships, 11,* 509 –534.

Holley, P., Yabiku, S. T., & Benin, M. (2006). The relationship between intelligence and divorce. *Journal of Family Issues, 27,* 1723–1748.

Homans, G. C. (1961). *Social behavior: Its elementary forms.* New York: Harcourt, Brace and World.

Insel, T. R. (1997). A neurobiological basis of social attachment. *American Journal of Psychiatry, 154,* 726–735.

James, W. H. (1974). Marital coital rates, spouses' ages, family size and social class. *Journal of Sex Research, 10,* 205–218.

James, W. H. (1981). The honeymoon effect on marital coitus. *Journal of Sex Research, 17,* 114–123.

Jasso, G. (1985). Marital coital frequency and the passage of time: Estimating the separate effects of spouse's ages and marital duration, birth and marriage cohorts, and period influences. *American Sociological Review, 50,* 224–241.

Keister, K. A., & Deeb-Sossa, N. (2001). Are baby boomers richer than their parents? Intergenerational patterns of wealth ownership in the United States. *Journal of Marriage and Family, 63,* 569–579.

Kinsey, A. C., Pomeroy, W. B., & Martin, C. E. (1948). *Sexual behavior in the human male.* Philadelphia: Saunders.

Kinsey, A. C., Pomeroy, W. B., Martin, C. E., & Gebhard, P. H. (1953). *Sexual behavior in the human female.* Philadelphia: Saunders.

Kravdal, O. (1999). Does marriage require a stronger economic underpinning than informal cohabitation? *Population Studies, 53,* 63–80.

Laumann, E. O., Gagnon, J. H., Michael, R. T., & Michaels, S. (1994). *The social organization of sexuality: Sexual practices in the United States.* Chicago: University of Chicago Press.

Laumann, E. O., Paik, A., & Rosen, R. C. (1999). Sexual dysfunction in the United States: Prevalence and predictors. *Journal of American Medical Association, 281,* 537–545.

Lawrance, K., & Byers, E. S. (1995). Sexual satisfaction in long-term heterosexual relationships: The interpersonal exchange model of sexual satisfaction. *Personal Relationships, 2,* 267–285.

Lehrer, E., & Chiswick, C. (1993). Religion as a determinant of marital stability. *Demography, 30,* 385–404.

Leridon, H. (1996). Coital frequency: Data and consistency analysis. In M. Bozon & H. Leridon (Eds.), *Sexuality and the social sciences: A French survey on sexual behaviour* (pp. 203–226). Aldershot, England: Dartmouth.

Levinger, G. (1979). A social psychological perspective on marital dissolution. In G. Levinger & O. Moles (Eds.), *Divorce and separation: Context, causes, and consequences* (pp. 37–60). New York: Basic Books.

Liu, C. (2000). A theory of marital sexual life. *Journal of Marriage and the Family, 62,* 363–374.

Michael, R. T., Gagnon, J. H., Laumann, E. O., & Kolata, G. (1994). *Sex in America: A definitive survey.* Boston: Little.

Milan, A. (1998). The impact of cohabiting on kin relations. Paper presented at the annual meetings of the International Sociological Association.

Morrison, D., & Ritualo, A. (2000). Routes to children's economic recovery after divorce: Are cohabitation and remarriage equivalent? *American Sociological Review, 65,* 560–580.

Nock, S. L. (1995). A comparison of marriages and cohabiting relationships. *Journal of Family Issues, 16*, 53–76.

O'Farrell, T. J., Choquette, K. A., & Birchler, G. R. (1991). Sexual satisfaction and dissatisfaction in the marital relationships of male alcoholics seeking marital therapy. *Journal of Studies on Alcohol, 52*, 91–99.

Oggins, J., Veroff, J., & Leber, D. (1993). Perceptions of marital interaction among black and white newlyweds. *Journal of Personality and Social Psychology, 65*, 495– 511.

Oppenheimer, V. K. (1988). A theory of marriage timing. *American Journal of Sociology, 94*, 563–591.

Perlman, S. D., & Abramson, P. R. (1982). Sexual satisfaction among married and cohabiting individuals. *Journal of Consulting and Clinical Psychology, 50*, 458– 460.

Rao, K. V., & DeMaris, A. (1995). Coital frequency among married and cohabiting couples in the United States. *Journal of Biosocial Science, 27*, 135–150.

Ren, X. H. S. (1997). Marital status and quality of relationships: The impact on health perception. *Social Science & Medicine, 44*, 241–249.

Rindfuss, R., & Van den Heuvel, A. (1990). Cohabitation: A precursor to marriage or an alternative to being single? *Population and Development Review, 16*, 703–726.

Risch, G. S., Riley, L. A., & Lawler, M. G. (2003). Problematic issues in the early years of marriage: Content for premarital education. *Journal of Psychology and Theology, 31*, 253–269.

Scanzoni, J., Polonko, K., Teachman, J., & Thompson, L. (1989). *The sexual bond: Rethinking families and close relationships.* Newbury Park, CA: Sage.

Smith, H. L., Morgan, S. P., & Gager, C. T. (1994). *Comparing spousal reports from the NSFH: Husbands' and wives' reports of coital frequency.* Paper presented at the annual meetings of the American Sociological Association, Los Angeles.

Smock, P. J. (2000). Cohabitation in the United States: An appraisal of research themes, findings, and implications. *Annual Review of Sociology, 26*, 1–20.

Smock, P. J., & Gupta, S. (2002). Cohabitation in contemporary North America. In A. Crouter & A. Booth (Eds.), *Just living together: Implications of cohabitation on families, children, and social policy* (pp. 53–74). Mahwah, NJ: Erlbaum.

Smock, P. J., & Manning, W. (1997). Cohabiting partners' economic circumstances and marriage. *Demography, 34*, 331–341.

Sprecher, S. (1998). Social exchange theories and sexuality. *Journal of Sex Research, 35*, 32–43.

Sprecher, S. (2002). Sexual satisfaction in premarital relationships: Associations with satisfaction, love, commitment, and stability. *Journal of Sex Research, 39*, 190– 196.

Sweet, J., Bumpass, L., & Call, V. (1988). The design and content of the National Survey of Families and Households. NSFH Working Paper No. 1. Madison, WI: Center for Demography and Ecology, University of Wisconsin-Madison.

Teachman, J. (2003). Premarital sex, premarital cohabitation, and the risk of subsequent marital dissolution among women. *Journal of Marriage and Family, 65*, 444– 455.

Thachil, A., & Bhugra, D. (2006). Literature update: A critical review. *Sexual and Relationship Therapy, 21*, 91–98.

Treas, J., & Giesen, D. (2000). Sexual infidelity among married and cohabiting Americans. *Journal of Marriage and the Family, 62*, 48–60.

Udry, J. R. (1993). Coitus as demographic behavior. In R. Gray, H. Leridon, & A. Spira (Eds.), *Biomedical and demographic determinants of reproduction* (pp. 85–97). Oxford: Oxford University Press.

Udry, J. R., Deven, F. R., & Coleman, S. J. (1982). A cross-national comparison of the relative influence of male and female age on the frequency of marital intercourse. *Journal of Biosocial Science, 14*, 1– 6.

Udry, J. R., & Morris, N. M. (1978). Relative contribution of male and female age to the frequency of marital intercourse. *Social Biology, 25*, 128–134.

Veroff, J., Douvan, E., & Hatchett, S. (1995). *Marital instability: A social and behavioral study of the early years.* Westport, CT: Praeger.

Waite, L. J., & Joyner, K. (1992). Emotional and physical satisfaction with sex in married, cohabiting, and dating sexual unions: Do men and women differ? In E. Laumann & R. Michael (Eds.), *Sex, love, and health in America: Private choices and public policies* (pp. 239–269). Chicago: The University of Chicago Press.

Waite, L. J., & Lillard, L. A. (1991). Children and marital disruption. *American Journal of Sociology, 96,* 930–953.

Westoff, C. F. (1974). Coital frequency and contraception. *Family Planning Perspectives, 6,* 136–141.

White, L., & Booth, A. (1991). Divorce over the life course: The role of marital happiness. *Journal of Family Issues, 12,* 5–21.

White, L., & Keith, B. (1990). The effect of shift work on the quality and stability of marital relations. *Journal of Marriage and the Family, 52,* 453–462.

Yabiku, S. T. (2004). Marriage timing in Nepal: Organizational effects and individual mechanisms. *Social Forces, 83,* 559–586.

Yeh, H., Lorenz, F. O., Wickrama, K. A. S., Conger, R., & Elder, G. (2006). Relationships among sexual satisfaction, marital quality, and marital instability at midlife. *Journal of Family Psychology, 20,* 329–343.

9

FEMINIST FAMILY THEORY

Bob and Alice Stephens were having dinner at a nice restaurant to celebrate their tenth wedding anniversary. Bob said to Alice, "Isn't this relaxing? A dinner alone without the kids. We should treat ourselves to this more often." Alice smiled politely but was not convinced that it was such a treat. It's true that Bob had suggested that they go out to dinner, but it was Alice who had made the reservations. In fact, Alice had also picked up Bob's suit from the cleaners on her way home from work. She had arranged for the babysitter, made dinner for the kids before she left, washed the basketball uniform that Bobby Junior needed for tomorrow's gym class, and helped little Alicia study for her spelling test before she drove downtown to Bob's engineering office, where he changed into his suit for dinner. She felt too tired and anxious to relax.

Alice had been feeling a great deal of stress lately. She enjoyed her job as a lawyer but was worried about making partner in her firm. Two men who had joined the firm after her had already achieved partner status. When she asked the senior partners about it, they explained that she was "off track" for partnership because of the maternity leave she had taken to have her children. They also indicated that her work with the Legal Aid fund was notable, but it did not bring in the kind of money to the firm that was expected of a partner. Alice worked with single mothers whose ex-husbands had failed to pay child support. But now she had to find ways to bring in clients who could afford to pay more money. And as much as she loved her husband, children, and her work, what Alice really wished for was an evening at home, soaking in a nice hot bath, with some peace and quiet to read a book.

HISTORY

Feminist family theory, not surprisingly, has its roots in the feminist movement. Feminism can be defined as the search for rights, opportunities, and identities women believe they deserve (Thomas 2000). Feminism in the United States might be said to have begun with the Seneca Falls Convention in 1848. Women—most notably Elizabeth Cady Stanton and Susan B. Anthony—fought for the right to vote, a battle that was not won until ratification of the Nineteenth Amendment to the U.S. Constitution in 1920.

This first wave of the feminist movement was focused on securing equal rights for women, with gaining the right to vote being their primary goal. They also sought equal rights with regard to education, employment, and politics. However, because there were some in the movement who had what were considered to be very extreme opinions, the suffragists separated themselves and focused more specifically on the right to vote (Osmond and Thorne 1993).

Perhaps the most notable feminist writer of the twentieth century was Margaret Mead, whose anthropological research was revolutionary at the time. She suggested that gender is socially constructed rather than biologically driven. Her cross-cultural research in Samoa, the South Pacific, and New Guinea led her to believe that whether a behavior is masculine or feminine is determined by the culture of which you are a part (Mead 1935). Thus, she proposed expanding our notions of gender and making home and places of employment more gender-neutral. The first wave of feminism extended into the Great Depression of the 1930s and then the rebuilding following the war, so feminist politics were somewhat quiet in the last few decades of the first wave.

The modern feminist movement, or the second wave of feminism, began in the 1960s, concurrent with the civil rights movement, the anti-Vietnam War protests, and the general cultural challenge to the established institutional authorities and the "status quo." Leaders in this movement, like Betty Friedan, Gloria Steinem, and the National Organization for Women (NOW), worked toward resolution of issues such as equal pay and job training for women, reproductive choice, maternity leave, subsidized childcare, and an end to sex discrimination (Okin 1997).

The feminist movement of the 1960s and 1970s was characterized by several branches, each with a slightly different emphasis. *Liberal feminists*, like Friedan, spoke out against the subjugation of women, particularly in terms of their career paths. They stressed the importance of challenging laws and customs that restricted women's ability to achieve significant roles in society. *Marxist feminists* focused on the exploitation of women in their reproductive roles and in household labor, which they felt maintained women as "second-class" citizens. They believed that, as long as women are solely responsible for the reproduction of children, this oppression will exist. *Radical feminists* emphasized male dominance as the problem with society, specifically male power and authority as oppressive to women. Radical feminists proposed that individuals should not be limited by masculine or feminine traits but should strive toward androgyny (a combination of both masculine and feminine traits). Families, as the source for patriarchy (male dominance) and oppression of women, could not be reformed into something positive and should therefore be avoided. *Socialist feminists* focused on women's liberation from the combined aspects of class oppression and patriarchy, particularly as found in families (Okin 1997; Osmond and Thorne 1993). *Cultural feminists* focused on bringing respect and value to those characteristics that are considered essentially feminine, rather than discriminating against those traits seen as masculine. In other words, they believed that we should acknowledge and celebrate the differences between men and women in order to bring equality to those feminine traits that are at present undervalued (Alcoff 1995). Most feminists in the United States today identify themselves primarily with the liberal branch of feminism (Shehan and Kammeyer 1997).

Within every field of study, knowledge is advanced by pioneers who propose cutting-edge ideas. Often we see that several extreme philosophies are presented, and after a time, a middle ground is reached that incorporates elements of each philosophy but is not as extreme as any individual one. This is also the case with feminism. By the 1980s, the distinctions among the feminist branches melted away. Feminists focused on issues related to women's second-class status in society and in families, reproductive rights, discrimination faced in the workplace, and how a gendered society affects the socialization of women (Okin 1997).

In the 1960s, one of the dominant theories of the family was structural functionalism. Structural functionalists proposed that roles in families should be divided in a "natural" way, generally based on sex. They proposed that families functioned best when men did the instrumental tasks of earning money and providing for basic needs, and women did the expressive tasks of caretaking for family members (Baca Zinn 2000). In 1972, sociologist Jessie Bernard wrote *The Future of Marriage*, in which she contradicted this perspective on marriage. Bernard found that there were two marriages—his and hers—and that his was better than hers. This finding was in direct opposition to the ideas presented in structural-functional theory.

Based on the work of Bernard and others, feminist family theorists began to consider status in families, causing them to analyze how males dominate family power, both intentionally and unintentionally. When male power dominates families, they said, males benefit but females do not, thus leading to two types of marriages. Feminist family theorists recognized that male power and dominance were the result of socialization and challenged the concept that male power was natural and inevitable, as suggested in structural functionalism. Feminist scholars examined how the family was influenced by social institutions and politics and how it was affected by the wider system of societal norms.

Feminist understanding was furthered in the 1980s by the groundbreaking work of Carol Gilligan, who analyzed the psychological and internal development of women's sense of self as being different from that of men's. In her book, *In a Different Voice*, Gilligan (1982) explored how women defined their identities and understood reality through relationships, particularly intimate relationships. Their experiences must be taken into account in the analysis of their development, she noted, particularly as they internalized their senses of self and their moral codes. She further clarified that, for women, nonviolence and caring for others dominated their views of justice and equality.

In the 1990s, feminist scholars sought to combine both the societal and individual perspectives of oppression, paving the way for a third wave of feminism, which is still a work in progress. This perspective focused on the multiple forms of oppression that might be experienced on an individual basis as a result of societal oppression. A "matrix of domination" (Hill Collins 1998, 2000) could include oppression based on gender, class, race, ethnicity, sexual orientation, religion, or physical ability. For example, although all women experience relatively less status than men, White women experience relatively more status than women of color, middle-class women have more status than poor women, and heterosexual women have more status than lesbians or bisexual women. Multiracial feminism (MRF) is one example of feminism that developed from this third wave of feminism. MRF focuses on the intersection of gender, race, and ethnicity and challenges the assumption that gender is the only issue that matters. It encourages us to understand "social location" as a more complex social phenomenon (Lorber 1998). We explore this concept a little further when we review literature on Black feminism at the end of this chapter.

BASIC ASSUMPTIONS

Although there have been many different forms of feminism, feminist family theorists generally base their work on the following basic assumptions (Baca Zinn 2000; Osmond and Thorne 1993; Sollie and Leslie 1994):

Women's experiences are central to our understanding of families. Feminist family theorists begin with the question "What is the perspective of women?" Other theories have investigated the structures, roles, and resources people bring to their relationships. Feminist family scholars focus on women's perspectives and feelings, how women have been left out of the social and historical dialogue, and how women's issues have been ignored. Gender becomes the organizing concept. For example, the concept of "work" used to mean only paid work, which used to mean only men's work. Adding women's experience to the conceptualization of the term expanded it to include the unpaid labor that women did for families and communities as well.

According to Katherine Ferguson (as cited in Osmond and Thorne 1993), "Feminist theory is not simply about women, although it is that; it is about the world, but from the usually ignored and devalued vantage point of women's experiences" (592–593). Osmond and Thorne go on to add:

> By making women's experiences visible, feminist scholarship reveals gaps and distortions in knowledge that claims to be inclusive but in fact is based on the experiences of Euro-American, class-privileged, heterosexual men. Starting with the life experiences of women, in all their diversity, opens new epistemologies or ways of knowing the world. (593)

Feminist family theorists "analyze gender as a central principle of social organization and as something that all people do in their daily activities in every institution" (Osmond and Thorne 1993, 593). Two related concepts are that people exaggerate differences between men and women and that they use "these distinctions to legitimize and perpetuate power relations between men and women" (Osmond and Thorne 1993, 593).

Feminist family theory also addresses the development of women across the lifespan. Because women have been oppressed, their development has been hindered. The theory investigates how their development might be different if society did not constrain them (Thomas 2000) and asks questions about the experience from a gendered perspective (Gilligan 1982). Think about Alice from the vignette at the beginning of the chapter. How would her life be different if her work environment had a different perception of her mothering role?

Gender is a socially constructed concept. When we talk about gender, we talk about something different from sex. Sex refers to biological assignment; gender refers to "the social meanings of masculinity and femininity that are produced through social processes and interactions that produce 'men' and 'women'" (Rutter and Schwartz 2000, 61).

Feminist family theorists make the point that gender roles are defined by society, not by biology. In the past, fathers went to work; mothers stayed home. Doctors were men; nurses were women. Business executives were men; secretaries were women. Boys were football players; girls were cheerleaders. These were socially constructed roles. In today's society, gender roles are changing, but there is still resistance. Women are members of the U.S. military, but they are not allowed in combat. Women are allowed on aircraft carriers, but they are not allowed on submarines. Contrast that with the Israeli army, in which women are drafted and fight alongside men.

Language is an important element in socially constructed gender roles. In French, for example, all nouns have a male or female gender, usually indicated by the article (le *pere*—father, la *mere*—mother). Although English is not so obvious, words still have gender connotations. Usages become so natural that the implications of words are not necessarily recognized. For example, using the term *mankind* instead of *humanity* implicitly excludes women.

A more subtle example is using the word *spinster* to refer to an unmarried, childless female. What word do we use to refer to an unmarried, childless male? There is no comparable word. We might use the word *bachelor*, but it doesn't have the negative connotation that the word *spinster* has. We define spinsters in terms of what they are **not**—they are not wives and not mothers (Allen 1994). Feminists pay attention to this kind of language use to ensure that women are not excluded from the social conversation.

Putting behaviors and labels together is termed *categorization*. Behaviors and roles are labeled and categorized according to gender. At a very early age, boys and girls learn what boys do, what girls do, what men do, and what women do. Behaviors by parents or other adults reinforce these categorizations. For instance, if a father were to see his three-year-old son dancing in a tutu at the daycare center, he might yell at the childcare provider, "Don't ever let my son wear that again! I want my son to grow up to be a real man!" Based on such comments, the boy might never play with a tutu again. The son's exploration in the fantasy play area of the daycare center had no social meaning *until* the father ascribed a gendered meaning to it.

Stratification is an outcome of categorization. Once tasks for men and women and boys and girls have been divided, people begin attributing value (even unintentionally) to those tasks. The value attributed to male tasks has always been greater than the value attributed to female tasks. People who are more highly valued have more power in society. Feminists refer to those with power as *privileged*. People with less value have less power (and are less privileged) and are oppressed because of this. In gender analysis, stratification is most commonly found when women's behaviors and roles are given less value than men's. For example, "women's work" like housework and childcare is unpaid, whereas men's work is given greater value and pay in society. Feminists seek to illuminate such status differences so that women can become empowered.

One way to do this is to bring attention to the ways in which language influences, and perhaps perpetuates, stratification. For example, a man believes himself to be an equal partner and proudly proclaims that he "helps around the house," as if this were an unusual behavior, and therefore notable. This implies that the woman is still in charge of, and ultimately responsible for, the housework, because the man is just "helping out." The old gender roles are still there. Privilege is also evident in race, ethnicity, sexuality, nationality, age, physical ability, and religion (Collins 1998). Recognizing the multiple levels where privilege is located and the language that distinguishes status is a complicated task. Many of the hierarchies we learned about were learned in our families (Collins 1998; Walker 1993), and challenging those beliefs is important but difficult.

Social and historical contexts are important. To understand women and families, we must understand the contexts in which they live. As they define women's roles in families, feminist family theorists look for meanings in both the sociological and the historical contexts. The analytical focus is not just on the individual and interpersonal relationships but also on the larger social forces that influence those relationships (Ferree 1990). Indeed, feminist family theorists contend that one must study the larger contexts to understand the position of women in the family. For example, the idealized concept of the nuclear family is still the norm in family research despite obvious demographic changes. The historical norm no longer applies to the new forms of family (which we investigate below). But if a researcher does not take into account the larger social changes that are occurring, the nuclear family might remain the norm by which to measure; this could lead to incorrect conclusions.

There are many examples of how society may negatively affect women—politically, economically, religiously, socially—and those ultimately impact the family. Some examples are women being paid less for doing the same job; women's standards of living dropping more significantly after divorce than men's; insurance paying for Viagra but not for birth-control pills (even when they are prescribed for noncontraceptive medical reasons); and the fact that in most states the maximum age limit for adoption is higher for men than for women. Many women face additional discrimination in terms of race, class, age, sexual orientation, and religion that adds burdens to their families.

Investigating the influences of religion on culture, families, and women's experiences provides a good example of taking the sociocultural context into account. In the early Judeo-Christian world, women were considered property and were exchanged from father to husband along with a dowry of land, money, and livestock. Although this practice is not acceptable in the United States, remnants of the subjugation of women are still evident in some religious perspectives. For example, predominant in the discussion of women's roles in certain Christian families is the question of whether the man is the head of the home (as Christ heads the Church), and how "head" is defined or understood. The issue of power, as influenced by religious conventions and beliefs, needs to be considered in this important social context and in how it affects women and girls within families.

Trying to understand the multiple levels of influence on women's experiences is the starting point for feminist family scholars. Analyzing these contexts is the basis for understanding how society developed particular views of what women and men should be. Feminist family scholars refer to the act of analysis as social deconstruction. The reflection on and discussion of that analysis forms the basis of the social discourse of gender roles.

There are many forms of families. Feminist family theorists broaden our view of families. The traditional view of the nuclear family is an inadequate description of families in today's society. Economic forces, divorce, and other social factors have changed the nature of the family in the United States. Today, families include long-term cohabiting couples, single parents and their children, multiethnic families, multigenerational families, same-sex families, stepfamilies, remarried couples, and fictive kin.

Research data indicate that the most successful family relationships are based on loving friendship, models of equality, intimacy, caring, and cooperation. These qualities are applicable to more than simply the traditional nuclear family (Allen and Baber

1992). Limiting families to the traditional nuclear definition restricts women's roles to a subordinate position and discounts the experiences of women in diverse family forms.

Emphasis is placed on social change. One goal of feminist family theory is an activist orientation—i.e., challenging the status quo. Feminists seek to empower the disenfranchised or those with less power (Sollie and Leslie 1994). They advocate examining diverse family forms, challenging sexism, and questioning aspects of our society that act against women and children, including homophobia and male violence, so that we can bring an acceptance of difference and diversity to human interactions. *Feminist praxis* refers to the feminists' struggle to put their beliefs into action.

Not only do feminist family theorists seek to uncover gender biases, they also work to change existing gender relations in society, in the economy, in education, and in families (Allen and Baber 1992; MacDermid and Jurich 1992; Osmond and Thorne 1993). They seek to bring public attention to what had previously been considered private issues, particularly with respect to families. Their slogan is "The personal is political." In other words, what happens personally to women has political and social impact. Given that much of a woman's experience is located within the family, one might also say that "The family is political" as well. You can see the dynamics of power in both society and in families, but power in families (whether of men having power over women or parents having power over children) has often been seen as "natural," and therefore less likely to be challenged. Although few in today's society would dispute the fact that family members should not use their power to the extremes of child or wife abuse, feminist family scholars have continued to uncover less obvious forms of power differentials, such as differing amounts of influence in decision-making, uneven divisions of labor in the household, and differences in anticipated costs when leaving a relationship (Okin 1997).

One example of the personal-made-political revolves around the issue of *sexual agency*. Sexual agency refers to the degree of control one has over one's own sexuality and reproductive activity, clearly a personal and a private issue. Early feminists pointed out how power over one's reproductive capacity led to power in one's life, both personally and economically (Baber 1994; Sollie and Leslie 1994; Thompson 1992). Prior to the advent of reliable birth control, women (married or not) who wanted an active sexual life had to be prepared for pregnancy. Until the Pregnancy Discrimination Act of 1975 was passed, women could be fired from their jobs simply because they were pregnant. Years after the federal mandate was passed, young married women were still discriminated against in hiring because employers feared that they would get pregnant and quit. Jobs, therefore, were more likely to be given to young men or single women. As birth control became more reliable and the women's movement opened the workplace, women who were pregnant and women who were mothers had increased access to economic opportunities, and therefore more power.

However, in the United States, women who are pregnant or have children still suffer economically and socially. Pregnant women cannot be fired, but the law does not require that they be paid for time taken off to have the baby. When they return to work, they often must pay for childcare, or miss out on a promotion like Alice, thereby reducing their resources. Compare this with several European countries that actually provide one-year paid maternity leave to women after childbirth and subsidize childcare so that all children receive the same quality of care when mothers return to work (Glazer 2006).

A subtler example of the personal-made-political may be seen in how women reflect on their roles. Many women believe that they need to stay at home with their children if they can. For economic reasons, most are unable to do that, and they often report feeling guilty about it. These women, and perhaps their families and society in general, interpret their inability to care for their children and work at the same time as a personal failure (Mahoney 1996). This guilt, generally not felt or expressed by men, is an indication of how subtle and pervasive the social inequality in our society is.

There is no objective, unbiased observation of humans. Our observations are influenced by social realities. This is implied by "the personal-is-political" slogan that we mentioned about above. Something that is personal is by definition subjective and not objective.

Feminist family scholars have challenged the traditional approach to scientific understanding. Even the questions that we ask are influenced by how we are trained to be scientists (Thompson 1992). Traditional science teaches objectivity and observation free of bias, with an emphasis on neutral "fact." Feminist family scholars challenge this perspective by saying that there is no neutral observation of humans. If our social realities are constructed based on a gendered perspective, then our perspective on reality, and therefore, the facts as we know them, are socially constructed. So, the real focus for feminists is not about obtaining objective facts, but rather about understanding how people's social realities are constructed by achieving insights into their experiences (Sollie and Leslie 1994).

Feminist family scholars believe that families should not be treated as a unitary whole. If they are, the lesser voices in the family are oppressed. For example, if an abuser is asked, "How is your family life?" he might respond, "Fine." His abused spouse probably views the state of the family differently. The question should not be "How is your family life?" but rather "What is your experience of this relationship?" Feminist family scholars seek to uncover the voices in families that have been oppressed or neglected by traditional social science. In order to uncover these voices, feminist researchers are more likely to use case studies, qualitative analyses, and ethnographic studies in addition to traditional survey data.

PRIMARY TERMS AND CONCEPTS

Sex

Sex refers to one's biological assignment as genetically defined at birth—i.e., male or female.

Gender

Gender refers to the social meanings and behaviors ascribed to one's sex, particularly with regard to roles and behaviors expected of someone because of one's sex. Gendered behaviors are learned as a result of socialization and are, therefore, the result of one's culture, not genetic predisposition. For example, we often give trucks to preschool boys and dolls to preschool girls as playthings, because that is what society, not genetics, deems acceptable. In our opening vignette, Alice performs a number of functions in her marriage (e.g., arranges for the babysitter, makes sure laundry is done, picks up her husband's suit from the cleaner) that appear to be "assumed" roles for women within marriage.

Categorization

Categorization is the process of applying labels to behaviors and roles according to one's sex. Certain behaviors, roles, words, and symbols are considered "male" (e.g., aggression, playing with trucks, "strong," the color blue), whereas others are considered "female" (e.g., being nice, ballet, "soft," the color pink).

Stratification

Stratification refers to the application of value to different categories. Assigning social value to categories ranks those categories within the social context. For example, is it better to be nice or aggressive? In the first-grade classes of most elementary schools, it is probably better to be nice, and girls may be treated more positively than boys by their teachers and peers in that social context. But in the social context of a Fortune 500 company, it is probably more highly valued to be aggressive than nice, so a woman who has been socialized to be only nice and never encouraged to learn any aggressive skills probably won't ever be hired as a chief executive officer, no matter how well educated she may be.

Privilege

Privilege refers to the social status given to one with more power and value in society. The concept of privilege requires feminists to ask not only who has power but who does **not**, and to ensure that those who have been previously marginalized and oppressed are now included in the matrix of voices represented.

Social Deconstruction

The first step in the analysis of how views of reality are constructed by social interactions, particularly in light of how gendered meanings are developed, is social deconstruction (see Figure 9.1). It involves the consideration of how society has categorized and assigned values to behaviors and roles according to sex.

Social Discourse

The next step in the analysis, social discourse, brings the analysis of social deconstruction into the "conversation" of gender expectations and behaviors. Social discourse raises awareness of the analysis into the work of social scientists by examining the ways in which we invite people to participate in the dialogue of deconstruction, ensuring that those who do not have privilege are included in the conversations. It challenges us to question how we focus our questions, and how we analyze the data.

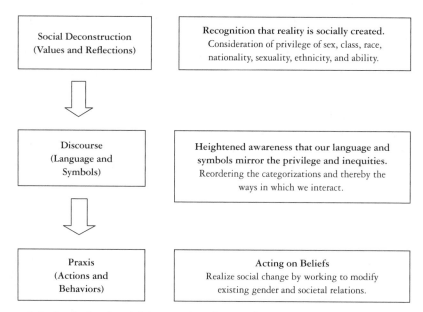

FIGURE 9.1 Analysis of social interaction from a feminist perspective.

Praxis

The step after analysis, in which beliefs and values are put into action, is praxis. For feminist family scholars, this includes advocacy for women, inclusiveness in language and behavior, and reflecting on one's own behavior with intention.

COMMON AREAS OF RESEARCH AND APPLICATION

Ferree (2010) addresses the plethora of research in the last decade that includes gender as one of its primary variables in her *Journal of Marriage and Family* decade review article on feminist theory. She points to areas such as household division of labor, work and family balance, and family diversity as being particularly inclusive, and areas such as social and family policy as being rejecting of this approach because of their feared effects on family function. Because of the exhaustive nature of the literature present in the field, this review touches on only a few examples of research done in the areas of division of labor, family violence, and Black feminist theory, or research that takes into consideration the intersection of more than one form of oppression.

Division of Labor

One of the major areas of feminist research is division of labor within the family. Labor divisions are often constructed according to gender, including both paid and unpaid labor in our society. The stereotypic family has been the traditional, idealized, nuclear family, in which the father is the breadwinner and the mother stays home to care for the house and children. Although the nuclear family is no longer representative of most families in the United States today, we still often see people reacting to women's labor outside the home as "intrusive" because of dated societal expectations that the woman's first responsibility is to home. Furthermore, unpaid work in our society is not considered "real work." The work that is done at home—maintaining the home, paying the bills, raising the children, tutoring the children, ferrying the children back and forth to their activities, nursing, getting up in the middle of the night, cooking, and cleaning—are not considered valuable work in our society because these jobs do not produce an income (Glazer 2006).

Even as women enter the workforce in increasingly higher-status, higher-income professional roles, they are still expected to be "wives" despite their work outside the home. Many high-level corporate jobs are structured according to the assumption that a worker has a partner for support, thereby creating what is essentially a two-person career. One partner, typically the male, is expected to work long hours, as if he does not need to worry about the needs of the children and the rest of the family because those needs will be met by the wife. The outcomes of this arrangement oppress both men and women and are perpetuated by social norms that feminist family scholars challenge. Furthermore, analyses of dual-earner couples show that women continue to do the majority of household tasks and childcare in addition to their full-time jobs (Noonan, Estes, and Glass 2007).

This is not a result of income, as it has been shown that even women who are the primary wage earners for their families do more housework and childcare than their husbands. This is a result of upholding societal gender role norms. In the extreme, it has even been shown that men who are financially dependent on their wives do even less housework than other men—this is how they "do gender." They exert their power by reverting to even more traditional gender roles at home, because they cannot fulfill the traditional role of breadwinner. Thus, the more money women begin to earn within a relationship, the more threatened gender roles become, and the more traditional gender roles within the household become (Mannino and Deutsch 2007).

In her analysis of this "second shift," Hochschild (1989) found that women in general not only did more housework and childcare but also often believed that it was their responsibility. Feminist family theorists analyze this division of labor from an equity perspective and also deconstruct the reality of why a woman would believe those jobs are her responsibility.

Family Violence

A second application of feminist family study is family violence. According to feminist family scholars, in our attempt to maintain privacy in the family, we have failed in our social obligations to identify injustices in the family (Wood 1998). Families are not always the "havens of love, goodwill, and affection" that we would like to believe, and families are not safe places for many women and children.

Although some homes are places that foster support for many of us, many other homes are places where "abuse, violence, exploitation, cruelty and persisting inequities fester for far too many citizens in our country" (Wood 1998, 129). By drawing attention to such abuse in families, feminist family scholars have identified facts about families that others have ignored. For example, a violent act against a woman is perpetrated every 12 to 18 seconds in the United States, and four women die each day because of family violence (Wood 1998).

It is important to recognize, however, that there are many types of intimate partner violence, just as there is more than one feminist interpretation of the reasons for partner violence (Johnson 2011). There has been a debate recently on the importance of clarifying definitions of partner violence, as the statistics vary from one form to the next and also vary from one data source to another. For example, Haselschwerdt, Hardesty and Hans (2010) note that feminist researchers are more likely to study violence perpetrated against women, whereas family violence researchers focus on research in the family most likely brought on by stress. The distinction is important. Feminist researchers are more likely to obtain their samples from social services aimed at supporting women who are survivors, to study intimate terrorism, which is the use of control over women through the use of violence, and to use smaller samples and more qualitative methodologies. In contrast, family violence researchers are more likely to study episodes of violence between family members that are situational in nature, which is more likely in the larger population, and to study it using data drawn from national surveys using large samples. These different foci lead to very different results. Intimate terrorism is most likely to have male perpetrators and female victims, whereas situational couple violence appears to have equal levels of instigation by men and women. Being specific about the type of violence you are studying or identifying is important for many reasons. Take, for example, people who are evaluating custody cases during a divorce. If they focus simply on situational violence, they might suggest that couples work together on a communication and parenting plan during the process. However, if the female was the victim of intimate terrorism, putting her in this situation would be risky to her overall psychological and perhaps even physical health (Haselschwerdt et al 2010).

Based on this, it seems obvious that much of the work in this area from a feminist perspective is focused on intimate terrorism. Paterson (2010) did an interesting study on the relationship between economic contributions to the family and the presence of intimate violence in the home. She suggests that, to put an end to violence in the home, we need to not only empower women within the home through their voices, but also enhance their ability to provide material resources to the relationship. Increasing women's economic standing can provide them with either an option for exiting a violent situation or an increase of power in the relationship that will allow them the voice they need to combat the oppressive situation.

Although much of the research in this area focuses on adult relationships, Burton et al. (2010) turned their attention to dating abuse in adolescent relationships. They found that adolescent girls stay in abusive relationships in order to fulfill socially constructed gender roles that suggest that being in a relationship is an important determinant of adulthood, and because they feel that they have no power in the relationship. They hope that staying in these relationships will help them develop a positive gender identity. It stands to reason that, if violence occurs in dating relationships for adolescents, it would also exist in relationships for adolescent girls who become mothers. This relatively unexamined area becomes even more unexplored when you add minority status to the mix. Dalla et al. (2010) studied Navajo adolescent mothers and their intimate partner relationships at two time frames: when the girls were 16–20 years of age and then again when they were 28–37 years of age. They found that this population had a long history of partner violence, as well as a culture that was supportive of male behavior that was at odds with the well-being of women. Furthermore, partner violence was often found in their families of origin, was shown to exist throughout the period of this study, and was discovered to be perhaps not supported by the culture but, at the very least, ignored because of their cultural beliefs.

The idea that culture influences domestic violence was also seen in a study by Xu et al. (2011), who assessed women's experiences with partner violence in urban Thailand. They found that domestic violence was shaped by religion, culture, and social norms. For example, Thai women are supposed to be selfless, devoted, and to put family and husbands before themselves. Their religion further reinforces these notions by stating that the status of women is secondary to that of men. These ideas are further supported in their political and cultural systems, which value the roles of men over those of women. Additional risk factors included inequalities in decision-making power and lack of access to outside resources.

Perhaps it is fitting to end this literature section with a study that focuses on the other end of the lifespan, or the physical, emotional, and sexual abuse of elders. It has been suggested that, as our elderly population continues to increase, the incidence of elder abuse will also increase. Brozowski and Hall (2009) found that risk factors for elder abuse include mental health issues, a history of abuse, being an unmarried female who lives alone, and dependence in the activities of daily living. Because of the shame associated with this type of abuse, it is suspected that it is greatly underreported, but it is a topic of concern for those interested in a feminist perspective on violence against women.

Although it is part of feminist family scholarship to identify the problems of oppression and inequities in our society, it is also imperative that it generates alternatives and seeks ways to empower the oppressed and disenfranchised. Feminist family scholars identify issues **and** also seek ways to advocate on behalf of women and their families through education and support.

Black Feminism

The three waves of feminist theory previously reviewed are based on literature that focuses more generally on the lives and experiences of women. However, many scholars believe it is important to recognize that gender is only one of many variables that can result in oppression. Other examples include race and class. Hill Collins (2000) suggests that one cannot "tease out" these various forms of oppression, and that instead we should focus on how they intersect. Black feminism is one example of research and practice that has emerged from this realization.

Black feminism takes the more general concepts of feminist theory and adds to them the element of the oppression of Black-ness in our society (Brock 2010). As Few (2007) has pointed out, this perspective allows Black women to simultaneously recognize both their sense of being a woman and their experience of being Black. This movement seeks to bring about an end to the oppression faced by Black women both historically and currently, to shape the image of Black women in today's society, and to promote activism on their behalf. They also recognize that, although they share struggles with other women based on their gender, they also face struggles similar to Black men because of their exposures to racism and classism.

Womanism is a term that came out of this movement. Alice Walker (1983) used this term because she did not want to have to use a descriptor for color, but instead wanted to create a word that was new and unique to the movement. She suggests that *womanism* is embedded in the feminist movement and is simply another layer that adds the importance of race and gender to the conversation. Interestingly, this word has been adapted by African feminists in a multitude of ways to reflect their desire to focus on family, mothering, and feminine expressions, to name a few (Jacobs 2011).

The entrance of Black feminism in its various forms into social science research and practice has been extensive in the last few decades. Few (2007) discusses the ways that it has been used in the field and provides an example of the integration of Black feminism into her own work. She suggests, for example, that while sharing insider status with the group under study can provide some insight, it also necessitates that scholars be aware of the ways they are different from their participants, as well, in order to remain true to the research process. The nature of qualitative research lends itself to continual analysis of the objectivity of the research process, but what about quantitative research? Harnois and Ifatunji (2011) suggest that quantitative research has not been as successful at recognizing the intersection of gender and race and at developing tools that can detect this nuanced relationship. It is not impossible, but more work needs to be done in this area to truly represent the lives and realities of women and men from a Black feminist perspective.

CRITIQUE

Feminist family theory can be used to analyze certain aspects of family relations. It includes a wide range of family types within its definition of a family unit. Other theories are narrower in their scope. Feminist family theory sheds light on other issues that are neglected or ignored by other theories, such as the male-oriented perspective of what was previously considered "objective" research. It attempts to lend more equal weight to women's issues in family interactions and to downplay the traditional gender roles of some other theories.

Feminist family theory is not without its critics, though. Feminism has been criticized as being oppressive to men by focusing only on issues that affect women. Feminist family scholars refute this by saying that issues that are important to women in families are important to men as well.

Feminist family theory has been criticized for working outside the parameters and paradigms of the traditional scientific base of knowledge. Critics say that, although science is not totally value-free, we should strive to present the information in the best and clearest way without becoming involved in the data. Feminist family scholars respond that, because it is impossible to be truly objective, the most truthful thing is to admit our subjectivity and work hard to reflect on our role as researchers, rather than deny subjectivity's influence in the research process.

Feminist family theorists have also been criticized for their activist position. Social scientists, maintaining an objective stance, have frequently preferred to be describers of events, rather than facilitators of change. Feminist scholars argue that it is impossible to fully embrace and understand the oppression of the disenfranchised without being ethically bound to do something to alter that reality. Issues of inequality, such as unfair division of labor in families, limited access to economic stability and support, and ways in which society devalues women's work and limits opportunities, should be addressed by those with power and privilege.

Feminist family theorists have also been criticized for working against traditional nuclear families. But the reality is that the traditional nuclear family is no longer the dominant norm. Feminist scholars argue that the inequality within families may actually lend itself to the dissolution of the traditional nuclear family, as power differentials enter into the conversations, economy, and distribution of labor in American families.

Finally, some have challenged feminist family theory because, they claim, it pays too much attention to the oppression of one group—women—to the exclusion of other forms of oppression (e.g., by race, ethnicity, age, disability, religion, etc.). Although helping women find their voices is paramount in today's multicultural climate, exploring dynamics related to race, culture, class, and sexuality are also increasingly important (Ashner 2007). For example, standards for motherhood are often based on a White middle-class norm that leads to the oppression of working-class and working-poor mothers in today's society (Jones 2007). Thus, while attempting to decrease the oppression of mothers, women of lower economic standing are simultaneously being oppressed. Race is another variable that needs to be disentangled. Black feminism has developed as a result of the need to recognize women who struggle with more than one type of oppression, as previously noted. It attempts to find a balance between raising consciousness based on race and raising consciousness based on gender (Few 2007). Exploring the diverse experiences of women across these many variables is a challenge worthy of our attention in the years to come.

So, what is the future of feminism? Some believe that the social activism that was so prevalent and powerful in the second wave of feminism has not existed in this third wave of feminism (White and Klein 2008). Why is that? It has been suggested that feminism is still something with which many people in the United States do not want to be associated (Ferree 2010). Mitra (2011) suggests that the stigma attached to the word "feminist" exists in other, developing countries as well, including India where her research is based. In addition, some men feel as though there is no place for them in feminist movements, but Alilunas (2011) notes that having a feminist movement **without** the involvement of men who are willing to explore their positions of privilege and work toward greater equality seems hopeless. Our culture needs the involvement of men for real social change to take place. Thus, although feminism has influenced a great deal of theoretical and empirical research in the last decade, it has yet to return to its former place of real social impact. So, who can decide the future of feminism? Only time and the work of many women, and men, will tell.

APPLICATION

1. Alice and Bob Stephens, from the vignette at the beginning of this chapter, seem to have a good marriage, a stable family, and two secure jobs. In many ways, they are part of a privileged class. But it is clear that, at least on this night, there are two marriages—his and hers. Bob relies on Alice to take care of the "little things" that keep their family life going smoothly, yet Alice is feeling overwhelmed by keeping up with all those "little things." Answer the following questions based on their situation:

    a. Compare Alice's experiences and Bob's experiences. What are some of the privileges they have? What are some of the inequities? Identify ways in which those inequities are intentional. Are there some inequities that are not intentional? If so, why do they exist?

    b. In what ways are their perspectives on their marriage different?

    c. How are Alice's and Bob's lives affected by social norms and expectations?

    d. What social and/or historical contexts should be taken into account when attempting to understand the Stephens family?

    e. Based on what you have learned about feminist family theory, what recommendations for change might you suggest if Alice and Bob consulted a counselor?

    f. If Bob and Alice were to divorce, how might the consequences of that divorce be different for each of them? What role would privilege play?

    g. If you wanted to study marriages like the Stephens', how might you design your research so that both men and women had equal voices in the study? What differences do you think you would find between the men and the women?

2. In the sample reading, Downing and Goldberg (2011) discuss the role of gender construction in the lives of lesbian mothers of children who are three-and-a-half years old.

    a. What are two assumptions of this theory that are illustrated in this reading?

    b. What are examples of categorization that are shown?

    c. What privileges do the participants have, and in what ways are they subject to oppression?

REFERENCES

Alcoff, L. (1995). Cultural feminism versus post-structuralism: The identity crisis in feminist theory. In *Feminism and philosophy: Essential readings in theory, reinterpretation, and application,* ed. N. Tuana and R. Tong, 434–456. Boulder, CO: Westview.

Alilunas, P. 2011. The (In)visible people in the room: Men in women's studies. *Men and Masculinities* 14: 210–229.

Allen, K. R. 1994. Feminist reflections on lifelong single women. In *Gender, families, and close relationships: Feminist research journeys*, ed. L. D. Sollie and L. A. Leslie, 97–119. Thousand Oaks, CA: Sage.

Allen, K. R., and K. M. Baber. 1992. Starting a revolution in family life education: A feminist vision. *Family Relations* 41: 378–384.

Ashner, N. 2007. Made in the (multicultural) U.S.A.: Unpacking tensions of race, culture, gender, and sexuality in education. *Educational Researcher* 36(2): 65–74.

Baber, K. M. 1994. Studying women's sexualities: Feminist transformations. In *Gender, families, and close relationships: Feminist research journeys*, ed. L. D. Sollie and L. A. Leslie, 50–73. Thousand Oaks, CA: Sage.

Baca Zinn, M. 2000. Feminism and family studies for a new century. *The Annals of the American Academy of Political and Social Science (AAPSS)* 571: 42–56.

Bernard, J. 1972. *The future of marriage*. New York: World Publishing.

Brock, R. 2011. Recovering from 'yo mama is so stupid': (en)gendering a critical paradigm on Black feminist theory and pedagogy. *International Journal of Qualitative Studies in Education* 24(3): 379–396.

Brozowski, K., and D. R. Hall. 2009. Aging and risk: Physical and sexual abuse of elders in Canada. *Journal of Interpersonal Violence* 25(7): 1183–1199.

Burton, C. W., B. Halpern-Felsher, S. H. Rankin, R. S. Rehm, and J.C. Humphreys. 2010. Relationships and betrayal among young women: Theoretical perspectives on adolescent dating abuse. *Journal of Advanced Nursing* 67(6), 1393–1405.

Dalla, R. L., A. M. Marchetti, E. A. Sechrest, and J. L. White. 2010. "All the men here have the Peter Pan Syndrome—they don't want to grow up": Navajo adolescent mothers' intimate partner relationships—a 15-year perspective. *Violence Against Women* 16(7): 743–763.

Downing, J.B., and A. E. Goldberg.. 2011. Lesbian mothers' constructions of the division of paid and unpaid labor. *Feminism & Psychology* 21: 100–120.

Ferree, M. M. 1990. Beyond separate spheres: Feminism and family research. *Journal of Marriage and the Family* 52: 866–884.

Ferree, M. M. 2010. Filling the glass: Gender perspectives on families. *Journal of Marriage and Family* 72: 420–439.

Few, A. L. 2007. Integrating black consciousness and critical race feminism into family studies research. *Journal of Family Issues* 28: 452–473.

Gilligan, C. 1982. *In a different voice: Psychological theory and women's development*. Cambridge, MA: Harvard University Press.

Glazer, S. 2006. Future of feminism. *CQ Researcher* 16(14): 313–336.

Harnois, C.E., and M. Ifatunji. 2011. Gendered measures, gendered models: Toward an intersectional analysis of interpersonal racial discrimination. *Ethnic and Racial Studies* 34(6) 1006–1028.

Haselschwerdt, M. L., Hardesty, J.L., and J.D. Hans. 2010. Custody evaluators' beliefs about domestic violence allegations during divorce: Feminist and family violence perspectives. *Journal of Interpersonal Violence* 26: 1694–1719.

Hill Collins, P. 1998. It's all in the family: Intersections of gender, race, and nation. *Hypatia* 13: 62–82.

———. 2000. *Black feminist thought: Knowledge, consciousness, and the politics of empowerment*. 2nd ed. New York: Routledge.

Hochschild, A. R. 1989. *The second shift: Working parents and the revolution at home*. New York: Viking/Penguin.

Jacobs, B. L. 2011. Unbound by theory and naming: Survival feminism and the women of the South African Victoria Mxenge Housing and Development Association. *Berkeley Journal of Gender, Law & Justice* 26: 19–77.

Johnson, M. P. 2011. Gender and types of intimate partner violence: A response to an anti-feminist literature review. *Aggression and Violent Behavior* 16: 289–296.

Jones, S. 2007. Working-poor mothers and middle-class others: Psychosocial considerations in home–school relations and research. *Anthropology and Education Quarterly* 38(2): 159–178.

Lorber, J. 1998. *Gender inequality: Feminist theories and politics*. Los Angeles: Roxbury.

MacDermid, S. M., and J. A. Jurich. 1992. Feminist teaching: Effective education. *Family Relations* 41: 31–39.

Mahoney, A. R. 1996. Children, families, and feminism: Perspectives on teaching. *Early Childhood Education Journal* 23: 191–196.

Mannino, C. A., and F. M. Deutsch. 2007. Changing the division of household labor: A negotiated process between partners. *Sex Roles* 56(5–6): 309–324.

Mead, M. 1935. *Sex and temperament in three primitive societies*. New York: Morrow.

Mitra, A. 2011. To be or not to be a feminist in India. *Journal of Women and Social Work* 26(2): 182–200.

Noonan, M. C., S. B. Estes, and J. S. Glass. 2007. Do workplace flexibility policies influence time spent in domestic labor? *Journal of Family Issues* 28: 263–289.

Okin, S. M. 1997. Families and feminist theory: Some past and present issues. In *Feminism and families*, ed. H. L. Nelson, 13–26. New York: Routledge.

Osmond, M. W., and B. Thorne. 1993. Feminist theories: The social construction of gender in families and society. In *Sourcebook of family theories and methods*, ed. P. G. Boss, W. J. Doherty, R. LaRossa, W. R. Schumm, and S. K. Steinmetz, 591–626. New York: Plenum.

Paterson, S. 2010. Rethinking the dynamics of abusive relationships: The implications of violence and resistenace for household bargaining. *Review of Radical Political Economics* 43(2): 137–153.

Rutter, V., and P. Schwartz. 2000. Gender, marriage, and diverse possibilities for cross-sex and same-sex pairs. In *Handbook of family diversity*, ed. D. H. Demo, K. R. Allen, and M. A. Fine, 59–81. New York: Oxford.

Shehan, C. L., and K. C. W. Kammeyer. 1997. *Marriages and families: Reflections of a gendered society*. Needham Heights, MA: Allyn and Bacon.

Sollie, L. D., and L. A. Leslie. 1994. *Gender, families, and close Relationships: Feminist research journeys*. Thousand Oaks, CA: Sage.

Thomas, R. M. 2000. *Recent theories of human development*. Thousand Oaks, CA: Sage.

Thompson, L. 1992. Feminist methodology for family studies. *Journal of Marriage and the Family* 54: 3–18.

Walker, A. 1983. *In search of our mother's gardens: Womanist prose*. San Diego, CA: Harcourt Brace Jovanovich.

Walker, A. J. 1993. Teaching about race, gender, and class diversity in the United States families. *Family Relations* 42: 342–350.

White, J. M., and D. M. Klein. Family theories 3rd ed. 2008. Los Angeles: Sage Publications.

Wood, J. T. 1998. Ethics, justice, and the "private sphere." *Women's Studies in Communication* 21: 127–149.

Xu, X., K. R. Kerley, and B. Sirisunyaluck. 2010. Understanding gender and domestic violence from a sample of married women in urban Thailand. *Journal of Family Issues* 32(6): 791–819.

SAMPLE READING

Downing, J. B., and A. E. Goldberg. (2011). Lesbian mothers' constructions of the division of paid and unpaid labor. *Feminism & Psychology* 21: 100–120.

This reading exemplifies many of the feminist assumptions and concepts discussed in the chapter. For example, a feminist perspective suggests that gender is socially constructed and that there is a difference between sex and gender. This article examines a traditional relationship issue of the division of housework and paid labor, but from the perspective of lesbian couples. The authors also discuss the historical and social contexts in which these relationships exist and examine how that affects these co-parenting relationships. They discuss the roles of gender, categorization, and privilege as well. The article was chosen as a sample reading because it represents one of the most studied topics utilizing feminist theory while, at the same time, presenting it from a different family orientation.

SAMPLE READING

Lesbian Mothers' Constructions of the Division of Paid and Unpaid Labor

Jordan B. Downing
Abbie E. Goldberg
Clark University

Do lesbian couples resist the (re)gendering of divisions of paid and unpaid labor within the context of biological and nonbiological parenting? In this study we explore how primarily Caucasian, North American lesbian mothers of three-and-a-half-year-old children construct divisions of paid and unpaid labor. We analyze 30 lesbian couples' narrative constructions of their labor arrangements, examining the ways in which they both transgress and accept traditionally masculine and feminine gendering. At the same time that biological mothers and nonbiological mothers often described differences in their contributions to paid and unpaid labor, they rarely invoked biology as a salient factor in explaining their work/family roles. Our analysis suggests that the 'egalitarian ethic' of lesbian women is an over-simplification of the multiple ways that women develop their divisions of labor.

Keywords: biology, division of labor, gender, lesbian, mothers, qualitative, social construction.

Jordan B. Downing, MA, is a doctoral candidate in clinical psychology at Clark University, USA. She is interested in how couples construct their identities within the context of alternative family forms that challenge traditional notions of the family. She is also interested in how same-sex couples navigate discriminatory discourses and practices in their efforts to become adoptive parents. She has published a number of articles in family and psychology journals. Her most recent work is focused on examining practices of transitioning and reconstructions of gender and sexuality for transgender individuals.

Abbie E. Goldberg received her PhD in clinical psychology from the University of Massachusetts Amherst, USA, and completed a predoctoral internship at Yale Medical School, USA. She is currently an assistant professor of psychology at Clark University. She is the author of Lesbian and Gay Parents and their Children: Research on the Family Life Cycle *(APA, 2009). She has received grant funds from sources such as the National Institutes of Health and the American Psychological Foundation. She has published in a variety of family studies and psychology journals and is on the editorial boards of* Adoption Quarterly, Family Relations, *and* Journal of Marriage and Family.

Corresponding author: Jordan B. Downing, Frances L. Hiatt School of Psychology, Clark University Worcester, MA 01610, USA. Email: jdowning@clarku.edu

An emerging body of research explores how lesbian couples negotiate their parental roles and identities (e.g. Dunne, 2000; Gabb, 2005; Goldberg and Perry-Jenkins, 2007; Patterson, 1995). Research pertaining to the division of labor in lesbian couples has tended to focus on the division of domestic labor, often highlighting lesbian women's 'egalitarian ethic'—that is, their tendency to value equality in their relationships and to share domestic labor more equally than heterosexual couples (Kurdek, 2007; Patterson, 1995). This study examines the larger work/family context that lesbian couples negotiate as they strive to create satisfying work/family arrangements.

Historically, research on the division of labor has focused on heterosexual couples, documenting that once they have children, their division of labor tends to become increasingly segregated into unequal work/family roles (e.g. Deutsch, 1999). Despite increases in women's paid employment over the last few decades, women continue to perform more domestic labor and to sacrifice more career opportunities than their husbands (e.g. Maume, 2006). Such inequalities continue despite the fact that many heterosexual couples claim to want more egalitarian roles and despite an increase in contemporary fathers' commitment to shared parenting (Nentwich, 2008).

Thus, the desire for an equal division of labor is not easily offset by the social pressures and structural inequalities that reinforce traditional gender roles. Further, the tendency for many heterosexual couples to 'default' to traditional roles may lead to the reification of gender norms and the essentializing of gender differences. When couples assume 'traditional' parental roles, the social construct of 'mother' becomes naturalized as an inherent outgrowth of women's maternal instincts. Similarly, the social construct of 'father' becomes equated with the idea that men naturally are more inclined to take on the role of family breadwinner (Carrington, 1999). Feminist scholars have long recognized the problems of reducing social phenomena to biological differences, and have pointed to the importance of examining how paid and unpaid labor are avenues through which individuals express, perform and substantiate their gendered identities (e.g. Kroska, 1997).

Comparative studies of heterosexual- and lesbian-parent families have highlighted similarities and differences in how heterosexual and lesbian parents construct family arrangements, often indicating that lesbian couples share childcare more equally (e.g. Patterson et al., 2004). For instance, Chan and colleagues' (1998) study of heterosexual and lesbian parents of children aged 5–11 found that both heterosexual and lesbian mothers desired equal divisions of childcare, but lesbians were more successful in enacting equality. Chan and colleagues' analysis suggests that equality is often preferred by women, and that a lesbian relationship may more easily allow for equal roles since both partners are of the same sex. Although all couples, regardless of sexual orientation (or sex), contend with the prevailing normative discourse of 'equal parenting' (Risman and Johnson-Sumerforrd, 1998), lesbians appear to be more effective in enacting this equality. Yet, in Chan and colleagues' analysis, sex differences are discussed as gender differences. They collapse any distinction between sex as a biological characteristic and gender as a constitutive process, thereby eclipsing how women may enact traditionally masculine and feminine gendering within a same-sex relationship.

Similar to comparative studies, research that focuses exclusively on lesbian couples has often emphasized lesbian women's 'egalitarian ethic' as strongly influencing equal divisions of domestic labor (Goldberg and Perry-Jenkins, 2007; Patterson, 1995). However, although lesbian couples tend to share housework equally, in couples with children, where one partner conceived the child, biological mothers often perform more childcare and nonbiological mothers often work longer hours in paid labor, at least when children are young (Bos et al., 2007; Goldberg and Perry-Jenkins, 2007; Patterson, 1995). Being in a same-sex relationship, therefore, does not necessarily ensure egalitarianism (Carrington, 1999). Biological mothers experience far more validation in their roles as mothers than nonbiological mothers, and may do more childcare as they embody the traditional role of 'mother' (Short, 2007). Moreover, relinquishing job opportunities or reducing time in paid work may not be perceived as 'sacrifices', but rather intentional decisions to redistribute paid work and family arrangements that evoke little perceived stress. Indeed, some biological mothers may resist the notion that because of their genetic relationship to their child, they should be more involved in unpaid labor.

Sullivan (1996) studied 34 lesbian two-mother families and found that most reported sharing domestic labor equally. She reported that among the few couples who did not equally share domestic labor, such role differentiations were regulated by 'personal preferences' rather than beliefs about gender. Sullivan, thereby, suggests that personal preferences can be distinguished from gender differences. Such a perspective differs from a social constructionist perspective (Erickson, 2005), which regards gender construction as an ever-present process that is not a clearly identifiable part of personality, but rather entwined with the very construction of identity. Even if women do not perceive their roles as gendered, their behaviors (and preferences) may reflect and potentially reinforce gendered expectations for behavior because there are no such gender-neutral grounds. For instance, some lesbian women may engage in divisions of labor where one mother is consistently the primary caregiver, and through such involvement in domestic labor (and perhaps reduced involvement in paid labor), that mother ultimately embodies the more stereotypical maternal role. Femininity, childcare and motherhood thereby are intertwined at a symbolic level, reinforcing each other such that unequal distributions of domestic and paid labor may inadvertently create traditional masculine/ feminine gender divides.

Parenting by two women refutes any differentiation of roles based on sex, illustrating the performative nature of gender (Butler, 1990). Research has tended to under-theorize the impact of gender processes impacting lesbian and gay parents' constructions of their family roles (Oerton, 1997). According to Oerton, this has led to an understanding of heterosexual relationships as 'gender-full' (1997: 421) and same-sex relationships as gender-absent. Lesbian mothers may enact gendered behavior that both instantiates the gender binary while at the same time discursively and materially exposing its artificiality. For instance, some mothers may engage in the traditional role of the masculine breadwinner at the same time that they shift what 'breadwinning' means to both their family and their personal identity, thereby challenging the presumed rigidity and 'naturalness' of gender stereotypes.

Researchers of lesbian mother-headed families have emphasized the radical potential of lesbian mothers in challenging heteronormative family practices. Dunne (2000), for example, posits that because of lesbian parents' similarities as two women, they are in direct contradiction to the traditional gender practices of heterosexual couples. Likewise, Sullivan (2004) argues that lesbian-and gay-parent families are free of socially sanctioned gender norms, whereby gender is a (negative) regulating practice that prevents more egalitarian family practices. However, when Dunne argues that egalitarianism is in the best interest of lesbian partners as compared to heterosexual couples, she seems to deny that lesbian partners may find it beneficial to divide labor unequally (but not necessarily inequitably). For example, one partner may have the capacity to make more money and may therefore be perceived by both partners as more suited for paid labor.

Our study expands on the existing literature by examining how lesbians may not only challenge traditional notions of the family but may also reproduce heteronormative gendering. This study examines how women discursively construct the complexities of balancing work and family, paying particular attention to how divisions of unpaid labor are embedded within divisions of paid labor. Data collected from 30 primarily Caucasian middle-class lesbian couples (60 women) living in the USA were analyzed, and two research questions were posed: (1) How do couples negotiate the balancing of work and family (e.g. to what extent do they describe having given up paid work commitments or time with family)? (2) How do they describe (both implicitly and explicitly) their own efforts to transgress, resist, or accept traditional masculine and feminine gendering?

THEORETICAL PERSPECTIVE

This study is informed by a feminist, social constructionist perspective that resists biological determinism and attends to the symbolic and material conditions of living in a heteronormative society. A social constructionist perspective highlights the ways in which individuals are in a continual process of gender construction through the roles they create, modify and maintain in varying contexts (Erickson, 2005). Although we discuss how women embody roles in constructing divisions of labor, we use the term 'role' with a critical perspective. We recognize that an overemphasis on 'roles' may suggest (1) that individuals voluntarily choose systems of behavior untethered by social structures; and (2) that such 'roles' are static enactments of behaviors that remain unchangeable temporally and situationally (Connell, 1987). This is not our position.

In addition to acknowledging that individuals are always engaged in the doing (and undoing) of gender (Butler, 1990; West and Zimmerman, 1987), we take a materialist feminist position that regards gender itself as a social structure that, like the economy, functions to stratify individuals into particular social positions (Risman, 2004). In a heteronormative society, the hierarchical relations ascribed to 'valuable' paid labor and the less valued domestic labor are deeply inscribed around stereotypes of male dominance and female submission. Even when personal perceptions change, basic presumptions about paid and domestic labor do not necessarily disappear. Because such inequalities are not products of nature or biology, but rather complex social and historical constructions, they can indeed be modified and resisted. Such resistance, however, is always enacted within, and therefore limited by, the very rigidity of long-standing societal and historical constructions.

Given that the women in this sample are predominantly well-educated, Caucasian, North American and middle-class (which is consistent with previous research on lesbian mothers), our interpretation represents a limited category of analysis (McCall, 2005). In both the design of the study and the following analysis, we recognize that our sample has specific parameters with regards to race, class and education that situate these women within a particular social position of privilege. In defining our focus of analysis we are constructing that very category of analysis (i.e. well-educated, Caucasian, middle-class lesbian mothers), and in doing so, potentially eclipsing the ways in which these women stretch the bounds of those very categories. Yet, given that one of the aims of this project is to provide an in-depth analysis of a previously understudied group (lesbian mothers), we construct the specific category of analysis (of well-educated, Caucasian, North American lesbian women) in order to fully explore the diversity within the category (Cole, 2009; McCall, 2005). Further, our analysis seeks to unravel some previously held assumptions concerning the supposedly monolithic group of 'lesbian mothers' (e.g. they are 'gender free' or prevailingly egalitarian in their enactments of divisions of labor). In so doing, our analysis views their narratives as contextualized within specific (privileged) class, race and educational social positions while at the same time situated within a marginalized position, given their same-sex minority status.

METHOD

Sixty first-time lesbian parents (30 couples) were interviewed as part of a larger study on lesbian couples' transition to parenthood. Inclusion criteria for the original study were: (1) women must be becoming parents for the first time; and (2) they must be in a committed same-sex relationship. Couples initially participated in interviews during the prenatal period and three months postnatally. They were re-contacted when their children were three years old and asked to participate in a follow-up. Given the lack of research on lesbian mothers of toddler-aged children, we focus here on this third wave of data. Telephone interviews (approximately one hour) were conducted with each partner separately, and were recorded and transcribed. Telephone interviews allowed us to reach a geographically diverse sample and despite not having face-to-face contact, effective rapport was built through researchers staying attuned to the participants' responses and appropriately probing vague or unclear responses (Burke and Miller, 2001). Interviews were transcribed closely verbatim to the participants' speech. We deleted minor 'fillers' (e.g. 'um,' 'ah') once we determined that such fillers were not critical to the meanings of the narratives (e.g. they were not indicative of moments of meaningful hesitation). Ellipses indicate pauses in the narratives. Pseudonyms were used to protect confidentiality. Individual interviews allowed us to elicit each participant's unique construction of her experience (as opposed to a co-constructed narrative with her partner).

The sample resided in the USA and had all had children by means of one mother giving birth to a child (i.e. she conceived via alternative insemination). Biological and nonbiological mothers' average age was 38 and 41 years old, respectively. Most women (94%) identified as White. Regarding the legal status of the families, in 78% of the sample, both parents were the legal (adoptive) parents, whereas in 22% of families, the biological mother was the sole legal parent (i.e. the nonbiological mother had not obtained a second parent adoption, typically because it was not legal in the couple's state). The sample was well-educated. Among biological mothers, four (13%) had a high school diploma, one (3%) had an associate's degree (typically a two-year degree after high school received prior to a bachelor's degree), four (13%) had a bachelor's degree, 16 (53%) had a master's degree, and five (17%) had a PhD/MD/JD (doctorate in law). Among nonbiological mothers, one (3%) had a high school diploma, three (10%) had an associate's degree, seven (23%) had a bachelor's degree, 10 (33%) had a master's degree, and nine (30%) had a PHD/JD/MD. The sample was financially secure, with a mean family income of $90,000. Biological mothers' mean income was $41,093 (SD ¼ 44,217; range $0–170,000) and nonbiological mothers' mean income was $78,721 (SD ¼ 113,321; range $12,000–$650,000).

The qualitative portion of this article focuses on data from the following open-ended questions:

1. Do you think that you and your partner approach parenting any differently than heterosexual parents? How?

2. What are the most difficult challenges you face in attempting to maintain a balance between work and family life?

3. Do you feel you've given up certain opportunities at work for your family? What about sacrificing time with family for work? If so, how?

4. (If division of domestic labor is unequal): Why do you do more/why does your partner do more housework/childcare? How do you explain this?

5. Is the division of domestic labor a topic of discussion or conflict between you and your partner? If so, how?

We utilized a qualitatively driven mixed-methods analysis of the data (Mason, 2006). In line with other feminist researchers utilizing a non-positivistic mode of mixed-methods analysis (Goldberg and Perry-Jenkins, 2007; Oswald and Suter, 2004), we present descriptive quantitative data in conjunction with the qualitative data to more fully illustrate the multidimensionality of human experience. Both modes of analysis are understood as capturing different facets of women's perceptions and providing a more thorough understanding of women's constructions of divisions of labor. A constructionist version of grounded theory (Charmaz, 2006) analysis was applied to the qualitative data. Framed by our feminist perspective, our analysis explores the various meaning-making processes that women invoke to represent their experiences, paying particular attention to unintentional and intentional gendered interpretations of their behavior. Although emphasis is given to the emergence of themes, we understand all such articulations and their theoretical implications as resulting from the researchers' constructed interpretations of the participants' discourse (Charmaz, 2006). Furthermore, our analysis is in accord with Charmaz's (2006) critique of the positivistic roots of grounded theory as a method of analysis that works to 'discover' reality. In this way, our study emphasizes how women discursively construct their lives, and how their narratives are linked to the material conditions within which they negotiate divisions of labor.

Applying grounded theory, we focused on patterns within the data, highlighting similarities and differences that emerged throughout the coding process (Charmaz, 2006). After applying line-by-line coding to the transcripts, Jordan Downing began to broadly categorize initial themes. This led to further differentiation of codes and refinement of categories. Abbie Goldberg reviewed the emerging coding scheme against the data at various points during the coding process. After numerous revisions to the initial coding scheme, transcripts were re-read and organized within the final schematic framework. In the presentation of our analysis, we differentiate between biological and nonbiological mothers. We also identify the number of individuals and couples within each category in order to illuminate levels of within couple agreement.

Several quantitative measures of the division of labor were administered to assess mean differences between biological and nonbiological mothers:

- Household tasks: Who does what? (Atkinson and Huston, 1984): Women were asked to rate their proportional involvement in 15 household tasks using a five-point scale, where 1 ¼ 'usually or always my partner' (0%–20% contribution), 3 ¼ 'shared about equally', and 5 ¼ 'usually or always myself' (80%–100% contribution). This scale is comprised of two subscales: 'feminine' tasks (eight items, including cooking and cleaning) and 'masculine' tasks (six items, including taking out the garbage and outdoor work). 'Feminine' tasks are those chores that women typically want more help with and are considered to be more repetitive and time consuming; 'masculine' tasks tend to be performed more quickly and less routinely (Dempsey, 1997).

- *Division of childcare chores* (Deutsch, 1999): Women reported on their contribution to 28 childcare tasks, including planning the child's activities, playing with the child and feeding the child. Women rated their proportional involvement in each task using the same scale as above.

- *Perceptions of satisfaction*: Two single-item questions were used to assess women's satisfaction with the division of unpaid labor: 'How satisfied are you with the division of household tasks? How satisfied are you with the division of childcare tasks?' Women rated their satisfaction using a five-point scale where 1 = very dissatisfied, 2 = somewhat dissatisfied, 3 = neither satisfied nor dissatisfied, 4 = somewhat satisfied, and 5 = very satisfied.

ANALYSIS

Table S9.1 presents means and standard deviations for women's childcare involvement, household task involvement, hours worked in paid labor and perceived satisfaction with unpaid labor. Paired t-tests revealed that biological mothers perceived themselves as performing more childcare than their partners perceived themselves as doing, $t(29) = 3.90$, $p < .001$, as well as more traditionally defined feminine tasks, $t(29) = 2.53$, $p < .05$. Nonbiological mothers worked more hours in paid employment, $t(29) = -4.71$, $p < .001$. No significant differences were found between biological and nonbiological mothers in their satisfaction with the division of housework and childcare; mean satisfaction levels for both groups of women were somewhat below 'somewhat satisfied'.

The quantitative data would seem to confirm stereotypical gender presumptions about the significance of biological mothering, but it does not shed light on the nuances of participants' experiences. Further, the fact that women in this study reported being relatively satisfied with divisions of domestic labor that were not always equal, as indicated by the quantitative data, is discrepant with what might be expected given research suggesting that lesbian couples strongly value equally shared parenting (Kurdek, 2007). The qualitative phase of this project aims to try to make sense of such discrepancies and explore a diversity of perspectives on the division of paid and domestic labor.

We first discuss those couples that reportedly divided paid labor equally, followed by those couples who divided paid labor unequally. Within each category of paid labor, we analyze how individuals (within couples) discursively constructed the division of domestic labor. The last two sections traverse all categories of labor divisions, focusing on women who presented discrepant perspectives with their partners, and those women who perceived themselves as challenging heteronormative stereotypes of work/family arrangements. We highlight how women's constructions of their work/family arrangements are explicitly or implicitly gendered in ways that embody or resist traditional gender categories.

PAID LABOR EQUALLY DIVIDED

Eight of the 30 couples divided paid labor relatively equally. Six of these couples consisted of partners who both worked over 40 hours a week, and two couples divided paid labor by having each partner work between 24 and 32 hours a week. The six couples who worked 40 hours a week or more tended to have strong work commitments, and they primarily worked high-skilled, professional jobs such as directors of programs and professors, whereas the two couples in which both women worked part-time had somewhat lower status jobs, such as social worker and sports trainer. Of the eight couples who divided paid work relatively equally, women acknowledged having to give up family time rather than time in paid employment, which sometimes caused stress. One biological mother, Lori, a journalist, was planning on quitting her job to stay home full-time:

> [It's] not that I have these delusions of grandeur that when I do quit, I'll have all the time in the world, because I know I won't. But I do think that between work

Table S9.1. Descriptive data for biological and nonbiological mothers (N=60)

	Biological mothers (n = 30)	Nonbiological mothers (n = 30)	
	M (SD)	M (SD)	t-test
Childcare chores	3.43 (58)	2.76 (.44)	3.90***
Household tasks	3.33 (.59)	2.95 (.58)	−1.80
Masculine tasks	3.19 (.98)	3.26 (1.05)	−.20
Feminine tasks	3.44 (.75)	2.80 (.76)	2.53*
Hours/week in paid work	22.84 (16.17)	45.16 (12.42)	−4.71***
Satisfaction – household tasks	3.37 (1.21)	3.89 (1.19)	−1.73
Satisfaction – childcare tasks	3.82 (1.06)	3.71 (1.18)	.33

$*= p < .05. ** = p < .01. *** = p < .00.$

and family time, it's hard to find enough time to do everything I want to do and find time for myself.

Such efforts to create less equal roles contrast with previous research indicating that lesbian women prefer equality within the domestic realm (e.g. Patterson, 1995). Not all women expressed this tension around not having enough time with family. Despite working full-time, four women discussed having to give up opportunities in paid work that they otherwise would have pursued if they did not have family commitments. Yet, women generally accepted these choices as worthwhile contributions to their family lives. As one biological mother, Patricia, stated:

> There are definitely choices that I make [at work] that I could be doing more and I know I don't do it. I consciously don't do some things that I know would help me to move along a little more quickly or maybe a little bit more…substantially. And I chose not to so we can spend time together.

Only one nonbiological mother expressed concern over being passed up for promotions as a result of family demands. However, she reported that she felt little regret about her decision to prioritize family.

Women's accounts indicate that equally divided paid labor did not necessarily determine equally divided domestic labor. Within reportedly equal paid labor arrangements, a few women (one biological mother, one couple) described creating unequal divisions of domestic labor. They described different attributions for the source of this inequality, discussing it as a function of hours in paid work or as a 'natural' result of 'personality' differences, thereby viewing this inequality as nevertheless equitable. Robyn, a nonbiological mother, believed that her partner 'sees' the dirt more readily, and she contended that their roles had developed from such personality differences:

> I think, having been married to a man before, it's really personality type. I don't think it's as much gender as it is personality. If you look at Maria and my relationship, if you saw us today, you would automatically assume Maria was more masculine and I was more feminine. But if you look at our sensitivities and our way of relating to the world, I'm more masculine and she's more feminine. So, we say, I'm the 'daddy' because I'm the one…that's how I am.…It's just kind of how it works. I'm more of the rough-housin', you know, more likely to say: 'Hey, pick that up.' Just what you might see a stereotypical thing in terms of parenting. In terms of housework, Maria…I don't know, she does most of it—she does all of the outside stuff. I don't do any of the outside stuff. You would think maybe a male would mow the lawn and I'd be more likely to do the deep cleaning types of stuff.

Robyn draws on gender stereotypes about what constitutes masculine and feminine roles. However, her narrative indicates a tension in accepting gendered interpretations of their lives at the same time that she articulates a resistance to a gendered lens that fails to capture the multidimensionality of their relationship, individual personalities and divisions of labor. In challenging the adequacy of traditional notions of masculinity and femininity to define their roles, Robyn also suggests that differences in 'sensitivities' may remain hidden under the more overt behavioral activities that carry gendered meanings. In this way, she may be 'doing gender' (West and Zimmerman,

1987) in ways that may mis-signify her more ingrained sense of self, which she views as 'more masculine' than what others might superficially perceive.

These women's narratives demonstrate that equality of paid work did not always interpellate into egalitarian divisions of domestic labor. Some women discussed how they desired greater equality, while others were striving for less equality. Further, some refuted the societal expectation that women must relinquish time spent in paid work in order to fulfill their parental duties. Others more thoroughly described a tension between paid work and family, involving themselves in activities more closely associated with stereotypical notions of the motherhood ideal.

PAID LABOR UNEQUALLY DIVIDED

Almost half of the sample (14 couples; 28 women) reportedly divided paid labor by having one partner work full-time and the other work part-time. In all but two of these couples, the biological mother was the one to cut back on paid work. Women described a variety of ways that they rationalized, accepted or resisted the obvious structural inequality. Unlike the couples that had relatively equal divisions of paid labor, solid patterns were evident, differentiating biological from nonbiological mothers. However, in only a few cases did women discuss how biology may have influenced their divisions of labor.

Women reported that in balancing paid work and family they either: (1) primarily relinquished involvement in paid labor; (2) primarily relinquished family time; or (3) relinquished both family and paid work. The first group, four biological mothers (all working part-time), discussed primarily giving up opportunities in paid work, although they did not describe these relinquishments as stressful. One biological mother perceived little stress around not investing time in her job because she was only 'temporarily' putting her job on hold. Another biological mother, Jeanne, who was employed as a part-time receptionist, stated: 'I really enjoy staying home with the kids, and I think that is really what I'm supposed to be doing.' Jeanne and three other biological mothers, who described decreasing their involvement in paid work and 'prioritizing' family time, indicated that embodying the traditional role of mother was not problematic despite inequalities in divisions of labor. Alternatively, two non-biological mothers described primarily giving up a certain level of family involvement because of full-time jobs, thereby 'missing out' on family time. However, they did not describe feeling like their jobs overly encroached on their work/family balance as to cause personal or relational conflict. Lastly, three women (all biological mothers) discussed having to give up both time spent in paid work as well as time with their family. All three women worked part-time and described tensions between paid work and family involvement.

Of the 14 couples who divided paid labor by having one partner work full-time while the other partner worked part-time, only nine women (four biological, five non-biological; three couples) stated that they were able to achieve equal divisions of domestic labor. One nonbiological mother described creating equal divisions by having one partner take the 'morning shift' with the children while the other took the 'evening shift.' For these couples, unequal involvement in paid labor was not perceived as threatening equality within the domestic realm. As Deborah explained, she and her partner drew on their 'strengths,' such that 'this is my responsibility and that's her responsibility.' These women may have perceived themselves as having differentiated roles in terms of the kinds of tasks they did, but they contended that the amount of work they did was equal. Thus, they viewed their roles as unequal, but nevertheless equitable – a common argument made by both heterosexual couples who may emphasize equitability over inequality (Nentwich, 2008) and gay and lesbian couples who are invested in representing their lives as egalitarian even if this is not always the case (Carrington, 1999).

Many of these women (10 biological, 10 nonbiological; nine couples) discussed having unequal divisions of domestic labor. Some of these women (six biological, six nonbiological; four couples) viewed their differences in paid work as causing unequal divisions of domestic labor. As Brooke, a nonbiological mother, stated: 'Samantha has been doing much more because she's home, and that's kind of the deal that we got right now. She has been the one who's expected to do the housework.' A few women also stated that personality differences, in conjunction with different amounts of involvement in paid work, led to unequal divisions of domestic labor. As Erin, a biological mother, stated: '[It's] more me taking care of things partially because I'm at home and partially because Sarah hates household stuff.' Narratives such as this suggest a conceptual separation between personality and the social construction of gender. That is, women discussed 'personality' differences as driving differences in division of labor. They did not view these daily enactments of differences as symbolically gendered (or gendering) behaviors. Only three women drew on biological explanations for understanding inequalities within the domestic realm. Nina stated:

> I kind of got the last say on things, and that's indicative of our relationship with [child], but I think that gets amplified by the fact that I'm the birth mom and that I've put probably quite a bit more time [in] than Joanne, and so I have a higher level of comfort in decision making about how to raise children, and kind of insider intuition about how it should be.

As a result of her biological 'connection', Nina perceived herself as having more decision-making power in the family.

Some women (one biological, three nonbiological; one couple) also discussed one mother—always the biological mother—as the 'primary caregiver' in explaining their unequal divisions of paid and unpaid labor. They thereby described an implicitly gendered understanding of their work/family roles. One nonbiological mother, Kari, stated:

> I've had to take a couple of sick days to take care of him when Rosanne was gone or something, but that's it. It hasn't been a problem. But I'm not the primary in-home caregiver and so when issues come up, I'm not the one who gets called out of work to go home, and so it hasn't been a problem.

Despite research indicating that lesbian women are invested in embodying an 'egalitarian ethic' (Patterson, 1995), such perceptions of primary parenthood suggest that they may also intentionally create inequalities (without necessarily challenging an investment in egalitarianism). These women may construct primary parenthood as a temporary role, which the biological mother takes on only in the beginning stages of raising their child. For example, Gertrude, a biological mother stated: '[My child]'s and my relationship was primary during that [early] period, and breast-feeding was both cause and symbol of that.' Significantly, none of the women explicitly viewed primary parenthood as linked to their status as biological mothers.

In eight couples (16 women) one partner worked in paid employment full-time while the other partner was not employed. In all eight couples, the non-employed parent was the biological mother. These couples most directly confront the hetero-normative stereotype of the traditional (male) breadwinner who leaves all the domestic chores to the domestic (female) housewife. Despite the social pressures of these ste-reotypes and the tendency for parental roles to develop along biological lines, these women mostly discussed divisions of labor without mentioning biological status. Instead, women often talked about inequalities as developing out of 'natural' person-ality differences or out of different levels of investment in, or time allotted to, paid labor.

Within this group, biological mothers generally described feeling positively about taking on more of the childcare and not being employed. They embraced their roles as primary caretakers, and they did not describe their unequal divisions in paid labor as particularly stressful or non-egalitarian. Nonbiological mothers expressed greater tension around work/family balance. As one woman, Ann, stated: 'My biggest problem is that I love both responsibilities, so sometimes it's hard to be away from one or the other. I love what I do at work, but it makes me sad to leave my kids in the morning. And then it makes me sad to leave my job at night because I love what I do.' Although four nonbiological mothers described their jobs as encroaching on family time, they did not typically experience this as stressful. Despite working full-time, three nonbiological mothers described their perception that they nevertheless had to primarily give up involvement in paid work as a result of parenting demands. For these women, work provided a respite from the stressful demands of parenting.

Within this context of unequal divisions of paid labor, nine women (six bio-logical, three nonbiological; three couples) described unequal divisions of domestic labor. These women similarly discussed the division of domestic labor as resulting from 'personality' differences, time spent at home, and gender differences. Women's interpretations of divisions of labor at times confronted the traditional roles that they might otherwise represent given these structural inequalities of paid labor differences. Delores, a non-employed biological mother, compared her experience with her partner to her marriage with her ex-husband: 'My wife seems to help me out a lot more than my first husband helped; she spends more time with the kids.' By turning to the par-ticularities of her personal history, she implicitly suggested that she may receive more help now precisely because she has a female partner. Delores further described: 'our friends tease us and say we are like the most heterosexual couple in the world. We live the typical straight life style. She's like the guy that goes to work and makes money, and I take care of the kids. People don't even look at us like we're gay.' Her partner, Faye, shared a similar perspective: 'she's definitely the mom, I'm kinda the dad. It's not a bad thing, it's just what it is.' For this couple, their differentiated roles were perceived as non-problematic, and they both expressed their comfort with embodying traditional gendered behaviors. Further, even though they are in a same-sex relation-ship, their enactment of gender norms within this context effectively extracted them, on a symbolic level, from their sexual minority status.

DISCREPANT PERSPECTIVES BETWEEN PARTNERS

Although there was generally high within-couple agreement amongst all women's descriptions of divisions of labor, six couples held discrepant perspectives. In all but one of these couples, the biological mothers described unequal divisions of domestic labor while the nonbiological mothers described relative equality. The biological mothers often emphasized either their satisfaction with being primary caregivers or the inevitabilities of doing more domestic work given that they spent less time in paid work. Women reported that these divergent perspectives did not usually cause relational conflict. Such satisfaction with unequal roles suggests that for some women the solidity of the relationship or healthy functioning of the family was not dependent on congruent perspectives. Perhaps similarly perceiving equal divisions of labor was less salient for these women than feeling that their individual needs and desires in the family and paid work domains were being met.

RESISTING HETERONORMATIVE STEREOTYPES

In all work/family arrangements, many women described resisting heteronormative stereotypes of the traditional family. Many women, particularly women with unequal divisions of paid labor, resisted an interpretation of their divisions of labor as being defined as either 'feminine' or 'masculine.' Fourteen women described altering heteronormative expectations for how they enacted divisions of labor, thus challenging the notion that inequalities in paid labor necessarily lead to inequalities in domestic labor. Some women (three biological, three nonbiological, no couples) described attempts to create equality despite unequal divisions of labor, explicitly constructing their relationships as not replicating traditional gender roles. As Joanne, a nonbiological mother, stated:

> I mow the lawn not because I'm butch necessarily, but because I like mowing the lawn, or not because I'm trying to be the man as much as, I like mowing the lawn. [These roles] get redefined for me....I try and have language to be able to share with other people, but I'm much more traditional dad about work and all that stuff than most people would think of a woman being, but what I've also realized is, I totally get to redefine what that feels like...it doesn't have to have all these other assumptions about not being home or not being engaged, or not being an active parent...it sort of triggers what are the assumptions and stereotypes about what it means as a parent to be a dad.

Joanne highlights the difficulty in giving meaning through language to her experience—one that she constructs as stretching the very bounds of how society conceptualizes parental roles and the gendered meanings attached to those roles.

Some women (six biological, three nonbiological, one couple) also described being less constrained by normative notions of family and gender norms than heterosexual couples. One biological mother, Nancy, stated:

> I think that we have more fluidity in our roles and there is no obvious role that each of us is supposed to take on or resist. So that gives us some freedom. I mean

I've seen the upside [positive aspect] of [having that kind of freedom]. When they were tiny, I really wished that we had this, like, male–female difference in career expectations, career advancement, money.

Nancy points to how she and her partner were able to construct roles that were not confined by masculine/feminine divisions of labor. Yet, this perceived 'fluidity' had caused tension because there was no easy solution for how to split up tasks in the absence of prescribed roles. Another biological mother, Nicole, had experienced distress over how much time her job required of her, leaving her to do less of the childcare. However, she emphasized how being in a same-sex relationship had allowed her a level of egalitarianism that she believed she would not have if she was in a heterosexual relationship. When asked about balancing her job with family, she explained: 'It's very hard. I don't think I could do it if I were married to a man. I think it makes a huge difference that I'm married to a woman.'

Consistent with some researchers' depictions of lesbians as challenging the traditional heteronormative family form (Dunne, 2000), almost half of the women constructed their work/family arrangements as challenging heteronormative masculine/feminine assumptions about family practices. When looking at biological and nonbiological mothers, our analysis suggests a tension, not typically discussed by participants, between the reported material inequalities of their divisions of labor (in ways that often mirror the heteronormative divisions of labor) and their personal constructions of these divisions. Such constructions expand the meanings attached to these inequalities. Thus, their narratives may be very similar to contemporary heterosexual parents who find them selves establishing unequal divisions of labor within the traditional gender divide, but who continually assert their contention that each partner is equally involved in parenting (Nentwich, 2008).

DISCUSSION

Interpreting women's perceptions of their divisions of labor within a structural framework of how they divided paid labor instantiates the theoretical and practical goal of examining subjective constructions of lived experiences as inherently imbedded within larger structural stratifications. The women's narratives in this sample suggest that they may construct symbolically gendered (and unequal) divisions of labor while challenging the salience of gendered interpretations of their roles. Thus, some of the women's narratives indicated daily activities in the work and family realm that carry gendered meanings, but were resisted at the level of identity (i.e. 'I may engage in more typical male behavior such as paid labor involvement, but I do not identify with the stereotyped male/father role') (Kroska, 1997).

For those couples who reportedly had equal divisions of paid labor, there was significant discussion of how their roles were egalitarian, suggesting the importance of perceptions of egalitarianism. Yet, women nevertheless discussed experiencing varying degrees of tension when both mothers worked in full-time or part-time employment. Thus, equality in paid labor did not necessarily lead to entirely satisfying roles, as different women were more or less desiring or striving for (even minor) shifts in labor arrangements. Further, women were constructing their work/ family arrangements within the context of prevailing heteronormative discourses and norms concerning divisions of labor and the salience of egalitarian parenting (Deutsch, 1999). As a result of such tensions, some of the women who had what could be considered an egalitarian division of labor were actually trying to establish less equal roles given one partner's greater desire to be the primary caregiver. Their narratives suggest that the 'egalitarian ethic' of lesbian women is an over simplification of the kinds of choices lesbian women actually reportedly enact. The women in this study challenge any singular interpretation of their roles and identities as essentially egalitarian. At the same time, they stretch the confines of the traditional (heterosexual) nuclear family. Even in the context of unequal divisions of labor, lesbian mothers reshape meanings tied to 'mothering' and 'fathering' (Dunne, 2000), and in so doing deconstruct any singular relationship between biological sex and gender enactments (Butler, 1990). Inequalities in labor arrangements within lesbian mother-headed families exist outside of male/female divisions, despite the reality that they must still contend with normative discourses concerning egalitarian parenting (Risman and Johnson-Sumerford, 1998). Thus, lesbian mothers can view inequalities in their relationships as nevertheless more egalitarian than inequalities in heterosexual relationships—where symbolic and material power (of paid labor) is more directly associated with systemic male privilege (Goldberg, 2009).

Equal divisions of paid and unpaid labor were not always constructed as satisfying arrangements. This does not mean that the women who divided labor relatively equally did not value egalitarianism. Rather, it may be that these women's discourses point to the complexities and struggles that are required in trying to create equal work/family arrangements. 'Equality' may not always feel so equal or fair if each partner has differing levels of personal investment in paid work or family life (Erickson, 2005).

Significantly, 22 of 30 couples reported unequal divisions of paid labor. Although greater education may account for the equal divisions of labor that some women discussed (e.g. Davis and Greenstein, 2004), women in this sample demonstrate more complex interpretations than can be explained by education levels alone. Most women who had cut back in paid work described little stress around this choice and few fears of long-term job consequences. Women, and typically biological mothers, were less concerned with supposed 'inequalities' of unequal divisions of labor, as they tended to more thoroughly embody traditional notions of intensive mothering (Nentwich, 2008). Women often described more concern over meeting the needs of each partner with regards to work/family roles, rather than arbitrarily creating equal divisions of labor. In this way, discourses of individualism (e.g. 'I prefer staying home given my personality') at times trumped discourses of equality. Many women did not thereby equate equality of labor with equality of needs. Thus, women may be invested in a perception of egalitarianism despite inequalities (Carrington, 1999). Unequal divisions of paid labor have often not been studied given the prevailing emphasis on divisions of domestic labor in lesbian mother families (Goldberg and Perry-Jenkins, 2007; Patterson, 1995).

Despite patterns delineating biological and nonbiological mothers in terms of how they constructed giving up time in paid work or family, their discourses also resist a dualistic interpretation of essential differences between biological and nonbiological mothers. Women rarely reported that they perceived their greater time spent performing domestic labor as related to their biological status. Biological mothers often embodied traditional notions of intensive mothering, a similar finding by other researchers concerning the greater involvement of biological mothers in childcare (e.g. Gabb, 2004; Patterson, 1995), indicated by their greater reported involvement in family life. Yet, they also challenged understandings of their roles as assimilating to heteronormative expectations of behavior (Weston, 1991). Thus, although biological connections appear to be salient in regulating divisions of labor, these women were often involved in processes that both reiterated traditional roles and subverted them.

Although some lesbian women described challenging heteronormative assumptions, their reportedly unequal divisions of labor suggest a more complex story. The discourse of egalitarianism (e.g. Dalton and Bielby, 2000; Ussher and Perz, 2008) often remained salient despite structural inequalities. Yet, in the realm of discursive constructions of practiced behaviors, the biological mothers described taking on more domestic labor and cutting back paid work. Thus, they may 'buy into' the assumed salience of biological motherhood, without overtly or consciously perceiving their roles as predicated on biology. Biology remained a 'silent marker' of difference that most women did not discuss as influencing their work/family arrangements. This remained the case even when biological mothers described less equality than their partners in the division of domestic labor. The silence of biology may also speak to the fact that these women were all mothers of toddlers and were no longer breastfeeding. Given most women's apparent desire to perceive themselves as equally invested in parenting, and the absence of a distinct behavior related to biology (i.e. breastfeeding), the importance of biology may have seemed irrelevant in understanding their current roles—even if breastfeeding may have initially led to a sequence of employment/family choices that increasingly set in motion unequal divisions of labor (Goldberg and Perry-Jenkins, 2007).

Women may not have mentioned biology as an important factor influencing divisions of labor precisely because they were invested in constructing their equal statuses as 'mothers' regardless of biological connection. Thus, in constructing their work/family arrangements, lesbian mothers may discursively resist the notion that biology is a salient aspect to their identities or mothering practices. Women may desire fitting into normative notions of egalitarian parenting whereby biology 'should not' differentiate parental roles. However, biological relatedness (particularly after termination of breastfeeding) may indeed have little personal significance to how lesbian mothers construct their personal and familial identities. Importantly, lesbian adoptive mothers may most fully succeed in the practice of egalitarian parenting precisely because there is no biological relationship between the child and either mother (Ciano-Boyce and Shelley-Sireci, 2002).

Even when couples described equal divisions of labor, some women's discussion of one mother as the 'primary parent' indicates that women could embrace both the notion of equality and primacy in parenthood. Despite differences in levels of 'primacy,' some couples interpreted various material inequalities as nevertheless symbolically egalitarian, thereby resisting readings of their work/family arrangements as either egalitarian or non-egalitarian. Their narratives contend that their divisions of labor do not necessarily fit within the gendered binary of the masculine breadwinner and the feminine housewife. Rather, gender is a contested terrain that many lesbian mothers challenged as an adequate interpretive lens for understanding the meanings and significance of their work/family roles. Some lesbian mothers were in the process of undoing gender at a subjective level at the same time that they were doing gender through reportedly enacting persistently unequal roles. While paid and unpaid labor continue to carry gendered meanings at a societal level, at a personal level these connotations may be constructed as irrelevant to lesbian mothers in their daily lives.

Thus, our analysis of both the quantitative and qualitative data indicates a dual process of enacting and subverting gender norms. The quantitative data suggest that biology may remain a significant factor in delineating divisions of labor; yet, the qualitative data elucidate women's diverse constructions of divisions of labor that extend far beyond biological determinism. This overlay of both analyses demonstrates the significance of biology, but challenges a reified dichotomy of biological and nonbiological parenting. Indeed, women's narratives demonstrate a range of interpretations for how they create divisions of labor. As they contend with the dominant discourses around egalitarianism/equality and masculinity/femininity in constructing divisions of labor, they may at times nevertheless find themselves engaging in traditionally masculine and feminine roles. Our analysis suggests a variety of constructions in how women rationalized, accepted, or refuted normative gendering, as they personally defined the importance of equality and egalitarianism to their individual lives, relationships and families.

This study extends previous research by providing an in-depth analysis of middle-class Caucasian North American lesbian mothers' perceptions of divisions of paid and unpaid labor. The women in this study contest narrowly defined understandings of how living and mothering in a same-sex relationship may or may not challenge normative gender ideologies. Their narratives suggest that lesbian mothers are continually involved in the doing and undoing of gender through their material enactments of the divisions of labor as well as through their symbolic interpretations of such divisions. This study demonstrates that the 'egalitarian ethic' is an over-simplification of the kinds of divisions of labor that lesbian women construct; biological kinship relations did not strictly determine lesbian women's interpretations of work/family roles; and lesbian women may both challenge and enact heteronormative constructions of the division of labor across a variety of paid and unpaid labor arrangements.

REFERENCES

Atkinson J and Huston TL (1984) Sex role orientation and division of labor early in marriage. *Journal of Personality and Social Psychology* 46(2): 330–345.

Bos HMW, van Balen F and van den Boom DC (2007) Child adjustment and parenting in planned lesbian-parent families. *American Journal of Orthopsychiatry* 77(1): 38–48.

Burke LA and Miller MK (2001) Phone interviewing as a means of data collection: Lessons learned and practical recommendations. *Forum: Qualitative Social Research* 2(2). Available at: nbn-resolving.de/urn:nbn:de:0114-fqs010271.

Butler J (1990) *Gender Trouble: Feminism and the Subversion of Identity.* New York: Routledge.

Carrington C (1999) *No Place Like Home: Relationships and Family Life Among Lesbians and Gay Men.* Chicago: University of Chicago Press.

Ciano-Boyce C and Shelley-Sireci L (2002) Who is mommy tonight? Lesbian parenting issues. *Journal of Homosexuality* 43(2): 1–13.

Cole ER (2009) Intersectionality and research in psychology. *American Psychologist* 64(3): 170–180.

Connell RW (1987) *Gender and Power.* Stanford, CA: Stanford University Press.

Chan RW, Brooks R, Patterson C and Raboy B (1998) Division of labor among lesbian and heterosexual parents: Associations with children's adjustment. *Journal of Family Psychology* 12(3): 402–419.

Charmaz K (2006) *Constructing Grounded Theory: A Practical Guide through Qualitative Analysis.* London: Sage.

Dalton SE and Bielby DD (2000) 'That's our kind of constellation': Lesbian mothers negotiate institutionalized understandings of gender within the family. *Gender and Society* 14(1): 36–61.

Davis S and Greenstein TN (2004) Cross-national variations in the division of household labor. *Journal of Marriage and Family* 66(5): 1260–1271.

Dempsey K (1997) Trying to get husbands to do more work at home. *Journal of Sociology* 33(2): 216–225.

Deutsch FM (1999) *Halving it All: How Equally Shared Parenting Works.* Cambridge, MA: Harvard University Press.

Dunne GA (2000) Opting into motherhood: Lesbians blurring the boundaries and transforming the meaning of parenthood and kinship. *Gender and Society* 14(1): 11–35.

Erickson R (2005) Why emotion work matters: Sex, gender and the division of household labor. *Journal of Marriage and Family* 67(2): 337–351.

Gabb J (2004) Critical differentials: Querying the incongruities within research on lesbian parent families. *Sexualities* 7(2): 167–182.

Gabb J (2005) Lesbian motherhood: Strategies of familial linguistic management in lesbian parent families. *Sociology* 39(4): 585–603.

Goldberg AE (2009) Lesbian parents and their families: Complexity and intersectionality from a feminist perspective. In: Lloyd S, Few A and Allen K (eds) *The Handbook of Feminist Family Studies.* Thousand Oaks, CA: Sage, 108–120.

Goldberg AE and Perry-Jenkins M (2007) The division of labor and perceptions of parental roles: Lesbian couples across the transition to parenthood. *Journal of Social and Personal Relationships* 24(2): 297–318.

Kroska A (1997) The division of labor in the home: A review and reconceptualization. *Social Psychology Quarterly* 60(4): 304–322.

Kurdek LA (2007) The allocation of household labor in partners in gay and lesbian couples. *Journal of Family Issues* 28(1): 132–148.

Mason J (2006) Mixing methods in a qualitatively driven way. *Qualitative Research* 6(1): 9–25.

Maume DJ (2006) Gender differences in restricting work efforts because of family responsibilities. *Journal of Marriage and Family* 68(4): 859–869.

McCall L (2005) The complexity of intersectionality. *Signs* 30(3): 1771–1800.

Nentwich JC (2008) New fathers and mothers as gender troublemakers? Exploring discursive constructions of heterosexual parenthood and their subversive potential. *Feminism and Psychology* 18(2): 207–230.

Oerton S (1997) 'Queer housewives?': Some problems in theorizing the division of domestic labour in lesbian and gay households. *Women's Studies International Forum* 20(3): 421–430.

Oswald RF and Suter EA (2004) Heterosexist inclusion and exclusion during ritual: A 'straight versus gay' comparison. *Journal of Family Issues* 25(7): 881–899.

Patterson CJ (1995) Families of the lesbian baby boom: Parents' division of labor and children's adjustment. *Developmental Psychology* 31(1): 115–123.

Patterson CJ, Sutfin EL and Fulcher M (2004) Division of labor among lesbian and heterosexual couples: Correlates of specialized versus shared patterns. *Journal of Adult Development* 11(3): 179–189.

Risman BJ (2004) Gender as a social structure: Theory wrestling with activism. *Gender and Society* 18(4): 429–450.

Risman BJ and Johnson-Sumerford D (1998) Doing it fairly: A study of postgender marriages. *Journal of Marriage and the Family* 60: 23–40.

Short L (2007) Lesbian mothers living well in the context of heterosexism and discrimination: Resources, strategies and legislative change. *Feminism and Psychology* 17(1): 57–74.

Sullivan M (1996) Rozzie and Harriet? Gender and family patterns of lesbian coparents. *Gender and Society* 10(6): 747–767.

Sullivan M (2004) *The Family of Woman: Lesbian Mothers, their Children, and the Undoing of Gender*. Berkeley, CA: University of California Press.

Ussher JM and Perz J (2008) Empathy, egalitarianism and emotion work in the relational negotiation of PMS: The experience of lesbian couples. *Feminism and Psychology* 18(1): 87–111.

West C and Zimmerman D (1987) Doing gender. *Gender and Society* 1(2): 125–151. Weston K (1991) *Families We Choose*. New York: Columbia University Press.

10

BIOSOCIAL THEORY

Ross and Roberta, both single parents in their early thirties, live across the hall from each other, and their children attend the same school. One day they were sitting with some other single parents as they watched their children play a soccer match. They started talking about how difficult it is to find a person to marry in today's society. After all, here are four adults who are attractive, funny, intelligent, and who could date all they wanted if they had the time. The problem seems to be that none of them can find long-term relationships that are satisfying and can lead to eventual remarriage and perhaps more children. Roberta stated that the problem was that men are raised differently than women and that they just don't understand what women want and need in a relationship.

Ross, being a scientist, said that mate selection, as it currently exists, is the result of thousands of years of evolution and the natural selection of traits that will allow the strongest of each species, in this case humans, to survive. Thus, for men to attempt to survive, it is better to have multiple mates to increase their chances of reproducing. For women, however, because they have to invest more time and energy in reproductive activities simply because they are the ones who give birth, it is imperative for them to choose mates wisely on the basis of who will provide the most resources. From this, Ross concluded that women have a greater need to select a good mate and marry than do men, which is why women are desperate to marry and men are desperate to avoid commitment and prefer to reproduce with multiple women. And men certainly **do not** want to waste their time and resources on other men's children! Roberta replied:

> I don't buy that genetic predisposition, evolutionary argument! What really matters is how a man and a woman feel about each other. If men would simply wake up and smell the java, they would realize what a great person I am and fall madly in love with me. I mean, really, what's not to love about me? Or any of us, for that matter? And how could they not love my child once they spent some time with him? The real problem is we just don't understand each other, we just don't appropriately value each other.

So, who's right? Is Roberta correct in assuming that society has created the differences between genders that lead to problems in mate selection, or is Ross correct in assuming that the problems that exist today are related to a genetic predisposition for certain male personality characteristics based on years of evolutionary selection and change? These questions and more are addressed in this chapter.

HISTORY

The history of biosocial theory is difficult to discuss with any certainty because there are so many variations. Variations that combine the ideas and beliefs of people from many disciplines are typical of a theory in its formative years, but they are also what make this theory both unique and exciting. Because there are many theories that are similar to biosocial theory—such as evolutionary psychology (Cosmides, Toby, and Barkow 1992), ethology and sociobiology (Thomas 1996), and psychobiology (Cloninger, Svrakic, and Przybeck 1993)—what you read here may not be the same as the treatment of this material in another text.

Although biosocial theory is in its beginning stages, it is based on ideas that have been around for some time. One of the earliest publications concerning evolution was *The Origin of Species* by Charles Darwin (1859). In this book, Darwin suggests that there is a struggle for survival among species, with nature "selecting" those individuals who are best adapted to the environment. This process occurs over generations, and as individuals are changing to fit the environment, the environment is also changing. Until the last several decades, Darwin's ideas were left basically untapped by social scientists in their understanding of human social behavior. In fact, there was a bias against his principles, with many in this field believing that biology and sociology were such opposites that they would never have a place in the same discussion.

Because of this opposition, much of the early work in this area was done in the medical arena, as biologists sought to discover biological causes of individual behaviors, as well as by ethologists who studied animal or human behavior from an evolutionary perspective. Perhaps the first to move the discussion of selection from biological pre-determination to possible influences of the environment was W. D. Hamilton (1964a, 1964b). Hamilton believed in the concept of inclusive fitness, which means not only that the individual changes and adapts over time in order to survive, but also that fitness includes those individuals who surround or are related to the individual. In other words, because we inherit our genetic material, it is in our best interest to support those to whom we are related, because this promises the survival of our own genes as well. This would help to explain such things as parental investment in children. This idea led other social scientists to consider the genetic nature of human relationships as they exist within a social environment.

Perhaps the most influential writing in this area was by Edward Osborne Wilson, who in 1975 published the book *Sociobiology*. In this writing, he posited that evolution was evident in people across time and that genes influence individual behaviors that have evolved in order to ensure survival. Although many in the field did not agree with his ideas, the book generated a great deal of discussion and research concerning the role of genetics in human behavior. Similarly, Hans J. Eysenck (1967; Eysenck and Eysenck 1985) sought to explain the role of genetic predisposition in introversion/

extraversion and stability/neuroticism and used this biological basis to explain how individuals interacted differently based on the social situation. These principles have been expanded upon in recent decades to explain human behavior in many areas, including mate selection, parenting, child development, behavioral and mental disorders, and the mind–body connection in the treatment of medical diseases. It is important to remember that this brief historical review is far from comprehensive but simply seeks to point out that the ideas of Darwin have been used as a basis for understanding modern behavior, although there is still much disagreement in the social sciences as to which is more powerful—nature or nurture.

BASIC ASSUMPTIONS

Because the assumptions of the theory depend on which version or writing you are discussing, it is important to note that these twelve assumptions were taken verbatim from a chapter on biosocial perspective written by Troost and Filsinger (1993).

"Humans have an evolutionary origin." This is based on the ideas of Darwin and the principle of natural selection. As Mayr (1991) states, "Change comes about through the abundant production of genetic variation in every generation. The relatively few individuals who survive, owing to a particularly well-adapted combination of inheritable characteristics, give rise to the next generation" (37).

"The family has played an important role in human evolution." Because survival of the individual is dependent on survival of the family, the existence of families across time has helped individual family members adapt and thus survive. An example of this is that people everywhere across cultures live in families of some sort, raise children, and attempt to make a living or a means to survive. These similarities are seen as a result of our specific evolutionary history (Fox 1989). Consider Ross and Roberta and the other single parents at the soccer game in the vignette at the beginning of the chapter. How has the single-parent family evolved, and what role does it play in human survival?

Some authors have suggested that families have thrived across times because they fit a *niche* within society. A niche is something that fulfills a function and is based on a set of stable activities or patterns of behavior. A niche can be filled by an individual or a unit or even a system. Thus, a mother in a family fulfills a certain niche related to nurturing and caregiving, while the role of a family in a social group might be to socialize children or to repopulate the culture. The roles or needs to be fulfilled by the niche depend on the social environment.

"The evolutionary origin of humans has an influence upon families today." Human behavior today is based upon the genetic and social adaptation of individuals and families since time began. Thus, reactions to current social issues, such as parental investment in children and gendered behavior, all have their basis in evolution. So, does this mean that Ross or Roberta is correct in the opening scenario?

"Proximate biology has an influence on the family, and the family has an influence on proximate biology and the health of its members." The word "proximate" refers to interaction between genetic predisposition and social interactions. This simply means that individuals are predisposed to some diseases or medical conditions, which influence how they interact within the family. Perhaps they are frequently tired

and thus not as active in family activities. In turn, the behaviors of family members influence the health of other family members (e.g., smoking, increased stress, physical abuse, or violence).

"Biosocial influences are both biological and social in character." One cannot discuss the social influences on behavior without also addressing the biological components. Teasing apart these two components is difficult because both are important. It is similar to the conundrum of the chicken and the egg: Which came first?

"The biosocial domain is concerned with three factors: the biological, biosocial, and social." Although most social scientists do not as yet have accurate ways to measure each of these factors, the best model is one that would take each of them into consideration. Problems arise when you try to disentangle one from the other.

"Human biological and biosocial variables do not determine human conduct but pose limitations and constraints as well as possibilities and opportunities for families." It is important to distinguish between biology **driving** human behavior and **influencing** it. The premise of this theory is that genetics sets the stage for certain behaviors but does not necessarily determine how, or even if, they will be exhibited.

"A biosocial approach takes an intermediate position between those who emphasize the similarity between humans and other animals (Wilson 1975) and those who emphasize the differences (Charon 1989; Mead 1964)" Although most who utilize this theory would agree that humans have evolved throughout time, most would also support the notion that we are also a unique species with our own culture and interactions. The reality lies somewhere in the middle.

"Adaptation is assumed to have taken place over a vast period of time. The hundreds to thousands of generations to reach Hardy–Weinberg equilibrium in adaptive evolutionary biology (Birdsell 1981) are vastly different than, for example, human ecology....Conjectures about biological adaptation in the span of one generation or over the course of the twentieth century or the computer age are dubious assertions." The Hardy–Weinberg law is the idea that if a system is at equilibrium, or in balance, the genetic distribution of alternative forms of a gene is also stable. In other words, genetic transitions do not take place until that system is no longer stable. At that point, genes may mutate or change so that some become more dominant than others. This is the basic principle of natural selection. Some mutation takes place to allow for greater fitness or to ensure adaptation that is necessary for survival. Because this process takes a great deal of time, it would be absurd to think we could study this change across just one or two generations; to understand behavior today, you must also understand the behavior of our ancestors.

"Adaptations in physiology or conduct vary by environment." Although we are born with our genetic structure (our *genotype*), the ways in which we express those genetic tendencies (our *phenotype*) will vary across different environments and situations. Furthermore, the interaction between our genotype and our phenotype necessitates a great deal of diversity across individuals, families, and cultures. This means that two different individuals with the same genetic composition, living in entirely different environments, will probably exhibit entirely different behaviors.

"Extant features of human biology can be used to reveal aspects of our adaptation in the past (see Troost 1988a; Turke 1988)." Obviously, we cannot go back in time and examine how people in other eras lived their lives on a day-to-day basis, although we do have a good deal of archaeological evidence that provides us with some

clues as to what their lives must have been like. Despite this inability to witness their experiences for ourselves, this theory posits that we can trace current features to their historical roots for at least a glimpse into why those biological features were adaptive at one point in time.

"Proximate, distal, and ultimate levels of interpretation can be approached separately; ideally they will be integrated." Definitions of proximate, distal, and ultimate levels will be given in the next section. At this point, it is important to note that, although you can focus on one piece of the equation at a time, the most fruitful explanations will come from an analysis of all three levels at once, because it is difficult to determine where one ends and the next one begins. Ross's argument at the beginning of the chapter is based on ultimate causes, whereas Roberta's argument is based on proximate causes. How would taking a distal approach help them?

PRIMARY TERMS AND CONCEPTS

Because this theory is called *biosocial*, the most logical place to start when discussing primary terms and concepts is with the theory's title itself. As mentioned earlier, biosocial describes the relationship between the biological and the social. Each component is seen as acting on its own behalf while also working together to produce human experience. The family is a perfect example of a biosocial entity, because its members share some genetic structure as well as the same social environment, with the purpose of advancing its individual members and its unified entity (Lovejoy 1981).

Adaptation

Based on these ideas, the family exists as it does because of adaptation. According to the principle of *ultimate causation*, the family has helped to reproduce the species because it provides the support or framework in which adaptation takes place. *Adaptation* is the ability to change or increase the level of fitness in order to improve the chances of survival with greater numbers of offspring.

Fitness

Fitness refers to the ability to fit within the environment. Generally, one would consider the fitness of an individual. However, Hamilton (1964a, 1964b) argued that we should also include the fitness of that individual's relatives as being important; he referred to this as *inclusive fitness*. For example, based on the idea of *reciprocal altruism*, individuals work together to better meet the needs of each person. An example of this is parenting, because it is in the best interests of both the mother and the father to work together to bear children and raise them until the children are old enough to have their own offspring. This process ensures the survival of the genetic and social structures of all parties involved. Therefore, the ultimate reason for families today is a history of adaptation that has led to the successful reproduction of fit children, which is best done within some sort of family unit. Simply put, you cannot analyze families today without recognizing this evolutionary past. Ross defends this notion of fitness in the vignette at the beginning of this chapter.

Proximate Causes

On the other end of the continuum are proximate causes. Proximate causes, literally meaning nearby or in close proximity, are the day-to-day interactions that take place during regular family life. This includes the interplay of biological and social forces, such as learning, language, and culture. If ultimate causes represent the past, and proximate causes represent the present, then *distal* or *intermediate causes* represent how the two interrelate. It should be noted, however, that not all who subscribe to this theory acknowledge this distal component. Rather, many assume that behaviors exhibited today are by necessity an interaction between some feature from the past that has been adapted and the current biological and social conditions. As noted above, perhaps it is most productive to approach studies or topics with the assumption that all three levels should be analyzed and/or considered.

Natural Selection

It is through natural selection that these terms and concepts come together. Natural selection explains our evolutionary past, because it is through adaptation that those genes most able to ensure survival were passed along to the next generation. This is known as *survival of the fittest*. In addition, it is through this evolutionary process that modern individuals behave as they do. An individual's genetic material must still interact with the environment. For example, although at conception the genetic material that is transferred controls the development of things such as the central nervous system, muscles, and other body functions and organs that influence behavior, how these genes develop also depends on the environment, which includes proper vitamins, minerals, and nutrients; lack of exposure to harmful toxins, gases, or drugs; and a harm-free environment. Thus, one cannot state that the biological is more important than the social, or vice versa, because both must work together to ensure that survival and adaptation take place.

As has been stated numerous times, biosocial theory has many forms and similar areas of research. Although this chapter covers terms most commonly found in readings concerning a biosocial perspective, it is by no means an exhaustive listing of terms associated with a biosocial approach. However, it is a comprehensive listing of those terms that are most necessary to have a working knowledge of this theory.

COMMON AREAS OF RESEARCH AND APPLICATION

The decade of the 2000s brought about a lot of growth in the development of this still- young theory for several reasons: new technologies that allow us to better measure biological influences; the advancement of basic neuroscience and the field's ability to study how biology and the environment behave when in a controlled environment; technological advances in our ability to study the brain; and more advanced quantitative statistical models that better enable us to test complex interactions (D'Onofrio and Lahey 2010). *The Journal of Marriage and Family* commissions articles every ten years for a special edition focusing on the decade in review. D'Onofrio and Lahey wrote an article on the biosocial influences on the family for the special issue in 2010 and focused on three primary areas: how genetics and the environment interact to influence family processes, current research in social neuroscience, and a critique of the research that had been done previously and that also offered suggestions for research in the future based on a biosocial perspective. The first two sections are briefly reviewed below. We then review current research using a biosocial perspective as it relates to the broad area of personality development, gender, and the role of testosterone. The importance of the new advances in testing and measuring brain activity will become apparent throughout this review. The sample reading at the end of this chapter also relies heavily on new brain- development research.

D'Onofrio and Lahey (2010) provide an overview of molecular genetics that informs their discussion of recent advances in biosocial theory. Differing methodologies that employ complex statistical designs have allowed us to explore the interplay between genetics and the environment in many areas: personality characteristics that affect alcohol dependency and marital status, risk factors for certain behaviors, and the relationship between genetics and environment in sibling and parenting studies.

One area that has shown tremendous growth over the last decade is social neuroscience. Research in this area has taken advantage of the new brain-imaging technologies to look at the relationship between genetics and environment, while also using animal studies and social psychophysiological methodologies. Research in this field has found that animal research can provide the basis for work in humans, especially with regard to parenting. However, there have been mixed results in this area. Research topics have included how people respond to stress and how it affects them, the body's response to marital conflict, the role of testosterone in multiple processes, and how to use brain imaging to better assess social processes (D'Onofrio and Lahey 2010).

Personality Development

Richter, Eiseman, and Richter (2000) have used a biosocial theory to determine the influence of genetic and environmental factors on personality development, especially temperament. Temperament, our automatic response to stimuli, is thought to be genetically predetermined. However, the environment in which one is raised, or the stimuli to which one has to react, influences how that temperament is displayed. Thomas and Chess (1980) support this idea through cross-cultural research on temperament. For example, they suggest that children will attempt to match their temperament to the standards of the culture in which they reside. Thus, although they may have a genetic predisposition toward certain behaviors, they will not engage in them if they are not seen as socially acceptable.

Udry (1994) did similar work on temperament, but in this case, he was studying adolescent problem behaviors. Traditionally, researchers assessed delinquency and other adolescent problem behaviors by studying the current environment, such as family and social situations. Udry suggested that you must also consider biologically based individual differences such as temperament. In fact, he stated that "you can make good predictions of who will use marijuana at age 14 by personality and environmental factors measured in the same children at age 4" (104). This is because children with different temperaments choose different environments that match those genetic predispositions.

Eysenck (1967) is another example of a researcher using a biosocial perspective at the individual level. At that time, his work was focused on developing a typology of personality that details the various traits and habits of different components of the personality. He identified two primary personality types: introversion/extraversion and stability/neuroticism. He later added the dimension of impulse control/psychoticism (Eysenck 1982). His plan was to first identify these dimensions, then to develop a test to measure them, and finally to develop a theory to explain why people have different levels of each of these traits. He did this by using brain research that showed how different people's brains reacted differently to the same stimuli. For example, extroverts' brains respond more slowly and weakly to stimuli, whereas introverts' brains react more quickly and strongly. Because of this, extroverts seek environments that provide a good deal of stimulation, and introverts seek to avoid chaotic environments (Ryckman 2000). Thus, the genetic predisposition of the personality trait, introversion/extraversion, is displayed differently depending on the social environment.

Eysenck (1997) continued to develop these ideas in order to utilize a biosocial approach. His current research assumes that biosocial influences are a given upon which additional empirical research should be built. He supports the movement within psychology of the acceptance of the mind–body connection as a standard from which to develop more scientifically based research. Although this idea has not been accepted by everyone within the field, it has spurred further thinking about basing future research on biosocial ideals (Brody 1997).

For example, Galang (2010) used the concept of Eysenck's personality types to study the relationship between the creative personality and antisocial behavior. This study combined biological components with environmental factors to determine whether individuals who are exceptionally creative are also more prone to antisocial behavior. It is suggested that, although there are genetic components that lead to more creative personalities, environmental influences are also critical in the development of the creative person. Perhaps there is more than one way of developing a creative personality, just as there is more than one way for genetics and environment to interact.

Biosocial theory has been used as the basis for multiple theories that assess some aspect of personality development. Al-Halabi and colleagues (2011) applied this theory to the study of four areas of temperament development. They conducted a cross-cultural study to determine if measurements of these four areas are applicable across samples from Spain and the United States. They suggested that, although we know genetics plays a prominent role in mental disorders, it is also important to consider the environments in which individuals live, and how these can also potentially influence the development of mental disorders.

Another study that assessed instruments used to measure some element of personality development looked at borderline personality disorder and how we measure two symptoms of it: emotional vulnerability and an invalidating environment (Sauer and Baer 2010). Because of the importance of these variables in the study of borderline personality development, the authors wanted to validate the measures typically used to assess these symptoms. They found support for the use of these instruments, which also lends support to the idea that biosocial constructs are important in the development of borderline personality disorder. The relevance of these symptoms was further tested by

Reeves and colleagues (2010), who also found support for their importance, but they also added the component of invalidation. Such research has provided important growth in the study of the development and symptoms of borderline personality development.

Gender

Another area of research that commonly uses a biosocial approach is that of the development of gendered behavior. Udry (2000) has used a biosocial model to explain how hormones, both present at birth and produced throughout adulthood, combine with the social expectations of each gender to form gendered behavior. Males and females are genetically driven at birth, but the effects of their hormones can be either strengthened or weakened based on the environment and social beliefs about what's masculine and feminine. Although you've probably heard about this with regard to the importance of hormones during adolescence and can perhaps remember what it felt like to experience hormone surges, Udry takes this one step further by suggesting that the environment also influences how these hormones affect us.

Specifically, in one study Udry measured hormone levels of females during early adolescence and then again when they were between the ages of 27 and 30. He also asked them questions about the types of behaviors their parents encouraged with regard to masculinity and femininity. What he found was that "if a daughter has natural tendencies to be feminine, encouragement will enhance femininity; but if she has below average femininity in childhood, encouraging her to be more feminine will have no effect" (Udry 2000, 451). Thus, although hormones obviously drive some of our behavior, it is also important to consider the social environment when examining why some people are more feminine or masculine than others.

The Role of Testosterone

Booth et al. (2003) studied the relationship between testosterone, child and adolescent adjustment, and parent–child relationships. This is easier to do now that testosterone can be measured using a saliva sample, which is simple to collect. Although there has been some research on the relationship between testosterone and behavioral problems in adults, research on children is in the beginning stages. Interestingly enough, it was found that high levels of testosterone alone did not create increased risk behaviors or symptoms of depression in children. However, the quality of the parent–child relationship did affect those variables. When the quality of the parent–child relationship was high, testosterone-related adjustment problems were minimized. This is important because it tells us that one has to include social context when trying to understand the relationship between hormones and behavior.

Rowe et al. (2004) found similar evidence of the existence of biosocial interactions in their study of adolescent boys. They found that testosterone is related to social dominance for boys during adolescence, particularly if they do not have deviant peers. This interaction between hormones and behavior is once again influenced by social context (with whom they associate).

Finally, Booth, Johnson, and Granger (2005) looked at the relationship between testosterone and marriage. Previous research found that married men have lower levels of testosterone than divorced men (Mazur and Michalek 1998). Current research suggests that testosterone can encourage both positive and negative behavior depending on the social context. For example, in this study testosterone was not shown to affect marital quality by itself. However, when you take into account the social contexts of men who feel overloaded by work and family roles, those with higher levels of testosterone reported lower marital quality than did men with lower levels of testosterone.

The role of testosterone was also assessed in the last decade with regard to its relationship to antisocial behavior, health outcomes, and environmental factors (D'Onofrio and Lahey 2010). In addition, Archer (2009) studied the relationship between testosterone and parental investment. He suggested that the cause of sexual differences in aggression can be explained by the interplay between proximal (immediate) and ultimate (evolutionary) factors. He suggests that aggression is more common in men because of the nature of their evolutionary roles and having less parental investment in children than women do. One cannot ignore, however, the role of biology in the development of these roles or the implications for them. Because testosterone levels are now easier to measure, we predict that the influence of testosterone will be increasingly studied across topics in the family field. It should be noted, however, that it is difficult, if not impossible, to establish a cause–effect relationship, or to disentangle the roles of biology, social context, and behavior.

CRITIQUE

The fact that there are many critics of biosocial theory may suggest that it has its limitations. However, the following criticisms are based on the assumption that one accepts the importance of both biology and environment in human behavior. That said, one valid critique of biosocial theory is that there is disagreement over the basic tenets of the theory and which of its principles are most important. As was mentioned in the **Basic Assumptions** section, where you get your information will determine what aspects of this theory are deemed to be of primary importance. Although this is perhaps not a huge stumbling block, it does make it more difficult than using structural functionalism, for example, because everyone agrees as to what that means. The relative newness of this theory is one reason for this disagreement, so we suggest that this will change over time.

Another problem with this theory is that, although it makes intuitive sense that both nature and nurture are important, it is very difficult to disentangle the two in research designs. In fact, in some cases it may even be unethical to attempt to determine genetic influences because of the intrusive and perhaps even experimental nature of that research. Thus, we are constrained by the measures that are currently available. There is also the issue of subjects' willingness to participate in a study on personality that requires blood and urine samples. In research of this nature, it may be more difficult to find and retain participants.

As you could probably guess from reading this chapter, biosocial theory cannot explain everything. Some research, and some human behavior for that matter, contradicts what we would predict based on genetics. One example of this is the fact that families today are moving toward having fewer, rather than more, children, to the extent of not having enough offspring to replenish the population. How does this fit with the evolutionary need to carry on your genetic material? Although there is a great deal of speculation, we don't exactly know.

Finally, there is a tendency to confuse a genetic predisposition with a value judgment—i.e., it is easy to say that because there is a genetic tendency toward a certain trait, then a certain behavior should follow. An example of that are the genetic and hormonal differences between males and females. Although we have said that women have more to be concerned with when it comes to mate selection than do men because they are physically responsible for bringing a child into this world, it doesn't mean that women should automatically be responsible for the care of that child for the rest of its life. Our cultural beliefs may prefer that to be true, but it is not entirely biologically based, as some have suggested.

Similarly, a good deal of previous research using this theoretical perspective suggests that rape is biologically driven, but this does not mean that individuals should not be held accountable for such behavior. Remember, one of our assumptions stated that human biological or biosocial drives do not determine human behavior. In other words, even though an individual may have a genetic predisposition toward violence, including sexual violence, this does not mean that he or she must act on that drive. Furthermore, we have strict social norms and laws that guard against and punish this behavior. Instead, we should use this information when we treat offenders or engage in prevention efforts. Recognizing the biological or social drives that possibly guide bad behaviors can provide another area of exploration as we strive to decrease crime.

Although most social scientists would support the use of a biosocial perspective when researching and explaining human behavior, there is still much work to be done in the development of this theory. It does seem, however, to be the wave of the future.

APPLICATION

1. Refer to the vignette at the beginning of this chapter. According to biosocial theory, whose argument is best supported—Ross's or Roberta's?

2. During exam week, a friend comes to you saying she's not sure she's going to make it through the next exam because she doesn't feel well. She needs to maintain a 3.5 GPA to keep her scholarship and has been studying very hard. You ask her what hurts and she replies, "I don't know, everything!" How would you use a biosocial approach to help her?

3. Think about the role of hormones in your life. What have you learned or been told about how they influence you physically? What about emotionally? Socially? How can you use a biosocial perspective to understand how hormones influence your behavior, as well as how your environment can affect your hormones?

4. List ways in which you are like one of your parents or a sibling. Now go through your list and write ways that each of these could be genetic or socially constructed. How can the interaction between genetics and your family environment be responsible for these similarities? How do these qualities ensure continuing adaptation and survival?

5. How does biosocial theory explain why adults might or might not be willing to raise nonbiological children?

6. The sample reading that follows provides an explanation for why cognitive-behavioral therapy will work to help rehabilitate criminal offenders. Try to apply the basic assumptions covered in the text to the article.

REFERENCES

Al-Halabi, S., R. Herrero, P. Saiz, M. P. Garcia-Portilla, J. M. Errasti, P. Corcoran, M. T. Bascaran, M. Bousono, S. Lemos, and J. Bobes. 2011. A cross-cultural comparison between Spain and the USA: Temperament and character distribution by sex and age. *Psychiatry Research* 186: 397–401.

Archer, J. 2009. Does sexual selection explain human sex differences in aggression? *Behavior and Brain Sciences* 32: 249–311.

Booth, A., D. R. Johnson, and D. A. Granger. 2005. Testosterone, marital quality, and role overload. *Journal of Marriage and Family* 67: 483–498.

Booth, A., D. R. Johnson, D. A. Granger, A. C. Crouter, and S. McHale. 2003. Testosterone and child and adolescent adjustment: The moderating role of parent–child relationships. *Developmental Psychology* 39(1): 85–98.

Brody, N. 1997. Dispositional paradigms: Comment on Eysenck (1997) and the biosocial science of individual differences. *Journal of Personality and Social Psychology* 73: 1242–1245.

Cloninger, C. R., D. M. Svrakic, and T. R. Przybeck. 1993. A psychobiological model of temperament and character. *Archives of General Psychiatry* 50: 975–990.

Cosmides, L., J. Toby, and J. H. Barkow. 1992. Introduction: Evolutionary psychology and conceptual integration. In *The adapted mind: Evolutionary psychology and the generation of culture*, ed. J. H. Barkow, L. Cosmides, and J. Toby, 3–15. New York: Oxford Univ. Press.

D'Onofrio, B. M., and B. B. Lahey. 2010. Biosocial influences on the family: A decade review. *Journal of Marriage and Family* 72(3): 762–782.

Eysenck, H. J. 1967. *The biological basis of personality*. Springfield, IL: Charles C. Thomas.

———. 1982. *Personality, genetics, and behavior: Selected papers*. New York: Praeger.

———. 1997. Personality and experimental psychology: The unification of psychology and the possibility of a paradigm. *Journal of Personality and Social Psychology* 73: 1224–1237.

Eysenck, H. J., and M. W. Eysenck. 1985. *Personality and individual differences: A natural science approach*. New York: Plenum.

Fox, R. 1989. *The search for society: Quest for a biosocial science and morality*. New Brunswick, NJ: Rutgers Univ. Press.

Galang, A. J. R. 2010. The prosocial psychopath: Explaining the paradoxes of the creative personality. *Neuroscience and Biobehavioral Reviews* 34: 1241–1248.

Hamilton, W. D. 1964a. The genetical evolution of social behavior. I. *Journal of Theoretical Biology* 7: 1–16.

———. 1964b. The genetical evolution of social behavior. II. *Journal of Theoretical Biology* 7: 17–52.

Lovejoy, C. O. 1981. The origin of man. *Science* 211: 341–450.

Mayr, E. 1991. *One long argument: Charles Darwin and the genesis of modern evolutionary thought*. Cambridge, MA: Harvard University Press.

Mazur, A., and J. Michalek. 1998. Marriage, divorce, and male testosterone. *Social Forces* 77(1): 315–330.

Reeves, M., L. M. Janes, S. M., Pizzarello, and J. E. Taylor. 2010. Support for Linehan's biosocial theory from a nonclinical sample. *Journal of Personality Disorders* 24(3): 312–326.

Richter, J., M. Eiseman, and G. Richter. 2000. Temperament, character and perceived parental rearing in healthy adults: Two related concepts? *Psychopathology* 33(1): 36–42.

Rowe, R., B. Maughan, C. M. Worthman, E. J. Costello, and A. Angold. 2004. Testosterone, antisocial behavior, and social dominance in boys: Pubertal development and biosocial interaction. *Biological Psychiatry* 55:546–552.

Ryckman, R. M. 2000. Eysenck's biological typology. In *Theories of personality*. 7th ed., 349–390. Belmont, CA: Wadsworth.

Sauer, S. E., and R. A. Baer. 2010. Validation of measures of biosocial precursors to Borderline Personality Disorder: Childhood emotional vulnerability and environmental invalidation. *Assessment* 17(4): 454–466.

Thomas, R. M. 1996. Ethology and sociobiology. In *Comparing theories of child development*, ed. R. M. Thomas. 4th ed., 394–412. Pacific Grove, CA: Brooks/Cole.

Thomas, A., and S. Chess. 1980. *The dynamics of psychological development*. New York: Brunner/Mazel.

Troost, K. M., and E. Filsinger. 1993. Emerging biosocial perspectives on the family. In *Sourcebook of family theories and methods: A contextual approach*, ed. P. G. Boss, W. J. Doherty, R. LaRossa, W. R. Schumm, and S. K. Steinmetz, 677–710. New York: Plenum.

Udry, J. R. 1994. Integrating biological and sociological models of adolescent problem behaviors. In *Adolescent problem behaviors: Issues and research*, ed. R. D. Ketterlinus and M. E. Lamb, 93–107. Hillsdale, NJ: Lawrence Erlbaum.

Udry, J. R., 2000. Biological limits of gender construction. *American Sociological Review* 65(3): 443–457.

Vaske, J., K. Galyean, and F. T. Cullen. 2011. Toward a biosocial theory of offender rehabilitation: Why does cognitive-behavioral therapy work? *Journal of Criminal Justice* 39: 90–102.

Wilson, E. O. 1975. *Sociobiology: The new synthesis*. Cambridge, MA: Belknap.

SAMPLE READING

Vaske, J., K. Galyean, and F. T. Cullen. 2011. Toward a biosocial theory of offender rehabilitation: Why does cognitive-behavioral therapy work? *Journal of Criminal Justice* 39: 90–102.

This article reviews research that was done using a biosocial perspective to study the effectiveness of cognitive-behavioral therapy on offender rehabilitation. The authors used the latest knowledge on brain development to assess which skills activate which portions of the brain in an attempt to determine the skills that should be targeted in therapy. Knowing how the brain reacts to certain stimuli allows us to teach people new strategies and techniques to use in response to these stimuli, rather than the previously ineffective or harmful responses. The reading provides a good overview of the regions of the brain, the specific terminology, and the skills associated with each brain region, which will aid in our understanding of the brain-development research covered.

SAMPLE READING

Toward a Biosocial Theory of Offender Rehabilitation: Why Does Cognitive-Behavioral Therapy Work?

Jamie Vaske[a],*, Kevan Galyean[b], and Francis T. Cullen[b]

Objective: The growing insights from neuropsychological research, including within biosocial criminology, have not yet been systematically incorporated into the study of correctional rehabilitation. Given developments in related fields, we argue that moving toward a biosocial theory of offender rehabilitation or neurocriminology will enrich our understanding and effectiveness of these interventions. A particularly promising area to investigate is cognitive-behavioral therapy (CBT). In this regard, we examine research on the neural correlates of skills that are addressed in correctional cognitive skills programs.

Results: A review of the literature reveals that social skills, coping skills, and problem-solving skills are consistently associated with activation in the medial prefrontal cortex, dorsolateral prefrontal cortex, dorsomedial prefrontal cortex, ventromedial prefrontal cortex, orbitofrontal cortex, cingulate cortex, insula, and temporo-parietal junction.

Conclusions: CBT programs that effectively target social skills, coping skills, and problem-solving skills should correspond to increased activity in these regions. The implications of this research are discussed.

INTRODUCTION

By the middle of the 1970s, correctional rehabilitation was in disarray. Martinson (1974) had published his review of the extant evaluation evidence suggesting that, in essence, "nothing works" reliably to change offender behavior. Liberals and conservatives, who

[a] Western Carolina University, United States
[b] University of Cincinnati, United States

agree on little else, had reached a consensus that rehabilitation was a failed enterprise (Cullen & Gilbert, 1982). Rehabilitation thus forfeited its status as the guiding paradigm of corrections, as the United States shifted dramatically to implement punitive policies that either denied the possibility of offender change (incapacitation) or linked offender change to fear of harsh sanctions (deterrence).

Over the past four decades, however, scholars have worked diligently to reestablish rehabilitation as a viable goal of corrections (Cullen, 2005). In large part, they have done so by embracing evidence-based corrections and by showing empirically that treatment programs achieve larger reductions in reoffending than do punitive sanctions (Andrews & Bonta, 2006; MacKenzie, 2006; Lipsey & Cullen, 2007). Further, efforts have been made—especially by Canadian psychologists Andrews, Bonta, and Gendreau—to develop a coherent theory of effective correctional treatment (Andrews & Bonta, 2006; Gendreau, 1996; see also Cullen & Jonson, 2010). A critical insight of this work is that offender treatments have heterogeneous effects; that is, some interventions reduce recidivism far more than other treatments.

In this regard, a substantial amount of research has been conducted in the last twenty years suggesting that cognitive-behavioral approaches are particularly effective in reducing recidivism. A large number of meta-analyses, which summarize these findings, suggest that cognitive-behavioral therapy (hereinafter "CBT") is the most successful treatment choice when working with offenders (Andrews, Zinger, Hoge, Bonta, Gendreau, & Cullen, 1990 Dowden & Andrews, 2000; Lipsey & Wilson, 1998; Pearson, Lipton, Cleland, & Yee, 2002). In large part, the effectiveness of CBT is rooted in the fact that it is "responsive to"—that is, is capable of changing—factors that are known to predict recidivism (e.g., antisocial attitudes) (Andrews & Bonta, 2006).

Our purpose is to extend current insights into the effectiveness of CBT by drawing on recent developments in neuropsychological research. For many years, criminologists were rightly skeptical of biological explanations of crime. These perspectives were often empirically vacuous, racist, and used to justify ill-conceived repressive crime control policies (Bruinius, 2006; Cornwell, 2003; Rafter, 2008). Today, however, advances in neuroscience, including brain imaging, make it possible—indeed, make it necessary—to explore the role of brain development and functioning in early conduct disorders and later criminal behavior. Moffitt's (1993) classic work on neuropsychological deficits in initiating life-course-persistent offending provided an impetus for this line of inquiry. Subsequent studies have shown that biological factors, when interacting with social relationships and context, are clearly implicated in antisocial behavior (Walsh & Beaver, 2009; Wright, Tibbetts, & Daigle, 2008).

Our project thus begins with the premise that biosocial theory and research may provide useful insights on how best to intervene with offenders. In the early intervention literature, it is now widely understood that efforts should be undertaken, such as through nurse-home-visitation programs, to help expectant mothers to avoid actions (e.g., ingestion of drugs) that would compromise their child's brain development in the womb (Farrington & Welsh, 2007; Olds, 2007). In a similar vein, as knowledge grows, it is increasingly likely that insights form biosocial criminology can help us unravel why interventions do and do not work. Let us hasten to say that we are not proposing that biosocial explanations of treatment effectiveness are rivals to or will trump current social and psychological explanations. At the same time, how or whether treatment interventions affect neuropsychological processes may play a salient role in shaping their effectiveness. Accordingly, moving toward a biosocial theory of offender rehabilitation is an avenue worthy of serious consideration. The integration of neurocognitive science and criminology is referred to as neurocriminology (Ross & Hilborn, 2008).

In this regard, it is noteworthy that some evidence exists that beyond crime, CBT is effective in reducing other cognitive and behavioral disorders because CBT corresponds to changes in brain functioning (Beauregard, 2007). Informed by this research, our efforts proceed along three steps. First, we identify three key skill sets that CBT attempts to improve through its programming (social skills, coping skills, and problem-solving skills). Second, we show that these three skill sets are related to specific areas of the brain, and that offending is linked to structural and functional deficits in these same brain areas. Third, we argue that CBT may be effective in reducing problem behavior, including crime, because the intervention affects specific areas of the brain; thus, CBT→changes in cognition↔changes in brain functioning→changes in behavior.

Our perspective suggests that the brain is dynamic rather than static; that is, the brain is capable of changing in both structure and function. The brain's ability to change its circuitry and function is referred to as brain plasticity. A large body of research has revealed that brain structures can change at multiple levels—from the synaptic level up to the cortex level (Buonomano & Merzenich, 1998)—and that metabolical changes also can occur. In addition, studies have shown that changes in brain structure and function can occur in childhood, adolescence, and adulthood (Leenders et al., 1990; Mahncke et al., 2006), with plasticity being most prominent in childhood (Müller-Dahlhaus, Orekhov, Liu, & Ziemann, 2008). Changes in brain structure and metabolic activity may result from social experiences, drug use, nutrition, disease, genetics, and hormones (Andersen & Teicher, 2009; Kolb, Gibb, & Robinson, 2003). Thus, the brain is a dynamic organ that may be susceptible to environmental and biochemical influences across the life-course.

We also suggest that, at least to a degree, interventions can shape neuropsychological processes (Doidge, 2007; Ross & Hilborn, 2008). Research has shown that the brain may "wire" itself in response to environmental factors (Kolb et al., 2003), including cognitive and behavioral interventions. For instance, stroke patients have shown short-term changes in brain function and motor skills in response to behavioral interventions (Johnston, 2009; Nelles, Jentzen, Jueptner, Müller, & Diener, 2001). Similarly, evaluation of language remediation programs, such as Fast For Word, have revealed that youths with language deficits experienced significant improvements in language skills and improved functioning in brain regions associated with language skills after completing the remediation program (Temple et al., 2003). These results converge to suggest that intervention programs have the ability to improve brain structure, brain function, cognition, and behavior.

Finally, we suggest that uncovering a biological basis for effective treatment has the potential to give added legitimacy to the treatment enterprise. Thus, showing that CBT changes brain functioning to overcome deficits and foster prosocial behavior provides hard scientific evidence for why offender treatment is effective. Phrased differently, such evidence would help to counteract claims that rehabilitation is a fuzzy, liberal enterprise which is inspired more by ideology rather than by a sober view of who offenders are and whether they are beyond redemption.

COGNITIVE-BEHAVIORAL TREATMENT
FOR OFFENDERS

Cognitive-behavioral programs assume that antisocial attitudes lead to higher levels of antisocial behavior. More specifically, CBT programs argue that high-risk situations lead to antisocial thoughts and feelings, which in turn increase the likelihood of antisocial behavior. Therefore, CBT programs attempt to decrease antisocial behavior by helping clients reduce their antisocial cognitive and emotional responses to high-risk situations.

Correctional CBT programs are implemented in a wide variety of ways. There are "home-grown" correctional CBT programs that focus on the broad goals of identifying and changing antisocial attitudes, and there are more structured CBT programs that have well developed curriculums, such as Yochelson and Samenow's (1977) Cognitive Self-Change program or Bush, Glick, and Taymans (1997) Thinking for a Change program. Despite the variation in how CBT programs are implemented, there are three key components that are emphasized in the majority of CBT programs: (1) identifying high-risk situations, thoughts, and feelings that may lead to criminal and antisocial behavior; (2) helping clients replace criminogenic thoughts with non-criminogenic thoughts; and (3) reducing deficits in cognitive processes that are linked to offending, such as deficits in problem-solving skills, coping skills, and social skills.

The first component, identifying high-risk situations/thoughts/feelings, is a core component of all CBT programs. This is a core component because CBT programs are predicated on the assumption that individuals must be able to identify the high-risk situations, attitudes, cognitive processes, and feelings that precede offending. The second component, helping clients replace their criminogenic thoughts with non-criminogenic thoughts, is a component that is characteristic of cognitive restructuring programs. Cognitive restructuring programs focus on identifying and changing the content of one's criminogenic beliefs (i.e., *what* they think).

Unlike the second component, the third component is characteristic of cognitive skills programs. Cognitive skills programs focus on reducing deficits in cognitive processes, or on changing how people think. More specifically, cognitive skills programs commonly target increasing self-control, increasing the ability to recognize short and long term consequences of behaviors, improving decision-making, and strengthening problem-solving skills. Additionally, these programs focus on increasing perspective taking, moral reasoning, meta-cognition, and coping skills. These skills are taught in correctional CBT programs such as Aggression Replacement Training (Goldstein, Glick, & Gibb, 1998) and Reasoning and Rehabilitation (Ross & Fabiano, 1985; Ross & Hilborn, 2008). The current review will emphasize the neural correlates of cognitive processes that are targeted in cognitive skills programs. Accordingly, the discussion here is most relevant to CBT cognitive skill programs.

Despite the effectiveness of correctional CBT programs, it remains unclear what are the neural mechanisms underlying the effectiveness of CBT programs among offender populations. It is very likely that changes in brain functioning underlie the relationship between changes in cognitive functioning and changes in criminal behavior. The next section will discuss which brain regions may be targeted in CBT programs for offender populations. More specifically, the section will discuss the neural correlates of three domains of skills: (1) social skills—cognitive empathy, emotional empathy, self-awareness, moral reasoning, and moral feelings; (2) coping skills—self-regulation, reappraisal, and thought suppression; and (3) problem-solving skills— planning, anticipating outcomes, decision-making, and sense of agency. It is important to identify which brain regions are associated with each of these skills, and then examine whether offenders show deficits within these same regions. If offenders have deficits in the same regions that are associated with each of these skills, then it may be hypothesized that correctional CBT programs (that target social, coping, and problem-solving skills) may reduce offenders' skill deficits and reduce offenders' criminal behavior because these programs improve functioning in the corresponding brain regions.

Finally, we realize that not all readers will be equally versed in the brain and its regions. Accordingly, for those wishing a primer in this information, we have provided a brief review of these issues in Appendix A.

NEUROPSYCHOLOGICAL RESEARCH AND SKILL SETS

Neuropsychological studies reveal that there is a substantial amount of overlap in the neural correlates of perspective taking, self-awareness, moral feelings, moral reasoning, self-control, reappraisal, thought suppression, planning, anticipating consequences, decision-making, and sense of agency. For instance, a wide range of studies implicate regions of the frontal cortex, parietal lobe, and temporal lobe in social skills, coping skills, and decision-making skills. More specifically, regions such as the medial prefrontal cortex (MPFC), dorsolateral prefrontal cortex (DLPFC), ventromedial prefrontal cortex (VMPFC) including the orbitofrontal cortex (OFC), cingulate cortex, temporoparietal junction (TPJ), and insula seem particularly important for a number of social skills, coping skills, and decision-making skills. This is not meant to imply that other regions are not relevant for these skills. Instead, it appears that these key areas are implicated in a wide range of skills, while other regions have a less pervasive effect on such skills. Thus, researchers who are interested in examining the neuropsychological changes that result from completing a correctional cognitive-behavioral program should, at a minimum, examine changes in the medial prefrontal cortex (BA 9, 10, 11, 14, 24, 25, 32), dorsolateral prefrontal cortex (BA 9, 46), ventromedial prefrontal cortex including the orbitofrontal cortex (BA 10, 11, 12, 24, 32, 47), cingulate cortex (BA 23, 24, 31, 32), temporo-parietal junction (BA 22, 39), and insula (BA 13, 14). Researchers may also examine changes in the dorsomedial prefrontal cortex (BA 8 and 32) (DMPFC), as this region has been implicated in individuals' ability to acknowledge how the external environment may be linked to one's internal states (Ochsner, Bunge, Gross, & Gabrieli, 2002). This skill, linking changes in the external environment to changes in individuals' internal processes, is the main skill targeted in cognitive-behavioral therapy with offenders.

Before describing the neural correlates of each skill targeted in cognitive-behavioral therapy (CBT), it is important to note that the definitions of skills targeted in correctional CBT programs do not exactly match the definitions of these skills in neuropsychology. For instance, the steps used to practice self-control in Aggression Replacement Training include skills such as meta-cognition, coping, and planning. In neuropsychology, the concept of self-control refers to controlling a prepotent or automatic response. Due to the differences in skills across CBT programs, the current review uses the conceptualization of each skill from neuropsychology rather than from CBT. Therefore, researchers and practitioners are encouraged to compare the definition of a skill found in CBTs to the definition of that skill in neuropsychology. If a treatment objective in a CBT program includes multiple skills, researchers should consult the neural correlates of each skill and expect changes in the brain regions associated with an individual skill.

NEUROPSYCHOLOGICAL STUDIES OF SOCIAL SKILLS

Neurologists have begun to investigate the neural correlates of a range of social skills, including the neural correlates of cognitive empathy, emotional empathy, moral feelings, moral reasoning, and self-awareness. Research has shown that empathy, moral judgment, and self-awareness are associated with activation in the amygdala, insula, posterior cingulate cortex (PCC), posterior superior temporal sulcus (pSTS), and the MPFC including the VMPFC, OFC, and DLPFC (Moll et al., 2002; Singer, 2006). While there is a substantial amount of overlap in the neural correlates of these three social skills, each social skill also has its own distinct set of neural correlates.

Cognitive Empathy and Emotional Empathy

Psychologists have differentiated between cognitive empathy and emotional empathy. Cognitive empathy is defined as one's ability to understand others' feelings, intentions, and beliefs. This form of empathy is commonly referred to as mentalizing or Theory of Mind (ToM). Cognitive empathy may allow individuals to predict how others will behave, and to plan their behavior accordingly. Research has shown that cognitive empathy is consistently associated with activation in the MPFC (including the ventromedial prefrontal cortex), cingulate cortex, pSTS, temporo-parietal junction (TPJ), and temporal poles (Amodio & Frith, 2006; Decety & Lamm, 2007; Lieberman, 2007; Mitchell, Banaji, & Macrae, 2005; Ruby & Decety, 2004; Singer, 2006). Theroleofthe MPFC in cognitive empathy tasks is not clearly understood, but it has been linked to a range of social skills including self-awareness, identifying others' emotions, and self-regulation (Lieberman, 2007). Activation in the TPJ is associated with identifying others' beliefs and feelings, identifying social cues, and processing the intentionality of others' behavior. Other regions have also been linked to higher levels of cognitive empathy. These regions include the OFC, DLPFC, DMPFC, and amygdala (Casebeer, 2003; Lieberman, 2007; Mitchell et al., 2005; Ruby & Decety, 2004). However, the research linking these latter regions to cognitive empathy is inconsistent and future research is needed to determine the functional significance of these regions to cognitive empathy.

Emotional empathy, in contrast, refers to one's ability to share or experience others' feelings and sensations. Emotional empathy has been linked to activation in the anterior cingulate cortex (ACC), posterior cingulate cortex (PCC), insula, TPJ, superior temporal sulcus (STS), amygdala, inferior frontal cortex, DLPFC, OFC, and superior frontal gyrus (Carr, Iacoboni, Dubeau, Mazziotta, & Lenzi, 2003; Jackson,

Brunet, Meltzoff, & Decety, 2006; Lamm, Batson, & Decety, 2007; Lieberman, 2007; Singer et al., 2004). Further, higher scores on empathy indices are associated with greater activation in the ACC and insula (Lamm et al., 2007; Singer et al., 2004). (For an interpretation of how these regions contribute to emotional empathy, see Carr et al. (2003) and Blair (2005)).

In sum, research suggests that cognitive and emotional empathy are associated with activation in the MPFC (including VMPFC), TPJ, and cingulate cortex. Cognitive and emotional empathy may activate many of the same neural networks, yet these also have very distinct neural processes. For instance, emotional empathy is associated with activation in the insula, amygdala, superior frontal gyrus, and ventrolateral frontal cortex, while cognitive empathy is not associated with activation in these regions (Blair, 2005; Singer, 2006; Völlm et al., 2006). Research suggests that cognitive and emotional empathy are somewhat distinct processes that may or may not co-occur. That is, someone may understand the types of thoughts another person is having, but he or she may not experience the same feelings or sensations as the other person. Further, research suggests that antisocial individuals do relatively well in mentalizing or knowing what someone else is feeling, but they may lack emotional empathy (Blair, 2005; Raine & Yang, 2006). Thus, there may be some overlap in the neural correlates of cognitive empathy and emotional empathy, but these are also distinct neural processes, and these differences may be important when dealing with offenders.

Moral Emotions and Moral Reasoning

Moral emotions are an integral part of moral judgments because emotions help attach value or meaning to thoughts and reasoning. Such emotions include feelings such as regret, shame, guilt, pride, embarrassment, anger, and admiration. These emotions can motivate individuals to engage in tedious or unattractive behaviors they would not otherwise engage in, even when there is a strong moral rationale that encourages or prohibits such behaviors. Given the importance of moral emotions in decision-making, cognitive neuroscientists have begun to investigate the neural correlates of moral emotions.

Research has shown that moral emotions may be a product of intricate connections between the frontal cortex, temporal lobe, and limbic system (Moll, Zahn, de Oliveira-Souza, Krueger, & Grafman, 2005). For instance, Ruby and Decety (2004) found that social emotions were associated with activation in the superior frontal gyrus, posterior cingulate gyrus, temporal poles, and amygdala. Other researchers have noted that moral and social emotions, such as regret, guilt, hostility, and embarrassment, are associated with activation in the OFC, MPFC, VMPFC, posterior superior temporal sulcus, temporal poles, ACC, and insula (Camille et al., 2004; Denson, Pedersen, Ronquillo, & Nandy, 2009; Heatherton & Krendi, 2009; Moll et al., 2002; Moll et al., 2005; Shin et al., 2000; Takahashi et al., 2004). Each one of these regions plays an integral part to the overall processing and execution of moral emotions. Some regions are important for perception of social stimuli (pSTS), while other regions, such as the amygdala, are responsible for generating emotions. As these emotions are generated, they may be linked to specific appraisals or memories and integrated into decision-making via the insula, OFC, temporal poles, and VMPFC. However, it may also be important for frontal regions to regulate emotions, especially negative emotions, and to resolve any conflict between emotional and cognitive processes via the ACC (Eisenberger, Lieberman, & Williams, 2003).

Studies have also shown that moral judgment is related to activation in the frontal and temporal lobes (Casebeer, 2003; Raine & Yang, 2006). More specifically, moral judgments and reasoning have been linked to activations in the MPFC, VMPFC, OFC, and temporal poles (Anderson, Bechara, Damasio, Tranel, & Damasio, 1999; Greene & Haidt, 2002; Greene & Paxton, 2009; Harenski, Antonenko, Shane, & Kiehl, 2009; Koenigs et al., 2007; Luo et al., 2006; Moll et al., 2005). There is some research that shows that the functional significance of these regions varies by the type of moral judgment. For instance, studies have found that moral judgments that are emotional in nature are associated with increased activation in "emotional" regions of the brain, such as the PCC, ACC, amygdala, and pSTS/TPJ (Greene, Sommerville, Nystrom, Darley, & Cohen, 2001; Greene & Haidt, 2002; Harenski et al., 2009). In contrast, moral judgments that are based on cognitive or utilitarian responses are related to greater activations in "cognitive" regions, such as the DLPFC and inferior parietal cortex (Greene, Nystrom, Engeil, Darley, & Cohen, 2004).

In sum, CBT programs that target moral emotions and moral reasoning should increase activations in the MPFC, VMPFC, OFC, temporal poles, and insula. While moral emotions and moral reasoning share a common set of neural correlates, they also have their own distinct neural correlates. For instance, programs that predominantly target moral emotions may see increased activation in the more emotional areas of the brain, such as the cingulate cortex, TPJ, and amygdala, while such activation patterns would be absent in moral reasoning programs. Programs that solely focus on moral reasoning, on the other hand, should expect increased activation in more cognitive regions, such as the DLPFC and inferior parietal cortex.

Self-Awareness

Individuals who lack self-awareness may be unaware of their feelings, engage in inappropriate behavior, overstate their goals or abilities, underestimate their cognitive and emotional problems, and ultimately frustrate those around them. Given the significance of self-awareness to social interactions, a number of studies have investigated the neural correlates of self-awareness of one's traits, abilities, and attitudes. These studies have consistently shown that the MPFC is associated with self-awareness of one's traits and attitudes (Johnson et al., 2002; Ochsner et al., 2005; Schmitz & Johnson, 2006). The MPFC has been linked to a variety of social behaviors, including mentalizing, monitoring one's thoughts and feelings, thinking about others' perceptions, and monitoring one's actions to make sure they are consistent with their intentions (Amodio & Frith, 2006). Other areas that have been linked to self-awareness of one's traits include the ACC, PCC, areas of the DLPFC, TPJ, insula, OFC, and hippocampus (Johnson et al., 2002; Kjaer, Nowak, & Lou, 2002; Ochsner et al., 2005; Schmitz, Kawahara-Baccus, & Johnson, 2004; Shimamura, 2000). Aside from the individual activations of each of these areas, studies have shown that connections between many of these areas underlie the process of self-attribution or self-awareness (Schmitz & Johnson, 2006).

Research has also examined the neural structures that underlie self-awareness of body states and emotions (Lane et al., 1998). These studies have shown that self-awareness of one's bodily states (i.e., heart rate) is associated with activation in the insula, somatosensory cortex, ACC, and prefrontal cortex (Critchley, Wiens, Rotshtein, Öhman, & Dolan, 2004; Pollatos, Gramann, & Schandry, 2007). Consequently, greater self-awareness of one's bodily states have been associated with greater intensity of and greater awareness of emotions (Herbert, Pollatos, & Schandry, 2007; Pollatos, Kirsch, & Schandry, 2005). It is important to be aware of one's bodily states because physiological states often accompany certain emotions and feelings. Without recognizing one's physiological states, individuals may make decisions without reference to emotions. As previously discussed, emotions can help motivate individuals to engage in or refrain from a behavior, even when a strong logical argument suggests otherwise. Thus, individuals who are more aware of their bodily states may be more aware of their emotions, and subsequently make more advantageous decisions than individuals who are less aware of their bodily states (Bechara & Naqvi, 2004).

In sum, self-awareness skills may be divided into two components that have very different neural correlates. The first component can be referred to as the "who am I" component. This component is associated with activations in the MPFC, DLPFC, OFC, TPJ, insula, and hippocampus. The second component can be referred to as the "what do my internal processes look like" component. This component is associated with activations in more sensory regions, such as the insula, somatosensory cortex, ACC, and portions of the prefrontal cortex.

NEUROPSYCHOLOGICAL STUDIES OF COPING SKILLS: DEALING WITH STRESS

There may be two basic domains of responses to stressful events: an immediate response and a non-immediate response. An immediate response may be the prepotent behavioral responses that one has to a stressful event, while a non-immediate response may include the cognitive and emotional responses that accompany the prepotent response. These cognitive and emotional responses may last for a couple of minutes or for a couple of days. Controlling the immediate response would involve a quick, "no-go" or stop strategy to prevent the individual from acting out. This may be referred to as "biting one's tongue." Controlling the non-immediate responses to stress, however, may generally involve more cognitive-based coping strategies, such as reappraisal and thought suppression. Reappraisal occurs when individuals reframe the stressful event in a less negative perspective or when they objectify the stressful event to mitigate any harm the event may cause. Thought suppression occurs when individuals try to avoid thinking a particular thought or when they consciously try to stop ruminating over a problem.

These coping or regulation strategies, while different in nature, all activate a common set of brain regions. For instance, response inhibition (i.e., controlling a prepotent response), controlling negative emotion, reappraisal, thought suppression, and coping with stress related cues are associated with increased activation in the MPFC, DLPFC, VLPFC, ACC, and OFC (Casey et al., 1997; Drabant, McRae, Manuck, Hariri, & Gross, 2009; Eisenberger et al., 2003; Garavan, Ross, & Stein, 1999; Gillath, Bunge, Shaver, Wendelken, & Mikulincer, 2005; Goldin, McRae, Ramel, & Gross, 2008; Li & Sinha, 2008; Ochsner et al., 2004; Ohira et al., 2006; Phan et al., 2005; Sinha

& Li, 2007; Wyland, Kelley, Macrae, Gordon, & Heatherton, 2003). In addition to these common neural correlates, there are some neural correlates that are more specific to one coping strategy than another. Controlling prepotent responses, for instance, activates the inferior parietal cortex and the superior frontal gyrus/premotor cortex (Dove, Pollmann, Schubert, Wiggins, & von Cramon, 2000; Garavan et al., 1999; Kawashima et al., 1996; Liddle, Kiehl, & Smith, 2001). Both of these regions are important for initiating and regulating motor responses.

There is some evidence that cognitive strategies, such as reappraisal and thought suppression, are successful in down-regulating brain regions associated with negative emotion. For instance, studies have shown that reappraisal is associated with decreased activation in the amygdala, nucleus accumbens, and insula (Drabant et al., 2009; Goldin et al., 2008; Ochsner et al., 2002; Phan et al., 2005). Thought suppression has been linked to decreased activation in the amygdala (Ohira et al., 2006). The amygdala, nucleus accumbens, and insula show increased activity during stressful or anxiety provoking events (Phan, Wager, Taylor, & Liberzon, 2004; Walker, Toufexis, & Davis, 2003). In addition to the negative correlations between cognitive coping strategies and emotional centers of the brain, studies have reported negative correlations between brain regions implicated in regulation or control and emotional centers of the brain. There is some evidence that increased activation of the VLPFC corresponds to decreased activation in the amygdala (Ochsner et al., 2002; Phan et al., 2005). Thus, reappraisal and thought suppression may decrease negative emotions because coping increases activation in inhibitory regions of the brain, and the inhibitory regions down-regulate activity in emotional centers (i.e., the amygdala).

NEUROPSYCHOLOGICAL STUDIES OF PROBLEM-SOLVING SKILLS: MAKING GOOD DECISIONS

Problem-Solving and Planning

Problem-solving is a general skill that consists of many sub-skills or individual skills. For instance, there may be at least seven sub-skills used in effective problem-solving: (1) articulating the goal or problem, (2) generating a plan, (3) keeping the goal and plan in working memory, (4) paying attention to pertinent issues (i.e., filtering out non-important issues), (5) listing all possible options, (6) evaluating and choosing an option or solution, and (7) implementing the solution. Effective problem-solving can be hindered if an individual fails to perform one sub-skill, or if they have an under-developed sub-skill.

Research has revealed that various regions of the frontal cortex are involved in many of the sub-skills used in problem-solving and decision-making (Burgess, Veitch, de Lacy Costello, & Shallice, 2000; Fukui, Murai, Fukuyama, Hayashi, & Hanakawa, 2005; Goldstein, Bernard, Fenwick, Burgess, & McNeil, 1993; Morris, Ahmed, Syed, & Toone, 1993; Owen, Downes, Sahakian, Polkey, & Robbins, 1990; Shallice & Burgess, 1991; Tranel, Hathaway-Nepple, & Anderson, 2007). The frontal cortex regions that are important for problem-solving and decision-making skills include the ACC, lateral prefrontal cortex, DLPFC, OFC, and VMPFC. More specifically, the ACC is primarily responsible for balancing competing goals. Further, the ACC has been implicated in learning task contingencies, keeping a plan in working memory, choosing an option, and execution of a plan (Baker et al., 1996; Burgess et al., 2000; Grafman, 2007). The lateral and ventrolateral prefrontal cortex are associated with generating plans, keeping the plan in working memory, sustaining attention, modifying the plan to fit context specific circumstances, paying attention to pertinent issues, switching from one cognitive task to another (i.e., task switching), and evaluating solutions (Channon, 2004; Dove et al., 2000; Grafman, 2007; Platt & Huettel, 2008). Similarly, the DLPFC has been linked to planning skills, such as generating a plan, generating the steps to fulfill a goal, keeping a plan in working memory, and following a plan (Baker et al., 1996; Barbey & Barsalou, 2009; Bechara, 2002; Burgess, 2000; Fincham, Carter, van Veen, Stenger, & Anderson, 2002; Grafman, 2007; Newman, Carpenter, Varma, & Just, 2003; Unterrainer & Owen, 2006). The OFC, unlike the other PFC regions, is particularly important for the motivational aspects of behavior. Research suggests that the OFC is responsible for anticipating the positive and negative consequences of one's behavior, and evaluating possible options or solutions to a problem (Bechara & Damasio, 2005; Hsu, Bhatt, Adolphs, Tranel, & Camerer, 2005; Lee, Chan, Leung, Fox, & Gao, 2009; O'Doherty, Kringelbach, Rolls, Hornak, & Andrews, 2001; Rahman, Sahakian, Cardinal, Rogers, & Robbins, 2001; Schoenbaum, Chiba, & Gallagher, 1998).

One region of the frontal cortex that has been heavily implicated in problem-solving and decision-making is the VMPFC. Studies have shown that individuals with VMPFC lesions score within the normal range on tasks that measure planning, listing possible solutions, and considering the consequences of choices. Individuals with lesions to the VMPFC, however, have trouble ordering the sequences of a plan, choosing any option (i.e., making a choice), choosing an advantageous option, and executing a plan (Adolphs, 1999; Barbey & Barsalou, 2009; Channon, 2004; Saver & Damasio, 1991; Tranel, Bechara, & Denburg, 2002; Tranel et al., 2007). Individuals with damage to the VMPFC also appear to focus only on the short-term positive and negative consequences of their behavior, while ignoring any long-term positive or negative consequences (Bechara, Damasio, Damasio, & Anderson, 1994; Clark et al., 2008). This disorder is commonly referred to as strategy application disorder, and researchers have used the somatic marker hypothesis to explain this disorder.

Briefly, the somatic marker hypothesis argues that the VMPFC is important for integrating cognitive information, physiological manifestations of emotions, and feelings into decision-making processes (Bechara, 2002). When presented with a choice or decision, individuals may keep the choice or goal in working memory systems such as the DLPFC. The act of choosing, however, is guided by emotions or somatic markers that are activated by signals from the amygdala (Bechara, Damasio, Damasio, & Lee, 1999). These somatic markers include changes in heart rate, skin conductance, endocrine and neurotransmitter release, smooth muscle contraction, and the musculoskeletal system (i.e., facial expression). All of these physiological changes prompt individuals to consciously or unconsciously prefer one option over another option; that is, these physiological changes help individuals develop "hunches." The physiological changes may also help bring feelings into one's consciousness via the insula (Augustine, 1996; Bechara & Damasio, 2005; Clark et al., 2008; Critchley et al., 2004; Paulus & Stein, 2006; Paulus, Rogalsky, Simmons, Feinstein, & Stein, 2003 Sanfey, Rilling, Aronson, Nystrom, & Cohen, 2003). All of this information—the cognitive representation of the goal, the physiological states associated with each goal and feelings associated with each goal—is integrated into decision-making via the VMPFC (Damasio, Everitt, & Bishop, 1996).

Sense of Agency

Individuals may plan out how to fulfill a goal, but they must also execute their goal directed behaviors to complete the sequence. Part of executing a goal directed behavior is recognizing that one is responsible for his or her own actions and attitudes leading up to the behavior. This self-awareness of the personal ability to generate one's own actions and attitudes is referred to as a sense of agency. According to Gallagher (2000, p. 15), a sense of agency is "the sense that I am the one who is causing or generating an action. For example, the sense that I am the one who is causing something to move, or that I am the one who is generating a certain thought in my stream of consciousness."

Neuroscientists have recently explored the neural correlates of agency, and they have found that the neural correlates are divided into two broad categories: one category corresponds to motor areas (i.e., physically performing the action), and the other category corresponds to cognitive areas (i.e., attributing actions to one's self or to others). The brain regions corresponding to physically performing an action include the premotor cortex and the supplementary motor area. In contrast, the regions corresponding to the cognitive aspects of agency include the DLPFC, TPJ, insula, and posterior parietal cortex (David, Newen, & Vogeley, 2008; Decety & Lamm, 2007; Farrer & Frith, 2002).

It should be noted that neuroscientists have conceptualized agency as recognizing that you are generating your own actions (i.e., moving your hand), rather than a third party generating your actions. This conceptualization of agency, as attributing your physical actions to your self, is somewhat distinct from criminologists' and psychologists' notion of agency (Laub & Sampson, 2003). Criminologists and psychologists conceptualize agency as a much broader concept that refers to one's ability "to influence intentionally one's functioning and life circumstances" (Bandura, 2006, p. 164). Thus, it remains open to empirical investigation whether the neural correlates of "physical" agency are the same correlates of behavioral human agency. As Bandura (2006) states, human agency includes forethought/planning, intentionality, self-regulation while executing a goal directed behavior, and self-awareness of one's abilities and performance. Given these components of human agency, it may be expected that additional brain regions (i.e., MPFC, VMPFC, ACC) are related to human agency.

SUMMARY

In sum, the empirical evidence suggests that the MPFC, DLPFC, VMPFC, OFC, ACC, PCC, TPJ, and the insula are important brain regions associated with social skills, coping skills for dealing with stress, and problem-solving skills. Some regions are associated with a specific type of skill, while other regions are generally involved in all three skill sets. For instance, the TPJ and its related structures (i.e., posterior superior temporal sulcus, superior temporal gyrus, angular gyrus) are more highly activated during socially relevant skills (such as perspective taking and moral reasoning) rather than during problem-solving or decision-making skills. Other regions, however, are related to a number of skills. The brain regions that are related to both socially relevant skills and analytical skills include the ACC, insula, MPFC, DLPFC, VMPFC, and OFC.

NEURO-IMAGING RESULTS FOR ANTISOCIAL GROUPS

As stated above, the skills targeted in correctional cognitive-behavioral therapies are associated with activation in the MPFC, DLPFC, VMPFC including the OFC, ACC, PCC, TPJ, and insula. Given empirical evidence that offenders lack many of the skills that are targeted in cognitive-behavioral programs (Goldstein et al., 1998), it is important to examine whether offenders also have deficits in the brain regions that are associated with the CBT skills. This is important to establish because if offenders show deficits in problem-solving skills and they also have structural or functional deficits in the MPFC (a region implicated in effective problem-solving), then we may expect that improvements in problem-solving skills during CBT programming will be accompanied by changes in the MPFC.

Indeed, studies have shown that offenders have structural and functional deficits in the MPFC, DLPFC, VMPFC, OFC, ACC, TPJ, and insula (Blair, 2004; Franklin et al., 2002; Laakso et al., 2002; Pridemore, Chambers, & McArthur, 2005; Raine, Buchsbaum, & LaCasse, 1997; Raine & Yang, 2006; Raine et al., 1994; Volavka, 1999; Yang et al., 2005). For instance, Raine et al. (2000) found that the volume of gray matter in the prefrontal cortex was significantly reduced among individuals with antisocial personality disorder, compared to healthy controls and individuals with substance dependency problems. In line with the somatic marker hypothesis, their results also revealed that individuals with antisocial personality disorder had lower mean levels of skin conductance and lower heart rate levels during a social stressor task. A recent fMRI analysis revealed that psychopaths had lower levels of activity in the amygdala, OFC, insula, somatosensory cortex, PCC, ACC, and supplemental motor area during a conditioning task, relative to healthy controls (Birbaumer et al., 2005). Psychopathic individuals and healthy controls did not significantly differ on conditioned responses, but psychopathic individuals exhibited lower levels of skin conductance and lower emotional valence ratings during the conditioning task. Finally, Sterzer, Stadler, Poustka, and Kleinschmidt (2008) found that gray matter volume in the insula and amygdala was significantly reduced among conduct disordered adolescent males, relative to healthy controls. Their analyses also revealed a positive correlation between insula gray matter and empathy scores for conduct disordered males.

In sum, studies have shown that antisocial individuals have structural and/or functional deficits in the same brain regions that are targeted in cognitive-behavioral therapies. Based on these findings, it may be hypothesized that cognitive-behavioral therapies that target social, coping skills, and problem-solving skills may be effective because these therapies cause changes in brain regions that are underdeveloped or dysfunctional in offending populations. It is not yet known whether correctional cognitive-behavioral therapies improve functioning in criminogenic brain regions. Yet, cognitive-behavioral therapies that target symptoms of mental disorders, such as depression and phobias, have been found to significantly improve brain functioning in areas linked to mental disorder (Paquette et al., 2003). In light of this evidence, it may be expected that cognitive-behavioral therapies for criminal behavior improve functioning in brain regions linked to criminal behavior.

NEURO-IMAGING STUDIES ON THE EFFECTS OF COGNITIVE BEHAVIORAL THERAPIES FOR MENTAL DISORDERS

Neuropsychologists have recently begun to explore whether cognitive-behavioral therapy is associated with changes in brain function. Schwartz and colleagues (1996) were some of the first researchers to examine the effects of cognitive-behavioral therapy on brain functioning. In their study, they measured brain activity in nine subjects with obsessive-compulsive disorder before and after the subjects completed a 10 week cognitive-behavioral program for obsessive compulsive disorder. Prior to treatment, there was a significant amount of activity between the OFC and the caudate nucleus, and between the OFC and the thalamus. After treatment, there was a significant reduction in activity between these structures, and the brain functioning of the patients resembled that of healthy controls. Further, the results revealed that treatment subjects who experienced a decrease in OCD symptoms after CBT treatment had lower rates of glucose metabolism in the caudate than subjects who did not experience a decrease in OCD symptoms after CBT. Additional studies have revealed that CBT improves functioning in additional regions, including the ACC, and improved brain functioning corresponds to fewer OCD symptoms (Saxena et al., 2009).

Since Schwartz et al.'s (1996) study, subsequent researchers have reported that cognitive-behavioral therapies for panic disorder, phobias, and depression are associated with changes in brain functioning (Beauregard, 2007; DeRubeis, Siegle, & Hollon, 2008; Paquette et al., 2003; Prasko et al., 2004). For instance, Goldapple et al.'s (2004) analysis of unmedicated patients with unipolar depression revealed that cognitive-behavioral therapy reduced depressive symptoms, and that reductions in depressive symptoms were associated with functional changes in the DLPFC, VLPFC, MPFC, PCC, inferior parietal lobe (BA40), and inferior temporal cortex. Treatment response was also associated with increases in glucose metabolism in the hippocampus and ACC. More recently, Fu et al. (2008) found that depressed patients had lower levels of activity in the ACC, superior frontal gyrus, PCC, inferior parietal cortex, and precuneus than controls prior to cognitive-behavioral treatment. After 16 weeks of CBT treatment, activity in these regions significantly increased among depressed patients, and depressed patients had activity levels in these regions that were comparable to healthy controls; thus, their activity levels in the frontal cortex, inferior parietal cortex, ACC, and PCC were normalized after receiving CBT treatment.

The results from the above studies suggest that cognitive-behavioral therapies may effectively treat a range of disorders because these therapies improve brain functioning. More specifically, cognitive-behavioral therapies for mental disorders may improve functioning in the frontal cortex, parietal cortex, cingulate cortex, hippocampus, and cerebellum. It remains open for empirical investigation whether cognitive-behavioral therapies for antisocial behaviors will also improve functioning within these regions. As previously stated, the skills targeted in cognitive-behavioral therapies for antisocial populations are associated with activation in the MPFC, DLPFC, DMPFC,

VMPFC including the OFC, ACC, PCC, TPJ, and insula. Thus, cognitive-behavioral therapies for antisocial populations should improve functioning in the MPFC, DLPFC, DMPFC, VMPFC, OFC, ACC, PCC, TPJ, and insula.

It should be noted that the above interventions ranged from intensive, four week treatments (i.e., three hour meetings once a week for four weeks) to moderate, twenty week treatments (i.e., one hour a week for twenty weeks). These studies reveal that a combination of short, intensive or long, moderate interventions can produce significant changes in brain function and behavior. Further, research suggests that interventions may produce both normalizing and compensatory effects among participants (Temple et al., 2003). That is, treatment participants may look more similar to healthy individuals in terms of brain functioning after treatment, but they may also develop alternative circuits or pathways to compensate for any remaining neural deficits associated with a skill. For instance, Paquette et al. (2003) found that individuals with spider phobia exhibited high levels of activity in the DLPFC and the paraphippocampus prior to treatment, but that participants' activity levels in these regions were comparable to those in healthy controls (i.e., normalized) after treatment. The authors also found, however, that participants exhibited an increase of activity in the inferior occipital gyrus, inferior frontal gyrus, and fusiform gyrus after treatment, while the healthy controls did not exhibit these activation patterns; thus, the emergence of new activation patterns among participants post-treatment relative to healthy controls indicates that additional regions may be recruited to complete a task.

A couple of caveats should be mentioned before proceeding to the discussion. It is important to note that the cognitive-behavioral programs that were administered in the studies above were administered by clinical psychologists in clinical settings. This amount of control over treatment integrity is often difficult to achieve in "real world" criminal justice settings; thus, researchers may find the greatest amount of change in brain functioning in high integrity or clinical programs. In addition, the studies examined brain functioning immediately prior to and after treatment; therefore, it is unclear whether any changes in brain activity persist for an extended period of time. It is hypothesized that the changes may persist if individuals continue practicing the cognitive-behavioral techniques they learned in treatment, but such changes will not be stable if they do not continue using a skill (i.e., neurons that fire together, wire together/ neurons that fire apart, wire apart).

DISCUSSION

The analysis of the extant literature provides solid ground to suggest that the effectiveness of CBT is likely rooted, in important ways, in how this prominent correctional intervention affect offenders' brain functioning. We have endeavored to identify the neural mechanisms that underlie why CBT programs work to reduce recidivism. As suggested by the empirical literature, it is expected that CBT for correctional populations will predominantly lead to changes in brain functioning in the MPFC, DLPFC, DMPFC, VMPFC, OFC, ACC, PCC, TPJ, and the insula. Neuroimaging research has shown that these regions are associated with a wide range of social skills, coping skills, and problem-solving skills. While other regions may be activated during social, coping, and problem-solving tasks, it is the above regions that are consistently activated during these tasks. Thus, researchers who are interested in the neural mechanisms of CBT's effectiveness should, at a minimum, examine changes in these eight regions. Other important regions may be identified during the course of investigation.

These results have three further implications. First, to the extent that CBT reduces criminal behavior because it improves brain functioning, it may be useful to use brain imaging technology to enhance CBT programs, especially for difficult to treat populations. For instance, the R&R2 program is a new strength-based curriculum that is grounded in research from the cognitive neuroscience discipline (Ross & Hilborn, 2008). The R&R2 curriculum encourages clients to develop various cognitive prosocial skills such as identifying others' emotions, emotional regulation, identifying and interpreting social cues, self-awareness, impulse control, and anticipating the consequences of one's actions. Clients who successfully practice and master such prosocial skills may build new neural pathways within their brain, which may foster prosocial behavior. The long-term effectiveness of R&R2 over other treatment paradigms remains an empirical question, but preliminary evidence suggests that the program is effective in reducing disruptive and antisocial behavior (Young, Chick, & Gudjonsson, 2010). Since the R&R2 program is predicated on research from cognitive neuroscience, it is important for future research to test whether there are functional changes in R&R2 clients after completing the program.

Before proceeding to the second implication, it is important to note that many CBT programs may not be able to employ brain imaging techniques in their programs. Programs may, however, use well-validated neuropsychological tasks and tests to examine whether CBT intervention is correlated with changes in brain functioning. As discussed above, researchers have found that neuropsychological tasks representing social skills, coping skills, and problem solving skills are related to brain activity in particular regions. Programs may include these tasks throughout treatment as one way to proxy changes in brain functioning. In particular, programs may employ the Go/No-go task (i.e., response inhibition), the Stroop task (i.e., cognitive control, response selection, monitoring performance), the Iowa Gambling Task (i.e., anticipating consequences and decision-making), the Tower of London or Tower of Hanoi (i.e., planning and problem-solving), and the Multiple Errands Task (i.e., planning and decision-making). Other tasks may also be integrated into the evaluation, such as identifying emotional facial expressions and thought suppression tasks. It may be hypothesized that programs that produce large improvements in task outcomes have the greatest effect on brain functioning, and that one could examine whether improvements in task outcomes were related to treatment effectiveness.

Second, understanding how CBT impacts brain functioning may be especially relevant when discussing the lack of CBT effectiveness for certain populations. For instance, Fishbein and colleagues have found that offenders with deficits in executive functions have poorer treatment outcomes in CBT than offenders without deficits in executive functions (Fishbein, Hyde, Coe, & Paschall, 2004; Fishbein et al., 2009). Given the extant literature on the neural correlates of executive functioning, it may be important to understand which CBT components have a greater effect on brain functioning than other components for this difficult to treat population. This information may then be pieced together to find an optimal set of treatments for this subgroup.

It is important to note that we have described the relationship between CBT and brain functioning as working in only one direction: CBT→brain functioning. It is very likely though that there are reciprocal relationships between CBT effectiveness and brain functioning (CBT↔brain functioning). Fishbein et al. (2004) recently put forth a conceptual model that explained how individual differences in executive functioning (which is associated with functioning in the prefrontal cortex) moderate the effectiveness of CBT for antisocial populations; thus, brain functioning may be a responsivity concern (Sakai et al., 2006). The conceptual model assumed reciprocal relationships between executive function and treatment response. While Fishbein and colleagues have not examined whether CBT leads to changes in brain functioning, their research group has found that antisocial individuals who have deficits in emotional regulation and executive functioning have poorer treatment outcomes in CBT programs than antisocial individuals who do not have such deficits (Fishbein et al., 2006; Fishbein & Sheppard, 2006; Fishbein et al., 2009). It has been suggested, therefore, that programs must first address offenders' deficits in key areas (i.e., anticipating consequences, self-regulation) before proceeding to other skills (i.e., perspective taking).

Third, and more broadly, our review shows the potential value in closing the gap that has traditionally existed between biosocial criminology and correctional intervention. Again, biological explanations of crime were long seen as hostile to notions of offender change. By depicting offenders as marred by immutable physical pathologies, biological thinking justified policing ranging from eugenics to prolonged incapacitation and "extirpation" (i.e., capital punishment). At present, however, progress in intervening with offenders cannot be held hostage by older, albeit legitimate, concerns about the repressive potential of imputing crime to biological defects. By contrast, the ability to show that interventions, such as CBT, activate if not reshape neuropsychological processes opens fresh vistas for demonstrating why treatments are capable of effective meaningful offender change. Accordingly, efforts to move toward a biosocial theory of offender rehabilitation may provide a powerful rationale for why treatment intervention must be a core goal of the correctional enterprise.

APPENDIX A. OVERALL ORGANIZATION OF THE BRAIN

Lobes

There are four lobes in the brain: frontal lobe, temporal lobe, parietal lobe, and occipital lobe (Walsh, 1978). The lobes primarily discussed in this manuscript include the frontal and temporal lobe, with some mention of the parietal lobe. The occipital lobe is not thought to be directly related to antisocial behavior. Each lobe can be further sub-divided into regions called Brodmann areas (BA). BAs are regions of similar cells that may perform similar functions.

The *frontal lobe* is located at the front of the brain, right behind the forehead, and it extends to the middle of the skull. The frontal lobe is responsible for a variety of functions including abstract reasoning, problem solving, planning, self-control, and some motor skills. It comprises a number of Brodmann areas including:

- Area 4 (Primary motor cortex)
- Area 6 (Premotor cortex and Supplementary Motor Area)

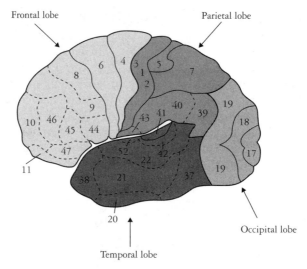

FIGURE S10.1. Lateral/side view of the brain by Brodmann areas.
Source: http://www.umich.edu/~ cogneuro/jpg/Brodmann.html.

- Area 8 (Frontal eye fields)
- Area 9 (Dorsolateral prefrontal cortex)
- Area 10 (Frontopolar area)
- Areas 11 & 12 (Orbitofrontal cortex)
- Area 44 & 45 (Broca's area)
- Area 46 (Dorsolateral prefrontal cortex)
- Area 47 (Inferior prefrontal gyrus)

The temporal lobe is located along the bottom section of the brain. The temporal lobe is responsible for functions such as perception and processing of auditory cues, formation of long term memories, language processing (i.e., identification of words, comprehension, organization of words, verbal memory), visual perception, and emotion-related functions (i.e., recognition of emotions, emotional memory). It includes the following Brodmann areas:

- Area 20 (Inferior temporal gyrus)
- Area 21 (Middle temporal gyrus)
- Area 22 (Superior temporal gyrus, posterior portion of 22 is Wernicke's area)
- Area 37 (Fusiform gyrus)
- Area 38 (Temporopolar area)
- Area 41 & 42 (Primary and auditory association cortex)
- Area 52 (Parainsular area)

The parietal lobe occupies the middle portion of the skull and it extends back towards the base of the brain. It is responsible for tactile perception, processing somatosensory information (i.e., pain, touch, heat), motor skills, and integrating visual and somatosensory information with motor skills (i.e., hand-eye coordination). It includes the following Brodmann areas:

- Area 1, 2, and 3 (Primary somatosensory cortex)
- Area 5 (Secondary somatosensory association cortex)
- Area 7 (Posterior parietal cortex)
- Area 39 (Angular gyrus, section of Wernicke's area)
- Area 40 (Supramarginal gyrus, section of Wernicke's area)
- Area 43 (Subcentral area)

The occipital lobe is located at the back of the brain, near the brain stem and cerebellum. It is responsible for the perception and processing of visual information. The occipital lobe includes the following Brodmann areas:

- Area 17 (Primary visual cortex)
- Area 18 (Lateral occipital gyrus)
- Area 19 (Lateral occipital gyrus)

Gyri and Sulci

The brain has ridges or bumps that are divided by grooves. The bumps are referred to as gyri (or gyrus for singlular) and they are separated by grooves called sulci (or a sulcus for singular). A lobe may contain multiple gyri and sulci. For instance, the frontal lobe has a superior frontal gyrus, a medial frontal gyrus, and an inferior frontal gyrus, with each gyrus separated from the adjacent gyrus by asulcus.

Directionality

One way the lobes and gyri can be divided up is by directionality. As shown below, areas that are closest to the front of the brain (or the forehead) can be labeled as anterior, and areas that are towards the back of the skull can be labeled as posterior. For instance, the cingulate cortex is divided up into an anterior portion (the section of the cingulate cortex closest to the forehead) and a posterior portion (the section closest to the back of the head).

The areas of the brain can also be labeled according to a vertical plane. That is, areas are labeled according to whether they are closest to the top of one's head (i.e., superior/dorsal) or whether they are closest to the bottom of the brain (i.e., inferior/ventral). For instance, the frontal cortex has three gyri: a superior frontal gyrus, a medial frontal gyrus, and an inferior frontal gyrus.

Finally, areas of the brain can be discussed from an inside-out approach. That is, neurons that are closest to the core or middle part of the brain can be labeled as medial, while areas that are closest to the sides of the brain are labeled as lateral. For instance, the prefrontal cortex can be divided into medial and lateral areas. Cells in the medial prefrontal cortex will be closer to the middle of the brain, while cells in the lateral prefrontal cortex will be closer to the side or wall of the brain.

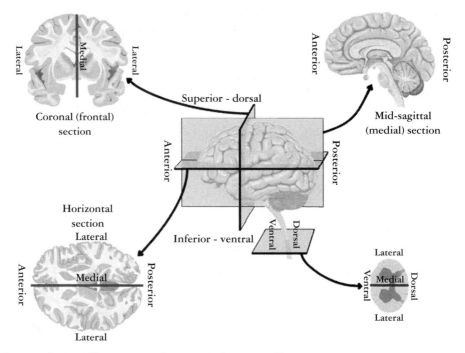

FIGURE S10.2. Illustration of anatomical terms of location.

Source: http://homepage.smc.edu/russell_richard/Psych2/Graphics/human_brain_directions.htm.

SPECIFIC BRAIN REGIONS

Frontal Cortex Regions

Medial Prefrontal Cortex

- Abbreviation: MPFC
- Brodmann areas that are included in the MPFC are areas 9, 10, 11, 14, 24, 25, and 32.
- Skills related to greater activation in the MPFC: Perspective taking, moral feelings, moral reasoning, self awareness, self-control, reappraisal, thought suppression, and anticipating consequences.
- Some of the more specific skills associated with the MPFC include perception of faces and objects, introspective thought, regulation of emotion, attention, working memory, self-awareness, and attributing the intent of one's behavior.
- Note: The MPFC is a large region that includes and overlaps with various other structures, such as the dorsolateral prefrontal cortex, ventromedial prefrontal cortex, orbitofrontal cortex, and anterior cingulate cortex.

Dorsolateral Prefrontal Cortex

- Abbreviation: DLPFC
- Brodmann areas that are included in the DLPFC are areas 9 and 46. Some scholars have a more liberal view on which areas comprise the DLPFC, and as such they include other Brodmann areas such as areas 10, 11, 45, and 47.
- Skills related to greater activation in DLPFC: Perspective taking, moral reasoning, self-awareness, self-control, reappraisal, thought suppression, planning, decision-making, and sense of agency.
- Some of the more specific skills associated with the DLPFC include self-evaluation, maintaining attention during a task, inhibiting behavioral responses, working memory, task switching, and the ability to form a plan and select a solution.

Dorsomedial Prefrontal Cortex

- Abbreviation: DMPFC
- The DMPFC includes BA 8 and BA 32.
- Skills related to greater activation in the DMPFC: Perspective taking, reappraisal, and thought suppression.
- Some of the more specific skills associated with the DMPFC include evaluating the emotional states of others, cognitive regulation, and understanding the link between one's external environment and one's internal state.

Ventrolateral Prefrontal Cortex

- Abbreviation: VLPFC
- The VLPFC includes BA 44, 45, and 47.
- Skills related to greater activation in the VLPFC: Perspective taking, self-control, reappraisal, thought suppression, and planning.
- Some of the more specific skills associated with the VLPFC include regulation of emotion, cognition, and behavioral responses.

Ventromedial Prefrontal Cortex

- Abbreviation: VMPFC
- The VMPFC may include BA 10, 12, 24, 32, and 47.
- Skills related to greater activation in the VMPFC: Perspective taking, moral feelings, moral reasoning, planning, anticipating consequences, and decision-making.

- Some of the more specific skills associated with the VMPFC include social emotions (i.e., guilt, shame), negative emotionality, executing a plan, considering multiple types of information during decision-making, efficiency of decision-making, anticipating long term positive and negative consequences, and assessing similarities between one's self and others.

Orbitofrontal Cortex

- Abbreviation: OFC
- The OFC may include BA's 10, 11, and 47.
- Skills related to greater activation in the OFC: Perspective taking, moral feelings, moral reasoning, self-awareness, self-control, reappraisal, thought suppression, anticipating consequences, and decision-making.
- Some of the more specific skills associated with the OFC include emotional regulation, motivational aspects of planning and behavior, anticipation and evaluation of rewards and punishments, and linking emotions to moral judgments.

Cingulate Cortex
Anterior Cingulate Cortex

- Abbreviation: ACC
- BA 24 and 32 correspond to the ACC.
- Skills related to greater activation in the ACC: Perspective taking, moral feelings, moral reasoning, self-awareness, self-control, reappraisal, thought suppression, planning, and decision-making.
- Some of the more specific skills associated with the ACC include attention, monitoring performance, self-awareness of internal and physiological states, resolving response conflict (i.e., a conflict between two goals, or a conflict between emotional and cognitive signals), following a plan, and emotional regulation during times of stress.

Posterior Cingulate Cortex

- Abbreviation: PCC
- Brodmann areas that are included in the PCC include 23 and 31.
- Skills related to greater activation in the PCC: Perspective taking, moral feelings, moral reasoning, self-awareness, self-control, and decision-making.
- Some of the more specific skills associated with the PCC include monitoring sensory signals, processing emotional cues, self-awareness of one's traits and abilities, emotional memory, and regulation of attention.

Premotor Cortex

- Abbreviation: N/A
- Premotor cortex includes BA 6.
- Skills related to greater activation in the premotor cortex: Self-control and agency.
- Some of the more specific skills associated with the premotor cortex include planning and regulating motor skills and responses.

Inferior Parietal Cortex

- Abbreviation: IFP cortex
- The IFP area that is focused on in this manuscript is found in Brodmann's area 40.
- Skills related to greater activation in the IFP cortex: Moral reasoning, self-control, planning, and decision-making.
- Some of the more specific skills associated with IFP cortex include spatial working memory, coordinating movements, processing symbols or words during reading, ability to filter out irrelevant information, evaluation of risk, and planning goal oriented actions.

Insula

- Abbreviation: N/A
- It is believed that the insula contains BA's 13, 14, and 15, and other researchers have considered areas 44, 45, and 52 as part of the insula. The insula relays sensory information and emotional signals to higher order structures (i.e., anterior cingulate), and from higher order structures to other areas of the brain (i.e., parietal cortex, amygdala).
- Skills related to greater activation in the insula: Perspective taking, moral feelings, self-awareness, self-control, anticipating consequences, decision-making, and sense of agency.
- Some of the more specific skills associated with the insula include evaluating risk, self-attribution, linking emotions with cognition, processing socio-emotional cues, and processing of pain and aversive sensory signals.

Temporo-Parietal Junction

- Abbreviation: TPJ
- The TPJ is a junction where the temporal lobe and the parietal lobe meet. This area includes various substructures. These substructures include: angular gyrus (BA 39), the posterior superior temporal gyrus (BA 22), and the posterior superior temporal sulcus (pSTS).

- Skills related to greater activation in the TPJ: Perspective taking, moral feelings, moral reasoning, self-awareness, reappraisal, and sense of agency.
- Some of the more specific skills associated with the TPJ include the perception of social cues, processing language and verbal cues, a sense of responsibility for one's actions, the processing of intentionality, and moral emotions such as embarrassment, pride, and regret.

Temporal Poles

- Abbreviation: N/A
- The temporal poles correspond to BA 38 or the anterior portion of the superior temporal gyrus.
- Skills related to greater activation of the temporal poles: Perspective taking, moral feelings, and moral reasoning.
- Some of the more specific skills associated with the temporal poles include retrieval of emotional memories, processing intentionality, and recalling social information.

Amygdala

- Abbreviation: N/A
- The amygdala is not identified by a Brodmann area.
- Skills related to greater activation of the amygdala: Perspective taking, moral feelings, moral reasoning, and anticipating consequences.
- Some of the more specific skills associated with amygdala include making crude emotional judgments about stimuli, regulating emotional memory, recognition of emotion and social cues, unconscious imitation of others' facial expressions during emotional events, and social emotions such as anger and empathy.

Walsh, K. (1978). *Neuropsychology: A clinical approach.* New York: Churchill Livingstone.

REFERENCES

Adolphs, R. (1999). Social cognition and the human brain. *Trends in Cognitive Sciences*, 3, 469–479.

Amodio, D. M., & Frith, C. D. (2006). Meeting of minds: The medial frontal cortex and social cognition. *Nature*, 7, 268–277.

Andersen, S. L., & Teicher, M. H. (2009). Desperately drive and no brakes: Developmental stress exposure and subsequent risk for substance abuse. *Neuroscience and Biobehavioral Reviews,* 33, 516–524.

Anderson, S. W., Bechara, A., Damasio, H., Tranel, D., & Damasio, A. R. (1999). Impairment of social and moral behavior related to early damage in human prefrontal cortex. *Nature Neuroscience*, 2, 1032–1037.

Andrews, D. A., & Bonta, J. (2006). *The psychology of criminal conduct,* 4th ed. Cincinnati, OH: LexisNexis/Anderson.

Andrews, D., Zinger, I., Hoge, R. D., Bonta, J., Gendreau, P., & Cullen, F. T. (1990). Does correctional treatment work? A clinically relevant and psychologically informed meta-analysis. *Criminology,* 28(3), 369–404.

Augustine, J. R. (1996). Circuitry and functional aspects of the insular lobe in primates including humans. *Brain Research Reviews,* 22, 229–244.

Baker, S. C., Rogers, R. D., Owen, A. M., Frith, C. D., Dolan, R. J., Frackowiak, R. S. J., et al. (1996). Neural systems engaged in planning: A PET study of the Tower of London task. *Neuropsychologia,* 34, 515–526.

Bandura, A. (2006). Toward a psychology of human agency. *Perspectives on Psychological Science,* 1, 164–180.

Barbey, A. K., & Barsalou, L. W. (2009). Reasoning and problem solving: Models. *Encyclopedia of Neuroscience,* 8, 35–43.

Beauregard, M. (2007). Mind does really matter: Evidence from neuroimaging studies of emotional self-regulation, psychotherapy, and placebo effect. *Progress in Neurobiology,* 81, 218–236.

Bechara, A. (2002). The neurology of social cognition. *Brain,* 125, 1673–1675.

Bechara, A., & Damasio, A. R. (2005). The somatic marker hypothesis: A neural theory of economic decision. *Games and Economic Behavior,* 52, 336–372.

Bechara, A., Damasio, A. R., Damasio, H., & Anderson, S. W. (1994). Insensitivity to future consequences following damage to human prefrontal cortex. *Cognition,* 50,7–15.

Bechara, A., Damasio, H., Damasio, A. R., & Lee, G. P. (1999). Different contributions of the human amygdala and ventromedial prefrontal cortex to decision-making. The *Journal of Neuroscience,* 19, 5473–5481.

Bechara, A., & Naqvi, N. (2004). Listening to your heart: Interoceptive awareness as a gateway to feeling. *Nature Neuroscience,* 7, 102–103.

Birbaumer, N., Veit, R., Lotze, M., Erb, M., Hermann, C., Grodd, W., et al. (2005). Deficient fear conditioning in psychopathy: A functional magnetic resonance imaging study. *Archives of General Psychiatry,* 62, 799–805.

Blair, R. J. R. (2004). The role of orbital frontal cortex in the modulation of antisocial behavior. *Brain and Cognition,* 55, 198–208.

Blair, R. J. R. (2005). Responding to the emotions of others: Dissociating forms of empathy through the study of typical and psychiatric populations. *Consciousness and Cognition,* 14, 698–718.

Bruinius, H. (2006). *Better for all the world: The secret history of forced sterilization and America's quest for racial purity.* New York: Knopf.

Buonomano, D. V., & Merzenich, M. M. (1998). Cortical plasticity: From synapses to maps. *Annual Review of Neuroscience,* 21, 149–186.

Burgess, P. W. (2000). Strategy application disorder: The role of the frontal lobes in human multitasking. *Psychological Research,* 63, 279–288.

Burgess, P. W., Veitch, E., de Lacy Costello, A., & Shallice, T. (2000). The cognitive and neuroanatomical correlates of multitasking. *Neuropsychologia,* 38, 848–863.

Bush, J., Glick, B., & Taymans, J. (1997). Thinking for a change: *Integrated cognitive behavior change program.* Washington, DC: U.S. Department of Justice, National Institute of Corrections.

Camille, N., Coricelli, G., Sallet, J., Pradat-Diehl, P., Duhamel, J. R., & Sirigu, A. (2004). The involvement of the orbitofrontal cortex in the experience of regret. *Science,* 304, 1167–1170.

Carr, L., Iacoboni, M., Dubeau, M. C., Mazziotta, J. C., & Lenzi, G. L. (2003). Neural mechanisms of empathy in humans: A relay from neural systems for imitation to limbic areas. *Proceedings of the National Academy of Sciences,* 100, 5497–5502.

Casebeer, W. D. (2003). Moral cognition and its neural constituents. *Nature Reviews Neuroscience,* 4, 840–847.

Casey, B. J., Trainor, R. J., Orendi, J. L., Schubert, A. B., Nystrom, L. E., Giedd, J. N., et al. (1997). A developmental functional MRI study of prefrontal activation during performance of a go-no-go task. *Journal of Cognitive Neuroscience,* 9, 835–847.

Channon, S. (2004). Frontal lobe dysfunction and everyday problem-solving: Social and non-social contributions. *Acta Psychologia,* 115, 235–254.

Clark, L., Bechara, A., Damasio, H., Aitken, M. R. F., Sahakian, B. J., & Robbins, T. W. (2008). Differential effects of insular and ventromedial prefrontal cortex lesions on risky decision-making. *Brain,* 131, 1311–1322.

Cornwell, J. (2003). *Hitler's scientists: Science, war, and the devil's pact.* New York: Penguin.

Critchley, H. D., Wiens, S., Rotshtein, P., Öhman, A., & Dolan, R. J. (2004). Neural systems supporting interoceptive awareness. *Nature Neuroscience,* 7, 189–195.

Cullen, F. T. (2005). The twelve people who saved rehabilitation: How the science of criminology made a difference—The American Society of Criminology 2004 Presidential Address. *Criminology,* 43, 1–42.

Cullen, F. T., & Gilbert, K. E. (1982). *Reaffirming rehabilitation.* Cincinnati, OH: Anderson.

Cullen, F. T., & Jonson, C. L. (2010). Rehabilitation and treatment. In J. Q. Wilson & J. Petersilia (Eds.), *Crime: Public policies for crime control,* 3rd ed. New York: Oxford University Press.

Damasio, A. R., Everitt, B. J., & Bishop, D. (1996). The somatic marker hypothesis and the possible functions of the prefrontal cortex. *Philosophical Transactions: Biological Science,* 351, 1413–1420.

David, N., Newen, A., & Vogeley, K. (2008). The "sense of agency" and its underlying cognitive and neural mechanisms. *Consciousness and Cognition,* 17, 523–534.

Decety, J., & Lamm, C. (2007). The role of the right temporoparietal junction in social interaction: How low-level computation processes contribute to meta-cognition. *The Neuroscientist,* 13, 580–593.

Denson, T. F., Pedersen, W. C., Ronquillo, J., & Nandy, A. S. (2009). The angry brain: Neural correlates of anger, anger rumination, and aggressive personality. *Journal of Cognitive Neuroscience,* 21, 734–744.

DeRubeis, R. J., Siegle, G. J., & Hollon, S. D. (2008). Cognitive therapy vs. medications for depression: Treatment outcomes and neural mechanisms. *Nature Reviews Neuroscience,* 9, 788–796.

Doidge, N. (2007). *The brain that changes itself: Stories of personal triumph from the frontiers of brain science.* New York: Penguin.

Dove, A., Pollmann, S., Schubert, T., Wiggins, C. J., & von Cramon, D. Y. (2000). Prefrontal cortex activation in task switching: An event related fMRI study. *Cognitive Brain Research,* 9, 103–109.

Dowden, C., & Andrews, D. A. (2000). Effective correctional treatment and violent reoffending: A meta-analysis. *Canadian Journal of Criminology,* 42, 449–476.

Drabant, E. M., McRae, K., Manuck, S. B., Hariri, A. R., & Gross, J. J. (2009). Individual differences in typical reappraisal use predict amygdala and prefrontal responses. *Biological Psychiatry,* 65, 367–373.

Eisenberger, N. I., Lieberman, M. D., & Williams, K. D. (2003). Does rejection hurt? An fMRI study of social exclusion. *Science,* 302, 290–292.

Farrer, C., & Frith, C. D. (2002). Experiencing oneself vs. another person as being the cause of an action: The neural correlates of the experience of agency. *NeuroImage,* 15, 596–603.

Farrington, D. P., & Welsh, B. C. (2007). *Saving children from a life in crime: Early risk factors and effective interventions.* New York: Oxford University Press.

Fincham, J. M., Carter, C. S., van Veen, V., Stenger, V. A., & Anderson, J. R. (2002). Neural mechanisms of planning: A computational analysis using event-related fMRI. *Proceedings of the National Academy of Sciences, 99*, 3346–3351.

Fishbein, D., Hyde, C., Coe, B., & Paschall, M. J. (2004). Neurocognitive and physiological prerequisites for prevention of adolescent drug abuse. *The Journal of Primary Prevention, 24*, 471–495.

Fishbein, D. H., Hyde, C., Eldreth, D., Paschall, M. J., Hubal, R., Das, A., et al. (2006). Neurocognitive skills moderate urban male adolescents' responses to preventive intervention materials. *Drug and Alcohol Dependence, 82*, 47–60.

Fishbein, D., & Sheppard, M. (2006). *Assessing the role of neuropsychological functioning in inmates' treatment response.* Washington, DC: National Institute of Justice.

Fishbein, D., Sheppard, M., Hyde, C., Hubal, R., Newlin, D., Serin, R., et al. (2009). Deficits in behavioral inhibition predict treatment engagement in prison inmates. *Law and Human Behavior, 33*, 419–435.

Franklin, T. R., Acton, P. D., Maldjian, J. A., Gray, J. D., Croft, J. R., Dackis, C. A., et al. (2002). Decreased gray matter concentration in the insular, orbitofrontal, cingulate, and temporal cortices of cocaine patients. *Biological Psychiatry, 51*, 134–142.

Fu, C. H. Y., Williams, S. C. R., Cleare, A. J., Scott, J., Mitterschiffthaler, M. T., Walsh, N. D., et al. (2008). Neural responses to sad facial expressions in major depression following cognitive-behavioral therapy. *Biological Psychiatry, 64*, 505–512.

Fukui, H., Murai, T., Fukuyama, H., Hayashi, T., & Hanakawa, T. (2005). Functional activity related to risk anticipation during performance of the Iowa gambling task. *NeuroImage, 24*, 253–259.

Gallagher, S. (2000). Philosophical conceptions of the self: Implications for cognitive science. *Trends in Cognitive Sciences, 4*, 14–21.

Garavan, H., Ross, T. J., & Stein, E. A. (1999). Right hemisphere dominance of inhibitory control: An event related functional MRI study. *Proceedings of the National Academy of Sciences, 96*, 8301–8306.

Gendreau, P. (1996). The principles of effective intervention with offenders. In A. T. Harland (Ed.), Choosing correctional options that work: *Defining the demand and evaluating the supply* (pp. 117–130). Thousand Oaks, CA: Sage.

Gillath, O., Bunge, S. A., Shaver, P. R., Wendelken, C., & Mikulincer, M. (2005). Attachment-style differences in the ability to suppress negative thoughts: Exploring the neural correlates. *NeuroImage, 28*, 835–847.

Goldapple, K., Segal, Z., Garson, C., Lau, M., Bieling, P., Kennedy, S., et al. (2004). Modulation of cortical-limbic pathways in major depression. *Archives of General Psychiatry, 61*, 34–41.

Goldin, P. R., McRae, K., Ramel, W., & Gross, J. J. (2008). The neural bases of emotion regulation: Reappraisal and suppression of negative emotion. *Biological Psychiatry, 63*, 577–586.

Goldstein, L. H., Bernard, S., Fenwick, P. B. C., Burgess, P. W., & McNeil, J. (1993). Unilateral frontal lobectomy can produce strategy application disorder. *Journal of Neurology, Neurosurgery, and Psychiatry, 56*, 274–276.

Goldstein, A. P., Glick, B., & Gibb, J. C. (1998). *Aggression replacement training: A comprehensive intervention for aggressive youth.* Champaign, IL: Research Press.

Grafman, J. (2007). Planning and the brain. In B. L. Miller & J.L. Cummings (Eds.), *The human frontal lobes: Functions and disorders* (pp. 249–262). New York: Guilford Press.

Greene, J., & Haidt, J. (2002). How (and where) does moral judgment work? *Trends in Cognitive Sciences, 6*, 517–523.

Greene, J. D., Nystrom, L. E., Engeil, A. D., Darley, J. M., & Cohen, J. D. (2004). The neural bases of cognitive conflict and control in moral judgment. *Neuron, 44*, 389–400.

Greene, J. D., & Paxton, J. M. (2009). Patterns of neural activity associated with honest and dishonest moral decisions. *Proceedings of the National Academy of Sciences, 106*, 12506–12511.

Greene, J. D., Sommerville, R. B., Nystrom, L. E., Darley, J. M., & Cohen, J. D. (2001). An fMRI investigation of emotional engagement in moral judgment. *Science,* 293, 2105–2108.

Harenski, C. L., Antonenko, O., Shane, M. S., & Kiehl, K. A. (2009). Gender differences in neural mechanisms underlying moral sensitivity. *Scan,* 3, 313–321.

Heatherton, T. F., & Krendi, A. C. (2009). Social emotion: Neuroimaging. *Encyclopedia of Neuroscience,* 9, 35–39.

Herbert, B. M., Pollatos, O., & Schandry, R. (2007). Interoceptive sensitivity and emotion processing: An EEG study. *International Journal of Psychophysiology,* 65, 214–227.

Hsu, M., Bhatt, M., Adolphs, R., Tranel, D., & Camerer, C. F. (2005). Neural systems responding to degrees of uncertainty in human decision-making. *Science,* 310, 1680–1683.

Jackson, P. L., Brunet, E., Meltzoff, A. N., & Decety, J. (2006). Empathy examined through the neural mechanisms involved in imaging how I feel versus how you feel pain. *Neuropsychologia,* 44, 752–761.

Johnson, S. C., Baxter, L. C., Wilder, L. S., Pipe, J. G., Heiserman, J. E., & Prigatano, G. P. (2002). Neural correlates of self-reflection. *Brain,* 125, 1808–1814.

Johnston, M. V. (2009). Plasticity in the developing brain: Implications for rehabilitation. *Developmental Disabilities Research Reviews,* 15, 94–101.

Kawashima, R., Satoh, K., Itoh, H., Ono, S., Furumoto, S., Gotoh, R., et al. (1996). Functional anatomy GO/NO-GO discrimination and response selection—a PET study in man. *Brain Research,* 728, 79–89.

Kjaer, T. W., Nowak, M., & Lou, H. C. (2002). Reflective self-awareness and conscious states: PET evidence for a common midline parietofrontal core. *NeuroImage,* 17, 1080–1086.

Koenigs, M., Young, L., Adolphs, R., Tranel, D., Cushman, F., Hauser, M., et al. (2007). Damage to the prefrontal cortex increases utilitarian moral judgments. *Nature,* 446, 908–911.

Kolb, B., Gibb, R., & Robinson, T. E. (2003). Brain plasticity and behavior. *Current Directions in Psychological Science,* 12, 1–5.

Laakso, M. P., Gunning-Dixon, F., Vaurio, O., Repo-Tiihonen, R., Soininen, H., & Tiihonen, J. (2002). Prefrontal volumes in habitually violent subjects with antisocial personality disorder and type 2 alcoholism. *Psychiatry Research Neuroimaging,* 114, 95–102.

Lamm, C., Batson, C. D., & Decety, J. (2007). The neural substrate of human empathy: Effect of perspective-taking and cognitive appraisal. *Journal of Cognitive Neuroscience,* 19, 42–58.

Lane, R. D., Reiman, E. M., Axelrod, B., Yun, L. S., Holmes, A., & Schwartz, G. E. (1998). Neural correlates of levels of emotional awareness: Evidence of an interaction between emotion and attention in the anterior cingulate cortex. *Journal of Cognitive Neuroscience,* 10, 525–535.

Laub, J. H., & Sampson, R. J. (2003). *Shared beginnings, divergent lives: Delinquent boys to age 70.* Cambridge, MA: Harvard University Press.

Lee, T. M. C., Chan, C. C. H., Leung, A. W. S., Fox, P. T., & Gao, J. H. (2009). Sex-related differences in neural activity during risk taking: An fMRI study. *Cerebral Cortex,* 19, 1303–1312.

Leenders, K.L., Perani,D., Lammertsma, A.A., Heather, J. D.,Buckingham, P., Healy, M. J. R., et al. (1990). Cerebral blood flow, blood volume, and oxygen utilization: Normal values and effect of age. *Brain,* 113, 27–47.

Li, C. R., & Sinha, R. (2008). Inhibitory control and emotional stress regulation: Neuroimaging evidence for frontal-limbic dysfunction in psycho-stimulant addiction. *Neuroscience and Biobehavioral Reviews,* 32, 581–597.

Liddle, P. F., Kiehl, K. A., & Smith, A. M. (2001). Event-related fMRI study of response inhibition. *Human Brain Mapping,* 12, 100–109.

Lieberman, M. D. (2007). Social cognitive neuroscience: A review of core processes. *Annual Review of Psychology,* 58, 259–289.

Lipsey, M. W., & Cullen, F. T. (2007). The effectiveness of correctional rehabilitation: A review of systematic reviews. Annual Review of *Law and Social Sciences,* 3, 297–320.

Lipsey, M. W., & Wilson, D. B. (1998). Effective intervention for serious juvenile offenders: A synthesis of research. In R. Loeber & D.P. Farrington (Eds.), *Serious and violent juvenile offenders: Risk factors and successful interventions* (pp. 313–366). Thousand Oaks, CA: Sage Publications.

Luo, Q., Nakic, M., Wheatley, T., Richell, R., Martin, A., & Blair, J. R. (2006). The neural basis of implicit moral attitude—An IAT study using event-related fMRI. *NeuroImage, 30,* 1449–1457.

MacKenzie, D. L. (2006). *What works in corrections: Reducing the criminal activities of offenders and delinquents.* New York: Cambridge University Press.

Mahncke, H. W., Connor, B. B., Appelman, J., Ahsanuddin, O. N., Hardy, J. L., Wood, R. A., et al. (2006). Memory enhancement in healthy older adults using a brain plasticity-based training program: A randomized, controlled study. *Proceedings of the National Academy of Sciences, 103,* 12523–12528.

Martinson, R. (1974). What works? Questions and answers about prison reform. *The Public Interest, 35*(2), 22–54.

Mitchell, J. P., Banaji, M. R., & Macrae, C. N. (2005). The link between social cognition and self-referential thought in the medial prefrontal cortex. *Journal of Cognitive Neuroscience, 17,* 1306–1315.

Moffitt, T. E. (1993). Adolescence-limited and life-course–persistent antisocial behavior: A developmental taxonomy. *Psychological Review, 100,* 674–701.

Moll, J., Oliveira-Souza, R., Eslinger, P. J., Bramati, I. E., Mourão-Miranda, J., Andreiuolo, P. A., et al. (2002). The neural correlates of moral sensitivity: A functional magnetic resonance imaging investigation of basic and moral emotions. *The Journal of Neuroscience, 22,* 2730–2736.

Moll, J., Zahn, R., de Oliveira-Souza, R., Krueger, F., & Grafman, J. (2005). The neural basis of human moral cognition. *Nature Reviews Neuroscience, 6,* 799–809.

Morris, R. G., Ahmed, S., Syed, G. M., & Toone, B. K. (1993). Neural correlates of planning ability: Frontal lobe activation during the Tower of London test. *Neuropsychologia, 31,* 1367–1378.

Müller-Dahlhaus, J. F. M., Orekhov, Y., Liu, Y., & Ziemann, U. (2008). Interindividual variability and age-dependency of motor cortical plasticity induced by paired associated stimulation. *Experimental Brain Research, 187,* 467–475.

Nelles, G., Jentzen, W., Jueptner, M., Müller, S., & Diener, H. C. (2001). Arm training induced brain plasticity in stroke studied with serial positron emission tomography. *NeuroImage, 13,* 1146–1154.

Newman, S. D., Carpenter, P. A., Varma, S., & Just, M. A. (2003). Frontal and parietal participation in problem solving in the Tower of London: fMRI and computation modeling of planning and high-level perception. *Neuropsychologia, 41,* 1668–1682.

O'Doherty, J., Kringelbach, M. L., Rolls, E. T., Hornak, J., & Andrews, C. (2001). Abstract reward and punishment representation in the human orbitofrontal cortex. *Nature Neuroscience, 4,* 95–102.

Ochsner, K. N., Beer, J. S., Robertson, E. R., Cooper, J. C., Gabrieli, J. D. E., Kihsltrom, J. F., et al. (2005). The neural correlates of direct and reflected self-knowledge. *NeuroImage, 28,* 797–814.

Ochsner, K. N., Bunge, S. A., Gross, J. J., & Gabrieli, J. D. E. (2002). Rethinking feelings: An fMRI study of the cognitive regulation of emotion. *Journal of Cognitive Neuroscience, 14,* 1215–1229.

Ochsner, K. N., Ray, R. D., Cooper, J. C., Robertson, E. R., Chopra, S., Gabrieli, J. D. E., et al. (2004). For better or for worse: Neural systems supporting the cognitive down-and up-regulation of negative emotion. *NeuroImage, 23,* 483–499.

Ohira, H., Nomura, M., Ichikawa, N., Isowa, T., Iidaka, T., Sato, A., et al. (2006). Association of neural and physiological responses during voluntary emotion suppression. *NeuroImage, 29,* 721–733.

Olds, D. L. (2007). Preventing crime with prenatal and infancy support of parents: The nurse-family partnership. *Victims and Offenders*, 2, 205–225.

Owen, A. M., Downes, J. J., Sahakian, B. J., Polkey, C. E., & Robbins, T. W. (1990). Planning and spatial working memory following frontal lobe lesions in man. *Neuropsychologia*, 28, 1021–1034.

Paquette, V., Lévesque, J., Mensour, B., Leroux, J. M., Beaudoin, G., Bourgouin, P., et al. (2003). "Change the mind and you change the brain": effects of cognitive-behavioral therapy on the neural correlates of spider phobia. *NeuroImage*, 18, 401–409.

Paulus, M. P., Rogalsky, C., Simmons, A., Feinstein, J. S., & Stein, M. B. (2003). Increased activation in the right insula during risk-taking decision making is related to harm avoidance and neuroticism. *NeuroImage*, 19, 1439–1448.

Paulus, M. P., & Stein, M. B. (2006). An insular view of anxiety. *Biological Psychiatry*, 60, 383–387.

Pearson, F. S., Lipton, D. S., Cleland, C. M., & Yee, D. S. (2002). The effects of behavioral/cognitive-behavioral programs on recidivism. *Crime and Delinquency*, 48, 476–496.

Phan, K. L., Fitzgerald, D. A., Nathan, P. J., Moore, G. J., Uhde, T. W., & Tancer, M. E. (2005). Neural substrates for voluntary suppression of negative affect: A functional magnetic resonance imaging study. *Biological Psychiatry*, 57, 210–219.

Phan, K. L., Wager, T. D., Taylor, S. F., & Liberzon, I. (2004). Functional neuroimaging studies of human emotions. *CNS Spectrums*, 9, 258–266.

Platt, M. L., & Huettel, S. A. (2008). Risky business: The neuroeconomics of decision making under uncertainty. *Nature Neuroscience*, 11, 395–403.

Pollatos, O., Gramann, K., & Schandry, R. (2007). Neural systems connecting interoceptive awareness and feelings. *Human Brain Mapping*, 28, 9–18.

Pollatos, O., Kirsch, W., & Schandry, R. (2005). On the relationship between interoceptive awareness, emotional experience, and brain processes. *Cognitive Brain Research*, 25, 948–962.

Prasko, J., Horácek, J., Záleský, R., Kopecek, M., Novák, T., Pasková, B., et al. (2004). The change of regional brain metabolism (18FDG PET) in panic disorder during the treatment with cognitive-behavioral therapy or antidepressants. *Neurology and Endocrinology Letters*, 25, 340–348.

Pridemore, S., Chambers, A., & McArthur, M. (2005). Neuroimaging in psychopathy. *Australian and New Zealand Journal of Psychiatry*, 39, 856–865.

Rafter, N. (2008). *The criminal brain: Understanding biological theories of crime.* New York: New York University Press.

Rahman, S., Sahakian, B. J., Cardinal, R. N., Rogers, R. D., & Robbins, T. W. (2001). Decision making and neuropsychiatry. *Trends in Cognitive Sciences*, 5, 271–277.

Raine, A., Buchsbaum, M., & LaCasse, L. (1997). Brain abnormalities in murderers indicated by positron emission tomography. *Biological Psychiatry*, 42, 495–508.

Raine, A., Buchsbaum, M. S., Stanley, J., Lottenberg, S., Abel, L., & Stoddard, J. (1994). Selective reductions in prefrontal glucose metabolism in murderers. *Biological Psychiatry*, 36, 365–373.

Raine, A., Lencz, T., Bihrle, S., LaCasse, L., & Colletti, P. (2000). Reduced prefrontal gray matter volume and reduced autonomic activity in antisocial personality disorder. *Archives of General Psychiatry*, 57, 119–127.

Raine, A., & Yang, Y. (2006). Neural foundations to moral reasoning and antisocial behavior. *Scan*, 1, 203–213.

Ross, R., & Fabiano, E. (1985). *Time to think: A cognitive model of delinquency prevention and offender rehabilitation.* Ottawa, ON: Air Training and Publications.

Ross, R. R., & Hilborn, J. (2008). *Rehabilitating Rehabilitation: Neurocriminology for treatment of antisocial behavior.* Ottawa, ON: Cognitive Centre of Canada.

Ruby, P., & Decety, J. (2004). How would you feel versus how do you think she would feel? A neuroimaging study of perspective-taking with social emotions. *Journal of Cognitive Neuroscience,* 16, 988–999.

Sakai, Y., Kumano, H., Nishikawa, M., Sakano, Y., Kaiya, H., Imabayashi, E., et al. (2006). Changes in cerebral glucose utilization in patients with panic disorder treated with cognitive-behavioral therapy. *NeuroImage,* 33, 218–226.

Sanfey, A. G., Rilling, J. K., Aronson, J. A., Nystrom, L. E., & Cohen, J. D. (2003). The neural basis of economic decision-making in the ultimatum game. *Science,* 300, 1755–1758.

Saver, J. L., & Damasio, A. R. (1991). Preserved access and processing of social knowledge in a patient with acquired sociopathy due to ventromedial frontal damage. *Neuropsychologia,* 29, 1241–1249.

Saxena, S., Gorbis, E., O'Neill, J., Baker, S. K., Mandelkern, M. A., Maidment, K. M., et al. (2009). Rapid effects of brief intensive cognitive-behavioral therapy on brain glucose metabolism in obsessive-compulsive disorder. *Molecular Psychiatry,* 14,197–205.

Schmitz, T. W., & Johnson, S. C. (2006). Self-appraisal decisions evoke dissociated dorsal-ventral aMPFC networks. *NeuroImage,* 30, 1050–1058.

Schmitz, T. W., Kawahara-Baccus, T. N., & Johnson, S. C. (2004). Metacognitive evaluation, self-relevance, and the right prefrontal cortex. *NeuroImage,* 22,941–947.

Schoenbaum, G., Chiba, A. A., & Gallagher, M. (1998). Orbitofrontal cortex and basolateral amygdala encode expected outcomes during learning. *Nature Neuroscience,* 1, 155–159.

Schwartz, J. M., Stoessel, P. W., Baxter, L. R., Martin, K. M., & Phelps, M. E. (1996). Systemic changes in cerebral glucose metabolic rate after successful behavior modification treatment of obsessive-compulsive disorder. *Archives of General Psychiatry,* 53, 109–113.

Shallice, T., & Burgess, P. W. (1991). Deficits in strategy application following frontal lobe damage in man. *Brain,* 114, 727–741.

Shimamura, A. P. (2000). Toward a cognitive neuroscience of metacognition. *Consciousness and Cognition,* 9, 313–323.

Shin, L. M., Dougherty, D. D., Orr, S. P., Pitman, R. K., Lasko, M., Macklin, M. L., et al. (2000). Activation of anterior paralimbic structures during guilt-related script-driven imagery. *Biological Psychiatry,* 48, 43–49.

Singer, T. (2006). The neuronal basis and ontogeny of empathy and mind reading: Review of literature and implications for future research. *Neuroscience and Biobehavioral Reviews,* 30, 855–863.

Singer, T., Seymour, B., O'Doherty, J., Kaube, H., Dolan, R. J., & Frith, C. D. (2004). Empathy for pain involves the affective but not sensory components of pain. *Science,* 303, 1157–1162.

Sinha, R., & Li, C. S. R. (2007). Imaging stress-and cue-induced drug and alcohol craving: Association with relapse and clinical implications. *Drug and Alcohol Review,* 26, 25–31.

Sterzer, P., Stadler, C., Poustka, F., & Kleinschmidt, A. (2008). A structural neural deficit in adolescents with conduct disorder and its association with lack of empathy. *NeuroImage,* 37, 335–342.

Takahashi, H., Yahata, N., Koeda, M., Matsuda, T., Asai, K., & Okubo, Y. (2004). Brain activation associated with evaluative processes of guilt and embarrassment: An fMRI study. *NeuroImage,* 23, 967–974.

Temple, E., Deutsch, G. K., Poldrack, R. A., Miller, S. L., Tallal, P., Merzenich, M. M., et al. (2003). Neural deficits in children with dyslexia ameliorated by behavioral remediation: Evidence from functional MRI. Proceedings of the *National Academy of Sciences,* 100, 2860–2865.

Tranel, D., Bechara, A., & Denburg, N. L. (2002). Asymmetric functional roles of right and left ventromedial prefrontal cortices in social conduct, decision-making, and emotional processing. *Cortex,* 38, 589–612.

Tranel, D., Hathaway-Nepple, J., & Anderson, S. W. (2007). Impaired behavior on real-world tasks following damage to the ventromedial prefrontal cortex. *Journal of Clinical and Experimental Neuropsychology, 29,* 319–332.

Unterrainer, J. M., & Owen, A. M. (2006). Planning and problem solving: From neuropsychology to functional neuroimaging. *Journal of Physiology, 99,* 308–317.

Volavka, J. (1999). The neurobiology of violence: An update. *Journal of Neuropsychiatry and Clinical Neuroscience, 11,* 307–314.

Völlm, B. A., Taylor, A. N. W., Richardson, P., Corcoran, R., Stirling, J., McKie, S., et al. (2006). Neuronal correlates of theory of mind and empathy: A functional magnetic resonance imaging study in a nonverbal task. *NeuroImage, 29,* 90–98.

Walker, D. L., Toufexis, D. J., & Davis, M. (2003). Role of the bed nucleus of the stria terminalis versus the amygdala in fear, stress, and anxiety. *European Journal of Pharmacology, 463,* 199–216.

Walsh, A., & Beaver, K. M. (Eds.) (2009). *Biosocial criminology: New directions in theory and research.* New York: Routledge.

Wright, J. P., Tibbetts, S. G., & Daigle, L. E. (2008). *Criminals in the making: Criminality across the life course.* Thousand Oaks, CA: Sage.

Wyland, C. L., Kelley, W. M., Macrae, C. N., Gordon, H. L., & Heatherton, T. F. (2003). Neural correlates of thought suppression. *Neuropsychologia, 41,* 1863–1867.

Yang, Y., Raine, A., Lencz, T., Bihrle, S., LaCasse, L., & Colletti, P. (2005). Volume reduction in prefrontal gray matter in unsuccessful criminal psychopaths. *Biological Psychiatry, 57,* 1103–1108.

Yochelson, S., & Samenow, S. (1977). *The criminal personality. The change process,* Vol. 2: New York: Jason Aronson.

Young, S., Chick, K., & Gudjonsson, G. (2010). A preliminary evaluation of Reasoning and Rehabilitation 2 in mentally disordered offenders (R&R2M) across two secure forensic settings in the United Kingdom. *Journal of Forensic Psychiatry & Psychology, 21,* 336–349.

Epilogue

In the **Introduction** to this book, we asked you to consider some fundamental questions about how individuals and families functioned—"Why do families do that?" and "Why do they behave that way?" In this book, we have explored ten different ways in which family scholars have explained family functioning. Each theory provides a unique set of lenses through which to view family functioning and offers different explanations as to why families behave the way they do.

The following figure "Summary of family theories" provides basic comparisons of the ten family theories that have been covered in this book. We have covered how families may be seen from both a broad, "macro" perspective as social institutions that function to maintain society and from an individual level to the specific "micro" perspective of individual analysis within the family system.

The purpose of social science is not to suggest there is only one truth about individuals and families, but rather to discover the many layers of their complex lives. Thus, depending on the question, the situation, and the outcome needed or expected, the theoretical perspective that is best to use will vary. In addition, knowing many theories gives us options to choose from in order to assess, analyze, and understand families better. Theories evolve over time, and these theories will continue to change and develop as research continues to challenge our understanding about families, increasing our knowledge of family issues, confronting our assumptions about how we define families, and expanding our perceptions of the complexities of family life.

The importance of knowing multiple theories can be seen in the following example. Let's say that you are investigating the factors individuals consider when choosing an intimate partner, with a specific focus on the importance of social practice. Structural functionalism or biosocial theory may provide a sufficient framework for your research questions. However, if you want to look at how particular couples make their decisions about becoming life partners, or how individuals choose one person over another, then you can probably get better insights and results by using the theory of social exchange. Conflict theory or even feminist theory would also help you decide why individuals choose the persons they do. Each theory provides you with different ways to focus your questions, which in turn reshapes your answers to those questions.

Let's say that you want to know not only **why** people pick the partners they choose, but also why they choose them **at a particular time**. In other words, if you had met this same person two years ago, would you still have fallen in love? The

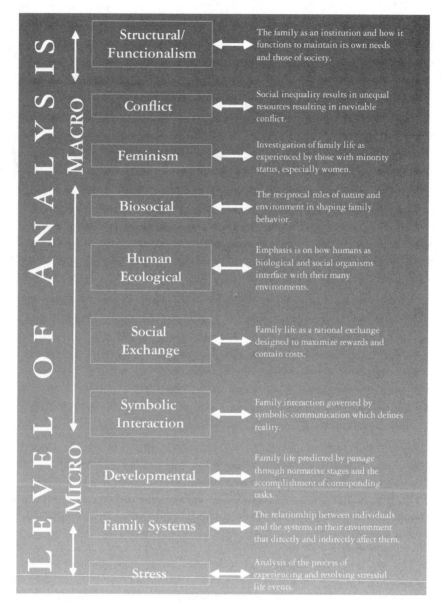

Summary of family theories

previously mentioned theories would not be as useful in answering this new question. Instead, you might turn to family development, symbolic interaction, human ecological theory, or even family systems theory to guide your research. Finally, you now decide that the most interesting questions have to do with the disagreements or tensions in relationships once they are formed. Conflict, feminist, or stress theory may best answer your new questions.

Knowing which theory to use is often a matter of preference, can be dictated by the situation, and sometimes is simply based on guessing. Theories speak to us because they resonate with what we believe to be important. You may have found, as you read these chapters, that you preferred some theories over others. That is a fairly typical experience. If you continue to work in this field, you will find that your colleagues will reflect theoretical orientations, either by training or by preference, in their work. The important thing to remember is that each theory has its usefulness. You may find, for example, that one theory explains 85 percent of the families with whom you work. However, there will inevitably be situations when that one theory will not explain a family as well as another theory might, and when you are faced with that family, in your office or in your life, it is always useful to have other theories in your repertoire.

Because a theory can change the way we view and understand the world—and families—theories can also help us know how to intervene. When we approach families in a systematic way, we can be certain that we have considered all possible avenues of understanding families, and therefore, the most effective ways of helping them achieve their best selves.

THE FUTURE OF FAMILY THEORIES

Although we have presented these ten theories as individual entities, you will soon have the opportunity to practice using them in a more integrated way. First, however, it's important that we briefly review what we anticipate will happen in the field in the years to come. Just as there are many ways of talking about and explaining families, there are also many differing opinions about the relevance of theory in family studies and its place in the field in the future. In 1990, Sprey stated that the field of family science is in critical need of theoretical development. However, as recently as 2008, it has been noted that journal articles written based on theoretical assessment are lacking, and surprisingly few family journal articles have even grounded their research in theory (White and Klein 2008). White and Klein suggest that family journals should require the use of theory in articles in order to advance both theory development and the quality of research in the field.

Although not all family scholars would agree with that stance, it is encouraging that The National Council on Family Relations, one of the premier family professional organizations, developed a journal called *The Journal of Family Theory & Review* in 2009. Their website states their purpose as "seeking to encourage integration and growth in the multidisciplinary and international domains of inquiry that define contemporary family studies. The journal publishes original contributions in all areas of family theory, including new advances in theory development, reviews of existing theory, and analyses of the interface of theory and method, as well as integrative and theory based reviews of content areas, and book reviews." This is an encouraging step in the advancement of theory development in the field.

At the most basic level, theory is used to either predict things or to explain things that have already happened, both of which are common goals of family science research, making theory integration applicable as well as informative. It is also true that families are not static entities, but instead are always being changed, tested, developed, and modified. The relevance of particular theories has also been shown to ebb and flow throughout this book. For example, although structural functionalism was an important theory in the early development of family studies, its use today is minimal at best. In contrast, biosocial theory has shown great strides in the last decade thanks to advancements in technology, methodology, and brain-development research and measurement. It is also true that the social and political environment shapes which theories emerge, as well as which theories will be most useful in explaining modern experiences such as the emergence of the second wave of feminist theory that was shaped by the social and political climate of the 1960s. Another way in which theory has been used in recent years is to serve as the basis for new theoretical developments. For example, conflict theory was the core for the development of parent–offspring conflict theory, which utilizes the concepts of conflict theory, but refines them to fit its particular area of study.

Another reason why theories must grow and change is because families themselves are changing. Adams (2010) traces families from their patriarchal roots prior to the 1900s to today's families, which are incredibly diverse. Examples of relevant modern influences on families include the education and employment of women, advances in technology, globalism, and changing family structures. Families now frequently have two breadwinners, can control fertility, are greatly influenced by what is happening around the world, and are experiencing tremendous demographic variation and change. These changes have led to the modification of some family theories and the development of others. Beck and Beck-Gernsheim (2010) call for the development of a family theory that is more reflective of the diverse family forms that exist today. Using marriage migration as an example, they suggest that our methodologies and theories need to recognize the globalization of our culture. Consequently, we need to conduct research on families while being mindful of these multiple cultural realities, rather than simply a Western ideology. This level of inclusiveness is one potential trend and challenge for family theory in the future.

White and Klein (2008) suggest that another challenge is to increase the inclusion of theory in family studies research, to test the theories that exist and their applicability to family topics, and to work toward more integration in the relationship between the theories we use, the methodologies we choose, and the data that are obtained. Stan Knapp (2009) agrees that the use of theoretical underpinnings is missing in the field of family studies. As he sees it, theory building in the future should be cognizant of the five functions of theories (as delineated in the beginning of this text). He also believes that we must use critical theorizing to advance our field. This entails taking the role of theory as seriously as we do the role of methodology, that we evaluate and analyze the assumptions that guide our use of theory, and that we think critically about the multitude of possible explanations for the phenomenon under study.

Knapp (2009) proposes that it is through "critical theorizing" that scholars scrutinize the grounding (explicit and implicit) assumptions of the theory and research methods they are employing to processes and events under consideration, and reflexively ponder "how the theory, method, and conceptualization of phenomena relate to other ways of theorizing, understanding, and studying the phenomena" (137). While critically theorizing, family scholars should engage in a dialogue with alternative perspectives, preventing prejudiced and premature acceptance of knowledge claims. Consequently, both methodological rigor and theoretical rigor are essential for the production of meaningful understandings about families. Daly (2003) also calls for examining theory and family processes in fresh ways, by paying attention to "negative spaces." Negative spaces represent the many everyday family activities that have yet to be considered in our theorizing about families. According to Daly, there are many areas of family life that need theorizing—like the realm of belief, feeling, and intuition; and the consumption and meaning of *things* within family life.

Klein and White (2008) offer two final challenges for family theory in the future. The first is that we need to ensure that "family" is a vital component of family theory. Most of the theories reviewed here discuss the family as a unit of interacting individuals, rather than as a unit unto itself. However, family groups differ from other groups in a multitude of ways, necessitating that we develop theories specifically focusing on them. Their final challenge for the future of family theories is the development of one theory of the family, or the integration of many of the principles of the other theories as discussed in this text into a single theory that seeks to explain families. Not all scholars would agree with this goal, but it is certainly interesting to contemplate

As you can see, the role of theory in the field of family science is fluid. The existence of a new journal focused on theory, the call for better and more consistent integration of theory into family research, and the development of new theories based on concepts of previously empirically tested theories are encouraging signs for the family field in the future. It is our hope that scholars will use theory as a guiding tool, empirically assess theories that currently exist so they may be continually modified, and develop strategies for better reflecting the diversity that exists in today's society.

USING THE THEORIES

Although the future is hopefully bright for family theory development and usage, this process is reliant on an understanding of how to utilize theories such as those that were reviewed in this text. You have had the chance in this book so far to consider each theory in its own historical context. It is important to practice using the theories in a more comprehensive way, in order to determine how each theory provides a focus for family issues. These theoretical lenses will give you different perspectives on a family's dynamics—its strengths, weaknesses, struggles, issues, challenges, and potentials.

Below is a complex case study of a three-generation family. Imagine that you are a helping professional, perhaps a family life educator or counselor, assigned to work with this family. Try to understand the family's situation and dynamics using each of the theoretical frameworks explained in this text.

For each theory, outline the major issues or crises facing the family from that perspective. Consider their strengths and weaknesses from that perspective as well. Find examples of basic assumptions in the case study. What roles do the family members play, if any? How do they enact their roles? How are societal and individual issues played out in the family? After considering each theory separately, consider them as a group.

THE MALDONADO FAMILY

Juan and Maria Maldonado have been married for 15 years. They were both born in Mexico and immigrated to the United States five years ago. Life was difficult for them in Mexico. Juan worked very long, labor-intensive days in the factory for little pay, which was barely enough to support his four children and wife. Maria worked as a nurse in the local village hospital. Despite all their hard work, they were still poor and did not see much hope for their future. Because they could not see a way out of their economic situation, they decided to move to the United States in hopes of finding a better life for themselves and, in particular, for their children. Maria's aunt, who was already living in the United States, offered to help Juan find a job there. Although they were filled with sadness at leaving their extended family behind, the Maldonados moved their family to the United States with hope for a brighter future.

Since they came to the United States, things have improved a little. Their children have learned English very well, although Juan and Maria still struggle with the language; this makes them depend a great deal on Marco, their eldest, for translation. Because Juan found a good job at a factory, their economic lives have improved. Maria cannot work as a nurse because her educational credentials are not recognized in the United States. As a result, she cleans houses to make extra money. Granted, they will probably never be able to buy name-brand clothes and fancy cars, but the children have decent clothes, shoes, medical care, and a dental plan.

Once Juan and Maria settled in the United States, both of their mothers came to live with them. The townhouse they rent is cramped with eight people living in it, but the two youngest children don't mind sleeping on the floor, and life is easier on Maria now that the older women are there, because they do all the cooking and cleaning for the family. She is free to do more paid housecleaning and to take English classes at the community college. Juan and Maria felt that bringing the grandparents to live with them was important. They missed the closeness of the family in Mexico, and they wanted their children to know their grandparents. They felt very sad that both of their fathers had died since they had left Mexico and they could not afford to go to their funerals. Having their mothers nearby meant they could also ensure that they had the best childcare. And Maria's mother could now be nearer to her own sister, who had been so instrumental in getting the Maldonado family to move to the United States in the first place.

Despite an improved living situation, the Maldonado family still has many problems. Both Juan and Maria worry about what will happen if Juan loses his job. They know that their inability to speak English puts them both at risk in their employment. Maria really wants a job at a hospital, but it costs money to take the special "English for Nurses" classes and the additional nursing courses required to work at the hospital. Besides, the classes are taught at night, when she needs to be at home with the boys helping them with their homework. Marco, who is now 14 years old, and his brother, Phillip, 12, are very little help around the house and seem to be getting into trouble more and more in the neighborhood. They used to come straight home from school, but now they hang out with friends Maria doesn't know and seem to defy her authority. Juan, who is working the night shift, is either sleeping or at work and sees his sons only on the weekends. Katrina, who is 10 years old, is a very quiet girl and very pleasant to everyone. She quietly does her homework and stays with her grandmothers when Maria must go out. Everyone thinks Katrina is a wonderful little girl, but Maria secretly worries that Katrina is perhaps a little too withdrawn.

Recently, Juan and Maria were called in for a parent–teacher conference to discuss Rosina, their 8-year-old daughter. They had to bring Marco along to be their translator. The school offered to provide one, but they felt more secure with Marco. But they were embarrassed by Marco's attitude when they got to the school because he was rude to the teacher instead of being respectful. He said it was because the teacher "talked bad" about Rosina. According to her teacher, Rosina's grades, which had never been great, were getting even worse. They found out that Rosina had been talking a lot in class and was frequently disruptive. They also discovered that other children in class teased her because of her clothes and her accent. When this would happen, she would yell at them and once she even attempted to hit another child, which is what had prompted this conference. The teacher suggested that perhaps Rosina needed to see the school counselor for some help. That is what made Marco angry, causing him to be rude to the teacher, because he believed that Rosina was provoked, and therefore, did not need any help from a school counselor. The teacher suggested that perhaps Marco needed some help as well. Juan and Maria went home from the conference feeling very upset and not knowing what to think.

In addition, Juan and Maria have been fighting more than usual since their parents came to live with them. When Juan and Maria first invited their mothers to live with them, they imagined the extended family in only positive ways—the larger family festivities, holidays with grandmothers present, traditional foods being taught to their daughters, the sense of honor toward women that the older women would instill in their sons. Both Maria and Juan know that their mothers are happy to be with them, but they also know that they miss Mexico. Although Maria appreciates their help around the house, she still feels overwhelmed by having to take care of four children while also working and going to school. She has to do all of this while under the watchful eyes of her elders and, naturally, she never seems to do anything up to their standards. She feels that they do not see the value of the sacrifices that she and Juan make for the sake of their children. For example, Juan works the night shift so he can earn more money. In fact, he wishes that Maria didn't have to work at all. He feels that he should earn enough money to care for her and the family. But his mother says that he should work while his children are in school, like his father did, so he can be *un papa verdadero*—a real father—to them in the evenings and set *un buen ejemplo*—a good example—for them. Maria and Juan never seem to have any time alone together.

Juan and Maria are finding it difficult to meet the expectations of their mothers while establishing new goals for their own family. Even though they see each other only between shifts or on weekends, those times are often spent arguing about the children or which bills to pay this month and which ones can wait a little longer. Occasionally, Maria thinks about the times in Mexico when she was poorer but had more family to support her, had more social status in the village, and fought less with Juan. She wants her children to have every opportunity, but she also wants her family to be happy. Perhaps, she thinks, they should consider moving back to Mexico and giving it another try there.

DISCUSSION

Which theories seemed to be most useful to you in understanding the Maldonado family? Why did you prefer one over another? What is it about that particular perspective that you find more reasonable or useful for the kind of work that you would eventually like to do with families? Use this case-study experience to illustrate for yourself not just the applicability of the theories but their relevance to your future career.

REFERENCES

Adams, B. 2010. Themes and threads of family theories: A brief history. *Journal of Comparative Family Studies* 41(4): 499–505.

Beck, U., and E. Beck-Gernsheim. 2010. Passage to hope: Marriage, migration, and the need for a cosmopolitan turn in family research. *Journal of Family Theory & Review* 2: 401–414.

Daly, K. 2003. Family theory versus the theories families live by. *Journal of Marriage and Family* 65: 771–784.

Knapp, S. J. 2009. Critical theorizing: Enhancing theoretical rigor in family research. *Journal of Family Theory & Review* 1:133–145.

Sprey, J. 1990. Theoretical practice in family studies. In J. Sprey (Ed.), *Fashioning Family Theory* (9–33). Newbury Park, CA: Sage Publications.

White, J. M., and D. M. Klein. 2008. *Family theories* (3rd ed). Los Angeles: Sage Publications.

Index